Henry Clay

Henry Clay *from a miniature by an unknown artist*

By Bernard Mayo

HENRY CLAY

SPOKESMAN OF THE NEW WEST

ILLUSTRATED

HOUGHTON MIFFLIN COMPANY · BOSTON

𝕿𝖍𝖊 𝕽𝖎𝖛𝖊𝖗𝖘𝖎𝖉𝖊 𝕻𝖗𝖊𝖘𝖘 𝕮𝖆𝖒𝖇𝖗𝖎𝖉𝖌𝖊

1937

E 176.8

The Riverside Press
CAMBRIDGE · MASSACHUSETTS
PRINTED IN THE U.S.A.

Sept 1378

37-28554

Clay was essentially, constructively, triumphantly American. . . . The impetuous impulse of Clay was to let the youth, the vigor, the creative spirit of triumphant America sweep in untrammeled activity whithersoever it would, secure that a beneficent Providence would guide it. . . . And in all these various phases Clay embodied the spirit of the West . . . its nervous vigor, its all-attempting courage, its undying enthusiasm.

GAMALIEL BRADFORD

Foreword

IN WRITING this story of young Henry Clay and of young America (the first of a trilogy on Clay), with some of the Kentuckian's optimism I have tried to meet both the standards of scholarship and the challenge in George Bancroft's remark, that 'neither in public nor in private did Henry Clay know how to be dull.' I have tried, also, to portray in objective manner the influence upon Clay of his environment, and the influence of Clay upon that environment. 'Readers might judge for themselves,' as Henry Adams said, 'what share the individual possessed in creating or shaping the nation; but whether it was small or great, the nation could be understood only by studying the individual.'

I should like to acknowledge here the many debts of gratitude incurred, and to mention particularly the following persons who have aided me: Lida Mayo, W. Stull Holt, Charles C. Tansill, Katherine Elizabeth Crane, Curtis W. Garrison, George Hudson Clay, Captain Thomas J. Clay, Mrs. Henry Clay McDowell, Mrs. Andrew Jackson Smith, Florine Taylor, William S. Hunt, Charles R. Staples, Mrs. Charles F. Norton, Mack Swearingen, John Wilson Townsend, J. Franklin Jameson and his staff of the Division of Manuscripts, Library of Congress, and the officers of the several local and state historical societies.

BERNARD MAYO

WASHINGTON, D.C.
  March 16, 1937

Contents

Illustrations

Chapter One. Henry Clay, Virginian

'Tis but the morning of the world with us. (Philip Freneau.)

A great revolution has happened... the appearance of a new state, of a new species, in a new part of the globe. (Edmund Burke.)

Rocked in the cradle of the Revolution... I was born a democrat — was raised and nurtured a Republican.... (Henry Clay.)

IN 1777 revolutionary battalions were marching, revolutionary ideas fermenting. At Saratoga, a colonial 'rabble-in-arms' defeated Burgoyne's Britons, Germans, and Indians, and turned civil strife into world-wide conflict. Within captured Philadelphia Sir William Howe tarried and frolicked. Outside the gay Quaker capital Washington's ragged insurgents endured the wintry bleakness of Valley Forge. At Paris, venerable, fur-capped Doctor Franklin negotiated an alliance with ill-starred Louis the Sixteenth. In Virginia, young Thomas Jefferson opened war to make his Declaration of Independence a reality, crusading against royal laws, landed aristocracy, and religious tyranny.

On April 12 of this revolutionary year Henry Clay was born. He was the seventh son of 'Sir John' Clay of Hanover Court House, Virginia, a tobacco planter and Baptist preacher whose activities in the cause of religious freedom reflected the American Revolution as a social movement.

'Sir John' was a popular title. While there was a family tradition of noble Welsh forbears, the first Clay to immigrate seems to have been Captain John, 'the English Grenadier,' who arrived at Jamestown a few years after the planting of British America. Charles Clay, the first of Henry's ancestors born in the New World, fought with Bacon's frontier democrats in Virginia's Great Rebellion of 1676. His revolt against Charles the Second's royal governor, like that of his grandson, Baptist John, against 'the servile train, the pimps and sycophants of George's reign,' was significant of the family's temperament and position: the democratic, strong-willed Clays of colonial Virginia were prosperous yeomen farmers, of the upper middle class but not of the ruling gentry. The Hudsons, Henry's maternal ancestors, were likewise substantial planters but not of the landed aristocracy.[1]

When John Clay, in 1765, married fifteen-year-old Elizabeth Hudson of Hanover he lived in neighboring Chesterfield, on the 'Southside' of Richmond and the James River. There he subsequently became a Baptist exhorter, a leader of lowly and despised dissenters from the politically and socially elect Church of England, the virtues of which had become obscured by parsons who babbled in the pulpit, roared in the tavern, guzzled, diced, wenched, and duelled. John Clay became an agitator for 'soul liberty.' He inveighed against 'diabolical, hell-conceived' religious tyranny, defying a tax-supported state church manned in large part by outcast English clerics — Old World refuse dumped by a mother country whose colonial policy was all too often in the Tory spirit of Doctor Samuel Johnson: 'Sir, they are a race of convicts, and ought to be thankful for any thing we allow them short of hanging.' [2]

---

[1] On Clay's ancestry, see Clay, M. R., *The Clay Family*; also, *American Historical Review*, V, 402–03; *Virginia Magazine of History and Biography*, XXI, 436; XXXIII, 395. The Virginia Archives, Richmond, reveal that Henry's ancestors had substantial middle-class holdings; that his father's popular title of 'Sir' sometimes appeared in court records (*MS. Hanover Records, 1783–92*, II, 418–19); that neither George Hudson, Henry's maternal grandfather, nor John Hudson, George's father, an English or possibly Welsh emigrant, were styled 'Gent.' (*MS. Vestry Book, Saint Paul's Parish, Hanover, 1705–85*); that 'founder' John Clay on July 13, 1635, was granted 1200A, 1100A for transporting 22 immigrants at his own expense, 100A for being an Old Planter resident in Virginia before August, 1611. Suggestive of genial good living is the inscription on the tombstone of Henry's great-grandfather: 'In Memory of Henry Clay who died at dinner with his Children & Grand Children at an annual Festival given to them, in August 1760.' (Stone at 'Morrimont,' nine miles southwest of Richmond.)

[2] *Boswell's Life of Johnson*, I, 560.

Notwithstanding his substantial property holdings and the qualities that inspired his title of 'Sir John,' Henry Clay's father aligned himself with the illiterate Murphy Boys, John Waller (once known as 'Swearing Jack'), and other evangels. They were men of the masses, of little learning and strong convictions, road-side revivalists given to 'yelping, barking, and whooping in odd tones.' With them he stirred the commoners of Virginia to a 'heavenly confusion' in the decade preceding Jefferson's Declaration of Independence. With them he scattered a leaven which hastened the Revolution and conditioned it as a people's uprising.

His disciples not only abandoned formal dogma for camp-meeting emotionalism, and authoritarian for democratic religion, but they rebelled against the Established Church of the rich man, its parasite priests, and its vestrymen, the twelve lords of parish government. The most radical of all dissenters, Clay's Baptists refused to compromise with religious toleration: they demanded as of right absolute religious freedom. Magistrates and mobs, priests and sheriffs, attempted to suppress their 'anarchy,' their 'howling Baptist mania.' They were haled into court as public nuisances, and arraigned for cramming Scripture down wayfarers' throats, for being 'unlicensed preachers of the gospel of Jesus Christ, and also strollers.' In Chesterfield County, a center of persecution, the Reverend John Clay was imprisoned for his fearless preaching. Henry's father was of 'the phalanx of Christian Spartans.' [1]

Eventually, however, the crusaders for 'soul liberty' won the support of the political libertarians. When all forms of protest merged into the general Revolutionary struggle the intransigent, 'outlandish,' and now patriotic Baptists achieved social and religious recognition. Jefferson, who had sworn to eradicate 'every fibre of antient or future aristocracy,' became their leader in overthrowing the Established Church of England and in enacting the famous Virginia Statute for Religious Freedom.

Unmolested, John Clay continued his voluntary and unpaid ministry after removing to Hanover, a few months before Henry was born. There he established himself on the Hudson homestead

---

[1] Thom, W. T., *Struggle for Religious Freedom in Virginia: The Baptists*, pp. 497, 502, *passim*; Leland, J., *Virginia Chronicle*.

some sixteen miles north of Richmond. Despite the cares of his five hundred acres and twenty slaves, and of another slave-worked plantation in neighboring Henrico,[1] he preached and baptized and founded Baptist meeting-houses on Black and Chickahominy Creeks. Kindly tradition has it that he was an eloquent exhorter, but his new ministry did not prosper. Fellow Baptists said his talents were of a plain order.[2] Yet even if he had ranted and whooped as violently as his fellows, the time had passed for 'heavenly confusion.' In Patrick Henry's Hanover, emotions had been diverted from revivalistic excitement to martial display.

Here in Hanover County Henry Clay was literally 'rocked in the cradle of the Revolution.'[3] In this frontier outpost of the British Empire as early as 1763 — the very year Britons acquired French America, exulted in world-wide conquests, and boasted of being 'heirs apparent to the Romans' — Patrick Henry, Hanover's 'Forest-born Demosthenes' (as Lord Byron called him), publicly defied imperial George the Third. Two years later this 'Trumpet of the American Revolution' made his famous Treason Speech. In 1775, two months before the fateful shots at Lexington, he had impelled royal Virginia to rebellion with the American classic ending, 'Give me Liberty or give me Death!'

When proud Hanover, 'with repeated huzzas,' sent its flaming orator to the Continental Congress, there went with Patrick Henry the fervent prayers of Henry Clay's parents. For John Clay, a rebel in politics as in religion, preached the godliness of revolt, assisted the county's committees, helped to recruit, and furnished supplies to the army.[4] Past his home on the Richmond Pike a never-ending stream of citizen soldiers with 'Liberty or Death' on their hunting shirts marched north to join General Washington. Later many of them returned for the desperate fighting in Hanover which preceded the final and glorious victory at Yorktown.

---

[1] Clay, *Clay Family*, pp. 53–58, 78; Geo. Hudson's will, *Henry Clay MSS.*
[2] Taylor, J. B., *Virginia Baptist Ministers*, s. II, 91–92; Semple, R. B., *History of . . . the Baptists in Virginia*, pp. 110–21.
[3] Clay, in a speech of 1842, Littell, J. S., *The Clay Minstrel*, p. 72.
[4] Clay, *Clay Family*, pp. 7–8, and receipts issued 1780–81 to John Clay, and to his estate, for foodstuffs supplied the army, *Hanover Public Claims*, Virginia Archives; also, for Revolutionary activities in Hanover, Force, Peter, compiler, *American Archives*, 4th series, vol. II.

Through Hanover in the spring of 1781 swept the terrifying cry of 'Tarl'ton's coming! Tarl'ton's coming!' Defeated at Saratoga, forced to evacuate Philadelphia, alarmed at the 'unnatural' alliance with France, the British had invested their war policy with frightfulness and desolation. Henry Clay's neighborhood became the seat of their operations. It was the arena for Lord Cornwallis, the raiding and looting ground for the fleet horsemen of Banastre Tarleton, who had given to ravaged Carolina 'Tarl'ton's quarter' — no quarter, no mercy.

While Jefferson, the war governor, vainly called for Continental troops, and the Treasurer of Virginia at his Hanover estate slept in his coach ready to be off in a twinkling, the brilliant and cruel Tarleton harried the land. His green-jacketed Dragoons mounted on Virginia race-horses were veritable birds of prey, 'falcons swift and fell.' A sudden dash on Charlottesville bagged Daniel Boone, Long Hunter from Virginia's District of Kentucky, and drove Patrick Henry and other legislators to the safety of the Blue Ridges and to the scorn of the mountaineers. To and fro in Hanover County galloped Tarleton's Dragoons, Hessian Yagers, and Simcoe's Queen's Rangers. Panic-stricken were the Clays and their Whig neighbors by the fire, rape, and carnage of the unimpeded invaders, and the vindictive and plundering Tory rabble in their train — 'enormities that fill the mind with horror... such terror and confusion... Governor, Council, everyone scampering.' [1]

While Virginia Light Dragoons at Hanover Court House were reporting to Jefferson that they had but sixty horse to oppose the enemy's five hundred, and that 'the mounted militia are all gone home except Capt. Royall, whose time is out next Thursday,' [2] the warehouse at Hanovertown, seven miles down the Pamunkey, with the greater part of the York country tobacco, went up in smoke. Then Tarleton with his usual secrecy and swiftness dashed into Hanover Court House, destroyed military stores, sacked houses, and applied the torch.

---

[1] Carrington, Mrs. Betsy Ambler (daughter of Treasurer Ambler), 'An Old Virginia Correspondence,' *Atlantic Monthly*, LXXXIV, 508–09, 538. Governor Jefferson was severely criticized, Eckenrode, H. J., *The Revolution in Virginia*.

[2] *Calendar of Virginia State Papers*, II, 118–19, May 26, 1781.

Amid this martial hubbub and terror, at Clay's Spring three miles away, a great personal sorrow had settled — John Clay, man of God and defiant crusader for freedom, had died. But even here Tarleton's cavalrymen wantonly ransacked the kitchen, broke open chests, and filled the air with the feathers of fat bedticks. Frightened slaves, turkeys, cattle, and whinnying horses were driven down the road. Roistering Dragoons even thrust their swords into the fresh grave of John Clay, thinking it held treasure. It was only then that the appeals of the widow caused Tarleton, 'Cornwallis's hunting leopard,' to order off his British marauders. Clinging to his mother, Henry Clay, a boy of four, witnessed these scenes with eyes that never forgot.[1]

Mars's hurricane had about spent itself. After a decade of protest and fighting, Britain's trans-Atlantic frontier had independence well within grasp. In the Pamunkey Valley of Hanover, which led down to Yorktown and Chesapeake Bay, Lord Cornwallis was outwitted time and again by blithe young Lafayette's marches and pseudo-marches. His lordship was forced to concede that the colonial rabble-in-arms, especially the Virginia militia, was 'not wholly contemptible.' [2] At Yorktown that fall of 1781 he found himself encompassed by a French fleet and by Washington's Franco-American army. It was then that the Whigs of Hanover — where Henry Clay, child of the Revolution, still mourned for his dead father — joined in the jubilant and victorious cry of the war-born young republic: 'Cornwallis is taken! Cornwallis is taken!'

In the days following Cornwallis's surrender the traveller going from Richmond to Fredericksburg and the north rode out Brooke Road and soon entered many-streamed, well-wooded, Hanover County where Piedmont merges into Tidewater. After pausing for a noggin of grog at Merry Oaks Tavern, he passed secluded manors of the gentry and rude cabins of the poor whites, skirted pine forests and pine 'slashes,' tobacco and corn clearings, forded Machump's Creek near the Clay homestead, and finally arrived at

---

[1] Clay, *Clay Family*, pp. 14–19; also, Littell, *op. cit.*, p. 72.
[2] Stevens, B. F., ed., *The Campaign in Virginia, 1781*, II, 34.

Hanover Court House. At the end of some twenty miles of execrable road, he gladly tarried at the large and comfortable inn facing the brick courthouse in this county seat of some seven or ten scattered houses.

The post-Revolutionary traveller found the tavern porch well plastered with miscellaneous notices, of runaway slaves, truant wives, and auctions. If it chanced to be court day perhaps he joined Hanover's judges in wines and other polite liquors — which often made Justice nod and drop her scales. If election day, he found the usual bucolic tranquillity shattered by partisan zeal and the free grog given by the candidates. A surging crowd surrounded the platform on the green on which sat the judges, candidates, and recording clerk. 'I vote for you, sir,' a freeholder would shout, naming his candidate. 'Thank you, sir,' would be the response. 'May you live a thousand years.' As the voting became close, and the whiskey sank in the barrel, disorders arose. All too frequently a trivial epithet such as 'thick Skull, Buckskin, or lubber' was enough to start brutal affrays — 'so loathesome and horrible!' — from which a citizen might emerge disfigured for life, an eye gouged out, the tip of his nose bitten off.[1]

Abandon and gusto characterized the infrequent gatherings of Henry Clay's rural neighbors — a people 'all very *learned* in horses & pedigrees & making Mint Slings & Juleps in the morning & toddy all day.'[2] Drinking was deep and prolonged. Cock-fighting was enjoyed by slave and gentleman. And as for horse-racing, earlier decreed a sport for gentlefolk only, everyone seemed to be grooming a winner for the quarter-mile straightaways and the Jockey Club meetings in Hanover, Bowling Green, Powhatan, or Richmond. Betting was heavy on horses and cocks, and at brag,

---

[1] For a particularly vivid account of election day in Hanover in 1778, see Watson, Elkanah, *Men and Times of the Revolution*, p. 71; also Munford, G. W., *The Two Parsons*, etc., pp. 208–11; and Munford, R., *Plays and Poems*, sketch entitled 'The Candidates, or the Humours of a Virginia Election.' All visitors commented upon 'the Diabolical custom of gouging' — 'biting, gouging, and [sometimes] Abelarding each other.' For contemporary life see Latrobe, B. H., *Journal*, pp. 1–64; the works listed under Chastellux, La Rochefoucauld-Liancourt, Fifthian, Schoepf, Brissot de Warville, Anburey, Davis, Weld, Sutcliffe, Melish, Smyth, Riedesel, Asbury, and the files of the *Virginia Gazette* and the *Richmond and Manchester Advertiser*. Of interest is Rosewell Page, *Hanover County — Its History and Legends*.

[2] Mrs. Wm. Thornton's diary of a Virginia tour, 1805, *William Thornton MSS.*

loo, and finger in danger, despite laws prohibiting losses at gaming of more than twenty dollars within twenty-four hours. Bluff free-livers, these Virginians, and boastfully independent. So commented Old World visitors, who invariably remarked that the men most meticulous of their own rights were the masters of enslaved Negroes, these republicans who but recently had won their seven years' war for 'life, liberty, and the pursuit of happiness.'

Slavery, the great paradox of the new Age of Liberty, was here firmly established. In Henry Clay's county there were eight thousand blacks to but six thousand whites. Yet foreign liberals who were shocked by slave huts at Mount Vernon and Monticello found the evils of the peculiar system fully acknowledged by Washington and Jefferson; by the men of Hanover who in 1774 cited the slave trade against George the Third; by John Clay's Baptists, who in 1789 resolved human bondage inconsistent with divine and natural laws; and by George Wythe, who at William and Mary College instructed Virginia's youth in the 'sacred cause' of gradual emancipation. Even so, the Old Dominion remained inactive under Wythe's preaching and Jefferson's prophecies of a God of 'exterminating thunder.'[1] Added to the perplexities inherent in the problem was alarm inspired by recurring slave revolts in the French West Indies. In 1793 slavery was definitely incised into Southern economy by a Yankee contraption separating cotton from its seed, which caused forest lands of the Lower South to give way to ever-widening white fields over which ruled King Cotton and his black minions.

Despite slave exploitation, Virginia's many-acred squires, for the most part, were congenial to the romantic libertarianism of this revolutionary epoch. Her exclusively agricultural economy induced her political theorists to regard the farmer as the one secure basis for republicanism, and to view with parochial distrust capitalistic exploiters and the mobs of great cities. A vigorous individualism was here fostered which found expression in Virginia's pioneer sons who conquered the frontier, and in her astonishing number of distinguished public men. Virginia's range was narrow, perhaps, yet within the field of law and politics, of oratory and

[1] Jefferson, *Works*, ed. P. L. Ford, V, 72, IV, 447–49.

statesmanship, she was supreme. Furthermore, her plantation society tended to induce fine manners, an open-handed hospitality, and a simple sense of truth untainted by the shoddy casuistry of the market-place. There was here a 'Virginia gentility' which young Henry Clay inherited, and which, 'as it ripened with his years, made him an idol among Northern and Western multitudes who knew neither the source nor secret of his charm.' [1]

'Here I find great vices, but greater virtues,' remarked a critical Yankee of this slave-supported Virginia commonwealth, in the tradition of the Greek and Roman republics. 'There is one single trait that attaches me... more than all the virtues of New England. They *love money less* than we do.... They are more disinterested. Their patriotism is not tied to their purse-strings.... Could I only take from the Virginians their *sensuality* and their *slaves*, I should think them the greatest people in the world.' [2]

In this post-bellum Old Dominion, where Henry Clay 'was raised and nurtured a Republican' in the agrarianism of Jefferson and the nationalism of Wythe, there were many contrasts — poor whites and rich planters, naked young Negroes and silk-gowned fine ladies, homespun gougers and duelling dandies, religious yelpers and deistic liberals in the vanguard of the Age of Reason. At the great houses, remarked the Marquis de Chastellux, you could count on a gracious welcome, elaborate wardrobes, gay sports of the turf and field; a sumptuous dinner, tea and syllabub in the afternoon, wines and agreeable conversation at an elegant little supper. If at Offley in Hanover, said this member of the French Academy, your sophisticated host was a rebel general and a signer of the Declaration of Independence who had been educated at Eton and Cambridge. If at Monticello in Albemarle, you were quite charmed with the author of the Declaration himself, most cultivated of humanitarians, most wide-ranging of intellectuals, who would discuss the poems of Ossian over a bowl of punch far into the night. Yet even in the manor houses, of a landed gentry patterned after old England's squirearchy, guests

---

[1] Adams, Henry, *History of the United States*, I, 134.
[2] Wm. Ellery Channing, 1798, then tutoring near Richmond; Channing, W. H., *Memoir of W. E. Channing*, I, 82–83.

complained of broken windows carelessly stuffed with rags, of crowded tables and bedrooms. Jefferson himself railed at leaky roofs and rats that ate his clothing and sheet music — his 'jemmy-worked silk garters, and half a dozen new minuets.'[1]

Though Virginia was famed for her blooded horses, travelling was a perilous adventure. Men flipped coins at crossroads, called for a compass, wandered all night lost in the woods between Alexandria and Mount Vernon; were marooned in snowdrifts, mired, upset, and bethumped in springless stages, and thought themselves fortunate at the end of a short journey if their saddle-horses had not been drowned or had their legs broken. The wise traveller went armed with pistols and bed-sheets, for often the road was infested by highwaymen, the water by Chesapeake and Potomac banditti, and the three-or-four-in-a-bed taverns with vermin.[2]

In Virginia, and throughout the former British colonies now loosely banded together in an American league of nations, the perils of travel were not less than the perils to which the New World experiment in republicanism was exposed. During Henry Clay's youth, America's Union, like her stages, seemed to be 'risking an upset at every step.'[3]

'"The times that tried men's souls" are over,' wrote Thomas Paine, Propagandist of the Revolution, on the eighth anniversary of Lexington. 'But to pass from the extremes of danger to safety — from the tumult of war to the tranquillity of peace,' he warned,

---

[1] Jefferson, *Works*, I, 68, 434; Chastellux, *Travels*, II, 19, 42, 201.

[2] The farmhouse taverns are in 'the Virginia Stile — the people decent & obliging but everything dirty, surrounded by filthy and half-naked blacks & offended with all kinds of disagreeable odors.' From Washington to Fredericksburg: 'Good beds at Stafford Court House. Intolerable at Herndon's. Bad at Harris's. Abominable at Palmer's. Travellers on this road ought to take sheets with them . . . if not Sheets take a long wrapper from head to foot.' Mrs. Wm. Thornton's diary, 1805, *Thornton MSS.* 'Such a road and such a conveyance!' wrote British critic Tom Moore in 1804. 'The mail takes twelve passengers, which generally consist of squalling children, stinking negroes, and republicans smoking cigars!' Moore, T., *Memoirs*, ed. by Lord John Russell, I, 161–62. Yet even near Philadelphia Vice President Adams reported himself mired — 'Pegged like Ariel in a rifted oak, we can only sprawl in the air with our arms and legs, and fill the atmosphere with our cries and clamors.' Adams, J., *Letters Addressed to His Wife*, ed. C. F. Adams, II, 224–25.

[3] Moore, Thomas, *loc. cit.* 'How often has it occurred to me that nothing can be more emblematic of the government of this country than its stages, filled with a motley mixture, all "hail fellows well met," driving through mud and filth, which bespatters them as they raise it, risking an upset at every step.'

with unconscious irony, 'requires a gradual composure of the senses.' [1] Composure was slow in coming. In these confederated thirteen republics, freshly transformed if not transmuted from isolated British provinces, conditions were such as to further provincial patriotisms and to hamper reforms aimed at bringing national order out of revolutionary turmoil. Paine himself, stormy agitator of Europe and America, contributed largely to fill these formative years in the life of Henry Clay with the varied manifestations of a prolonged post-war psychology.

Conservatives lamented the general breakdown of authority in this new America of some four million 'free and equal' republicans — the emphasis upon rights rather than duties, the recklessness of the younger generation, the extravagance of war profiteers, the licentious spirit and disorganizing principles of the masses. No longer in Hanover were the bewigged vestrymen of Clay's parish of Saint Paul accorded homage as superior gentlefolk. At the Governor's Victory Ball after Yorktown the cotillion was led by a shoemaker's daughter! Religious freedom had been won, but there was now remarkably little religion. 'Iniquity abounds,' wailed Henry's cousin, the Reverend Eleazer Clay of Chesterfield. 'Deism prevails, and the spirit of the world comes in like a flood.' [2]

While the poets urged 'Columbia! Columbia! To glory arise!' General Washington on his princely Potomac estate three times put off the tax-collector; and General Nelson of York, with estates in Hanover of Offley (twelve thousand acres) and Bullfield (thirteen hundred acres) and lands in Saint Paul's Parish, now lived in a comparatively frugal manner. Such men agreed that America's ills came from too much democracy: the country which had thrown off King George was likely to be ruled by hydra-headed King Mob. They were alarmed by populist legislation. They were panic-stricken in 1786 when Shays's Rebellion of debt-ridden farmers in western Massachusetts seemed a prelude to a general proletarian revolt.

To check the disorganizing forces unleashed by the Revolution,

---

[1] Paine, T., Selections from... Thomas Paine, ed. C. Van Doren, p. 112.
[2] E. Clay, Baptist preacher, in Hovey, A., Rev. Isaac Backus, p. 293. See also, in general, the essays of J. Franklin Jameson, The American Revolution Considered as a Social Movement.

to replace the 'imbecilic' Confederation of bumptiously sovereign American republics by a national government acting directly with and upon the people, to weld an American Union that could command respect at home and abroad, a conservative counter-revolution was fought until the Constitution of 1787 was ratified. All-important was the assent of Virginia, greatest of the republics in area, population, and public men. In spite of Patrick Henry's magnificent States' Rights speeches, such national republicans as James Madison, George Nicholas, and George Wythe obtained Virginia's ratification. And in so doing they inspired the hopeful tidings: 'Arrived safe in port, the ship FEDERAL CONSTITU-TION, Perpetual Union, commander. In her came Flourishing Commerce, Public Faith, Confidence, Justice, General Prosperity, and National Energy.' [1]

Echoes of Virginia's famed Ratifying Convention of 1788 — with its masterly if logomachic discussions of the new Constitution's compromises as to political theories and sectional economic interests, and its possible sources of conflict between 'sovereign states' and a 'sovereign' federal government — drifted back from Richmond to Hanover when Henry Clay was a boy of eleven, a boy who was growing up on the Hudson homestead near Hanover Court House.

His childhood dwelling was a story-and-a-half frame building flanked by two massive stone chimneys, with slave quarters adjoining, situated on a gentle slope rising from Machump's Creek. It was typical of his family's middle-class stake in Virginia society. It was not comparable, to be sure, to General Nelson's Offley or to Scotchtown where dwelt Patrick Henry, and later Dolly Madison, yet it was far removed from the mud-chinked cabins of Hanover's poor whites. Here in these post-Revolutionary days young Henry did the chores common to country boys. Perhaps he sometimes rode astride a corn-laden farm-horse to the grist-mills on the Pamunkey River.[2] But he was neither an indentured miller's

---

[1] 'Ship News — Extra' of *Pennsylvania Packet* (Phila.), July 14, 1788. It was also announced: 'the sloop *Anarchy*... is ashore on the Rock of Union,' and 'the same day sailed the scow *Old Confederation*, Capt. Imbecility,' carrying away 'paper money, pine barren and tender acts — local prejudices, jealousies, and seeds of discord.'

[2] There are, however, the ruins of a grist-mill on the Hudson-Clay farm.

THE BIRTHPLACE OF HENRY CLAY

apprentice nor in the dire poverty of those possessing only 'the widow's and orphan's God' later ascribed to him, in poor-boy-to-greatness legends, by political admirers of 'Harry Clay, the Mill Boy of the Slashes.' [1]

Henry's mother did not long remain a widow nor he an orphan. Scarcely a year after Tarleton's raid and Sir John's death, his mother married Henry Watkins, a twenty-six-year-old planter and militia captain, the brother-in-law of her sister Mary. Elizabeth Clay was then about thirty-three, a widow in comfortable circumstances, still attractive despite the nine children she had borne her first husband, and the many tasks she performed as the mistress of five hundred fertile acres, thirty-two cattle, and a score of slaves. Small, well-rounded, dark of hair and eyes, engaging and friendly, with a good share of spirited independence, she was a kind and indulgent mother. As a child Henry learned from her of his father's struggles for 'soul liberty' and received elementary instructions which complemented his meagre Hanover schooling.[2]

In an abandoned clearing near the courthouse stood his Old Field School — a dirt-floored log cabin with pine slab benches and a huge fireplace which belched choking smoke on windy days. It was presided over by Peter Deacon, an Englishman more distinguished by his fondness for Virginia peach brandy than by his teaching. Under this bibulous itinerant sat Henry, clad in rough osnaburgs, his hair tied down his back in a pigtail; a flaxen-haired little boy, with a high forehead, alert, grayish-blue eyes, and a wide mouth that gave him difficulty in whistling. Aided by occasional thrashings from Master Peter he learned the three R's

---

[1] Elizabeth Clay from 1782 on was taxed, in Hanover, for 2 vehicles, 32 cattle, and (an average of) 16 slaves, in addition to the 464A Hudson homestead (of which she acquired the half interest of her sister Mary, the wife of John Watkins). Her land in the slashes, so-called, was unusually rich, being taxed at double the average rate. *Hanover Tax Lists, Tax Books, 1782–1792*, Virginia Archives. Legends as fallacious as the campaign biographers' poor, orphaned 'Mill Boy of the Slashes' are those which place Clay in an elegant Virginia 'Cavalier' setting: for example, see works listed under Z. F. Smith.

[2] From 1784 on, Elizabeth Clay's taxable property is listed under Henry Watkins, and the first of the seven children she bore Watkins was born in October, 1785 — disproving the story that for ten years she remained a widow and Henry an orphan. Only three of the nine Clay children lived beyond maturity: John, Henry, Porter; a son also named Henry was born before 1770 and died before 1777. Clay, *Clay Family*, pp. 18–30, 90; McIlhany, H. M., *Some Virginia Families*, p. 183.

as far as 'practise.' The drudgery of *Dilworth's Speller*, of ciphering and memorizing, was relieved by mimic Indian and Revolutionary battles, oratorical contests, and pranks played upon Peter Deacon. For three years Henry attended this Old Field School, completing during this brief period all of the formal education he was to receive.[1]

More significant than these scanty years of formal training was Hanover's tradition of great orators, of such notable spell-binders as Samuel Davies, the Presbyterian divine, William Winston, the uncle of Patrick Henry, and of course, the great Patrick himself. According to Virginians, Patrick Henry was 'the greatest orator who ever spoke.' His voice still hovered about Hanover's little brick courthouse where he had argued and won his lawsuits, and where he had sounded the trumpet of the Revolution. His ability to sway the people with his wizard words, to inflame them by his oratorical 'pillar of fire,' had made him Virginia's first republican governor and twice reelected him thereafter. Speakers on the courthouse green, the county's 'College of the Stump,' endeavored to win the highest praise Hanover could bestow — 'He is almost equal to Patrick Henry.' [2] Here, under the influence of the greatest of all Revolutionary orators, in a day when the speaker disseminated information and directed public opinion, when eloquence was the key to legal and political honors, young Henry Clay could not help being stimulated and guided in the choice of a career.

Declamation early became a passion with him. He recited, read aloud from political and historical works, and even practiced in the barn before the horses and oxen. He frequented Hanover's court and election-fields, and at home listened to the gossip of men to whom politics was the staple of conversation as tobacco was that of trade. He admired such neighbors as Colonel Thomas Tinsley, Hanover's delegate to the Virginia Assembly, and Major Parke Goodall, who had sat in the famous Virginia Ratifying Convention. But it was Patrick Henry whom he sought to emulate; it was Hanover's, and America's, great Demosthenes he held constantly before him as a model when he declaimed on the banks of

[1] Colton, Calvin, *Life and Times of Henry Clay*, I, 18–19.
[2] Wirt, Wm., *Patrick Henry*, p. 46; Henry, Wm. Wirt, *Patrick Henry*, I, 6, 12–16.

Machump's Creek, in silent pine forests, and in sun-bathed fields.

Throughout his youth this self-directed training continued, encouraging not only a fluency of speech, a passion for words and their magic, but an unusual self-confidence. Later, describing to a class of law graduates how ardently and persistently he had devoted himself to the study of oratory in Patrick Henry's Hanover, he paid tribute to 'this practice of the art of all arts.' To it, he said, 'I am indebted for the primary and leading impulses that stimulated my progress and have shaped and moulded my entire destiny.'[1]

A lively, sociable lad, Henry joined with his brothers and companions in the sports of the neighborhood, became an expert horseman, a good swimmer, and made some acquaintance with the fiddle, that popular instrument beloved of Jefferson and Patrick Henry. Tranquil yet pleasantly varied was his life on the Clay-Watkins plantation, a little community unto itself dozing in the Virginia sunshine, with its waving green fields and fragrant peach and apple orchards, its spirited horses, lowing cattle, and score of chattering blacks who responded to such names as Caesar and Bob, Dinah, Dilce, Annaka. He assisted Captain 'Hal' Watkins in conveying their prime York River tobacco — 'sweet-scented, the best in the world' — to the warehouse at Hanover-town where Grandfather George Hudson had been inspector. With Little Sam and Jim, two servants willed to him by Sir John Clay as his very own, tow-headed, slender, and wiry Master Henry tramped the woods, hunted, and fished. Once, according to tradition, he discovered a runaway slave in hiding, became fond of him, smuggled him food; when the likable fellow later was killed in resisting arrest, he wept disconsolately.[2] Such an incident brought home to a sensitive boy the human elements interwoven through the runaway notices in the Richmond journals, each embellished with a woodcut of the Devil, pitchfork in hand, chasing fugitive black Caesars, Pompeys, and Catos.

---

[1] Peck, C. H., *The Jacksonian Epoch*, p. 17.

[2] Rogers, Joseph M., *The True Henry Clay*, p. 30. Also, for boyhood reminiscences by Clay: Colton, *Clay*, I, 27; and Clay, Henry, *Works*, ed. Colton, VIII, 197.

When the hue and cry over runaways, and the excitement of election and court day, had subsided, and the little hamlet had resumed its habitual drowsiness, he frequented Mr. Tilghman's Hanover ordinary — in the taproom of which Patrick Henry had once assisted his innkeeper father-in-law.

Travellers of all conditions here arrived, gossiped, and departed. Tall, freckled, and dignified Mr. Jefferson, so Henry learned, was by easy stages and with a pleasantly observant eye making his way to the Federal capital at Philadelphia; stern-faced, psalm-singing Bishop Asbury was planting Sunday Schools and nursing his infant Methodist Church; while jovial, roguish Mason Weems, fiddle-playing parson turned author and book-seller, from his Jersey wagon was dispensing synthetic patriot-lore and melodramatic tracts entitled *God's Revenge Against Gambling, The Drunkard's Looking-Glass,* and *Hymen's Recruiting Sergeant,* or *The New Matrimonial Tattoo for Bachelors.* General Washington, the great hero himself (not yet embalmed in Parson Weems's cherry-tree story), often put up at the Hanover tavern, staying the night, leaving with impressive military precision at sunrise, and arriving at the Virginia capital at noon. To his guests one and all Mr. Tilghman told how he had lodged Lord Cornwallis without his lordship's making the least recompense, and how his Whig patrons in the spring of 1781 had scattered to the four winds when a wild-eyed Negro galloped up shouting, 'Tarl'ton's coming! Tarl'ton's coming!' [1]

Henry's Pamunkey Valley country was rich in varied lore. It had been the setting for Powhatan and Pocahontas; for Captain John Smith who planted, and Lord Cornwallis who relinquished, Britain's first overseas colony. Yet tales of the War for Independence most appealed to this child of the Revolution, who with his own eyes had seen in dreadful activity Simcoe's Queen's Rangers and Tarleton's Dragoons. In his war-ravaged neighborhood there were many vivid reminders of the British invader — and of the French ally, for when swimming at the Pamunkey Henry could trace out 'l'Avocat' and 'le Démoniaque' on the French brass cannon thrown there by Tarleton at the time of his father's death. [2]

---

[1] Chastellux, *Travels,* II, 14.

[2] These cannon were noted by Schoepf, J. D., *Travels,* II, 46.

At the Clay hearth, over a hot toddy, veterans on their way to Richmond recounted to Henry and his brothers tales of that 'prodigy of nature,' Patrick Henry, and of Lord Dunmore, Virginia's last royal governor, with his Indian incitements and Loyal Ethiopian Legion of runaway slaves. They told of Morgan's Virginia Rifles at Quebec and Saratoga, and of the peerless George Rogers Clark, whose backwoods Virginia army had conquered the Northwest from the British and their Indian allies. Not to be outdone by mere soldiers, John Kilby spun yarns about Virginia's navy under Commodore O'Brien (now, alas, imprisoned by Barbary corsairs); the daring exploits of young Joshua Barney; and especially about that prince of sea-fighters, John Paul Jones (who had lived near Fredericksburg), under whom Kilby himself had fought and carried the American flag into the very chops of the British Channel — ''twas Jones, brave Jones, to battle led, as bold a crew as ever bled.' [1]

Current happenings, also, were stimulating to an impressionable boy. A neighbor's son, Lewis Littlepage, after having fought England at the siege of Gibraltar was then adventuring about Europe — a warrior against the Turks, a paramour of Catherine the Great, chamberlain to Stanislaus (last king of a Poland that was being criminally swallowed up by the monarchs of Russia, Prussia, and Austria), and colleague of Kosciusko, the gallant but ill-fated Polish nationalist. From far-off Cathay the *Empress of China* and the *Grand Turk*, flying the colors of the New World republic, had returned with fantastic tales of the Celestial Empire, and of fabulous profits there for America's seafaring pioneers. On the Potomac a marvellous new boat propelled by steam was being demonstrated. From the capitol at Richmond the balloon of M. Busselot, pioneer aeronaut, had recently sailed through the skies as far as Captain John Austin's Hanover plantation. [2]

Henry Clay, child of the Revolution and of Jefferson's Old

---

[1] Kilby, J., 'Narrative,' *Scribner's Magazine*, XXXVIII, 23–41; and Henry, W. W., *P. Henry*, for war stories popular in Hanover — the giant Tory-killer, Peter Francisco; Captain Jack Jouett's famous ride from Cuckoo Tavern to warn the legislators of Tarleton's advance; the ludicrous figure cut by Captain John Symes, Patrick Henry's half-brother, when Tarleton captured him in his nightshirt; etc.

[2] Henry, W. W., *op. cit.*, II, 267–69, on Littlepage; Stanard, M. N., *Richmond, Its People and Its Story*, p. 54, on Busselot, in 1785–86.

Dominion, was growing up in an age of gestation, of revolt, transition, and varied pioneering in both the New World and the Old.

Europe was then on the eve of the French Revolution — disgusted with the picture of its parasite rulers drawn by Voltaire; agitated by *philosophes* vehement for the glories of reason and peace; stirred by the anarchism of Godwin, 'the greatest happiness of the greatest number' of Bentham, the economic liberalism of the French physiocrats and Adam Smith; inspired by the roseate picture of America's republic drawn by Tom Paine, and by the levelling ideas and brilliant sophistries of Jean Jacques Rousseau. The social pioneers of France were about to unfurl the banners of a romanticized Age of Reason. New rulers, 'the counterparts of Aristides and Cato, Brutus and Cicero,' were to spread new ideas and faiths, in theory democratic and pacific, at the point of French bayonets and in the shadow first of Robespierre's guillotine and, later, of a modern Caesar who was to bestride Europe like Colossus.

America, socially adventurous also, was impatiently forming new institutions to replace the British colonialism she had so gloriously wrecked. Revolutionary romantics, who emphasized States' Rights and individual liberty, were being balanced by Constitutional realists, who insisted upon national duties and social order. A new federal empire was being constructed, capable of continental expansion. A new national government, vitalized by the administrative genius of Hamilton, was beginning to counteract the centrifugal forces that had prevailed against the former British imperialism. Territorially adventurous, America was beginning the conquest of the wilderness empire at her back door. An unprecedented mass migration was just then getting fairly under way; a surging westward flood of peoples which was to roll onward for generations to come. While the Old World was convulsed with the tumult of pen and sword, this great conquering wave of men against Nature — and against Indians, Britons, and Spaniards as well — was to flow over mountains and spread over a continent, leaving in its wake flourishing farms and towns, a new society, the America of the future, conditioned by the wilderness which it subdued and conquered.

To the West, as Henry Clay well knew, lay the land of promise.

Descriptions of Kentucky's bluegrass meadows made Hanover's long-tilled tobacco lands appear barren and desolate. Within a few years of his migration Captain John Watkins, Henry's uncle, had become a wealthy proprietor of the Kentucky town of Versailles, a large landholder, and a legislator. Every day Hanover neighbors were striking out. They were advised to avoid the Ohio River route because of the Indian wars then raging. But they were told that the roads west from Hanover Court House were generally good and crossing the mountains not too difficult, although a particularly sharp watch must be maintained in Cumberland Gap and along Boone's Wilderness Trace for marauding redskins and border outlaws. Once at the Crab Orchard they were safe. And when they arrived in the Western metropolis of Lexington, in the famed Blue Grass, they were in a position to survey and to begin their individual conquests of the vast and virgin Western World.[1]

Succumbing to this contagious Western fever, Elizabeth and Henry Watkins in 1791 decided to pull up their Virginia stakes and try their fortunes in the fertile fields of frontier Kentucky. Young Henry was to be left behind in the Old Dominion. He was now a good-sized boy of fourteen, ambitious and self-reliant, with a predilection for the law and a passion for oratory. It was arranged that he would be placed as a clerk in Richard Denny's store in Richmond, but only until Colonel Tinsley could get him an assistantship under his brother, Peter Tinsley, Clerk of the Virginia High Court of Chancery.

While his family prepared for the great adventure westward, Henry in 1791 went on to Richmond hopeful and eager.

Canvas-topped, gaudily painted Blue Ridge wagons joggled briskly through the little town of Richmond, Virginia's capital, where Henry Clay, rustic lad from the Hanover slashes, had become a mercantile clerk. High-stepping horses bedizened with bearskin mantillas, jingling harness-bells, and rosettes of red and

---

[1] For post-Revolutionary migrations from Hanover, see Journal of William Brown, in Speed, T., *Wilderness Road*, pp. 17–20; and the account of John Watkins's journey to Kentucky in 1785, in Harper, L.D.V.C., *Colonial Men and Times*, pp. 129–33.

yellow galloon were noisily hallooed by bearded, whip-cracking wagoners over muddy thoroughfares to the stores on Main Street, Richmond's Brick Row. Before crossing the pontoon bridge spanning the James, some of these lumbering land schooners had been weeks on forest roads with their cargoes of hemp, furs, ginseng, beeswax, and whiskey. Sometimes they brought in dried rattlesnakes which were used, so Denny's new clerk discovered, for a medicinal brew called viper's broth. Even more fascinating to Henry was the miscellany brought in by West Indian brigs, Baltimore schooners, and tall-masted ships from the Old World — all of them in quest of Virginia tobacco — to Richard Denny's, to Hugh Hayes-near-the-Bridge, and to William Waddell at the Sign of the Thirteen Stars.

After arranging their shelves, Clay and other clerks attended to the wants of Richmond's ladies who came to Brick Row on the river's edge, billowing gowns in full sail, silk shoes protected by wooden clogs, their curiosity whetted by notices in the *Gazette* and the *Advertiser*. For them there were bell-hoops and Italian stays, ribands, exquisite perfumes, and Parisian bonnets; for their husbands and brothers Merry Andrew playing cards, approved London books and apparel, fine old Boston rum, and imported wines and brandies which kindled the eye of Virginia epicures. Seldom did Henry and his fellow clerks receive cash, and that commonly in foreign coins — Spanish doubloons and pieces of eight, French écus, Dutch florins, Arabian sequins. Customers generally paid in tobacco warehouse receipts and produce, sometimes in warrants and public securities at a reasonable discount. In the fall, trade was brisk when planters and legislators with their families arrived for the social season and the opening of the Virginia Assembly.[1]

An unusual bustle and stir then animated the little metropolis. Lawmakers and lawyers gathered in groups on Main Street below, and Broad Street above, the pillared Greek-temple capitol Jefferson had designed. Tidewater aristocrats in smallclothes and lace furbelows rubbed elbows with homespun farmers and shirted

---

[1] Mordecai, S., *Richmond in By-Gone Days*, pp. 51–56, *passim*; Stanard, M. N., *Richmond*, pp. 69–70; Munford, G. W., *The Two Parsons*, etc., pp. 83–84, *passim*; files of *Virginia Gazette* and *Richmond and Manchester Advertiser*. For a reference by Clay to his storekeeping days, Smith, M. B., *Forty Years of Washington Society*, ed. Gaillard Hunt, p. 207.

frontiersmen. There were saddled horses at every turn, with centaur-like Virginians mounting and remounting 'if only to fetch a prise of snuff from across the street.' The Eagle Tavern on Main Street, where one found the best accommodations in the South, the Swan, and Formicola's were filled with 'Generals, Colonels, Captains, Assemblymen, Judges, Doctors, Clerks, and crowds of Gentlemen of every weight and calibre and hue of dress.' Late arrivals slept on the floor, undisturbed, apparently, by the tosspots who made merry in the sanded barroom, 'drinking, smoking, singing, and talking ribaldry.' [1]

When Henry called at the capitol upon Thomas Tinsley, Hanover's delegate, he found the anteroom crowded with gossiping and bargaining people who freely criticized their assembled representatives. Within the Hall of Delegates there was a hum of voices, laughter, inattention, and the calling of members' names by the stentorian doorkeeper. Only a few of the legislators, as the sharp-eyed boy noted, proposed and debated measures. Yet the speeches he heard furnished him with excellent oratorical models. 'I have listened to these speeches with a great deal of pleasure,' commented a young New England divinity student, himself later a public speaker of national renown. 'The Virginians are the best orators I have ever heard.' [2]

More conscious than ever that politics and law, not huckstering trade, were the royal highroads to fame and fortune, Henry eagerly awaited his release from Richard Denny's emporium. And release came after several months as a clerk with yardstick and scales. Just before his family began their long trek to Kentucky, he obtained the desired post under Peter Tinsley, the Clerk of Chancery. For one ambitious to become a lawyer, this was a promising connection. Yet Henry's first appearance in the Chancery office in the basement of the Virginia capitol was such as to provoke derisive laughter.

He had dressed himself in his best suit of Virginia ('figinny') pepper-and-salt cloth, and his linen was starched to a brave yet

---

[1] Schoepf, *Travels*, II, 55–65; see, also, the interesting account of Richmond at this time by La Rochefoucauld-Liancourt, *Travels*, II, 31 ff.

[2] Channing, W. H., *Memoir of Wm. E. Channing*, I, 96.

uncomfortable stiffness. To the Chancery clerks, however, he appeared as a gawky country boy of fifteen, with a mouth that seemed split from ear to ear, ludicrous in unfashionable homespuns, his breeches ill-fitting, his broad-tailed coat flapping about his lanky frame. They were disposed to haze the newcomer, but they soon discovered that he had a ready tongue that could be both witty and caustic. It was dangerous to ridicule Harry Clay. Their tendency to do so was disarmed, moreover, by his friendliness and exuberant spirits. Two of the copyists, Thomas Williamson and William Sharp, were from Hanover. With their help the newcomer quickly adapted himself to the dress of Richmond and to life in this legal and political center of the Old Dominion.[1]

Here in the Chancery office at the Virginia capitol young Henry (as he declared) for some years was to be immersed, 'to live,' in an atmosphere of oratory and electioneering, of speech-making and legal debating.[2] Virginia's high courts and legislative halls were to be his preparatory school, giving him a training far more congenial than that of musty books and studious drudgery. He came into daily contact with Virginia's public men, and heard the gossip of lawyers and legislators — not only as to clients and voters but as to summer outings at Green or Sweet Springs; the latest in *bons mots* and cravats; the proper and the unpardonable in social address; the Richmond season of balls, christenings, weddings, and Jockey Club races. Most of his companions were studying law, some as assistants in the courts, others as apprentices in law offices. In their social activities they reflected the holiday mood of the planters and public men who made the most of their visits to the Virginia metropolis, as well as the convivial tone of Richmond's distinguished bar. These embryonic lawyers and politicians were noted for their gaiety and sometimes for their 'excessive dissipation.'[3]

When free of their duties Henry and his new companions played brag and billiards, bet on the races and smoked cigars, had beer-

---

[1] Colton, *Clay*, I, 20.

[2] Henry Clay to Ninian Edwards, July 9, 1800, Edwards, N., *Papers*, ed. E. B. Washburne, p. 23.

[3] Jos. Cabell to John Breckinridge, May 20, 1800, *Breckinridge MSS.*; also, on Clay's companions, Grigsby, H. B., *Littleton W. Tazewell*, pp. 37 ff.

and-oyster junkets, and displayed their skill in parlor games: in Copenhagen, says pleasant tradition, the tow-headed, provocative boy from Hanover was singled out to be kissed by the girls more often than his fellows.[1] The son of the Reverend John Clay embraced the prevailing deistic rationalism: conventional religion was neglected, unfashionable, regarded as base superstition or gross hypocrisy, incompatible with the new republican Age of Reason and its revolt against 'the crimes of tyrants and the fanaticism of priests.' [2] Far more exciting, and genteel, were the high stakes hazarded at the taverns by John Marshall, James Monroe, and other lawyers; the rope-walking Great Saxon at the Shockhoe Hill Theatre; and such plays as *The Beggar's Opera* and *The World's Ups and Downs* — which Henry and his friends thoroughly enjoyed even if the strolling players sometimes were tipsy, read their parts, or were loudly cursed by the prompter. They huzzaed General Washington and acclaimed his Roman valor and constancy when he arrived in 1791 in his ornate coach-and-four to inspect the new canal at the falls of the James. They cheered Fourth of July orators who extolled Parisian *sans-culottes* as well as the heroes of the late war against George the Third. On the anniversary of Independence they accompanied the blue-jacketed, black-helmeted, Richmond Light Infantry to Buchanan's Spring, and there helped them empty their famous thirty-two-gallon punch bowl, while the grove rang with repeated huzzas and the blowing of bugles.

In this gay and hospitable Richmond, young William Ellery Channing, although disturbed by the loose Deism which contrasted so sharply with Massachusetts' taut Puritanism, said he could not but prefer as against the selfish prudence of the Yankee the Virginian's generous if sometimes imprudent confidence in his fellow man and the warm friendliness of his social relations. 'They

---

[1] Rogers, *Clay*, p. 23.

[2] 'The pure Deism' which prevailed 'contributed no small degree to the Revolution and' to America's 'unfettered constitutions of freedom and tolerance.' Chastellux, *op. cit.*, II, 197. Also, Channing, W. H., *op. cit.*, I, 122–26. The Reverend Devereux Jarratt (*Life, written by himself*, p. 124 ff.), attributed the 'noxious weed of infidelity' less to Voltaire and Paine than to ignorant, whooping, shirt-sleeved Baptists, an opinion deriving support from the character of the Reverend John Clay's successors in Hanover (see Semple, *op. cit.*, pp. 110 ff.).

address each other and converse together with the same familiarity and frankness which they used to do when they were boys. How different from our Northern manners! There avarice and ceremony at the age of twenty graft the coldness and unfeelingness of age on the disinterested ardor of youth.' [1] Swiss-born, French-speaking Albert Gallatin long remembered how warmly he had been welcomed in Richmond. 'Every one with whom I became acquainted appeared to take an interest in the young stranger,' said Gallatin. 'Every one encouraged me and was disposed to promote my success.' [2] Henry Clay's reception was similar. Not long after his appointment as an assistant Chancery clerk he received material encouragement from the great George Wythe, sole Chancellor of Virginia.

To the mean surroundings of Virginia's High Court of Chancery in the basement of the capitol impressive dignity was given by this man of whom Jefferson, his student and foster-son, said, 'His virtue was of the purest tint, his integrity inflexible, and his justice exact.' Mr. Wythe was a small, erect old man, with keen blue eyes above a beaked nose, his domelike head entirely bald except for a fringe of crisp gray curls that lightly fell upon the standup collar of his Quakerish drab coat. He was Virginia's most distinguished jurist, yet about him was none of 'the coldness and unfeelingness of age.' To young Clay, the Chancellor's countenance was always full of 'blandness and benevolence.' [3]

About this time, however, there flared up in Wythe the hot blood of his colonial youth. Justice Pendleton, an old rival, had reversed some of his decisions. He proceeded to write a counterblast, but his trembling hand was unequal to the task, and young Henry was selected to take his dictation. An intimate, and for

---

[1] Channing, W. H., *op. cit.*, I, 82.

[2] Gallatin, A., *Writings*, ed. Henry Adams, II, 659–60.

[3] Clay to Benj. B. Minor, May 3, 1851, a long letter on his association with Wythe, in Minor, B. B. ed., *Decisions of Cases in Virginia by the High Court of Chancery*, pp. xxxii–xxxvi of the introductory sketch of Wythe. See also, Jefferson, *Writings*, I, 165–70, *passim*; and sketches of Wythe (1726–1806) by L. G. Tyler, L. S. Herrink; obituaries in *Virginia Argus* and Richmond *Enquirer*, June, 1806; and Munford, G. W., *The Two Parsons*, etc., chaps. xxii, xxviii. Wythe has never received adequate attention: 'The truth is,' wrote St. George Tucker to William Wirt in 1813, 'that Socrates himself would pass unnoticed and forgotten in Virginia.' Kennedy, J. P., *William Wirt*, I, 352–55.

GEORGE WYTHE

Clay a most significant, connection was thus formed. Henceforth much of his time was spent with the Chancellor as his private secretary, writing down his decisions and his correspondence with the great men of the day. A likable boy, eager and quick to learn, attentive and courteous, he soon became a protégé of George Wythe, the noblest and one of the most influential men in Virginia's Golden Age.

From a spendthrift colonial rake, the boon companion of Fauquier, the dice-rattling royal governor, Wythe had become a republican sage, most learned, most respected. A signer of the Declaration, an able member of the Continental Congress, he had helped to frame the Constitution of 1787 at Philadelphia and then, at Richmond in 1788, had helped to overcome a strong States' Rights opposition. With Pendleton he had led the colonial bar: the youthful Jefferson had spent five years in his law office. As Professor of Law at William and Mary he had taught not only Jefferson and Marshall, but James Monroe, Spencer Roane, and John Wickham, George Nicholas, John Breckinridge, the Browns of Kentucky, and a host of public leaders. He had disseminated the English and French liberalism which had permeated and given tone to America's Revolutionary generation. A profound scholar of catholic tastes, as Chancellor he was fearlessly independent in a transitional period when the people carried over into the new epoch colonial antagonisms to central control, governors, and judges. In more than one notable decision he had boldly restricted overweening legislators to their constitutional limits. He was popularly known as 'The American Aristides.'

In private life Judge Wythe was shy, reserved, somewhat eccentric; a childless widower noted (despite his niggardly republican salary) for his charities and for his interest in young men who aspired to legal and political honors. The fatherless Thomas Jefferson, among others, had profited by his paternal instructions. Now, by singular good fortune, the fatherless and untutored Henry Clay had become the object of his affectionate guidance. From his sixteenth to his twenty-first year the ambitious and impressionable boy had in George Wythe a counsellor and a mentor.

A new world was opened up to the former pupil of Peter Deacon, although the road he travelled was hard beset by the Greek and Latin quotations with which the Chancellor salted his dictation. Wythe fortified legal points with Juvenal's *Satires*, Quintilian's *Rhetoric and Oratory*, and the Whig *Essays* of the great John Locke; with Rutherford on Grotius, Archimedes on mathematics, Tooke and Purley on grammar. He freshened and vivified his decisions by anecdotes, often satiric, drawn from Petronius Arbiter's tales of decadent Rome, the amusing experiences of Tristram Shandy, and the schemes of Peter, Martin, and Jack in Dean Swift's *Tale of a Tub*. His new secretary was undergoing not only a course in law but one in history and literature.

Often the venerable judge would have the tow-headed youth rest from his copying while he explained some literary reference, pointed out the merits and defects of a particular work, or held him enthralled by reading Homer in sonorous Greek. He would discuss for Henry's edification the classical orators, compare the historians Thucydides and Herodotus, the dramatists Sophocles and Euripides, and expound his ideas on international relations, the Admirable Crichton, and the Epistles of Saint Paul. Once, when confronted with a petty suit in which the Widow Beverley claimed a carriage, the cap and boots provided for the coachman thereof, as well as a pipe of wine, Wythe petulantly exclaimed: 'Fine subjects for a HIGH Court of Chancery, are they not?' Always he found amusement in classical analogies to the tribulations of Virginia litigants. Sometimes he expressed mock chagrin because his published decisions were not best-sellers in the bookstalls of Richmond.[1]

Despite his 'compleat knowledge of the dead languages and all the sciences,' [2] Wythe, ever the student, was then learning Hebrew

[1] Wythe's decisions (dictated to Clay), in Minor, *op. cit.*; and Clay's letter to Minor of May 3, 1851 (*ibid.*, pp. xxxii–xxxvi) on his intimate association with Wythe.

[2] Major William Pierce of Georgia, describing Wythe in the Constitutional Convention of 1787, at Philadelphia: 'Mr. Wythe is the famous Professor of Law... confessedly one of the most learned legal Characters of the present age... of general learning he has acquired a compleat knowledge of the dead languages and all the sciences. He is remarked for his exemplary life and is universally esteemed for his good principles. No Man, it is said understands the history of Government better than Mr. Wythe, nor any man who understands the fluctuating conditions to which all societies are liable... yet from his too favorable opinion of Men, he is no great politician. He is a neat and pleasing Speaker, and a most correct and able Writer.' Tansill, C. C., compiler, *Documents Illustrative of the Formation of the Union*, p. 104.

under his friend, Rabbi Seixas. He was ever the teacher. Not content with having at William and Mary instructed and moulded future presidents, justices, senators, and governors, he even taught Greek and Latin to one of his Negro boys. He encouraged his young secretary's interest in law and politics, and directed his reading. Upon Henry and other law students of Richmond, who were privileged to use his extensive library, the Chancellor urged careful, serious study. 'Don't skim it,' he would admonish. 'Read deeply and ponder what you read. They begin to make lawyers now without the *viginti annorum* lucubrations of Lord Coke. They are mere skimmers of the law, and know little else.' [1]

Perhaps, as one of Clay's fulsome biographers states, the Chancellor beheld in his secretary 'the genius of an aspiring, all-grasping mind'; he had only to name a book to Henry and the next day or so he would find the boy 'not only possessed of its contents but ... extending his thoughts far beyond his instructors.' [2] One suspects, however, that Wythe's protégé often 'skimmed.' Although diligent and hard-working, he was a lively, pleasure-loving boy, well acquainted with those scions of Virginia's tobacco aristocracy, those 'young bloods of the metropolis,' who for a brief period 'smoked segars in a lawyer's office in Richmond' and thus obtained their 'bird's-eye view of Blackstone and the Revised Code.' [3]

In truth, Henry was not destined to be a Wythe, a painstaking scholar, a calm and impartial judge. Rather he was to be an active partisan, a leader of men and causes, a maker of history, not a commentator. His talents, like those of untutored Patrick Henry, sprang naturally from the lush soil of the Old Dominion. They were nourished by the stirring events and Ciceronian declamation of the age — an age revolving about such public men as Washington and Jefferson, Hamilton, Adams, and Madison; Pitt and Fox,

---

[1] Munford, George Wythe, *The Two Parsons*, etc., pp. 363–64.
[2] Colton, *Clay*, I, 22–23.
[3] Kennedy, J. P., *Swallow Barn*, p. 28 — a sketch (by a Whig novelist and friend of Clay) of 'Frank Meriwether,' a Richmond law student at the turn of the century: 'He was a member of a Law Debating Society, which ate oysters once a week in a cellar; and he wore, in accordance with the usage of the most promising law students of that day, six cravats, one over the other, and yellow-topped boots, by which he was recognized as a blood of the metropolis.'

Sheridan, Burke, and Nelson; Mirabeau and Danton, Robespierre, Talleyrand, and Bonaparte. He was a child of his environment, a true son of this romantic and revolutionary epoch. He was ambitious, precocious even. Yet what fired him most was the personalities and issues of the day. He would rather debate them with his fellows, or listen and learn upstairs in Virginia's Assembly and superior courts, than read abstract treatises. He was much more interested in men, in lawyers and politicians, than in books on law and politics.

Of great moment, nevertheless, were these years of intimate association with the scholarly, and inspiring, George Wythe. For the first time the spirited boy from Hanover received training in disciplined study. Upon the foundations laid by bibulous Peter Deacon the Chancellor was erecting an invaluable, if somewhat irregular, superstructure. And Henry, who often recalled these days, 'when I was a white-headed boy in Mr. Wythe's office,' [1] was appreciative. 'To no man,' he would say, 'was I more indebted by his instructions, his advice, and his example.' [2]

As an example, an ideal, Wythe contributed much. The son of Sir John Clay was deeply impressed by the courtliness of this former colonial dandy, this republican sage of aristocratic breeding and manners. Mr. Wythe, Henry would often say, had the most graceful bow he had ever seen. He admired the suavity with which the scrupulous Chancellor returned gifts — on one occasion when he returned a demijohn of arrack and an orange tree to a neighbor, a West Indian nabob, Wythe courteously explained that his niece had no conservatory for the orange tree and that he himself had long ceased to have any use for arrack. Henry well remembered that bland 'ineffable smile' which lighted up his face when he mildly but firmly rebuked Bushrod Washington, then a Richmond attorney, for urging him to grant an injunction of questionable justice. Henry was flattered by the attentions of so great a man. He felt elevated, even if he did not always comprehend, when the good old gentleman would bring forth his phil-

---

[1] [Preston, Mrs. Wm. C.], 'Diary,' *The Land We Love*, III, 420. Clay often paid tribute to Wythe; for example, see Richmond *Enquirer*, Feb. 9, 12, 1822.

[2] Minor, *loc. cit.*, Clay to Minor, May 3, 1851.

osophical apparatus and conduct experiments for the instruction of his devoted band of young students.

Even the Chancellor's eccentricities — his early morning cold shower and four-mile walk, his absent-mindedness, his old-fashioned dress, his daily trips from the baker's to his home on Grace Street with a loaf of bread under his arm, his vegetarianism, his air-and-sun baths, his attempts to write with his left hand — all these only further endeared him to his hero-worshipping secretary and to a Richmond that taught its children to venerate Mr. Wythe as the very incarnation of justice and benevolence.

Not without its direct influence upon Henry was the sweet reasonableness which was the touchstone of the great man's character and philosophy. His rationalistic Deism, compounded of compassionate irony and brotherly love, strikingly contrasted with the 'heavenly confusion' of the Reverend Eleazer Clay. That gruff and 'aged saint' who lived over the river in Chesterfield would have been shocked to see Henry's Mr. Wythe of a Sunday at chess with Jefferson and Edmund Randolph; or to hear his remarks on contentious zealots who were given to 'beating their heads and embittering their hearts with disputes about forms of baptism and modes of faith.' [1] Impressed also upon the plastic youth were the Chancellor's views on gradual emancipation. Judge Wythe not only advocated the 'sacred cause' but put his ideas into practice, for he freed his Negroes and even bequeathed his property to them.

Often would he satirize mankind's veneration for outworn tradition, which even in America seemed 'so deeply rooted that the man who can rationally expect to live until it is eradicated ought to have antediluvian stamina.' A Revolutionary Father, he was also a Constitutionalist, a national republican, and far from being a half-cocked leveller. Yet he was convinced that the people were capable of self-government, in republican fashion; that national as well as sectional rivalries could be settled amicably; and, as he would say to young Clay, that republican America was pioneering a road to human betterment along which, eventually, would advance the oppressed peoples of the Old World. Already America

---

[1] Munford, *op. cit.*, pp. 466–67; Taylor, J. B., *Virginia Baptist Ministers*, s. I, 202–05; Conway, M. D., *Edmund Randolph*, p. 157.

had set an example to mankind by the bloodless, the refreshingly rational, manner in which she had transformed her nest of rival republics into a Constitutional Union. Other examples would be set by the progressive measures of the younger generation, Henry's generation of New World republicans.[1]

With characteristic independence, Wythe in one of his decisions declared void certain acts, in conflict with the Treaty of Peace, which permitted Virginians to evade payment of pre-Revolutionary British debts. Bitter protests were voiced. Had not 'perfidious Albion' violated the treaty from the very day she signed it? She had failed to restore Virginia's stolen slaves, or to evacuate British forts on American soil from Lake Champlain to Detroit, which made much of a presumably sovereign United States a British-Indian protectorate. Were not British agents at this very moment arming and inciting the Ohio Valley Indians, and 'British savages habited as Indians,' to those barbarous wars which had afflicted the West ever since 1775? George Wythe well deserved his title of 'Aristides' when he held that the sovereign state of Virginia must pay her British debts at a time when Henry Clay and other Virginians, incensed by ghastly 'British-Indian hostilities,' were demanding 'that spirit which of yore the British thunder stay'd, forbade their lion huge to roar, and low his fury laid.'[2]

Young Clay managed to squeeze into the crowded Federal courtroom at Richmond in May of 1793 when this burning issue was fought out before Chief Justice Jay by John Wickham, who headed the attorneys for the British creditors, and by Patrick Henry and John Marshall, who argued for States' Rights. It was one of the last of the great Patrick's oratorical efforts. Hanover's Demosthenes eloquently portrayed the plight of Virginia's patriotic debtors brought on by British wartime ravages, and then, most dramatically, ended his emotional storm by suddenly stop-

---

[1] Minor, *op. cit.*, pp. 283–84, *passim*.

[2] Munford, Wm., *Poems and Compositions in Prose*, p. 18; and, on British Debts, Minor, *op. cit.*, pp. xxi, 211–18; Harrell, I. S., *Loyalism in Virginia*; Bemis, S. F., *Jay's Treaty*. A British view of Clay's fellow Virginians was expressed by Thomas Moore, *Works*, II, 280:

> 'Those vaunted demagogues, who nobly rose
> From England's debtors to be England's foes,
> Who could their monarch in their purse forget,
> And break allegiance, but to cancel debt.'

ping and stretching forth his hands in mute appeal. In that tense moment one of the judges cried out: 'Gracious God! He is an orator indeed.' The Countess of Huntington, a spectator, effusively remarked that not only Patrick Henry but every lawyer who spoke that day would, in England, have deserved a peerage for his eloquence. Justice Iredell said the arguments he heard were unequalled for their ingenuity of reasoning and splendor of eloquence. Young Henry Clay thrilled with pride and admiration for the distinguished Virginia bar and the soul-stirring Patrick Henry.[1]

Such oratory as this aroused emulation in the debating society of which he had become a member.[2] Here in rivalry with the Virginia capital's budding lawyer-politicians, a lively and often tumultuous group, he got experience in rapidly organizing and presenting his ideas, and in making a naturally good voice a more flexible and effective instrument. He acquired a facility in speaking on a wide range of subjects. Mr. Wythe's instructions and the reading pursued under the Chancellor's supervision gave him a background in politics and history. But the distant past, outside of some attention to the orators of the Greek and Roman republics, received scant notice in the debating clubs of the roaring seventeen-nineties, when in both hemispheres history on a grand scale was in the making.

About the time Patrick Henry argued the British Debts cause, news came that George the Third had joined the allied monarchs of Europe in war upon the people of France. And this was followed by further accounts of the all-engrossing French Revolution: of the titanic Danton, who had thrust aside indecisive 'eunuch politicians,' inspired a hard-pressed France with his superb audacity, and saved it from the fate of Poland; of Robespierre's 'virtuous purging' of the nation in the Reign of Terror; of a French Republic consecrated to Liberty, Equality, and Fraternity.

Like the shot at Lexington in '75, the fall of the Bastille in '89

---

[1] *U.S. Supreme Court Reports*, Dallas, III, 256; Henry, W. W., *P. Henry*, II, 474–75; Beveridge, A. J., *John Marshall*, II, 186–92. In 1796 the Supreme Court upheld Wythe's view: the treaty of 1783 was part of the fundamental law, and 'sovereign' states could not evade national obligations.

[2] Among the members were Littleton W. Tazewell, Edwin Burrell, Walter Jones, John C. Herbert, Bennett Taylor, Philip Narbonne Nicholas, Edmund C. Root, Thomas R. Robinson. Colton, *Clay*, I, 25.

had resounded throughout the world. 'The Great Revolution' long predicted by Voltaire intensified political passions, and gave a mighty impetus to American democracy. The great wars it engendered were to enrich neutral America, to strengthen her by distracting Europe from territorial aggrandizement at the republic's expense, to weaken her by nurturing internal divisions, and to humiliate her by unparalleled assaults upon neutral and national rights. Until the cannon smoke lifted from Waterloo, the United States was to be blown hither and thither by gusts from the Old World. For years she was to stand on the brink of Mars's swirling whirlpool — a monstrous world-wide vortex which threatened to engulf the pacific America of Jefferson, and which at length sucked into its maw the nationalistic Young America of Henry Clay.

Since 1789 — when Washington was quietly inaugurated and the keys of a sacked Bastille were sent to Mount Vernon by exultant Tom Paine — Americans had become divided into pro-French Jeffersonians and pro-British Hamiltonians. With Jefferson and his fellow Democratic-Republicans young Clay rejoiced that America had pollenized fruitfully Old World aspirations for a new order, a new deal. Their own 'trumpet of freedom' had inspired 'Gallic heroes' to fight forward against Britain and Europe to the Republican Utopia and that 'great and unparalleled aera' in which 'all nations will form one vast society of brethren.' [1]

Henry and his Richmond companions cheered each French victory, aped French fashions, hailed each other as 'Citizen,' and sometimes dated their letters from the birth of the French Republic. They wildly acclaimed young Citizen Genêt, dapper and impulsive French Minister, when he passed through Richmond on his way to Philadelphia. Roundly did they condemn Gouverneur Morris, American Minister to Paris, and all Federalist aristocrats

---

[1] Munford, Wm., *Poems and Compositions in Prose*, pp. 153–62, an oration of July 4, 1793, typical of a young Virginian's reaction. See also *Virginia Gazette* and *Richmond and Manchester Advertiser*, 1793 ff.; Cobbett, Wm., *Works*, I; Hazen, C. D., *Contemporary American Opinion of the French Revolution*; Fäy, B., *Revolutionary Spirit in France and America*; Jones, H. M., *America and French Culture*; Parrington, V. L., *Main Currents in American Thought*. For 'Jacobinism' in Massachusetts, see the diary of Dr. Nathaniel Ames of Dedham, the arch-democrat brother of arch-Federalist Fisher Ames, in Warren, Chas., *Jacobin and Junto*.

who sympathized with Louis the Sixteenth, George the Third, and other despots. In their debating club, armed with Paine's *Rights of Man* and his *Age of Reason*, they made florid speeches affirming their faith in majority rule, the essential goodness of the common man, and the power of human reason to build a better world; and ended their meetings in the fervent emotionalism of such songs as *Freedom's Sons Are Frenchmen All* and Philip Freneau's *God Save the Rights of Man*.

For Citizen Henry Clay and many another American the French Revolution had ushered in a brave new world. How quickening it all was! Fellow republicans in France were breaking feudal chains of state and church, beating back monarchical invaders from Britain, Prussia, Austria, Italy, and Spain, suppressing civil war at home, and casting down as a gauntlet of battle the head of a traitorous king. A republic of freemen against the combined despots of Europe! A people's army against royal parasites and hirelings; an army of gallant youths, ragged *sans-culottes*, yet knights errant of Liberty, apostles of Freedom, crusaders for the inestimable Rights of Man, who marched and conquered with the exaltation that vibrated in every note of the *Marseillaise*.

From Boston to Savannah and from Baltimore to Nashville 'Citizen Farmers and Mechanics,' the 'plain, homespun people,' gave way to a 'Jacobinic phrenzy.' Jefferson himself declared that the Revolution was justified even if it left on earth, and free, but an Adam and an Eve.[1] Liberal clerics said they could hug the very whores of Paris who contributed to 'this cause divine.'[2] Recalling French aid that had ensured America's independence, impassioned democrats urged aid to 'dear France allied' so that Britain, 'The Universal Robber and Arch Foe of Liberty,' never more could rape and rob America, Europe, and Asia. 'O happy moment for America to be revenged the Millions of insults.... This is the time to put it for ever out of British Power to insult her more: drive them out of Canada; leave no such troublesome Pirates near her.'[3] At turbulent Civic Feasts red-capped Sons of

---

[1] Jefferson, *Works*, VIII, 202–06, Jan., 1793.

[2] Graydon, A., *Memoirs*, p. 329.

[3] Joshua Barney to his brother, Bordeaux, Dec. 21, 1794 — a letter intercepted by the British and sent to Minister Hammond at Philadelphia by Lord Grenville, June 5,

Liberty stuck knives into roast pigs, yelling 'Down with Tyrants!' And they did not fail to threaten Federalist 'aristocrats' — for surely those defenders of king-craft and priest-craft, Americans who put profits above the Rights of Man and like swine grunted and swilled unmindful of British cuffs and kicks, 'ought to be made food for a Guillotine.' [1]

Appalled and frightened were conservative Americans by this 'Gallo-democratic-Tom Paine mania,' this outburst of 'anarchic and infidel French Mobocracy' which was 'as powerful and destructive as the swords of the Goths and vandals.' [2] Federalist merchants, squires, and clerics, self-styled 'the rich, wise, and well-born,' called for an 'ordered liberty' and grimly opposed plunging America into this international crusade of '*sans-culottes*, armed cap-a-pe, to force the nations to be free.' They regarded peace with England as morally desirable and as economically essential. For under Hamilton the infant nation nursed at the breast of commerce, and commerce was dominated by England. It was England who controlled the ocean highways travelled by Federalist importer-shippers; England who bought about half of America's exports — the produce of Republican farmers; England who supplied ninety per cent of America's imports, the revenue from which — sobering reality! — vitalized and sustained the new national government and precarious Union.

To Federalists, Citizen Henry Clay's 'Jacobinic phrenzy' was far more reprehensible than Baptist John Clay's 'heavenly confusion.' Democratic Clubs such as Henry's were hotbeds of atheism, immorality, and sedition; nurseries of 'this hellish Cerebus of Jacobinism,' of designing Robespierres who preached 'the Commandments of Faction and the impervious Dogmas of Popularity.' Intoxicated by gaudy shibboleths, the Jeffersonians

---

1795, No. 12, Public Record Office, London (Library of Congress transcripts), *Foreign Office*, 115: 4. A Revolutionary naval hero while still in his teens, a very popular Baltimore captain and shipowner, Barney in 1793–94 had been 'robbed' by the notorious West Indian privateers of several vessels; for recapturing one of them, he had been threatened in Jamaica with a pirate's death, until a tremendous agitation in America had brought about his release. He became a commodore in the French navy and served until Bonaparte overthrew the republic.

[1] Joshua Barney, letter cited above.

[2] James A. Bayard, Dec. 30, 1797. Bayard, J. A., 'Papers,' ed. Elizabeth Donnan, *Ann. Rept. of the Amer. Hist. Assoc. for 1913*, II, 47.

were fetish worshippers of a bloody Goddess of Reason, a ruthless guillotine, and the whole witches' broth of 'French Democracy.' According to John Adams, they had become deluded slaves to 'the Tyranny of Clubs and Majorities,' which was as terrible 'as the Tyranny of Hurricanes and Tornadoes or the raging waves of the Sea.' [1]

Jeffersonian though he was, Chancellor Wythe tempered his enthusiasm for France and the great benefits of the French Revolution with his good sense. He did not submerge his Americanism in the Gallican sea of universal liberty. A national Republican, he was quick to resent French as well as British outrages. In 1793 a Richmond mass meeting, called by Federalist John Marshall, censured Citizen Genêt's interference in domestic politics as fraught with danger to the Union, perhaps 'leading to the introduction of foreign gold and foreign armies, with their fatal consequences of dismemberment and partition.' It was a meeting attended largely by 'Federalist aristocrats.' Yet it was presided over by none other than Henry Clay's patron and teacher. Wythe's example then, and throughout these years, tended to chasten his young secretary's emotional Jacobinism.[2]

This 'Gallophobia,' however, was no more pronounced than America's 'scripomania' — the fever for speculation in Continental paper, Secretary Hamilton's funding system, the semi-public United States Bank, the proposed Federal City, and most of all in Western lands. Speculation, life-blood and curse of the new country, was in full swing among a people who were, according to Vice President Adams, 'more avaricious than any other Nation that ever existed, the Carthaginians and Dutch not excepted.' [3]

In Richmond's taverns and in the Greek-temple edifice on Capitol Hill, where vast areas in Trans-Allegheny were bartered, young Henry often fell in with Kentuckians who vented their ire

---

[1] Vice President Adams to Chas. Adams, Feb. 14, 1795, Kent, Wm., *James Kent*, pp. 65–66; also, on Virginia Jacobinism, Channing, W. H., *Memoir of W. E. Channing*, I, 86–93.

[2] Wythe to Jefferson, Aug. 17, 1793, *Jefferson MSS.*; White, E. B., *American Opinion of France*, p. xv; Madison, *Writings*, ed. G. Hunt, VI, 179 n. In this connection it might be well to note that Clerk Peter Tinsley was a moderate Federalist, with friends in all parties, and (like Wythe) widely beloved. Richmond *Enquirer*, July 24, 1810.

[3] Adams to Dr. Benj. Rush, Apr. 4, 1790, *Old Family Letters*, p. 57.

upon Eastern 'aristocratic neebobs' and the Washington-Hamilton 'British' administration. These coonskin Jacobins saw in Citizen Genêt's schemes to attack Spanish Louisiana and British Canada an opportunity to gain an outlet to the sea through New Orleans and to end British dominance in the American Northwest.[1] With them came accounts of Indian incitements by Spain as well as Britain, and rumors that the trans-Allegheny rim of the new federal empire might soon revolt against the seaboard, just as in '76 the trans-Atlantic rim of Britain's empire had revolted against England.

In its weak infancy young Clay's nation was wracked by internal dissensions, imperilled and despoiled by foreign aggressions. Even the Barbary corsairs levied annual tribute and (like England's 'bloody sea-robbers') seized ships and enslaved seamen, clapping them into Tripolitan dungeons or putting them at the oars of Algerine galleys. France, with Genêt's plots and privateers, had insulted America's sovereignty — yet, as George Nicholas wrote a fellow Republican, the cause of the French 'is so good and their conduct in general so great that I am naturally inclined to overlook their imprudences.'[2] Not so with Royal Britain! 'A general great indignation against that proud imperious nation'[3] had been incited to a war crisis, in the spring of 1794, by the same maritime and territorial grievances which in 1812 were to impel long-suffering America into 'Mr. Clay's War.'

Federalists as well as Republicans were enraged when Britain climaxed her plundering of ships and impressing of seamen by the sudden seizure, without warning, of two hundred and fifty American vessels under a secret order-in-council which declared foodstuffs contraband and subject to British preemption. This indefensible naval policy struck not only at America's commerce but at the very roots of her agriculture. Moreover, seized ships meant impressed sailors, or stranded crews which were a prey to the first

---

[1] To gain these objectives they in vain demanded of Washington a display of force, if not joint action with France. England would not dare burden her people with an American war; Spain would not dare 'stake the Silver Mines of Mexico against the Wild Woods of Kentucky.' Alex. White to Madison, Dec. 28, 1793, *Madison MSS.*

[2] *Ibid.*, Nicholas to Madison, from Kentucky, Nov. 15, 1793.

[3] *Ibid.*, John Dawson to same, Dec. 22, 1793.

short-handed British captain. Yet 'the most hostile and cruel,' to Washington no less than to Kentucky democrats, was a territorial policy which also came to a climax in 1794, when Britain's Canadian officials (notably Governor Simcoe, formerly of the Queen's Rangers) openly incited American Indians and garrisoned another British post in Ohio — near which Wayne's troops that summer fought (and captured) both 'white and red savages.' [1]

No wonder was it that Henry Clay and fellow Americans angrily demanded a second war to secure their independence against a Britain so openly committed to might-makes-right; to an 'Algerine code' on land as on sea, in Trans-Allegheny as within the very capes of the Chesapeake. Yet in their anger was mingled shame — shame at their nation's impotence against a Tory Britain that yielded nothing but to necessity, that was only too well represented at Philadelphia by a minister who termed America's grievances 'preposterously magnified' and America's rights 'ridiculous.' To British Minister Hammond, as to the Dey of Algiers, all sufficient was it that these '*rights*' were 'asserted by a nation that has not the *means* of enforcing them.' [2] Alas, America could but entreat.

In 1795 Clay's Democratic Club, the great and seething mass meeting presided over by Chancellor Wythe, and the Richmond press were funnels for popular abuse of the British treaty negotiated by 'that damned Arch Traitor, John Jay,' who had yielded American rights to British might on impressments, neutral trade, stolen slaves, and British Debts. The uproar was tremendous and nation-wide. Jay in effigy was guillotined from Portsmouth to Charleston, Hamilton was stoned at New York, the British Minister was threatened at Philadelphia, and a British privateer was burned at Boston. Threats of secession were made by Republican farmers against Hamilton's 'be-Britished fiscal crew,' and the Virginia Assembly debated George Washington's wisdom and patriotism.[3]

---

[1] Washington to Jay, Aug. 30, 1794, Jay, John, *Correspondence*, ed. H. P. Johnston, IV, 55–56; *American State Papers, Indian Affairs*, I, 471, 491; *A.S.P., Foreign Relations*, I, 429, 461, 474; Bemis, *Jay's Treaty*.

[2] Geo. Hammond to Burges, Apr. 28, 1794, Hutton, Jas., ed., *The Bland Burges Papers*, p. 247; also, Hammond's dispatches, 1791–95, *F.O. 5*.

[3] *Richmond and Manchester Advertiser*, July 30, 1795 ff.; Beveridge, *Marshall*, II.

The Federalists jibed at these Jacobinic 'dark clubs and riots fell,' and said 'the *old dominion* frets because she has to pay her debts.' [1] But they themselves, at the very moment they defended a humiliating treaty, were sorely handicapped by fresh British outrages — sudden wholesale captures of grain vessels as in 1794, and in home waters confiscations, impressments, the firing on a revenue cutter, gross insults and threats by British blockaders at New York and Newport. Washington and Hamilton privately fumed at this most untimely outburst of 'the domineering spirit of Great Britain.' [2] Secretary of State Pickering, perforce, protested against Britain's 'plunderers' and corrupt vice-admiralty judges, an insatiable greed which disregarded 'all evidence of American property and fair trade,' and a more than Algerine 'cruelty and brutality' as had been exhibited on July 4, 1795 (Independence Day!) when the British frigate *Hermione* off Hispaniola 'stripped upwards of twenty American vessels of their crews; impressing all the men, excepting the Captains and Mates.' [3] Posterity will not credit outrages 'so brutally shocking,' it was said — yet 'our Government hugs the British the closer for it, while the people are bursting with indignation!!!' [4]

In the end Jay's Treaty was ratified, and a British war averted. Yet in thus yielding to Britain, and to prudence, the Federalists incited aggressions from France, failed to stop those from Britain, and only augmented a violent anti-British opposition. How clamorous Henry Clay's 'French party' was could be judged from the opinion of England expressed by the Federalists themselves.

The 'British party' from now on emphasized the captures by France, but Britain's captures and her 'wanton impressment of our seamen' caused Hamilton himself, privately, to upbraid Pitt's 'overbearing Cabinet... as great fools or as great rascals as our Jacobins.' [5] Pickering, as before, protested against 'ruinous'

---

[1] Fessenden, T. G., *Democracy Unveiled*, I, 137–38.

[2] Washington, *Writings*, ed. W. C. Ford, XIII, 99, Aug. 31, 1795; Hamilton, *Works*, ed. H. C. Lodge, X, 113–14, Aug. 10, 1795.

[3] Pickering to Deas, Sept. 12, 14, Oct. 22, 1795; to Samuel Bayard, Nov. 6, 1795, State Department Archives, *U.S. Ministers, Instructions*, 3.

[4] Ames, Dr. N., Warren, *Jacobin and Junto*, p. 66.

[5] Hamilton, April 20, 1796, *Works*, X, 161–62.

British 'outrages daily committing,' especially the 'tyrannical and inhuman' impressment of bona fide citizens [1] — which the new British Minister, Robert Liston, termed truly a grievous and growing evil, meriting 'redress and a change of conduct,' the greatest obstacle to a possible Anglo-American alliance. Yet Britain's naval officers, enraged by the popular aid given in American ports to their deserting sailors, continued 'to make reprisals by impressing American Seamen,' putting into effect the blunt dogma of the commander of the British warships in American waters: 'It is my duty to keep my Ship manned, and I will do so wherever I find men that speak the same language with me.' [2] So humiliated by the ruling Tories was John Quincy Adams, at London in 1796, that he declared America had 'not upon earth more rancorous enemies.' [3] 'His wrath and indignation' overcoming prudence, the son of John Adams, in private, 'breathed nothing but war, and was content to run into it at the hazard of our finances, and even of our Constitution.' [4]

Yet with the Federalists publicly stressing French captures and attempting to make it 'seem that the British were doing us no injury,' Citizen Clay and his fellow Republicans in this same year of 1796 were convinced that the election of 'be-Britished' John Adams meant war with France. War with Republican France! — even though 'the British are daily Capturing our vessels, impressing our seamen and Treating them with the utmost severity and brutality'; even though of the ships seized by the two belligerents 'the British Capture 20 to one.' [5] There were torrents of coarse invective in the campaign of '96, cries of foreign gold, shouts of 'Liberty, Equality, and No King!' Nevertheless, 'Gallicized' Thomas Jefferson was defeated by three electoral votes. And in March of 1797, amid the still swirling fumes of partisan and

---

[1] Pickering to Bond, May 19, 1796, State Dept. Archives, *Domestic Letters*, 9; to King, Sept. 10, 1796, King, Rufus, *Correspondence*, ed. C. R. King, II, 115–16.

[2] Robt. Liston to Grenville, May 12, 1797, *F.O.* 5: 18; Commodore H. Mowat to Liston, Hampton Roads, Mar. 27, 1797, *Admiralty*, I, 494.

[3] Adams to John Adams, London, Feb. 10, 1796, Adams, John Quincy, *Writings*, ed. W. C. Ford, I, 477.

[4] Morris, Gouverneur, *Diary*, ed. A. C. Morris, II, 157, Feb. 22, 1796.

[5] Andrew Jackson, Phila., Dec., 1796. Jackson, A., *Correspondence*, ed. J. S. Bassett, VI, 420–21.

foreign prejudice, 'King' Adams became President, and 'Jacobin' Jefferson Vice President, of the weak, divided, and harassed American Union.

Despite all the debates and mass meetings of these clamorous years, these formative years for him and his young nation, Henry Clay had given a good account of himself at the Chancery office as clerk and private secretary. George Wythe recognized the boy's promise. He predicted for him 'a high destiny.' Better still, the Chancellor himself arranged his transfer, late in 1796, to the office of the Attorney General of Virginia that he might better prepare himself for that destiny.[1]

In Robert Brooke, Virginia's attorney general and but recently (December 1794 to November 1796) her governor, Henry found a new teacher and patron. Educated at the University of Edinburgh, a soldier in the Revolution, a lawyer of thirty-five with a brilliant record at the bar and on the hustings, young 'Governor' Brooke was more Clay's type of man than the scholarly and venerable Wythe. Like Jefferson, he was a Virginian of family, one of those 'aristocratic-democrats' whom the Washington-Marshall Federalists derided as traitors to their class, whose boasted Rights of Man had impoverished their own landed gentry, done little for the yeomanry, and nothing for the slaves. Though far from a 'ranting Jacobin,' he nevertheless had heeded 'the impervious Dogmas of Popularity' and mastered the democratic art of manipulating voters and jurors. [2]

Of Henry's apprenticeship under Robert Brooke, William Wirt, the Richmond lawyer and littérateur, might well have written (as he did of Clay's friend, Littleton Tazewell, who was studying under John Wickham): 'He had the advantage of a most extensive and judiciously selected library; he heard the daily and hourly counsel given by this eminent advocate in every variety of cases; he learned all the technical and practical parts of the profession, acquired the best system of arranging his papers and going through the routine of professional duties, and, being in the

---

[1] Ritchie, Thomas, *Reminiscences of Henry Clay*, etc., p. 2.

[2] Brooke, Francis T., *Narrative of My Life*, pp. 7–9; Smith, M. V., *Executives of Virginia*, pp. 295–97. A brother, Lawrence, also educated at Edinburgh, was surgeon on John Paul Jones's *Bon Homme Richard*.

metropolis, he had before him not only the most finished models of forensic argument and eloquence in the superior courts of the State, but he had the opportunity of lighting his genius at the altar of a Henry and a Lee in the Virginia Legislature.' [1]

Six years of intimate contact with the Old Dominion's public men in high courts and Assembly had quickened Henry's wits and ambition, 'lighted his genius.' His schooling in Patrick Henry's Hanover had been supplemented by training in the Virginia metropolis under such eminent teachers as Attorney General Brooke and Chancellor Wythe. While irregular, his education was above the average of the day — comparable to that of John Marshall and Patrick Henry. Later, Clay with oratorical license (and the ardent orator was never as nicely discriminating as Wythe, the judge) would sometimes deplore his 'imperfect and neglected education,' picturing himself in Richmond as a poor struggling orphan, deprived of a father's smile and warm caress.[2] He early displayed this trait of dramatizing himself. It contributed to the favorable impression he made upon 'Governor' Brooke, who was so taken with Wythe's protégé that he had Henry live at the Brooke home, and treated him like a son. Moreover, as Grand Master of Virginia's Masons, he saw to it that Henry (although under age) was inducted into this fellowship of prominent Virginians.[3] Like Wythe, and many others, Robert Brooke helped to smooth the path of the 'orphan' boy — and Henry, characteristically, was always grateful.

As a member of the Brooke family, he formed an intimate and life-long friendship with Francis Brooke, Robert's younger brother, a rising lawyer-politician of thirty-three, who became a famous Virginia judge. Tom Ritchie, Robert's brother-in-law, a boy of eighteen, was also appreciative of Henry's 'fine talents and agreeable temper.' With these friends he would debate the grave issues of the day. Yet years later, when Ritchie was the famous

---

[1] Wm. Wirt, in Edwards, N. W., *Ninian Edwards*, pp. 417–18.

[2] Clay, *Works*, IX, 356, 363. While in Richmond he received some money from his stepfather, which came out of his share of John Clay's estate. Railey, Wm. E., 'Woodford County Notes,' *Register of the Kentucky State Historical Society*, XIX, 98–100.

[3] Information kindly furnished by Mr. Wm. S. Hunt, of the New Jersey Historical Society, who has made a study of Clay as a Mason.

editor of the Richmond *Enquirer*, the reminiscences in which they delighted were not of politics but those of gay and ungoverned youth, of 'the frolics which had amused us in Richmond.' [1] For Henry these frolics were now less boisterous, for the son of Baptist John Clay, the 'Mill Boy of the Slashes,' was blossoming forth the Virginia gentleman.

As the protégé of Virginia's revered Chancellor and popular Attorney General, he had become a member of a Richmond society the warmth and graciousness of which disarmed Yankee and British critics of Virginia's slavery and 'Gallic democracy' — 'that nauseous slaver of our frantick times.' [2] It was a society 'liberal, friendly, and sensible' in which versatile Benjamin Latrobe happily busied himself in designing public and private buildings, sketching lawyers and judges, birds and insects, and scribbling light verse, tragedy, and Italian songs.[3] It was a romantic Richmond which 'absolutely enchanted' young Washington Irving, with its daybreak rides and moonlight strolls, its Harmonic Society and Jockey Club Balls, its 'tender-hearted fair ones' who expected a man 'to talk sentiment and act Romeo, and Sir Charles, and King Pepin, all the while.' [4] One met not only belles and beaux from all Virginia but distinguished men, 'polished, sociable, and extremely hospitable,' whom even Tom Moore thought genteel enough for the London of Beau Brummell. At the assemblies young Clay and other gentlemen appeared not in the new-style French pantaloons but in the short clothes of the *ancien régime*: with the ladies they bowed and scraped and tiptoed in the *Minuet Ordinaire*, with *Pas Grave*, and at dawn ended with contra-dances, jigs, and the spirited Congo.

Henry was now twenty years old. He was tall and slender, some six feet in height, with long arms, small hands, lively blue-gray eyes, and a wide mouth which often quirked at the corners into a quizzical smile. Poise and self-confidence were in his bearing and manner. They were reflected in his carefully knotted linen

---

[1] Ritchie, *op. cit.*, pp. 2–9. Also, Ambler, C. H., *Thomas Ritchie*, pp. 23 ff.

[2] Moore, Thomas, *Works*, II, 300; Channing, W. H., *op. cit.*, I, 79–131.

[3] Latrobe, *Journal*, p. xv, and ff.

[4] Irving, Pierre M., *Life and Letters of Washington Irving*, I, 159–64.

cravat; in the cut of his cloth breeches, polished yellow-top boots, and high-collared, eagle-buttoned, blue cutaway coat; in the fashionable disorder of his fair, almost white, hair, which was un-queued and tousled, cut short à la mode Brutus in French Republican style. He was attractive but not handsome; at times there was a faint suggestion of the grotesque in his gangling arms and wide mouth.[1] When animated, in conversation or debate, his eyes flashed and sparkled; he was a vibrant personality, and his expression and appearance were then distinctly pleasing. Henry was usually animated.

Often with Tom Ritchie and Francis Brooke as his audience he would declaim on the era of reform and progress ushered in by the American and French Revolutions, arguing with infectious enthusiasm that young men like themselves should make governments bold, energetic, alive to the needs of the people and the changing times. A favorite book, which he would read and expound, was Mackintosh's *Vindiciae Gallicae*. With whole-souled conviction, foot out-thrust, and gesturing like a Patrick Henry, he would often end his orations with his favorite passage from this gospel of enlightened progressivism: 'Legislators, instead of the narrow and dastardly *coasting* which never ventures to lose sight of usage and precedent, should, guided by the polarity of reason, hazard a bolder navigation and discover in unexplored regions the treasure of public felicity.' [2]

Of buoyant temperament, emotional and quick to excitement, was this son of the Revolutionary Epoch spawned by an Age of Reason: he lived in the present, preferring action, incisive and vigorous, to 'narrow and dastardly *coasting*.' Warm-hearted, companionable, trustful, with the promising talents and likable personality which had won him rich friendships, Henry himself was

---

[1] 'Though his long limbs were loosely put together, yet his manner was neither awkward nor uncouth, nor ever embarrassed; on the contrary, it was easy and natural, and wholly unpretentious... he was never in the slightest degree, even in his early youth, awed by the presence of any one...' Harrison, J. O., 'Henry Clay, Reminiscences by His Executor,' *Century Magazine*, XXXIII, 178. (The original, and somewhat fuller, manuscript memoir of Clay is in the *James O. Harrison MSS.*)

[2] Ritchie, *op. cit.*, p. 2; also, Mackintosh, James, *Vindiciae Gallicae — Defence of the French Revolution and its English Admirers against the Accusations of the Right Hon. Edmund Burke*, p. 52.

about to venture boldly for fame and fortune in a new region and among a new people.

In November of 1797, after being duly examined and admitted to practice,[1] the twenty-year-old attorney decided to do no '*coasting*' in a Richmond (albeit friendly) of eminent jurists, or in an Old Dominion filled with veterans of law and politics — some of whom, like Chancellor Wythe, had grown old in judicial honors and Roman poverty. The growing Western country, especially the lusty five-year-old state of Kentucky where his mother and family were settled, offered fresh and exciting opportunities. The fees of five years there were said to equal those of a lifetime in the Old Dominion. Indeed, 'in the soil of Kentucky everything flourishes with rapidity,' remarked William Wirt, himself attracted by 'the ardent character of the State' and the choice it gave a man as to modes of life. 'Land being cheap and fertile, he may farm it on his country seat, or dash away, when his wealth will authorize it, in the circles of the gay, or float his commercial speculations down the Mississippi.'[2]

The new and glamorous Western World invited. Kentucky distinctly appealed to young Henry Clay of Richmond. Shortly after his admission to the Virginia bar he bade farewell to his friends on Capitol Hill and the debating society, and to his patrons, Robert Brooke and the venerable George Wythe. He turned from the Old Dominion of his fathers to follow the rising star of Trans-Allegheny. Henry Clay, Virginian, henceforth was to be Harry of the West.

---

[1] Admission certificate, Nov. 6, 1797, of 'Henry Clay, Gentleman,' signed by Judges Spencer Roane, H. Carrington, Wm. Fleming, *Clay MSS.*

[2] Kennedy, J. P., *William Wirt*, I, 93–97.

Chapter Two. The Western World

Behold! along yon western plains,
Where wild Misrule with Mischief reigns. .
  (Richard Alsop.)

Henry is like a lion's whelp; who shall rouse him up? The sound of his
voice is terrible; yea, it is like the voice of many waters. (William Littell.)

Europe stretches to the Alleghenies; America lies beyond. (Emerson.)

OVER Blue Ridge and Allegheny rode young Clay in November of
1797 to the Western World of the Revolutionary pioneer, a wilderness backwoods stretching from mountains to Mississippi, hemmed
in by Britain on the north and Spain on the south and west. Out
of it during his Richmond days had been carved the states of Kentucky and Tennessee — two outposts of the future continental
United States. He was entering the Land of the Western Waters,
a virgin territory vibrant with fresh life, growth, and challenges,
which invited men from the seaboard and overseas, and fused
them into a distinctive American race. A new society was here
evolving, conditioned by its rich opportunities and by its raw environment; a brisk new country believing in a material progress
manifestly destined, possessing an idealistic faith in a glorious
future.

Only a generation separated the young adventurer from Kentucky's first settlers. For not until the eve of the Revolution had

Thomas Hart, James Harrod, and other promoters, in defiance of George the Third's closure of Trans-Allegheny to colonization, succeeded in planting palisaded stockades in the Great Meadow, this beautiful land of luxuriant forests and lush bluegrass. A wilderness paradise was this Dark and Bloody Ground long contested by Shawnees and Cherokees, British and French. To gain it, the few primitive adventurers with epic courage had withstood British-savage onslaughts during the Revolution, and for years after Yorktown had doggedly repelled inhuman foes, 'treacherous in peace, tremendous in war, and diabolical in revenge.'[1] By 1797 their numbers had swelled to almost two hundred thousand. And still the flood tide of immigrants streamed over Boone's Wilderness Road and down the winding Ohio; a mass movement of peoples for which men could find parallels only in the Crusades or the migrations of the Germanic tribes.

> 'Our soil so rich, our clime so pure,
> Sweet asylum for rich and poor —
> Poor, did I say! — recall the word,
> Here plenty spreads her gen'rous board;
> Base poverty must stay behind,
> No asylum with us she'll find —
> Avaunt, fell fiend! we'll know thee not,
> Thy mem'ry must forever rot;
> Dame Nature, by a kind behest,
> Forbade you ever here to rest.'[2]

Stay-at-homes ridiculed fancied Elysiums in 'the Wild Woods of Kentucky,' but men disgruntled by the reaction from Revolutionary idealism to post-war realities visualized a republican El Dorado in the free and open West. Young men especially succumbed to this 'Kentucky fever.' Some of those who accompanied young Lawyer Clay ('Henry Clay, Gentleman,' as his bar certif-

---

[1] Littell, Wm., *Political Transactions*, etc. (1806), p. 11. For early conditions, see *Calendar of Virginia State Papers*, III, IV; Robertson, J. R., *Petitions of the Early Inhabitants of Kentucky... 1769–1792*. 'Perhaps no Adventureor Since the days of donquicksotte or before ever felt So Cheerful & Ilated,' wrote Felix Walker, of the 'Rapturous appearance of the plains of Kentucky' in 1775. 'A new Sky & Strange Earth... So Rich a Soil we had never Saw before; Covered with Clover in full Bloom, the Woods alive abounding in wild Game... it appeared that Nature in the profusion of her Bounties, had Spread a feast for all that lives, both for the Animal & Rational World.' Henderson, A., *The Conquest of the Old Southwest*, pp. 233–34.

[2] *Kentucky Gazette*, April 1, 1797.

icate read) as he rode westward were the poorest of the poor, modern 'Pilgrims,' on foot, possessing a faith as moving and as distressing as that of the Children Crusaders of old — men, women, and children 'Travelling a Wilderness Through Ice and Snow passing large rivers and Creeks with out Shoe or Stocking, and barely as maney raggs as covers their Nakedness, with out money or provisions except what the Wilderness affords... Travelling hundreds of Miles, they Know not for what Nor Whither, except its to Kentucky, passing land almost as good and easy obtain'd... but it will not do its not Kentucky its not the goodly inheratence the Land of Milk and Honey.' [1]

Kentucky! An enchanted Eden west of mist-hung mountains, 'where principalities are acquired and real Lords of Creation will arise.' [2] A virgin land 'uncontaminated with Atlantic luxury' and 'untainted by the pampered vultures of commercial countries,' it was here that 'the genuine Republican, the real Whig,' could find 'a safe asylum, a comfortable retreat.' Eastern America under Washington's 'Mock Republicanism' was 'Scuffling Shifting, wreathing and distorting itself to keep up an appearance of Plenty & Greatness.' But Kentucky, 'endowing naturally its owners with ease & affluence as well as preserving them from the infection of prodigality & the poison of Aristocracy,' gave promise of freedom from a corrupt and enslaving past.[3] Here was the Promised Land where the future smiled and the past was unknown. On its bounteous plains 'the superabundant sons and daughters' of an oppressive Old World could 'wipe away the tear of tyrannical toil, and join the Children of America in the easy labours of comfort and plenty.' [4] On Western Waters mankind could make a fresh beginning. Far 'from Europe's proud despotic shores' and the seaboard's 'Anglo-aristocrats,' the common man could fashion an ideal commonwealth, a republican Utopia —

'What wonders there shall freedom show!
What mighty states successive grow!' [5]

---

[1] Austin, Moses, 'Journal, Dec., 1796–March, 1797,' *Amer. Hist. Rev.*, V, 525–26.

[2] John Taylor to ——, Richmond, June 23, 1790, *Clay MSS.*

[3] Samuel Hopkins to John Breckinridge, March 29, 1794, *Breckinridge MSS.*

[4] Quoted in James, J. A., 'Some Phases of the History of the Northwest, 1783–1786,' *Proc. Miss. Valley Hist. Assoc.*, VII, 186.

[5] Freneau, Philip, 'On the Emigration to America, and Peopling the Western Country,' *Ky. Gazette*, Feb. 1, 1797.

Alas, ideal commonwealths are not easy of achievement. The twenty years of Kentucky before twenty-year-old Henry Clay appeared were filled with sacrifice and tumult — a story of bloody Indian wars and feverish land speculation, of strident demands for independent statehood and a free Mississippi, of rebellious Jacobin Clubs and opportunist private diplomacy. Virginia and the impotent Confederation 'Union,' absorbed in their own grave problems, had allowed the Western World to go through its birth throes and perilous infancy unassisted. Neglected, thwarted, unprotected, the 'Children of America' had pleaded and threatened and intrigued and fought for their rights and aspirations. Desperate conditions had nurtured desperate men. For years the forests of Kentucky had flamed high with fires lighted by a race of hereditary rebels.

Virginia's District of Kentucky was a bastion thrust out into an American West much of which was dominated by Britons or Spaniards, who with the Indians sought to retard America's expansion. It had been baptized in blood and continually 'harassed by the most savage enemies.' [1] Against barbarous Indians, 'formally hired' by Britain 'year after year to inflict agony and torture, death and destruction,' [2] isolated pioneers had been compelled to act for themselves 'upon the principles of *revenge, protection,* and *self-preservation.*' [3] The Northeast had been indifferent — even scornful of these Indian-killing, land-stealing, 'inoffensive Kentucky Lambs,' who, most probably, would soon secede from the Union.[4] Aid had finally come from the new national government. But the Federal armies, incompetently led

---

[1] *Ky. Gazette,* Aug. 18, 1787 (the second issue of the *Gazette*), and ff.

[2] Littell, *op. cit.,* pp. 7–11. Alluding to the incitement of the savages, and the aid given them against Wayne, by the British of Canada, John Breckinridge declared: 'Unassisted common sense & common honesty tell us, it is as criminal & treacherous in a British Subject to hire an Indian to murder our wives and children, as if he had committed the act himself, and that the deed is no less atrocious because perpetrated on the *west* side of the Allegheny.' Breckinridge to Samuel Hopkins, Sept. 15, 1794, *Breckinridge MSS.* Although much abused for his alleged indifference and neglect, Washington himself was no less convinced that Britain's agents were the source of 'all the hostilities, the murders. . . there does not remain a doubt. . . we have a thousand corroborating evidences.' Washington to Jay, Aug. 30, 1794, Jay, *Corres.,* IV, 55–56.

[3] Harry Innes to Sec. of War Knox, July 7, 1790, *A.S.P., Indian Affairs,* I, 88. Since the Peace of 1783, stated Innes, 1500 Kentuckians had been killed, 20,000 horses stolen, £15,000 in property plundered.

[4] Alsop, R., *The Echo,* pp. 32–34.

and composed (sneered Kentuckians) of 'wretched, broken-spirited creatures... obliged to conceal their posteriors with ragged blankets,'[1] had suffered appalling defeats. Not until 1794, with its threat of war with Great Britain, when Kentuckians in alarm pointed out that the British of Canada 'are advancing towards us, and have sent a regiment or two as far as the rapids of the Miami' in Ohio,[2] had the victories of Mad Anthony Wayne removed the menace of Indian reconquest. And not until 1797 were Kentuckians, hopeful for the first time since 1775 of a real peace with their redskin neighbors, singing in happy anticipation:

> 'Rejoice ye Freemen of the West!
> Secure from foes, with plenty blest;
> Hail, happy day! no savage wild
> Disturbs the husband, wife or child;
> Each in his cot secure may sleep,
> Nor longer in his block-house keep.'[3]

For years Kentucky's deep-rooted agitation for home rule — for separation from Virginia and admission into the Union as a sovereign state — had been voiced in numerous conventions and in petitions modelled after the Declaration of Independence. Continued vassalage, it was said, was repugnant to common sense and to republican principles. The great distance, and wilderness isolation, from Richmond entailed legal and economic inequalities. Above all, the Old Dominion did nothing but bid her frontier colonials 'sit still and receive the stroke of the Tomahawk.'[4]

Thwarted, the people came to consider themselves treated as 'enemies or aliens,' not only by Virginia but by the Confederation, which seemed hostile and envious, averse to admitting into the Union a Western World which in time might be more potent than the original thirteen Atlantic States. Like the Indians, the East did not treat Kentucky as 'a part of the thirteen fires.' A crisis occurred when the Confederation, tempted by Spanish commercial favors for the Northeast, backed John Jay's attempt 'to Barter away the first and greatest blessing of the Western Country... the naviga-

---

[1] *Ky. Gazette*, Dec. 1, 1792.
[2] Breckinridge to Smythe Payne of Virginia, June 20, 1794, *Breckinridge MSS.*
[3] *Ky. Gazette*, April 1, 1797.
[4] *Ibid.*, Aug. 18, 1797; also, *Cal. Va. State Papers*, III, IV.

tion of the Mississippi, our inalienable right.' [1] With their rights
not only unprotected but endangered, it seemed as though the
pioneers would secede from both Virginia and the East, and maintain themselves by their own rifles or by their own negotiations.

Both Britain and Spain fished in these troubled Western Waters,
tempting harassed Kentuckians (and Tennesseans) from the
Confederated Union — which even Easterners decried as 'imbecilic,' a mere 'rope of sand' — with promises of protection and of
an ocean outlet for their bumper crops. In 1788 General James
Wilkinson, a secret pensioner of Spain, attempted to direct them
into secession; but Congressman John Brown, to whom Spanish
proposals had also been made, refused to support his maneuvers.
Even after Kentucky entered the new Constitutional Union in
1792, the frontier cauldron continued its furious boiling. The
people still regarded themselves 'sacrificed to the narrow, local
policy of the Eastern States'; sacrificed to Federalist aristocrats
'who make money their God,' who 'brighten their ideas & pockets
with British guineas,' and who for some trifling benefit to their
codfish and molasses trade would allow Britain or Spain to
strangle the infant Western World.[2] If their just demands were not
speedily heeded, regretfully yet firmly declared George Nicholas in
1793, it was debatable indeed 'whether America shall continue
united or whether a division shall take place.' [3]

Almost to a man did turbulent Kentucky rally to the Demo-
cratic-Republican party, agreeing with Jefferson that the ruling
Federalists were 'Anglican, monarchical, & aristocratical... timid

---

[1] Innes to John Brown, April 4, 1788, *Harry Innes MSS.*, 19.

[2] Hubbard Taylor to Madison, Jan. 13, 1794, *Madison MSS.*; Breckinridge to Hopkins, Sept. 15, 1794, *Breckinridge MSS.* 'I wish the Rulers of Ama. revered the British as
little as we do,' wrote Breckinridge. 'Neither their policy nor their guineas are current
here. Our statesmen here have not yet learnt how to draw from them those materials
which brighten both their ideas & their pockets. Is this the case in Eastern Ama.?
... But we may be wrong, for we are too distant from the grand seat of information, all
too much hackneyed in old fashioned principles of 1776, to receive much light, from the
banking, funding & other new fashioned systems and schemes of policy which are the
offspring and ornament of the present administration.'

[3] George Nicholas to Madison, Nov. 15, 1793, *Madison MSS.* Singularly revealing as
to the motives of the pioneer leaders are Nicholas's letters to Madison (*ibid.*, May 8,
Nov. 2, 1789, and ff.) — a strong Constitutionalist in 1788, in 1789 he reaffirmed his
Unionism, but, now a Kentuckian, he declared that if the just and reasonable demands
of the frontiersmen were denied he himself was 'ready to join in any other mode of obtaining our rights.'

men who prefer the calm of despotism to the boisterous sea of liberty, British merchants & Americans trading on British capital, speculators & holders in the banks & public funds...their heads shorn by the whore England.'[1] Plunging into Jefferson's boisterous sea, the pioneers refused to pay Secretary Hamilton's Whiskey Excise, burned in effigy John Marshall's father, the tax-collector, and assaulted his deputies. They persisted in their violent anti-Federalism even after an army of fifteen thousand had crushed Pennsylvania's Liberty Men and Whiskey Boys. Yet from 1794 to 1801 the fear was general that a Federalist army, upon the slightest pretext, might be hurled against Kentucky's Jacobins.[2]

No place in the New World offered more combustible material for 'French Democracy.' Henry Clay's Jacobinic phrenzy was but child's play to the *sans-culottism* of the Children of America. They acclaimed the Goddess of Reason, cheered the guillotining of tyrants, priests, and nobles, erected Liberty Poles, formed Jacobin Clubs, and flaunted the tricolor in their coonskin caps. In the name of the Rights of Man, missionaries from Revolutionary France exhorted them to crusade with George Rogers Clark, their own great Revolutionary leader, in a 'superb & truly Holy Expedition' against monarchical Spain, with New Orleans the modern Jerusalem. In spreading the blessings of republicanism to 'Louisiana and its wretched inhabitants,' said one agent of Citizen Genêt, their French brethren could be relied upon, for they too, 'freed from the yoke of Despotism, Superstition, & religious fanaticism, burn with the Divine fire & sacred enthusiasm which Liberty inspires.'[3]

Through the Lexington Democratic Society, headed by Citizen John Breckinridge, these frontier Jacobins had attempted to force Washington's administration either to 'abandon or protect the

---

[1] Jefferson to Mazzei, April 24, 1796, Jefferson, *Works*, VIII, 237–41. To his friend Innes, May 23, 1793, Jefferson had expressed his fear that the crushing of Republican France might lead Britain and her allies, the American Indians, to make war upon the United States in real earnest; and, further, that the defeat of Republican France might encourage the Federalists forward to despotism, perhaps to an American monarchy. *Innes MSS.*, 21.

[2] *Ky. Gazette*, Aug. 17, 1793, ff.; *Innes MSS.*, 19.

[3] Auguste Lachaise to the Citizens of the Lexington Democratic Society, May 19, 1794, *Innes MSS.*, 19.

Western Country.' In flaming manifestoes they had demanded
immediate action — removal of the British garrisons north of the
Ohio, relief from Indian murder and rapine, and above all freedom of the Mississippi from the exactions, 'the humiliating and
degrading tribute,' extorted by Spain.[1] In 1794 they had supported Genêt's scheme to conquer Louisiana with General
Clark's 'French Revolutionary Legion on the Mississippi.' With
Clark they had 'bled and acquired' the Western Country, *their*
country; with Clark they would again 'fight and bleed, while any
appendage to its complete enjoyment remains to be procured.'[2]
The French project proved abortive. But their manifestoes continued to be so fiery that Easterners in alarm now charged them
with seeking disunion and alliance with either Britain or Spain.
Citizen Breckinridge retorted that the British were too 'odious' for
allies, the Spaniards too 'contemptible.' Yet he warned the East
that patience was exhausted.

'Nature has done everything for us; Government everything
against us,' he declared. 'As distant however as our thoughts may
be from a connection with the British or Spanish, at the present
time, let Government take care they do not drive us to it. The
Missi[ssippi] we *will* have. If Government will not procure it for
us, we must procure it for ourselves. Whether this will be done by
the sword or by negociations is yet to scan.'[3]

At this critical juncture Spain offered the freedom of the
Mississippi to the threatening and intriguing frontiersmen. But
George Nicholas and Judge Harry Innes shied away from obtaining the grand object at the price demanded — Kentucky's secession from the Union. Governor Carondelet of Louisiana persisted.

---

[1] *Ky. Gazette*, Oct. 12, Nov. 11, 1793, May 31, 1794; also, *Innes MSS.*, 19; *Breckinridge MSS.*, 1793–94.

[2] *Ky. Gazette*, Feb. 8, 1794. The project was openly advertised, and was unhindered by Gov. Shelby of Kentucky, who was advised by James Brown, his Sec. of State (in a letter typical of the frontiersman's opportunism; his willingness to threaten, cajole, and intrigue on all sides to obtain his objectives), that Clark should not be punished for try-ing to do 'what government ought long ago have done for us'; that Kentucky's defiant attitude might compel action from the neglectful Federal Government, since it 'may be alarmed at the idea of our detaching ourselves from the Union at so critical a period.' Turner, F. J., ed., 'Corres. of Clark and Genêt,' *Ann. Rept. Amer. Hist. Assoc. for 1896*, I, 1041.

[3] Breckinridge to S. Hopkins, Sept. 15, 1794, *Breckinridge MSS.*

In 1795 he assured General Wilkinson of preeminence as the Washington of Western America should Wilkinson succeed in corrupting by pensions Innes, Nicholas, Benjamin Sebastian, and 'the famous Brakenridge, whose talents and writtings in my opinion Will be very useful to bind the minds of the western People in favour of our Plan.' As late as 1797, through Wilkinson and Sebastian, Carondelet made glittering offers to Kentucky leaders — but in 1797 Spanish lures to disunionism were not only futile but absurd; and by Nicholas and Innes they were 'unequivocally' rejected.[1]

Fortunately for the continued union of West and East, Washington's much-abused administration had negotiated treaties at Madrid and London. Pinckney's Treaty of 1795 (which Spain did not fully effectuate until 1798) obtained the right of navigation and the right of deposit at the Mississippi's mouth for goods awaiting trans-shipment. At London Jay did succeed, at least, in removing the British forts from American soil. Together with General Wayne's pact with the Indians in 1795, these Federal (and Federalist) treaties did much to arrrest the centrifugal force of Western discontent.

The British treaty, however, incited more abuse on the intransigent frontier than in Clay's Richmond. For Chief Justice Jay, 'the Evil Genius of Western America,' had not only yielded to Britain's 'Algerine' maritime code, and affronted France, but had granted trading privileges which seemed to portend continued British control over America's Indians and a British monopoly of Mississippi commerce. The treaty was 'the offspring of a vile, aristocratic few' who planned to deliver America into the 'voracious clutches of that insatiable and iniquitous George the Third of Britain.' Senator Humphrey Marshall, against whom young Clay was soon to be pitted, suffered gross indignities for having supported it. Never again did Kentucky send to Congress this

---

[1] Whitaker, A. P., 'Harry Innes and the Spanish Intrigue; 1794–1795.' *Miss. Valley Hist. Rev.* XV, 248; and, by the same writer, *The Spanish-American Frontier, 1783–1795*; also *A.S.P., Miscellaneous*, I, 922–24. Severely criticized by Humphrey Marshall's Federalists from 1806 on, Innes, supported by volumes of depositions from pioneer associates, defended himself for not having made these private negotiations public on the ground that this would have caused (*a*) acceptance by Kentucky or (*b*) a Kentucky attack upon New Orleans or (*c*) the dispatch by Washington or Adams of a Federalist army against the Republicans of 'Jacobin Kentucky,' *Innes MSS.*, 19.

'Anglicized' Federalist, who 'would sell his country for foreign gold.'[1] Curiously enough, this charge of foreign gold was to be employed by the embittered Marshall against Kentucky's 'Gallicized' and 'Espaniolized' pioneer leaders, after years had tightened the bonds of union between West and East, and thrown a veil over conditions which had prevailed before the arrival of Henry Clay.

Thus, in 1797, the young Virginian was entering a Western World of powerful and elemental forces, turbulent, aggressive, defiant. In 1796 Tennessee had followed Kentucky into the still precarious, experimental, Union; thinly settled Ohio was to follow in 1803. Some four hundred thousand pioneering Children of America were scattered throughout the vast wilderness reaches from the Great Lakes to Spanish West Florida, from the mountain wall to the broad Mississippi. About half of them were in the dominant state of Kentucky. Among them the democratic ferment continued, and young Henry upon his arrival in Lexington became involved in its yeasting process.

Lexington, in the heart of the fertile Blue Grass, within the encircling bend of the Kentucky River, was the political and economic center of Western America. Two years before Clay's birth, Long Hunters had here named a wilderness camp in honor of Massachusetts' rebel Minute Men. When the twenty-year-old Virginian first rode down its Main Street, Lexington had become the largest town west of the mountain barrier, with a population approaching sixteen hundred and some three hundred log houses, which were rapidly being replaced by frame and brick dwellings. Only Pittsburgh at the head of the Ohio rivalled it in size and importance. Young Mr. Clay of Richmond was astonished, as were all visitors, by the bustling activity of this booming pioneer metropolis, by 'the immense amount of business' transacted in this 'Philadelphia of Kentucky.'[2]

---

[1] *Ky. Gazette*, Sept.–Oct., 1795, ff.; H. Taylor to Madison, Sept. 12, 1796, *Madison MSS.*; Quisenberry, A. C., *Humphrey Marshall*, pp. 59–60.

[2] Condict, Lewis, 'Journal of a Trip to Kentucky in 1795,' *Proc. New Jersey Hist. Soc.*, n.s., IV, 120. In 1800, when only 200,000 of America's total population of 5,300,000 lived in towns of 10,000 or over, Lexington had 1797 people, Pittsburgh 1565, Frankfort 628, Cincinnati 500, Nashville 355.

Into Lexington trekked immigrants from the Wilderness Road and from Limestone on the Ohio — to buy supplies, attend land and slave auctions, and to seek rest and conviviality at the Sheaf of Wheat, the Crossed Keys, and the Sign of the Indian King. To the stores, taverns, and bawdy-houses, to the public square with its Cheapside market and its stone courthouse, where countless disputes sharpened the lawyers' wits and filled their purses, came farmers, hunters, jobbers, Indian traders, planters, drovers, and brawling 'Kentuc' boatmen who described themselves as half-horse, half-alligator, tipped with snapping turtle. There was noise and confusion — creaking, heavily laden emigrant wagons; tethered saddle-horses that shied as droves of bellowing cattle were shouted past; incessant bartering; an excited clamor over mercantile ventures going downriver to New Orleans, and land caravans returning from the Atlantic seaboard via Pittsburgh and Limestone.

Kentucky's hemp, tobacco, and foodstuffs were here exchanged for English manufactures and Parisian luxuries, for Virginia-born Negroes and town lots. Near the Stray-Pen for wandering hogs and horses, Apothecary McCalla accepted wheat and whiskey for 'Just Imported French Medicines & Paints, copper stills, needles, wines, teas, and razors.' McGuire & Connelly, Patrick McCullough, MacBean & Poyzer likewise bartered their diversified wares. On Cheapside, Trotter & Scott had everything a Kentuckian or a passing immigrant could desire, from divinity books to Dutch scythes. Commercial news filled the *Kentucky Gazette* and the *Kentucky Herald*, along with intelligence from Virginia, from the capital at Philadelphia, and from far-away London, Paris, and Vienna.

Many of the residents were Virginia-born, yet to Clay they seemed younger, hardier, more enterprising, than the people he had left behind. From the plank and flat-stone sidewalks men in homespun and buckskin boisterously hailed the incoming traveller, offered him a hospitable glass of raw whiskey, and then asked him a thousand questions.[1] They offered to swap horses or wrestle, to take his money at cards or at the popular and unlawful device

---

[1] Michaux, F. A., *Travels to the Westward... 1802* (in Thwaites, R. G., ed., *Early Western Travels, 1748–1846*, III), pp. 247 ff., an excellent description of Lexington and of Kentucky.

known as the Wheel of Fortune. They offered to make his fortune in land ventures, or sell him lottery tickets issued by the town fathers in lieu of tax notices. They appeared (even to a Virginian) to be speculation-mad; to be free of the restraints of older, more settled, Atlantic communities; to be imbued with Elizabethan qualities — heartiness, gusto, and bombast, a reckless aggressiveness, a childlike candor and cunning, an easily aroused emotionalism.

In their frontier press they advertised that large sums of money had been found; that they should not be entrusted with money while intoxicated; that 'It is No Joke, and those indebted to the subscriber will be assured of it'; that the return of a runaway slave, such as Negress 'Siner, thick, trunchy made, flabby breasts, her buttocks stick out more than common,' would bring high rewards; that runaway white apprentices would bring 'One cent, with no thanks from me,' or 'The Full Reward of Four Pence and a Chaw of Tobacco.'[1] In the surrounding forests they killed as many as five thousand squirrels in one day's shooting, and wagered that twice that number could be killed on the morrow.[2] Indian-killing was more creditable than otherwise: there were frequent accounts of raids by the Indians, especially in the Southwest, where a hostile Spain seemed determined not to put Pinckney's Treaty into effect; yet young Clay did not find in the *Gazette* the warnings of a few years back that food 'impregnated with Arsenic and other Subtil poisons' had been placed to exterminate marauding redskins.[3]

Squirrels and Indians were pests, but no less a menace were enemies of the Rights of Man. Lexingtonians drank grandiloquent toasts to Thomas Jefferson, to Irish Patriots, English Whigs, and French Republicans. Frequently harking back to the days when over America 'the proud hand of a British tyrant shook the iron rod of despotism,' they were elated at the stirrings of liberty among the British masses and at the widespread mutinies of 1797 in a

---

[1] *Ky. Gazette*, June 20, Feb. 21, 1798; Aug. 2, 1803; Feb. 5, 1802; *passim*.

[2] *Ibid.*, May 18, 1801; Michaux, *op. cit.*, pp. 235–36.

[3] *Ky. Gazette*, March 22, April 8, July 5, and ff., 1797; and, for warning as to poisoned food, May 15, 1788. Also, for white as well as red savagery in 'the settlement of Kentucke' when 'the Indians, constantly stealing horses and frequently killing individuals,' kept the settlers 'in a perfect state of war,' see Beatty, E., 'Diary of Major Erkuries Beatty, Paymaster of the Western Army, 1786–1787,' *Mag. of Amer. Hist.*, I, 435; 177.

British navy of intolerable hardships, neglect, and brutality.[1] With fervor they shouted out such popular songs as *God Save the Guillotine* — save it ' 'till England's King and Queen, her power shall prove,' 'till the 'annointed knobs' of George the Third and all enemies of Liberty, Equality, and Fraternity were clipped off into the bloody basket, ' 'till all the world like France, o'er Tyrants' graves shall dance, and Peace begin.' [2]

Peace, the humdrum serenity of a fixed pattern of life, was not characteristic of Henry Clay's new environment. This Western World was dynamic. With its mass immigration of divers people and sweaty exploitation of virgin resources, it had all the movement and change and emotionalism of great social upheavals. Democracy was native to its soil, to its uncharted acres of cheap or free land, and here gave a new validity to Jeffersonian theories. And with all its rough strength, crudities, and inconsistencies, this frontier democracy was to be the determining factor in the nationalism young America was slowly and painfully creating.

More than a geographical term, the frontier was an evolutionary condition; a matter of feeling and state of mind; a tangible promise of betterment for the common man. It was a refuge for those who with Robbie Burns rebelled against the old order — 'A fig for those by law protected! Liberty's a glorious feast, courts for cowards were erected, churches built to please the priest!' It was a haven of hope for those who with Burns believed that 'it's coming yet, for a' that, that man to man the whole world o'er shall brithers be,' and with Freneau, who was not only the Poet of the American Revolution but the Poet of Jeffersonian Democracy, that the new order would 'Reason's laws restore, Man to be Man in every clime ... debased in dust no more.'

The frontier was youth, venturous, credulously brash. In its crude and as yet unordered society there was a rude individualism that tended toward anarchy; and, paradoxically, a rough equality that tended toward a depressing standardization. In the eyes of critical realists the Children of America often failed to justify their grandiose sentiments, surcharged with emotionalism, of Liberty,

---

[1] *Ky. Gazette*, Dec. 2, July 5, Jan. 7, 1797.
[2] In Bradford, John, *Kentucky Almanac for 1795*.

Equality, and Fraternity. Yet their zeal was not thereby weakened. No less dynamic than the forces springing naturally from the frontier soil were the pervasive ideas, the romantic conceptions, which the 'Freemen of the West' had of themselves and their destiny.

Young Clay was to find that life in Kentucky was not wholly the transformation of a wilderness into a utopia by idealistic 'real Lords of Creation,' nor entirely sordid exploitation by liberty-bellowing, Indian-killing mobocrats, dregs of the East and Europe, who were further debased rather than ennobled by raw primordial realities. There was some truth in the rose-colored romances of land promoters and perfervid Republicans who sang of 'the gay fertile soil on the banks of the Kentuck . . . far from tyrannical power removed'; [1] some truth, also, in the homely and biting satires of Thomas Johnson, the frontier's Villon, who professed to see in his fellow adventurers boastful, selfish exploiters, permeated with a crass materialism.[2]

Despite the din of exploitation and the motley nomads who thronged the streets, Lexington by the time of Clay's arrival was evolving into a settled community — horse-racing in the streets had been forbidden, as were wooden chimneys, the lighting of fires with rifles, and the keeping of pet panthers. Lexington, indeed, was 'The Athens of the West' — the seat of Transylvania Seminary, two newspapers, a public library; of jockey clubs,

---

[1] 'On the Banks of the Kentuck,' *Ky. Gazette*, Aug. 19, 1797.

[2] In his *Kentucky Miscellany*, 1788, Johnson criticized all classes; a sample follows (from Townsend, J. W., *Kentuckians in History and Literature*, p. 94):

'I hate Kentucky, curse the place,
And all her vile and miscreant race!
Who make religion's sacred tie
A mask thro' which they cheat and lie.
Proteus could not change his shape,
Nor Jupiter commit a rape,
With half the ease these villains can
Send prayers to God and cheat their man!
I hate all Judges here of late,
And every Lawyer in the State.
Each quack that is called Physician,
And all blockheads in Commission —
Worse than the Baptist roaring rant,
I hate the Presbyterian cant —
Their Parsons, Elders, nay the whole,
And wish them gone with all my soul.'

churches, schools of fencing, French, and dancing; and of a group of public-spirited men who would have done credit to any town in the East. Its preeminence was further enhanced in 1799 when Transylvania (somewhat pretentiously) became a university, with colleges of law, medicine, and the arts. Debating societies were active; dramas were given in the Fayette County courthouse; and young men strove to excel at public speaking, the fiddle, and in writing verses to the fair. In the Blue Grass, moreover, frontier hurly-burly was beginning to give way to the more refined (if more deadly) 'Specific' of the Southern gentleman — the leaden pill of the Code Duello.

Not only did the young bucks of Lexington echo the shibboleths of French libertarianism, but they aped the manners and fashions brought in by French immigrants — the frizzled hair daubed with pomatum and powder, 'the pudding round the neck,' side-whiskers, and pantaloons so tight that difficulty was had in sitting down. Frenchified dandies smoking 'Spanish seegars' sauntered along the plank sidewalks, in review before uncouth pioneers, farmers, land-jobbers, and visiting Indian chiefs who lounged at the Eagle, the Free and Easy, the Swan, and the Fried Meat Taverns. With studied gallantry these frontier beaux escorted to Cheapside ladies in ginghams and muslins, with yard-long trains, red morocco slippers, and hair fluffed with powder or tucked under turbans à la mode.[1] No less surprising than this frippery and penchant for display was the thriving book trade in this 'Athens of the West.' Merchants advertised lists of over a hundred titles — Fielding, Sterne, Smollett, Chesterfield's *Letters* and Plutarch's *Lives*, Watts's *Life of Christ with Psalms and Hymns*, and the popular works of Voltaire, Rousseau, Godwin, Franklin, and Thomas Paine. Editor John Bradford of the *Gazette* not only printed the verses of Freneau and Burns but published and sold Thomas Johnson's satiric *Kentucky Miscellany*, grammars and primers, religious tracts, the laws of Kentucky, anti-slavery pamphlets, and such works of the day as *Monarchy No Creature of God's Making*.

---

[1] *Ky. Gazette*, Dec. 23, 1797; McAfee, Robt. B., 'Life and Times... written by Himself,' *Reg. Ky. S. Hist. Soc.*, XXV, 135, *passim*, for Lexington life at this time.

Socially, Lexington impressed buckskinned frontiersmen for miles around. They marvelled at the fine furniture and carpets in the brick houses of John Breckinridge, the lawyer, and Thomas Hart, the merchant-manufacturer.[1] Easterners were informed that in this 'flourishing, agreeable place' there were 'a number of very genteel families, affording very agreeable society.'[2] Virginians, who like Clay ventured over the Indian-infested Wilderness Road, were also impressed with this backwoods Philadelphia, and enjoyed 'the gaiety and eclat of its inhabitants.'[3] Visitors from Europe to the Western World — to this great social laboratory in which the Children of America were pioneering on many frontiers — usually arranged to tarry amid the comforts of Lexington. They commented upon the rustic affluence of their hosts, their spirited character, their Celt-like emotionalism. The people of this little Western metropolis with whom Henry Clay of Richmond was now throwing in his lot were pronounced to be 'frank, affable, polite, and hospitable in a high degree; they are quick in their temper, sudden in their resentment, and warm in all their affections.'[4]

There was a merry family reunion at Versailles, twelve miles from Lexington, when Henry, the tow-headed boy of fifteen whom Elizabeth Clay Watkins had left behind in Virginia, arrived a man of twenty, changed and grown, ambitious to hang out his shingle as an attorney. His family's Western venture had prospered. At Versailles, the seat of Woodford County, Captain Henry Watkins was a justice of the peace, the owner of a commodious stone tavern, of slaves, farmlands, and town lots.[5] But it was at Lexington, not Versailles, that Henry had decided to win his own fortune.

---

[1] McAfee, *op. cit.*, pp. 127–28.

[2] Morse, Jedidiah, *The American Gazetteer* (1798), p. 275.

[3] Robt. Breckinridge to John Breckinridge, Aug. 9, 1794, *Breckinridge MSS*. He stated that he was about to return to Virginia by the Wilderness Road — 'notwithstanding a poor fellow lossed the skin of his head two or three days past.'

[4] Melish, J., *Travels*, II, 185–90, 208.

[5] Henry Watkins in 1792 (the first year in which he was listed) was taxed for 11 slaves, 6 horses and cattle, no land; in 1796 for 11 slaves, 7 horses, 11 cattle, 126 acres of land and 2 Versailles town lots; in 1797 for 11 slaves, 5 horses, and 950 acres of land. *Woodford County Tax Lists*, Ky. S. Hist. Society, Frankfort. See also sketch of the Watkins family, and picture of the Versailles tavern, in Railey, *Woodford County Notes*, pp. 98–100.

There his brother John was a merchant, and his younger brother, Porter, was soon to establish his residence.

In Lexington, when Henry presented himself, the former secretary of the Virginia Chancellor came well recommended to John Breckinridge, George Nicholas, James Brown, and other lawyers who had once studied under George Wythe. He did not, however, immediately apply for admission to the bar. From his arrival in December, 1797, to March, 1798, he studied Kentucky's laws and court usages, spent some time with his mother at Versailles, and assisted Brown, Breckinridge, and other attorneys in preparing cases and in collecting debts.

His ready speech and quick wits were soon called into play. Sent to collect a debt in the frontier country south of Lexington, where collectors were as unwelcome as Whiskey Excise agents, he discovered his man attending a political meeting. Called upon to give his views of the candidates, Henry hesitated, not knowing on which side his truculent debtor stood. But he took the stump and made an impromptu speech — on the exploits and heroism of Daniel Boone. Both sides applauded, and in the end he collected his debt.[1]

It was by oratory also that he first won the approval of Lexington. Upon his arrival he had joined the Junto, successor to the earlier Kentucky Society for Promoting Useful Knowledge, but he did not speak until he had familiarized himself with the great question then agitating Kentucky — the revision of the state constitution. One day his whispered remark that all had not been said on the subject was overheard, and he was urged to speak. Henry arose — and made a blundering beginning. Apparently the fledgling lawyer had been rehearsing in an imaginary courtroom, for he began with a loud 'Gentlemen of the Jury!' Recovering himself, he launched into a fiery oration which established his reputation. Lawyer James Hughes, who was present at his oratorical debut, remarked that the thin, fair-haired newcomer from Richmond had a fluent colloquial style, an uncommonly good voice, and sound republican principles.[2] All these were ad-

---

[1] Rogers, *Clay*, p. 28. There are references to Clay's activities in the *Breckinridge MSS*.
[2] [Clay, Henry] *Speeches of Henry Clay, with a Biographical Sketch*, Anonymous (Phila., 1827), pp. vi–x; Prentice, George D., *Henry Clay*, p. 9; Colton, *Clay*, I, 78.

mirable assets in a land of incessant agitation where the passion
for public speaking was even more pronounced than in Virginia.

Henry's Junto was but one of the Lexington debating societies
which held forth at the taverns — at Captain Postlethwaite's low
and rambling log inn, at Satterwhite's Eagle, Benjamin Kiser's
Sign of the Indian King, and the Free and Easy, where the Democratic Society had framed its revolutionary manifestoes. Politics
and everything under the sun were here discussed — the justice of
imprisoning a man for debt, 'the influence of the Inquisition on the
growth of Atheism and Deism,' the relative virtues of Red Jacket,
the Indian chief, and the Reverend Mr. Cram, the Indian mission-
ary from Boston. They propounded such questions as: 'Is the
existence of God deducible from nature, without Revelation?' and
'Is the colour of the Human species attributable to the climate and
local circumstances?' Instruction as well as amusement was
furnished by these debating and literary societies, said a writer in
the *Gazette*. They went far 'in ameliorating manners, establishing
the decencies of debate, and forming more and more a correct taste
in literature.' [1]

Helpful, also, to the young orators was the influence exerted in
countless ways by the Virginia-bred lawyers who headed the
Lexington bar and dominated Kentucky — and Western —
politics. Students of Wythe, colleagues of Jefferson and Madison,
such men as Breckinridge, James Brown, and Nicholas manifested
the traditional helpfulness of Virginia lawyers to those aspiring for
a place at the bar and in politics. They fostered debating, instructed in Coke and Blackstone, held moot courts, and encouraged
their young Republican friends, the future leaders of Kentucky
and other frontier commonwealths, to take a lively interest in
current issues. [2]

Young and most susceptible to his environment, Henry Clay
was to enter into intimate relations with these Kentucky founding

---

[1] *Ky. Gazette*, Feb. 6, 1810; Jan. 23, 30, 1810; and Nov. 24, 1807 ff. Also McAfee, *op. cit.*, pp. 219–27 (for subjects discussed, 1797–1800).

[2] McAfee, *op. cit.*, pp. 217–20. McAfee was then a student of Breckinridge. For George Wythe's influence on Kentucky's pioneer leaders see Breckinridge's Common-place Book of his student reading (*Breckinridge MSS.*, 1799), and Brown, John, 'Glimpses of Old College Life' (letters of James Brown's brother from William and Mary College), *Wm. and Mary Coll. Qtrly. Hist. Mag.*, IX, 18–23, 75–83.

JOHN BRECKINRIDGE

JAMES BROWN

FELIX GRUNDY

JOHN BRADFORD

fathers, especially with James Brown. The ageing Nicholas, a man of powerful frame and strong-fibered mind, and the tall, spare, brown-eyed, thoughtful Breckinridge were to be his political mentors — but not until he had bearded these leaders of the Western Democracy in the fight then brewing over the revision of Kentucky's first constitution. Clay's opposition followed shortly after his admission to the Kentucky bar, which took place on March 20, 1798, when he presented his Virginia certificate signed by Spencer Roane and other judges, took the oath prescribed, and from the Lexington District Court received his license to practise.[1]

On that day Fayette's courthouse and Lexington's public square had been thronged with a motley crowd in holiday dress and mood, a gossiping, bargaining, frolicking people, many of whom at daybreak had saddled their Kentucky horses, 'the hardiest in the world,' taken a stiff slug of rye whiskey and perhaps slung a jug over the saddle, and then ridden to town 'with a fury and celerity incomprehensible to . . . folks on the other side of the Allegheny.' [2] Court day, long anticipated, had been given an additional fillip by the case of the Reverend Francis Barrett, fluent, affable Baptist preacher, whose six months' career of shoplifting in Lexington had come to an abrupt end when he made so bold as to stagger off with a heavy saddle from Nathaniel Burrows's emporium. Barrett's escape from jail, the raising of the hue and cry, his capture in a rye field near town, his appearance in court 'with leather laggons on & . . . wet above the knees,' the jury's verdict of guilty, his plea of benefit of clergy, and his dismissal after being branded (with the letter R on his hand) a robber, had set tongues a-wagging and given the people of Fayette County a Roman holiday.[3]

Other cases were heard, typical of those young Clay would soon handle, involving forgeries, various felonies, land titles, delinquent debtors, and the keeping of 'disorderly Gambling houses.' But with the conclusion of the sensational Barrett case the people had turned their attention to the great question of the day — whether

[1] *Order Book A, Lexington District Court, 1796–98*, p. 94.
[2] Alex. Wilson, describing Lexington court day, in Ord. G., *A. Wilson*, p. cxxiii.
[3] McAfee, *op. cit.*, pp. 138–39; *Order Book A, Lexington Dist. Court*, p. 94 ff.

or not a convention should be called to revise Kentucky's constitution. No one was more interested in the subject than Henry Clay, who now plunged into his first political adventure.

Great strides toward democracy had been taken by George Nicholas and his colleagues six years before in fashioning Kentucky's first constitution. Yet their liberal reforms, which seemed so radical to the East, had failed to satisfy the equalitarian individualists of the frontier. No sooner had Isaac Shelby, the first governor, taken the oath of office in the log-cabin capitol on Lexington's Main Street, and retired to his temporary home at the Sheaf of Wheat, than a people disliking all restraint had termed him as despotic as George the Third and his administration 'a self-created Kentucky nobility.' Since 1792 they had attacked all branches of the state government. They had clamored against 'court rule' and 'the aristocratic few,' demanded direct election of governor and senators, ousted judges for unpopular decisions by having compliant legislators reorganize the courts, and denounced the legislators for being base enough to raise their pay from one to one and a half dollars a day.[1]

In May of 1797 the people in irregular yet pointed fashion had called for a convention to bring about manifold constitutional reforms. In December, when Clay arrived from Richmond, the agitation was in full swing, and among the many proposed changes being discussed was that of the gradual emancipation of Kentucky's slaves. It was this aspect of the revision movement that most interested the young lawyer who had but recently been private secretary to Chancellor Wythe.

While slavery was less suited to Kentucky than to the Lower South it was becoming intrenched, aided by the constitution of 1792, which allowed individuals to free their slaves but prohibited any general emancipation law. A respectable minority would remove this constitutional bar to a general, gradual, compensated system of emancipation. Somehow, sometime, they hoped to see the extinction of this blight of human bondage. Such were young Clay's views, carried with him from the Old Dominion of Jefferson and Wythe — where the 'sacred cause' had been frustrated. In

---

[1] *Ky. Gazette,* June 23, Aug. 25, 1792; June 8, 1793, and ff.

Virginia's daughter state, in this New West, the chances of success
were hopeful and worth fighting for. With Wythe, Henry would

> '. . . haste the day,
> When man shall man no longer crush!
> When reason shall enforce her sway,
> Nor these fair regions raise our blush;
> Where still the African complains,
> And mourns his, yet unbroken, chains.' [1]

It was a cause which appealed to the young Virginian's good
sense, to his emotions — and to his courage, for among the many
reforms agitated he selected and stressed that which was distinctly
the cause of a minority, favored by few persons of position.
Henry's own assets, save the horse that had carried him from
Virginia, then consisted only of native ability, a large share of
self-confidence, and a burning ambition to distinguish himself.
Both Breckinridge, fresh from leading the anti-convention fight in
the legislature at Frankfort,[2] and Nicholas were bitterly opposed to
emancipation in any form. And the good will of these leaders was
considered all but essential by young men ambitious for legal and
political advancement.[3] Regardless, Clay plucked a lance from
the armory of George Wythe and boldly advanced to the fray.

His great cause, unfortunately, was intertwined with the varied
phases of discontent, hampered by wild talk of immediate abolition
without compensation to the slaveowners, weakened by anarchic
attacks upon all existing institutions. The leaders of both political
parties were alarmed. Humphrey Marshall, chief of Kentucky's
few Federalists, declared 'a menacing voice had been whispering
in the regions of popularity, stimulated by some with, and others
without sinister design, against slave holding, land holding, and
money holding, in too great quantities by *some people*.' [4] Citizen
John Breckinridge regarded emancipation as but one symptom of

---

[1] Freneau, Philip, 'On the Emigration to America, and Peopling the Western
Country,' *Ky. Gazette*, Feb. 1, 1797.

[2] *Ibid.*, Feb. 14, 21, 28, March 14, 1798. On this agitation, in addition to the general
histories of Kentucky, see the special studies: McDougle, I. E., *Slavery in Kentucky, 1792–
1865*; Martin, A. E., *Anti-Slavery Movement in Kentucky Prior to 1850*.

[3] McAfee, *op. cit.*, pp. 142, 217 ff.

[4] Marshall, H., *History of Kentucky*, II, 246–47.

an incipient social and economic revolution. 'If the envious, the discontented, or the needy . . . can by one experiment emancipate our Slaves,' he wrote Isaac Shelby, 'the same principle pursued will enable them at a second experiment to extinguish our Land titles, for both are held by rights equally sacred.' [1]

Meanwhile, as the May elections of 1798 approached, when the people would express their will as to a convention, Fayette County in the heart of the populous, slaveholding, Blue Grass had become the center of agitation. Public feeling in Lexington was excited to fever pitch by the debating clubs, by pamphlets and newspaper articles. On the eve of the election Breckinridge with all of his prestige and ability attempted to silence the clamor. 'Are you a large Land holder?' he asked. 'I suspect not . . . Are you a slave holder? No, I will give you my right hand if you are. This is the Canker that preys upon you. This is what produces all your bellowings about Conventions, Conventions. This is what stirs up your envy, wounds your pride, & makes you cry out *aristocracy*.' What is the difference, he demanded, 'whether I am robbed of my horse by a highwayman, or of my slave by a set of people called a Convention?' [2]

He was answered by young Clay. Writing in the *Kentucky Gazette* under the pen-name of 'Scaevola,' Henry took pointed issue with Breckinridge, stating that his anti-republican arguments struck at the basis of representative government, and made necessary a grave refutation. He had been a member of the Lexington bar but a month; only a few days before he had celebrated his twenty-first birthday. Nevertheless he boldly picked out as his first political opponent, and boldly assailed, none other than the great Citizen Breckinridge, the leader and spearhead of the Western Democracy, and charged him with being a reactionary in Kentucky politics, an enemy of the Rights of Man, a proponent of the Tory doctrine of the status quo, of 'whatever is, is right.'

'Has it ever been known that the cause of truth was hurt by en-

---

[1] Breckinridge to Shelby, Mar. 11, 1798, *Breckinridge MSS.*

[2] *Ibid.*, MS. article dated April 20, 1798, signed 'A Friend to Order,' which presumably appeared in James Stewart's *Kentucky Herald.*

quiry and investigation?' asked Clay of the electors of Fayette.[1] Free and critical discussion was vital to republicanism, he said, pointing out the obvious difference between highwaymen and constitutional delegates. He denied that the people were content with the existing system. 'The true question with the philosopher and statesman,' declared Wythe's young disciple, 'should be not whether men are contented, for there is a tranquillity of the mind which has the countenance of happiness, but can the sum of human happiness, by the reform of corrupt institutions or the change of licentious manners, be increased.' The endungeoned prisoner, the bereft parent, after a while, cease their unavailing complaints. 'The subjects of the most despotic prince, the African who has the most ruthless and inexorable master, seem contented and happy, and rarely heave a sigh of misery ... It is not, however, true that the people of Kentucky are contented and happy under the present government. The vote of so large a number in favor of a convention at the last election, and the present stir in the country, prove the contrary.

'Can any humane man be happy and contented,' continued Clay, 'when he sees near thirty thousand of his fellow beings around him deprived of all the rights which make life desirable, transferred like cattle from the possession of one to another; when he sees the trembling slave under the hammer surrounded by a number of eager purchasers, and feeling all the emotions which arise when one is uncertain into whose tyrannic hands he must next fall; when he beholds the anguish and hears the piercing cries of husbands separated from wives, and children from parents; when, in a word, all the tender and endearing ties of nature are broken asunder and disregarded; and when he reflects that no gradual mode of emancipation is adopted either for these slaves or their posterity, doubling their number every twenty-five years? To suppose the people of Kentucky, enthusiasts as they are in the cause of liberty, could be contented and happy under circumstances like these, would be insulting their good sense.'

---

[1] *Ky. Gazette*, April 25, 1798. As to Clay's authorship, see Colton, *Clay*, I, 187 (Colton wrote under Clay's supervision). The *nom de plume* of 'Scaevola' was used later by Clay, in 1799, 1803, 1808.

An immediate and unqualified abolition of slavery, 'however just such a measure might be,' was proposed neither by himself nor his friends, said Clay. This and other radical motives were being ascribed only 'to awaken the prejudices, and mislead the judgment of the public. But it is the wish of some of them that a gradual plan of emancipation should be adopted,' he asserted. 'All America acknowledges the existence of slavery to be an evil, which, while it deprives the slave of the best gift of heaven, in the end injures the master too by laying waste his lands, enabling him to live independently, and thus contracting all the vices generated by a state of idleness. If it be this enormous evil,' he concluded, 'the sooner we attempt its destruction the better ... The first dawn of disease is the moment for remedy. The longer it continues, the more difficult is the cure. ... Fellow citizens, the present is the moment for coming forward — it is impossible to foresee the consequences of inactivity.' [1]

It was a creditable performance, this Scaevola letter of the pamphleteer of twenty-one. Henry's arguments for a safe and cautious liberation of the blacks, similar to the system adopted in Pennsylvania and other states to the north, were temperate and cogent, appealing to the sensibilities and to the mind. But he only intensified the agitation in Fayette. All those opposed to change, the slaveholders, the propertied, the timid and ignorant, resented the intrusion of a youngster fresh from Virginia, and denounced him as a bumptious 'beardless boy,' a non-propertied stranger who advocated the confiscation and redistribution of all forms of property.

According to his opponents, young Clay had allied himself with visionary busybodies, demagogic firebrands, and meddlesome preachers — smug individuals who had no stake in society yet sought to govern society; who concerned themselves not with

[1] Another, and secondary, reform which Clay advocated in this same article was the abolition of the state senate. It was unnecessary, since the old distinction between nobility and commons had ceased; it was 'against the spirit of democracy' to suppose that fifteen senators were better qualified than the fifty-six representatives. 'If it be true that the farther we go from the people we get men better acquainted with, and more competent to decide upon, the affairs of the republic, why stop at fifteen, why not descend to two or one?' As to the senate's checking 'the impetuosity and precipitancy of the lower house,' Clay believed the people themselves, through the ballot, could sufficiently control their elected representatives.

what they should do but what the substantial, property-owning, slaveholding citizens of Kentucky ought to do. 'Scaevola' and his colleagues would throw the state into anarchy, hoping that 'in the general scuffle those who are now at the bottom will rise uppermost.' We appreciate, said the sarcastic conservatives, 'your extreme condescension in communicating to us your bright ideas on a subject in which we are so deeply interested; for awakening us from our lethargic stupid state; for pointing out the necessity for innovation in our affairs; for your willingness to judge for us, and your desire to establish a perfect system of government.' [1]

Nevertheless, at the May elections of 1798 Clay's reformers were victorious.[2] A constitutional convention was called for July of 1799. Breckinridge and Nicholas were chagrined at their defeat, but they determined to carry the fight into the nomination and election of delegates. In the meantime, however, the convention issue was dwarfed (and, ironically enough, the 'sacred cause' given a severe setback) by the storm of protest which greeted the enactment of the Alien and Sedition Laws. Differences within Republican Kentucky were subordinated as the frontier democracy prepared to battle against John Adams's Federalist administration.

Young Henry Clay had boldly plunged into the boisterous sea of Kentucky politics. He was now to win his spurs as an Anti-Federalist, a Jeffersonian subaltern of most promising talents.

In the spring of 1798 the Federalist party swung into popular ascendancy to the cry of 'Millions for Defence But Not One Cent for Tribute!' when the French Directory under Talleyrand capped its maritime aggressions by demanding bribes through secret agents 'X, Y, and Z.' War measures, taxes, and loans were rushed through a Hamiltonian 'War Hawk' Congress. Hamilton himself, under Washington, headed a greatly increased army — which, presumably, was to prevent an invasion by General Bonaparte. And though war was not declared, from 1798 to 1800 American

---

[1] Handbills in *Breckinridge MSS.*; and *Ky. Gazette*, May 2, Feb. 28, April 11, 1798.

[2] Fayette in 1797 cast 560 votes for, 253 against, a convention; in 1798, 1357 for, 622 against. *Ky. Gazette*, Jan. 31, May 9, 1798.

privateers and John Adams's gallant little navy fought the ships of the French Republic.

The Republicans cried up British aggressions on seamen and vessels, and contended that France was only applying to American vessels British principles to which the Federalists themselves had submitted, in that 'insulting, cringing, and ignominious Jay's Treaty.' They ridiculed the necessity of the increased army. True Republicans had no fear of 'Jacobinic' Bonaparte, then menacing the English coast; indeed, 'should Bonaparte make a landing on the English shore,' said a Western senator, 'tyranny will be humbled, a throne crushed, and a republic will spring from the wreck, and millions of distressed people restored to the rights of man by the conquering arm of Bonaparte.' [1]

But it was extremely difficult for the Republicans to apologize for the 'imprudences,' maritime and diplomatic, of the corrupt and rapacious Directory then ruling France. Many who had once worn the tricolor and sung *Freedom's Sons Are Frenchmen All* now donned the Federalist (British) black cockade and sang out the new song of *Hail Columbia*. Even the 'Virtuous Minority' in Congress was falling away from Vice President Jefferson when the Federalists, made overbold by the patriotic war frenzy, committed their stupendous folly. Repressive laws were enacted which put them in the light not of patriotic nationalists but of men maddened by power, intent upon riding roughshod over the Constitution, and in erecting a centralized despotism.

Although America was officially at peace, President Adams at his own discretion could now imprison or banish 'Alien Enemies.' Naturalization was now possible only after fourteen years' residence for 'wild Irishmen,' 'English renegadoes,' and other exiled European liberals who had a way of becoming Jeffersonian politicians and editors. Most detestable was the Sedition Act, which attempted to make political opposition a crime. Similar to the measures of British Toryism, it made the slightest criticism of Federalist officials or policies punishable by fine or imprisonment.

Tactless Federalists! They had given their opponents the best of weapons. Casting aside their poor rôle as apologists for France,

---

[1] Andrew Jackson, Jan. 11, 1798, Jackson, *Corres.*, I, 42.

the Democratic-Republicans became the vociferous champions of the Constitution and the Bill of Rights, of the sovereign states and of personal liberties. French insults and aggressions were obscured by a roaring campaign, against Federalist consolidation, aristocracy, and militarism, which was to end only in 1800 with the election of Thomas Jefferson.

In Kentucky, most anti-Federalist of the states, well-oiled machinery of agitation at once began to operate against John Adams's 'Asiatic Tyranny,' against an anti-French hysteria incited (it was said) in order to bind America to Britain, involve her in Britain's wars, and establish a Tory despotism at home. A new country which clamored for settlers, through such agencies as the Lexington Emigrant Society, deeply resented the Alien Laws. Kentucky had too long enjoyed the freedom, and the license, of unbridled expression to submit to the Sedition Act. A decade of accumulated hatred was easily inflamed against the ruling Federalists who, emulating Britain's Anti-Jacobins, in the East now carried on a Tory 'Reign of Terror' — mobbing or clapping into jail carping ('seditious') Republican editors; mobbing or forcing from America's shores English and French scholars of liberal leanings; fining and imprisoning Congressman Matthew Lyon for 'seditiously' charging President Adams with 'a continual grasp for power, an unbounded thirst for ridiculous pomp'; and even fining one poor wight one hundred dollars for expressing the hope that the wadding of a cannon fired in holiday salute might strike the rear bulge of Johnny Adams's velvet breeches.

Clay and his fellow Kentuckians solemnly resolved the Alien and Sedition Acts to be unconstitutional, 'dead letters,' 'absolute nullities,' 'political monsters.' They loudly toasted 'Trial by Jury, Liberty of the Press, the Militia — the only mode of national defense, No Standing Army and No British Alliance.' Men would next be exterminated, they said, for saying 'Boo!' to a collector of Adams's 'odious Stamp and Still taxes,' for having an Irish Republican in for dinner, or for kissing a French girl. With voice and pen they inveighed against 'the hellish aristocratic junto' that sought to crush out the Rights of Man — at home, by General Hamilton's standing army; in Republican France (and in Britain

as well, where English riots, Irish revolts, and widespread mutinies
in the British navy gave promise of an uprising of the common
people), by allying Republican America with Europe's despots,
headed by 'the corrupt and tottering British Monarchy.' Could
anything be more abominable to the genuine Republican, the real
Whig? —

> 'If not the cause of France we aid,
> O never may the words be said,
> That, we to royal factions prone,
> *Made not the cause of Man our own.'* [1]

Nothing more impressively revealed their detestation, and fear,
of Hamiltonian Federalism than their repulse of propaganda
which sought to make a French war popular by calling for conquests from Spain, since 1795 the ally of France. Strong as was
their expansionism, their desire to own the Mississippi outlet,
they refused to be ensnared by Federalist-British stratagems.
Their answer to the schemes of Senator Blount of Tennessee, and
especially to those of Hamilton and Pickering, by which with the
aid of the British navy New Orleans and the Floridas were to be
taken, and perhaps Mexico and beyond, was given in the toast of
Kentucky's militia officers at Lexington — 'Harmony with France
and Spain.' [2] A few hotheads talked of secession. But in public
remonstrances the people took care to sound a note of loyalty, to
'the Union, the independence, the Constitution, and the Liberty
of the United States.' [3] They dared domestic foes to attack their
constitutional liberties and foreign foes to 'pluck a feather from the

---

[1] *Ky. Gazette*, July 22, 1797; and, especially, June, 1798 ff.; Nicholas, George,
Letter... to His Friend in Virginia. Jefferson advised his lieutenants that the acts were
'only an experiment on the American mind' — if successful, the way was paved to a
monarchy under Hamilton or Adams, Jefferson, *Works*, VIII, 450.

[2] *Ky. Gazette*, Oct. 17, 1798; also, July 26, 1797; Feb. 7, June 6, 1798 (on Blount),
and issues of June, 1798 for articles by 'A Friend of Peace.' Referring to 'the malignant
use which the democratick faction' made of the Blount disclosures, the British Minister
reported that the great mass of people had an 'extreme Aversion... to any measure
that might risk involving the United States in a quarrel with Spain — while that
country was connected with France.' Liston to Grenville, Aug. 30, 1797, *F.O.* 5:18.
Yet Federalist officials, in face of a public opinion which (they said) was always 'not
yet ripe for a close connection with us,' and in face too of 'perpetual complaints'
against British aggressions, continued to 'have their views fixed on the conquest of the
Floridas and Louisiana for themselves and the acquisition of St. Domingo (if not other
French Islands) by Great Britain.' Same to same, May 2, 1798, *F.O.* 5:22.

[3] *Ky. Gazette*, Aug. 1, 8, 1798; also, *Breckinridge MSS.*, 1798.

American Eagle.' They toasted Jefferson and 'the Sixteen United States one and indivisible: May no link of that chain be broken, but new ones added' — but added not under Hamilton, at the price of a French war and a British alliance, and at the expense of American democracy.[1]

Lexington as usual was the storm center of the Western World. When the news came of the Alien and Sedition Acts in July of 1798, about a thousand people from the Blue Grass region gathered at Maxwell's Spring, the field ground south of the town. George Nicholas, heavy-set and grimly determined, took the lead in denouncing laws that violated the Constitution which he had so staunchly championed in the Virginia Ratifying Convention ten years before. When he had concluded his long and weighty speech, amid the noise and confusion young Clay was pushed to the wagon that served as the speakers' platform. Henry willingly mounted, and while waiting for the shouts to subside, surveyed the surging mass of frontiersmen who encircled him. It was a splendid opportunity for a born orator. The setting, the issues, the mood of the people, all inspired young Clay to thrill Lexington as young Patrick Henry had thrilled Hanover.

Continuing the attack begun by Colonel Nicholas, he marshalled his arguments and thundered his defiance. Spiritedly did he express his abhorrence of Federalism's attempts to dragonnade the republic into an unnecessary French war and an alliance with Britain; bitterly did he denounce the un-American measures which portended class-rule and military despotism. Here was not the reasoned argument of Nicholas or of Clay's Scaevola letter but a tumultuous flood of emotion. His fiery invective was as remarkable as it was unexpected. A frontier audience accustomed to clamorous protests was held enthralled by the slender, tow-headed young orator on the cart-tail rostrum, so erect, so passionately defiant.

With moving eloquence Citizen Clay voiced the sentiments of these backwoodsmen — their hatred of the aristocratic Adams, of the monarchy-loving Hamilton; their sympathy for France and scorn of Britain; their faith and hope as Children of America in that utopian republic they had envisioned for themselves and

---

[1] *Ky. Gazette*, Oct. 24, 1798.

posterity, the promise of which was now directly threatened by Federalist Toryism. His voice penetrated to the outskirts of the crowd — a frontier crowd that was strangely silent. It was now soothing and caressing as he spoke of Revolutionary sacrifices and Republican aspirations; now high and strident as he condemned the soaring ambitions of power-infatuated Federalism. Finally he ceased — but there were no shouts. Then a low rumbling sound gathered momentum and crashed into prolonged applause.

'It would be impossible,' said one of that rapt audience, 'to give an adequate idea of the effect produced.' 'An orator indeed!' exclaimed men of a region devoted to public speaking and public speakers. This stripling had been a torch inflaming all who heard him with his fire. For the moment he had impressively, dramatically, symbolized the democratic protest of this young and vigorous Western World.

In face of this remarkable demonstration, William Murray climbed upon the wagon, determined to defend indicted Federalism. He was a courageous man, a forceful speaker, and a lawyer of reputation. When he attempted to speak the angry crowd booed and threatened; they would have seized him had it not been for Nicholas and Clay, who put into effect the liberty of speech they preached against Federalism. Then Mr. McLean, another courageous Federalist, climbed upon the speakers' wagon. But the crowd would have no more. There was a wild rush from all directions, and it was only by a hurried flight that the hapless Federalists escaped being tarred and feathered.

Then, with 'King' John Adams rhetorically guillotined, the minions of Aristocracy put to flight, and a right manly protest registered against the Alien and Sedition Acts, the good citizens turned to and paid civic honors to the Tribunes of the People, their peerless orators. From the cart they took the heroes of the day, carried young Clay and old Nicholas on their shoulders to a carriage, unhitched the horses, and back from Maxwell's Grove and through the streets of Lexington pulled the vehicle amid the shouts and huzzas of the assembled people. Henry Clay, within a few months of his arrival from Virginia, had scored a great personal triumph. Already he had won his first triumphal procession through the streets of Lexington, the metropolis of the Western World.[1]

From this time on Henry was conspicuous among the 'Wagon and Stump Orators' who in turbulent mass meetings in almost every town and hamlet voiced and augmented Kentucky's strident protest. He helped to incite a tremendous popular uproar — in August as many as five thousand citizens gathered in Lexington to defy Sedition Act and Standing Army. Provoked, Eastern Federalists assailed Kentucky's 'Jacobinic Demagogues,' who 'feed the Multitude with Sedition,' threatened them with Mat Lyon's fate, and called for an avenging Federal army to crush the backwoods Robespierres. Led by William Cobbett of Philadelphia (the notorious British editor who headed the Federalist press), they jeered at Lexington's unwashed 'hordes,' as more savage than Indians or 'wild Irish,' coonskin barbarians 'just civilized enough to be the tools of faction,' who, incited by old Nicholas and young Clay, had resolved: 'wee doe beleev that our leebeerte es in daingur . . . wee will defende um agenst awl unconstetushonal ataks.' [2] Senator Humphrey Marshall, who had voted for the unpopular laws and written an atrociously rhymed poem, *The Aliens*, led Kentucky's few Federalists in courageously pledging their loyalty to President Adams and the quasi-war against France. But among a people almost wholly given to riotous Mobocracy their resolutions, complained Marshall, were but 'drop-shot against cannon-balls.' [3]

In November of 1798 the agitation was concentrated into the famous Kentucky Resolutions, inspired by Jefferson, and sponsored

[1] Prentice, *Clay*, pp. 23–24; also, Warfield, E., *Kentucky Resolutions*, pp. 42–43; McElroy, R. McN., *Kentucky in the Nation's History*, pp. 224–25.

[2] Cobbett's *Porcupine's Gazette* (Phila.) and other Federalist journals, q. in *Ky. Gazette*, Oct. 17, Nov. 28, 1798; also, Arthur Campbell to Timothy Pickering, Nov. 23 (inclosing letter of Samuel McDowell of Ky., of Oct. 29), Dec. 4, 23, 1798, *Pickering MSS.*, 23; Nicholas, G., *Letter*.

[3] Marshall, H., *History of Kentucky*, II, 283–85. Marshall's *The Aliens* expressed in bad verse what Tom Moore phrased (*Works*, II, 298):

> 'Did heaven design thy lordly land to nurse
> The motley dregs of every distant clime,
> Each blast of anarchy and taint of crime,
> Which Europe shakes from her perturbed sphere,
> In full malignity to rankle here?'

by Breckinridge, after Governor Garrard had called upon the legislators for such action as would convince all friends of the Rights of Man that Kentucky, 'remote from the contaminating influences of European politics, is steady to the principles of pure republicanism, and will ever be the asylum of her persecuted votaries.' The Constitution was avowed to be a compact between sovereign states. When the Federal Government, their agent, their servant, exceeded its constitutional limitations the sovereign states should declare such acts void and of no effect. In keeping with Jefferson's 'pure republicanism,' which held power to be the enemy of liberty and that government best which governed least, Kentucky was determined 'tamely to submit to undelegated and consequently unlimited powers in no man or body of men on earth.' [1]

With such 'solemn official protests' in Kentucky, and in Virginia, the astute Jefferson kindled a backfire of agrarian States' Rights against Federalist centralization — and in partisan fashion further capitalized the discontent among his embattled, and office-hungry, Republicans.

There now came a lull, an interlude. Attention was deflected, temporarily, from national issues to the July convention which would give Kentucky a new constitution.

In January of 1799 Fayette's conservatives nominated as delegates Breckinridge, Judge Buckner Thruston, Hezekiah Harrison, and others on a ticket pledged to the protection of property and opposed to emancipation either immediate or gradual.[2] Again they encountered the opposition of young Lawyer Clay. To Breckinridge and Nicholas he reappeared in his former rôle of an upstart, a presumptuous youth 'in the plentitude of puppyism.' And his words carried a sting. The wagon orator who had joined with these mighty champions of 'Jefferson and Liberty' once again ridiculed them as reactionaries who defended an inhumane status quo. In home affairs, Nicholas and Breckinridge were resorting to that 'narrow and dastardly *coasting*' against which at Richmond George Wythe's protégé had so often declaimed.

---

[1] *Ky. Gazette*, Nov. 14, 1798; Warfield, *op. cit.*, and see *Breckinridge* and *Innes MSS.*, 1798–1799.

[2] *Breckinridge MSS.*, Jan. 1799; *Ky. Gazette*, Jan. 31, Feb. 7, March 21, 1799.

A slaveholders' clique, asserted Clay,[1] was secretly attempting to thwart the will of the people. 'Truth seeks not the prop of combination; her strength is internal,' admonished the young reformer. 'It is error alone that demands the support of intrigue and of external force.' Their argument runs like this, he said: 'We will not put the posterity of the present race of negroes in possession of their rights, because if we do, we are not sure but we may afterwards proceed farther and emancipate all the hogs in the state, or divide them amongst ourselves. We will therefore tye up our hands. We have no confidence in ourselves.'

Once again Citizen Clay stressed the Rights of Man, in reasoned, hard-hitting arguments. The slavery issue had to be faced, he said, and better now than in the future. Yet he was no radical abolitionist: 'Thirty thousand slaves, without preparation for enjoying the rights of a freeman, without property, without principle, let loose upon society would be wretched themselves, and render others miserable.' These objections, however, would not apply to the posterity of the present slaves under the system which he and his friends proposed, for under it they would be treated as deserving orphans, educated, prepared for ultimate freedom and citizenship. So it is, he asserted, 'that a man may advocate a gradual and oppose an immediate emancipation (as is actually the case), upon principle.' In such a sacred cause he was certain that enlightened, liberty-loving Fayette would elect its own delegates, 'undismayed by the insidious cry of alarm, and undeluded by the whine of interest.'

With the shrewdness of an experienced politician, he insinuated that the anti-slavery men, in their fear and greed, intended to consolidate their power by substituting for Kentucky's cherished universal and unrestricted suffrage a property, freehold, qualification. Black slavery might thus in time lead to white slavery! 'Turn out, therefore,' urged reform broadsides, 'and snatch your dearly bought liberty from the devouring jaws of despotic power. There is a secret conspiracy now forming to deprive you of the inestimable right of suffrage, deep laid, and like a threatening cloud, ready to burst over your heads.' When Henry's friends

---

[1] Scaevola to the Citizens of Fayette, *Ky. Gazette*, Feb. 28, 1799.

nominated delegates — among them Editor John Bradford and Lawyer James Hughes — they were pledged to gradual emancipation for the blacks and to unrestricted suffrage for the whites.[1]

Meanwhile, the battle raged in Lexington's newspapers. 'Clergyman' took laymen to task for advocating slavery on Christian principles. 'Emancipator' hotly denied that his colleagues were 'robbers stealing leather from the rich to make shoes for the poor,' or that they 'broke the laws of God and man — and are composed of beardless boys.' 'Slaveholder' would restrict voting to owners of land and slaves; he scoffed at all this 'talk about humanity,' declaring 'that the slaves are better off in Virginia where I come from, than if they were turned loose to gain their own livings or starve.' George Nicholas was forced to defend himself on the charge made by Clay and others that his pro-slavery views were inconsistent with the principles he advocated against Federalist tyranny. Contending that the reform party embraced 'most of your political characters who are known to be in search of popularity,' Colonel Nicholas admonished Fayette 'not to take counsel from *beardless boys.*'[2]

If beardless Henry Clay, as Nicholas charged, was a mere popularity-seeker, he showed extraordinarily poor judgment in continuing the fight in such hard-hitting, uncompromising fashion. For public opinion had undergone a decided shift since the victory of the year before, and the cause of emancipation was doomed. In leading the vociferous crusade against the Federalist Reign of Terror, Breckinridge and Nicholas had recovered their former prestige. Moreover, 'the steady part of the Community' had come to believe that the violent forces unleashed by the Alien and Sedition agitation might impel Clay's 'enthusiasts in the cause of liberty' into too many and too radical constitutional revisions.[3]

[1] Broadside in *Durrett Collection*, quoted in Kerr, C., ed., *History of Kentucky*, I, 398–99; *Ky. Gazette*, March 28, 1799.

[2] Nicholas, in *Ky. Gazette*, April 11, 1799 (also in *Kentucky Broadsides*, Library of Congress), and, *ibid.*, March 14, 21, Feb. 28, March 7, 1799.

[3] We have 'great apprehensions of too great a change being attempted... with great violence,' such as 'the abolition of slavery & the Senate, the Representation by Counties, and I fear the destruction of the Compact with Virginia [made at Kentucky's separation, re public lands, debts, etc.]... & [also they will try] to Gag the Judges' from declaring 'a Law unconstitutional.' Hubbard Taylor to Madison, Jan. 3, 1799, *Madison MSS.*

'Let us not liberate others at the expense of our own freedom,' was the watchword of Citizen Breckinridge's conservatives. Postpone the emancipation question, advised John Taylor of Caroline, sage and mentor of Virginia Republicanism: 'take care of yourselves in the first instance.' Do not exclude slaveholding immigrants, cautioned others: this will prevent men of wealth and breeding from refining by their influence the 'rude and indigested mass' of backwoodsmen. The flaming Rights of Man could very properly be flung against the 'Asiatic Tyranny' of Federalism, but, at home, caution must be taken to insure stability, men should coast along with the status quo — if for no other reason, contended Samuel Hopkins, than to sustain Kentucky's reputation as 'the ultimate refuge of those in the atlantic states who will not Submit to the Oppressions ... of Federal Measures.' [1]

In view of these circumstances, Clay's reformers in Fayette County failed to send one emancipator to the constitutional convention. Indeed, from the whole state of Kentucky only one delegate pledged to emancipation was elected.[2] Some few reforms were made, but in the new constitution of 1799 the objectionable slavery articles of the constitution of 1792 were identically repeated. The 'enthusiasts,' the 'beardless boys,' the liberal Republicans, who sought to make gradual emancipation constitutionally possible, had been most decisively defeated. The state which was to shape Henry Clay's destiny had decided, most definitely, to be a slave state.

Thus did young Clay, disciple of Wythe, and fledgling reformer, see his Tom Paine-Jefferson-Rousseau idealism go down to defeat before the economic and social realities of slave exploitation. 'The whine of interest' had overcome loudly trumpeted libertarianism. The romantic idealism of the Rights of Man applied no more to enchained blacks than to redskinned occupants of desirable Western lands. Clay's fellow Kentuckians had made their decision. Their democracy, it seemed, could be as rigidly exclusive and as righteously intolerant as the grim Calvinism of Jonathan Edwards

---

[1] Hopkins to Breckinridge, July 15, 1799, W. Lewis to same, July 18, 1799, *Breckinridge MSS.*; John Taylor to Innes, April 25, 1799, *Innes MSS.*, 21.

[2] Purviance, L., *David Purviance*, p. 40; *Ky. Gazette*, May 16, 1799.

or the snobbish Federalism of the self-styled 'rich, wise, and well-born.' Even among these Jacobinic Children of America the dead hand of the past rested heavily. For years to come, critics less understanding than Clay of the grave perplexities of the slavery problem were to jeer at the inconsistencies of theory and practice in this America of 'bastard freedom,' of 'slaving blacks and democratic whites.' [1]

The slavery issue in Kentucky was long to remain quiescent; and Henry Clay was not to stir it up. He quickly took on the color of his environment, finding life exciting, diverting, and on the whole agreeable. Like others who had participated in the emancipation struggle he was to own slaves, treat them considerately, and employ them on his farm in the manner of the country. Like Jefferson and other disciples of Wythe's 'sacred cause,' he was to lay himself open to the criticisms of both abolition and pro-slavery zealots. He continued, however, consistently to hold the reasonable and liberal views which at the beginning of his career he had advocated, in favor of gradual emancipation. [2]

With the minority accepting the majority's decision on the vexatious subjects of slavery and constitutional reform, Kentucky once again presented a solid phalanx in the campaign to elect Jefferson president, the opening guns of which were formally fired in January of 1800. By the end of the year the speech-making at courthouse and tavern, at militia musters, barbecues, and the

---

[1] Many and persistent were the jibes at Indian-killing and Negro-enslaving democrats, who were not above wooing 'some black Aspasia's charms,' and dreaming of freedom in their 'bondsmaid's arms' — a theme much capitalized by Federalist critics: Fessenden, *Democracy Unveiled*, II, 16–25, *passim*, has verses on 'Mr. Jefferson and his black Sally' which plumb the depths of vileness. Wrote British Tom Moore in 1804 (*Works*, II, 291):

'Oh! Freedom, Freedom, how I hate thy cant!
Not Eastern bombast, not the savage rant
Of purpled madmen, were they number'd all
From Roman Nero down to Russian Paul,
Could grate upon my ear so mean, so base,
As the rank jargon of that factious race,
Who poor of heart and prodigal of words,
Form'd to be slaves, yet struggling to be lords,
Strut forth, as patriots, from their negro marts,
And shout for rights, with rapine in their hearts.'

[2] 'Clay's private dealings with the institution were always consistent with his political principles on the subject of slavery... Among the mass of the slaveholders of the State, Clay was one of the very few who held a perfectly consistent attitude on gradual emancipation.' McDougle, I. E., *Slavery in Kentucky, 1792–1865*, pp. 104–05.

raising of Liberty Poles (termed by Federalists 'anarchy poles' and 'wooden gods of sedition'), had 'Blown Kentucky into a Flame.' As in 1798 the wagon and stump orators thundered their defiance of the Federalist East — 'Kentucky! In vain the Harpy's Claw is extended over thee.' And few of them, said one of Breckinridge's law students, 'were more noisy than Mr. Clay.' [1]

Henry was engaged in the great 'Political Revolution of 1800.' Against 'Anglo-monarchic-aristocratical Federalism' the masterful Jefferson had welded Southern and Western farmers with Eastern proletarians into a hard-hitting party committed to state and personal rights, majority rule, retrenchment and reform, economy and peace. It was a revolt of 'the People,' of homespun against broadcloth. And material aid was given by Federalist dissensions. For President Adams by putting country above party, and accepting the peace overtures of France, had deeply antagonized the War Hawk Hamiltonians and Pickeronians.

Divided, despondent, the once-proud Federalist party, splendidly capable for all its faults, fought hard to retain control of the national government it had established and put into operation. It would preserve the nation from Jefferson, whom Hamilton termed 'an atheist in religion and a fanatic in politics,' who might bring about 'a REVOLUTION, after the manner of BONAPARTE.' [2] It would preserve the Union from men whom it termed 'original opposers of the Constitution, British debtors, and Frenchified Jacobins,' and, less elegantly, 'thieves, traitors, Irish renegadoes, scape-gallowes, and desperadoes.' Republican orators and editors, however, only increased their attacks upon Federalism's direct taxes, against which Pennsylvanians in 1799 had vainly revolted; the costly army and navy; and especially the Sedition Act, under which men were indicted for erecting Liberty Poles, and Federal judges (even Chief Justice Ellsworth) openly electioneered, solemnly charging grand juries to extirpate 'Jeffersonian anarchy.'

In Kentucky the agitation was given an impetus by the im-

[1] McAfee, *Life and Times*, p. 219; also, *Ky. Gazette*, Dec. 12, 1798; Jan. 16, 1800 ff.
[2] Hamilton to Jay, May 7, 1800, in Beard, Chas. A., *Economic Origins of Jeffersonian Democracy*, p. 370.

migration of the Reign of Terror's most famous victim, Matthew Lyon, radical Vermont democrat. Of tempestuous career and curious oaths, Lyon was notorious not only for 'seditiously' lampooning President Adams but for his recent encounter in Congress with Roger Griswold, Connecticut Federalist. Insulted, he spit in Griswold's face; then, attacked in cowardly fashion by Griswold, who wielded a cudgel, he had nobly defended himself with the congressional fire-tongs. Although termed by Federalists 'a strange offensive brute, too wild to tame, too base to shoot,' a roaring Lyon of Hibernian breed, 'the brogue still hobbling on his tongue, his brows with rank rebellion hung,' Colonel Lyon was warmly welcomed by the frontier democrats and acclaimed as 'The Scourge of Aristocracy' and 'The American Martyr to Liberty.'[1]

Regardless of the Reign of Terror, Clay's neighbors familiarly referred to President Adams as a tyrant, an aristocrat who itched for an American crown; and to Hamilton as a confessed adulterer, an unprincipled West Indian Creole who aspired to be an American Caesar. In striking contrast was the homage they lavished on Thomas Jefferson. He was the Sage of Monticello, the incorruptible Roman, the pontifex maximus of pure republicanism, the father of the Declaration of Independence and of American Liberty. They were proud of Jefferson's scientific experiments, his interest in the bones of the American mammoth, his generous (if somewhat hazy) ideas of ameliorating the common lot of humanity. Attacks upon him as atheist, libertine, Jacobinic terrorist, and demagogic visionary were indignantly repelled — 'the arts of malice and the rude voice of faction assail him in vain.' Like Cato, they said, Jefferson was attached to his country; like Socrates, his affections embraced the universe; like Jupiter from Olympus, he surveyed with serenity and silence the awful fate of corrupt empires.[2]

Young Henry Clay and his fellow Kentuckians all but deified

[1] Alsop, R., *The Political Green-House for 1798*, pp. 3–10; letters on Lyon's arrival in *Breckinridge MSS.*, April–May, 1799 (which reveal that George Nicholas and other Lexingtonians were cool to the idea of Lyon's settling as their close neighbor); also, McLaughlin, J. F., *Matthew Lyon, the Hampden of Congress*.

[2] *Ky. Gazette*, May 29, 1800, and *passim*.

Thomas Jefferson, 'The Man of the People,' 'The Mammoth of Democracy.' They could not wholly forgive General Washington for being his opponent, for being a Federalist. In the midst of their riotous campaign, news reached Lexington of the death of America's Revolutionary commander and first president. At the Presbyterian meeting-house there was a respectful eulogy by Professor James Brown of Transylvania University. Yet at the political rallies, when Henry and his friends drank to young Bonaparte, the new French leader and regenerator who had overthrown Talleyrand's corrupt Directory; and to 'No Army, No Navy, and the repeal of (their inevitable consequences) direct tax laws,' their toast to Washington was sharply qualified — 'George Washington: down to the year 1787 but no farther.' [1]

It seemed as if the election of Jefferson was vital to the safeguarding of rights and liberties won by the Revolution. In this spirit Colonel Thomas Hart, Breckinridge, Editor Bradford, and other town fathers planned a great Civic Feast, an impressive Republican Festival, on the Fourth of July, 1800. For the signal honor of orator of the day they chose the twenty-three-year-old Henry Clay. And on the twenty-fourth anniversary of 'blood-bought' independence, in Lexington's public square 'a considerable concourse of citizens' with militia companies of horse and foot heard from the courthouse steps 'an elegant oration on the occasion . . . delivered by Henry Clay, Esq.'

Thus did the *Gazette* (with its usual economy) summarize Orator Clay's soaring tributes to the Revolutionary Heroes, his spirited defense of American Democracy, and his vehement arraignment of Federalist Toryism. It was another glorious opportunity for the young lawyer to impress himself upon Blue Grass Kentucky as a bold and generous Republican, keenly attuned to the sympathies and aspirations of the common man, and by the speaker's art of subtle flattery to transform rough Kentucs into high-souled patriots, and restless 'mobocrats' into gallant 'Freemen of the West.'

Following Clay's 'elegant oration' the procession formed and marched to Mr. Maxwell's Spring: the Fayette Troop of Horse in

---

[1] *Ky. Gazette*, Jan. 9, 23, Feb. 6, 1800; McAfee, *op. cit.*, p. 217.

front, the Lexington Light Infantry in the rear, Revolutionary veterans, farmers, merchants, artisans, women and children in the center, and ahead of all a proud citizen in homespun carrying a long pole topped by a Liberty Cap. At Maxwell's Grove the company toasted 'the tree of LIBERTY . . . while we enjoy its fruits, may we never forget its planters,' and 'Destruction to all combinations against the rights of man'; Kentucky's rich agriculture, aspiring manufactures, and booming Mississippi trade; and, with gallant gestures and much clinking of glasses, 'The American fair — Although last toasted, the first in our hearts.' [1]

Between his 'elegant' orations and 'noisy' stump speeches young Clay kept pace with Eastern political developments, particularly those of the pivotal state of New York.[2] There was no question as to Kentucky's vote — it was solid for Jefferson. At length, in January of 1801, rolling drums and clanging bells announced the thrilling news: Thomas Jefferson had been elected president! With the jubilant citizens of Lexington Henry attended 'the Grand Festival' presided over by Colonel Thomas Hart, drank 'half a hundred toasts with ten thousand acclamations,' and participated in 'the innocent amusement of the Sprightly Dance.' [3]

But it was not until March of 1801 that he was certain that Jefferson had been made president. Aaron Burr of New York, the Republican vice-presidential candidate, had received the same number of electoral votes. And a Federalist House seemed intent on declaring Burr president and Jefferson vice president, or on calling a new election. The uncertainty was most trying to true Republicans. It gave the Federalists a chance to jeer at premature celebrations of Jefferson's elevation to the throne as 'Monarch of the People':

> 'Stop — ere your civic feasts begin,
> Wait 'till the votes are all come in;
> Perchance, amid this mighty stir
> Your Monarch may be — Col. BURR!
> Who, if he mounts the sovereign seat,
> Like BONAPARTE will *make you sweat*,

---

[1] *Ky. Gazette*, July 10, 1800.
[2] Clay to Ninian Edwards, July 9, 1800, Edwards, N., *Papers*, p. 23.
[3] *Ky. Gazette*, Jan. 26, 1801.

Your Idol then must quaking dwell,
Mid *Mammoth's* bones at *Monticelle,*
His country's barque from anchors free,
On "Liberty's tempestuous sea,"
While all Democrats will sing —
THE DEVIL TAKE THE PEOPLE'S KING.' [1]

Would Aaron Burr, noted for his intrigues in New York politics, bargain with the Federalists and rob the people of their triumph? Would the vindictive aristocrats thus take revenge for their defeat at the polls? Would the Federalists thus dare precipitate a civil war which might well lead to disunion or to a dictator for republican America, Hamilton, perhaps Burr, just as the recent Eighteenth Brumaire (November 9, 1799) in republican France had installed First Consul Bonaparte? Anxious days and months passed. The drums of civil war were beating in the distracted, ill-coordinated Union as Clay and his friends waited, waited, 'all on the tenters about Jefferson's election.' [2]

'The federalists will die hard,' reported John Fowler, Lexington's congressman, from the new Federal City of Washington, 'but must and will give way to the Majesty of the People.' [3] Having lost control of executive and legislature they now appeared to be not only plotting Burr's election but 'of a settled determination to enforce their high-handed measures through the Judiciary.' Kentuckians saw proof of this in the horde of 'Midnight Judges' and other court officials appointed by Adams in the last days of his administration; in the appointees who afterward appeared at the Federal Court in Frankfort in unrepublican dress, 'with their Judicial gowns & cocked hats on, in imitation of the British judges.' [4]

Meanwhile young Clay and his fellow Westerners in great suspense awaited the verdict of the long-drawn-out balloting on Jefferson and Burr. It made Henry realize how isolated Kentucky

---

[1] Alsop, R., *The Echo,* pp. 281–82.

[2] Breckinridge to Jas. Breckinridge, Dec. 21, 1800, *Breckinridge MSS.*

[3] *Ibid.,* Fowler to Breckinridge, March 5, 1801.

[4] McAfee, *op. cit.,* p. 219; G. Thompson to Breckinridge, Dec. 28, 1801, and Sen. S. T. Mason of Va. to same, Feb. 12, 1801, *Breckinridge MSS.*; *Ky. Gazette,* March 30, 1801. 'The Judges Sit on the Bench Cocked hats on there heads Made Every body Stand about. I had rather the Indians would fall on us than to have this federal Court,' wrote George Thompson to Breckinridge, *supra,* from Shawanee Springs.

was from the East. Ice choked the Ohio and great rains had gutted
the Wilderness Road. In desperation Editor John Bradford said he
could as well predict the return of a comet, an earthquake, or an
eruption of Mount Vesuvius as the arrival of the next Eastern
mail.[1]

At length the glorious news came to Kentucky — Jefferson had
been elected on the thirty-sixth ballot.[2] The Political Revolution
of 1800 had triumphed over Adams and Aristocracy. It was a
turning point in the evolution of Clay's Western World. For the
first time Americans on the frontier periphery of the new Federal
Union felt they would be treated henceforth on an equality with
Easterners; no longer regarded as 'enemies or aliens.' For the
first time they became unqualifiedly devoted to the general government — now most happily administered by their own Jefferson
and by men genuinely republican, truly American. No longer
would the Children of America impatiently agitate; rather, they
would buttress their own Republican national administration.

The Federalist Reign of Terror was no more. In 1801 Lawyer
Henry Clay of Lexington joined with his fellow Republicans of the
Western World in triumphant toasts — 'The United States: May
their republican government endure while the earth revolves on
its axis,' and in triumphant song —

> 'Rejoice! Columbia's sons rejoice!
> To tyrants never bend the knee,
> But join with heart, and soul, and voice,
> For JEFFERSON and LIBERTY.'

---

[1] *Ky. Gazette*, April 13, 1801; also Feb. 21, 1799, March 16, April 6, 1801.

[2] At this crisis Hamilton powerfully exerted his influence against Federalists (including Chief Justice Marshall) who would elect Burr; he believed that Jefferson, while
'a contemptible hypocrit,' would not destroy the governmental foundations laid by
Federalism; on the other hand, Aaron Burr, his bitter rival in New York, was the very
'Catiline of America.' Hamilton, *Works*, X, 392, 395.

Chapter Three. A Frontier Lawyer

*With a great deal of native talent, and a little smattering of law . . .
Mr. Clay went into the wilderness . . . and with a good address, natural
eloquence, perseverance, boldness, and all those qualities that are admired by
a new people, he became an influential man.* (Daniel Webster.)

Well, neighbor, the court has decided against you?
Yes, but if I could have got Harry Clay *to my side things would not
have been so.* ('*Citizen*' *in* Lexington Reporter.)

'BEARDLESS Henry Clay's advocacy of Jefferson and Liberty, and
of the Rights of Men both white and black, did not solve his own
compelling problems; did not pay for his board and lodging, or for
convivial evenings at the taverns, or for the beaver hats and colorful waistcoats supplied by Tailor Paddy McCullough. In March
of 1798 he had hung out his shingle and looked about for business.
New to the country, and just turned twenty-one, he faced the
prospect of competing for a livelihood with able, well-established
lawyers and a host of aggressive younger rivals.

Yet Kentucky, as Clay would say in after years, was most
generous to him — a penniless boy newly arrived from Richmond,
'without patrons, without the favor or countenance of the great
and opulent. . . . I remember how comfortable I thought I should
be if I could make one hundred pounds, Virginia money, per year,
and with what delight I received my first fifteen shilling fee. My
hopes were more than realized,' he said, with no great exaggera-

tion: 'I immediately rushed into a successful and lucrative practice.' [1]

Although he faced formidable competition 'in the midst of a bar uncommonly distinguished by eminent members,' he soon discovered that Fayette and the surrounding Blue Grass counties yielded an amazing amount of litigation. John Breckinridge would often declare that if he were cut into four pieces each would have more than enough legal employment.[2] The 'beardless boy' was no less eager to relieve Citizen Breckinridge of his burden than he was to oppose him on the slavery issue. Breckinridge, indeed, early availed himself of his services. Virginia friends, even before he was admitted to the Kentucky bar, entrusted Western lands to his care. In his first year of practice he became the agent for William Taylor, famed Baltimore merchant. And in short time he was the attorney for prominent Kentuckians, including Nathaniel Hart, a former proprietor of Transylvania Colony, who like most citizens refused to pay the hated Federalist excise on whiskey and even threatened an enemy who reported him to United States Attorney Daveiss that he would have Lawyer Clay bring suit against him for 'Malacious prosecution.' [3]

Henry 'rushed' into practice, and steadily progressed. 'Two words,' he said to one of his law students in 1807, 'will make any man of sound intellect a lawyer, industry and application; and the same words with a third, economy, will enable him to make a fortune.' [4] Such platitudes, however, did not explain his own rapid climb to fortune at the bar. In his own career there entered other elements — his knowledge of human nature, intuitive sense of what affected men, an instinctive dramatic flair, and his gift of speech. Then too there was the element of luck, of happy accident. The fair-haired youth in Kentucky as in Virginia was (as a Lexington companion stated) 'Fortune's darling son.' [5]

---

[1] Speech at Lexington, 1842, Clay, *Works*, IX, 363.

[2] McAfee, *Life and Times*, p. 215.

[3] Hart to Breckinridge, Nov. 19, 1801, Nath. W. Price to same, March 11, 1798, *Breckinridge MSS.*; Clay to Wm. Taylor, 1799 ff., *Clay MSS.*; *Ky. Gazette*, Aug. 22, 1799 (re his handling of Francis Brooke's lands), and ff.; and Edwards, N., *Papers*, p. 25 ff.

[4] Clay, *Private Correspondence*, ed. Calvin Colton, p. 15.

[5] William T. Barry to Clay, Jan. 29, 1809, *Clay MSS*. For a keen analysis of Clay's character see the sketch of him by Gamaliel Bradford, *As God Made Them*, pp. 43–85.

Of 'superior talents,' as Federalist Humphrey Marshall remarked, and of independent spirit, his natural forwardness had been polished to some degree by mingling with Virginia's great men at Richmond. In Lexington, as in the Virginia capital, he won friends quickly, and soon had patrons among the great and opulent. It was hard not to like young Harry Clay — lively, warmhearted, frank, easy of manner, with an air of deep interest and personal regard. From his arrival in Lexington James Brown was not alone in wishing Henry (as he so often did) his 'measure of felicity filled to the brim.'

This bustling frontier country sharpened his wits, developed self-reliance, and called forth a remarkable energy. It did not demand or encourage any deep or prolonged introspection; rather, it was congenial to his emotional temperament, to a proneness to 'skim' in his general reading and to make impulsive judgments. He came to rely very largely upon his shrewd observations of men and events, his intuitive knowledge and personal charm, and upon his fluent tongue which could persuade others, and often himself. He was ever sanguine about the subject immediately before him, and absorbed in its successful presentation.

Yet at the very beginning of his career law and politics found a stronger rival in a subject far removed from wagon-tail speeches and jury harangues. During the tumult over the constitutional convention and the Federalist Reign of Terror, Henry's emotional life had indeed been richly full and varied. The irrepressible young orator and pamphleteer had fallen in love. To his desire to defend outraged humanity and distinguish himself as a Tribune of the People by his Scaevola letters and his anti-Federalist declamations was added the hope that he would make a good impression upon Lucretia Hart.

Soon after his arrival from Virginia he had won the countenance of Colonel Thomas Hart, and of his family. A native of Clay's county of Hanover, the Colonel in early life had migrated to North Carolina, and had become an influential Revolutionary Whig. Still active though approaching seventy, he had been a proprietor of the Transylvania Company, which a generation before had staked out Kentucky and much of Tennessee as a feudal domain, hired Daniel Boone as a road-blazer, and financed the first settlers in the short-lived Transylvania Colony. In Hagerstown, Maryland, he had been the partner of Nathaniel Rochester (the great merchant, founder of the city in New York bearing his name) until 1794, when he had come to Lexington to look after his thousands of Western acres and his town of Transylvania near Louisville, and had become a prominent merchant-manufacturer.

Public-spirited, Colonel Hart was connected with everything in Lexington from the subscription library over McCalla's apothecary shop to the Masonic Lodge and the Emigration Society. He was a Jeffersonian, and enthusiastic over Henry's Republican orations. His law cases were many, but the townspeople had soon become aware that the impelling cause of Lawyer Clay's frequent visits was Lucretia, the Colonel's youngest daughter.

Lucretia, born in Hagerstown in 1781, was affectionately called by the Colonel his 'Little Marylander.' [1] She was a lively, dark-eyed, dark-haired girl of eighteen, good-looking but not of uncommon beauty. Although she may have studied 'reading and needlework' at Mrs. Walsh's School for Little Misses,[2] her book knowledge was no more extensive than that of other young ladies, of Lexington or of Jane Austen's England. She nevertheless possessed much of the acumen and common sense that had made her father one of the West's great entrepreneurs, and shared to some degree Colonel Hart's robust sociability. Lucretia was not gushing or demonstrative, but her sympathies were deep and generous. She was broad-minded (as Henry well appreciated) about a gentleman's gaming and drinking, and was as little in-

---

[1] George H. Clay, grandson of Henry, to the writer, Lexington, Sept., 1929. On Lucretia, see Harrison, James O., *Reminiscences*, and his MS. Memoir of Clay in *Harrison MSS.*; Kendall, Amos, *Autobiography*, pp. 115–49; Smith, *Forty Years of Washington Society*, p. 84 ff. On Thomas Hart, see Young, S. S., *Hart Family*; Henderson, A., *Conquest of the Old Southwest*; Williams, T. J. C., *History of Washington County, Maryland*, I, 89, 94, 136–38; and the many references in *North Carolina Colonial* and *State Records*. J. F. D. Smyth, *A Tour* (1784), I, 246–48, describes 'the humane benevolent... polished... accomplished' Thomas Hart, who in North Carolina had 'received and entertained me with the greatest hospitality and kindness... The refreshments, comforts and consolation he bestowed on me with a liberal hand, appeared to afford even a superior degree of satisfaction and felicity to him, than to me...'

[2] See Mrs. Walsh's notice, *Ky. Gazette*, March 22, 1797. Lucretia's older sister, Elizabeth (Mrs. Pindell), had studied at a boarding-school in Philadelphia, where she had been under the care of the celebrated Robert Morris. Nathaniel Rochester's memoir, Williams, T. J. C., *op. cit.*, I, 138.

clined to conventional religion as Citizen Clay himself. Had she been more assertive, and possessed of more intellectual qualities, she might better have balanced Henry's emotional and impulsive nature. She was capable of unselfish devotion to those she loved, and she accepted them as they were; if she had been of different temperament it is not likely that Henry Clay would have fallen so deeply in love.

His courtship was ardent and brief. Lucretia, on her part, was enchanted with this tall suitor whose pale hair (he had, she would say, 'the whitest head of hair I ever saw'[1]) was tousled so fashionably and whose courtly bow and wide smile were so disarming. She liked his Richmond manners, his Virginia gallantry, and was flattered at being singled out by this young hero of the Maxwell's Spring oration and the triumphal procession through Lexington. They were often seen together during the winter and spring of 1799, at the dancing assemblies, at tea and syllabub parties, and at the courthouse where (in February and March) such dramas were presented as *All the World's a Stage* and *Love à la Mode*.

On April 11, 1799, a day before Henry's twenty-second birthday, he and Lucretia were married at Colonel Hart's home with all the spirited festivities of a Blue Grass wedding. In a small brick house on Mill Street, adjoining the dignified dwelling of the Harts on the corner of Mill and Second Streets, they established their first home.

It was a happy marriage — and a fortunate one. By it Clay became intimately connected with the ruling families of Kentucky, with the clannish society of transplanted Virginians that was fast developing in the Blue Grass. It facilitated his initiation into the group of men whose leadership in law, politics, trade, and manufacturing made Lexington the frontier metropolis, made 'Lexington influence' and 'Lexington dictation' felt not only in Kentucky but throughout the Western World. In this group his father-in-law was a commanding figure.

Colonel Hart was a true empire-builder, in contrast with his old friend, nomadic, anti-social Daniel Boone. His creative energies

---

[1] Harrison, J. O., *Reminiscences*, p. 179.

left a deep impress on Western development. Less than a year after removing to Lexington he wrote to Governor William Blount of Maryland of the many irons he had in the fire — a rope-walk, a smithy with four forges, an extensive wholesale and retail mercantile business, and a nail factory which was 'a very pretty thing in this country' since '25 hands net me a clear profit of 20 dollars a day.' A genial soul who loved to have his friends about him, the Colonel attempted to induce the Blounts to join him, praising the society of Lexington — where 'not a day passes over our heads but I can have half a dozen Gentlemen to dine with us, and they are from all parts of the Union' — and painting a glowing picture of 'what pleasure we should have in raking up money and spending it with our friends.' [1]

Of the jovial old Colonel's many friends and relatives, James Brown, the husband of Lucretia's sister Nancy, was most helpful in aiding young Henry to get a start in Kentucky. A man of thirty-three, one of the West's ablest lawyers, Brown was Professor of Law and Politics at Transylvania University, having succeeded George Nicholas upon the latter's death a few months after the wedding of Lucretia and Henry.[2] Handsome, 'towering and majestic in person,' was this well-educated, well-mannered, son of Virginia. A Kentucky founding father, young as he was, he had commanded a company of sharpshooters in the Indian wars and had been Kentucky's first secretary of state. He was to be the first secretary of Louisiana Territory, Federal senator from Louisiana, and minister to France under Monroe and Adams. The brother of John Brown, Kentucky's pioneer statesman, now a senator at Philadelphia, and of Doctor Sam Brown, Lexington's noted physician, he was related to the Breckinridges, Prestons, and Cabells of Virginia. Successful at the bar, distinguished, suave; a Jeffersonian democrat who often confounded frontiersmen with

---

[1] Hart to Blount, Feb. 15, 1795, Kerr, *Hist. Ky.*, I, 504–05, 525. See also, Henderson, A., 'Creative Forces in Western Expansion,' *Amer. Hist. Rev.*, XX, 86–107, for an appreciation of Thomas Hart as an empire-builder.

[2] Brown's studies at Wythe's William & Mary, his 12 years' practice, 'and the number of law students who already crowd his classes, give the most decided proof of the propriety of the appointment.' *Ky. Gazette*, March 6, 1800. 'A man of large fortune, respectable talents, handsome person, polished manners, and elegant deportment.' Adams, J. Q., *Memoirs*, ed. C. F. Adams, VI, 123. See, also, Taul, Micah, 'Memoirs,' *Reg. Ky. S. Hist. Soc.*, XXVII, 356.

his knowledge of French, German, and Spanish; courageous, and with an independence which his enemies often considered egotistic arrogance, James Brown was a man of parts, whom impressionable Henry Clay warmly admired.

Regarding Henry as a younger brother, Brown assisted him in acquiring a practice, steered him through Kentucky's legal mazes, and turned over to him cases which he had formerly handled for their common father-in-law. He took delight in recommending his young colleague to his many friends in Western America as 'an attorney of the most promising Talents and amiable disposition.' [1]

Audacity and ingenuity availed young Henry in an early case in which he was called before an untutored Kentucky magistrate to defend a man accused of stealing hogs. Although the evidence was conclusive against his client, Henry's eloquent tongue, it was said, and his quotation from memory of a lengthy English decision he had once copied for Chancellor Wythe, finally convinced the bewildered justice of the peace that the hog-stealer should have his freedom.[2] In August 1799 at Frankfort, however, this sort of daring ingenuity failed to win an arrest of judgment for wife-killer Henry Fields; but Clay's efforts in attacking the indictment as faulty, and his defiance of a mob that threatened to lynch Fields, caused favorable comment.[3] Not long after, he won a solid victory and much public acclaim when pitted against James Hughes, veteran Lexington lawyer who was considered by many to be 'undoubtedly the first attorney in this State,' [4] in a case involving rival mills on North Elkhorn Creek. The battle of the water wheels 'made a great deal of noise' and was hotly contested before Mr. Hughes acknowledged his defeat. 'This event at once established Mr. Clay's practice,' said Robert McAfee, who attended the trial, 'and

---

[1] Brown to Colonel Thomas Bedford of Nashville, Oct. 8, 1799, Ky. S. Hist. Society, *Misc. MSS.* Brown stated that Clay 'goes down on a visit to your Country and... may probably become an Inhabitant.' It is possible that Clay contemplated a visit to Tennessee in the interests of Colonel Hart or of some other client, and thought it politic to go in the character of a prospective settler.

[2] Rogers, *Clay*, pp. 28–29.

[3] Johnson, L. F., *History of Franklin County*, pp. 11–12.

[4] Hubbard Taylor to Madison, Jan. 15, 1803, *Madison MSS.*

in a little while he was at the head of the Bar, and employed on one side of almost every suit in the Fayette courts.'[1]

Crumbling legal records in the Fayette courthouse support McAfee's statement, as well as Henry's assertion that he 'immediately rushed into a successful and lucrative practice.' They also tend to confirm the encomiums of Clay's contemporaries and the Kentucky tradition that it was exceptional for him to lose a lawsuit. A random selection of some thirty cases from the number in which he was engaged from March of 1798 to March of 1802 reveals that in only one did the young attorney meet with defeat. They concerned Negroes illegally enslaved by rapacious whites; debts owed Colonel Hart and other merchants ranging from '328 dollars Kentucky currency' to as high as £10,000; damages for broken covenants regarding slaves, '£76 worth of good geldings,' hemp, tobacco, whiskey, and Kentucky broadhorn boats; and several intricate land-title suits.[2] His letters written during this early period reveal a hard-working, forthright youngster who seemed to have a clear and confident grasp of affairs, especially of devices resorted to by delinquent debtors who had 'a talent for lying.' He was diligent, courteous, boldly individual, and eager for advancement.[3]

In face of strong competition from the bar's younger members, Henry fell heir to much of Breckinridge's practice when that 'Atlas of Republicanism' went to Washington in 1801 to become the Jeffersonian leader of the Senate. He profited likewise by the removal to Louisiana in 1803 of James Brown and other lawyers. He early became the Kentucky agent of such Baltimore merchants (in addition to William Taylor) as John Comegys and Luke Tiernan. He looked after the lands of Judge Francis Brooke, Matthew Clay, and other Virginians; of Secretary of the Navy Robert Smith and of the creditors of Robert Morris, 'Financier of the Revolution,' whose colossal land speculations brought him to

---

[1] McAfee, *Life and Times*, p. 218.

[2] *Order Books*, and file records, Fayette Cir. Court, Lexington.

[3] See Clay's letters 1800–1801, directing action on Colonel Hart's legal affairs, to Ninian Edwards of Russellville, Ky., Edwards, N., *Papers*, pp. 17–27; also his letters to Wm. Taylor, et al., 1799–1804, *Clay MSS.*; and to Breckinridge, 1800 ff., *Breckinridge MSS.*

the debtors' prison. He handled at least one case for General Andrew Jackson, merchant of Nashville; and he was urged by Noah Webster to look after the copyrights and royalties in the West of his famous spelling books.[1]

In 1803 Major James Morrison, an executor of the George Nicholas estate, considered it good insurance to retain young Clay and thus prevent claimants from employing him.[2] As early as 1800 Elijah Craig, Baptist preacher and shrewd business adventurer, seeking aid from the Lexington bar to protect his 'ferry road' across the Kentucky River at Frankfort, called upon, in the order named, 'John Brakenridge, James Brown, and Henry Clay.'[3]

Without much loss of time, the 'beardless boy' who had won huzzas and a triumphal carriage ride for his prowess as a Jeffersonian orator was acquiring a reputation as a lawyer. And this, too, without ever inserting a card in the *Kentucky Gazette*. Unlike most attorneys, including Breckinridge, he did not deem it necessary, apparently, to advertise that his Lexington office was open. Business came to him — even from Humphrey Marshall. When his large landholdings were endangered, Marshall overcame his political repugnance to 'noisy' Henry Clay, whom he regarded as a Jacobinic upstart whose 'anti-Federalism had been bred in his bones,' and requested his aid. As the Federalist leader remarked, young Lawyer Clay in no time at all had made himself as conspicuous in Kentucky as the state house in Frankfort or the Cheapside market in Lexington.[4]

His success was achieved among a frontier people uncommonly litigious, yet pervaded by a democratic equalitarianism that made them resent any assumption of superiority by reason of wealth or talents, especially by the lawyer, with his title of Esquire, and his gaining as if by intrigue the important public offices.[5] While they

---

[1] *Clay MSS.*, 1798 ff.; Jackson, *Corres.*, I, 151 (Oct., 1806).

[2] [Morrison] to Wilson Cary Nicholas, Nov. 30, 1803, *W. C. Nicholas MSS.*

[3] Craig's letter, June 17, 1800, *Breckinridge MSS.*

[4] H. Marshall, in *Ky. Gazette*, Jan. 28, Feb. 18, 1832.

[5] 'Who shall represent us?' asked 'A Plain Simple Peasant' at the beginning of the state government. 'A dire dilemma! On all sides there is danger — Farmers, perhaps, are too ignorant; Lawyers too full of quibble and mischief, and Magistrates too aspiring and designing. The Lawyer whose business is chicanery will make laws to perplex and deceive. The Magistrate can fix the pay for his own services as high as he pleases, the Lawyer inhances his own fees; but the Farmer none of these.' The honest, though ignorant, farmer should guide the ship of state. *Ky. Gazette*, April 27, 1793.

filled his coffers the buckskin pioneers inveighed against the lawyer as knavish and artful, 'enveloped in mystery, chicane, and subtlety.' [1] From early days the Children of America had agitated for a legal code devoid of foreign phrases and English common-law precedents, plainly worded and 'adapted to the weakest capacity' — one which would 'happily supersede the necessity of attorneys.' [2]

Their antipathy to a 'Lawyer Aristocracy' and to 'Judge Rule' had brought about the sanctioning of legal arbitration by laymen outside of court.[3] In 1802 they revolutionized the judiciary and set up circuit courts, one in each county, each with one judge and two assistants. Significantly, the backwoods democracy (led by 'cunning and intriguing' Felix Grundy) which triumphed over a protesting Blue Grass expressly provided that the new assistant judges must be men 'not learned in the law.' [4] In the new circuit courts where cases were decided by majority rule the two assistants, local politicians and ignorant of the law as required, would often arrive late from the pothouses and card tables and undo everything the judge had done. Gruff Judge Broadnax despised his associates as judicial excrescences. On the bench he would sarcastically inquire first of one, 'What do you *guess*?' and then of the other, 'What do you *guess*?' [5]

There were some distinguished judges, like Thomas Todd of Frankfort and the uncommonly well-educated, Wythe-trained Buckner Thruston of Lexington, but many were rough-moulded pioneers, intellectually handicapped, men who were known to adjourn court to witness strolling magicians, to comb their unkempt hair in court, and to fall victims to their favorite beverage. It was notorious that the bar 'in every county of the state was superior to the bench.' [6] So often were the judges outwitted, 'out-

[1] *Ky. Gazette*, April 24, 1810; and *passim*, for similar articles.

[2] *Ibid.*, Oct. 15, 1791, Bourbon County Resolutions.

[3] 'And thus,' said Lawyer Humphrey Marshall (*Hist. of Ky.*, II, 176), 'by a side wind, and under the specious pretense of expediting and cheapening... justice, was the trial by jury dispensed with; and a door thrown open by law, for every species of irregularity.'

[4] *Ky. Gazette*, Jan. 25, Feb. 1, 1803; *Breckinridge MSS.*, Nov.–Dec., 1802.

[5] Little, Judge Lucius P., *Ben Hardin*, etc., pp. 468–69.

[6] *Ky. Gazette*, April 17, 1804; one of several articles by 'Hibernian.'

guessed,' and even browbeaten by the lawyers that continual, and unavailing, pleas were made of a backwoods legislature for salaries sufficiently attractive to fill the bench with men 'enlightened, virtuous, and independent' — salaries which would enable the judges of Kentucky to afford at least 'one nine pence per annum for a patriotic glass of whiskey.' [1]

The many inferior judges, together with overcrowded dockets and protracted litigation, legislative meddling with the judiciary, the chaos as to legal organization, procedure, and precedents then prevailing (not only in Kentucky but in the states of the East),[2] and the disorders of court day, brought about the generally low calibre of the courts in which Henry Clay practiced.

As in rural Virginia, the three-or-four-day session of court was a time of 'drinking, fighting, & jollifying.' [3] To the court towns came backwoods farmers on horseback or in lurching country wagons: 'some plaintiffs, some defendants, some going there to wrestle, fight, shoot at a mark with the rifle for wagers, gamble at other games, or drink whiskey... prepared for any kind of a frolick.' On the green they competed in snuffing the candle, barking the squirrel, or driving the nail into the target; they raced horses, fought cocks, threw long bullets, pulled the old gander's head off, ran foot-races, drank each other under the table, and, in brutal gouging affrays, compelled the bully or 'roarer' of the neighborhood to make good his bellicose vauntings.[4]

Even in the metropolis of Lexington, court day was carried on with the abandon of frontiersmen happy in their release from months of bucolic monotony. Around the public square, on Main, Upper, Short, and Market Streets, as many as a thousand

---

[1] *Ky. Gazette*, Aug. 23, 1803; July 3, Nov. 13, 1804; Jan. 23, 1810; *passim*.

[2] 'When James Kent went upon the bench in New York in 1791, he could say with entire truth: "There were no reports or state precedents. The opinions from the bench were delivered *ore tenus*. We had no law of our own and nobody knew what [the law] was."' Pound, Roscoe, *The Spirit of the Common Law*, chap. V, 'The Pioneer and the Law,' p. 113. See also Paxson, F. L., 'Influence of Frontier Life on the Development of American Law,' *Proc. of the State Bar Assoc. of Wisconsin*, 1919–1921, pp. 477–89; and Warren, Chas., *History of the American Bar*.

[3] Taul, Micah, *Memoirs*, p. 363. Taul was then Clerk of Clark County.

[4] *Ibid.*, p. 359 *passim*; Cuming, F., *Tour to the Western Country* (in Thwaites, R. G., ed., *Early Western Travels*, IV), p. 136; Audubon, John J., *Delineations of American Scenery and Character*, pp. 56–63.

saddle-horses (reported an Easterner in 1810) would be tethered by the jostling crowd which milled about, questioning lawyers and judges, frequenting courtroom, taverns, and houses of pleasure.[1] On these gala days Lexington exhibited 'an unfavorable example of republican order,' said a British visitor of 1804, whose accuracy was vouched for by the *Gazette*. Clad in buckskin breeches, homespun jeans, or striped linen pantaloons much the worse for wear, Henry Clay's compatriots had gathered not so much for the sake of business as to display their 'noisy, democratical notions of independence.' Fayette courthouse presented a Hogarthian scene: 'judges sitting as silent spectators, attorneys wrangling and disputing among themselves within the bar, parties often clamorous, witnesses pertinacious and contemptuous, and what may be called the people — some sober, and others drunk, laughing, talking, sometimes shouting, and not unfrequently brawling or fighting in the presence of the court.'[2]

Against this tumultuous background young Clay, bold, adroit, and resourceful, magnified his knowledge of fundamental legal principles by adept management and splendid acting, made effective use of his native wit and eloquent tongue, and in the courtroom early attained a dominance which frequently exceeded that of the presiding judge. Henry Clay was well equipped, and the frontier Kentucky setting perfectly adapted, for the exercise of the maxim that 'Law is whatever is boldly asserted and plausibly maintained.'

His reputation in criminal causes, a field in which his oratorical talents had full swing and sweep, really began with the murder trial of Mrs. Doshey Phelps at the September 1801 term of Fayette Court. In an argument over stolen money Mrs. Phelps had engaged in a cudgelling brawl with her husband's mother and sisters. At length, when the ladies were resting, Doshey grimly appeared with a musket: one of the sisters fell dead with 'one bullit and ten buck shot lodged in her.' The killer fled, was captured, and brought into Lexington for trial, with the Attorney

---

[1] Alex. Wilson, in Ord, *A. Wilson*, p. cxlviii.

[2] *Ky. Gazette*, March 27, 1804, article by 'Hibernian' and editorial note vouching for its accuracy.

THE COURTHOUSE AND PUBLIC SQUARE, LEXINGTON, KENTUCKY

THE KENTUCKY STATE HOUSE, FRANKFORT, KENTUCKY, 1793–1813

General of Kentucky, 'Little Jemmy' Blair, confidently demanding a verdict of murder in the first degree. It looked black for Doshey — Kentucky juries before this had sent members of the weaker sex to their death. To save her from the gallows Clay was compelled to bring into play all his ingenuity and histrionic powers.

This was an exceptional case, he informed the jury. The deed was shocking, but most assuredly Mrs. Phelps had committed it in a moment of mental aberration, a moment of 'temporary delirium.' Dreadful was her recollection of that awful moment when reason was unhinged. Her life, hitherto unblemished, was now in the balance. Phelps had forgiven her, though his own sister was her unfortunate victim. Surely these twelve Kentuckians, good men and true, would find in their hearts the same quality of Christian mercy, would rescue the poor female from the arbitrary provisions of the common law, and make possible her ultimate restoration to husband and family. He insisted upon the validity of his defense, 'temporary insanity,' which was then a novel theory, a new device of the criminal lawyer. Aroused by his stirring appeals, the compassionate and chivalrous jurors returned a verdict of manslaughter. Instead of being hanged by the neck, Doshey Phelps was given the least possible punishment — five years in the new penitentiary at Frankfort.[1]

Crimes of violence offered a large and lucrative field for the defender of unfortunate Mrs. Phelps. This raw backwoods, peopled by brawling, anarchic adventurers, seemed to breed a distinct race, so visitors reported, much taller and leaner, more restless, excitable, and ruthless than the men of the humdrum, law-abiding East.[2] Courage, physical courage, was a prime essential among these Children of America — some of whom, alas, were 'but a remove from Indians in their manners or moreals.'[3]

As near Lexington as the Sign of the Reap-Hook tavern on the

---

[1] *Ky. Gazette*, Aug. 17, 24, Sept. 28, 1801; *Order Book B, 1801–03*, Fayette Circuit Court, pp. 173, 186; Prentice, *Clay*, pp. 12–13.

[2] Espy, J., *A Tour* (1805), p. 24; Flint, T., *Recollections of the Last Ten Years*, ed. C. H. Grattan, p. 61.

[3] Austin, Moses, *Journal*, p. 525.

Frankfort Pike immigrants and circuit-riding lawyers were waylaid, with a volley of bullets and the command: 'Stop, you damned buggers!' Frequent were admonitions in the *Gazette* of 'Travellers Beware!!' More dangerous than the redskins (whom the whites fleeced and even killed with impunity) were wanton desperadoes — sometimes disguised as Indians, sometimes as Methodist preachers — who often terrorized whole districts. Along the Ohio, the Cumberland, and the Green Rivers, and along the Natchez Trace leading to New Orleans, roamed the Mason gang and the infamous Big and Little Harpe, land and river pirates, robbers and assassins, until relatives of their victims finally tracked them down and brought back their bloody heads to expose as impressive public warnings.[1]

On one occasion young Lawyer Clay of Lexington took the lead in breaking up a 'Banditti of Horse-thieves and Murderers.' A man named Russell appealed to him, after having been terribly beaten and warned to leave the country, his home, and lands, by desperadoes who called themselves 'Regulators.' At considerable personal hazard Clay took up his cause, sounded a clarion call to public sentiment, and succeeded in bringing the outlaws into court. He not only obtained justice for poor Russell but helped to rid Kentucky of a 'sett of Gallows Villains.' [2]

For all its cultural prestige as 'The Athens of the West,' Henry's Lexington had its full share of shooting, stabbing, and gouging affrays — so much so in fact that James Bliss, a lawyer recently arrived from England, publicly advertised that for safety's sake he felt compelled to go heavily armed in Lexington as well as on the circuit because of fellow citizens who wantonly fought with pistols and dirks, fists, feet, and teeth.[3] Sometimes, however, differences were fought out in the newspapers and in broadsides. There was the incessant brawling of Clay's client, William Foley, with Isaac

---

[1] *Ky. Gazette*, June 12, July 10, 31, Nov. 3, 1800; Nov. 13, 1801, *passim*; correspondence of Federal Judge Innes and Gov. Wm. H. Harrison of the N.W. Territory (*Innes MSS.*, 21) about Indian-murdering whites; Rothert, O. A., *Outlaws of Cave-in-Rock* and Coates, R. M., *The Outlaw Years*; and *Breckinridge MSS.* for many references to 'setts of Gallows Villains.'

[2] Colton, *Clay*, I, 39.

[3] *Ky. Gazette*, July 11, 1798, March 28, 1799, March 23, 1801.

Welles, occasioned in part by Foley's attacks upon 'Cock's Comb Welles' in handbills and torrid tavern speeches as a politician in petticoats, an old woman without 'the real merrit,' however, of such females of history as Helen of Troy, Queen Bess, and Madame Roland.[1]

Then, too, there was the much-publicized race to Frankfort and back between Doctor Champney's mule, Jenny, and Spunky, a horse belonging to Leon Claiborne, the gambler. Jenny lost, and was forfeited; but Champney, not a sportsman, in the dead of night retrieved his mule, pleading the law against gaming. For months thereafter the principals and their friends informed Western America through the *Gazette* of the merits of Jenny and Spunky, and of their respective owners, under headlines of 'Beware of the Scoundrel Champney!' and 'Beware of the Scoundrel Claiborne!' The former, it appeared, was a quack and no gentleman; while the latter was an itinerant blackleg who victimized the good citizens of Lexington at horse-races, cards, dice, and 'pharo,' a tavern lounger who did nothing but 'strut about the house, stretch upon the sopha, ride out on horseback, with a trisling knife in his hand . . .'[2]

Young Lawyer Clay, with his affable manner and pleasant word for all, got along well with his frontier neighbors. They liked him, accepted him as one of their own, and turned to him when they ran afoul of the law, bringing him disputes provoked by whiskey and politics, and suits involving slander, theft, bastardy, and homicide. He was the friend of the man in trouble; his sympathetic and understanding counsellor; his ardent defender before the bar of justice. There were no frills about Mr. Clay, even though he dressed in the finest broadcloth and was connected with 'the best families.' In the courtroom he fought the cause of the rough Kentuc with just as much determined vigor as he did when handling a case for Colonel Thomas Hart or Senator John Breckinridge. Long a topic of conversation was his colossal audacity and uncommonly effective eloquence in the case of Willis, who had

---

[1] *Order Book, 1803–04,* pp. 321, 468; and File Box 59–61, Fayette Circuit Court. Clay won Foley's assault and battery suit against Welles.

[2] *Ky. Gazette,* July 23, Oct. 19, Nov. 2, 1802. Papers in File Box 59–61, Fayette Circuit Court, connect Clay with the dispute, but the outcome in court is unknown.

been indicted by a Fayette grand jury for what was said to have been a peculiarly cold-blooded murder.

At the trial Henry succeeded in creating a division among the jurors, and a new trial, the object he aimed at, was requested by the prosecuting attorney. When Willis was again brought into court Clay argued that the jury should pay no further attention to the evidence, or to the question of his client's guilt. They must only consider, he warned, the appalling fact that the state was attempting to do what the law emphatically forbade — to place a man's life in jeopardy twice for the same offense!

When the court peremptorily ordered him to desist from this startling procedure, Henry affected great astonishment, then high indignation. His blue eyes blazing, he strenuously protested that a man's life was in danger, that as his lawyer he was compelled to defend him, and the judge must listen. Did not the court realize, he asked in most solemn tone, its grave responsibility? Was poor Willis, looking death in the face, to be deprived of his rights? If so, woe to the judge when he came before the awful judgment seat of the Almighty! The court refused to yield, refused to be intimidated. Henry then picked up his papers and books, made a stiffly formal bow to the bench, and stalked from the courtroom, leaving behind spellbound spectators and a judge who was not a little befogged by such boldness and casuistry.

Still under the spell of Clay's vivid portrayal of the Nemesis of Retribution, the judge, as he reflected, became more and more impressed with the idea that perhaps Mr. Clay was correct after all. A messenger hurriedly summoned Henry from his office. With a grave demeanor he at once pressed home his point that the first trial was equivalent to an acquittal, carried the day, and won Willis a complete discharge. It was a striking commentary on Kentucky judicial conditions and on the defender of Willis; on the audacious Henry Clay, who made his own laws to fit the occasion, enforced them on a timid judge, and persuaded a jury enchanted by his oratory of the correctness of his views.[1]

There were other cases long remembered by Kentuckians in which he bullied judges and seduced juries — and appeared to his

[1] Prentice, *Clay*, pp. 14–16; Colton, *Clay*, I, 86.

clients as a delivering angel. In Harrison County, defending two Germans, father and son, accused of murder, he struggled and strained in a famous five-day oratorical battle before he won a verdict for manslaughter. He then surprised the court with a motion for an arrest of judgment. After another day of protracted argument he succeeded in winning the complete freedom of the accused. Warmly did the two men express their gratitude. They were joined by an old woman, ugly and perspiring, who waddled down the aisle to the bar beaming with joy. She was the mother of one, the wife of the other. Throwing her arms about Clay, clasping him to her ample bosom, she repeatedly smacked kisses upon him, much to the amusement of the crowded courtroom. 'She bounced upon him with irrepressible emotion,' and gave him what he afterwards said was 'the longest and strongest embrace he ever encountered in his professional practice.' [1]

Such victories as these not only increased his criminal practice but gave him, even while a young lawyer, the reputation of being able to ensure the freedom, at least freedom from the gallows, of those indicted for murder. Not one of his many clients in capital cases, it was said, was ever sentenced to death. [2]

Quite as remarkable, in view of such cases as that of Willis, was the fact that he usually won the verdict of the people. Unlike some of his colleagues, he was never burned in effigy or threatened with tar and feathers by disappointed and indignant frontiersmen. [3] That he never incurred such public opprobrium, despite the nature of many of his victories in criminal causes, must be considered a peculiarly noteworthy tribute to his personal popularity and 'amiable disposition,' to his courtroom technique and eloquent tongue that beguiled judge, jury, and spectators as well.

He was an advocate in the grand tradition, according to contemporaries. He fulfilled the popular conception of the great trial lawyer — dominating, hypnotic, ingratiating, with a church-organ voice and unlimited command over tears and laughter; one who

---

[1] Prentice, *Clay*, pp. 13–14; Colton, *Clay*, I, 85–86; Clark, L. G., 'Henry Clay, Personal Anecdotes,' *Harper's Magazine*, V, 393–94.

[2] Prentice, *op. cit.*, pp. 18–19; Colton, *op. cit.*, I, 86.

[3] On such mob displays, see Taul, *Memoirs*, p. 498.

could shrivel up witnesses with a flash of the eye, convince jurors that black was white, and elevate a petty case into a drama of such intense human interest that it was worth coming miles to see.

In truth, Clay had the advocate's quick mind and understanding heart; the ability to express himself simply and eloquently; the élan, the force and sweep, which enabled him to win causes where a more timorous if more learned competitor might have lost. In a day when the citizen 'found his theater in the courthouse,' and frontier conditions subordinated law and judge to the wordy duels of eloquent counsel,[1] he always managed, even in the most involved and technical case, 'to throw in some amusing episodes.' [2] Men long remembered and liked to recall his retentive memory and adroit tactics, his 'speaking eye' and 'killing countenance.' His manner was usually friendly, confiding; but he knew as if by intuition when to confine himself to severe argument, when to indulge in humor or the dialect of the backwoods and the Ohio-Mississippi riverman's idiom, when to frighten simple souls, when to soften imperious tones into mellow persuasiveness, when to soar into heart-stirring rhetoric.

Henry was at his best as attorney for the defense — the advocate of the unfortunate, the oppressed, the downtrodden, and the maligned. On such occasions he was truly magnetic, fascinating; his voice, person, and manner, his expressive mobile face and 'catamount eyes,' all contributed to make him impressively commanding. Tall and erect, head and shoulders thrown back, foot out-thrust, his lean and sinewy frame vibrating, as it were, with human sympathies and aspirations, he seemed a knightly champion, a Saint George against fearful dragons (which his fancy had readily conjured up for his drama-loving audience), a chivalrous son of generous and noble Kentucky who well merited acclaim as a popular idol.

Never, according to his early biographers, did he take a criminal cause without first satisfying himself that the charge was unfounded or that there were palliating circumstances. Never did he appear in court to defeat the ends of justice or for the sake of a

---

[1] Pound, Roscoe, *Spirit of the Common Law*, pp. 124–25.
[2] Preston, Mrs. Wm. C., *Diary*, p. 420.

personal triumph. This, of course, was an egregious fiction. Yet he seems to have been troubled, in some degree, by such cases as that of Willis in which he had been the means of restoring to society men who richly deserved to swing at the end of the hangman's noose. Some years after that almost incredible Willis affair, he was hailed on the streets of Lexington by the cry of 'Here comes Mr. Clay, who saved my life!' Clay stopped. Before him was Willis, drunk as usual, and effusively cordial. Regarding the worthless creature, the killer whom he had rescued from the gallows, he shook his head, and remarked: 'Ah! Willis, poor fellow, I fear I have saved too many like you, who ought to be hanged.' [1]

His conscience also troubled him about a case he argued during his very brief period as Fayette's prosecuting attorney. He had reluctantly accepted the appointment, and did so only with the idea of transferring the office to a friend. Before this could take place he was called upon to prosecute a slave, hitherto of good repute, who in self-defense had killed a ruthless overseer. Goaded beyond endurance by the fellow's brutality, the black had seized an axe and hacked him down. Admitting that if a white man had done the deed he would be guilty only of manslaughter, Clay said he was duty-bound, as attorney for the commonwealth, to sustain the indictment for murder in the first degree. He pressed the charge and the Negro was hanged. In disgust, Clay immediately resigned. He had acted in accordance with the letter of the law and the spirit of the times, but ever afterwards he felt ashamed of himself, confessing to his friends that he had violated his own sympathies and principles. Never again did Henry Clay act as criminal prosecutor.[2]

Adhering to private practice, he appeared in the state house at Frankfort before the Court of Appeals and the Federal District Court.[3] He rode in the cavalcade of lawyers, with the judges riding

---

[1] Colton, *op. cit.*, I, 96.

[2] *Ibid.*, I, 86–87; Prentice, *op. cit.*, pp. 16–17.

[3] In Dec. of 1802 the lawyers practicing in the U. S. District Court petitioned for a reduction in the terms of court from three to two. Nine lawyers signed: Joseph H. Daveiss (U. S. Attorney), James Hughes, James Blair, James Brown, Henry Clay, John Allen, Isham Talbot, John Rowan, and Humphrey Marshall. (*Breckinridge MSS.*)

in front, which went from one county court to another, stopping for the session at each court town, fighting again at night in the tavern and boarding-house the legal battles of the day, and then departing for the next county seat. It was a hard-riding existence, with long stretches of poor roads, inclement weather, and nondescript lodgings. After several days spent in arguing and bickering in some mud-chinked palace of justice, said a frontier lawyer of these early days, we mounted our horses 'and rode one and two hundred miles to a Court, and then to another, and another yet, and through the woods, following merely a bridle-path, crossing the swollen streams . . .' How welcome to the saddle-sore cavalcade were 'the comforts of the evening, when the hospitable cabin and warm fire greeted the traveller! — when a glorious supper was spread before him — turkey, venison, bear's meat, fresh butter, hot corn bread, sweet potatoes, apple sauce, and pumpkin butter . . . and then the animated conversation succeeded by a floor and a blanket, and a refreshing sleep!'[1]

An indefatigable circuit-rider, Clay accepted the tedium and hardships of constant travel as a part of his profession. There were many compensations — the warm friends he made throughout Kentucky, the intimate companionship of his fellow lawyers, and the popular fame which in the Ohio Valley West tended to become legendary. Many were the stories told of Lawyer Henry Clay.

Sometimes he would appear in court entirely unprepared, it was said, and study a case while his opponent argued. Then, with a few pointed and daring remarks he would dissipate the clouds of bombast and pedantry raised by the opposition, bring the discussion around to his mode of reasoning, clarify matters by a commonsense presentment, and clinch matters by an oratorical appeal. He had his own methods. 'You must let me have my own way,' he once remarked to an apprehensive lawyer who had entrusted him with an important personal case. While in the saddle riding to the court town where the case was to be heard, young Clay slowly and thoroughly read over the papers, and then returned them to the lawyer's saddle-bag. Upon arrival he at once joined some convivial

[1] Cass, Lewis, *France, Its King, Court, and Government*, pp. 63–65 — describing his early days (in Ohio) as a frontier lawyer.

friends and did not leave them until after dawn. His lawyer-client wrung his hands in despair. Yet when court opened that morning Clay, as fresh as if he had slept the night, argued the case in masterly manner, covered every point, reduced complexities to a few simple principles, and won the suit.[1]

On one occasion, it was obvious that a stubborn countryman was reluctant to join the rest of a jury in favoring his cause. At length, in the midst of an impassioned outburst, Henry, always sensitive to his audience, dramatically stopped short, and in the breathless silence slowly turned, pointed his finger at the obdurate juryman, and most politely requested: 'A pinch of snuff, if you please.' The old farmer was overcome by the concentrated attention of the courtroom, and by the personal interest evinced in him by Lexington's noted young attorney. After twisting and squirming, he finally blurted out: 'I don't snuff, Mr. Clay, but I chaws.' Whether or not Clay took a bite from the juror's hunk of tobacco, the verdict was in his favor.[2] Equally effective were his tactics with witnesses. He often put words in their mouths. A man on the stand was explaining that Clay's client was not a good financial risk. 'He is *slow* ——' the witness began, in hesitant fashion. 'He is *slow* ——' 'And *sure*,' interposed Clay. 'Yes, sir, slow and sure,' agreed the witness, committing himself, and glad to find himself relieved from further questioning.[3]

Not always was he successful. At Mount Sterling one day, at the place outside of town where litigants gathered to select their favorites from the incoming cirucit-riding lawyers, he was hailed by one of the town's wealthiest, and most pompous, citizens. Henry agreed to defend him against a charge which the man considered monstrously malignant, that of stealing a neighbor's beehive or 'bee-gum.' But the righteous worthy embarrassed him by failing to gather character witnesses: no one in town would vouch that it was not likely he would steal his neighbor's honey. As a consequence Clay was defeated. As he left the courtroom, nettled by his failure, his peckish client grabbed him by the coattails and cried: 'Mr. Clay! Mr. Clay! We've lost our case!' Clay

---

[1] Colton, Calvin, *The Last Seven Years of the Life of Henry Clay*, pp. 266–67.
[2] Rogers, *Clay*, pp. 36–37.   [3] Colton, *Clay*, I, 96.

turned upon him. Drawing himself up very stiffly, and fixing his 'catamount eyes' upon the man, he said: 'Yes, we've lost our case, but, by God, we've got our bee-gum!' [1]

A tendency displayed even in these early professional years to become imperious and domineering was encouraged by his train of legal victories. When the old Fayette courthouse, a small, two-storied, stone structure, was being replaced, between 1806 and 1808, by a modern brick edifice, and court was being held in Adam Rankin's meeting-house, he was called upon to defend a prisoner in the jail. Demanding that he be shown the warrant of arrest, he scrutinized it in the presence of the court, then turned abruptly to the prisoner and said to him: 'Go home, sir.' The man hesitated. 'Go home!' thundered Clay. The prisoner no longer hesitated. More frightened of the tall young lawyer with the blazing eyes and commanding voice than of sheriff and judge, he jumped up and ran from the courtroom without an effort being made to stop him.[2]

In view of such incidents it was not surprising to find that in 1802 Henry Clay, Esquire, was fined ten pounds for contempt of court by the Fayette Quarter Sessions. Even less surprising was Henry's action in the matter. He immediately brought suit against the Quarter Sessions judges, and on a writ of error to the Kentucky Court of Appeals so argued his case that the superior tribunal decided that the ten pounds, with costs of court, should be returned to him.[3]

Much of Clay's income as a lawyer came from land-title suits. The most absorbing topic in Western America was land, its ownership, sale, and settlement. It lay at the root of the feverish speculation characterizing this sprawling hinterland which doubled its population with each census, advertised for emigrants, sold huge wilderness tracts, and boomed town sites (which often existed only on paper, on the banks of mythical rivers). No man escaped being influenced by the sense of bigness which came from

---

[1] Rogers, *op. cit.*, p. 36.

[2] Ranck, G. W., *History of Lexington*, pp. 211–12.

[3] *Kentucky Law Reports:* Sneed, Achilles, *Reports of the Court of Appeals, 1801–05*, pp. 189–90, Nov. 3, 1802.

the territorial vastness of the Western World, the sense of newness, and the quickening hope of rapid material progress. Henry was so affected; as was his brother John, a young Lexington merchant-broker who pursued fortune in dare-devil manner, being noted for his 'wild and extravagant ideas.' [1] All his neighbors and friends breathed in the heady air of future wealth and greatness which, most assuredly, were to result from their speculations and rising land values. In Henry's Kentucky and throughout the Western World there was a peculiar appositeness to the saying that one looked upon an acorn not as an acorn but as a forest of oaks.

With the earliest settlement had begun that scramble for land which 'distressed and desolated society in Kentucky almost as calamitously as pestilence or famine.' [2] Early adventurers had been unable to decide between the proprietary rights of the Cherokees and the Six Nations, the Transylvania Company and Virginia, the Continental Congress and the British Crown. Most of them cared little about the matter and took possession by squatter and tomahawk rights. Virginia's land policy for her District of Kentucky had been most haphazard. Lands were settled, then surveyed. Thousands of acres in vaguely described regions were granted to Revolutionary veterans and to speculators. Overlapping surveys — crudely done with the pioneer's compass (his 'land-stealer,' as the Indians called it), rapid settlement, legal technicalities, unscrupulous land-jobbers, all combined to bring about ceaseless litigation, the dispossession of early pioneers such as Boone and Kenton, and widespread confusion. Young Clay found Kentucky, he said, 'literally shingled over with conflicting claims.' [3] Never before had there been such an El Dorado for lawyers, such an inexhaustible source of tedious and expensive lawsuits.

Yet in land litigation it little availed the lawyer to present only 'rambling thoughts, impertinences, and long hollow harangues

---

[1] On John Clay see Henry Clay to Breckinridge, Dec. 30, 1803, *Breckinridge MSS.*; James Brown to Clay, March 12, 1805, *Clay MSS.* In Oct., 1799 Henry stood security for John in a debt case, *Order Book A, 1798–1803*, pp. 262, 331, 515, Fayette Circuit Court.

[2] Butler, M., *Hist. Ky.*, pp. 137–38.

[3] Clay, *Works*, VII, 491–92; see also, Michaux, *Travels*, pp. 225–28; McAfee, *Life and Times*, pp. 113, 220, on land litigation, frauds, etc.

from empty heads,' said Justice Bibb of the Court of Appeals: all
but the most acute minds were hopelessly enmeshed in Kentucky's
land laws, which were almost as confusing and contradictory as her
land titles.[1] Clay's land-title suits were weighed down with plats
and maps, and depositions of early Long Hunters as to innumerable 'Paint Licks,' 'Clay Licks,' and 'Buffalo Crossings,' as to
vague boundary lines which ran so many poles and chains between
such debatable objects as blazed white oaks, stunted pawpaws
or buckeyes, or three hickories in a glade. Sometimes Henry
uncovered what he termed 'Chimney-corner surveys — that is
surveys made without ever going upon the ground and marking
corners and boundary.'[2] New surveys, 'on some fair day,' would
be ordered by the court, or by the arbitrators appointed by the
judge, who usually held forth at some convenient tavern over
pipes, 'segars,' and whiskey jugs. Cases dragged on for years with
no one benefiting, apparently, but the gentlemen of the bar.

The young lawyer who in criminal causes displayed a dramatic
adroitness and an almost mesmerizing power over juries worked
hard and persistently at these complicated, tedious, yet lucrative
title suits. Even in this type of case he found opportunities to play
his rôle of champion of the weak, contending in county courts and
in the Court of Appeals for 'the old settlements and preemptions,
the most meritorious claims in our country; which, having been in
part erroneously surveyed, have been swallowed up by the young,
but large sweeping entries of the speculators.'[3] Many of these
title suits were settled by compromise, and the Fayette order books
reveal that Clay was a good bargainer. Significantly, Senator
John Breckinridge, a shrewd judge of members of his own profession, as early as 1800 turned over to Henry some of the land cases
of his clients. By 1803 Clay had so securely established his

---

[1] *Kentucky Law Reports:* Bibb, Geo. M., *Reports of the Court of Appeals, 1808–09*, preface,
p. 6.

[2] Clay to Robt. Smith (Jefferson's Sec. of the Navy), Aug. 7, 1805, *Samuel Smith MSS.*;
also, Clay's many land-title suits in Fayette order books, Lexington. In the *Clay MSS.*
there is an interesting letter from Richard Anderson to Maj. John Swan of Baltimore,
May 19, 1788 on pioneer surveying; and one from Daniel Boone to Colonel Thomas
Hart, Aug. 11, 1785, in which Boone stated that 'for good Reasons of past favors and
good friendship the Exspencis of Locating your Land is payd to my Satisfaction.'

[3] *Kentucky Law Reports:* Hardin, Martin D., *Reports of the Court of Appeals, 1805–08*, p.
483.

reputation in this class of litigation that Breckinridge employed him whenever his own extensive lands were threatened, giving him full power to proceed at his discretion against James Hughes and other veteran land lawyers.[1] In 1805, when it seemed as if Lexington might be deprived of a part of its public square, the town fathers in their quandary turned to young Clay to defend Lexington's title to the land.[2]

Impressed by the apparent ease with which he won his cases, especially criminal causes, the casual observer was likely to overlook Henry's cultivation since boyhood of the potent art of oratory ('the art of all arts'), his study of men as well as the law, his sustained drudgery in a hundred cases of ordinary interest to one of dramatic possibilities. Critical Easterners, pallid from poring over musty legal authorities and somewhat abashed by Clay's Western glibness and insouciant self-confidence, might contend — as later did Daniel Webster, Henry's slow-moving, somewhat pompous, somewhat envious, political-legal colleague and rival — that his knowledge of the law was superficial.[3] This, however, was not the opinion of the Western bench and bar or of such competent authorities as Joseph Story and John Marshall. When Clay came to practice before the Supreme Court, Marshall rated him high and Story praised his ability in legal argument, regretting that Clay, who 'might attain great eminence at this Bar,' preferred politics to law — 'the fame of popular talents to the steady fame of the Bar.' [4]

Eastern lawyers who ventured among Clay and his colleagues soon came to acknowledge their forcible reasoning, dexterity, and cleverness of management in criminal and particularly in intricate land-title causes, and the stiff competition they provided. 'I went to Kentucky expecting to be a great man there,' frankly confessed James Buchanan of Pennsylvania (whose legal, political, and

---

[1] Clay to Breckinridge, Aug. 27, 1803, and ff.; and Chas. Morgan to same, June 22, 1800, *Breckinridge MSS.*

[2] *Lexington Trustees' Books*, 1805; information kindly furnished by Charles R. Staples, Esq., of Lexington.

[3] Harvey, Peter, *Reminiscences... of Daniel Webster*, pp. 217–18.

[4] Story, Wm. W., *Joseph Story*, I, 423; Greeley, Horace, *Henry Clay* (to 1848 by Epes Sargent, edited and completed by Greeley), p. 315.

diplomatic career was to end with the presidency), 'but every lawyer I met at the bar was my equal, and more than half of them my superiors, so I gave it up.' [1]

Whatever the depth of Henry's legal learning, that which he possessed, and was compelled to augment as necessity arose, was most effectively employed. He possessed the 'great deal of native talent' credited to him by Webster, and he brought to Kentucky somewhat more than 'a little smattering of law.' Yet by no means was he a Wythe, profoundly versed in the refinements and niceties of jurisprudence. His triumphs were those of the advocate, the trial lawyer, facile, perceptive, eloquent, with methods admirably adapted to the problems immediately before him and to the courts in which he practiced — and made his fortune. He made skilful use of the lore he had gleaned from his distinguished Virginia tutors, from his boyhood years in Virginia's high courts where he had 'lived' and 'lighted his genius,' and from experience, his greatest teacher. He employed his 'great native talent' (his un-common 'common sense') and his forensic magic to the utmost: after all, quick wits and eloquent presentation were more im-portant to him in this Western World of the highly emotional Children of America than the closet scholarship of Wythe. Having satisfied himself as to what the result of a cause ought to be, he moved heaven and earth to make court and jury see it in the same light. While he never burdened himself with unnecessary labor, his early and striking success, his immediate 'rush' into a lucrative practice, argued adequate legal research, adequate preparation in manner and method peculiar to himself and to his environment.

For one endowed with the gifts of a Patrick Henry he wasted surprisingly little energy in mere rhetoric. His style was fluent, forceful, colloquial rather than Ciceronian, as James Hughes noted when he first appeared in Lexington. There was about him a refreshing directness, an uncommon virtue in a day of Eighteenth-Century pomposities and circumlocutions. He well knew how to gratify a jury or a political audience with oratorical pyrotechnics, but seldom did he mar his speeches, and never his letters, by the

---

[1] Little, *Hardin*, pp. 352–53.

elephantine verbosities and hackneyed classical allusions which characterized so many of his colleagues in that so-called Age of Reason and of Jeffersonian Simplicity.

His letters on legal matters expressed his ideas simply, lucidly. They went directly to the heart of the matter, were clear-cut, understandable, well-considered as to the facts, the law, and the possible maneuvers of opposing counsel. He was sure of himself; confident of his ability and worth. Yet even in business-like communications to his clients there ever appeared his warm personal interest and engaging friendliness. 'You ought to call on me when you next come to Town relative to this business,' concluded a characteristic letter, to Doctor Ridgley, who had removed to a country seat in Woodford. 'It will at the same time afford me the pleasure of seeing you, and learning what sort of a farmer the physician makes.' [1]

The famed mantle of George Nicholas had fallen on his young and capable shoulders. When he arrived from Virginia people would say that to have Nicholas take one's lawsuit was to ensure victory. They were now saying that litigants considered 'their causes as gained in every part of the state, if they are fortunate enough to get the cock of the walk, the Nicholas or the Clay of the court on their side.' [2] In Lexington, the metropolis of the Western World, 'in the midst of a bar uncommonly distinguished by eminent members,' he stood foremost in the number of causes and in their successful management although still in his twenties and but some few years removed from his student days in Richmond. At the beginning of the century, said the Clerk of Clark County, Henry Clay, George Bibb, and Jesse Bledsoe had become the great favorites at the Kentucky bar — 'Mr. Clay however took the lead, and kept it.' [3]

Significant was his substitution for the signature of the legal novice, the 'Henry Clay' underscored with elaborate flourishes, of the plain 'Henry Clay' and, more frequently, the simple 'H.

---

[1] Clay to Dr. Frederick Ridgley, Jan. 31, 1804, *Ferdinand J. Dreer Collection*, Hist. Society of Pennsylvania.

[2] *Ky. Gazette*, June 27, 1809 — 'Stubborn Facts' by 'Republican.'

[3] Taul, *Memoirs*, p. 356.

Clay' of the young lawyer of assured position and increasing prestige. And sweet music to his ears was popular acclaim of his legal prowess and competence, of his profitably employed talents. 'On all hands it seems agreed by such of your countrymen as visit us,' wrote James Brown from New Orleans in 1805, 'that you are at the head of your profession, and are rapidly growing rich. Indeed some accounts assure us that you are acquiring money "as fast as you can count it." All that I infer from this is that you are *doing extremely well.*' [1]

[1] Brown to Clay, Oct. 31, 1805, *Clay MSS.*

Chapter Four. Henry Clay, Kentuckian

I love Kentucky; I am charmed by her republican spirit; I am delighted by the energy with which she sustains her rank in the Union. (William Wirt.)

We who have been from our very hearts Western men, *who have seen our Country grow, and have grown with our Country, can now view its unforeseen and unparalleled prosperity with pleasure and with pride. (James Brown.)*

DURING these years at the turn of the century, young Clay was becoming rooted in the Blue Grass, and taking on the color of his Western environment: the Virginian was becoming the Kentuckian. He was now a man of family and property, whose worldly assets kept pace with a law practice which was 'successful and lucrative.'[1] Well might he say, on those occasions in later life when he paid tribute to his adopted state of Kentucky, that 'scarce had I set foot upon her generous soil when I was embraced with parental fondness, caressed as though I had been a favorite child, and patronized with liberal and unbounded munificence.'[2]

As early as 1800, when but twenty-three, he was in a position to propose buying Satterwhite's very respectable Eagle Tavern. A

---

[1] In 1799 he was taxed for one horse; in 1802 for 2 horses, 5 slaves, 2 vehicles, 2 Lexington town lots; in 1803 for 5 horses, 6 slaves, 2 town lots, and 8,000 acres of land in Mason County; in 1805 for 8 horses, 6 slaves, [4] town lots valued at $1000, and 6525 acres of land: 2000 acres in Greenup County, 4400 acres in Montgomery and Clark, 125 acres on Hickman Creek in Fayette. *Fayette Tax Lists*, Ky. S. Hist. Society.

[2] Mallory, Daniel, *Life and Speeches of Henry Clay*, II, 565.

few months later he informed Ninian Edwards that he was 'engaged in a very expensive building.' His ventures in Kentucky lands and Lexington real estate were many and profitable. In 1802 he bought eight thousand acres in Mason County (for one thousand dollars, and sold them before 1804) and acquired from Colonel Hart the lot on Mill Street on which he resided, adjoining that owned by James Brown; in 1805 he bought three town lots, and was building a brick house on 'Jordan's Row' (Upper Street) opposite the courthouse on land purchased from John Jordan, the merchant.[1]

In contrast with his ability in these transactions and in his law practice was a warm and generous faith in the financial integrity of his friends. Clay's sympathies and loyalties were easily enlisted, often to his financial loss. It was characteristic of him, also, that he should not forget his Virginia benefactors. It gave him genuine pleasure to be able to make a request, in December, 1801, of Judge Francis Brooke: it was that the Judge should send to him the orphaned son of Henry's former patron and 'much regretted friend,' the late Robert Brooke.

'We have in this place an university in a very flourishing condition,' wrote Henry, pointing out the advantages awaiting the son of the Attorney General. 'Could you not spare him to me in this country for two or three years? I live at a short distance from the buildings, have a small family, and need not add that from the cheapness of living in this country, his expenses to me would be extremely inconsiderable.' Nothing could make him happier than discharging in this manner heartfelt obligations of gratitude incurred during his Richmond days.[2]

If young Brooke adventured to the Western Country (it does not appear that he did) he would have found Lawyer Clay's family at this time small indeed, since there was but one child, a girl, born in June of 1800, named Henrietta. In 1802 was born a son, named

---

[1] Clay to Wm. Taylor (who held a mortgage on Satterwhite's), Aug. 31, 1800, *Clay MSS.*; Edwards, N., *Papers*, pp. 24–25; Fayette County *Deed Book F*, May 7, 1802, at the Kentucky Capitol, Office of the Clerk, Court of Appeals, Frankfort; Lex. Dist. Court *Deed Book D*, pp. 13–15; Fayette County *Deed Book A*, p. 500, and *Deed Book B*, pp. 419, 529; also, *General Index to Deeds* etc., Fayette Courthouse, Lexington, for Clay's many transactions.

[2] Clay to Brooke, Dec. 30, 1801, Clay, *Corres.*, p. 10.

Theodore Wythe; Thomas Hart Clay followed in 1803, and Susan Hart Clay in 1805.[1] In the early years of the century young Brooke of Richmond would have found Mr. Clay of Kentucky a man of family devoted to his children, a man of property who was of Lexington's little ruling circle and a leader in its many enterprises.

He was a shareholder and the attorney of the Kentucky Insurance Company, the first bank in Western America. He was the attorney and one of the backers of the Kentucky Vineyard Association, a project financed by Lexington capital and conducted by a colony of Swiss emigrants, which was typical (said a French visitor of 1802) of the reigning spirit that made Kentuckians 'greedily seize hold of every plan that tends to enrich the country by agriculture and commerce.' With his fellow entrepreneurs Clay drank Kentucky-produced wines, toasting 'The Virtuous and Independent Sons of Switzerland, who have chosen our country as a retreat from the commotions of war,' and recommending 'the juice of the Kentucky grape as a solace for all their misfortunes.'[2]

A shareholder of Lexington's public subscription library, the first of its kind in the West, he could supplement from its seven hundred volumes his own collection of books, including the well-thumbed *Plutarch's Lives of the Noble Grecians and Romans* which was his constant companion on the circuit.[3] Henry was much interested in Transylvania University, where James Brown taught law and Doctor Sam Brown lectured in the Medical School. With these good friends he attended the students' debates and dramas, heard the papers and discussions of their philosophical societies, and at public meetings heartily and most loyally toasted this institution, a pioneer on the cultural frontier, as 'the cradle of Genius and the nursery of Patriots.'[4]

---

[1] On Clay's children, eleven in all, see Clay, *Clay Family*, pp. 127–28; Winthrop, R., *Memoir of Henry Clay*, p. 39. Henrietta died in infancy.

[2] Michaux, *Travels*, p. 207; Dufour, P., 'Early Vevay,' *Indiana Mag. of History*, XX, 2 ff.; *Ky. Gazette*, Jan. 10, 1798, July 3, 1800, Jan. 26, 1801, Feb. 1, March 22, 1803.

[3] *MS. Records*, Lexington Public Library. For Clay's attachment to Plutarch, see Jos. R. Underwood, q. in Greeley, *Clay*, p. 373.

[4] *Ky. Gazette*, Jan. 26, 1801; and Peter, R. and J., *Transylvania University*.

Soon after his arrival from Virginia, Henry had become Junior Warden of Lexington's Masonic Lodge, which had on its roster almost every Kentuckian of note, including a host of young men who gave him vigorous competition in politics and at the bar — Jesse Bledsoe, his good friend, and his greatest rival as an orator; Benjamin Howard, soon to be Lexington's congressman and then governor of Upper Louisiana; Richard Mentor Johnson, of flaming declamation and reckless courage, whose colorful career was to end with the vice-presidency under Van Buren; George Bibb (later Federal senator, and chief justice of Kentucky) and Fielding L. Turner, who as prosecuting attorneys for Fayette attempted to offset Clay's judge-bullying and jury-seducing. There were other young lawyers — Joseph Hamilton Daveiss, John Pope, Isham Talbot, John Rowan, William T. Barry, John Allen, and Felix Grundy; all rivals of Lawyer Clay, and all well on the road to legal and political distinction in Kentucky and in new American commonwealths yet to be carved out of the Western World.[1]

They were high-spirited and convivial, these ambitious young lawyer-politicians with whom Henry spent so much time, linked together by common aspirations and animated by a spirit of bluff camaraderie. On the circuit, riding from one county court to another, they were not unlike a band of strolling players. Their undress freedom, jests, witty sallies, and droll anecdotes contrasted with the grave and even tragic seriousness they assumed when combatting each other before the bar of justice. A visitor to Lexington who spent some time with the lawyers, alternating with them between Fayette courthouse and the pothouses on Main Street, said they were 'as happy and as jovial a set of fellows as I ever saw collected together.'[2]

On Christmas Day, around a cockpit in the public square of Winchester, eighteen miles from Lexington, the same observer noted his jovial friends placing large bets on their favorite fighting fowls. Gaming, of course, was popular not only on Christmas Day in this country, which itself was a grand gamble in future wealth

---

[1] [Norwood, J. W.], *Concise History of Lexington Lodge, No. 1, F. & A. M., 1788–1913,* has portraits and brief sketches of members. Clay was Junior Warden, 1802; State Representative, 1803–09; Grand Master, 1820.

[2] Taul, *Memoirs,* pp. 357, 358.

and prestige. Chief Justice Robertson was not alone in saying that he might have starved in his early years at the bar had it not been for his skill at cards. Often briefless attorneys who studied Hoyle rather than Blackstone carried off the fees of their hardworking colleagues. On court days lawyers and planters and traders engaged in exciting games of loo, brag, old sledge, all-fours, whist, euchre, and twenty-deck poker. On the turn of a card, and with a princely flourish, Kentuckians would stake their blooded horses, their plantations, even their entire fortunes.[1]

The feverish gambling of 'Legal Characters' and their immoderate drinking provoked frequent criticism, even in those robust days. The *Gazette* in 1804, however, took up a cudgel in their defense. If an occasional passing of the convivial glass makes our lawyers sots, scoffed Editor Bradford, there are 'not one hundred citizens of the same age in the state of Kentucky who will not be equally liable to the odious charge.' The subject had become stale, said Doctor Sam Brown, who was not fond of righteous fault-finders: those who attacked our public men on such puerile grounds 'forfeited all pretensions to talents of a preeminent grade.' [2]

In those spacious days 'Mr. Clay, himself, was rather a wildish fellow,' said one who had studied law under Henry.[3] His enemies early alluded to his fondness for 'the card table and the punch bowl.' [4] Extremely sociable, a boon companion, after a hard day in court or on the hustings he occasionally cut loose and displayed the most exuberant spirits. Kentuckians fully appreciated his amiability and humor, his superb story-telling, his charm and color and warmth of feeling — the very humanness of his virtues and of his defects. He was hot-tempered yet warm-hearted, egotistical yet most sympathetic. There were times when he was headstrong and incautious; when his assumption of leadership, his sharp tongue, and impulsive acts provoked justified resentment.

---

[1] Taul, *Memoirs*, pp. 366–67; Robertson, G., *Autobiography*, p. 35; and Little, *Ben Hardin*, pp. 32–34, *passim.*

[2] *Ky. Gazette*, May 22, 1804; Sam Brown to Jas. Brown, June 12, 1804, *Jas. Brown MSS.*

[3] Coleman, R. T., 'Jo Daveiss, of Kentucky,' *Harper's Mag.*, XXI, 351.

[4] Lexington *Reporter*, July 2, 1808.

But Harry Clay could be depended upon to make amends — and graciously. He went out of his way, and often his twinging conscience so compelled him, to assuage the feelings of those whom he had offended. 'I swear by Clay, for I know him as a boy may know his companion,' once said a friend, 'and I believe a more noble being does not live; still he has a copious chapter of faults, but they are *les plus beaux défauts de la nature humaine,* and such as are almost always found allied with great parts and a generous nature.' [1]

Living intensely, playing hard and working hard, he loved activity and craved excitement, whether it came from lawsuits, politics, real estate deals, or the card table. Gaming was with him a passion, prominent in his 'copious chapter of faults,' and, in a broad sense, a passion which influenced his boldly aggressive attitude toward life in general. 'When Mr. Clay was in doubt about what course to pursue,' once said General Preston of Kentucky, 'he acted on the principle of Hoyle, and took the trick.' [2]

Clay pursued and courted Dame Chance most ardently: sometimes he found her a scowling, ill-favored jade; often, however, a smiling beneficent lady worthy indeed of his continued homage. 'You know,' he once remarked, 'that I have always paid peculiar homage to the fickle goddess.' [3] Great was his prowess in the West, among a race of gamblers. Some Kentuckians even went on record that they would sit at cards with Harry Clay but only if they played with him, and not against him.[4]

Among his intimate friends the stakes were sometimes too extravagant to cause him serious concern. This was true of the brag he played at the taverns with John Bradford — 'Old Wisdom,' as he was often affectionately called. One morning, after a game in which Clay had won $40,000, Bradford hailed him on the street.

'Clay,' said the editor, 'what are you going to do about the money you won last night? My entire fortune, you know, won't pay the half of it.'

---

[1] Christopher Hughes to Sir Chas. Bagot, May 30, 1825, Bagot, J., ed., *George Canning and His Friends*, II, 286.

[2] Little, *Hardin*, p. 349.

[3] Clay to Caesar A. Rodney, Dec. 29, 1812, *Simon Gratz Collection*, Hist. Society of Penna.

[4] Little, *op. cit.*, pp. 34, 355.

'Oh, give me your note for $500,' was the nonchalant reply, 'and let the balance go.'

The note was executed. A few nights later, in a game which ended at dawn, Clay found himself a loser to Bradford to the sum of $60,000. When they next met the conversation was almost identically repeated — but with young Clay questioning Old Wisdom.

'Oh, give me back that note I gave you the other day for $500,' said Bradford, 'and we'll call it square.' [1]

Editor of the first newspaper west of Pittsburgh, publicist of the Western World's early struggles and aspirations, ardent Jeffersonian and public-spirited citizen, John Bradford was 'The Benjamin Franklin of the West.' With young Clay he was one of those Lexingtonians who frequented Colonel Hart's brick mansion on Mill Street and helped their genial host realize his ambition of 'raking up money and spending it with our friends.' There, of an evening, with the great log fire crackling, the candles shedding their glow on the Colonel's set of Robbie Burns and his beloved *Tristram Shandy*, with decanters well filled and prime Kentucky tobacco tamped in long-stemmed churchwardens, Clay's father-in-law gathered his friends about him.

Stout of body and strong of jaw, Bradford overflowed with news that came to him as editor of the *Gazette*, publisher, justice of the peace, cashier of the bank, and promoter of varied enterprises. Chairman of the Transylvania trustees, he discussed the prospects of the arts and sciences on Western Waters; secretary of Lexington's Emigration Society, of which Colonel Hart was president, he showed the latest broadside extolling Kentucky's attractions. Lawyer Clay and Doctor Sam Brown joined in denouncing rumors of a smallpox epidemic as hurtful to Lexington's reputation.[2] Toasts were drunk to the doubling of the town's population. Senator Breckinridge, and Senator John Brown of Frankfort, talked intimately of Mr. Jefferson and the Federal City. James Brown and young Clay regaled the company with anecdotes of

---

[1] Perrin, W. H., *Pioneer Press of Kentucky*, pp. 15–16. Also, for John Bradford, see Jillson, W. R., *The First Printing in Kentucky*.

[2] A smallpox disclaimer signed by Lexington's four doctors and some twenty-five prominent citizens, including Clay, appeared in the *Kentucky Gazette*, June 8, 1801.

bench and bar; of truculent jurors, evasive witnesses, daydreaming judges, and of their fellow lawyers: crafty, aggressive Felix Grundy; one-armed, long-winded John Pope; profane, tempestuous Isham Talbot; handsome, demagogic Dick Johnson; and that eccentric Federalist, Jo Daveiss, whom Mr. Jefferson somehow allowed to stay on as United States Attorney.

Pausing now and then to have the glasses refilled, old Colonel Hart drew generously from his stories of the Revolution and of colonial days. His son, Thomas, junior, and his son-in-law, Samuel Price, told of recent mercantile adventures: of fur-trading in the Indian country; of trips downriver to New Orleans, returning by way of the redskin-and-outlaw-infested Natchez Trace; of sea voyages from New Orleans with Western flour and foodstuffs to the West Indies, to Philadelphia and Baltimore, returning overland with their Atlantic merchandise as far as Pittsburgh in gaudy red and blue Conestoga wagons. There were discussions about the efficiency of Negro artisans, many of whom were employed in Colonel Hart's rope-walk, nail factory, brickyard, and other enterprises; about the scarcity of hard money and the high wages demanded by white artisans; about the 'rheumatic rings' and labor-saving devices of Edward West, who on the Town Branch of the Elkhorn had recently demonstrated his new-fangled steamboat.[1] But most interesting was the extraordinary religious revival which about the turn of the century convulsed Kentucky and the West; an emotional epidemic appalling in its elemental force and hysterical abandonment.

As Clay and Nicholas and Breckinridge had roused the people against 'King' John Adams, itinerant prophets were rousing them to revolt against Satan, against authoritarian religion, and against the agnostic Deism and the liberalizing secular culture of the Age of Reason. It was a movement radical and in many respects reactionary, which stressed personal conviction of revealed religion and Biblical literalism, which appealed to emotion rather than to reason by means of mass enthusiasm, violent oratory, and

---

[1] *Ky. Gazette*, Dec. 19, 1799, Aug. 10, 1801, May 14, 28, 1802, as to West's brick-moulding and nail-cutting machines, his steamboat, etc.; and *Ky. Gazette, passim*, for the Harts' varied activities.

an ideology attractive to the common man in its simplicity and sentimentality. It was a revolt even more perhaps against the greedy materialism of a new country, against the limited interests of laborious pioneer lives, often sordidly primitive, filled with the outward and obvious, starved of the inner and hidden. Whatever its motivation, the 'Great Revival' presented a spectacle awesome and ignoble.

In congregations numbering thousands — 'lovely hosts of Israel, all in one joyful field of pleasure' — men and women camped in forest groves for days listening to preacher after preacher until, wrought to a high pitch of excitability, they gave way to primitive and grotesque exhibitionism. They rolled on the ground, flogged themselves, hugged and kissed, treed the Devil, laughed the Holy Laugh, barked like dogs, and danced like dervishes. Most common were 'the jerks,' a spasmodic twitching with the head jerking so violently that women's bonnets were snapped off and their loose flowing hair (so exultant preachers reported) 'would crack almost as loud as a waggoner's whip.' [1] Nothing was lacking at night meetings to break down mental and emotional control — the burning billows of hell pictured by the shouting exhorters, the yelling, singing, clapping, and stamping, the flickering shadows cast on tents and wagons by camp fires and pine torches, the dense aphrodisiac darkness of the surrounding forest where men and women groaned and writhed and shrieked in torment and ecstasy.

Women were especially responsive to this 'mighty Stir of Religion.' Sometimes one-third of the congregation, said an amazed and perplexed Frenchman, would be carrying out 'hysterical and deluded females,' putting them under trees where they would lie twitching and tossing and heaving lamentable sighs.[2] When George Nicholas's widow attempted to revive afflicted ladies by rubbing their faces with vinegar-soaked bread she was rebuked for interfering with the Lord's work.[3] Tipsy men who prodded the afflicted with nail-pointed staffs were them-

---

[1] Cartwright, Rev. Peter, *Autobiography*, pp. 48–49.
[2] Michaux, *Travels*, p. 249.
[3] Cleveland, C., *Great Revival in the West, 1797–1805*, pp. 176–181.

selves, according to the evangels, stricken down by an Unseen
Hand. Nothing could stop this volcanic Great Revival — its lava
'flowed from the fountain of life, and was poured from Heaven, as
a benign flower, to fertilize our wilderness, and make the desert
rejoice and blossom like a rose.' [1]

Monster 'sacramental meetings' in the Blue Grass region about
Lexington, especially the famous Cane Ridge meeting in Bourbon
in which a score of preachers for six days maintained their 'heavenly confusion' in a congregation estimated at twenty thousand,
gave the exhorters a peculiar satisfaction. They regarded the little
metropolis as a wilderness Gomorrah, with its upper classes, 'the
well-informed and wealthy, immersed in infidelity and dissipation.'
Yet Lexington's well-informed, both cleric and lay, continued to
disdain 'the Religious Maniacs' and to regard their meetings as
marked more often by alcoholic relaxations and amorous pleas-
antries than by love divine. The Reverend Adam Rankin inveighed against the self-appointed apostles, lay tutors of religious
anarchy, whose Great Revival was a satanical snare and delusion,
offensive to a God of order and intelligence, compounded of lewd
witchcraft, Stygian darkness, and manifold egregious disorders.[2]

At first Doctor Barry and other rationalistic Republicans
suspected the Federalists of inciting this volcanic eruption to dis-
tract attention from political issues: it seemed to be 'more of an
Electioneering than an Apostolic Mission.' [3] Yet it was soon noted
that 'the lovely hosts of Israel' were the same farmer-democrats
who had applauded the Goddess of Reason, damned John Adams,
huzzaed Thomas Jefferson, and who now between sacramental
meetings bibulously celebrated the repeal of Alexander Hamilton's
Whiskey Excise.[4]

Humphrey Marshall and Jo Daveiss regarded these irrational
excesses as symptoms of vicious unrest among a people given to

---

[1] Thomas, D., *The Observer trying the Great Reformation*, etc., p. 7.

[2] Rankin, A., *A Review of the Noted Revival*, etc.

[3] Dr. Redmond D. Barry to Breckinridge, Nov. 26, 1800, *Breckinridge MSS*. See also
same to same, Oct. 25, 1803, *ibid.*, on the 'Religious Maniacs . . . Jerkers and Butters,'
some of whom had 'to be closely confined.'

[4] Michaux, *op. cit.*, p. 144; *Ky. Gazette*, July 2, 1802; and Cuming, F., *A Tour*, p. 223,
who remarked on the people's alternation between 'the orgies of Bacchus' and 'the
dogmatick lectures of some fanatick dispenser of the gospel.'

'the brutalizing tenets of French Mobocracy.' Sarcastic Federalists declared that Kentucky, in religion as in politics, with her 'bawling, itinerant field and barn preachers' and their disciples, 'wretches wild and sad, like gloomy wights in Bedlam mad,' gave conclusive proof of the futility of Jeffersonian doctrines as to the nobility and intelligence of the common man. Even more edifying, they said, than 'the Jacobinic phrenzy' of the 1800 campaign was this spectacle offered by the greasy mob, the puissant vulgar, the anarchic multitude which Hamilton had quite rightly called 'a great beast.' The many-headed monster called the people, for all its heads, was sadly lacking in brains. And yet these bedlamic New Lights, these Jacobins in politics and fanatics in religion, call this the Age of Reason! Our times, said former President Adams, should be named 'the Age of Folly, Vice, Frenzy, Fury, Brutality, Daemons, Buonaparte, Tom Paine, or the Age of the burning brand from the bottomless Pitt; or any thing but the Age of Reason.' [1]

All this 'heavenly confusion' appealed no more to Henry Clay than to Humphrey Marshall or John Adams. The son of Baptist John Clay, the disciple of Wythe and Jefferson, was indifferent if not openly hostile to the clamorous zealots and their new rival churches of mushroom growth and insistent dogmas, which made the fair and fat land of Kentucky the scene of 'universal Strife and irritating animosities.' [2] He was one of the 'Bad Folks,' the 'Lynx-eyed Illuminati' and Deists. His intimate friends, Colonel Hart, John Bradford, William Morton, and others, were nominal Episcopalians; and with them Henry in 1808 aided gentle Parson Moore in organizing Christ Church; yet he did not formally become a member even of this, 'the gentleman's church.' [3]

With his colleagues of the bar young Clay was immune from revivalism: 'the sectaries' fanatick cant, where all is blasphemy

---

[1] [Adams, John], *Statesman and Friend — Corres. of John Adams with Benj. Waterhouse*, ed. W. C. Ford, p. 31; Fessenden, T. G., *Democracy Unveiled*, II, 173–76; Quisenberry, *H. Marshall*, p. 18; Bishop, R. H., *Hist. of the Church in Kentucky*, p. 216 (re Daveiss).

[2] Rankin, *op. cit.*, p. 5. Rankin himself, however, had led a secession movement among the Presbyterians over the question of using Watts's *Psalms and Hymns* instead of the version by Rouse.

[3] *Hist. Sketch of Christ Church Cathedral*, pp. 16–18, 56–57; and for deistical views of Clay's family, Kendall, *Autobiography*, p. 119.

and rant.' He and his fellow lawyers continued to prefer Voltaire, Volney, and Tom Paine's *Age of Reason* to such tracts as *Infernal Conferences, or Dialogues of Devils* and *A Short and Easy Method with the Deists*, or such current diversions as hell-fire threats, jerks, and Holy Laughs. 'It was firmly impressed on my mind,' said Robert McAfee, then a Lexington law student, 'that a person could not be religious and a Lawyer at the same time.' Only one lawyer in all Kentucky, reported this disciple of John Breckinridge and Thomas Paine, had been spiritually slain; only one had ventured to profess religion ('and he was looked upon with jeers and derision') during the period of the Great Revival.[1]

When the religious tornado had spent its force, and the prophets had gone on to greener pastures, visitors to Lexington commented on the dilapidated condition of many of the recently erected meeting-houses. 'The birds of heaven,' it was said, 'find a hundred passages through the broken panes; and the cows and hogs ready access on all sides.' [2] In 1804 the *Gazette* sharply rebuked Lorenzo Dow, one of the most notorious of roving exhorters, when he preached fire and brimstone and terrorized Lexington's ladies by predicting their deaths within the month.[3] The Blue Grass became a less inviting field for the itinerant prophets. Nevertheless, intermittent revivals continued; Baptist and Methodist circuit-riders patrolled and 'fertilized' the Western Wilds; and the tendency of pioneers to rush to extremes was reflected in the saying 'that in Kentucky everybody was either a bigot or an atheist.' [4]

The Great Revival was a striking illustration of the democratic frontier's uncoordinated and unreflecting energies. The camp-meeting, like the political rally of Clay and his fellow 'Wagon and Stump Orators,' served socially as a psychological outlet for the

---

[1] McAfee, *Life and Times*, p. 222; and see pp. 221–232.

[2] Ord, *Alex. Wilson*, p. cxxiii.   [3] *Ky. Gazette*, Oct. 9, 1804.

[4] Quincy, Josiah, *Figures of the Past*, p. 71. 'The state of society in Kentucky I did not admire,' wrote an Easterner, who visited Lexington in 1805 (where he found that his younger brother 'had made considerable progress in the dead languages and in general science' at Transylvania University). 'The great body of the well-informed and wealthy were immersed in infidelity and dissipation, while the more illiterate were downright fanatics and zealots in religion. However, they are generally an hospitable people, fond of society and polite to strangers. With a few exceptions, they are more sprightly and fonder of conversation than the Pennsylvanians, and have a remarkable attachment to all public meetings and amusements, particularly to horse-racing, where they assemble in vast crowds.' Espy, *A Tour*, pp. 24, 8.

isolated and individualistic pioneers; as a vent for the pent-up emotionalism of the Children of America. These emotional torrents flooded forth at intervals. Sometimes their crests were bright with democratic idealism and constructive if impassioned young nationalism. Sometimes they were darkly sinister and hissing with destruction, undermining rational social progress, bearing little or no hope of rebuilding a society they would tear apart.

'Citizen' Henry Clay rode the crest of the wave of Jeffersonian Democracy. He was to ride foremost on the crest of nascent nationality which led to the 'Second War for Independence.' Later, as he matured into a statesman sobered by power and broadened by views as wide as the Union, he was to realize increasingly the social dangers that lay in mass enthusiasm little restrained by reason and blinded by passion and prejudice. Most poignantly, perhaps, was he to realize such dangers when he championed his 'American System' against the shouting legions of Andrew Jackson.

In the first issue of the *Gazette* for the year 1801 Editor Bradford congratulated his fellow pioneers upon entering the Nineteenth Century, and voiced the prevailing optimism as to Kentucky's glorious future.[1] 'From dirty stations, or forts, and smoky huts,' remarked another early adventurer, Kentucky 'has expanded into fertile fields, blushing orchards, pleasant gardens, luxuriant sugar groves, neat and commodious houses, rising villages, and trading towns. Ten years have produced a difference in the population and comforts of this country, which to be portrayed in just colours, would appear marvellous.'[2] With understandable pride, Blue Grass Kentucky was referred to as the garden spot of the Western World. It was a farmer's Eden, said a sarcastic Easterner —

'A country which they tell us vies,
In point of soil with paradise,

---

[1] *Ky. Gazette,* Jan. 5, 1801. There was some question as to whether the century began with 1800 or 1801; Bradford held to the latter.

[2] Imlay, Gilbert, *Topographical Description of the Western Territory of North America,* p. 168. Imlay had taken up lands in Kentucky, *Ky. Gazette,* Feb. 6, 1800.

> Where turneps, beets, and carrots, grow,
> Until they reach the shades below,
> And thus the gifts of Ceres yield
> To tenants of Elysium field;
> And parsnips stretch their roots with ease,
> Quite through to our antipodes,
> And Chinese thieves, if fame says true,
> To rob our farmers pull them through.' [1]

Lexington, in the heart of this frontier garden, with a Main Street having 'all the appearance of Market Street in Philadelphia on a busy day,' was well on its way to rivalling 'the most populous inland town in the Atlantic states.' [2] The prosperity of its lawyers and merchants was steadily enhanced by the influx of emigrants to 'the fat and prolific vales of Kentucky,' to 'this best part of the world.' In the fall of 1801, in two months more than nine hundred emigrant wagons lumbered in over 'the Wilderness,' while down 'the bewildering curves of the Ohio,' *La Belle Rivière*, continuously came motley newcomers to the rollicking tune of 'Hi-O, away we go, floating down the river on the O-hi-o.' Truly it appeared 'as if these immense and fertile regions were to be the asylum common to all the inhabitants of the globe.' [3]

Although farming and stock-raising predominated, observers of the hinterland scene discovered society in all stages of evolution, noted the great amount of household manufacturing, and were particularly impressed by the number of mills and factories that enlivened 'the universal woods of Kentucky.' They found that all pioneers were not to be conceived in the image of Daniel Boone or the shirted Long Hunter of romance, for there were here enterprising and ingenious men who pioneered on many frontiers.

> 'We'd better trade, we all must own,
> For beaver scalps than for our own.' [4]

Even before they had subdued the Indians some of Clay's compatriots dreamed of Kentucky as the commercial and industrial center of the Mississippi Valley. 'If ever we are to become

---

[1] Fessenden, T. G., *Pills, Poetical, Political*, etc., p. 111.

[2] Espy, J., *A Tour* (1805), p. 8.

[3] Michaux, *op. cit.*, p. 161; and, on emigrant wagons, G. Thompson to Breckinridge, Dec. 28, 1801, *Breckinridge MSS.*

[4] *Ky. Gazette*, April 1, 1797.

a great and happy people,' declared Harry Innes as early as 1788 (even while raging at almost daily Indian raids, and at Eastern neglect and hostility), 'it must arise from our industry and attention to manufactures.' Two years later Innes, John Brown, and others, at Danville erected the first cotton mill in the West. Other establishments followed — paper and fulling mills, hat and tobacco factories, salt and iron works, and extensive rope-walks, such as those of Clay's father-in-law, which converted hemp, Kentucky's chief crop, into cordage, bagging, and sailcloth. As early as the tumultuous year 1793 this industrial pioneering was 'almost beyond conception,' wrote Hubbard Taylor: 'if I live to see ... the Indians ... at peace, the Mississippi open, & the titles of our Lands adjusted ... I shall behold the happiest & richest Country in the world.' [1]

It was only natural that Henry Clay of Lexington, the economic metropolis of the West, should become the political champion of these pioneer industrialists, the advocate of economic independence for Kentucky — and for the United States. His people generally contended that native manufactures would end Kentucky's unfavorable balance of trade with the importing merchants of the East, stop the drain to them of the hard money received for produce at New Orleans, and lessen her dependence upon the British, who supplied 'seven-tenths of the manufactured articles consumed in Kentucky, as well as in the other parts of the United States.' [2] Henry's friends launched their infant industries with fervid patriotic appeals, formed boycott associations against imported (i.e., British) goods, and toasted their hopes of 'blowing the manufactures of Kentucky all over the Western World.' [3] They petitioned and received some aid from the state government;

---

[1] Taylor to Madison, May 23, 1793, and Geo. Nicholas to same, May 8, 1789, *Madison MSS.*; Innes to John Brown, Feb. 20, 1788, and to same, Dec. 7, 1787, *Innes MSS.*, 28; and, for Danville mill, *Innes MSS.*, 24; also, letters in *Breckinridge MSS.* and *Ky. Gazette*, Aug. 18, 1787 ff. In Lexington, in 1802, the Harts had large cordage and bagging contracts, and supplied the Georgia and Carolina markets; the sail duck factory of Bastrop & Nancarrow was large enough for the 160 ladies and 500 gentlemen who celebrated Jefferson's election; the fire loss at the Hart & Dodge rope-walk in 1806 was estimated as high as $7000. *Ky. Gazette*, Jan. 26, 1801, June 24, 1806.

[2] Michaux, *op. cit.*, p. 203; also, on home manufactures, Marshall, *Hist. of Ky.*, II, 322; *Ky. Gazette*, Aug. 29, 1789, Nov. 10, 1800, *passim*.

[3] *Ky. Gazette*, July 8, 1806; and *passim*.

and they looked increasingly to the Federal Government for paternal assistance. Ultimately, when sponsored nationally by Clay, this demand for aid was to clash with Jeffersonian theories of a static agricultural society, and of a general government simple and frugal, of limited powers literally interpreted and strictly construed.

Even in these early days there was a demand for a protective tariff, especially by the hemp interests with which Clay was identified. In this boom period of war-time profits, Kentucky's cordage, sail duck, and rigging materials were supplied to the ships of America's great and increasing merchant marine. In 1802, however, the general fall in prices caused by the Peace of Amiens, with the prospect of a home market glutted by European competitors, caused the apprehensive hemp farmers and manufacturers to petition the national government (in vain) for higher tariff protection.

'Rushey supplies cheap hemp because of despotism of emperor & nobility, paying only a penny a day wages,' wrote preacher-manufacturer Elijah Craig to Senator Breckinridge. To exclude foreign hemp products, to guarantee a market for those produced under Kentucky's higher standard of living, and to lessen America's dependence upon the Old World, Congress should immediately enact duties as high as possible. 'Will the wisdom of the union remain inactive, and suffer a very promising part of the states to pearish away in Poverty,' asked Craig, 'and the value of the millions of acres of unsold Continental lands also sink to nothing, while the Despots of Urop suck our wealth from us, or will they Instantly interfear? The time, Sir, is extreamly Critical.' [1]

Internal improvements, especially good roads, were also demanded by Clay's compatriots. Exports overland to the East, other than horses and cattle on hoof, were restricted by costly carriage charges to furs, ginseng, and whiskey. Imports were expensive, pointed out advocates of roads to tidewater Virginia, Carolina, and Georgia, because 'the Lexington merchants purchase their goods in Philadelphia — waggon them 320 miles to Pitts-

---

[1] Craig to Breckinridge, Dec. 30, 1801 (also, Feb. 25, 1802), *Breckinridge MSS.*; and the general Kentucky petition, *A.S.P., Finance*, I, 732.

burgh — boat them 400 miles to Limestone — waggon them again to Lexington 65 miles.' [1] National roads would materially aid merchant and emigrant, develop the states and Federal territories of the West, and tighten the bonds of national union.

In these early demands, and in this feeling of dependence upon the national government, of an isolated American hinterland — all of which except Kentucky and Tennessee was to undergo a period of Federal territorial control, with men looking to Washington for authority, direction, and aid — were to be discerned the roots of Henry Clay's economic nationalism, of his later American System of a planned national economy. The West's very weakness and youth tended to promote a spirit of national unity. With the Jeffersonian triumph of 1800 this nascent nationalism, based on economic realities as well as political sentiments, came to predominate over the rampant sectionalism of Confederation and Federalist days. Despite a continuing resentment of Eastern financial dominance and a continuing homage to the rights of 'sovereign states,' this spirit was to persist and flourish, particularly in Clay's Kentucky, which claimed and exercised a tremendous influence over the entire Western World.

Within this nationalistic frontier country — so distinctly American in its outlook, its melting-pot of varied peoples, its lack of the seaboard's colonial traditions, and its democratic virtues and defects which in time were to stamp themselves upon the nation at large — were common problems and aspirations which brought about a solidarity of interests. A 'Solid West' was further unified by the merging of navigable streams, the natural highways in a day when roads were few or non-existent, into one mighty river system. The Mississippi was still the key to frontier economy, more important to this Land of the Western Waters than 'the Hudson, the Delaware, the Potomac, and all the navigable rivers of the atlantic States formed into one stream.' [2]

---

[1] *Ky. Gazette*, Jan. 9, 1800, and *passim*; also Robt. Barr to Breckinridge, Feb. 4, 1802, Jan. 4, Nov. 22, 1803, *Breckinridge MSS*. It took 35 or 40 days from Philadelphia or Baltimore at a cost of $7 to $8 per cwt. The merchants of Bedford, Penna., found it cheaper to ship goods 2200 miles to Philadelphia via New Orleans than to send them overland 200 miles. Michaux, *op. cit.*, pp. 145, 202. Yet Robt. Barr (Nov. 22, 1803, *supra*) contended that good roads to Southern seaports would bring about the export by land of horses, cattle, and pork twenty times the value of produce exported by water.

[2] Sec. of State James Madison, in 1802, Madison, *Writings*, ed. G. Hunt, VI, 460.

Until the steamboat puffed and chugged against the current of the Mississippi and the Ohio the river trade was almost exclusively one of export, moving to the south, bound for the port of New Orleans, down 'two of the longest, and one, for navigation, of the most difficult rivers in the Universe.'[1] Innumerable obstacles confronted those who pioneered in this traffic. Kentuc boatmen were compelled to wait for high water to carry them over the falls of the Ohio at Louisville; treacherous Mississippi snags, bars, and storms accounted for many losses; and there was inevitable friction with the Spanish port authorities. Moreover, there was a dearth of capital, of financial credit, banking, and marketing facilities — until 1802, when these primitive handicaps were in part overcome by the capitalistic pioneers of Lexington with their Kentucky Insurance Company, which not only insured boats on Western Waters and at sea but carried on a general banking business.[2]

As the frontier's agricultural surplus mounted in ratio to the rising tide of immigrant farmers, foreign control of the Orleans outlet to the ocean became more and more a cause of irritation and discontent. Young Clay of Lexington could well understand the intensity of purpose and desire in John Breckinridge's declaration: 'The Mississippi we *will* have.' And why Kentucky's pioneers had raged at John Jay's East, which treated them as 'enemies or aliens,' and why they had acclaimed General Wilkinson as a benefactor when that enterprising, smooth-quilled adventurer in 1787 obtained a private monopoly and for a few years sent their produce downriver in an uncertain and restricted traffic complicated by Spanish intrigue.[3] And why the Democratic Societies had threat-

---

[1] Kentucky petition for tariff aid, *A.S.P.*, *Finance*, I, 732, which went into the 'obvious disadvantages' of the West as compared to the East — the distance from markets, delay in receiving news of market conditions, etc. 'No Arabs or Tartars travel farther and wider in pursuit of... a market.' Butler, M., *Hist. Ky.*, p. 453.

[2] *Ky. Gazette*, Feb. 5, 12, 1802, Jan. 11, 18, 1803.

[3] Wilkinson had dispatched a 'squadron under the Kentucke colors' of 25 armed boats, 'the first Armada that ever floated on Western Waters.' Verhoeff, M., *Kentucky River Navigation*, pp. 57–58; also, his advertisements in *Ky. Gazette*, Dec. 15, 22, 1787, Sept. 13, 1788. The trade languished (but not Wilkinson's Spanish pension) after the General's return to the American army. His amazing career of intrigue was long concealed: Lexington in 1803 toasted 'General Wilkinson — Let us not forget the man who first adventured as an exporter of produce to New Orleans.' *Ky. Gazette*, Aug. 16, 1803.

ened and schemed for the freedom of the Mississippi highway —
'the great Road of Nations — its Waters run free, so ought its use
to be.' [1] Henry could well appreciate, also, why the public square
of Lexington had flamed with the bonfires of jubilant Kentuckians
when news had come of Pinckney's Treaty, with its right of un-
loading, storing, and reshipping at Spanish New Orleans.

Within young Clay's own time the river trade, stimulated by the
abnormal demands of war-torn Europe, had grown by leaps and
bounds. In 1799 it was astounding in extent, with the quantity of
exports 'almost incalculable,' the number of boats 'incredible to
relate.' Within a few years, if favored by a liberal Federal Government, this fruitful Western World 'would or might administer
to the wants of North & South America and their dependencies.' [2]
During the first six months of 1801, Western America sent to the
outside world, via the Spanish outlet on the Gulf of Mexico, no
less than four hundred and fifty flatboats, twenty-six keelboats,
two schooners, one brig, and seven pirogues loaded down with
flour, hemp, tobacco, pork, pig lead, cordage, apples, and other
articles ranging from saltpetre and whiskey to millstones and
onions.[3]

Coonskin frontiersmen became shipbuilders. In the very heart
of the continent, thousands of miles from the sea, the sound of axe
and hammer rang out in shipyards along the Ohio and its tribu-
taries. In 1800 the brig *St. Clair* of 110 tons was being built at
Marietta, Ohio; the *Monongahela Farmer* of 250 tons was nearing
completion at Elizabethtown, Pennsylvania; a three-master was
on the stocks at Pittsburgh; the brig *Kentucky* was ready at Louisville, below the falls; while along the Kentucky River, which
pierced the fertile Blue Grass, scores of flatboats and broadhorns
were being launched. 'Vessels built on our waters, calculated for
transporting our commodities to the most distant quarters of the
globe,' proudly declared the governor of backwoods Kentucky in

---

[1] John Rhea to Breckinridge, Sept. 10, 1794, *Breckinridge MSS.*

[2] Samuel Hopkins to Breckinridge, May 3, 1799, *Breckinridge MSS.*

[3] Pelzer, L., 'Economic Factors in the Acquisition of Louisiana,' *Proc. Miss. Valley Hist. Assoc.*, VI, 109–28; Michaux, *Travels*, pp. 239–47; Hulbert, A., 'Western Ship-Building,' *Amer. Hist. Rev.*, XXI, 720–33; *A.S.P.*, *Miscellaneous*, I, 344–56; Channing, E., *History of U.S.*, IV, 311; and the excellent general account by Whitaker, A. P., *The Mississippi Question, 1795–1803*.

1802, 'afford us a flattering view of the resources and future greatness of our country.' [1]

Many of Clay's lawsuits were concerned with the cargoes and
carriers of this expanding river and ocean trade, this 'Golden
Commerce of Western America.' His relatives and friends played
a large part in its development, individually and through their
Kentucky Insurance Company, of which he was the attorney and
a shareholder. His father-in-law's Mississippi ventures were
miscellaneous and many. Colonel Hart and his associates had
flatboats built annually, and exported not only foodstuffs but
cordage, rigging materials, nails, bagging for cotton and rough
cloth for slaves in the Lower South, and other manufactures.
Henry's younger brother, Porter, was early engaged in shipbuild-
ing on the Kentucky River, while brother John in 1800 migrated
to New Orleans and there became the agent for the Harts and
other upcountry entrepreneurs.

It was a trade which unified the Jeffersonian frontier north and
south and, at the same time, helped to break down its geographical
isolation. It was a trade which tended to liberalize the ultra-
agrarianism inherited from the Virginia planter-democracy, and
to give the enterprising Ohio Valley section a wider outlook, a
more varied economy. It compelled an awareness, often painful,
of economic interdependence with the East — which took money
so gained for its imports, and of the impact of international conditions — which in the spring of 1802, by the Peace of Amiens,
brought flour down from five to three dollars at Orleans.[2] It ran
threads of finance and commerce through the pattern of a region
predominantly yet not exclusively agricultural; complex threads
which were gathered in by the business pioneers of Lexington.
Together with the conditions which gave rise to demands for internal improvements and tariff protection, this New Orleans
commerce with its financing, insuring, marketing, and shipbuild-
ing had a decided influence in shaping the politico-economic
ideas of Henry Clay.

---

[1] Message of Gov. Jas. Garrard, *Ky. Gazette*, Nov. 9, 1802.

[2] Benjamin Howard to Breckinridge, April 30, 1802, *Breckinridge MSS.* — 'the
quantity of provisions taken from this Country during the winter and spring is almost
incalculable. Considerable losses have been sustained on the river.'

In public life he represented not only the farmer but the business pioneer. During these early years, in the Kentucky Assembly he led the movement to align politics, despite a prejudiced agrarian liberalism, with this new capitalistic liberalism, the forces of which were most essential in developing a frontier economy that was limited, raw, primitive. A few years later, in Congress he was to shock doctrinaire Jeffersonians by advocating a navy, contending that commerce was not exclusively a Northeastern (Federalist) interest but a national interest, inseparable from agriculture, and as such entitled to national protection. Clay's arguments were novel for a Republican, a member of a States' Rights agrarian party considered unfriendly, if not maliciously hostile, to commerce. His reasoned appeals were buttressed, however, with an eloquent portrayal of an adventurous Western commerce; of indomitable seafaring pioneers in America's great Inland Empire who on Western Waters built their own ocean-going ships, loaded them with the products of their own lush frontier soil, and first voyaged one thousand miles down the Ohio, then another thousand miles down the Mississippi, before heading for the West Indies or eastward across the broad Atlantic to the markets of the Old World.[1]

At the turn of the century Clay and his fellow Kentuckians echoed Eastern America's toast — prompted by British interference with America's neutral trade — of 'Free Bottoms Make Free Goods!' Public meetings which Clay attended, and addressed, voiced such sentiments as 'The Mississippi — Success to the public-spirited merchants who are endeavoring to turn our trade into its proper and natural channel,' and 'The Navigation of the Mississippi — May it ever remain free and undisturbed.'[2] Henry shared the enthusiasm of his fellow Westerners of the Ohio Valley when the brig *St. Clair* majestically sailed on her maiden voyage to the Gulf of Mexico and the great waters beyond. Commodore Abraham Whipple, Revolutionary sailor and master of the ship, 'hath Oped the way to Commerce,' exulted a frontier poet. As the *St. Clair* emerged from the Mississippi's mouth into the ocean

[1] *Annals of Congress*, 12th Congress, 1st session, pp. 916–19.
[2] *Ky. Gazette*, July 10, 1800, Jan. 26, 1801.

trade routes, her sails bellying with fair winds, Neptune himself
would come on board and welcome this white-winged harbinger of
Western seafaring —

> 'Sirens attend with Flute and Lyre
> And bring your Conks, my Trittons;
> in chorus Blow to the Aged Sire
> in welcome to my Dominions.' [1]

All this commercial pioneering only emphasized Spain's grip at
New Orleans on the Western jugular vein. Nowhere could
produce be floated to the Gulf without paying tribute to His
Catholic Majesty. Yet America was expanding and Spain was
over-expanded. It seemed only a matter of years before her un-
tenanted provinces of Louisiana and the Floridas, and perhaps
Mexico with its silver mines, would be seized by the dynamic sons
of the Western World. So thought Moses Austin in 1797, who
predicted that by the time his son (the destined founder of American Texas) reached manhood the Spanish Louisiana he had just
visited, and found 'in a state of Nature,' would 'be overspread
with Towns and Villages, for it is Not possible that a Country
which has with in its self everything to make its settlers Rich and
Happy can remain Unnotice'd by the American people.' [2]

But there were others who had 'noticed' Louisiana — which to
Spain was an adopted French daughter that had become not only
a luxury but a liability. In the midst of their paeans of Western
enterprise, Clay and his fellow Kentuckians were rudely shocked
by rumors that Spain (in exchange for European spoils) in 1800
had secretly retroceded to France the port of Orleans and the vast
Louisiana colony stretching from the Mississippi to the Rockies. [3]

---

[1] Hulbert, *Western Ship-Building*, p. 724.   [2] Austin, M., *Journal*, p. 542.

[3] There had been vague rumors, but little alarm, of a retrocession since the Franco-
Spanish Alliance of 1795. John Brown to Innes, June 27, 1795, *Innes MSS.*, 19; *Ky.
Gazette*, Feb. 4, 1797. Since that time Spain, secretly, had been bargaining to rid herself of Louisiana. Whitaker, *Mississippi Question*. Of interest are the letters (in *Breckinridge MSS.*) of Colonel Samuel Fulton of the French Army in Haiti, a former colleague
of Clark and Genêt — on May 7, 1801 (in 1802 volume) he informed Breckinridge of
the cession; on March 22, 1802 he doubted 'whether this will be as agreeable to the
Western people as it would have been had we succeeded in '94,' and, expecting war
with France, sought service in the American army; yet on Aug. 22, 1802 from New
Orleans he wrote Breckinridge: 'be assured it will be the greatest thing imaginable in
favour of the Western Country, it will assure the independence of the Western World
ten years sooner than it would otherwise happen,' especially if the able and independent General Bernadotte should be the head of French Louisiana.

First Consul Bonaparte, after overturning the Old World, was now to be master of the Mississippi Valley! Taking advantage of the brief lull in the great war, this modern Caesar was to re-establish a French empire which might easily swallow up British Canada, Spanish Mexico, and Spanish South America — ulti-mately, perhaps, the entire New World.

In October of 1802 the grasping hand of the invincible Bona-parte seemed stretched across the Atlantic when at New Orleans the Spanish Intendant struck a sudden and staggering blow at Western prosperity (already depressed by the Peace of Amiens) by proclaiming the cessation of 'the privilege which the Americans had of bringing and depositing their goods in this capitol.' [1] Here was a foretaste of what Kentuckians might expect when mighty France controlled their great highway to the sea.

'The shutting that port has given a great shock,' reported a Blue Grass planter: 'the farmer is discouraged, the Millers think themselves Grimed, and everything seems to be floating on a sea of uncertainty.' [2] Loaded boats piled up along the Mississippi, the Ohio, the Cumberland and Tennessee; exports ceased and stagna-tion ensued. 'The proclamation ... has Cast a damp on the Com-mercial pursuits of this once prosperous land' [3] — 'given a general and serious alarm here, no kind of produce will sell.' [4]

The Western World quivered with excitement. There were rumblings of protest premonitory of a volcanic eruption which might well mean foreign war or Western secession. Incensed at 'the wretched state of our Western Country,' frontiersmen declared Spain's action equivalent to war. America could not, would not, be robbed of rights gained by Pinckney's Treaty. 'The whole country was in commotion,' said Clay, 'and, at the nod of Govern-ment, would have fallen on Baton Rouge and New Orleans.' [5]

Alarming reports reached Washington. 'The voice of the

---

[1] *Ky. Gazette*, Nov. 30, 1802.

[2] Chas. Smith, Jr., to Breckinridge, Feb. 1, 1803, *Breckinridge MSS.*

[3] *Ibid.*, F. L. Turner to same, Dec. 8, 1802 — at the same time he noted that goods might still be exported, but only in Spanish bottoms, for Spanish ports, at a Spanish duty of 12 per cent.

[4] *Ibid.*, Christopher Greenup to same, Dec. 27, 1802.

[5] *Annals of Congress*, 12th, 1st, p. 916.

people becomes serious,' Senator Breckinridge was informed: they 'begin to mesure their strength' — a Kentucky militia 'about 30,000 strong.' [1] In Lexington everyone expects war: 'it will be impossible for the U. S. to steer Clear of a warr with France, provided they mean to protect this Western Country in its Natural & Political Rights.' [2] The most serious consequences are in prospect: 'the Kentuckians are all in a Hubbub, all ready and waiting to step on board & sail down and take Possession of New Orleans.' [3]

Take possession now, negotiate after, urged hot-tempered pioneers, willing to risk war with both Spain and France. 'Condine punishment' must be inflicted upon 'the arrogant and imperious Intendant and his Reptile Spaniards.' A bold stroke now, and an end would be put to foreign control of the Mississippi. A quick blow now, and we would annex 'one of the fairest countries under Heaven.' [4] New Orleans must not be left 'to the yoke of any Nation on Earth — the port must be opened or Kentuckyans will Fight!' [5]

Cooler counsel prevailed, however. It was far easier to conquer Orleans from decadent Spain than to hold it against the superb veterans of Bonaparte. Old Judge McDowell pointed out how one of the enemy's seventy-fours could blockade the port, regretted the Republican prejudices that had all but destroyed John Adams's army and navy, and lamented the weakness of the young republic — 'I fear we Shall be insulted by other nations and not have it in our Power even to make an attempt to Repell the Insult. No Army, No Navy and worst of all an Empty Treasury. (O America).' [6]

In the past such realistic considerations had not dampened impetuous, direct-action frontier romantics, or arrested their volcanic protests against Federalist 'British' administrations.

[1] Wm. Stevenson to Breckinridge, Jan. 29, 1803, *Breckinridge MSS.*
[2] *Ibid.*, John A. Seitz to same, Feb. 17, 1803.
[3] *Ibid.*, Robt. Barr to same, Jan. 4, 1803.
[4] *Ky. Gazette*, Jan. 11, Feb. 14, 1803; also, Nov. 30, Dec. 7, 1802.
[5] Chas. Smith, Jr., to Breckinridge, Feb. 1, 1803; and, of same tenor, Achilles Sneed to same, Dec. 30, 1802, *Breckinridge MSS.*
[6] *Ibid.*, Samuel McDowell to same, Dec. 15, 1802.

Prudence, a careful canvassing of consequences, was a rare virtue among the Children of America. Yet, significantly, 'the Wild Men of Kentucky' were willing to trust to Jefferson, to mark time, to await 'the nod of Government' before rushing forward. At this grave national crisis, when so much depended upon the West, supreme confidence was placed in Thomas Jefferson and the Republican administration. And it was this that capped and restrained the frontier volcano.

Sharp indeed was the swing in Kentucky sentiment from the days of separatist intrigues, Clark-Genêt filibusters, and clamorous Democratic Societies. Surprisingly moderate in tone was the memorial to the Federal Government of the Kentucky Assembly that had but recently issued its famous States' Rights resolutions. A Lexington citizen who agitated for immediate Western action was imprisoned for disturbing the peace. In Frankfort the advocate of an independent West, or a West allied with France, was brought to trial for sedition. A Republican mob, composed of the same men who during the Alien and Sedition furor had roundly cheered Henry Clay and other 'seditious Wagon and Stump Orators,' set upon this anti-Jefferson and anti-American wretch, burned him in effigy, and with righteous indignation shouted 'Perpetuity to the Union! Confidence in Government! Free Navigation of the Mississippi!' [1]

Similar nationalistic sentiments were voiced in Lexington by Clay and his fellow townsmen. The Vineyard Association not only toasted 'That Most Pleasing Union — The Myrtle of Venus with the Vine of Bacchus,' but condemned 'those who seek war or a separation from the Union' — May they 'never taste the juice of the grape.' Punishment equally as terrible was threatened by Clay, James Brown, and Editor Bradford against partisan Eastern Federalists who asserted that Kentucky was up in arms, hostile to Jefferson, and ready to secede from the Union in order to gain New Orleans. Clay and his associates pointed out that such 'war-whooping' came from New Englanders who had once voted to

---

[1] *Ky. Gazette*, March 1, 15, 22, 1803. 'But a single man in this state ventured to oppose the general sentiment.' Breckinridge to Monroe, July 9, 1803, *Breckinridge MSS*. 'The project of a conceited and crack'd brained individual.' Harry Toulmin to Madison, April 5, 1803, *Madison MSS*.

barter away the Mississippi; from the same Federalist aristocrats who were endeavoring, as in 1797–99, to bring about their cherished alliance with Tory England.[1]

'Our Country is in a State of perfect tranquillity,' reported one of Henry's friends in February of 1803 (although he had reported only two months before that 'most people Calculate on a war'). 'The confidence of the people here in the president, and I may add, in Congress too, are so firmly fixed that they will not move in any direction but that pointed out by the general government.' Should Jefferson through diplomacy fail to get them justice, then, and then only, would Kentuckians consider marching on New Orleans. Jefferson, the Man of the People, must first speak; and 'no State in the Union will attend with more firmness and Composure for the *Word*.'[2]

While Kentuckians strained at a seldom-imposed leash, Jefferson negotiated for the purchase of Orleans and a strip of East Florida. Although elected in opposition to an 'entangling alliance' with 'the corrupt and tottering British Monarchy,' the leader of the so-called French party went so far as to threaten France that the moment she took New Orleans the United States would marry themselves to the British fleet and nation. The anxiety of Kentucky was little eased when Intendant Morales, who had permitted evasions of his provocative proclamation, in May of 1803 restored the right of deposit. Such a restoration was 'of very little importance,' as Breckinridge remarked, when continued foreign control of the Mississippi's mouth meant 'the perpetual fear of similar & more violent outrages on our commerce.'[3]

At length the suspense was broken by news from Paris — glorious news! Even Jefferson was entirely unprepared for the startling and providential turn of events which gave the republic not only Orleans but the whole province of Louisiana, a vast empire equal to the combined area of France and Germany, a vast wilderness world which doubled the area of the nation, removed grave dangers to its independence, ensured to it the

---

[1] *Ky. Gazette*, April 16, Aug. 20, Oct. 1, 1802; March 29, May 3, June 14, 1803.

[2] Judge John Allen to Breckinridge, Feb. 15, 1803, and Dec. 18, 1802, *Breckinridge MSS.*; also, H. Taylor to Madison, Jan. 15, March 6, 1803, *Madison MSS.*

[3] Breckinridge to Monroe, July 9, 1803, *Breckinridge MSS.*

essential Western outlet to the sea, and made possible its greatness as a continental power!

Young Henry Clay and his fellow Westerners gave way to unbounded joy. Monster Louisiana Purchase celebrations were held in Lexington, in Frankfort, and in every hamlet in the state. Fervid were the impromptu speeches, jubilant the public addresses, numberless the toasts. For months to come Clay and his compatriots could talk of little else but of 'America's Extension of Empire' and of 'The Immortal Jefferson.' [1]

The Purchase Treaty was duly ratified. Jefferson cast aside his dogma of a government of expressed powers literally interpreted, and did not insist upon a constitutional amendment giving Congress the specific power of purchasing territory. Senator Breckinridge with the same commendable common sense forgot about the Kentucky Resolutions. New England Federalists in vain opposed this grand, this unprecedented, real estate deal as unconstitutional and prophesied the rapid dissolution of the enlarged Union. Overjoyed at the glittering prospects before them, and welcoming the idea of future Republican states from the new territory, frontiersmen consigned all treaty opponents to 'the shaving mill of the Guillotine,' and hailed the dawn of a new day for the Western World and for 'the United States one and indivisible.'

But the cession was not yet an accomplished fact. Jubilation soon gave way to fresh apprehension, for Spain, resenting Bonaparte's cavalier treatment, was reluctant to yield Louisiana.

In answer to her protests Jefferson ordered the Western militia to be in readiness to descend the Mississippi by December 20, 1803, and to take New Orleans by force if need be. At Jefferson's '*Word*' Kentucky flamed with excitement. And this time the volcano erupted, spreading far and wide its lava of molten patriotism.

'Our Western Country [is] all on fire!' exclaimed old General Russell of Lexington.[2] 'Nothing but war is the topick of the day,' reported William Stevenson: Kentuckians were not to be thwarted of the grand object for which they had so long pleaded and agitated.[3] 'The magnitude of the Louisiana question keeps us all

---

[1] *Ky. Gazette*, Aug. 2, 9, 16, 1803, ff.
[2] Wm. Russell to Breckinridge, Nov. 18, 1803, *Breckinridge MSS.*
[3] *Ibid.*, Wm. Stevenson to same, Nov. 21, 1803.

on tiptoe,' wrote James Brown to Breckinridge, 'and our anxiety will continue until we are informed of the result.' [1] With Clay and other fiery orators Brown made war-whooping speeches at courthouse and muster ground. A few days spent with Henry on the stump convinced him that the citizens were as eager as young Clay to take up musket and sword; that Kentucky's quota of four thousand volunteer militiamen would not only be quickly filled but that as many as ten thousand could be easily raised.[2] Frankfort, the state capital, was a bedlam of patriotic bustle. Through Lexington's streets and public square to rolling drum and shrilling fife paraded Captain Wyatt's Company and the bluecoated Light Infantry. 'The *Spirit* here is highly Wrought,' wrote Samuel Hopkins, 'and nothing but the possession of Orleans will quiet it.' [3]

No one was more enthusiastic over this welling up of patriotism than young Henry Clay. 'Armies, Sieges and Storms completely engross the public mind,' he reported to Senator Breckinridge. 'The first interrogatory put on every occasion is — Do you go to New Orleans? If all who answer in the affirmative should really design to go, Government will find it necessary to restrain the public Ardor.' He enjoyed the hubbub, the military preparations, the exciting talk of storms and sieges. No one seemed more eager to meet the Spanish Dons amid clanging sword and roaring cannon. Was Lawyer Clay going to Orleans? Yes, decidedly! He was a member of the gallant Louisiana Volunteers. Major General Hopkins, commander of the Kentucky contingent, had made him an aide-de-camp. 'I shall go with the crowd,' Clay informed Breckinridge, 'to endeavour to share the glory of the expedition.' [4]

As an aide Henry was engrossed in martial duties, in the problems of men and arms. There were maps and charts and in-

---

[1] Jas. Brown to Breckinridge, Oct. 21, 1803, *Breckinridge MSS.*

[2] *Ibid.*, same to same, Nov. 21, 1803. Indignant at 'the crooked policy of the capricious Court of Spain... I overcame my usual dislike of mob-oratory — mounted the rostrum and addressed the multitude... Having engaged to accompany the expedition as aid de camp to General Adair, I felt the more entitled to address the people and to urge their embarking in the enterprise.'

[3] *Ibid.*, Hopkins to same, Nov. 17, 1803; and see *Ky. Gazette*, Nov. 22, 1803, and ff.

[4] Clay to Breckinridge, Nov. 21, 1803, *Breckinridge MSS.* Clay, like Hopkins and others, only hoped that Tennessee, where the people were distracted and divided by the disputes and duels of Andrew Jackson and Gov. John Sevier, would be as prompt in taking the field.

ventories, conferences as to river garrisons and the forts at Orleans, questions as to transportation, mounted infantry, powder and ball, travelling forges and armorers — all the varied gear and accouterments of Mars. His chief did not take his responsibilities lightly. General Hopkins assured Breckinridge that the Army of Kentucky would be a competent fighting force, capable of sustaining the state's reputation, and ready to take the field even if unaided by the sister states. He had taken 'Great Pains . . . in choosing the officers for the Service,' and he appeared to be undaunted by the squabbling for rank and place in his ill-disciplined citizen army drawn from a Kentucky militia of some thirty thousand men only half of whom possessed arms. But the good General was distressed by the lack of a most important item — 'Gold Epaulets' for his officers' uniforms. These were essential for appearance and morale. Would not Senator Breckinridge from Washington immediately send gold epaulets for himself, for Mr. Henry Clay, and other members of his staff? [1]

'Spanish fever' had seized the Children of America. 'The Tocsin of War resounds,' reported a Virginian visiting Lexington — such a fervor! Everyone was preoccupied with the one topic — the glory awaiting the Louisiana Volunteers. Private business could no longer be transacted. Lawyer, sheriff, surveyor, and merchant — all talked and dreamed of gunpowder and bayonet. The Spirit of '76 had flamed up in the woods of Western America.[2] Yet such devoted patriotism, such brisk recruiting, such 'alacrity and zeal with which men volunteer in this war for the purpose of maintaining our rights,' was to be expected of the gallant state of Kentucky. 'It is not known the bounds that zeal or ardour for one's country will carry a man!' [3] Young Clay and his fellow Volunteers

---

[1] Hopkins to Breckinridge, Nov. 22, 1803, *Breckinridge MSS.*; also, on militia, *Ky. Gazette*, Nov. 10, 1800.

[2] Francis Preston to same, Nov. 29, 1803, *Breckinridge MSS.* 'Ask a Sheriff if there are any taxes due on your Land, he will answer: they *will seize* the town of Orleans *instanter* and *execute* the rascals without bail or main prize. Ask a Lawyer to prosecute a suit for you, & he will answer that it is *doubtfull* whether it is better to make a *forcible entry* on the fort or take it by *Surprise*. Ask a Surveyor whether your platt is made out. He will answer that it is a cursed *plott* in the Spaniards to withhold possession of Orleans, but has no doubt that on a *Survey* of the *premises* such *courses* will be pursued as to effect our *right*.'

[3] *Ibid.*, Wm. Stevenson to same, Nov. 27, 1803.

appeared in the guise of embattled patriots, Republican Sons of Liberty, who would 'cause the despots of the earth to tremble like Belteshazer of old at the thoughts of violating the rights of man.' [1]

Perhaps at far-away Madrid His Catholic Majesty saw the handwriting on the wall. Perhaps Don Carlos IV appreciated the hornets' nest he had stirred up in Henry Clay's Kentucky, and like Belshazzar of old trembled at the threatening approach of these modern Medes and Persians, these American frontiersmen whom his Louisiana governors described as predatory semi-savages. For Spain, fortunately, gave up the idea of resorting to arms and, still protesting, accepted the bargain made by Napoleon Bonaparte and Thomas Jefferson which transferred from her possession the port of New Orleans and 'the limitless province of Louisiana.' In December of 1803, Louisiana was formally and peaceably handed over, first to France, then to the United States.

The war flurry was over; the excitement subsided; and Kentucky was 'like a Ship, after being wrecked by the violence of a hurricane, and is becalmed.' [2] Young Clay and his friends were deprived of the opportunity of going 'with the crowd,' of seeking glory under the banners of the Louisiana Volunteers, of storming Spanish redoubts and carving out careers as Kentucky Bernadottes or Bonapartes. Such brazen glories were not for Henry; he was to be one of Kentucky's few public men who did not boast a military title. 'It would have given me individual pleasure to visit New Orleans,' he wrote Breckinridge, 'but I nevertheless sincerely rejoice that the affair has terminated pacifically.'

He rejoiced, too, that Kentucky's patriotic restraint as well as ardor had raised her in the estimation of critical Easterners. He speculated upon the extent and richness of Louisiana, queried Breckinridge as to policies to be pursued, and was interested in the distribution of Federal territorial offices, of 'the Loaves and Fishes.' While he modestly recommended his brother John of New Orleans for a post he did not seek any preferment for himself. Unlike James Brown and other friends, Henry had no intention of quitting Kentucky.[3]

---

[1] *Ky. Gazette*, May 22, 1804.
[2] Wm. Stevenson to Breckinridge, Jan. 29, 1804, *Breckinridge MSS.*
[3] *Ibid.*, Clay to Breckinridge, Dec. 30, 1803.

In the meantime, freed from tasks involving sieges and storms, and gold epaulets, he joined with his jubilant compatriots in Grand Festivals celebrating the splendid and unprecedented stroke of fortune that had given the young republic half a continent. Orator Clay was conspicuous at public dinners and rollicking tavern parties which usually ended in the town square with eighteen rifle salutes — seventeen for the states of the Union, and one whopping big volley for America's 'Extension of Empire.' Most fittingly did his friends Senator Breckinridge and Federal Judge Innes preside over the Jubilee at Maxwell's Spring on Saint Tammany's Day, a glorious day with bugles blowing, cannons booming, and orators acclaiming America's ownership of the Father of Waters, President Jefferson, and Kentucky's pioneer statesmen who had long labored to gain the great highway to the sea. Most happily, that evening at Mr. Bradley's Travellers Hall, 'amidst a brilliant assemblage, beauty presided, and joy beamed from every eye.'[1]

Like Henry, James Brown cast aside the trumpet and epaulets of Mars and sincerely rejoiced that the crisis had terminated pacifically. No one was more elated by the Louisiana Purchase — it was a reality compounded by some fortuitous magic out of dreams which he and other pioneer leaders had long cherished. 'We who have been from our very hearts *Western men*, who have seen our Country grow, and have grown with our Country,' wrote Brown to Breckinridge, 'can now view its unforeseen and unparalleled prosperity with pleasure and with pride; and perhaps our enjoyment is not a little heightened by a recollection of the part we took in favor of our Country at an early period; and of the immediate consequences, bold I admit, and proscribed by aristocracy, but well calculated to alarm an unfriendly administration into a respect for our neglected rights.'[2]

Nor would Senator Breckinridge, formerly Citizen Breckinridge

---

[1] *Ky. Gazette*, May 15, 1804; *passim*.

[2] Brown to Breckinridge, Jan. 13, 1804 [misdated Jan. 13, 1803; in 1803 volume], *Breckinridge MSS.*: 'With what joy have we received assurances that the Country is to be peaceably and honorably incorporated with our Union, that its citizens are cheered by the exhilarating prospect of liberty, and that you are rapidly advancing in the formation of a government which will promote the happiness, encourage the population, and secure the affections of the Inhabitants of the fairest portion of the United States!'

of the 'seditious' Democratic Society, ever forget the exultation of these days. 'The magnitude of the acquisition,' he wrote Jefferson, 'is not more important than the manner in which it was acquired. To add to our empire more than two hundred millions of acres of the first portion of the earth, without a convulsion, without spilling one drop of blood, without impairing the rights or interest of a single individual, without damaging in the slightest degree the fiscal concerns of the country, & without, in short, the expence of a single dollar (for the port of Orleans will of itself reimburse the 15 millions of dollars in the 15 years) is an achievement of which the annals of no country can furnish a parallel.

'As to the Floridas,' continued this spokesman of the Western Democracy, 'I really consider their acquisition as of no consequence for the present. We can attain them long before we want them, & upon our own terms . . . We certainly discharged the duty imposed on us, and have nothing to answer for to our posterity . . . leaving remote, & to us incalculable events, to be governed by those whose immediate duty it becomes to watch & to detect them.'[1]

John Breckinridge was soon (in December of 1806) to pass off the political stage. But from his own state, and from those to be carved out of the Louisiana Territory, were to come successors who would carry on this tradition of growth and expansion. Within a few years his mantle of Western leadership was to be worn by Henry Clay of Kentucky, his fellow townsman and political lieutenant, one of those younger Americans destined 'to watch & to detect' what now seemed remote and incalculable. Like Breckinridge, Clay of Kentucky was to be a Republican expansionist, a Jeffersonian imperialist. But he was also to distinguish himself as a nationalist capable of conserving territory acquired, of defending the independence of the enlarged Union against foreign aggressions, of compromising sectional rivalries, and of advancing the interests of a unified nation.

And the spirit which animated Henry Clay of Kentucky, soon to be hailed nationally as 'Harry of the West,' was perhaps best expressed in a toast of 1804 given by his frontier compatriots at a Louisiana Purchase celebration: 'The 17 confederated States of

---

[1] Breckinridge to Jefferson, Sept. 10, 1803, *Breckinridge MSS.*

America and territorial appendages — the aggravated punishment of Tantalus and Prometheus be the portion of him who shall dare weaken the golden ligaments which bind them together.' [1]

[1] *Ky. Gazette*, May 22, 1804.

Chapter Five. Blue Grass Politician

Now Henry was an exceeding learned counselor, the spirit of discretion and eloquence was in him; and when he spake all the people marvelled at his wisdom: So the merchants and people of Lexington chose Henry to be their chief. (*William Littell.*)

The glorious uncertainty of the law is a proverbial expression; and why may we not speak of the glorious uncertainty of politics? It gives . . . ample scope for all your genius, experience, sagacity, and eloquence. (*John Adams.*)

IN AUGUST of 1803 the men of Fayette descended upon their county seat, invading Lexington's taverns and stores and market-place, crowding its courthouse square, filling the little town with their bustle and swagger. A noisy political campaign was in progress: the sovereign people were about to elect Fayette's four representatives in the Kentucky Assembly. Candidates circulated about, shaking hands most cordially, treating the voters to free grog and unlimited promises, making florid speeches on their own transcendent merits. A militia muster contributed to the general confusion with the rolling of drums, firing of rifles, and drinking of drams usual on such occasions. Little knots of men gathered here and there, and a recurring question among them was how young Lawyer Clay would fare in competition with the many candidates who had offered. It was his first campaign for elective office, and his prospects were none too bright.

Even Henry's friends were becoming apprehensive, although a few days before when they had placed his name on the lists they had considered him certain of election. But now the third and last day of the balloting had dawned, competition had become intense, and Clay had yet to make his appearance. He had been at Olympian Springs when his friends, 'without my knowledge or previous consent,' he later said,[1] had nominated him; and he was still tarrying at this fashionable Blue Grass watering-place some distance from town. In the meantime, with the polls about to close, votes were being diverted from him by rivals who asserted that young Mr. Clay was indifferent to the election, did not wish politics to interfere with his law practice, and preferred the social pleasures of Olympian Springs to the heat and burden of campaigning.

In the midst of such speeches they were confounded by Henry's sudden appearance. It is more likely that he had been cocksure of his election than indifferent to it. Perhaps he had arranged this dramatic eleventh-hour appearance. Whatever the circumstances or motives, he mounted the stump, refuted arguments that he was uninterested — far from it! — gave his views on state affairs, and made his first eloquent appeal for office to the citizens of Fayette. His whirlwind finish delighted his frontier neighbors; he had injected an element of the unusual, of the spectacular, into the campaign. They were particularly impressed by the flair for electioneering he revealed when he canvassed for votes among the riflemen attending the militia muster.

After haranguing this group he was approached by one of the militiamen — a leather-faced, heavily bearded backwoodsman dressed in buckskin breeches, hunting shirt, and coonskin cap, with knife, hatchet, and bullet pouch at his belt, a huge powder-horn slung across his tanned and hairy chest. 'Young man,' said the fellow, 'you want to go to the legislature, I see.' Clay admitted that he did. 'Are you a good shot?' 'The best in the country,' was the prompt reply. 'Then you shall go to the legislature. But first you must give us a specimen of your skill. We must see you shoot.' Henry now regretted his hasty assurances: he was a poor shot, and

---

[1] Clay in speech at Lexington, June 9, 1842, Mallory, *Clay*, II, 572.

he knew it only too well. 'I never shoot any rifle but my own,' he lamely said. 'No matter,' replied the hunter, handing him his long Kentucky rifle. 'Here is Old Bess; she never fails in the hands of a marksman. She has often sent death through a squirrel's head one hundred yards, and daylight through many a redskin twice that distance. If you can shoot any gun you can shoot Old Bess.'

For a moment Henry was taken aback; then his gambling instinct asserted itself. 'Well, put up your mark!' he cried. The target was set at eighty yards. With an air of great assurance Lawyer Clay put Old Bess to his shoulder, quickly sighted, and fired. The target was pierced near the center! There were cheers; yet not one of the crowd could have been more surprised than the young candidate who held smoking Old Bess in his hands. 'Oh, a chance shot!' shouted an onlooker. 'He might shoot all day and not hit the mark again. Make him try it over.' Another hit, however, would have been asking too much of Henry's beloved Goddess of Chance. Turning to the unfriendly fellow, Clay hotly retorted: 'No. Beat that; beat that, and then I will.' His challenge was unaccepted, and as the heckler withdrew, another roar went up from the crowd. Chance shot or not, this young lawyer was a man of spirit, a candidate after their own hearts. So reasoned Old Bess's buckskin owner and his comrades as they marched noisily off to the polls.[1]

It was not so much the hunters and small farmers, however, as the business men and planters of Fayette who were interested in sending the resourceful young attorney to the Assembly. At the session of 1802 the radical agrarians from south of the Kentucky River, under the leadership of Felix Grundy, had revolutionized the judiciary with their ultra-democratic Circuit Court Bill. This hotly contested issue had revealed in Kentucky a cleavage between the Blue Grass and the less developed and exclusively farming South Country comparable to that in Virginia between Tidewater and Piedmont, and, in many ways, to that between Eastern and Western America. To defend their varied economic interests the business pioneers of Lexington wanted Clay, whose prowess at the

---

[1] In after years Clay would say: 'I had never before fired a rifle, and have not since.' Mallory, *op. cit.*, I, 18–19; and Prentice, *Clay*, pp. 25–26.

bar was now well established, as their legislative champion. In Henry's absence at the Springs these friends and associates had brought about his 'unsolicited nomination.'

With their backing, and with the support of the crowd gained by his personal popularity and his adept performance on the stump, young Lawyer Clay was elected.[1] In November of 1803, the year of the great Louisiana Purchase, he rode over to neighboring Frankfort, took his seat as a representative from Fayette County, and began his political career.

Having 'lived' his Virginia boyhood in the atmosphere of practical politics, Henry had few illusions as to the Kentucky Assembly and its 'good democratic majority' which, according to Federalist Humphrey Marshall, was unexcelled in furnishing 'precedents for every species of irregularity and incorrect legislation.'[2] He shared to some degree the disdainful superiority his fellow Lexingtonians assumed toward the homespun legislators who annually gathered at the state capital. A session there, said his friend Benjamin Howard, meant only 'a dreary two months among the wise men of the State.'[3] And Henry himself, in 1800, with all the cynicism of his twenty-three years, had observed to Mr. Breckinridge that 'our assembly... have indeed attempted much and done little; but I have heard it remarked, perhaps not improperly, that this is the best evidence of their superior wisdom.'[4]

He had hardly taken his seat when Frankfort was seized by the 'Spanish fever.' Everything was directed, he reported, to the acquisition of Louisiana, 'this great National concern.'[5] Throughout the three-storied stone state house, from the basement to the square roof with its cupola and bell, in the hall of the representatives on the second floor, the senate chamber on the third, and in the courtrooms and offices, men talked of nothing but the conquest of Orleans — and of getting coveted commissions under General Hopkins for themselves and friends. The excitement subsided

---

[1] *Ky. Gazette*, Aug. 9, 1803. Fayette elected as representatives Wm. Russell, James Hughes, James True, and Henry Clay.

[2] Marshall, *Hist. Ky.*, II, 323–24.

[3] Howard to Breckinridge, Oct. 30, 1802, *Breckinridge MSS.*

[4] *Ibid.*, Clay to same, Dec. 18, 1800.

[5] *Ibid.*, Clay to same, Nov. 21, 1803.

only when the news came that General Wilkinson had run up the American flag over Louisiana. It was then that the session got under way with the members 'hammering at almost everything' in the vigorous and zestful manner of Kentucky politicians.

Jockeying for votes and offices promptly engaged the best political minds: as many as forty candidates applied for the office of Registrar of Lands before the late registrar could be decently interred, with all the funereal pomp of a state burial. Sectionalism early revealed itself: Governor Garrard was most careful to select the chief officers of the gallant Louisiana Volunteers from each side of the Kentucky River. More than two-thirds of the House, it was said, proposed utopian 'innovating schemes.' Yet at this session Felix Grundy was absent, and the 'thinking members' from the Blue Grass were not unduly alarmed.

Among the usual bills pertaining to divorce petitions, removal of corrupt officials, aid to victims and veterans of Indian wars, bounties on wolves, and postponement of payments due on state lands in the Green River region, there were local measures which Clay advocated, and carried, for the town of Lexington. Along with his friend Judge John Allen of Bourbon, he was nominated a reviser of Kentucky's legal code. Both Henry and Allen joked about their failure to get this profitable political plum, but the 'Coldest Stroke' of the session in Allen's opinion was the long and righteous sermon inflicted on the House by preacher-politician David Purviance, who admonished his fellow representatives on 'profane Swearing, Sabbath Breaking, fornication, etc., etc.' [1]

Clay himself at his first session caused 'considerable commotions.' He introduced a bill, extremely partisan in nature, for reducing from six to two the number of districts from which electors would be chosen for the presidential contest of 1804. By thus merging into two districts, one on each side of the Kentucky, all those regions where Federalists and lukewarm Republicans might coalesce, he would eliminate any possibility of a single anti-Jefferson vote. Such gerrymandering in a state so ardently Re-

---

[1] Judge John Allen to Breckinridge, Dec. 24, 1803; also accounts of the session given Breckinridge by Henry Clay, Dec. 30, Harry Innes, Nov. 15, Wm. Stevenson, Nov. 21, James Brown, Nov. 21, Dec. 10, James Blair, Dec. 5, 1803, *Breckinridge MSS.*

publican seemed hardly necessary. Yet there were circumstances which Henry, zealous Jeffersonian, magnified into threatening importance.

The grave uncertainty of the Louisiana crisis had 'enlivened the hopes of federalism and warmed its venomous abettors into a momentary existence.' [1] Led by Humphrey Marshall and Jo Daveiss, they had attempted to capture some of Kentucky's congressional seats (which the census of 1800 had increased from two to six). But the 'aristocratic party' had been thwarted, and Clay, reappearing as 'Scaevola,' the pamphleteer, had effectively crushed Daveiss's aspirations.[2] With the cession of Louisiana thereafter Kentucky seemingly was unitedly Jeffersonian. Yet here, as in the country at large, there were dangers in Republicanism's very unanimity. The Assembly was faction-ridden, and Henry feared intra-party strife might lead to coalitions with the Federalists. He became apprehensive when John Rowan, bosom friend of Daveiss yet a nominal Republican, dared to vote against resolutions praising Jefferson's Louisiana negotiations. In the Senate, also, according to Thomas Todd, 'Federalism had its influence with several members & induced a strong suspicion that more of it exists in our Assembly than has been heretofore supposed.' [3]

---

[1] Jas. Brown to Breckinridge, Jan. 13 [1804], *Breckinridge MSS*. 'They began, even here, to reassume the tone of insolence which they adopted under the auspices of the black cockade in 1798. The prospect of war was cherished as their last resort, and was never abandoned until within a few days.' Also, on the few 'aristocrats... the Marshalls, J. H. Daveiss, etc.,' *ibid.*, others to same, 1802–03; and Harry Toulmin to Madison, Aug. 12, 1803, *Madison MSS*. However, as Levi Todd wrote Breckinridge, the real 'mischief is that excepting 15 or 20 all the Kentuckyans think the same way.' The 'friends of Government... are abundant, nay, superabundant,' wrote James Morrison; yet in state politics there is much friction: Garrard, 'the Governor, is as unpopular with our Assembly, as John Adams would be with Congress if now President.' Todd, Feb. 22, Morrison, Feb. 27, Dec. 20, 1802, to Breckinridge, *Breckinridge MSS*.

[2] *Ky. Gazette*, Feb. 1, 1803 — Daveiss, taking 'infinite pains to secure popular approbation,' did not openly campaign as a Federalist. Clay ('Scaevola'), however, assailed his apparent turncoat maneuvers and recalled his past Federalism. You must inform the people of your true principles, said Clay, 'whether you are displeased with Mr. Adams because he is out of office, or pleased with Mr. Jefferson because he is in office... I am well aware, sir, that it is natural with *some* characters to worship the rising sun; but I do not therefore conclude that it is generous to kick at the fallen.' Clay succeeded in labelling Daveiss an irreconcilable Federalist — and in Kentucky, said Wm. Littell (*ibid.*, May 3, 1803) Federalism was as ruinous politically as sheep-stealing was morally.

[3] Todd to Breckinridge, Dec. 1, 1803, *Breckinridge MSS.*; *Ky. Gazette*, Dec. 27, 1803 (condemning Rowan); *Session Acts, 1803*, pp. 100–102, for Clay's bill.

In face of these symptoms, these very faint symptoms, of dissidence, 'Citizen' Clay felt justified in presenting his redistricting bill. It was passed after some discussion and 'commotions.' And in the ensuing presidential election of 1804 Kentucky, as usual, voted solidly for Thomas Jefferson.

Returning from his first legislative session, Henry resumed his law practice, took part in Louisiana celebrations (at which, incidentally, there were toasts to the nation-wide dissolution of 'the foul fiend of modern Federalism'), and later in the summer visited Olympian Springs for a round of gaiety, cards, and gossip. With his friends he rejoiced in the Jeffersonianism of the new state of Ohio; hailed the impeachment of the notoriously partisan Justice Samuel Chase of the Supreme Court; and denounced Britain's execution of brilliant young Robert Emmet. They discussed John Philpot Curran's orations on Irish Freedom, the Reverend Mr. Lyle's *New American English Grammar*, and Lewis and Clark's exploration of the new imperial domain of Louisiana, where such marvels were said to exist as mountains of salt and of massy gold, and white Indians descended from Welshmen. At Mobile and Baton Rouge, in a West Florida claimed by the United States but still occupied by Spain, American emigrant settlers had unsuccessfully revolted; in the Mediterranean young Stephen Decatur and the tiny American navy were winning renown against the pirates of Tripoli; in French Haiti the freed blacks were committing frightful atrocities and setting up a Negro republic. Henry and his friends gossiped about Jerome Bonaparte's marriage to Miss Patterson of Baltimore, the niece of Mrs. George Nicholas of Lexington; about his famous brother's plan to conquer England with Fulton's torpedoes and 'subaqueous boats'; and they were considerably excited when the same issue of the *Gazette* reported Bonaparte's coronation as Emperor of the French and Alexander Hamilton's death in a duel with Vice President Burr.[1]

Of peculiar interest to young Clay, now fairly launched on his

---

[1] *Ky. Gazette*, May–Oct., 1804. Harry Toulmin, preacher-politician, did much to propagate stories of Welsh Indians. *Ibid.*, Jan. 1, 1805; Janson, C. W., *Stranger in America*, pp. 270–77. The Osage chiefs who passed through Lexington in June to visit White Father Jefferson were unmistakably red; 'their size and uncommon beauty excited universal admiration.' Sam Brown to Jas. Brown, June 12, 1804, *Jas. Brown MSS.*

political career, was the attack made that summer upon Senator Breckinridge, one of Jefferson's most prominent lieutenants. Despite his popularity, in his home town Breckinridge was excoriated, slandered, and grossly abused by a clique headed by Editor Dan Bradford of the *Gazette*, in scurrilous newspaper articles which cut him to the heart.[1] The controversy was typical of Kentucky's intensely personal politics, and of a press so licentious that seemingly only the most adroit and tough-fibered of public men could survive, let alone rise to high office. To young Henry, who was so blithely embarking on his political career, it might well have served as a warning of turbulent seas ahead. Like John Breckinridge, he was to encounter squalls and heavy seas of abuse — abuse which was to provoke from James Brown the bitter comment that such was the inevitable fate of brains and independence in a democracy. 'Republicanism demands that a man of talents should be kept down by detraction. Too much genius, like too much wealth, destroys equality, the very soul of democracy.' [2]

Henry's frontier democracy was notorious for newspapers that were 'scenes of war, vehicles of scandal,' for 'Quarrels, libels, Calumnies, and Duels,' for family feuds, bitter and bloodstained. That between the Marshall and Brown clans dating back to the beginning of Kentucky was a classic example. Through family connections, friendships, and political principles, Henry had fallen heir to loyalties and hatreds. In his many tilts with Humphrey Marshall and Jo Daveiss (both of whom had married sisters of Chief Justice Marshall) he could not help being influenced by the long-standing and ever-fresh feud of his relatives and friends with these Federalist leaders. When he opposed them his voice was shriller, his pen more vitriolic.[3]

In electioneering, one advantage which he possessed and they

---

[1] *Ky. Gazette* and *Breckinridge MSS.*, July–Sept., 1804. Dan Bradford, successor to his father, attacked Breckinridge's alleged vice-presidential ambitions as unwise and selfish; actually, he was incensed because James Brown, and not his brother, James Bradford, was recommended by Breckinridge for secretary of Louisiana Territory.

[2] Brown to Clay, Sept. 1, 1808, Clay, *Corres.*, p. 16.

[3] Since Jefferson's election James Brown in vain had tried to oust Daveiss as U. S. Attorney; only recently he had forced Daveiss to apologize for his attitude at Olympian Springs to Mrs. Brown, Henry's sister-in-law. Brown-Daveiss letters to Breckinridge, Dec. 1801, *Breckinridge MSS.*; Brown to Daveiss, March 25, 1803, *Jas. Brown MSS.*

lacked was a record of opposition to Jay's Treaty, Adams's 'odious Stamp and Still taxes,' the Alien and Sedition Acts, and other 'excrescences of aristocratical legislation.' Yet even with this essential to success, Henry soon realized that the Jeffersonian frontier with its keenly competitive politics demanded much of the candidate — red-hot stump speeches, effusive back-slapping and baby-kissing, generous grog-treating, democratic easiness of approach, and the courage to fight if need be with pen, fist, or pistol.

'Drink whiskey and talk loud with the fullest confidence' was a sure way to popularity in Kentucky, said the Yankee tutor of Clay's children.[1] An effective campaigner was one who 'could drink Grog all day without getting drunk,' according to County Clerk Taul.[2] King Mob was regnant, said one of Henry's lawyer friends, who in his *Political Primer* of 1802 satirized the obsequious candidate who frequented 'taverns, tippling houses, gambling tables, dram shops, and every hole and corner where their Majesties,' the sovereign people, were to be found, flattered, and cajoled.[3] Election crowds were rude, noisy, tipsy, quarrelsome: the wise traveller spurred his horse to escape being challenged 'to run a race with them, or to amuse the company with a game of rough and tumble.'[4] Vote-bribing whiskey and apple toddy flowed through the streets 'like the Euphrates through ancient Babylon,' remarked a Kentucky editor: each faction kept 'half a dozen bullies under pay, genuine specimens of Kentucky alligatorism ... A half a hundred mortar would scarcely fill up the chinks of the skulls that were broken.'[5]

Among these robust partisans, these ebullient Children of America, young Clay 'rushed' into his political career with the same audacity, energy, and resource he employed at the bar. He had, as James Brown remarked, a 'rage for electioneering.'[6] He became adept in the wiles of the candidate, as the Old Bess incident of his first campaign had promised, and in 'the artful management' of the legislative leader. Eloquent, quick-witted,

---

[1] Kendall, Amos, *Autobiography*, p. 126.   [2] Taul, *Memoirs*, pp. 364–65.
[3] Littell, Wm., *Festoons of Fancy*, pp. 142–79.   [4] Cuming, *A Tour*, p. 199.
[5] George D. Prentice, in Perrin, *Pioneer Press*, pp. 77–79.
[6] Brown to Clay, Sept. 1, 1808, Clay, *Corres.*, p. 17.

persuasive, he seemed destined by temperament and training for the great game of politics with its glorious uncertainties, exciting turmoil, and challenges to mastery over men and events.

The plant of public favor demanded constant watering, and Henry did not neglect the chore. In Blue Grass Kentucky he built up an enduring popularity: not once in his long and often stormy career did the Lexington District send Henry Clay down to defeat.

His unbroken record was particularly noteworthy in a district where the intelligence quota of 'the numerical majority' was relatively high, where the candidate had to win over not only 'the puissant vulgar' but also 'the more solid part of the Community.' In Lexington a certain degree of scepticism had early displayed itself toward the candidate who trifled with the dignity and good sense of the electorate.¹ Less discriminating, however, than the planters and merchants of the Blue Grass were the coonskin democrats of the South Country, who in Colonel Matthew Lyon possessed one of the most energetic and colorful candidates on the hustings of the Western World.

'Democratic Mat' had won his seat in Congress from Kentucky, which he held from 1803 to 1811, by posting himself (as he very frankly boasted) 'at a cross-roads by which everybody in the district passed from time to time, and abusing the sitting member.' ² A 'Roaring Lyon' on the stump, he out-shouted and out-drank his rivals, and assured his supporters he would make them all squires, sheriffs, and justices of the peace. By his vigorous campaigns the 'Scourge of Aristocracy' confirmed Easterners in their notion that Kentucky was truly a paradise for barbarous Yahoos.³ The

---

¹ '*Yes, he says so now*,' remarked a Lexingtonian of such a candidate. 'But what was his conduct before the election came off? Did he then shake hands with every man he met, stop and talk with me, care about any man's affairs but his own, pull off his hat to everybody, enquire about our good health and families' and endeavour to conciliate our good will?' *Ky. Gazette*, July 31, 1810.

² Quincy, E., *Josiah Quincy*, pp. 327–29; also, Taul, *Memoirs*, pp. 364–66 on Lyon's prowess as 'a good Electioneerer.'

³ On the stump in 1806 when one Cofield reminded him how in Congress he had replied to Griswold by spitting in that gentleman's face, 'Mr. L[yon] immediately cracked away at Mr. C, but Mr. C so completely defended himself that he parried off the blow, and the "scene of action" commenced hot and hard. Mr. C at last knocked the honourable gentleman down, and made an essay to gouge him — in the attempt however, the honourable gentleman got Mr. C's thumb in his mouth and completely amputated it at the first joint.' N. Y. *Herald*, Nov. 29, 1806, 'from a Virginia paper.'

Republican gentry of the Blue Grass disliked his *sans-culotte* manners, his shady government contracts and trimming politics. Moreover, they had come to regard him as an unbridled demagogue who fostered discontent in the Green River section where the frontier farmers, extremely reluctant to pay the state for their lands, were then agitating for secession from Kentucky and annexation to Tennessee.[1]

Infinitely more alarming to Lexingtonians, however, than Lyon's schemes 'for rending our State asunder' were the threats then being made by Felix Grundy, that other idol of the backwoods democracy. In the summer of 1804 Grundy was stumping the South Country, demanding the utter destruction of the Kentucky Insurance Company — and setting the stage for a mighty conflict with Henry Clay.

When the legislature without opposition in 1802 incorporated the Kentucky Insurance Company, firmly imbedded in the charter (which was to run until 1818) was a clause making its notes negotiable. This pregnant clause had enabled the Insurance Company to transform itself into the 'Lexington Bank.'[2] Thus indirectly established, this pioneer bank (it was the first west of the Alleghenies) had become a profitable concern, a facilitating factor in the frontier's economic evolution. Lexingtonians, especially Henry Clay and his fellow investors in the company's stock, were proud of this burgeoning capitalism; proud of the bank's new brick building on Main Street, and of the business acumen of its president, William Morton, its cashier, John Bradford, and its board of directors, composed of such solid citizens as Thomas Hart, Jr., and John Jordan, which had made possible after a year's operation dividends 'equal to 18 and 15/18% interest.'[3]

---

[1] Wm. Russell to Breckinridge, Nov. 5, 1802, and others to same, 1802–03, *Breckinridge MSS*.

[2] Although both Mann Butler and Humphrey Marshall regarded banking as first smuggled into Kentucky 'by a fraud upon her legislative understanding,' later and specialized writers (Duke, B. W., *Hist. of Bank of Ky.*; Griffith, E. C., 'Early Banking in Kentucky,' *Proc. Miss. Valley Hist. Assoc.*, II, 168–81) believe that more than a few legislators were aware of the pregnant clause.

[3] *Ky. Gazette*, Jan. 10, 1804; and, *ibid.*, Jan. 18, 1803, for the incorporating act of Dec. 16, 1802.

It was only natural that the profits of the infant institution should have attracted more attention than its high significance in organizing and developing a new society. Yet its contribution to social finance was invaluable: the Western need for capital and credit was second only to the need for good-titled land. In this preeminently debtor section men borrowed, or wanted to borrow, for initial payments on land, for its maintenance until self-supporting, for more land, and for varied speculations in the new country's rich opportunities. Money-lending, obviously, was an important social function. Yet even more important were credit and currency. The frontier, and the world at large, was currency-hungry; and the paper of the newly devised commercial bank seemed heaven-sent to overcome financial deficiencies — in a United States which lacked media of exchange, investment capital, and stores of specie; and in a Western World which cried out for the exploitation of its boundless resources.

A token of Lexington's business pioneering, an indication of the maturing frontier, the institution established by Clay's friends and associates, small though it was (its capitalization was only fifty thousand dollars), materially helped to supply this need. It financed Kentucky's infant industries, promoted her mercantile transactions, and facilitated the exporting of her agricultural surpluses. It was enterprising and well managed: its notes were accepted in the East without discount losses; they were even preferred in Kentucky to drafts on a straitened state treasury. All classes benefited by using its paper as a circulating medium — the farmer who had formerly bartered his crops; the lawyer whose fees had often been in cattle and land; the merchant who had exchanged his goods for inconvenient produce; the editor who had received subscriptions in bacon or country linen; the clergyman whose contributions had been almost exclusively in hemp or whiskey.[1]

Nevertheless, this new and progressive institution encountered

---

[1] Wm. Morton was justly proud that his bank had 'not yet experienced one solitary loss by Discount.' Morton to Thomas & John Clifford of Phila., Dec. 8, 1805, *Clifford MSS.*, Hist. Soc. of Penna. Newspaper and manuscript sources are replete with instances of crude barter, 'cut money,' scarcity of bank notes and specie, etc. See Paxson, F. L., *History of the American Frontier*, chap. XXVI, 'Frontier Finance.'

the general opposition against banking of an isolated rural people, influenced by the prejudices and ignorance of their primitive society, and by the shibboleths of doctrinaire agrarianism which Jefferson had used against Hamilton's semi-public United States Bank. The Children of America were inclined to view the bank as a symptom of Eastern and Old World aristocracy, monopoly, and special privilege; of 'the pampered vultures of commercial countries,' abhorred by 'the genuine Republican, the real Whig.' The farmer-democrat believed in the private property of land, cattle, crops, whiskey, and furs; yet he suspected the private property of commercial paper, bank and insurance stock, franchise rights, and other business intangibles. The principles of money and credit, like those of the 'Lawyer Aristocracy,' seemed to be 'enveloped in mystery, chicane, and subtlety.' Did the banker toil and sweat, fell trees and plough virgin land? Then why permit him fat profits from the farmer's labor by the mere juggling of 'rag-money'?

Banking on Western Waters! It smacked of the seaboard's stock-jobbers and Federalist 'neebobs.' It seemed wickedly undemocratic to coonskin equalitarians, isolated on their log-cabin clearings, who associated the pioneer bank with Lexington's shrewd merchants, enterprising manufacturers, and rich planters; with her lawyers, professional men, tax-collectors, and land speculators; with the superior social life of the Kentucky metropolis — in short, with the 'monied aristocracy' that was rearing its sinister head in the Blue Grass region of which Lexington was the center.

This age-old suspicion of the metropolis, this backwoods distrust and envy, had become a formidable weapon in the hands of Felix Grundy. That Lawyer Grundy could not have been unaware of the banking powers granted in 1802, when he dominated the Assembly and pushed through his Circuit Court Bill, mattered not at all. For he was now violently demanding the repeal of the contract which the state had made with the Kentucky Insurance Company.

In face of this attack, Lexingtonians in August of 1804 re-elected Lawyer Clay, placing him at the head of Fayette's successful candidates.[1] His selection was described by William Littell, lawyer and littérateur, who in Biblical style reported the ensuing legislative battles with Felix Grundy.

'And it came to pass that when the merchants of the city of Lexington heard that the wrath of Felix was kindled against them, they were sore afraid. And they assembled the people together, and said unto them, evil will surely overtake us — yea, it will come suddenly upon us like a whirlwind, unless we choose some mighty man to be our chief.

'Then all the people looked on Henry.

'Now Henry was an exceeding learned counselor, the spirit of discretion and eloquence was in him; and when he spake all the people marvelled at his wisdom: So the merchants and people of Lexington chose Henry to be their chief.' [2]

The session of 1804–05 was opened by Governor Christopher Greenup, a plain, respectable, much-esteemed old gentleman, in a message which extolled Kentucky's high rank in the Union, her rising commerce, and her arts and sciences that sweetened human intercourse in a land which within living memory had truly been a Dark and Bloody Ground. Formalities over, the legislators 'in a very defiant tone' and with 'great animosity' [3] proceeded to the first test of strength between Clayites and Grundy men — the election of a United States senator. Ever since statehood the Blue Grass had furnished Kentucky's senators. And now, with John Brown of Frankfort up for reelection, Grundy's South Side members loudly and confidently supported General John Adair.

The Clayites pointed to Brown's distinguished record as Kentucky's national representative since 1787, his soldiering under Lafayette, his studies under Wythe and Jefferson, his anti-Federalism as one of the famous 'Kentucky Triumvirate of Nicholas, Brown, and Breckinridge.' They charged Adair with favoring

---

[1] *Ky. Gazette*, Aug. 14, 1804.

[2] *Ibid.*, Jan. 23, 1806; also in Littell, *Festoons of Fancy*.

[3] Wm. Russell, Nov. 28, Robt. H. Grayson, Nov. 18, 1804, and others to Breckinridge, *Breckinridge MSS*. Alarmed by their reports of Grundy's power and of its threat to his own seat in the Senate, Breckinridge sought to have Grundy appointed a Louisiana Land Commissioner. *Ibid.*, Breckinridge to Albert Gallatin, April 25, 1805, and Gallatin's reply, July 11, 1805.

Federalist Charles Pinckney of his native South Carolina in the presidential election of 1804, and with opposing the constitutional amendment which would prevent any future contests like the Jefferson-Burr tie-vote of 1801. No less aggressive, the agrarian radicals assailed the monopoly of senate seats long enjoyed by Frankfort and Lexington. Grundy, whose 'Talent for Plot and Management,' it was said, equalled that of the Cardinal de Retz,[1] after conferences with Jo Daveiss resurrected Humphrey Marshall's hackneyed charge that Brown in 1788 had been party to a 'treasonable' Spanish conspiracy respecting the navigation of the Mississippi. Two years later, amid sensational developments, this partisan accusation was to be revived. Yet in 1804, lamented Federalist Daveiss, Grundy 'went all over town & told it: but . . . Brown did not loose one Vote by it.'[2]

Nevertheless, there was a feeling even in the Blue Grass that Clay's candidate, a veteran of eighteen years' national service, should now make way for a younger man. After much 'juggling' and 'combinations,' Judge Buckner Thruston of Lexington was also nominated.[3] This split the Blue Grass vote, greatly to the exultation of the backwoods democrats. For six ballots Adair led his opponents, Thruston being a poor third. But Clay would not acknowledge victory for the South Country. Although he must have been chagrined at Thruston's entrance into the race, he was on friendly terms with the Judge — his fellow Lexingtonian. On the seventh ballot, seeing no hope for John Brown and anxious to have a North Side man chosen, he threw the Brown votes to Thruston and elected him. From the homespun party he had snatched an almost certain victory.

'You have no gues how much . . . mortified' Grundy and Adair were, reported Captain Jack Jouett from Frankfort. The Kentucky capital was fairly buzzing with talk of how John Adair 'got work'd out of his Election by the artful management of H. Clay.'

---

[1] Murphey, Archibald D., Papers, ed. W. H. Hoyt, I, 258–59 — in 1822.

[2] Daveiss to Jefferson, March 28, 1806, Jefferson MSS. In 1803 Grundy, old schoolmate of both Daveiss and John Rowan, had resigned as Commonwealth Attorney rather than prosecute Rowan for killing Dr. Chambers in a duel, in which Daveiss had been Rowan's second. Coleman, Daveiss, pp. 348–49; Little, Hardin, pp. 178–79.

[3] Dr. Sam Brown to Jas. Brown, Nov. 10, 1804, Jas. Brown MSS. — 'George Bibb is to be Judge if Thruston can be [thus] got out of the way.'

In his first legislative contest with the leader and party so long dominant in the Assembly, 'Clay has proved entirely too hard for Grundy.' [1]

Following Adair's defeat and Thruston's election to the Senate, where he would join Breckinridge, his fellow Lexingtonian, it was with increased resentment against the Blue Grass metropolis that the South Country members rallied about Grundy in his attack upon the Lexington Bank. The importance of the issue, the clash of bold personalities, the warm and animated speeches, the comprehensive field for debate, all attracted unusual attention.

Citizens of Frankfort and neighboring towns filled the gallery. Senators and officials crowded the floor. Even the courts adjourned, despite overcrowded dockets. Evening sessions were held: when twilight dimmed the chamber, candles stuck in tumblers on members' desks were lighted, and more wood was thrown into the huge fireplace. Never before had the little frontier capital witnessed such exciting or important debates as now ensued between Henry Clay and Felix Grundy — both of whom were lawyers of reputation; both twenty-seven years old, having been born in Virginia in the same year; and both ambitious to increase their political standing. Under their handling the arguments on banking, and on the state-chartered Lexington Bank, 'assumed every variety of untried being.' [2]

Both men were inspired by the occasion and by the conflicting forces they represented. Grundy, short, thick-set, red-faced, rough and ready, embodied the older forces of the primitive frontier, the emotional coonskin individualism of pioneer farmers who believed in an exclusively agrarian laissez-faire and a simple and frugal government. Clay, tall, slender, supple, and fiery, embodied the newer and progressive forces of the maturing frontier, the middle-class individualism of pioneer merchants and bankers and manufacturers who believed that government should be a positive agency in aiding the people (i.e., their enterprising leaders) in ex-

---

[1] Jouett (of Cuckoo Tavern fame) to Breckinridge, Dec. 24, 1804, *Breckinridge MSS.*; also, *Journal of House, 1804*, p. 30.

[2] *Ky. Gazette*, Dec. 18, 1804, and ff.; *Breckinridge MSS.*, Nov. 1804–Jan. 1805; and, also, Prentice, *Clay*, p. 27.

ploiting the resources of the new country, fostering its growth, promoting its general welfare.

The conflict was fundamental: the lines here drawn continued to divide the people, becoming most marked in the later battle between Henry Clay and Andrew Jackson. Each side here had a capable champion: in Grundy, who would retard, even destroy, the pioneering forces of capitalistic liberalism; in Clay, who from boyhood had declaimed against that 'narrow and dastardly *coasting* which never ventures to lose sight of usage and precedent.' Perhaps Henry, confronted by Grundy's radical conservatism, now recalled that oft-quoted passage which urged a progressive course 'guided by the polarity of reason,' which called upon timid or prejudiced legislators to 'hazard a bolder navigation and discover in unexplored regions the treasures of public felicity.'

Arguing for the repeal of the banking clause in the compact made two years before, Grundy violently declaimed against banking in general as a dangerous novelty which threatened economic enslavement and the destruction of republicanism. Already every shilling in Kentucky was swallowed up by the Lexington financial octopus which the legislators in 1802 had unwittingly helped to spawn. The circulating medium of the state was concentrated and controlled by a Blue Grass 'monied aristocracy.' The purses of the few were being fattened at the expense of the many. The bank was unrestricted, he said, and here he trod on more rational ground; from its great profits one must conclude that it issued notes over and above its resources. There was nothing to hinder it from issuing an unlimited amount of bank notes; from foisting upon an unsuspecting or deluded citizenry its corrupt and corrupting rag-money. Banking, and the Lexington Bank in particular, must be crushed before it strangled the farmer-democrats of Kentucky.

Clay answered on two grounds. First, repeal was unconstitutional because it violated rights vested by the state in the company; it would undermine confidence in government and blemish Kentucky's fair name. Second, the bank was not only legal but eminently useful and helpful to the farmer and every class of citizen.

His arguments on the inviolability of charters so granted won the praise of Federal Judge Harry Innes, and were later confirmed by the Supreme Court. But more effective was his advocacy of the bank on the ground of its great utility. Such an institution was essential, he declared. Kentucky was growing, her commerce was expanding, her agricultural produce was being exported to the four corners of the globe. It was absurd, it was against reason and human nature, to insist that she remain forever in the wilderness stage of crude barter and primitive exchange. Would Mr. Grundy prevent Kentucky from attaining her high destiny as a great and powerful commonwealth? That banking in Kentucky was a novelty, Clay contended, was no evidence of its being a menacing evil. That it was profitable only confirmed the people's need of it.[1]

'Thus did Felix and Henry assail the chiefs of the people with cunning speeches for many days,' reported William Littell, 'insomuch that the chiefs were astonished and confounded; and the wise men and all the people marvelled at their wisdom and subtlety.'[2]

Lexington's *Gazette* reported that Grundy's attacks upon the company had forced insurance premiums up from four to eight per cent; that the shareholders faced ruin; and, indeed, that the very prosperity of the Western World was endangered. 'To diminish the rising prosperity of Lexington, by the destruction of the Insurance Company, was the great object in view,' it was said. Felix Grundy of Bardstown was 'a complete demagogue' who led his mob of ignorance and prejudice 'by the nose, at will.' Opposed to him, a very Galahad for truth and justice, was 'Henry Clay, esquire, a youthful patriot, uniting in his character a most accomplished elocution, with an understanding comprehensive and acute, and a heart as mild and honest as ever glowed in the human bosom.'[3]

At Frankfort the debates finally gave way to a decision. Despite

---

[1] *Journal of House, 1804*, pp. 100–03; Innes to Breckinridge, Dec. 20, 1804, and others to same, *Breckinridge MSS*.

[2] In *Ky. Gazette*, Jan. 23, 1806 — 'The counsel of Felix is not good at this time,' said Henry. 'The merchants of Lexington have bought this authority from you with a price, and it becometh not the chiefs of the people to take away what they themselves have sold. And if ye do this thing, ye will become a reproach among all the nations of the earth!'

[3] *Ky. Gazette*, Jan. 29, 1805, 'A Poor Farmer,' and Dec. 5, 11, 18, 1804.

Grundy's whetting of frontier prejudices, the bank was saved — by the narrow margin of one vote. 'The attempt to repeal so much of the Charter granted to the Insurance Company as authorized a Bank,' Clay reported to Breckinridge, 'occasioned much struggling — its discussion occupied in all nearly a week, and was at length negatived by a very small majority.' The institution 'had to encounter and at length subdued the most unheard of prejudices. The ignorance of members on the subject was truly astonishing.' [1]

Nevertheless the Grundy men scored a partial victory. They succeeded in depriving the company of its insurance monopoly, and they limited the notes it could issue to the amount of money in its vaults, the value of debts due, its property and capital stock. To this extent, said Littell, because of the 'elaborate custom that the greatest number shall always prevail over the less,' Grundy was victorious. In effect, however, the Lexington Bank was strengthened. For its banking rights were thus reconfirmed by the Assembly, and the limitations imposed could only have a salutary influence upon its operations and upon public confidence in its paper. [2]

Clay had thwarted the attempt upon the life of the bank. He had been the means, remarked James Brown, who from New Orleans sent Henry his congratulations and praise, 'of resisting that unprincipled demagogue Grundy.' [3] But, having driven an opening wedge into its charter, the 'indefatigable Felix' looked forward to the complete destruction of the bank at the session of 1805.

Meanwhile this violent contest over banking was continued in the press by numerous articles written in the language of high excitement. 'Mechanic' charged that the bank originated in deception, enriched Lexington, and defrauded the rest of the state. 'Poor Farmer' echoed Clay's arguments, urged its expediency,

---

[1] Clay to Breckinridge, Dec. 22, 1804, *Whelpley Collection*, Hist. & Phil. Society of Ohio.

[2] *Session Acts, 1804*, pp. 23–24; Littell, in *Ky. Gazette*, Jan. 23, 1806. This action in 1804 'hardly seems compatible with the idea that such [banking powers, in 1802] had been unconsciously and unintentionally given.' Duke, *Hist. of Bank of Ky.*, pp. 11–12.

[3] Brown to Clay, March 12, 1805, *Clay MSS.*

general utility, and the stimulus it gave to every phase of economic life. Pro-bank men lauded Clay to the skies and, in what the South Country termed 'indecent, illiberal, and scandalous attacks,' condemned Grundy for his arts of intrigue, and his self-confessed ignorance of money and credit; his eagerness to win a seat in Congress, they said, had made him assail legitimate bankers as 'a band of aristocratical monopolizers,' and to see 'a Frightful Bugbear' in the Lexington Bank. 'More from the pertinacious obstinacy of Mr. Grundy than from the solidity of his objections, the decision in favour of the company was made by ONE VOTE! Upon *such* a question, how disgraceful to all the representatives of the people!' [1]

Yet the violence attending the introduction of banking into Western America was mild compared with the extraordinary disturbances of 1805 over the Federal direct tax on land — disturbances which were to give a new turn to the bank fight.

Defects in the Federal act, the frontier's repugnance to direct taxation, the activities of land speculators, and the great scarcity of specie to pay the tax, had brought about state-wide confusion and distress. From one-third to one-half of all the land in Kentucky, it was estimated, had been confiscated for non-payment. In the Blue Grass county of Bourbon alone more than six hundred farms had been acquired by the land scavengers who swarmed about the Lexington office of Major James Morrison, supervisor of the tax, and George Mansell, his deputy. Collectors were as unpopular as in the days of President Adams. Men complained that 'old Devil John Adams and his aids hang on us yet,' and cried out: 'Exterminate them from the globe, together with all the purchasers!' [2] Although accused of extortion and collusion, Major Morrison for months had warned that the Federal tax must be paid.[3] His

---

[1] *Ky. Gazette*, Jan.–June, 1805, especially Jan. 29, Feb. 26, March 5, 12, 16. So fiercely did the battle rage that Grundy requested Clay (Feb. 4, 1805, *Clay MSS.*) to aid him in denying some of the more extreme statements attributed to him.

[2] *Ky. Gazette*, Feb. 5, 1805; G. Thompson to Breckinridge, Feb. 2, 1805, and others to same, Dec. 1804–March 1805, *Breckinridge MSS.*

[3] 'For the direct tax Major Morrison will Make his Jack, I am told, a hundred dollars a day he Makes Clear...' G. Thompson to Breckinridge, Feb. 2, 1805, but see Morrison to same, Nov. 30, 1804, *Breckinridge MSS.* One of Morrison's handbills (*ibid.*, Jan. 3, 1805) read: 'AWAKE! AWAKE! AWAKE! ROUSE! ROUSE! ROUSE! CITIZENS OF KENTUCKY. You will be RUINED! RUINED! Yes, irretrievably

admonitions had gone in one ear and out the other, Senator Breckinridge was informed: now the people are 'all Cussing and Swearing about the Business, and it did appear Like we should have a little warr in the state.' [1]

When Clay returned to Lexington he found, in the words of his father-in-law, that 'a devil of a rumpus has been kicked up here.' The uproar increased when a group of shaggy Green River men descended upon the town, roistered drunkenly about, and regardless of the extra police threatened to burn the tax records and to kill Morrison and Mansell. A few days later at Paris, the county seat of Bourbon, Deputy Collector Mansell was burned in effigy, his tax-book hanging from his coat-tails, decorated with skull and cross-bones and labelled with large letters: 'Mansell the Peculator & Destroyer of the property of Bourbon County.' No sooner was this baleful ceremony concluded, said old Colonel Hart, than '(as the Devil would have it) up comes Mansell in person.' The mob seized him, 'got him into a room and turned thickly upon him, and had it not been for Judge Allen and some other influential characters, would have burnt him in reality.' [2]

As legislator and lawyer Clay was vitally interested in this all-absorbing question of land and land taxation. At each session he introduced a bill (until it was passed in 1806) making it possible for landowners, within a fixed period of time and by paying interest, to redeem the millions of acres seized for non-payment of the Kentucky tax on land.[3] He was a constant and caustic critic of inept and often corrupt land legislation, which, together with uncertain land titles and incessant land litigation, kept the state in a turmoil. As a result of such conditions, emigrants were diverted to

---

RUINED! and UNDONE!' — if you do not at once redeem lands sold for non-payment. 'BE ALARMED, fellow citizens, when you are informed that at this late period not one Tract out of fifty is yet redeemed.'

[1] Jesse Richardson to Breckinridge, March 8, 1805, *Breckinridge MSS.*

[2] Hart to Jas. Brown, Jan. 27, 1805, *Jas. Brown MSS.*; also, W. Moore to Breckinridge, Jan. 23, 1805, *Breckinridge MSS.*

[3] This was a matter of moment: in 1800 more than 15,000,000 acres belonging to non-residents alone had been confiscated and offered for sale. Clay's bill had been defeated in 1804 (by the land scavengers, it was said) yet it caused favorable comment, and many requested a similar Federal law. *Ky. Gazette*, Feb. 5, 1805; *House Journal* and *Session Acts*, 1806, for Clay's bill; and, on confiscated lands, J. H. Daveiss to R. & S. Smith, Nov. 16, 1800, *Samuel Smith MSS.*, Breckinridge to Jas. Breckinridge, Nov. 21, 1800, *Breckinridge MSS.*

Ohio and the Northwest Territory, where the Federal Government had first surveyed the land and then opened it for settlement.[1]

Most notorious was legislation concerning state grants south of the Green River. These grants, which were offered for sale before being surveyed, had been limited to two hundred acres a person. Since the laws, said Clay, 'were somewhat loosely worded, the keen eye of the speculator soon discerned the defects, and he took advantage of them.' Thousands of acres had been entered under fictitious names. Lands had been obtained in the names of slaves by their owners: 'to conceal the fraud, the owner would add Black, or some other cognomination, so that the certificate would read Tom Black, Jack Black, and so forth.' Yet when the entries came to be indexed, as Clay on occasion called to Grundy's attention, 'the truth would be told, whatever might be the language of the record; for the alphabet would read *Black* Tom, *Black* Harry, and so forth.' [2]

Not only had thousands of acres of public lands been fraudulently obtained, but the payment due the state had been deferred time and again, year after year, until Kentucky's 'Green River Debt' had become a byword of reproach. The debt had now 'become enormous.' The 'great burthern' of it, according to Judge Innes, was not on settlers or prospective settlers but 'on Speculators,' [3] who had for years been represented in the Assembly by the powerful, log-rolling, 'Green River Band.' The votes of this group, as Humphrey Marshall remarked, 'were for barter and exchange—"You vote for my law; we want indulgence; we want something done for Green River; and we will vote for yours"— caring in fact but little what it was' as long as the debtors were not forced to pay into the treasury the money long due on their lands.[4]

This notorious log-rolling among the most radical of agrarians,

---

[1] 'All this fall the roads have been lined with waggons and travellers, and all of them are inticed to the Northwest of the Ohio by the delightful certainty of a peaceful home.' F. L. Turner to Breckinridge, Dec. 20, 1805, *Breckinridge MSS.* James Morrison advised Breckinridge (*ibid.*, Dec. 20, 1802) to oppose decreasing the price of Federal territorial lands to prevent emigrations from Kentucky.

[2] Clay, speech on Public Lands, 1832, Mallory, *Clay*, II, 61.

[3] Innes to Breckinridge, Dec. 24, 1805, *Breckinridge MSS.*

[4] Marshall, *Hist. Ky.*, II, 179.

and the most ardent of Felix Grundy's supporters, was a legislative factor the power and the weakness of which Henry Clay, as a practical politician, fully realized. And he was to make dramatic use of it in the next phase of the Lexington Bank fight.

At the 1804 session Henry had cited the aid given by the bank to many citizens who had redeemed their lands by borrowing from it the hard money required by Morrison's collectors. Only such an agency could supply the necessary and extremely scarce hard money. Upon his return from Frankfort, he found many distressed pioneer farmers unable to borrow because of their lack of security. Clay and his friends of the bank now planned to relieve them, and to arrest the wholesale confiscation and sale of forfeited lands, by a spectacular maneuver. Through John Bradford, its cashier, the bank tendered, and Major Morrison accepted, a lump sum of five thousand dollars in payment of the Federal taxes and obtained thereby the redemption of all the houses, lots, and lands which had been seized in Bourbon and all the counties south of the Big Barren and Green Rivers.[1]

By this timely intervention the bank quieted the land-tax agitation. No longer were Lexington's streets thronged with wild-eyed frontiersmen. Major James Morrison breathed a deep sigh of relief. From New Orleans, writing in March of 1805, James Brown congratulated Clay and his friends of the bank for withstanding Grundy's onslaughts in the Assembly, and for 'defeating the villainous speculations of that nest of rascals who have fattened under the auspices of Morrison's office.' [2] The utility of the Lexington Bank had been strikingly revealed. But the question involving its continued existence was not as yet settled.

In thus saving thousands of improved acres from the land scavengers, Bradford, Morton, Hart, and other officials of the bank had done so with no security save the honor of those whom they

---

[1] Certificate signed by Morrison, Jan. 18, 1805, *Breckinridge MSS.* Although aided by six extra clerks, Morrison could not make out receipts for all before the payment period expired, and some were made out thereafter but dated back. Doubt arose as to the legality of such receipts, even among Lexington's lawyers, but Clay with characteristic decisiveness assured one and all of their unquestionable legality. *Ibid.*, W. Moore, Jan. 23, John Kercheval, Feb. 2, 1805, to Breckinridge.

[2] Brown to Clay, March 12, 1805, *Clay MSS.* 'Mansell was originally destined for the gallows and nothing but a premature death will disappoint him of the pomp of an execution.'

had benefited.[1] Even so, the South Country enemies of the Lexington Bank, and of all banking, were most obdurate. 'It ought not be admitted,' said a spokesman for the agrarians, 'that because a man has rendered me a service, that I am under obligations to continue him in a situation in which he may at some future period ruin me.' [2] The bank must be destroyed! For there must be something wrong, some sinister financial chicanery, when Morton and his associates merely by the manipulation of printed paper — bank notes and insurance policies — could make their hundred-dollar shares yield as high as the eight-dollar half-year dividend announced in January of 1805.[3] The bank's very success had drawn upon it 'the horrorific denunciation of being a "monied aristocracy," and therefore to be put down.' [4]

As the session of 1805 approached, William Morton was most fearful that the legislators 'from the basest motives, envy, & ignorance' would repeal the company's charter — 'tho' they prostrate our State constitution & their plighted faith.' [5] Henry Clay, however, was sanguine, confident, as he prepared to meet Felix Grundy once again. In August he was reelected. On the third of November he mounted his horse and galloped over the Frankfort Pike for the final battle which would decide the life or death of Kentucky's — and Western America's — first bank.

Grundy's increased strength was shown at the opening of the Assembly when John Adair was elected to the United States Senate to fill the seat vacated by Breckinridge, who had become Jefferson's Attorney General. At once the indefatigable Felix attacked the bank, 'exerting his utmost eloquence.' The Lexington Bank, and all banks, he declared, were 'inimical to a free Government as they indirectly tend to move the ballance of wealth out of the hands of the people. . . . The law establishing a bank

---

[1] Sen. Breckinridge, in Plumer, Wm., *Memorandum of Proceedings in the United States Senate 1803–1807*, ed. E. S. Brown, p. 296.

[2] *Ky. Gazette*, Feb. 26, 1805.

[3] *Ibid.*, Jan. 9, 1805.

[4] Marshall, H., *op. cit.*, II, 374–75. No institution or individual 'against which or whom that denunciation, coming from the soul and body of democracy,' was aimed could face the future without fear.

[5] Morton to Thomas & John Clifford, Aug. 31, 1805, *Clifford MSS.*

in Lexington was unconstitutional, as it gave a certain class of individuals an exclusive privilege.' [1]

Rallying his 'thinking members' from the Blue Grass, Clay for two weeks fought Grundy and his aggressive South Country majority. 'Lengthy and warm' were the debates. 'With words sharper than two-edged swords' Henry parried and thrust. But he was outnumbered two to one, and at length he went down to defeat.

Felix Grundy, 'whether by the power of reason or party spirit the spectators will determine,' sourly remarked Judge Innes, had at last succeeded in repealing the charter. Both houses passed his bill, which completely deprived the company of its banking powers. [2]

Then, to the consternation of the South Country, Governor Christopher Greenup, hitherto a silent spectator, promptly issued a veto message. Repeal of the charter he held to be unconstitutional and unwise: it violated the contract of 1802, impugned the good faith of Kentucky, and was against the 'true interest of the state. Blessed with a country of wide extention, of unequalled fertility, and of growing commerce, have we not much to do,' asked Greenup, 'roads to open, turnpikes to erect, and does not the experience of our sister states prove that those great objects are best effected through the agency of incorporated companies?' [3]

His veto provoked a storm of abuse. It was unusual, audacious. Seldom did a Kentucky governor dare employ this counteracting power. The legislative branch of government was predominant; it was poor politics to interfere with the puissant senators and representatives. Indignant at what they termed Greenup's 'executive pretensions,' the anti-bank men immediately, and with four additional votes, passed the bill over the Governor's veto and sent it to the Senate for similar action. [4]

Despair now settled upon Lexington. 'Sensational!' and 'Highly Important!' were headlines over accounts from Frankfort.

---

[1] Wm. Stevenson to Breckinridge [Jan. 1806], *Breckinridge MSS.*; also, Littell, *Festoons of Fancy*, p. 35.

[2] Innes to Breckinridge, Dec. 24, 1805, *Breckinridge MSS.*

[3] *Journal of House, 1805*, pp. 83–87.   [4] *Ky. Gazette*, Jan. 2, 1806.

It was all over with 'the little Bank at Lexington,' reported Fielding Turner and others: Grundy's 'mob of ignorance and prejudice' had carried the bill in the House over Greenup's veto by a vote of 40 to 18. It was a 'shameful violation' and would 'prostrate all confidence,' wrote embittered William Morton to his Philadelphia business associates. 'Every Gentleman of legal knowledge does say the honor, the faith, & the Constitution is implicated, and all violated.' Throughout the Blue Grass, men discussed 'Grundy's attack upon the Kentucky Bank and his success in destroying the Charter.' [1]

At the courthouse in Lexington, at the bank's new brick building on Main Street, at Travellers Hall, and the Indian King and the Side of Bacon Taverns, citizens asked each other, 'What will become of our poor little institution?' Doctor Sam Brown sent the gloomy tidings to his brother James. Backwoods envy had struck a great blow at Lexington, her economic pioneering, her prestige as the business pathfinder of Western America. Accepting the inevitable, yet with the courage to pioneer anew, the citizens of the little frontier metropolis in public meeting resolved to petition for a branch of the United States Bank to replace their doomed institution.[2]

Within a few days, however, public opinion underwent a startling change. The pall of gloom was suddenly dissipated. 'I am still, I find, a stranger to Kentucky politics,' wrote Doctor Brown. 'Billy' Morton's face had brightened; there was jubilation at the bank building and the taverns. There was a new appreciation of Lawyer Clay's ability. Even Lexington had been unprepared, in face of Grundy's two-to-one majority, for what Fielding Turner called Clay's skilful 'maneuvering of legislative parties.' At Frankfort, Henry's 'artful management' and powerful speeches had brought about a complete reversal and lifted friends of the bank up from the depths of despair.[3]

Upon its prompt repassage by the House the repeal bill had been sent to the Senate, and there it was carried on its first reading.

[1] Morton to T. & J. Clifford, Dec. 8, 1805, *Clifford MSS.*; Turner, Nov. 22, and others to Breckinridge, Nov. 1805–Jan. 1806, *Breckinridge MSS.*

[2] *Ky. Gazette*, Dec. 5, 1805.

[3] Sam Brown to James Brown, Dec. 13, 1805, *Jas. Brown MSS.*

But before it could come up for its second reading, Clay, in the House, routed the anti-bank men as they stood on the threshold of victory. He introduced a bill which would compel payment of the notorious Green River Debt, and mustered up strong support for its passage among members from the other sections of the state. This, reported Lawyer Turner, 'This was a paralyzing stroke!' [1]

The Green River Debt was the Achilles' heel of the Grundy men, and at it with unerring aim Orator Clay let fly his bolt.

Never before had he displayed such eloquence, such invective, as when he charged into the ranks of the anti-bank men; or such persuasive talents as when he mustered up votes behind the scenes. On the floor of the House with scathing sarcasm he exposed the fraud and corruption which permeated the Green River land grants. He flayed the Green River Band — the most tireless and vociferous foes of the bank — for its annual bartering of votes. He cited the numerous relief laws postponing payments on these public lands, which, in effect, defrauded the rest of the state and made the mass of Kentuckians bear the burdens imposed by this one section. He vigorously maintained that if his coercing bill were enacted, and the debt paid, Kentucky's empty treasury would be replenished and taxes lowered throughout the state.

His unexpected onslaught, his searing accusations, and his well-founded arguments, presented so powerfully, and so plausibly, caused consternation among the members from Green River. It appeared that Clay, forceful orator and shrewd manipulator, would command enough votes to coerce the payment of their long-standing debt. This was to be prevented at all costs. Since Clay could be persuaded from his purpose only by assurances that the Lexington Bank would not be destroyed, the South Country majority split asunder and 'the repealing bill stopped short in its progress.' [2]

'The Green River people,' reported Doctor Brown, 'suppose that if their representation had let the Bank alone, Clay would not have brought in his coercing bill. The popularity of these Patriots

---

[1] F. L. Turner to Breckinridge, Dec. 20, 1805, *Breckinridge MSS.*

[2] *Ibid.*, Turner to Breckinridge, Dec. 20, 1805, Wm. Russell to same, March 1, 1806.

being in danger, the log-rolling system has been resorted to with singular cordiality.' [1] Fearing the consequences attending Clay's bill, they 'flew the way into the Senate, and joined the banking institution, which formed a party sufficient to lay the law asleep.' [2] Greenup's veto of Grundy's bill was sustained. The bank was saved, and Lexington rejoiced.

'Henry is like a lion's whelp; who shall rouse him up? The sound of his voice is terrible; yea, it is like the voice of many waters.' Thus commented William Littell on Clay's unexpected victory over Grundy and the South Country, in an article entitled 'Lexington's Song of Triumph.' Henry had vanquished the terrible Felix, 'the man of Bardstown,' who for two years had roared and snorted fire like a Bull of Bashan; 'he hath brought to naught the devices of the subtle, and hath humbled the mighty in the dust.' [3]

Writing to Breckinridge, and apparently taking his great triumph modestly since he did not refer to his adroit maneuvering and his savage thrust at the Green River Band, Henry remarked that 'the attempt to Repeal the Lexington Bank is no doubt made known to you through our papers. The measure finally failed in the Senate.' [4]

His speeches in defense of banking, of its legality, its value and necessity, had been educational. They had informed and clarified public opinion. The Frightful Bugbear brandished by Grundy before the excitable and ignorant had been dispelled. Moreover, the eyes of prejudiced legislators had been opened to the handsome profits to be derived from banking. And these dangled temptingly before the Grundy men when, at this same session, a bill was introduced providing for a state bank.

'When this Bill reached the House of Representatives,' reported a Lexington lawyer, 'Mr. Grundy, the enemy to Banks, strange to tell, became the leader for preparing it, and his party was so strong that he new-modelled the whole Bill.' [5] The man who for

---

[1] Sam Brown to Jas. Brown, Dec. 13, 1805, *Jas. Brown MSS.*

[2] Russell to Breckinridge, March 1, 1806, and others to same, Dec. 1805–Jan. 1806, *Breckinridge MSS.*; and *Ky. Gazette*, Dec. 12, 26, 1805.

[3] Littell, *Festoons of Fancy*, pp. 35–37.

[4] Clay to Breckinridge, Jan. 5, 1806, *Breckinridge MSS.*

[5] *Ibid.*, F. L. Turner to same, Dec. 20, 1805.

two sessions had incited coonskin legislators to a fierce hostility against 'the Bank, or any Bank,' now shifted ground with celerity and aplomb. According to Littell, 'Felix showed unto the chiefs of the people *his* manner of making money out of rags,' informing them that 'inasmuch as ye will go a-whoring after this thing, I will counsel you how this money shall be made, for verily the manner which the wise men [the Senate] have devised is not a good one.' [1]

Again 'there arose a great strife between Felix and Henry.' Opposing the issuance of bank notes solely on the credit of the state, Clay insisted that they be backed by money and securities. In the end he defeated Grundy's new-modelled State Bank Bill.[2] It was not until the following session that Kentucky entered the banking business, operating a central bank at Frankfort with branches in the larger towns. Clay's fellow legislators honored him by electing him one of its directors. The Lexington Bank, however, successfully continued its course. It was profitable; its notes were conspicuously sound in an era of wildcat banking; and in 1818 its charter was extended for two additional years.

And so the first bank in the Western World was not destroyed by a hostile frontier legislature: the two years' defensive battle Clay had waged had at last ended in 'the defeat and consequent mortification of that unprincipled upstart Grundy.' [3] 'Thus was the counsel of Felix and all his cunning speeches at last set at naught,' concluded the contemporary historian of the great bank fight. 'And he prevailed not against the merchants of Lexington. And when the merchants saw that Felix was discomfited they rejoiced with an exceeding great joy, and gat them every man to his own house.' [4]

This great stir about banking alarmed, however, some of the older, doctrinaire, Jeffersonians. They were shocked by the speeches of Henry Clay which might well have been drawn from

---

[1] *Ky. Gazette*, Jan. 30, 1806.

[2] *Ibid.*, Jan. 1806, and *Breckinridge MSS.*, Dec. 1805–April 1806. The State Bank Bill of Senator Green Clay (a distant relative) provided that half the stock should be state-owned, bought out of money derived from Henry's bill to coerce payment of the Green River Debt.

[3] James Brown to Clay, Feb. 27, 1806, *Clay MSS*.

[4] *Ky. Gazette*, Jan. 30, 1806.

the Treasury Reports of Alexander Hamilton, that 'most high-toned,' arch-Federalist. 'I believe that our Legislature in Kentucky are getting higher-toned every year,' complained old General Russell, senator from Fayette, who, because of 'the manner in which the banking System is relished in this State,' gloomily looked forward to Kentucky's fall from Republican grace and her ultimate ruin.[1]

Russell, a plain-spoken, honest, hospitable man, a planter of means, a veteran of King's Mountain and of Indian campaigns under Wilkinson and Wayne, was well-liked and respected. But he had lost standing in Fayette by his refusal to follow Clay's leadership. He had even made a speech against banking as 'impolitick and ruinous,' a speech of which it was said: Felix Grundy was 'the Granny who brought it forth.' As a result, wrote a friend, 'General Russell has been much abused' by irate Lexingtonians, charged with having his 'politics horsed,' and told that 'none but fools or rascals were or could be opposed to the Bank.'[2]

Upon his return to Lexington Henry directed his attention to Russell and all others who disapproved of 'the Bank, or any Bank,' and wrote a 'very lengthy circular' to his constituents. Compelled to write a defense of his views and conduct, Russell in answering Henry's pamphlet confessed himself 'at a great loss for the want of Grundy and his talents.'[3] Lawyer Clay had become dominant in Blue Grass politics. In August of 1806 when Fayette held its annual election his name was at the top and General Russell's at the bottom of the list of successful candidates.

The prejudice against banking subsided. Indeed, banking now began to appear in the rôle of a frontier hero, generous and helpful; it was not until some years later that economic depression, uncritical Western optimism, and wildcat methods were to transform the hero into a frontier villain. In 1806 Felix Grundy became a judge of the Circuit Court of Appeals; a year later he migrated to Andrew Jackson's Tennessee. No one then remained to dispute young Henry Clay's leadership in the Kentucky Assembly.

---

[1] Wm. Russell to Breckinridge, March 1, 1806, *Breckinridge MSS.*
[2] *Ibid.*, Wm. Stevenson to same [Jan. 1806].
[3] *Ibid.*, Russell to same, March 1, 1806.

Political success such as his demanded dexterity and strength; constant attention to aggressive rivals, to the jockeying for votes, and the many requests for favors by supporters. One had to coax, to compel, and to inspire personal loyalty. Varied temptations had to be faced: in 1806 outraged citizens demanded the removal of a Pendleton County justice, a wretched fellow who had peculated and defrauded, shamelessly made over his property to his concubine, and, moreover, offered 'Henry Clay, esq. (a respectable member of the Kentucky legislature) a bribe to use his influence ... to obtain a bill or act of divorce for the purpose of repudiating his lawful wife — which offer Clay rejected with disdain.' [1]

Heatedly debated in 1805 was a bill empowering the courts to grant divorces, thus freeing the legislators from prurient and time-wasting inquiries into domestic relations. Lobbying preachers had defeated it, insisting that marriages were made in heaven. This had provoked pamphleteer William Littell to declare that the marriages prompting the bill were most assuredly made by the Devil. The chief cause of the descent upon Frankfort in the year 1805 of 'a great multitude of women, wives of eunuchs and other sons of Belial,' he said, was that 'many of the fair daughters of Kentucky find themselves in the noontide of life, married to men who have made themselves eunuchs, not verily for the sake of the Kingdom of Heaven, but for the sake of Ethiopian women and strong drink. And these women lament and bewail their calamity *on the evening* of every day.' [2]

Littell's satires, particularly this very frank one on divorce (which revealed the great freedom then allowed on slavery problems), helped to relieve the tedium of legislative routine.[3] Yet the Kentucky Assembly could never be entirely dull.

Young Clay must have held tongue in cheek when voting to suppress gaming by the seizure of 'A B C and E O tables,' or to remove justices of the peace for fighting duels and administering oaths on a wolf's scalp in lieu of the Holy Bible. He found human

---

[1] *Journal of House, 1806*, pp. 35–36.　　[2] Littell, *Festoons of Fancy*, pp. 46–51.
[3] When Clay opposed aid for Littell's *Opinions of the Court of Appeals*, since statements of cases were not included, Littell in a special article complained that 'Satan entered into Henry' and prevailed against me. *Ky. Gazette*, March 1, 1806.

interest in the many private bills: in 1804 warm-hearted legislators had confirmed Deacon Payne's questionable land titles primarily because the Deacon had recently fallen into the boiling kettle at Robinson's salt licks; and they had granted Clarinda Allington a three years' pension because she, poor woman, had endured twelve years' captivity among the red savages and been forced to bear children to a Cherokee chief.[1]

Each session saw the galleries crowded with importunate petitioners and excited partisans. Sometimes a shaggy frontiersman, violently objecting to the course of legislation, would jump to the floor, throw the chamber into confusion, and frighten timid members under their desks. At the 1804 session such an unruly constituent was haled before the bar of the House and sentenced to an hour in jail for using 'abusive, scurrilous, and scandalous' language to the representatives of the sovereign people.

On occasion the House tried its own members. In an interval between the Grundy-Clay debates of 1805 a white-haired pioneer was arraigned for stealing a few copies of James Hughes's *Law Reports*. 'This necessarily took up several days,' and 'the sensibility of the house was prodigiously excited.' Yet when the worthy legislator proved, to the satisfaction of all, that 'he never kept any Books in his house — the Bible, psalter and hymn Books excepted — & these two only for the use of his family, not being able to read himself . . . he was acquitted with credit to himself and country.'[2]

Illiterate legislators, good Jeffersonians, to be sure, but manifestly ill-equipped, gave point to Federalist laments that the country locally and nationally was ruled by 'demagogic Jacobins' and their ignorant puppets. 'Your *half-wits* are by nature formed for Democracy,' declared a pamphleteer for 'the rich, the wise, and the able.'[3] Kentucky's 'good democratic majority' only confirmed Humphrey Marshall's disgust, which he fearlessly voiced, at bedlamic government by 'the nether end of society.'[4]

---

[1] *Journal of House, Session Acts*, 1804. 'Miss Allington sais the Indian used her as Cruel as a Devil. She is hansom & retains her mother Tongue very well — will Congress give me leave to take her as my wife.' Geo. Thompson to Breckinridge, Dec. 12, 1804, *Breckinridge MSS.*

[2] John Smith to Breckinridge, Jan. 16, 1806, *Breckinridge MSS.*

[3] Fessenden, *Democracy Unveiled*, I, 123 n., *passim*.

[4] Marshall, *Hist. Ky.*, II, 316, *passim*.

Clay himself found the ignorance of many legislators 'truly astonishing.' As one of those whom Judge Innes termed 'the thinking members,' he found himself frequently in opposition to 'innovating schemes.' Yet he himself advocated many changes — in addition to the 'innovation' of banking. Especially did he strive for reforms making for a more stable judiciary.

Henry introduced a bill increasing the salaries of the state's superior judges. He opposed repealing the pension granted to Judge Muter after a lifetime on the bench at starvation wages. He took the lead in attempting to correct the deplorable conditions in the United States District Court, where Innes, the only judge, enfeebled by fifteen years on the bench, wrestled with an overcrowded docket and with duties (said Clay) 'too vast for one man, altho' he possessed the head of Holt or Mansfield.'[1] In 1804 the legislature unanimously adopted his resolution for an extension of the Federal circuit system to Western America. Thereafter Henry beseeched Breckinridge to use his influence in effecting this much-needed innovation. 'Our State has been too long held in a kind of vassalage,' he declared; 'in no other State in the Union is the Federal Court more important. . . . It is what the Bar have much at heart: and Mr. Innes, who is so much esteemed by us all, is anxious for the change.'[2]

He also advocated a constitutional amendment restricting Federal Courts to cases arising under Federal laws. This was of great concern in Kentucky, where the devices of 'artful and wealthy land claimants' had brought state and Federal jurisdictions into sharp conflict.[3] Such an amendment was called for by a joint resolution of 1804. It was most desirable, wrote Clay, even if at

---

[1] Clay to Breckinridge, Jan. 5, 1806, *Breckinridge MSS.* Of Breckinridge — who had been prominent in repealing the Judiciary Act of 1801, which had added 16 Federal (and Federalist) judges — Clay asked: 'Could you not lend a hand in getting this Court new modeled so as to impose a greater degree of confidence, and divide the enormous power now exercised by a single individual? The honesty and many good qualities of Judge Innes are unquestionable. But the duties assigned him are too vast for one man . . .'

[2] Clay to same, Dec. 22, 1804, *Whelpley Collection.*

[3] To avoid a decision in the courts of Kentucky men would temporarily vest their titles to disputed lands in friends outside the state, and have them, as non-residents, insist that the title suits be tried in the Federal District Court. In that tribunal, with its one judge and overcrowded docket, the cases would not come to trial for years. See resolution of Assembly, Nov. 27, 1804, *Ky. Broadsides.*

this moment unattainable. For 'it is evident, upon the least reflection, that unless the amendment contemplated does take place, a dissolution of the union must be the ultimate consequence. Two independent Judiciaries, neither acknowledging the superiority of the other, may for a time subsist without inconvenience, but in the end they will come into collision, and the concussion which they will produce must destroy one or the other or the government.' [1]

Of internal improvements he was a strong champion. He was not in agreement with legislators under whom, complained James Brown, 'economy has long ago degenerated into parsimony.' [2] The most important project which he advocated during these early political years was a canal around the falls of the Ohio at Louisville. In 1805 Clay and his colleagues chartered the Ohio Canal Company, appropriated fifty thousand dollars, and solicited aid from the adjoining states and from the Federal Government. But the cutting of the canal was a stupendous task for that day. The Kentucky company, slow in organizing, competed with a rival Indiana Canal Company to which prestige was given by such men as George Rogers Clark, John Brown, William Henry Harrison, and Aaron Burr. And the Jefferson administration had constitutional prejudices on internal improvements. Then too, though it had the almost universal approval of the Ohio Valley West, it was further hindered by a depreciation of public faith because of the legislators' attempt to repeal the charter they had granted to the Kentucky Insurance Company.[3]

The Ohio Canal, the extension of the Federal Circuit Court system, and other improvements desired by the West were to have Clay's advocacy and leadership later, in Congress.

Dear to his heart was a measure local in character which he urged at every session as long as he represented Fayette. Each November as he rode over to Frankfort, Henry meditated upon

[1] Clay to Breckinridge, Dec. 22, 1804, *Whelpley Collection*. The issue was settled in 1821–23, in Green *vs.* Biddle, in which Clay appeared for Kentucky, by the Supreme Court decision in favor of Federal supremacy. Warren, Chas., *The Supreme Court in United States History*, I, 636–42.

[2] Brown to Breckinridge, Nov. 21, 1803, *Breckinridge MSS.*

[3] Dr. Sam Brown to James Brown, Dec. 13, 1805, *Jas. Brown MSS.*; and *Ky. Gazette*, Feb. 13, 1806.

ways and means of persuading his fellow legislators to make
Lexington Kentucky's capital. Rivalry between these two Blue
Grass towns was intense, and had been ever since 1792 when
Robert Todd, an overscrupulous commissioner who had large
land holdings in Lexington, gave the deciding vote which had
transferred the state house to Frankfort. For years Lexingtonians
had carried on a campaign of alarums and excursions. Earlier the
Gazette had broadcast rumors that Cherokees or Shawnees had
raided exposed Frankfort and massacred the legislators. Now, un-
ceasingly, it was said that no public man of sensibility could prefer
Frankfort because of its climate and general unloveliness, its
location in a deep dank hole cut by the raging Kentucky River,
and its gloomy, fearsome, state penitentiary.

At his first session Henry all but succeeded in overcoming the
constitutional two-thirds vote necessary to remove the seat of
government. Year after year he tried, keeping Lexington hopeful
and Frankfort on tenterhooks. 'Its agonized and breathless inhabitants,' said Humphrey Marshall of Clay's 1805 speech, 'were
made to hear its site depressed below overwhelming floods; its
adjacent hills elevated to the clouds and broken into precipices;
the country round about described as the fit haunts of wolves and
bears — while a crack in the plaster of the state house, and a cobweb on the ceiling, were magnified into objects but little less portentous than comets — or less dreaded than a volcanic irruption
— of which they might be taken as the certain auguries.' [1]

The Lexington orator was in fine fettle that day. 'We have,'
said Henry, 'the model of an *inverted hat* — Frankfort is the body of
the hat, and the lands adjacent are the brim. To change the
figure, it is *nature's great penitentiary*; and, if the members of this
house would know the bodily condition of the prisoners, let them
look at those poor creatures in the gallery.' As he spoke he turned
and pointed to the gallery above where half a dozen idlers,
nondescript Frankfort town characters, happened to be moving
about. With the tall orator's catamount eyes gleaming at them,
his long finger pointing at them, and all the members focussing
their attention upon them, the men dodged behind the railings or

---

[1] Marshall, *Hist. Ky.*, II, 9–10.

scampered off in confusion while the House roared with laughter.[1]

'Mr. Clay,' recorded historian Humphrey Marshall (who lived near Frankfort), 'probably never made greater exertions, or a more illiberal display.' Although he failed to win the required two-thirds vote, great as usual was the effect of his oratorical storm. Many good citizens of 'ill-fated, devoted Frankfort' were convinced that Kentucky's state house would soon be on the road to Lexington.[2]

In the summer of 1805, while Henry was enjoying the varied delights of Olympian Springs, John Adair sought his aid in quieting attacks upon him, because of alleged views 'inimical to Mr. Jefferson and republicanism.' These attacks upon Adair had begun at the 1804 session — when Thruston was sent to the Senate and General Adair 'got work'd out of his Election by the artful management of H. Clay.' Henry's reply was a model of suavity and polite discretion. He regretted a memory which did not recall the details. He did remember that Mr. Adair, about the time Grundy and Daveiss were maligning Senator John Brown, had expressed doubts as to the propriety of certain Jeffersonian measures. 'Whether your opinion was matured or not I can not say, but I do not think you expressed one decisively,' wrote young Clay. 'When I saw the handbill to which you allude, I was surprised at some of the sentiments there ascribed to you; and I am inclined to think had they been avowed in my presence and hearing, that they would have made an impression which would be still fresh.'[3]

It was not a statement Adair could use either as a shield or as a weapon to counter-attack Clay and his Blue Grass supporters. There was about it none of the blunt frontier yes or no. While he frequently did lay about him with the broadsword of partisan vituperation, the young Lexington politician could when necessary make skilful use of the political rapier. His deft handling of

---

[1] Prentice, *Clay*, p. 28.

[2] Marshall, *op. cit.*, pp. 9–10. 'It was a subject befitting the orator,' said Marshall, who, with reference to what he called Clay's 'illiberal display,' added: 'but as he did not exceed thirty years of age, and has delivered several greater speeches since, this is merely mentioned for the sake of historic justice.'

[3] Adair to Clay, Aug. 15, and Clay's reply, Aug. 24, 1805, *Clay MSS*.

General Adair's request revealed a mastery more subtle than that of mere rough-and-tumble, 'Old Bess,' electioneering, just as his bank victory over the South Country majority revealed his boldness, eloquence, and, above all, his adroitness.

'Artful management,' uncommonly effective oratory, zest for 'the glorious uncertainties of politics,' a commanding personality, and an ability to drive through measures even though they aroused 'considerable commotions,' had definitely established his political leadership. In 1807 he was elected Speaker of the House. As a presiding officer, whose powers and duties he combined with those of a party leader, Speaker Clay was eminently successful in maintaining order and in dispatching public business in a representative body noted for its brawls and uproars.

In the Kentucky Assembly during these early years young Henry Clay was acquiring an invaluable political and parliamentary experience, preparing himself for his future national career. His interest in banking, a stable judiciary, internal improvements, and manufacturing gave some inkling of the course he would later pursue in national politics. Clay's politico-economic ideas contrasted in many ways with those of Felix Grundy (a lieutenant, later, of Andrew Jackson), and other representatives of the primitive and exclusively agrarian frontier. His views were those of his Lexington environment, the ideas of progressive pioneers of a Blue Grass frontier which was maturing economically — and socially.

Chapter Six. The Goshen of the Western World

I need hardly tell you that Lexington . . . is the seat of wealth and refinement of the western country. (James McBride.)

'Tis one dull chaos, one unfertile strife
Betwixt half-polish'd and half-barbarous life. (Thomas Moore.)

It is true there are gamblers, and gougers, and outlaws, but there are fewer of them, than from the nature of things and the character of the age and the world, we ought to expect. (Timothy Flint.)

'You may sit down and tax your fancy to the extent of her powers, which I know are fruitful, and she cannot create such a Country as borders on the Mississippi,' wrote James Brown to Clay in the spring of 1805 in one of many letters urging Henry to quit Kentucky and to join him at New Orleans. Brown was now the Federal Attorney, with a very profitable private practice; the vivacious Creole society was much to his liking, and his country seat outside Orleans was a most delightful retreat in a neighborhood of genteel families. Yet he warmly assured Henry, in the romantic style of the period, that only 'the hope of a rapturous meeting with you shortly consoles me under an absence which, without this delightful expectation, would be insupportable.' He was certain that this gay Latin metropolis, this thriving seaport of Western America, would appeal to one of young Clay's lively temperament and afford him a much richer field for his legal and political talents.[1]

[1] Brown to Clay, March 12, 1805, *Clay MSS.*

His invitations were tempting. Henry felt the pull of those forces which gave the Western World a high mobility; which caused the restless Children of America ever to be moving on to fresh frontiers. Many Kentuckians had migrated to Upper Louisiana about St. Louis and, in greater numbers, to Lower Louisiana about New Orleans. His wildish brother John was now (according to Brown) an Orleans merchant of 'steady habits, industry, and obliging temper.' His brother Porter was planning to move to the Bayou Sarah settlement. James Bradford had become editor of the *Orleans Gazette*, and young Doctor Watkins, Henry's cousin of Versailles, was soon to be mayor of New Orleans. From Allan Magruder, formerly of Lexington, and from other Louisianans, he was receiving long and glowing reports on the influence and affluence already attained by Kentucky emigrants, and on the glorious future of this commercial mart of America's vast inland empire.[1]

Yet Henry was reluctant to forsake Blue Grass Kentucky. Brown's Creole city had its exotic attractions, its gay and pompous Mardi Gras, its cathedral and fine Old World buildings, its semi-tropical colorfulness and cosmopolitan air. Undeniable were its opportunities. But there were deterrents: the dread yellow fever, the imminence of war with Spain, the threat of civil disorders arising from friction between swashbuckling, hard-bargaining Kentucky adventurers and the quiet-paced French and Spanish Creoles.

To Clay, the climate was an important consideration — though Brown in sprightly and affectionate letters assured him that Orleans was as salubrious as Fayette and more favorable to longevity. In February of 1806, however, James himself admitted that the horrors of yellow fever were only too evident. 'Much as I wish to see you display upon a new theatre talents which from frequent

---

[1] A. Magruder to same, Jan. 7, March 6, 1806, *Clay MSS*. A warm friend of Clay's, Magruder was now a Louisiana Land Commissioner and publicist, who regarded the Louisiana Cession as putting an end to Spanish and French intrigues, giving the United States a charter of economic independence, and offering an opportunity for Americans to abolish slavery by colonizing their Negroes in the new territory. Rusk, R. L., *Literature of the Middle Western Frontier*, I, 212. On March 6, 1806, he wrote Clay: 'The French are remarkably Civil; but they do not like the Americans, who are too fond of Speculation, & often take advantage of their ignorance in making a Bargain.'

experience of their powers I have learned to respect,' he wrote, 'I cannot *yet* advise you to change your establishment.' Meanwhile he and his wife, Nancy, were hoping that Henry and Lucretia would, at least, soon 'change the scene and spend a winter among the gay, unthinking, dancing inhabitants of Louisiana.' [1]

Like Henry, old Colonel Hart was proud of James Brown's success in Louisiana 'among the most polite, gay, friendly, and hospitable people on earth,' where he had 'got in the way of receiving 20 doubloons a fee.' But he too was deterred by the 'ugly fashion' at fever-ridden Orleans of precipitously bidding farewell to this life. 'I should like very well to be with you,' he wrote his son-in-law, 'but to form my connections with a man to-day, and tomorrow he goes off without giving me the least notice ... is too troublesome.... I should like the Old Gentleman to give me two or three days notice at least in order to settle my debts.'

Kentucky, after all, was the best part of the world, wrote the Colonel, in letters savoring of the buoyant optimism, the hearty hospitality, the robust delight in food and drink which character-ized Henry Clay's social environment. Many 'will run all the risques' and venture to Orleans, yet we in Kentucky 'have had a greater Emigration from Virginia and Carolinas than were ex-perienced in two years before ... our numbers will double before the next Census.' Despite Tristram Shandy's assertion that 'the french manage these matters better than we can,' he doubted whether James's French chef could equal the Blue Grass cuisine. 'I am fond of French cooking ... but upon the whole I think I would give [it] up sooner than be deprived of the fine Stall-fed Beef and Cabbage, fine fat Veal, fine bacon hams with the fine red gravy to relish the turnip greens in spring running out as you cut it, our fine pastry of every description swimming in fine fresh butter ... If your French cook has the art of dressing up a sheeps-head without butter, you must have a great bargain in him, even at 240$ a year.'

Of this he was certain: Brown's efforts were doomed to failure. Clay was too busy making his fortune in law and his fame in

---

[1] Brown to Clay, Oct. 31, 1805, Feb. 27, 1806, *Clay MSS.*; also, James Brown–Sam Brown letters on migration, 1804–05, *Jas. Brown MSS.*

politics. Thomas Hart, Jr., and Doctor Sam Brown had just purchased a saltpetre cave in Madison County, and were already
counting an expected thirty thousand dollars a year from the sale
of gunpowder. No, said the bluff old Colonel, all the luxuries and
gaieties of Orleans, all of James's 'black supes and fricasses,'
oysters and sheepsheads, could not induce them to forsake the
Blue Grass.[1]

In hearty agreement were Henry and his father-in-law with the
preacher who, exhorting outside the state and finding himself at a
loss to describe the joys of the hereafter, thus concluded his sermon:
'In short, my brethren, to say it all in a word, heaven is a Kentuck
of a place.' [2] Kentucky was the garden spot of the frontier, and
Lexington, according to fulsome accounts in the *Gazette*, was truly
'the Goshen of this Western World.' [3]

Henry's friends later recalled these flush times as a golden age,
when 'every independent farmer's house was a house for all, and a
temple of jollity,' when every young man with his horse, gun, and
violin had unparalleled pleasures at the 'round of frolics,' fish-
feasts, barbecues, 'races, shooting-matches, squirrel hunts, and
what were dearer than every other enjoyment, the dancing parties.'
Perhaps memory's picture of halcyon days, when man's 'great
business was to pass life off with as little care as possible,' was more
roseate than truth warranted.[4] Yet an old Indian-fighter as early
as 1802 found much fault with the social season because there were
only 'three or four balls in Lexington, and one play acted.' [5]

This Kentucky and this Goshen of the Western World, which
were moulding young Henry Clay into Harry of the West, variously
impressed visitors in the years following the eventful Louisiana
Purchase. They remarked upon Lexington's uncommonly wide,
stone-paved streets with spacious footways guarded by hitching-
posts; the some 'six hundred houses mostly brick, which appear to
have neatness, elegance, and convenience combined'; the stores,

---

[1] Thomas Hart to Brown, Jan. 27, 1805, *Jas. Brown MSS.*
[2] Flint, Rev. Timothy, *Recollections*, p. 63.
[3] *Ky. Gazette*, Feb. 13, 1809, *passim*.
[4] Butler, Mann, *Hist. Ky.*, pp. 455–56 — on life in Kentucky about 1806, the year Butler arrived there.
[5] Levi Todd to Breckinridge, Feb. 22, 1802, *Breckinridge MSS.*

with their swinging signboards, filled with varied merchandise; the clean and commodious inns with their cherry or walnut furniture and panelling, and bells on the roofs which summoned guests to an excellent and bounteous table; and the many thriving industries in this 'singularly neat and pleasant town.' Visitors from adjoining Western states looked up to Lexington as 'the seat of wealth and refinement of the western country.' [1] Those from the East, however, were often hypercritical: amid the din of exploitation they grudgingly discerned some elements of refinement but many more of rawness and crudity.

Such a hypercritical observer was Mr. Alexander Wilson of Philadelphia, the poet-naturalist, who arrived at Satterwhite's Eagle Tavern one day weary and saddle-sore. At first he was pleased to record that Lexington's 'numerous shops piled high with goods, and the many well-dressed females I passed in the streets, the sounds of social industry, and the gay scenery of "the busy haunts of men" had a most exhilarating effect on my spirits after being so long immured in the forest.' After disposing of his luggage, pistol, and dirk, he set forth on an extended survey of the Athens of the West which, alas, failed to confirm his first impressions.

'Restless, speculating set of mortals, here, full of lawsuits, no great readers,' he noted. 'The sweet courtesies of life, the innumerable civilities in deeds and conversation, which cost one so little, are seldom found here. Every man you meet with has either some land to buy or sell, some lawsuit, some coarse hemp or corn to dispose of; and if the conversation do not lead to any of these he will force it. Strangers receive less civilities than in any other place I have ever been in.'

It was court day, recorded the splenetic Mr. Wilson, and there were 'not less than one thousand horses in town, hitched to the sideposts — no food for them all day. Horses selling by auction. Negro women sold the same way: my reflections while standing by and hearing her cried: "three hundred and twenty-five dollars for

---

[1] McBride, James (of Ohio), 'Journey to Lexington, Kentucky, 1810,' *Qtrly. Pub. Hist. and Phil. Soc. of Ohio*, V, 24–25. Cuming, *A Tour*, pp. 182–89 (1807) has an excellent description.

this woman and boy! Going! Going!" Woman and boy after-wards weep. Damned, damned slavery.' The citizens were 'rude and barbarous,' sadly in need of razors, scissors, and soap. Fay-ette's new and expensive courthouse was a curious pile of bricks with 'all the gloom of the Gothic, so much admired of late,' where-in sat the judges 'like spiders in a window corner, dimly discern-ible.' In the unfinished brick Cheapside Markethouse one sank ankle-deep in mud and slime, and saw there displayed products which in quality and variety sharply belied the boasted reputation of this 'metropolis of the fertile country of Kentucky.' [1]

These caustic comments on Lexington, and on the 'savage ignorance, rudeness, and boorishness' of Henry Clay's fellow townsmen, were deeply resented. Given to boasting, to the breezy, highly colored, and uncritical optimism peculiar to a new country, Westerners (and Clay not the least) were unusually sensitive to real or fancied jibes. Brash and callous as they might appear, the Children of America were remarkably thin-skinned. They fumed at the criticisms of Easterners and, especially, of Tory Britishers who seemed ever to delight in rancorous assaults upon 'the National Character.' Some of these 'Munchausen gentry' had never crossed the Alleghenies, yet they portrayed 'Jacobinic' Ken-tucky as a region inhabited by savage Yahoos or strange creatures half-man, half-ape; as a frontier alembic which made men nar-rowly intolerant politically, intellectually, spiritually; as a refuge or dumping-ground for the lawless and incompetent of the sea-board and of Europe.[2] Under the circumstances the reply made to carping Mr. Wilson was in surprisingly good temper and good taste.

'Thirty years ago we had no right to expect that literature and science would so soon appear among us,' wrote a Lexingtonian to the arch-Tory *Port Folio* of Philadelphia, which had published Wilson's critique. 'We hardly dreamed, by this time, to have been exempted from the necessity of exciting our youth to savage war-

---

[1] Ord, G., *Alex. Wilson*, pp. cxx–cxxiv; cxlvii–cxlviii (in 1810).

[2] There were frequent sharp reviews of 'the lies and stuff' of Thomas Ashe, Isaac Weld, and 'sing-song Thomas Moore' — these 'modern Mandevilles' doubtless, it was said, had been hired by George III and his Tory ministry to delude the oppressed com-moners of England and prevent their emigration to America, the poor man's paradise.

fare, by making an enemy's scalp the diploma of their merit.' It
was surprising, to say the least, to hear the Blue Grass described as
'"sequestered wilds."' Perhaps the Fayette courthouse was '"a
heavy labour'd monument of shame,"' but never had there been
exposed at Cheapside '"skinned squirrels cut up into quarters."'
Mr. Wilson should heed Washington Irving's advice to English
travellers: because one Jerseyman is fat all Jerseymen are not.
Because some Kentuckians were in filthy guise it should not be
assumed that to all Kentuckians soap was an article unknown.[1]

In truth, the amenities of life had measurably increased since
young Clay's arrival from Virginia in '97. His Goshen of the
Western World had become 'as handsome, as far as it extends, as
[Mr. Wilson's] Philadelphia.' [2] His adopted state, especially the
central Blue Grass region, was maturing socially: there had been a
steady growth, a quickening development.

Kentucky, 'the chicken hatched by Virginia,' seemed to present
more of a cross-section of the stratified seaboard society than the
one-class society common to a frontier in its first stages of development. While it was a 'mixing bowl' of divers peoples, domestic and
foreign, and while it was frequently remarked that Kentuckians
were like the Irish in their high independence, quick temper, and
frank generosity, indeed, that Kentucky was 'the Ireland of
America,' [3] tribute was generally paid to 'the considerable tone'
which the many Virginia emigrants of education and property had
given to 'the happy and cultivated state of Kentucky,' to the
'genial atmosphere of our great western garden.' John James
Audubon, the naturalist, early fell under the romantic spell of the
Kentuckian as he came to be typified nationally by Henry Clay, of
'the free, single-hearted, Kentuckian, bold, erect, and proud of his

---

[1] *Port Folio*, Phila., Aug. 1811, VI, 109–11.

[2] Melish, John, *Travels*, II, 182–208 (Lexington in 1810–11).

[3] *Ibid.*, II, 208. Clay, the orator and politician, often paid tribute to the Irish
emigrants and their descendants. 'Kentucky has been sometimes called the Ireland of
America . . . the same open-heartedness; the same generous hospitality; the same care-
less and uncalculating indifference about human life; characterizes the inhabitants of
both countries.' One might imagine 'that Ireland was originally part and parcel of this
continent, and that, by some extraordinary convulsion of nature, it was torn from
America, and, drifting across the ocean, was placed in the unfortunate vicinity of
Great Britain.' Speech in Defence of the American System, Feb., 1832, Mallory.
Clay, II, 18.

Virginian descent.'[1] Neither Audubon nor Timothy Flint could praise too highly the 'frank and cordial Virginian spirit of hospitality,' which in the case of Flint was impressed 'the more forcibly, for being unexpected' by one who in the Northeast had imbibed prejudices against the backwoodsmen of Republican Kentucky.[2]

Strong was the Virginia influence, along with other factors racial and geographical. Yet even among those Kentuckians who like Clay had come from the Old Dominion, distinguishing traits had developed: the chicken hatched by Virginia had become a young Western rooster, lusty, loud-crowing, far more aggressive than the mother hen. When young Clay went back East, to Congress, there was a peculiar appositeness in the term, 'The Cock of Kentucky,' applied to him by John Randolph. In the same spirit Virginia cousins stated that their frontier relatives had 'lost a portion of Virginia caste and assumed something of Kentucky esteem, an absence of reticence and a presence of presumptuousness.'[3]

There were distinguishing traits, in temperament as well as in politics, religion, economics. For it was not true, said Timothy Flint, that the Kentuckians as a whole were 'too recent, and too various in their descent and manners, to have a distinct character as a people.' Already there was 'a distinct and striking moral physiognomy to this people; an enthusiasm, a vivacity, and ardour of character, courage, frankness, generosity, that have been developed with the peculiar circumstances under which they have been placed. These are the incitements to all that is noble in a people,' said the Reverend Mr. Flint. 'Happy for them, if they learn to temper and moderate their enthusiasm, by reflection and good sense.'[4]

In Clay's Blue Grass country, as in Virginia and in England, the term 'Gentleman' had come to be associated with landed estates. Success at the bar or in trade was signalized by the purchase of a country seat. John Breckinridge had early removed from Lexing-

---

[1] Audubon, J. J., *Delineations of American Scenery and Character*, pp. 241, 259, *passim*. Audubon, incidentally, had a sharp encounter with his fellow naturalist, testy Mr. Wilson.

[2] Flint, *Recollections*, p. 70. 'The Kentuckians, it must be admitted, are a high-minded people, and possess the stamina of a noble character.'

[3] Preston, Wm. C., *Reminiscences*, ed. M. C. Yarborough, pp. 11–12.'

[4] Flint, *op. cit.*, p. 70.

ton to Cabell's Dale, where, in 1806, he had 128 horses, 70 head of cattle, and Negroes so numerous that he hired them out to Peter January, John Nancarrow, and other merchant-manufacturers.[1] General William Russell had his Mount Brilliant, Thomas Irwin his Mansfield, and General Levi Todd his Ellerslie — to mention a few of the estates which gave to Clay's section of the West a rustic opulence and made the beautiful country about Lexington a region of 'finely cultivated fields, rich gardens, and elegant mansions.'[2]

Some of these Blue Grass plantations and stock-farms, it was said, resembled estates in Languedoc and Provence.[3] Unique, however, was David Meade's Chaumière du Prairie near Lexington, in Jessamine County, a mansion composed of rustic cottages grouped together, with a drawing-room draped in silk brocades, flower gardens after those at Versailles, serpentine walks, and a lake presided over by a Greek temple and statuary. Colonel Meade, eccentric and charming, was an old-school Virginian who dressed in smallclothes and periwig, had the manners of a grandee, and delighted Clay and others with his hospitality.[4]

To the north, on an island in the Ohio near Marietta, lived Harman Blennerhassett, a rich young Irish exile who in his elegant rural retreat (as Clay called it) dwelt like a feudal lord, entertaining lavishly and with taste, experimenting with his chemical apparatus, playing his fiddle, and innocently dreaming of future greatness. Blennerhassett and his accomplished wife made a brave display: Harman in his scarlet breeches, blue coat, and silver-buckled shoes; his wife in French gowns, with her head turbaned in richly colored silk. Occasionally they would drive into Lexington, in coach-and-four with outriders, call at the Harts', Mortons', and Browns', stop at Chaumière, and sometimes draw up with a flourish before the law office on the public square of H. Clay, Esquire.[5]

---

[1] Breckinridge to his overseer, John Payne, Oct. 18, 1806, *Breckinridge MSS.*

[2] Melish, *op. cit.*, II, 183–84.   [3] Cuming, *A Tour*, pp. 180–81.

[4] Terhune, M. V. H., *More Colonial Homesteads*, pp. 65–98; Caldwell, Chas., *Discourse on Rev. Horace Holley*, p. 152; and, in general, Simpson, E. M., *Bluegrass Houses and Their Traditions.*

[5] Safford, W. H., *Blennerhassett Papers*; Cuming, *op. cit.*, pp. 128–30; and references in *James Brown MSS.* and *Blennerhassett MSS.*

In the spring of 1806 Henry established himself upon his own country seat, which he called Ashland from its wood of native ash, situated on slightly rising ground about a mile and a half south of Lexington. From it he could see the spire of Christ Church and the cupola of Fayette courthouse. Quarters were simple when he and his family removed from town. It was not until a few years later that he built the spacious brick mansion, designed by Benjamin Latrobe, with its projecting ells, its wooded paths and shrubbery, which became associated with the name of Ashland. At intervals he purchased adjoining lands, including the estate of Mansfield, until he possessed some six hundred fertile acres.[1] It pleased him always to be able to say that Ashland had been acquired by his own labors; that no part of it was hereditary except one slave, who would oblige him if he would accept his freedom.[2]

Thus young Clay, the erstwhile 'Mill Boy of the Slashes,' had become the landed gentleman, a many-acred squire, with a country seat commanding flourishing fields and rolling blue-grass meadows where his blooded cattle and horses peacefully grazed. Before he was thirty Henry drank of this 'brimming cup of felicity.'

Like Jefferson and others who favored gradual emancipation, he farmed his estate with slave labor — and the slaves of Kentucky, said a visiting British Whig, were 'better fed, better lodged, and better clothed, than many of the peasantry in Britain.' [3] Henry's slaves increased from six in 1805 to fourteen in 1808 and to eighteen in 1811; his horses from eight to forty and thence to sixty-five during the same years.[4] He planted hemp and corn and rye, but

---

[1] Clay lived on Mill Street in 1805 (Charless, J., *Directory of Lexington for 1806*); his house and lot there were advertised for sale, by James Condon, in the *Gazette*, June 24, 1806. The 255-acre (Ashland) farm was advertised for sale in the *Gazette*, Nov. 28, 1805, with the sale set for Jan. 18, 1806. Clay apparently was a tenant until Nov. 16, 1811, when he bought the tract from Geo. Nicholas's heirs, Samuel Smith of Md., and Wilson Cary Nicholas of Va., for $25 an acre (Fayette *Deed Book G*, p. 124). An adjoining tract of 123 acres was obtained from Thomas Bodley, Oct. 11, 1811 (Fayette *Deed Book F*, p. 120). The Latrobe-designed brick dwelling (Kimball, S. F., *Domestic Architecture*, etc., p. 274) was insured by Clay, Sept. 25, 1812, for $8000, though valued at $10,000 (Policy No. 16, Ky. Mutual Assurance Society Against Fire, Jas. Morrison, president, in *Clay MSS.*).

[2] *Niles' Register* (Baltimore), June 28, 1828, a letter from Clay to Robert Wickliffe, May 24, 1828.

[3] Melish, *op. cit.*, II, 206–07.

[4] *Fayette Tax Lists*, Ky. Historical Society.

ASHLAND

he was mainly interested in stock-breeding. Shortly after he moved to Ashland, with Judge Thomas Todd and three other gentlemen he purchased 'the Celebrated Imported Turf Horse Buzzard,' at 'the extraordinary price of 5500 Dollars.' This splendid stallion, the pedigree of which commanded a full column in the *Gazette*, stood at Ashland, where it served the mares of the owners and of all those who wished to improve the stock of the Blue Grass.[1]

It was a horse country, a sporting country, already in a fair way to surpass Virginia and South Carolina in blooded animals, high racing stakes, and colorful Jockey Club meetings. John Breckinridge in Washington was probably as much interested in the forty mares being served at Cabell's Dale by his stud, Speculator, and in the slanderous stories of Speculator's unsatisfactory performance, as he was in the Lexington Bank struggle. Wherever the young squire of Ashland and his friends congregated one heard horse talk — 'the most astonishing animal of the age, sir,' 'no horse on the Continent stands higher in the public estimation,' 'of great size, fine bone, symmetry and action,' 'she easily distanced the field,' 'able to run with any horse in the world.' All classes, even the slaves, had the 'Kentucky mania' — indeed, wrote a citizen to the *Gazette*, it is said throughout the Union that 'horse-jockeying and tippling is [our] chief employment.'[2]

To the contrary, there were now many polite diversions for a gay Blue Grass society that had its own musical clubs and theatre company, enjoyed travelling exhibitions, sojourned in summer at Olympian Springs, and accepted the fashionable dictum that 'cold water and ice cream are extremely pernicious.' Both Henry and Lucretia were fond of society; Henry passionately so. Many occasions demanded their presence — dancing assemblies and tea parties; the gala launching on the Kentucky of Mr. Jordan's two-hundred-ton brig, the *General Scott*; the marriage of gay and talkative Doctor Warfield to Maria Barr, that of Lucretia's dashing

---

[1] *Ky. Gazette*, April 5, 1808. A good stud was profitable: Spread Eagle made about $6000 the first season. Wm. Baker to Breckinridge, Jan. 10, 1805, *Breckinridge MSS.*; and see the 'horsy' letters in *Jas. Brown MSS.*, 1807.

[2] *Ky. Gazette*, Sept. 11, 1806, article by 'A Kentuckian.'

young brother, Nathaniel, to Ann Gist of Frankfort, and the wedding at Cabell's Dale of Alfred Grayson and Letitia Breckinridge.

When young people were 'put into the same alphabet,' Henry's good friend, Doctor Sam Brown, would doubtfully shake his head. Himself a most eligible bachelor, Sam Brown added much to the social tone by his attractive person and by his scientific dabblings — his pioneering in smallpox inoculation, his improvements in cleaning ginseng, his scheme to heat the whole town of Lexington by steam. Educated at Edinburgh and at Philadelphia, he was often irked by Western manners. Yet always when he returned from 'the wilderness parts of the state,' from those 'comfortless regions' outside the Blue Grass, he rejoiced in the metropolitan civilities of Lexington.[1]

As a pioneer on the frontiers of science, who contributed to the *Medical Repository* at New York, who made reports to the Philosophical Society at Philadelphia on Kentucky's fossils, Indian mounds, and limestone caverns, and who was interested in all aspects of the natural world, Professor Brown appreciated the unusual educational opportunity of 1805 when an 'African Lion' was shown at Satterwhite's Tavern. At Travellers Hall, competing with this exciting exhibit, was Mr. Rennie, the magician, who promised Lexingtonians that he would cut off their fingers, slash their clothes, and smash their watches — and then restore all with his 'Magic Cement.' When a 'Living Elephant' arrived in town the event was so unusual that Editor William Worsley of the Lexington *Reporter* exhorted his readers to see the mammoth beast: 'Perhaps the present generation may never have the opportunity of seeing an Elephant again, as this is the only one in the United States, and perhaps the last visit to this place.' [2]

In the new dining and assembly room of Mr. Bradley's Travel-

[1] Samuel Brown to James Brown, Sept. 14, 1805, and letters, 1804–06, in *Jas. Brown MSS*. The scholarly Michaux (*Travels*, pp. 205–06, in 1802) thought highly of Brown as a pioneer scientist. See also sketch by Dr. R. LaRoche in Gross, S. D., ed., *Eminent American Physicians* etc., pp. 231–46. A Western business associate, however, termed him 'a man entirely ignorant of accounts... in short a man only versed in books calculated to spend hours time and money in unprofitable discoveries (to wit, heating a town with steam)... actera at cetera ...' Nath. Cox, Oct. 19, 1806, 'Letters of Nathaniel Cox to Gabriel Lewis,' *Louisiana Hist. Qtrly.*, II, 180.

[2] Lex. *Reporter*, Dec. 22, 1808; *Ky. Gazette*, April 30, June 11, 1805.

lers Hall — a fine hostelry which Clay in 1808 purchased, renamed
the Kentucky Hotel, and leased out [1] — the Musical Society
gathered for 'Songs, Glees, Rounds, Marches, etc.' These concerts,
with the liberal servings of spiced Sangaree punch, often inspired
poems which appeared in the *Gazette's* column titled 'Sacred to the
Muses' — alongside debates on the morals of the ancients, Baptist
pleas for the education of the Indians on Mad River, perhaps
letters on monsters born from unnatural unions, and robust,
Rabelaisian anecdotes in the spirit of *Humphry Clinker* or *Tom Jones.*
At the taverns assembled the Bachelors Club for the Promotion of
Marriage and the debating societies. It was here that the Amusing
Club, the Tomahawks, the Frogs, and the notorious Free and Easy
Club 'cut up didoes' and planned escapades alarming to the night
watchmen as they went their rounds crying 'in a shrill, unearthly
tone, the time of night, and the weather.' [2]

Sometimes the young bloods would take the town fathers to task.
'We have had Hog Laws, Dog Laws, Theatre Laws, and Laws
about the Hay Scale . . . Kitchen Slops, Soap Suds, and Filth of
every kind,' read an open letter from the Frogs, 'and in no single
instance have they been executed.' [3] Attempts to regulate their
whiskey aroused a manly opposition — 'Ain't this a free country?
My father fought for liberty against the British, and I'll get drunk
whenever I please.' [4] What a dreary world if a free-born son of Old
Kentuc couldn't take his gum-tickler (about a gill of spirits) of a
morning or his phlegm-cutter (a double dose) before breakfast;
his anti-fogmatic (a similar dram) before dinner; and a few gall-
breakers (about a half pint) during the day? [5] A decent respect

---

[1] In June of 1808 Clay exchanged some real estate in Louisville for Travellers Hall;
leased it June 24, 1808 to Cuthbert Banks, and in 1811 to Wm. Satterwhite. *Ky. Law
Reports,* Dana, J. G., *Reports of Select Cases Decided in the Court of Appeals . . . 1833,* I, 585–
86; C. Banks's receipt, Nov. 26, 1809, and other papers, *Clay MSS.; Ky. Gazette,* June 26,
1811. This hotel on the public square, with an assembly room seating 200, was
Lexington's chief social center. Bradley advertised its attractions fully in the *Gazette* of
June 12, 1804 — the proprietor, who caters to 'Genteel Guests only,' has splendid
furniture, 'domestics and servants of the most faithful dispositions . . . a constant supply
of the best stable forage, imported and country provisions, imported liquors, &c., of the
best quality, foreign newspapers, &c., &c., and his ice will, most probably, last through
the hot weather.'

[2] *Ky. Gazette,* Nov. 21, 28, 1805; Reynolds, J., *My Own Times,* p. 77.
[3] *Lex. Reporter,* Aug. 26, 1809.   [4] *Ky. Gazette,* Dec. 3, 1810.
[5] Drinks noted by Lambert, John, *Travels,* II, 299.

for society usually restrained them, however, when they frequented the public gardens which Captain John Fowler, on retiring from Congress in 1807, had opened. Or when at Monsieur Terasse's Vauxhall, where, in the grape arbor under the moon and the glow of variegated lanterns, they danced to the shrill fiddling of *Roy's Wife* and *Jefferson's March* or listened to the black fiddlers scrape away at *Just Like Love is Yonder Rose*, a sentimental piece much in demand among Lexington's belles, in their silks and muslins, and Lexington's gallants, spruced and essenced with pomatum.[1]

Since Henry's arrival from Richmond Mr. Weber had built his 'Warm and Cold Baths for Both Sexes,' and lotteries — promising '600 DOLLARS FOR $5!!!' — had paved Main Street and erected the brick building of Sam Brown's Lexington Medical Society.[2] There was now a Coffee House, a club for gentlemen only, where Henry could select his favorite newspaper or magazine from the file in the reading-room, play billiards, chess, or back-gammon, and drink the best of wines and spirits.[3] At their ease, after tedious saddle journeys to county court towns, he and his friends drank, exchanged snuff, smoked Spanish seegars, and swapped stories. They discussed Henry Fenk's alleged discovery of Perpetual Motion (which British agents, it was rumored, were attempting to steal),[4] and congratulated Editor Dan Bradford on his pioneer Western magazine, *The Medley, or Monthly Miscellany*. Armed with *The Medley's* essays, poems, and moral tales, said Brad-ford, one was safe from embarrassment in any company — 'such a company amongst whom you could easily discover the phiz of the profound sage, the learned divine, the deep philosopher, the well-read politician, the subtil casuist, the fluttering coxcomb, and the snarling critic — the pious matron, the prudent wife, the sprightly maid, and the gay coquette.' [5]

---

[1] Cuming, *A Tour*, p. 188; McBride, *Journey*, p. 26.

[2] *Ky. Gazette*, June 7, 1806, Jan. 3, 1809, Feb. 14, 1804.

[3] *Ibid.*, March 19, 1811; Cuming, *op. cit.*, pp. 188–89 (in 1807).

[4] *Ky. Gazette*, April 11, 1809, and ff. Serious attention was given such devices: in 1813 shrewd Moses Austin ordered his agent to 'git a Drawing [of a Philadelphia model]; the advantages... of such an invention in the Western Country passeth all the Ideas and imagination of man.' 'The Austin Papers,' ed. E. C. Barker, *Ann. Rpt. Amer. Hist. Assoc. 1919*, II, pt. I, 223.

[5] Bradford, D., ed., *The Medley, or Monthly Miscellany for the Year 1803*, introduction.

Bradford's venture on the frontiers of culture was proudly considered an answer to current British criticisms of America as a land where material values exclusively prevailed; a greedy bartering land where neither mind nor spirit 'blooms, nor rises, nor expands, nor flows.' [1] Only in blind local pride, however, could Clay rank Lexington's magazine with Philadelphia's *Port Folio* or New York's *Salmagundi*, to say nothing of the British reviews. Servile to Eastern and English modes, *The Medley* scorned the simple, expressive idiom of the frontier and lacked the homely strength and gusto of the native works that Bradford published: the diaries of Early Adventurers, Johnson's *Kentucky Miscellany*, and that Defoe-like Lexington autobiography of 1807, the *Life and Travels of John Robert Shaw, the Well-Digger*.[2] To the homespun realism of Johnson and Shaw, it preferred foreign romances and sentimental moral tales. In literature, as in politics, it was a day of reaction from an ordered and unemotional neo-classicism: like many other ventures, Lexington's *Medley* came well within the purview of the Federalist wit who wrote —

> 'Our *learned* world is chiefly fed
> With flummery and gingerbread
> Whipped syllabub and pepper-pot
> By Jacobins served piping-hot,
> Vile fricasses of foreign trash,
> Sour krout and gallimaufry hash
> And stuff more gross than what the group
> Of Macbeth's witches formed for soup.' [3]

Not only did Clay's little frontier town with less than five thousand inhabitants have its own literary magazine, its own authors, publishers, and critics, but in the first decade of the century it had its own repertory theatre. A company of strolling players, meeting with enthusiastic audiences, had acquired some

---

[1] Moore, Thomas, *Works*, II, 314–15, *passim*.

[2] Shaw told of his adventures as a British deserter during the Revolution, in which he saw British atrocities 'sufficient to melt the heart of a Turk or Tartar'; as an Ohio Valley Indian-fighter; a soldier-vagabond who at the taverns cavorted with 'the brisk lasses de bonne humeur' and 'the Mother Carey's chickens'; and as a well-digger with divining rod and spade, who alternately skirmished with John Barleycorn's 'bottle-fever' and the camp-meeting's jerks and Holy Laughs. In the *Gazette* of June 20, 1798 he warned that he would in the future refuse to pay all debts contracted while drunk.

[3] Fessenden, T. G., *Pills, Poetical, Political*, etc., pp. 94–95.

'very splendid scenery' and were now providing regular entertainment which met the taste of that Age of Romanticism. Their plays plumbed the depths of sentimentalism and scaled the heights of blood-and-thunder melodrama; they were tender and awful, melting and gory, replete with horrid villains, saucer-eyed heroines, and Falstaffian humor. Lawyer Clay warmly appreciated the Lexington Players: in his own way he himself was an actor in the spirit of his times. And his little frontier community, which relished two, four, and even six hour orations, responded with great éclat.[1]

The Lexington Theatre usually gave a tragedy or comedy followed by an uproarious farce. *Animal Magnetism, or the Doctor Outwitted* was accompanied by *No Song, No Supper*; *The Revenge* was followed by *The Village Lawyer*; Kotzebue's *Pizarro*, with Mr. Vos of the Montreal Theatre as the Peruvian hero, was followed by *The Honest Thieves*. Most popular of all was John Home's *Douglas, or the Noble Shepherd* — 'fast came the Douglas with his Scottish spears.' Native talents were encouraged: the Thespian Society gave *Columbus, or a World Discovered*, and the Military Society, to equip themselves with rifles (for a probable British war and a quick and glorious conquest of British Canada), gave *The Rivals*. Aspiring Blue Grass playwrights were not neglected: a gentleman of Lexington wrote *The Reformed Gamester, or the Wedding*, and Mr. Abram Jones of Paris, in Bourbon, wrote the local success, *Love in Jeopardy, A Tragic Comedy.*[2]

Female rôles were played by smooth-cheeked boys until an unusually poor performance of Lady Macbeth overcame moral scruples against actresses. Popular approval was won by Mrs. Cipriani as the 'Genius of the Wood' and Miss Cipriani as 'Cupid' in *Harlequin's Vagaries*. Beyond this daring innovation Lexington was not prepared to go. When Mr. Cipriani, 'ballet-master from Boston,' between *The Reconciliation, or the Birthday* and the farce, *The Weathercock, or Love Alone Can Fix Him*, attempted to give a

---

[1] Lexington's audiences were no less excitable than those of Baltimore, where, when Coriolanus was killed, voices from the pit yelled out: 'That's not fair, by God! Three to one is too much. Let him up again and have a fair chance. One at a time, I say, by God!' Janson, *Stranger in America*, pp. 255-56, in 1806.

[2] *Ky. Gazette* and Lex. *Reporter*, particularly 1809-11.

fancy dance from Kreutzer's overture to *Lodoiska* he met with open rebellion. Ballet-dancing on Western Waters! And by a man! This was Old World degeneracy; aristocratic corruption. It was too much for the frontier romantics, too much even for the Athens of the West. By no means would the republican citizens of Lexington allow their stage to be disgraced by a male dancer's 'Baboon capers.' [1]

Cupid, the Genius of the Wood, and Mr. Cipriani fluttered about where but recently had stood a rude wilderness hamlet in the Dark and Bloody Ground. In the audience were middle-aged men who had here fought Indians and Tories — to save their scalps from the 'Hair-Buyers' of British Canada; who had here been Long Hunters when buffalo thunderously stamped their way to the salt licks and bear and panther prowled in the canebrake on what was now Lawyer Clay's elegant seat of Ashland. This older generation was beginning to pass away,[2] but the spirit of canebrake days persisted.

Men might still open the *Gazette* and find statements of their indebtedness printed as warnings to other merchants. A newborn infant found on Major Morrison's doorsteps inspired an advertisement offering the mother two hundred dollars if she would return, claim the child, and thus clear the names of several innocent Lexington females. Commenting upon the disputes with members of the bar of a lawyer named Mason, Mrs. John Breckinridge informed her husband that 'Mason & Allen has settled all their matters without a duel, also Turner & Mason has maid up, tho' Mason and Murray has some disputes on hand yet — how bad he has conducted himself, good god!' [3]

Lawyer Henry Clay had yet to fight his first duel — although early in his practice he had come dangerously close to it: after a

---

[1] *Ky. Gazette*, Oct. 9, 16, Dec. 25, 1810; Jan. 8, Feb. 19, 1811.

[2] 'The Old Gentleman may call me off suddenly, perhaps,' wrote old Colonel Hart, 'as he has done several in this place within a few days past. To wit Old Adams, Old January, and Old Paddy McCullough. They have all gone and left me, but I did not request any of them to wait for me, for I was not very fond of their company in this world, and God only knows whether I should be in the next.' To James Brown, Jan. 27, 1805, *Jas. Brown MSS.*

[3] Mrs. Mary Breckinridge to husband, Dec. 22, 1806, *Breckinridge MSS.*; *Ky. Gazette*, April 2, 1805, Feb. 7, 1804.

warm exchange with Jo Daveiss in the Frankfort court, he had
been challenged, had promptly accepted, and would have taken
the field had not mutual friends interposed.[1] Affairs of honor were
frequent. At Henry's first session two of his fellow legislators had
given 'An Unhappy Display of Courage,' and John Rowan had
killed Doctor Chambers. The press gave full attention to noteworthy duels, among them Andrew Jackson's harrowing dispatch
of Dickinson; the George Canning-Lord Castlereagh encounter in
which (it was reported) His Lordship lost a button from his coat;
the Irish doctor who single-handedly fought, and wounded, two
British officers; the namby-pamby New York Hectors who had
exchanged seven shots without a hit; and the Delaware slaves who
had set an example for timid white men by a duel 'fought with
courage and . . . worthy of record.' [2]

In theory, duelling was mildly condemned. Yet when James
McDowell (the former Federalist United States Marshal), acting
like a Kentuc boatman rather than a gentleman accustomed to the
Code, pummelled James Brown on the streets of Frankfort, and
then refused to meet him on the field, Brown had little difficulty in
bringing down upon him the scorn of the Blue Grass gentry.[3] The
Code Duello, while regrettable, was held to be absolutely necessary
if a gentleman would support a reputation for 'courage, honor, and
propriety.'

Along with its acceptance as the correct social arbiter there was,
in this heavenly 'Kentuck of a place,' a reputation for show and
expense as well as for 'a self-important deportment, expressive of
conscious superiority.' [4] The 'bold and erect' Kentuckian, it was
proudly said, bowed in homage only to God and the ladies. He
had, said critics, a surpassing appetite for Eastern and Old World
fashions, which he professed to detest as undemocratic; and a
handsome opinion of himself, partaking of 'the pride of an

---

[1] Philip Bush, Frankfort tavern-keeper, of advanced age but of vigorous opinions,
had sued Daveiss for assault and battery, retaining Clay. At the trial, Clay sharply
warned Daveiss to desist from abusing his client, old Bush. Incensed, Daveiss challenged. Prentice, *Clay*, pp. 29–30.

[2] *Ky. Gazette*, July 22, 1797, March 20, 1804, June 17, 1806, Sept. 2, 12, Nov. 21,
Dec. 19, 1809, *passim*.

[3] Nath. Hart to Breckinridge, Nov. 19, 1801, *Breckinridge MSS.*

[4] McBride, *Journey*, p. 25.

Englishman and the vanity of a Frenchman' against which he so often raged.[1]

Self-confidence and adaptability were traits most striking to observers. 'This perfect repose of self-confidence is in fact their good star,' said a New Englander, who had so often seen young Kentuckians quickly rise to leadership in the new Western states. 'With no other qualifications than that ease and perfect command of all that they knew,' they would immediately 'step down into the "moving water," before the tardy, bashful, and self-criticizing young man from the North had made up his mind to attempt to avail himself of the opportunity. "Sua dextra" is the constant motto,' and self-confidence 'the guardian genius of the Kentuckian.'[2]

Often, however, 'this perfect repose of self-confidence' had its unpleasing side. The spirit of equality rampant in the West, wrote the handsome and pious Mrs. John Brown of Frankfort to Mrs. Josiah Quincy of Boston, tended to produce the same effect as did unprincipled wealth in the East — 'it makes men arrogant.' After years in New York and Philadelphia she found even the Blue Grass sadly inadequate. She lamented the comparative cultural barrenness; the preoccupation of professional men which allowed them little leisure for general development; the superficiality of their wives, who married young, had many children, read a few romances, and devoted what free time they had to dress, 'in which they display a great deal of taste.' Nevertheless, as compared with the seaboard American, the Kentuckian had by nature 'a universal ease of manners,' and 'more genuine politeness and hospitality.'[3]

Both Henry and Lucretia were frequent guests of Senator and Mrs. Brown at Liberty Hall, their Georgian mansion in Frankfort, which Jefferson had designed, with its gardens which terraced down from Wilkinson Street to the Kentucky River. Possibly Mrs. Brown had Henry in mind when writing her observations on Ken-

---

[1] 'Hibernian,' in *Ky. Gazette*, Jan. 24, 1804. Also, Cuming, *op. cit.*, p. 212.

[2] Flint, *Recollections*, p. 72.

[3] Mrs. Brown to Mrs. Eliza Quincy, Dec. 22, 1804, in Quincy, E. S. M., *Memoir of Eliza S. M. Quincy*, pp. 97–99.

tucky politeness and arrogance. She was not alone in thinking him too hard on little Frankfort — few of its inhabitants ever quite forgave Clay for his 'inverted hat' speech in which he likened them to inmates of a natural penitentiary. To Mrs. Brown, Frankfort was 'extremely pleasing,' quite romantic, surrounded by 'high and beautiful hills on whose luxuriant and varied foliage the eye is never weary of gazing, and whose summits afford interesting and delightful prospects.' No doubt Henry agreed with her when at Liberty Hall; and he was there often, since he spent much of his time in Frankfort.

Although considerably smaller than Lexington, Frankfort since 1786, when its streets were laid out by the affable, enterprising, if sinister General Wilkinson, had acquired a social tone and distinction worthy of Kentucky's capital. In 1807 most of its ninety houses were of a dusky cream-colored marble veined in red and blue. The streets, while unpaved, were pleasantly shaded, and were named after Wilkinson and his Revolutionary colleagues — St. Clair, Clinton, Montgomery, Washington. One was called Miro, after the General's Spanish friend. Drinking-water was conveyed in two miles of wooden pipes from Cedar Cove Spring. A rickety pontoon bridge spanned the high-banked and crooked Kentucky River, but public-spirited John Brown was planning to replace it with as fine and strong a bridge as any in the East. In Frankfort resided the public officials, including Judge Thomas Todd, co-owner with Clay of the celebrated horse Buzzard. Not far from Todd's house on Wapping and Washington Streets were the four commodious taverns, preeminently the social centers for Kentucky's lawyers and legislators.[1]

Most popular was Daniel Weisiger's, the Sign of the Golden Eagle. Here in the large dining-room, seventy-two feet long, with the genial host at the table's head, and with a Negro pulling at strings attached to green silk ceiling fans which waved away flies and tobacco smoke, Clay and his colleagues often gathered for food and entertainment. Dinners were sumptuous, yet limited in cost to thirty-seven cents; wines, brandies, imported and country-made

---

[1] Cuming, *op. cit.* (1807), pp. 191–94; also, see Jillson, W. R., *Early Frankfort and Franklin County*; Trabue, A. E., *A Corner in Celebrities*.

gins were also restricted by court order to a reasonable price.¹
After a day in court or Assembly the cards were dealt, the bottle
passed, and the inimitable story-telling of Clay's Kentuckians got
under way. Their 'nocturnal frolics' were often 'noisily and even
riotously mirthful,' and often their 'bibomania' led to lamentations
the morning after that they 'must have drunk all the liquor in
Frankfort.'

Towards the end of one of these 'nocturnal frolics' Henry Clay,
Esquire, announced his intention of bringing the festivities to an
appropriate close by giving a dance, a solo dance. He would
finish off the entertainment, so the story goes, by 'a grand Terp-
sichorean performance on the table.' This Henry 'accordingly did,
executing a *pas seul* from head to foot of the dining-room table,
sixty feet in length, amidst the loud applause of his companions,
and to a crashing accompaniment of shivered glass and china; for
which expensive music he next morning paid, without demur, a
bill for $120.' ²

Perhaps Henry was trying to outdo Mr. Cipriani's 'Baboon
capers.' At least this and other incidents show him throwing himself into the amusements of his day with the same spirit and nervous
energy which characterized him in law and politics.³ Friends
marvelled at his endurance in the saddle, the courtroom, the
House chamber; at his ability to appear fresh and unjaded after a
night's convivial bout. One of his law students went to his room at
a Frankfort tavern early one morning to remind him that he was to
appear that day before Kentucky's superior judges. To his surprise Mr. Clay was just then bidding good-night to a large and gay
company. The student was agitated; the suit was to be argued by
some of the best appeals lawyers. But Clay reassured him and,
calling for a basin of water and a cup of coffee, flung himself on the
sofa for an hour's rest. Shortly after the court bell rang Lawyer

---

¹ Johnson, *History of Franklin County*, p. 62.
² Coleman, *Jo Daveiss*, pp. 351–52.
³ To be sure, said one of Clay's contemporaries, he was 'a little given in his early days
to such wild pranks, as your full-blooded Kentuckian is prone to; but [he turned] his
hot spirit, as he grew, into stump-speaking, and into strong pleas before Western juries;
and, finally into such fierce debate, so strong and fresh, and so big with his whole-
souled humanity, as kindled not only the Senate, but the whole Union, into applause.'
Editorial, *Harper's Magazine*, VI (Jan., 1853), 270.

Clay appeared in the Court of Appeals, argued the case with his
usual energy and eloquence, for twelve hours (according to the
student's account), and came off victorious.[1]

More relaxing were Henry's amusements at Olympian Springs,
forty miles from Lexington, which early in the century had become
'The Bath of Kentucky,' a reflection in the Western World of
England's Bath and Brighton, her Corinthians and Bucks, and the
fashions of Beau Brummell and the Prince Regent. The creator and
owner, that versatile pioneer, old Colonel Hart, had discarded the
earlier name of Mud Licks, and built cabins, lodges, and a dining-
room seating one hundred; had the waters praised by Doctor Sam
Brown and other physicians, and the varied attractions lauded by
the *Gazette*; and urged all to come to his olympian resort, with its
'romantic and picturesque scenery' and its 'most pure and salubrious air,' who might be 'prompted by disease or pleasure.' [2]
Promptly at four o'clock in the morning each Thursday during
the summer season the driver of the Olympian Springs stage
cracked his whip and with a great clattering and blowing of horns
departed from Travellers Hall for the playground of the Blue
Grass — and Western — gentry. After being jounced and jostled
from Lexington to Winchester and through Mount Sterling, one
arrived tired yet eager to join the 'most distinguished personages'
who frequented 'this place of very fashionable resort.'
Henry Clay was there, as usual, meeting old friends and making
new ones, 'revelling in the enjoyments of ease, mirth, and engaging
society.' [3] Old Judge Sebastian found the waters 'indispensably
necessary.' Other gentlemen got 'well steam'd out by the salt
water.' Mr. Breckinridge developed a hearty appetite for the
venison steaks provided by Cuthbert Banks, who managed the

---

[1] Coleman, *loc. cit.*
[2] Col. Hart attributed his own good health to the waters, which equalled the
European baths in efficacy, and anticipated, 'with the permission of Providence, an
addition to his years, upon which, at the age of upwards of 74, he had never calculated.' At the Springs everything conspired 'to restore the invalid and amuse those
who seek relaxation... Music, Dancing, Bathing, Swinging, Riding, Hunting, and
other exercises.' *Ky. Gazette*, April 2, 1805, *passim*; also, Michaux, *op. cit.*, pp. 205–06;
T. Hart to Jas. Brown, Jan. 27, 1805, *Jas. Brown MSS.*
[3] James Brown to Clay, Sept. 16, 1804, Clay, *Corres.*, p. 10.

Springs for Colonel Hart. Lovers strolled through wooded paths, and pledged each other in a glass of pale sherry. Planters and lawyers canvassed politics, trade, and war, discussed the proper way of making a mint julep, noted such items in the *Gazette* as the revival of Connecticut's Blue Laws, the advertisement of 'T. Jordy, French teacher and best French Cognac Brandy, 4th proof,' and with Editor Bradford deplored the fact that Lexington's two fire engines had been out of order for twelve months past. On the verandah matrons gossiped about the latest Philadelphia styles in bonnets and spencers, the activities of 'Dr. Essex, Physician, Surgeon and Man Mid Wife,' and the dislike Mrs. Breckinridge had for Washington society. At the long dining-table there was much 'dashing conversation,' perhaps of the wrecked romance of Betsy Patterson and Jerome Bonaparte, or of adventurous young Kentuckians who fought under Napoleon. All were pleased and flattered by the *Gazette's* prose and poetry on the charming people who annually sojourned at these 'celebrated springs.' [1]

It was indeed a gay place — more given to 'cards, billiards, horse-jockeying, &c. than to the use of the waters for medicinal purposes.' [2] The Springs 'are no more visited by merely invalids than an ordinary tavern is resorted to for necessary accommodations,' said a Kentucky critic. There was here much flirting, sometimes by 'married charmers, thirsting for universal dominion.' At times, alas, there were disputes between ladies in which use was made of 'pillows, bolsters, finger nails, and the poignant sarcasm of the tongue.' And, at times, the duelling pistols of sensitive gentlemen shattered the tranquillity of 'the romantic and picturesque scenery.' [3]

Then, too, professional gamblers sometimes entered these olympian precincts, although Colonel Hart did his best to keep out the blacklegs. On one occasion he found a worthy avenger in son-in-law Clay. Coming across a distrait and ruined friend, a man who had unwittingly engaged one of the gamesters and had lost farm, Negroes, and given large I O U's, Henry in silence heard his story. He made no reply, yet at the first opportunity he

---

[1] *Ky. Gazette*, Sept. 10, 1805, *passim*; *Breckinridge MSS.*, 1804–06.
[2] Cuming, *A Tour*, pp. 211–12.   [3] *Ky. Gazette*, Sept. 17, 1805.

managed to meet the blackleg at cards. 'Being an adept, as is well known, in the science,' he succeeded in beating the fellow at his own trade. Then, perhaps with a word of advice on the 'pernicious practice' of gambling, he returned the winnings to his guileless friend.[1]

At this Bath of Kentucky in 1806 a notable group of veterans celebrated their victories over the Ohio Valley Indians a decade before. Reflecting upon the many and rapid changes since they had fought under Wayne and Wilkinson for this country of theirs, they toasted Olympian Springs, its hospitable proprietor, and its 'uninterrupted harmony and refined social intercourse.'[2]

In this same summer of 1806 Clay had an opportunity to reflect upon the changes in his personal fortunes since 1797, nine years before, when he had left Chancellor Wythe and Governor Brooke of Virginia and turned to the West.

Lexington's Fourth of July that year held a note of sadness for Henry. Yet the occasion was festive as usual, with the Light Infantry in blue uniforms faced with red, and jaunty black helmets with red cockades; the Rifle Sharp Shooters in blue hunting shirts and coonskin caps; the Free Masons in blue and red sashes and lambskin aprons. At Maxwell's Spring, to the booming of a swivel gun, the citizens drank to 'The Fair of our country, but for the command of God we should fall down and worship'; to the stirrings of liberty in Spain's American colonies; to Republican victories, even in Federalist Massachusetts. There was a toast to Henry Clay — 'The Orator of the day, our worthy representative,' and one, also, to 'The Memory of George Wythe — a faithful laborer in the vineyard of the republic.'[3]

Henry's address was 'short and impressive' — for the news of Wythe's death had just reached Lexington, and the orator of the

---

[1] Little, *Hardin*, p. 33. In 1804 when Jemmy Payne, a professional gambler who operated a Wheel of Fortune or Spanish Needle, assaulted Judge Thruston near Downing's Sign of the Buffaloes Tavern, and later protested in the press when Thruston fined him $25, Clay in a public letter defended Thruston: the Judge had been actuated solely by his duty 'of preserving the morals of society and suppressing [the] pernicious practice' of gambling. *Ky. Gazette*, July 3, 24, 1804. Judge Thruston himself was or had been addicted to gambling, Innes to John Brown, March 5, 1800, *Innes MSS.*, 28.

[2] *Ky. Gazette*, Aug. 25, 1806.

[3] *Ibid.*, July 5, 1806; also, McCullough, S., *Reminiscences*, p. 414.

day was deeply affected. His adopted Kentucky and his native Virginia eulogized 'The Wise and Modest Wythe,' the just, benevolent, and learned Chancellor, whose republican virtues were unequalled even by 'the best of the worthies of ancient Greece and Rome,' whose efforts as the preceptor of youth were perhaps 'the most remarkable instances of his genuine patriotism.' [1] Warm-hearted Henry Clay mourned the passing of the great and noble man who had been his patron and teacher, who had predicted for him 'a high destiny' and inspired him to attain it.

Before his death Wythe had occasion to note with pride a new rôle Henry had begun to play in the evolving society of Western America. Visitors to Lexington attributed its 'considerable taste and refinement' to its bookstores, theatre, circulating library (now with two thousand volumes), academies for both sexes, and to its Transylvania University. Transylvania, which even critical Mr. Wilson termed 'a well endowed university under the superintendence of men of learning and piety,' contributed most to sustain Lexington's title as the Athens of the West. And it must have been of singular interest to Chancellor Wythe to note Henry's unanimous election by the trustees of Transylvania in October of 1805 to succeed James Brown as Professor of Law and Politics.[2]

Lawyer Clay was then twenty-eight. In age, in manner, and in conventional 'learning and piety' he afforded a contrast with his academic colleagues — with the Reverend James Blythe, president of Transylvania, who taught Natural Philosophy, Mathematics, Geography, and English Grammar; the Reverend Robert Bishop, Professor of Moral Philosophy, Belles Lettres, Logick and History; Mr. Ebenezer Sharpe, who taught the Languages; and Doctor James Fishback, Professor of Medicine.

For two years Professor Henry Clay lectured in the brick college building, not far from the public square, to classes drawn from an enrollment of some fifty to seventy students. His teaching was

---

[1] *Ky. Gazette*, July 8, Aug. 11, 1806; *Virginia Argus*, and Richmond *Enquirer*, June 10–20, 1806. Wythe had been poisoned, it was said, by George Sweeney, a disinherited relative, who was incensed that Wythe should deed his property to his freed Negroes.

[2] *MS. Records of Trustees*, I, 295, in Transylvania Library, Lexington; also, Peter, R. & J., *Transylvania University*; Cuming, *op. cit.*, p. 184.

successful, inspiring; in keeping with that of his predecessors, George Nicholas and James Brown, both Wythe-trained, in this pioneer university which for a generation was 'the only organized center of legal education west of the Alleghenies.' [1] In October of 1807, a few weeks before he resigned his professorship — in favor of John Monroe of Virginia — he was unanimously elected a member of the board. This proved to be a lifetime position.

As a trustee of Transylvania young Mr. Clay was regular in attendance at board meetings, served on committees which examined the students, and in every way was zealous in advancing the institution. Like many men whose education had been irregular, he took pains to see that his sons had college training. He enjoined them, when they became old enough, to read widely, particularly in history and biography, with 'some systematic course as to time, that is, to read so many hours out of the twenty-four.' [2] As for himself, he seemed too preoccupied with the pulsating life about him to engage in any profound research. Activity, 'constant employment,' according to Henry, was 'the great secret of human happiness.' [3] But in his case it was an activity outside of the library.

Obviously his absorption in the world of action was at the expense of what he might have gained from the world of thought. Undoubtedly a deeper and more systematic study would have balanced his intuitive knowledge and tempered his impulsive reactions. Yet his independence, great driving force, and buoyant confidence might have suffered in the process. 'He consults nobody, he leans upon nobody, he fears nobody,' later remarked a nephew of Humphrey Marshall. Mr. Clay 'is independent alike of history, or the schools; he knows little of either, and despises both. His ambition, his spirit, and his eloquence are all great, natural, and entirely his own. If he is like anybody, he does not know it. He has never studied models, and if he had, his pride would have

---

[1] Reed, A. L., *Training for the Public Profession of the Law*, p. 118.

[2] Clay to his son, James Brown Clay, Dec. 18, 1837, Clay, *Corres.*, pp. 421–22. He recommended Gillie's *Greece*, with Plutarch's *Lives*; Gibbon's *Rise and Fall of the Roman Empire* [sic]; Tacitus; Hume; Russell's *Modern Europe*; Hallam; Marshall's *Washington*; Robertson's *Charles V*; Botta's *American Revolution*.

[3] *Ibid.*, p. 425, Clay to same, Jan. 22, 1838.

rescued him from the fault of imitation.' [1] This same quality of vital individuality was stressed by an intimate friend, James O. Harrison. Objecting to the view held by some 'that Mr. Clay was but an impulsive orator — dashing and reckless — always ready for a speech, a frolic, or a fight, and never taking time for preparation however difficult or weighty the subject, or the occasion,' Harrison declared that 'he was exceedingly painstaking in the ascertainment of facts' and in his own peculiar way 'one of the most laborious and methodical of men.' His knowledge was adequate, 'though he was no scholar, though he had no knowledge of the metaphysics or rhetoric or logic of the schools, and in fact had a hearty contempt for all three of them.' [2]

Contempt for the schools and their metaphysics appealed with peculiar force to the frontier jurors and electors with whom Clay dealt and upon whom he depended for legal and political success. Their distrust of 'trained statesmen and official classes,' of the expert in all fields — political, legal, financial, religious — was a democratic defect which in time was to plague all America. To admit the need of special and acquired skill seemed like treachery to their faith in the common man. They affected to jeer at the book-learning of an effete East and a decadent Old World. And yet, at the same time, they prided themselves upon their 'Athens of the West,' their schools and literature.

Strikingly paradoxical were the traits of these romantic Children of America. They were arrogantly self-sufficient; yet wistfully, even pathetically, dependent upon the older society from which they had sprung. They were anarchically individualistic; yet enamored of an equalitarianism which tended to bring about a depressing uniformity and which provoked Federalist jibes at the puerile Rousseauism of untutored natural man —

> 'I am for Nature, unadulterated, pure . . .
> Nor spelling-book, nor primmer, well I wot,
> Had mother Eve or Father Adam got,

---

[1] Marshall, Thomas F. (son of Dr. Louis Marshall), *Speeches and Writings*, ed. W. L. Barre, p. 425.

[2] Harrison, Memoir of Clay in *Harrison MSS.*, and his printed *Reminiscences* of Clay, p. 182. This same note is stressed in the early, campaign, biographies.

> When shame first introduced the taylor's trade,
> And taught how fig-leaf Overalls were made,
> While all so blithely, mid the sun and rain,
> They strutted *sans-culotte* around the plain.' [1]

As a public man, Clay of Kentucky found it expedient at times to ward off the impression that 'book-larnin'' had elevated him above democratic mediocrity. 'Yet it is far from being true that he is not a scholar, and that he is not possessed of classical taste and discernment,' said Timothy Flint, Harvard-educated, a keen, critical, yet sympathetic Western observer. Although Mr. Clay is generally conceded to be 'an orator nature-taught,' holding his diploma from the school of experience rather than the cloistered college, 'a great and intellectual man he undoubtedly is.' [2]

It might have been of interest to nature-taught *sans-culottes* that during these early years Mr. Clay built up a library, 'a multitude of miscellaneous books,' which was one of the chief inducements that led a Yankee boy from Dartmouth to become the tutor of Clay's children.[3] Politician though he was, Clay was ever the devoted, self-sacrificing, friend of Transylvania University. He was proud indeed of this 'first temple of science erected in the wilds of the West,' [4] which in truth was extremely influential in the evolution of the frontier. The national prestige which Transylvania later attained was in a great degree directly traceable to Clay's efforts in strengthening it financially and in bringing to it teachers of established reputation.

His experience as a teacher must have been congenial. He got along famously with young men; he captured their imagination, cherished their affection, and was particularly helpful in preparing

---

[1] Alsop, R., *The Echo*, p. 150.

[2] Flint, *Recollections*, pp. 76–77 (in 1815). At the same time he warned the 'hundreds of idle and arrogant young men in the West,' who from Mr. Clay's lack of formal education 'draw a most preposterous conclusion against classical training,' that 'brilliant and successful as he may be, it does by no means appear, that he would not have been more so, had he added to his native vigour, feeling, eloquence, tone, and manner, the high finish, polish, and discipline of classical instruction. If he now thrills his audience at Washington, what limits could have been assigned to his success, had he grafted upon his own fine stock the perennial scions of the Greeks and Romans.'

[3] Kendall, Amos, *Autobiography*, pp. 115, 122 (in 1814).

[4] Clay to J. S. Johnston (U. S. Senator from Louisiana, who received his A.B. degree from Transylvania in 1802), Jan. 12, 1830, Clay, *Corres.*, p. 251; also, Clay's letters, *Transylvania College MSS.*, on the affairs of the institution.

them for public life.[1] As a lawyer and teacher he gave with a free hand that invaluable sort of encouragement which he himself had received from such men as James Brown and George Wythe — and in turn he received warm expressions and acts of gratitude.[2] As an orator he inspired their emulation: among Kentuckians and Westerners generally it was said of Henry Clay that 'in the depth and sweetness of his voice . . . he has no compeers; and in the gracefulness of his enunciation and manner, few equals.' [3]

On the circuit as a lawyer, and on the hustings as a canvasser of votes, he was usually accompanied by a cavalcade of youthful admirers, disciples as spirited as their Kentucky saddle-horses.[4] These 'free-born sons of the Western World' (as they toasted themselves) were proud indeed that Mr. Clay called them by their first names. They dreamed of following in his footsteps — of being 'an eloquent lawyer, defending the cause of innocence, basking in the sunshine of popularity, getting rich, and then thundering with Ciceronian eloquence into the Congress of the United States.' [5]

With the national laurels which in a few years he was to win, Clay's influence came to be of incalculable importance in the social and psychological development of the Kentuckian — and of the Westerner. 'They have one star, at least in the estimation of every genuine son of the West, of the first magnitude,' said Flint in 1815, commenting upon the great influence exerted upon his Kentucky environment by Clay as an individual. At the same time, with other discerning observers, Flint recognized the great influence which Clay's Kentucky exerted upon Western America.

'Kentucky is proudly exalted as a common mother of the western states,' he said. 'It seems to be generally understood, that

---

[1] His aid was not confined to law students. Discovering the talents of Joseph Bush, grandson of Philip Bush, the Frankfort tavern-keeper, Clay, after persuading the father, took Bush, a boy of seventeen, to Philadelphia in 1811 and placed him under the artist Sully. Price, S. W., *Old Masters of the Blue Grass*, pp. 75–76.

[2] Letters to Clay bear eloquent witness to this. Young Robert Wickliffe (for example) who was handling some lawsuits for Clay, while the latter was in Washington, stated: 'I hope you will permit [me] to declare to you that I should reproach myself were I to take one cent for closing them for you. No, my dear fellow, I wish it were in my power to show you how much I consider myself your debtor in something else than closing a few plain suits.' Wickliffe to Clay, Jan. 9, 1811, *Clay MSS*.

[3] Flint, *loc. cit.*   [4] Birney, Wm., *James G. Birney and His Times*, p. 29.

[5] Kendall, *op. cit.*, p. 125.

birth and breeding in that state, constitute a kind of prescriptive
claim upon office, as formerly birth in Old Spain did, to office in
her colonies. Hence, from the falls of St. Anthony to the gulph of
Mexico, and from the Allegany hills to the Rocky Mountains, the
character of this state has a certain preponderance. Her modes of
thinking and action dictate the fashion to the rest. The peculiar
hardihood, energy, and enthusiasm of her character, will tend long
to perpetuate this empire.' [1]

About the time Clay was Professor of Law and Politics, there
were at Transylvania young men from every part of the far-flung
Western hinterland. And a surprisingly large number of these
students (some of whom afterwards read law in Clay's office) later
attained prominence — such as George Robertson, senatorial colleague of Clay and chief justice of Kentucky; Robert P. Letcher,
Robert P. Henry, Thomas Washington, Robert A. Sturgess,
and John Speed Smith, all of whom became lawyers; James G.
Birney, father of the anti-slavery Liberty Party; James McChord,
who became a preacher after leaving Clay's law office, and then the
president of Centre College; Matthew Harris Jouett, who deserted
law for painting, studied under Gilbert Stuart, and became
'Kentucky's Rubens'; Robert Todd, father-in-law of Abraham
Lincoln; and Stephen F. Austin, 'the Father of Texas.' Transylvania in some measure lived up to the ideal which in these early
days Clay and his friends had hopefully toasted — 'the cradle of
Genius and nursery of Patriots.'

The students gave Lexington an atmosphere of youthful fresh-
ness and gaiety. They fought duels, broke the rules against
'tippling, gaming, and other licentious and unprofitable amusements,' engaged in battles of town and gown, and made life trying
for Mrs. Beck, preceptress of the Lexington Female Academy.[2]
Young Professor Clay soon realized that there were stronger at-

---

[1] Flint, op. cit., pp. 72, 76.

[2] Mrs. Beck's in 1807 was one of three creditable female academies. When opened in
1806 the Gazette hailed 'the dawn of the day when science shall establish her universal
empire over the inhabitants of the Western World — when sisters shall vie with their
brothers in their knowledge of every useful part of literature.' Encouraging, too, was
the founding of a Female Society for Promoting Knowledge. Ky. Gazette, July 19, 1806;
May 29, 1810.

tractions for them than law, logic, and moral philosophy. They enlisted under Cupid's banners, had their 'Amorettos,' and admitted that before they 'pushed for degrees' they would most certainly be 'crossed in love and bedeviled by the girls.' They paid court to such reigning beauties as Eliza Parker and Eliza Price, the latter Clay's niece by marriage. At Samuel Price's house on Mill Street George Robertson and his messmates often fiddled and danced by moonlight on the velvet lawn. Verses were composed — 'My heart Eliza turns me all to thee; to thee sweet girl who hast my bosom warm'd, to nobler views than int'rest ever formed.' Stephen Austin and other rivals for the hand of Eliza Parker at length yielded to Robert Todd, who, leaving Mr. Clay's law classes in 1807 for the office of Thomas Bodley, Clerk of Fayette Court, was 'studying Law like a house afire.'

At times students regretted having left their 'Mississippi Backwoods' for this center of Western culture and the famed Blue Grass society — in Lexington there were 'so many things to puzzle a fellow's Brain and restrain his actions.' Yet they stayed on, paying some attention to the lectures, 'taking a small breezing' to the theatre, to Vauxhall, or to Captain Fowler's Gardens, and engaging in 'amorous conflicts too delicate for pen to describe.' They admired the eloquence and bearing of Mr. Clay and patterned their politics after his. They paid calls upon the Prices, Bradfords, Parkers, Russells, Breckinridges, and Clays, and congratulated that popular alumnus, young Captain Nathaniel Hart of the Lexington Light Infantry, upon the fine appearance of his son, Henry Clay Hart. They commiserated with Matthew Jouett when old Captain Jack Jouett, disliking his son's concern with sketches and miniatures, would declare that he had sent Matthew to college to make a gentleman of him and not 'a damned signpainter.' And they frequently remarked that Mrs. Beck, the vigilant guardian of her pretty female academicians, was 'still crazed.' [1]

---

[1] Students' letters, 1810–11, to Stephen F. Austin, *Austin Papers*, II, pt. 1, 172–90; Robertson, G., *Autobiography*, pp. 27–28; Birney, *op. cit.*, p. 11; Townsend, W. H., *Lincoln and His Wife's Home Town*, p. 44; *Transylvania College MSS.*; and, on Jouett, sketch in Price, S. W., *Old Masters of the Blue Grass*, and Berryman, F. S., 'Kentucky's "Rubens" and Some of His Subjects,' *D.A.R. Magazine*, LXIV, 220–28, 414–22.

These carefree young Transylvanians gave point to a growing opinion that the equality of pioneer days no longer existed in the Blue Grass. 'Who claim the uppermost seats?' in 1809 demanded an Early Adventurer, who had not realized the early hope of becoming a ruler of principalities, a real Lord of Creation. 'Who established their privileged societies and companies; their privileged balls and assemblies from which the mechannick, however respectable by virtue or industry, is excluded?' The Mechannick of Lexington and the Farmer òf Fayette were called upon to preserve their 'liberties' from a self-created Kentucky aristocracy.[1] In the same year violent protests were lodged against a new Lexington militia company to be composed exclusively of 'Gentlemen.' [2] Another token of the social and economic maturing of the Blue Grass frontier was the formation of workingmen's unions.[3] In one of his rhymed advertisements John Robert Shaw, the well-digger, complained that —

> 'The great men are determin'd,
> All the negroes to have;
> To work in their factories,
> The poor men to starve.' [4]

The pioneers still railed at the lawyer's wealth and power, even though, as James Brown remarked to Clay, they 'vie with each other in filling the coffers.' [5] Colonel Hart, himself a liberal contributor to such coffers, in 1805 was inclined to believe that a 'New Religion' which would have an Arbitration Society settle outside of court all disputes among its members might succeed in quieting Kentucky's incessant litigation. Such ideas of a lawyerless utopia were being spread by the pamphlet *Samson Against the Philistines* and the levelling articles of Editor Duane of

---

[1] Lex. *Reporter*, July 29, 1809. The writer described the founding of Lexington in 1775 and the great changes since.

[2] *Ibid.*, Jan. 30, 1809.

[3] *Ky. Gazette*, Feb. 26, 1811. Some twenty 'Journeymen Cordwainers' united.

[4] *Ibid.*, Feb. 12, 1811. Shaw at this time was not only a well-digger and mason but the owner of the Weary Travellers Rest or Kentucky Volunteer Inn, drill-master of the Lexington Rangers (training them for a possible British war), and forthright social critic.

[5] Brown to Clay, Sept. 1, 1808, Clay, *Corres.*, p. 17.

the Philadelphia *Aurora*, whom Federalists hotly denounced as 'an Irish renegado,' the 'Wat Tyler of Jeffersonian Mobocracy.'

'In Duane's paper,' wrote Colonel Hart to James Brown, 'is published a dialogue between a lawyer and a parson ... wherein the Parson has so much the advantage of the Lawyer that Clay, after receiving the paper from me for perusal, refused to return it, fearing perhaps that it may be made too publick.' Henry did not take kindly to the old Colonel's teasing offer of twenty thousand dollars for drawing up a creed or constitution for the New Religion, with 'a certain salary as Arbitrator and 2,000$ a year for Preaching to us.' Lawyer Clay in characteristic fashion expressed in no uncertain terms what he thought of William Duane — 'a Damn'd unprincipled wretch who would wish to see anarchy and confusion prevail throughout the Union.' [1]

The democratic idea of every man his own attorney — his own judge, doctor, preacher, etc. — was as repugnant to James Brown as to Henry. Like Jefferson and their common teacher, Wythe, he too believed in the sovereignty of the people; yet he was likewise a republican, a believer in representative government rather than in direct government by 'the nether end of society.' It was this *sans-culotte* equality, among other considerations such as 'the number of lawyers, the ignorance and insolence of the Judges, the scarcity of specie, and the instability of the Judiciary systems' under Grundy's disorganizing South Country legislators, which had induced Brown to migrate to Orleans. [2] That young Clay, who had preferred to stay behind, was prospering at the bar gave him much pleasure. He was happy to hear Henry describe his prospects as flattering, and to note that his rage for electioneering had not made him neglect his law practice, which was 'the main point.' [3]

Lawyer Clay was now in a position to turn down cases for want of time and to command fees which some of his Virginia clients,

---

[1] Hart to Brown, Jan. 27, 1805, *Jas. Brown MSS.*; also, on Duane's 'Godwinian schemes,' Fessenden, *Democracy Unveiled*, II, 197, *passim*.

[2] Brown to Breckinridge, Jan. 13, [1804], *Breckinridge MSS.*

[3] Brown to Clay, Feb. 27, 1806, *Clay MSS.*; and, to same, Sept. 1, 1808, Clay, *Corres.*, p. 17.

among them John Taylor of Caroline, regarded as remarkably high.[1] Among the Kentuckians whose legal affairs he handled were Breckinridge, Jefferson's Attorney General, and Thomas Todd, who in 1807 was elevated from the Court of Appeals to the United States Supreme Court. The death in 1808 of Colonel Hart — that gallant adventurer who 'lived long and lived well' — followed by the death of Thomas Hart, Jr., in 1809, increased his responsibilities, since he became executor of both estates, which comprised miscellaneous enterprises and many tracts of Western lands.[2]

In the superior courts Clay by no means repeated his sweeping triumphs in the county courts. Yet in the first decade of the century he stood in the front rank of the attorneys who appeared in the Court of Appeals, in the number of cases argued and in the number won. Some of the appellate suits which he argued were long remembered by Kentucky lawyers for the 'luminous and versatile talent' displayed.[3]

The position at the bar which he had attained was perhaps best revealed by the article of 'A Citizen' in the Lexington *Reporter*. Meeting with one of his neighbors, and understanding that he had lost a just cause, the writer thus accosted him:

' "Well, neighbor, the court decided that the law was against you."

' "Yes," replied he, taking me sorrowfully by the hand, "but if I could have got *Harry Clay* to my side things would not have been so."

'Not so long afterwards in going home from another court, I fell in with a young Lawyer who was regretting the undue influence of the elder Lawyers of his District. Upon enquiry I found that the immediate cause of his regret was this: The two associate Judges (and I know them to be men as highly respected as any others in the state) had undone in the evening what they had done

---

[1] Taylor to Clay, Jan. 4, Feb. 5, 12, 1807, June 26, 1809, *Clay MSS.*

[2] *Will Book A*, p. 480, Fayette County Court; Lex. *Reporter*, June 25, 1808; *Ky. Gazette,* Nov. 28, 1809.

[3] Levin, H., ed., *Lawyers and Lawmakers of Ky.*, p. 47. At the spring term, 1808, of the 114 cases recorded which give the names of the attorneys, Clay appeared in 57 and won 33. *Ky. Law Reports*, Hardin.

in the morning — and from all that he could learn, because this same *Harry Clay* happened to say, he did not think the opinion of their honors could be supported.' [1]

With such prestige and power, happy in his friends and in his interests, which were now deepened in root and widened in range, flattered by the prospects before him in this Goshen of the Western World, in this heavenly 'Kentuck of a place,' young Harry Clay (now one of Kentucky's 'elder Lawyers') did not regret his decision to forego James Brown's 'merry dancing country' of New Orleans.

After his friend's departure he looked after James's Kentucky lands and unfinished lawsuits. For this he received warm thanks: Brown hoped that Henry could discover some method by which he could make more substantial expressions of gratitude than those which flowed from the point of his goose quill. Knowing Clay's tastes, and remembering his own days among the bench and bar of Kentucky, James meanwhile was putting on board at Orleans 'some good wine to be drank by the Judges at the June session of the Court of Appeals.' Tell my good friends Todd and Sebastian, he wrote, 'that they must invite the bar and sit as president and Vice President of the Club.' Judge Caleb Wallace was too strict a Presbyterian to preside over the festive gathering, he warned; and as for old Judge Muter, he should be sorry to force Muter to drink as much as a presiding officer, on such occasions, should drink to a man's health and happiness.[2]

About the time Henry and his colleagues of bench and bar were toasting James Brown in the wine forwarded from New Orleans, the young Lexington attorney looked not very different from the miniature, a small locket miniature, Lucretia had of him. Probably, as family tradition has it, Henry had given this to Lucretia during his courting days or as a wedding present. Perhaps it was painted a few years later. The artist is unknown, although at this period in Lexington Waldemand Mentelle, a French *émigré*, was making portraits with his 'Physiognotrace' (similar to the Parisian device then being used in the East by Saint-Mémin, another French

---

[1] Lex. *Reporter*, April 22, 1809.
[2] Brown to Clay, Feb. 27, 1806; also, to same, March 12, Oct. 31, 1805, *Clay MSS.*

émigré); young Matthew Jouett was trying his hand at miniatures on ivory; and Edwin Smith was not only directing a corps of house-painters but was advertising himself as a first-class artist.[1] Whoever did it caught the self-assured tilt of Henry's head, the frank steadiness of his grayish-blue eyes, and the good-humored smile curling about the corners of his wide full mouth. His blond hair was ruffled and frizzled in true republican fashion; an arranged disorder, with the studied nonchalance of the Romantic Era. About the eyes and mouth of this engaging young Western lawyer was an alert, an expectant and quizzical, expression.

In the spring of 1805 the young man of the miniature could be seen in the crowded assembly-room of Mr. Bradley's Travellers Hall examining an exhibition of waxworks, the first ever to visit Lexington.[2] While the organ played 'elegant music,' Henry with his fellow citizens inspected these reproductions of historical characters and events remote and recent. Those of Mr. Jefferson, General Washington, and other worthies were remarkably lifelike. Most conspicuous, and most exciting, was that of the Aaron Burr–Alexander Hamilton duel of the summer before. Over long, levelled pistols the famous New York politicians and rivals glared at each other — so hotly it seemed the very wax would melt. Attached to Colonel Burr's coat-tails was a card which, with poetic license, imparted the following information —

> 'Oh, Aaron Burr, what hast thou done?
> Thou hast shooted dead great Hamilton.
> You got behind a bunch of thistle
> And shot him dead with a big hoss-pistol.'

Not two months later Aaron Burr himself, in the flesh, rode into Lexington and in this same assembly-room of Mr. Bradley's Travellers Hall attended the Sacred Concert of the Musical Society.[3]

The famous Colonel Burr, recently Vice President of the United States and victor in the notorious duel with the great Hamilton,

---

[1] *Ky. Gazette*, June 12, 1804, Nov. 10, 1807.
[2] *Ibid.*, March 19, 1805.
[3] *Ibid.*, May 28, 1805.

had arrived in the Western World! With his arrival there came about a succession, a cumulative series, of most startling rumors of 'conspiracies, plots, and combinations' — rumors which convulsed Western America, alarmed the nation, and threatened to shake the Union's precarious structure from foundation to turret; rumors which led to a most sensational legal battle, in which Henry Clay of Lexington appeared as counsel for the defense.

Chapter Seven. Counsel for Aaron Burr

Enterprises of great Pith may be in a State of Coction ... and great Results, whether good or bad I will not conjecture. (John Adams.)

Did I entertain the remotest idea of Colonel Burr's guilt ... I should spurn the thought of appearing as his advocate. (Henry Clay.)

But surely he is a very extraordinary man ... it is impossible to say what he will attempt — or what he may obtain. (William Plumer.)

'IF THE twentieth year from this should find an Emperor enthroned in America,' wrote William Wirt in 1805 to one of Clay's friends, it would not be more surprising than that a few years 'should have conducted France through a complete revolution, from despotism, through anarchy, democracy, and aristocracy, back to despotism again!'

An Emperor of America! Was it possible, when Republicanism appeared so triumphant, so solidly intrenched? In 1804 Jefferson had even carried New England with the sole exception of Connecticut. Wirt, however, was disturbed by strife within the huge and unwieldy Republican party and by dire Federalist prophecies that the 'disease of Democracy' would inevitably as in France give rise to a Bonaparte. 'Is there not some reason,' he asked Ninian Edwards, 'to dread State jealousies, faction, corruption, ambition, may then disturb the halcyon sea on which we are riding, and change our peaceful elections into a military operation; then dis-union, anarchy, civil war, and the fate of divided Greece — subjugation to some Macedonian Philip, Corsican usurper, or some other foreign martial tyrant, or perhaps some Caesar or Cromwell at home?' [1]

Similar inquiries in 1805 agitated other citizens of the ill-coordinated Union. Nationalism was weak; localism strong. Which would be first to split off, the Northeast or the West?

In the Northeast, Federalist extremists chafed at a general government dominated by the agrarians of the slave South and backwoods West. Led by Senator Timothy Pickering of Massachusetts, they hoped and schemed to effect '*a new confederacy*, exempt from the corrupt and corrupting influence & oppression of the *aristocratic democrats* of the South' — a new empire protected by England, bounded by the Hudson or the Potomac, which would embrace the Canadas, since 'the British Provinces, even with the assent of Britain, will become members of the *Northern Confederacy*.' [2] In 1804 Pickering's 'Essex Junto' had asked aid of a willing British Minister at Washington; and at the same time, be it noted, Vice President Burr's relations with these Yankee conspirators (and with the British and Spanish ministers) were not above suspicion.[3]

The idea of a Western Confederacy, even now, 'almost continually presented itself,' said a Pennsylvanian touring Kentucky in 1805. Geographical separation will in time lead to political separation: whenever the Children of America *will* it, 'force from the Atlantic states to restrain them would be madness and folly.' [4]

The fate of divided Greece? An Emperor of America within twenty years? So asked William Wirt in 1805. Within less than two years Mr. Wirt of Richmond was prosecuting Aaron Burr, former Vice President, for schemes of Napoleonic aggrandizement.

---

[1] Wirt to Edwards, Sept. 17, 1805, Edwards, *N. Edwards*, p. 414.

[2] Pickering to Federal Judge Rich. Peters, Dec. 24, 1803, Peters, R., 'Correspondence,' *Penna. Mag. of Hist. and Biog.*, XLIV, 330.

[3] If successful, the Pickeronian-Burr intrigue of 1804 (which Hamilton, nationalist, and expansionist, had opposed) would have made Burr governor of New York and perhaps Emperor of the Northern Confederacy. Burr's requests in 1804–05 of both British and Spanish ministers for aid to revolutionize the West were not fully revealed until 1889; and have been variously interpreted. See Adams, H., *Hist. U. S.*, and *Docs. Rel. to New-England Federalism*; McCaleb, W. F., *The Aaron Burr Conspiracy*; Beveridge, *John Marshall*; Brown, C. R., *Northern Confederacy*, etc.; Prentiss, H. P., *Timothy Pickering*, etc.

[4] Espy, J., *A Tour*, pp. 25–26.

What was passing in the mind of Colonel Burr as he sat in the
new room of Mr. Bradley's Travellers Hall in Lexington, in May
of 1805, gravely attentive to the Sacred Concert?

It was less than a year since his fateful duel with Hamilton, the
turning-point in a devious and brilliant career. In the East he was
politically, financially, and morally bankrupt, detested by Federalists as a 'murderer,' denounced by Republicans as a 'trimmer,'
generally regarded as a man of great talents but 'designing, intriguing, dangerous.' Yet this 'libertine' grandson of the Reverend
Jonathan Edwards, the grim Puritan, was still in the prime of life,
charming and unmoral, magnetic and unscrupulous; still capable
of winning and retaining intense personal loyalty. As Vice
President he had presided over the Senate 'with the dignity and
impartiality of an angel' and kept order 'with the rigour of a devil.'
Just two months ago his farewell address, replete with exhortations
to personal morality and love of the Union, had melted senators to
tears by its 'tenderness, knowledge, and concern.' [1]

A character to fascinate was Aaron Burr, so elegantly formed, so
fastidiously dressed, so impressive with his steady dark eyes and
pallid face; a personage who rivalled the angels in tenderness and
the devil himself in 'formal, insolent manner.' Like Lucifer he had
been plunged down into darkness and 'can never, I think, rise
again. But surely he is a very extraordinary man, & is an exception
to all rules,' remarked Senator Plumer, New Hampshire Federalist,
in December of 1804. 'And considering of what materials the mass
of men are formed — how easily they are gulled — & considering
how little restraint laws human or divine have on his mind, it is
impossible to say what he will attempt—or what he may obtain.' [2]

'Mr. Burr's career is generally looked upon as finished,' reported
French Minister Turreau in March of 1805; 'but he is far from
sharing that opinion, and I believe he would rather sacrifice the

[1] Plumer, Wm., Memo of Procs. in Senate, pp. 440, 540, 313–14; Mitchill, S. L. (N.Y.
senator), 'Letters from Washington, 1801–1813,' Harper's Magazine, LVIII, 749–50;
Davis, M. L., Memoirs of Burr, II, 360; Taggart, S., 'Letters . . . 1803–1814,' Proc.
Amer. Antiquarian Soc., XXXIII, 159.

[2] Plumer, op. cit., p. 213. He thought America had come to a pretty pass with a
'murderer' Vice President and an 'infidel' President.

interests of his country than renounce celebrity and fortune. ...
Louisiana is therefore to become the theatre of Mr. Burr's new
intrigues; he is going there under the aegis of General Wilkinson.'
Now commander of the army and Governor of Upper Louisiana,
James Wilkinson had been with Burr and Benedict Arnold at
Quebec in '75. 'Ambitious and easily dazzled, fond of show,'
critical, when in his cups, of a republican government 'which
leaves officers few chances of fortune, advancement, and glory,' he
was, according to Turreau, Colonel Burr's 'most intimate friend ...
most devoted creature.' [1]

To recover fortune and fame Burr in 1805 had turned to
Western America. By saddle-horse and river-boat he toured from
Pittsburgh to Orleans. He dined with Mrs. Blennerhassett on her
island domain, conferred with Governor William Henry Harrison
of Indiana Territory, and with Senator John Smith of Ohio, was
'magnificently lodged' in Liberty Hall at Frankfort by former
Senator John Brown; he passed through Lexington, tarried with
Andrew Jackson in hospitable Nashville, and received an effusive
welcome in New Orleans. In August of 1805 he spent a fortnight
in the Blue Grass before returning East from a Western tour that
was an impressive social triumph.

Henry Clay and his fellow Kentuckians, especially, felt the
romantic glamor about this gallant 'Little Burr' of Revolutionary
fame, this brilliant politician who in 1800 had swung New York
and elected Jefferson, this duellist who in a fair field had killed
Hamilton, only to be hounded in the East, threatened (as Burr
remarked) with disfranchisement in New York and a gallows in
New Jersey.[2] In him Lord Chesterfield and all the graces were
combined, wrote a fascinated Kentuckian. 'Never were there
charms displayed with such potency and irresistible attraction.'
At first sight he seemed 'reserved, mysterious, and inscrutable,'
yet there was about him 'such apparent frankness and negligence
as would induce a person to believe he was a man of guileless and

---

[1] Turreau to Talleyrand, March 9, 1805, Adams, H., *Hist. U. S.*, II, 406–07.
[2] 'In New York I am to be disfranchised, and in New-Jersey hanged. Having substantial objections to both, I shall not, for the present, hazard either, but shall seek another country.' Burr to Alston, March 22, 1805, Davis, *Burr*, II, 365.

ingenuous heart.' Colonel Burr was 'passionately fond of female society'; his fine eyes glowed 'with all the ardor of venerial fire.' To the ladies of Lexington and Frankfort he was 'all attention — all devotion. . . . He gazes on them with complacency and rapture, and when he addresses them it is with that smiling affability, those captivating gestures, that je ne sais quoi, those desolating looks, that soft, sweet and insinuating eloquence which takes the soul captive before it can prepare for defence. In short, he is the most perfect model of an accomplished gentleman that could be found, even by the wanton imagination of poetry and fiction.' [1]

In Clay's Blue Grass country Aaron Burr aroused curiosity, compelled admiration, and invoked sympathy.

Nevertheless, Editor Dan Bradford declared himself suspicious of the former Vice President. His political career had been 'fraught, perhaps, with a degree of duplicity which can never be satisfactorily defended,' and his Western tour had already inspired rumors of an American Catiline — a possible Emperor Aaron the First. Bradford reprinted 'queries' from an Eastern Federalist journal which asked how long it would be before Burr revolutionized Western America, carved out an empire for himself between the Alleghenies and the Rockies, and with the help of the British navy conquered Spanish America. The frontier Jacobins would heartily support Burr, it was asserted, for 'they will gain the Congress lands, will throw off the public debt, will seize their own revenues, and enjoy the plunder of Spain.' Dan Bradford avowed he knew nothing to substantiate such 'queries,' and he expressed his certain belief that if the mischievous author 'calculated on withdrawing the affections of the people of the Western States from their

---

[1] *Ky. Gazette*, Sept. 17, 1805 (from Frankfort *Palladium* of Aug. 30, 1805). Burr was the victim of circumstances, said the writer; his Nemesis the duel with Hamilton. 'Yes, my friend, even Burr, the inimitable, the incomparable Burr, is disturbed, is unhappy! Often did I mark the perturbation of his mind, the agonizing sensations which wrung his too susceptible heart, and which in spite of his philosophy and sprightliness, wrote themselves in the darkest shades on his countenance. And when I beheld the melancholy, the saturnine clouds, which often enveloped his bleeding, his magnanimous soul, my feelings were melted with a thrilling, a sublime sympathy — the tears started in my eyes, and could I have given them the efficacy of the angela, I would have expiated his crime — I would have blotted out the imputation from the memory of man and the records of Heaven!'

Government, he will find himself deceived, if he has not already made the discovery.' [1]

When questioned as to the object of his tour, whether he was (as rumor stated) to cut a canal at the falls of the Ohio, to be returned to Congress from Tennessee, or to be appointed by Jefferson Governor of Lower Louisiana, Colonel Burr had replied that he was merely seeking 'information and amusement.' [2] His reconnaissance revealed the West to be a theatre congenial to his peculiar talents. Relations with Spain had reached the breaking point over unpaid spoliation claims and the disputed boundaries of Louisiana. Even a casual visit was enough to convince him that a war with Spain, or a private filibuster against her domains, would be a popular venture among the aggressive sons of the Western World.

Clay's compatriots not only claimed West Florida, with its Gulf coast and Mobile outlet, as a part of Louisiana, but they had 'noticed' (as Moses Austin would say) and had 'squinted at' (as Alexander Hamilton would say — when Federalism was in power) the East Florida peninsula and the silver mines of Mexico.[3] Their expansionism, their agricultural imperialism, they rationalized and justified with the arguments of 'Manifest Destiny' and an emotional 'Spread-Eagle-ism' —

> 'Then let Columbia's Eagle spread her tail,
> And on her hovering wings adventurous sail . . .
> Where Spanish silver — Spanish gold is made,
> Their southern settlements to us will fall,
> For heaven intends that we shall have them all.' [4]

Interwoven was a romantic republicanism, in itself a robust and dynamic force, harking back to the American Revolution and to

---

[1] *Ky. Gazette*, Sept. 3, 1805.

[2] *Ibid.*, May 28, 1805. It was a characteristic remark. Of Burr Senator Plumer (*Memo*, p. 540) said: 'As a conspirator — or as a politician — he has a fault; he is too cunning — too secret — even . . . [his] lawful business always appeared enveloped in mystery.' On March 29, 1805 to his daughter, the famed Theodosia, Burr wrote: 'The objects of this journey, not mere curiosity or *pour passer le tems*, may lead me to Orleans, and perhaps farther.' Davis, *Burr*, II, 366–67.

[3] 'Besides eventual security against invasion, we ought certainly to look to the possession of the Floridas and Louisiana, and we ought to squint at South America.' Hamilton to Sec. of War McHenry, June 27, 1799, Hamilton, *Works*, ed. J. C. Hamilton, V, 283.

[4] Alsop, *The Echo* (written in 1793), p. 108.

the French Revolutionary crusade of '*sans-culottes*, armed cap-a-pe, to force the nations to be free.' Typical and significant in its timeliness was the flamboyant declaration of James Bradford's *Orleans Gazette* upon the eve of Burr's arrival in Lower Louisiana. The hour had struck to dispatch an Army of Liberation, asserted Editor Bradford (Dan Bradford's brother), which would give the wretched subjects of despotic Spain the blessings of American republicanism. Once in the possession of the Floridas and Mexico, the United States would have 'the key to the southern continent; and the soldiers of Liberty, animated by the spirit of '76 and the genius of their Washington, would go to the field, not with a hope of plunder, but to avenge the cause of their country, and to give freedom to a new world.'[1]

The time was ripe; the crusading Children of America were ready for war or filibuster; and it seemed that Aaron Burr was destined to scourge the Spaniards from the New World.

During the exciting winter of 1805–06 Clay and his friends again talked of 'Armies, Sieges and Storms,' with 'On to Mobile!' now their cry, and discussed imperial events and men of imperial cast. Though the United States was then on the verge of war with Britain over maritime aggressions, as it was with Spain over territorial claims, and though the air was filled with denunciations of England and plans for a retaliatory conquest of her Canadian provinces, they paid handsome tribute to Nelson for his victory at Trafalgar.[2] They admired even more the unparalleled genius of Bonaparte, who at Austerlitz had put an end to the Holy Roman Empire. They rejoiced at the continued blows he struck at the *ancien régime*, the mainstay of which was a detestable Tory Britain that seemed intent upon goading America into Europe's 'furious War.'[3]

---

[1] *Orleans Gazette*, May 24, 1805, in McCaleb, *Burr Conspiracy*, pp. 52–53. 'The innocent blood... so lavishly spilt by the merciless Cortez and Pizarro, yet calls aloud for vengeance,' said Bradford; 'the descendants of Montezuma and Mango Capac would draw the avenging sword... [and assist the] invading army... Thus in eighteen months would the two continents own the dominion of laws.'

[2] It 'gives me pain,' but Nelson's victory over the combined French and Spanish fleets is 'the most splendid & glorious on record.' Thomas Roberts to Breckinridge, Feb. 2, 1806, *Breckinridge MSS*.

[3] 'BRITISH OUTRAGE!' and 'BRITISH MURDER!' were headlines in the *Gazette* over accounts of Britain's seizures and impressments. Clay heard men talking in

As yet, to many Republicans, Napoleon still seemed to symbolize and to embody the French Revolution, to be the agent chosen to spread its great benefits and reforms to Europe's oppressed peoples.[1] Unquestionably this self-made emperor and marvel of the age, this audacious son of destiny, was the *beau idéal* of adventurers. And in Western America, a new country peopled by adventurous youth, the 'Little Corporal' of the Old World stirred the imagination — just as 'Little Burr' inspired grandiose New World visions.

Given favorable circumstances, surely a man of Burr's undoubted talents could adventure mightily against the Spanish Dons — aided by those (in James Bradford's words) eager to 'fight for the cause of rational liberty, and the dignity of the human species.'

Favorable indeed seemed circumstances when in December of 1805 President Jefferson called upon Congress to take vigorous measures against Spain. His message, applauded by all parties and sections, was generally regarded as preliminary to war.

Kentuckians, especially, became 'all fired with the hope of being permitted to chastise the insolence of the Spaniards.'[2] They acclaimed Francisco Miranda, who, unhindered by Jefferson, had just sailed from New York to revolutionize South America. They discussed claims against Spain for ships seized and for the closure of the deposit in 1802. They were incited by the presence of Spanish troops on American soil. And they vowed that they must now enforce their 'unquestioned right' to West Florida. No part of the Louisiana Cession except New Orleans was more important: if Spain was 'so foolish as to oblige us to demand it by force,' if war was once begun over West Florida, even Jefferson himself 'after-

---

this strain: 'Are we to Suffer the English Nation to do as they please with our Ships & Country Men... I hope the people of Canada will petition Congress to receive them as a State in the union... I hope the French people will destroy the English Nation. I hate the English, I mean their government, More than I do the Devil. I had rather have the Indians to reign over me.' G. Thompson to Breckinridge, Feb. 13, 1806; also, A. Campbell, Jan. 11, 1806, and others to same, *Breckinridge MSS.*

[1] For example, *ibid.*, F. L. Turner to Breckinridge, Jan. 19, 1806. If as yet undeceived by Bonaparte, Turner and others found little to admire, then or later, in England's Tories, who were harshly repressive of parliamentary reform, Catholic Emancipation, suffrage even for the middle class, ruthless in suppressing ('democratic,' 'seditious') protests from the wretched working people.

[2] *Ibid.*, Samuel G. Hopkins to same, Dec. 23, 1805.

wards could not prevent the americans from overrunning both the Mexicos.' ¹

Spanish Fever and the Spirit of '76 once again animated the gallant patriots of Kentucky. Indian-fighters who had not fought 'an open and civilized People' since they had clanged their steel against Banastre Tarleton, against Ferguson at King's Mountain and Burgoyne at Saratoga, prayed that 'those in Power will Act with firmness and despatch So that our Enemys may not get too far the Start of us.' Old Judge McDowell lamented Jefferson's woeful lack of military and naval preparations, yet he asserted with great fervor that old as he was he 'would not think it hard to march from Kentucky to the Sea Shore to oppose any Invading Enemy, whether of Spain, France, or any other Nation.' ² Young Henry Clay spiritedly declared that this seemed to be 'a fortunate moment to repress European Aggressions; and to evince to the world that Americans appreciate their rights in such a way as will induce them, when violated, to engage in War with alacrity and effect.' ³

Yet engaging in war with alacrity and effect, regardless of young and spirited Mr. Clay of Kentucky, was not the method of pacific and prudent Thomas Jefferson. Despite his public message, the President secretly asked Congress not for arms and men to take West Florida but for two million dollars to buy it through the agency of Napoleon. The money was granted — but the involved negotiations came to naught. This indirect policy alienated John Randolph of Roanoke, who henceforth rallied discontented Republicans to his insurgent 'Quid' standard. It greatly disappointed the Federalists, who had calculated upon a war with Spain and France leading to an Anglo-American alliance. Terming Jefferson 'a smooth, sly, cunning, underhanded, hypocritical

---

¹ Judge Thomas Rodney, Miss. Ter., to C. A. Rodney, Oct. 20, 1804, Rodney, T., 'Letters,' *Penna. Mag. of Hist. and Biog.*, XLIV, 61. Said Rodney (*ibid.*, p. 172): Spain, despite her former practice, denies West Florida is part of Louisiana only to force a war or a purchase. 'A. sells his farm to B. and B. sells it to C. who pays him in full; but A. still remains in possession and tells C. he will not give it up... Unless C. will pay him also for it. What would any honest Man think of such Conduct in an Individual? Are not Nations as much bound as individuals to act justly and uprightly with Each other?'

² McDowell to Breckinridge, Dec. 27, 1805, *Breckinridge MSS*.

³ *Ibid.*, Clay to same, Jan. 5, 1806.

devil,' and his administration one distinguished 'only by weakness and hypocrisy,' the merchant-Federalists clamored against a Republican economy and pacifism which had stripped America of her army and navy, paralyzed her spirit, and degraded her national character.[1]

In the West throughout 1806 the Spanish situation threatened war, and the 'Burr fever' steadily mounted. Negotiations had failed; but the sword remained. And the former Louisiana Volunteers were rattling their scabbards, adjusting their gold epaulets.

At New Orleans James Bradford demanded 'the avenging sword' against Spanish 'injuries and insults almost beyond human endurance.' An independent Mexico would make Orleans 'the deposit of the countless treasures of the South, and the inexhaustible fertility of the Western states: we should soon rival and outshine the most opulent cities of the world.' Surely, 'we may sincerely rely that our President,' Author of our own Independence, 'will seize with eagerness and exultation an honorable occasion that may offer for conferring on our oppressed Spanish brethren in Mexico those inestimable blessings of freedom which we ourselves enjoy.' [2]

At Lexington, at the Independence Day celebration of which Henry Clay was the orator, to the booming of a swivel gun and the crackle of militia rifles, the 'free-born sons of the Western World' toasted 'The Genius of Liberty — driven from the shores of Europe — may her empire extend over the American continent,' and (much to the point in Jefferson's republic of bellicose yet all but unarmed farmer-imperialists) 'The Militia of the United States — to be useful they must be disciplined.' [3] In Tennessee, Major General Andrew Jackson ordered his militia to be in instant readiness for 'avenging our countrie's wrongs.' [4] In Mississippi

---

[1] Taggart, *Letters*, pp. 172–73; also Bayard, Jas. A., *Papers*, pp. 164–69.

[2] *Orleans Gazette*, Sept. 23, 1806, McCaleb, *op. cit.*, pp. 125–26.

[3] *Ky. Gazette*, July 8, 1806.

[4] Jackson, *Corres.*, I, 150, Oct. 4, 1806 — A menacing Spain has climaxed acts 'degrading to our national Character' by taking 'an unjustifiable and insulting position on the East side of the river sabine and within the Territory of New Orleans!!!.... but one voice will be heard... *preperation and decipline.*'

Territory, at Natchez, young George Poindexter called the Mississippi Blues to arms, and marched them off to join General Wilkinson, who (as if to provoke hostilities) had moved the little American army to the Sabine River on the disputed Mexican border.[1]

In September Wilkinson secretly sent word to Senator John Adair of Kentucky that the hour had come for 'subverting the Spanish government in Mexico' and for carrying 'our conquests to California and the Isthmus of Darien.'[2] In that same month the fascinating 'Little Burr' reappeared in the metropolis of Lexington.

Western America was restive, expectant, favoring either open war with Spain or a secret filibuster, when in September of 1806 Aaron Burr returned to Lexington, took up headquarters at John Jordan's house, and gave to rumor some degree of fact.

Aided by funds entrusted to him by the guileless Harman Blennerhassett,[3] Burr in Lexington bought a vast tract of land on the Washita River, near the Mexican border, with the announced purpose of planting a colony and recouping his fortune from Indian trading, furs, and land sales. It was generally and tacitly understood, however, that his project might easily become a filibuster; that at John Jordan's house on Upper Street imperial adventurers like Cortez of old planned to seize the throne of Montezuma. War with Spain was imminent, and hostilities could easily be provoked on the disputed border by Burrite General Wilkinson. In the meantime, should government inquire into any warlike expedition against a nation with which America was still officially at peace, Burr could assert that his object was solely colonization. Should Spain repel his 'Army of Liberation,' he could retreat in safety across the border to his Washita colony in Louisiana Territory.

While these plans were going forward briskly if mysteriously, a storm broke on the 'New Empire Plotters,' a storm which had

---

[1] Swearingen, Mack, *Early Life of George Poindexter*, pp. 75–76.

[2] Wilkinson to Adair, Sept. 28, 1806 (and similar letter of same date to Sen. John Smith of Ohio), McCaleb, *op. cit.*, pp. 128–31.

[3] In 1805 Blennerhassett had been swindled out of $1160 by a prepossessing youth named Harte. Jas. Brown to Blennerhassett, [Aug.], 1805, *Blennerhassett MSS.*; Sam Brown to Jas. Brown, Sept. 14, 1805, *Jas. Brown MSS.*; Safford, *Blennerhassett*, pp. 109–11.

been brewing ever since July of 1806 when at Frankfort a weekly newspaper called the *Western World* had been established by John Wood, a notorious New York hack writer, and Joseph M. Street, a pugnacious young Virginian from Richmond. Two adventurers in printer's ink and scandal had arrived on a stage set for some romantic drama, Knights of the Pen to joust with the modern Cortez and his frontier Conquistadores. The press in the person of Wood, 'the writing editor,' wizened and furtive, and Street, 'the fighting editor,' bold and swashbuckling, had made its sinister appearance —

> 'And lo! in meretricious dress,
> Forth comes a strumpet call'd "THE PRESS" —
> Whose haggard, unrequested charms,
> Rush into every blackguard's arms.' [1]

With the first issue it became apparent that the *Western World* was to be the mouthpiece of Jo Daveiss and Humphrey Marshall. Since January, Daveiss, still the United States Attorney, had been writing Jefferson about some mysterious conspiracy being concocted by Burr which, to his mind, might well be a continuation of the old 'Spanish Conspiracy.' This was the text taken by Wood and Street.

Supported and advised by their Federalist coadjutors, supplied first to last with essays by 'historian' Humphrey Marshall, the newly arrived editors immediately began to ransack and muckrake Kentucky's turbulent past. Their circulation climbed to unprecedented heights when in issue after issue they subjected Kentucky's pioneer statesmen not only to the foulest of personal abuse but also, indiscriminately, to the imputation of treason. Treasonable had been their home-rule agitation of the seventeen-eighties; treasonable their Democratic Society manifestoes and private Spanish negotiations of the seventeen-nineties. These self-same Espaniolized and Frenchified conspirators, declared the *Western World*, now planned to separate the West from the Union, add to it Mexico and the Floridas, and weld the whole into an empire under the scepter of Aaron Burr. [2]

---

[1] Alsop, *The Echo*, p. 273.
[2] *Western World*, in *Ky. Gazette*, July 8, 1806, and ff.

Thus did Marshall and Daveiss begin a general and sensational campaign against the long-dominant Republicans. By branding the Jeffersonian pioneer leaders as Spanish pensioners (on par with Wilkinson and Sebastian, who had received Spanish gold), they might erect a strong political party. By striking down Burr, they would avenge their great Hamilton. By stirring up fears of disunion, they would embarrass Jefferson, whose silence they construed as official sanction of Burr's project. It was a splendid opportunity, in the name of patriotism, to wreak revenge and obtain power. And it was fully capitalized by these able Federalist leaders.

With his lashing tongue and trenchant pen Marshall had long carried on war, unsuccessfully. A rugged man of forty-six years, over six feet in height, with the hard jaw, piercing black eyes, and coal-black hair of the Marshall clan, he was a Kentuckian of means, a shrewd and not too scrupulous land speculator, lawyer, and an unrivalled controversialist. Daveiss, his brother-in-law, a fair-haired, stern-faced, handsome man of twenty-nine, was his equal in energy and courage, but 'his manner, his style, his tactics at the bar, were all his own.'

Both were uncompromising rebels against democratic uniformity: scornful of 'the impervious Dogmas of Popularity,' contemptuous of 'the Tyranny of Clubs and Majorities,' openly derisive of the body politic's 'nether end' and of frontier toasts demanding 'Equality in society.' [1] Both were rugged individualists, yet Daveiss, although extremely ambitious, had a mania for dissent.

He would appear in court resplendent in colored broadcloth one day and in frayed buckskin the next; on the circuit he would trudge the dusty road while his Negro boy rode his saddle-horse; on the streets of Lexington and Frankfort he would lapse into deep abstraction, mutter, gesticulate, and declaim to the sky above. 'A most abstemious student,' according to Marshall, 'he (for he was very eccentric) would use no other pillow than a hew'd block, and a bed equally rigid and anti-voluptuous.' Yet his strong mind,

---

[1] At Lexington's Independent Grove, July 4, 1806, men toasted not only 'Equality in society' but their loyalty to the Union, and — 'May republicans enjoy peaceful alliance with the free born sons of the Western World.' *Ky. Gazette*, July 8, 1806.

HUMPHREY MARSHALL

JOSEPH HAMILTON DAVEISS

HARMAN BLENNERHASSETT

AARON BURR

according to William Wirt, was 'as undisciplined and illy regulated as a raw body of militia.' So passionately did he worship Alexander Hamilton, said Clay, that 'after he had attained full age' he made Hamilton's name a part of his own. In spite of his eccentricities, his dour egotism, and his repellent haughtiness (which in Philip Bush's recent lawsuit Henry Clay had resented in terms so strong as nearly to provoke a duel), Joseph Hamilton Daveiss possessed qualities which won respect if not admiration. George Nicholas, under whom he had studied, thought highly of him; despite political differences Nicholas had made Daveiss an executor of his estate.[1] Clay characterized him as 'a man of genius, but of strong prejudices.' [2] And now, these Federalist prejudices were finding a vent through the *Western World*.

Indignant were Kentuckians at the 'Wonderful Conspiracy' conjured up by the poison-pens directed by Daveiss and Marshall. Chagrined and mortified were they when Eastern America reprinted the new editors' 'Absurd and improbable' charges — their 'Tissue of the grossest falsehood and abominable slanders ever uttered,' which 'implicated and denounced as Conspirators and Traitors' almost every Republican prominent in the founding of the state.[3] A people 'bigoted to Jefferson' could only construe such

---

[1] John Wood later asserted that Daveiss as an executor (with James Morrison) of Nicholas's estate had obtained the fullest information of the pioneer 'Spanish Conspiracy,' but 'chose to conceal the treason' until the Burr affair gave him a chance to wreak revenge upon Judge Innes and the Republicans of Kentucky. Wood, in the *Atlantic World* (Wash., D.C.), Jan. 19, 1807; he quoted in substantiation a letter from Daveiss to Street, Oct. 9, 1806, in which Daveiss stated: 'Judge Innes has a very distressed conscience, and I am one of the very few who knows it: and he knows I know it — and each night when he prays, he beseeches God to take me off somehow. This man has been at the head (nominally) of all this devilment, tho' in fact he has been only the creature of the more sensible villains, who to tickle his vanity and serve him, gave him the apparent commands. . .'

[2] Clay to Dr. R. Pindell, Oct. 15, 1828, Clay, *Corres.*, pp. 206–08; and, Wirt, in Edwards, *N. Edwards*, p. 432; H. Marshall, in N.Y. *Evening Post*, March 4, 1812; Coleman, *Jo Daveiss*; and introduction to Daveiss, J. H., *A View of the President's Conduct Concerning the Conspiracy of 1806. From the Press of Joseph M. Street, 1807*, reprint, edited with introduction by I. J. Cox and H. A. Swineford, *Qtrly. Pub. of the Hist. and Phil. Soc. of Ohio*, XII, 53–154. Although it seems generally to have been believed, as Clay stated, that Daveiss took the name Hamilton in honor of the great Federalist, Judge Samuel M. Wilson, the Kentucky historian, has informed the writer that Daveiss took the name from his mother's family.

[3] Jas. Morrison to Sen. Samuel Smith of Md. (brother-in-law of George Nicholas), long postscript of Oct. 6 to his letter of Sept. 29, 1806, *Samuel Smith MSS*. Morrison, an executor with Daveiss of Nicholas's estate, said there were documents ('known only to 3 or four persons — and I presume not to the Editors of the W. World, or to their Co-

a wholesale indictment of their Republican leaders as an indictment
of themselves. Their sympathy went out to Aaron Burr; for Burr,
after all, was a Republican, and without doubt the attacks upon
him were inspired by the same partisan malice.

Clay's Kentuckians demanded an end to this flood of calumny,
and drank such toasts as 'May the seventeen states be welded into
one united empire by the hammer of peace, on the anvil of reconciliation; and may he that attempts to blow the bellows of discord be burnt up by the sparks!' [1] Alas, the *Western World* continued to blow up its foul bellows. And in self-defense the people
countered with sharp goose quills; and with stronger weapons
against 'fighting editor' Street, who with pistol and dirk stalked
through Frankfort inviting assaults from the victims of his pen.[2]

'Early Inhabitant' and many others reviewed conditions when
Kentuckians, treated by the East as 'enemies or aliens,' had been
compelled to act by and for themselves. They abhorred this
stirring up of the muddy sediment of the past, now, when conditions had changed, Republicanism was triumphant, and frontier
rights and aspirations were close to the heart of their own Republican President. In a history of pioneer Kentucky, William
Littell assailed the *Western World* as 'an engine of depravity, in the
hands of a prostituted Junto.' It had revived transactions 'half-
veiled in antiquity' to stain unspotted reputations, 'by accusations
boldly made, and resolutely persisted in, and from the nature of
things not easily disproved.' How wonderful that the people for
years had been 'so utterly devoted to a band of traitors,' even
though for years 'the "still small voice" of *purity* speaking through

---

adjutors') to prove not only that Spain had made overtures to the pioneer leaders but
that these had been 'rejected with detestation & contempt.' Since any attempt to
refute the *Western World* Junto would only cause further misrepresentations, 'these
documents will not be brought forward.' Innes was forced to bring these documents
forward in December. See, also, Morrison to W. C. Nicholas, Dec. 11, 1806, and to
Robt. Smith, same date, *Wilson Cary Nicholas MSS.*

[1] *Ky. Gazette*, July 8, 1806; also, Aug. 25, 1806.

[2] There were several affrays — and only Daveiss and Marshall would go bail for
Street. Greatly to popular satisfaction, when George Adams (with Clay and young
John Allen as his counsel) was tried for the attempted murder of Street, he was at once
released — Jemmy Blair, the prosecutor, most conveniently forgot to charge that
Adams intended to kill when he fired his pistol at Street! Lex. *Reporter*, July 23, 1808;
and references in *Innes MSS.*, 22.

the lips of Humphrey Marshall' had been uttering these self-same tones of 'disappointed ambition and detected villainy.' [1]

Less elegant than Littell were the many other defenders of Kentucky's fair name. John Wood & Company were 'lumps of deformity and corruption,' vipers, blackguards, character-assassins. They were 'Skunks whose effluvia has drenched Frankfort' and engendered abusive reports throughout the Union that Kentuckians under Colonel Burr were ripe for revolt, eager for secession. [2]

Meanwhile young Henry Clay by 'artful management' was attempting to silence the noxious journal, which, as yet, had not pulled him into its vortex of calumny. One day at Philip Bush's Frankfort tavern he came across Wood and Street engaged in a violent quarrel. He helped to separate them. Wood afterward told him that the cause of their fight was the ascendency which Daveiss and Marshall had acquired over his partner and over their *Western World*. Henry was exceedingly sympathetic. And to him Wood confided that he had ventured West because of his 'strong passion' for young Street, who, alas, had now formed a deep attachment for Jo Daveiss. 'By every art of which he was master' the Federal Attorney had succeeded in making Street his devotee and willing tool. When Clay contended that Daveiss, although eccentric and prejudiced, was a man of integrity, Wood passionately declared that as long as he lived he would hold Jo Daveiss in the highest contempt. [3]

Despite his estrangement, and despite Clay's efforts to induce him to withdraw, Wood continued at the 'bellows of discord,' which were now being pumped so vigorously by Street and his

---

[1] Littell, Wm., *Political Transactions*, etc., pp. 3, 58, 59, *passim*.

[2] *Ky. Gazette*, Sept. 22, 1806, and *passim*. The Burrite-Spanish affair revived so many old feuds, some entirely unrelated, between the Marshall clan and its foes, that the *Gazette* on Nov. 13, 1806 announced that thereafter it would charge advertising rates for any polemics inspired by the 'Wonderful Conspiracy.'

[3] John Wood to Clay, Oct. 9, 1806; and, to same, Dec. 4, 1806, *Clay MSS*. Also, Wood to Wm. Hunter, editor of the Frankfort *Palladium*, June 22, 1807, *Innes MSS.*, 22; Safford, *Blennerhassett*, pp. 372–73; and Wood's address to the citizens of Franklin and Woodford counties in the *Atlantic World*, Jan. 19, 1807, in which he said that after the second issue of the journal 'I viewed Mr. D[aveiss] as a most dangerous character, and . . . I endeavoured to break off every connexion between him and my partner,' to whom I had been attached by 'more than common ties of affection.' Street 'had for several years been the first in my regard and the nearest to my heart.'

Federalist coadjutors. The older man's fortune was invested in the paper; and he was still hopeful of regaining the affections of his youthful partner. Henry, however, had won his confidence and respect; and had obtained conclusive proof of the partisan motivation of this sensational attack upon the Jeffersonian pioneers of Kentucky, and upon the ill-starred Aaron Burr.

With other citizens Clay had joined in welcoming the former Vice President, 'the inimitable, the incomparable, Burr,' to the hospitable Blue Grass. He scoffed at the specter of disunionism raised by Marshall's Junto — it was absurd to contend that Burr or anyone else could wean Kentuckians from Jefferson into secession. A Mexican filibuster upon the outbreak of the imminent war with Spain — that was an entirely different matter. As a prominent land lawyer, Henry had examined and pronounced valid the rather involved title to the Washita lands; and he was given to understand by Colonel Burr and his associates that the proposed colonization was known to Jefferson and had the President's approval. The young frontier attorney marvelled at Little Burr's self-possession under the most startling of accusations: silence under such circumstances was beyond the ken of Clay of Kentucky. Burr assured him, however, that silent contempt was ever the best policy; that time and time alone would set all things right.[1]

This had now become the opinion of Editor Dan Bradford, who the year before had been so suspicious. 'Publick curiosity is still on tiptoe relating to the object of Colonel Burr's visits to the Western country,' stated Bradford in October of 1806. 'That some grand object is in contemplation we have no doubt; and we are disposed to think that object not unfavourable to the interests of the union. At present it would be improper to publish our opinions; but if our suspicions are well-founded, a few months will probably lay his plans before the publick.'[2] A few months, however, was too long a time for Joseph Hamilton Daveiss.

'We have traitors among us,' he had been informing President

---

[1] Clay's account of Burr, Dec. 29, 1806, Plumer, *Memo*, p. 549; Clay, *Corres.*, pp. 206–08; and articles by Clay under pseudonym of 'Scaevola' and 'Regulus' in Lex. *Reporter*, June–July, 1808.

[2] *Ky. Gazette*, Oct. 30, 1806.

Jefferson in confidential and hysterical letters. In February
Daveiss had forwarded a long list of prominent Western Republicans which at first included Attorney General Breckinridge and
Henry Clay, although later he withdrew both, believing both to
be 'wholly innocent.' He assured Jefferson that he would 'soon
know all about it without *suspecting*.' Yet suspicion throughout
remained the basis for his fears and varied surmises: perhaps Spain
was again attempting to disunite and weaken America; perhaps
Burr planned an extensive Western Empire; again, it might be
merely a 'swindling trick played off on the Spaniards by our
countrymen.' [1]

His letters and frenzied labors were curtly acknowledged by
Jefferson, who advised him to send further and definite information. The President seemed reluctant to credit Federalist suspicions of treason levelled at Western Republicans, among them
governors of territories, state and Federal judges, several United
States senators, militia generals, and the commander of the American army.

'Good God!' cried the overwrought Daveiss, 'was ever anything
so astonishing! so unaccountable! That ... the government should
still keep me profoundly in the dark, never order me to do or
forbear anything, or give me one hint of their views!' He had
tried 'to awake this *snoring* administration; but to no purpose.' [2]
However, Joseph Hamilton Daveiss was still the United States
Attorney for Kentucky. And he was independent enough, and
indiscreet enough, to disregard official Washington. He went
ahead on his own responsibility to arrest this Wonderful Conspiracy, which he believed was intended to revolutionize the Western

---

[1] Daveiss wrote seven letters to Jefferson, Jan. 10–July 14, 1806, and two, Aug. 14,
Nov. 16, 1806, to Sec. of State Madison. The letters (originals in the *Jefferson MSS.*)
were printed by Daveiss in his *A View*, etc. The names of his suspects, deleted in the
original pamphlet, are given in the reprint edited by Cox and Swineford. His list of
Feb. 10, 1806 bore the names of Breckinridge, John Fowler, Wilkinson, Adair, Sen.
John Smith, Sebastian, Innes, Burr, Clay, and Wm. Henry Harrison. Later he
added Andrew Jackson and many others, including the French general, Moreau,
whom Bonaparte had exiled. On March 28 Daveiss professed doubts about the 'lawyer
of Lexington,' i.e., Clay; on July 14 he removed both Clay and Breckinridge from the
list; on Aug. 14 he doubted his action; but on Nov. 16, 1806 he declared them 'wholly
innocent.'

[2] Daveiss, *A View*, etc., p. 96.

states as well as Mexico, and to bring about a Napoleonic empire
ruled by Emperor Aaron the First.

On Wednesday, November 6, 1806, before the Federal Court
at Frankfort, Daveiss moved that a compulsory process be issued
for Aaron Burr's immediate apprehension, charging him with
preparing a warlike expedition against a friendly power. This, he
asserted, 'can and will be fully substantiated.' Proof equally conclusive could also be obtained for Burr's treasonable project for
separating the West from the Union, he added. But at present he
would confine himself to the formal charge of high misdemeanor.

So extraordinary, and so questionable, was his motion that
Judge Innes delayed giving his opinion until he had consulted with
Daveiss as to the law on specific and probable causes of action.
On Saturday, November 9, Innes denied the motion, holding
Daveiss's own affidavit insufficient and advising him to abide by
the regular procedure: to obtain legal evidence sufficient for a
warrant, or else to call for a grand jury investigation.[1]

Just as he finished reading his opinion, Aaron Burr entered the
courtroom and dramatically confronted Daveiss. This was entirely unexpected, for rumor had it that Burr had fled Lexington.
Instead, Burr had taken the offensive. Accompanied by such
respected men as General Samuel Hopkins and General Thomas
Posey (both Revolutionary colleagues of Burr); by Henry Clay,
and other legislators, he now presented himself, and to Daveiss's
surprise asked for an immediate investigation. Accordingly, a
grand jury was impanelled which was to meet the following
Tuesday.

'Fame had now full hold of the subject,' said Humphrey
Marshall, 'and seldom has she been more profuse in the use of her
many tongues, or impelled her messengers on more rapid wings.'[2]
Both Lexington's *Gazette* and Frankfort's *Palladium* reported that
Burr's voluntary appearance, along with his 'dignified, concise,

---

[1] Innes's opinion, and Innes–Daveiss letters, Nov. 5, 6, 1806, *Innes MSS.*, 18. Daveiss
admitted suspicion to be his basis, and that there was danger of false imprisonment, yet
he insisted upon a process to ascertain whether Burr was innocent or guilty of 'illegal
design.'

[2] Marshall, *Hist. Ky.*, II, 396.

and impressive' request for an inquiry, gave 'his enemies evident chagrin,' but 'to the impartial, that is, to nine-tenths of the house, it gave the utmost satisfaction.' It was agreed that 'publick opinion in Frankfort appears very much in favour of Col. Burr.' [1]

To assist him, Burr requested and obtained the services of Henry Clay and of young John Allen of Frankfort. That he should select Clay as his chief counsel was not surprising, said the sarcastic Marshall: 'When in Lexington who could not find the market-house of a Wednesday, or Saturday morning? In Frankfort, who could not find the state-house? Was not Mr. Clay equally conspicuous?' [2]

Both attorneys were fully convinced that Burr was innocent, and that Daveiss's prosecution was grounded solely on his Federalist prejudices and fanatical admiration for Hamilton. 'Such was our conviction of the innocence of the accused,' said Clay later, 'that, when he sent us a considerable fee, we resolved to decline accepting it, and accordingly returned it. We said to each other, Colonel Burr has been an eminent member of the profession, has been an Attorney General of the State of New York, is prosecuted without cause in a distant State, and we ought not to regard him in the light of an ordinary culprit.' [3]

Supported by these two young lawyers, Aaron Burr on the following Tuesday entered a courthouse crowded with citizens eager to learn which of the many sensational rumors and charges were to be pressed. But no sooner was the court called to order than Jo Daveiss arose and requested the grand jury's dismissal! Of the thirteen witnesses summoned all were present but Davis Floyd, reputed quartermaster of Burr's armada, who was then attending the Indiana Legislature. Because of this one man's absence Daveiss refused to go ahead. The jury was accordingly dismissed — but not before Burr himself asked that the reason be recorded, and assured the people that Mr. Attorney's suspicions would prove quite groundless if ever they were put to the test. His 'moderation and firmness,' his 'earnest desire for a full and

---

[1] *Ky. Gazette*, Nov. 10, and Nov. 17 (quoting *Palladium*), 1806.
[2] Marshall, in *Ky. Gazette*, Jan. 28, 1832.
[3] Clay to Pindell, Oct. 15, 1828, Clay, *Corres.*, pp. 206–08.

speedy investigation,' inspired 'the strongest sensations of respect and friendship.' Public sentiment in Burr's favor 'now burst forth without disguise.' [1]

Thus the first attempt to indict 'Emperor Aaron the First' had collapsed, and in a manner which subjected Jo Daveiss to popular condemnation. 'The disappointment and chagrin of a crowded audience may be conceived, but the ridicule and laughter which followed was universal,' reported the Frankfort *Palladium*. 'The people,' complained Daveiss, 'seemed to vie with each other in folly, and a zeal to distinguish and caress this *persecuted patriot*.' Like some magician, Burr had captivated Kentucky *en masse*, 'wrought a spell or enchantment on the whole people and their magistracy.' [2] Despite his malignant machinations, said the *Western World*, he 'is courted and regarded in Frankfort and Lexington more in the capacity of a supernatural being, than a wandering conspirator.' [3]

Aaron Burr's spell was less potent, however, in Eastern America, where alarming rumors filled the press. The notorious General Eaton, former consul to Algiers, publicly stated that Burr had asked him to join in a disunionist plot. Widely reprinted were two essays from the *Ohio Gazette*, attributed to Blennerhassett, advocating the secession of Trans-Allegheny. National attention was commanded by the *Western World's* accounts of Burr's 'immense revolution.' Undeterred by Daveiss's abortive action, it declared its 'certain belief' that the plot was as extensive as the Western Hemisphere. Miranda would revolutionize South America, Burr the Western states and Mexico. One mighty empire from the Arctic to Cape Horn 'headed by a man of the enterprise and talents of Colonel Burr, will present a phenomenon in the political history of the globe perhaps only equalled by the modern Empire of France.' [4]

Maintaining his pregnant silence, the alleged American Bonaparte continued his preparations, his recruiting of men and supplies, his building of boats at Blennerhassett's Island. President

---

[1] *Palladium*, Nov. 13, in *Ky. Gazette*, Nov. 17, 1806.
[2] Daveiss, *A View*, p. 102.   [3] *Western World*, in N.Y. *Herald*, Dec. 17, 1806.
[4] *Loc. cit.*; also N.Y. *Herald* and Phila. *Aurora*, Nov. 1806 ff.

Jefferson also remained silent, taking no public cognizance of the rumors which perplexed and enfevered the nation. Conjectures 'actually swarm around us,' said the *National Intelligencer* of Washington; many are such 'that it might be criminal either to treat them with indifference, or to receive them.' [1] Surmises 'as various as the Camelion's colours' filled Tom Ritchie's Richmond *Enquirer*; yet Ritchie, like his friend Clay, regarded Burr as too sensible a man to be credited with these 'monstrous tales' of disunion.[2] No one but a maniac, said the *Virginia Argus*, would try to alienate from the Union 'the hardy Republicans of the West.' [3]

This was the general opinion in Kentucky. Aaron Burr would surely adapt the means to the end. 'Can it be supposed he has done so,' asked Editor Hunter of the Frankfort *Palladium*, 'if his object is to attack Mexico, dismember the Union, and erect an independent empire, by building a few boats on the Ohio and by a few secret emissaries scattered over the Western Country? The physical force to do this lies with the people, and to command it, public opinion must be with him.' The people, especially the warm-hearted patriots of Kentucky, would immediately and emphatically oppose any project that might in the least endanger the American Union.[4]

Meanwhile in his opening message to the Assembly Governor Greenup, whose patriotism not even Jo Daveiss dared question, had disdained to take the slightest notice of the Wonderful Conspiracy. Indeed, both he and the legislators paid marked honors to Colonel Burr. The Governor ceremoniously dined him, members of both chambers visited him, he was invited to sit in the House, and on his strolls about Frankfort he was accompanied by legislators who had been his fellow soldiers in the Revolution.[5] All this further inflamed Daveiss. He was impressed by the 'great abundance of mysterious whispers' in the Assembly that Jefferson

[1] In Phila. *Aurora*, Nov. 17, 1806.

[2] Richmond *Enquirer*, Dec. 9 and Dec. 13, 1806.

[3] *Va. Argus*, Nov. 28, 1806 — a filibuster was more likely: 'artfully to rouse the resentment of the western people against... Spain, to insinuate by *innuendo* the backwardness and timidity of the government, to tamper with the military, to allure them by delusive prospects of the plunder of Mexican treasures... seem to present to... disappointed ambition a prospect at once more dazzling and less hopeless.'

[4] In *Ky. Gazette*, Nov. 17, 1806.   [5] Lex. *Reporter*, July 9, 1808.

sanctioned Burr's expedition; indeed, that Jefferson had instigated it. 'How wonderfully numerous the friends or neutrals of this infernal scheme!!!' [1]

Three days later Daveiss was given striking proof of how numerous in the Assembly were the friends of young Henry Clay. A week to a day after he appeared as Burr's senior counsel, the Lexington lawyer was overwhelmingly elected to the United States Senate. The term of John Breckinridge which Adair was completing was to expire in March of 1807. When John Pope of Fayette defeated him for the coveted six years' term, Adair angrily resigned. To serve out the remainder of his term, Clay on November 19 was elected over George Bibb, Fayette Circuit judge, by a vote of 68 to 10. Even Felix Grundy voted for him.[2] On that same day Henry gave up his seat. Yet before he could arrange his affairs and leave for Washington he was once again called upon to serve as Burr's counsel.

Certain that the crisis was at hand, Jo Daveiss on November 25 had moved for another grand jury to indict the elusive Burr. Mingled with motives he attributed to patriotism was a resentment of Jefferson's 'negligent and flagitious' conduct, a hatred of Hamilton's 'murderer,' and a smarting sense of the ridicule he had suffered from a people who seemed to be supporting 'this Catiline's conspiracy' to a man. He was further encouraged to renew the attack by a legislative investigation, instigated by Humphrey Marshall, into old Judge Sebastian's Spanish pension.

Although Sebastian resigned before the committee reported on December 6, and although he protested that his object in 1795-97 was not disunion but a commercial treaty opening up the Spanish-estopped Mississippi, the fact remained that a Kentucky judge had been receiving a Spanish pension.[3] First blood had been drawn

---

[1] Daveiss to Madison, Nov. 16, 1806, Daveiss, *A View*, p. 98; also, p. 79.

[2] *Journal of House, 1806*, pp. 60–66. Adair regarded his defeat as evidence of non-confidence; yet not one vote did he lose, said Clay, because of his connection with Burr. Clay told Plumer 'that Adair was never popular — that Pope was always so — & had a great advantage over Adair by being a member of the legislature who elected the senator.' Plumer, *Memo*, pp. 552–53; Dec. 31, 1806.

[3] *Journal of House, 1806*, p. 84 ff. [Sebastian, B.], *Report of the Select Committee* etc., on Sebastian, 1806; also, *Annals of Congress*, 10th, 1st, 2760–90. Daveiss and a few others had known of Sebastian's pension since 1804, when papers of the Judge had been intercepted.

by the Federalist Junto! Furthermore, the testimony of Judge
Innes as to Sebastian's Spanish proposals, which he and George
Nicholas had 'unequivocally' rejected, tended to confirm the
Junto's charges of a pioneer 'Spanish Association' and to increase
the confusion attending Burr's enterprise.[1] To avoid misrepresentations, the Assembly on December 3 unanimously resolved
that Kentuckians were devoted to the Union, and would to a man
oppose 'any individuals or sets of individuals' who might attempt
to dissever it.[2]

Meanwhile, on November 27, two days after Daveiss had moved
for another grand jury, Colonel Burr from Louisville had requested
Clay to delay his journey to Washington and to continue in the
case.[3] That the former Vice President should request him, even
entreat him, was flattering to the young frontier lawyer. But
Henry was now a United States senator-elect and there was the
question of propriety in opposing the United States Attorney.
His loyalty to his clients was appealed to by Burr; a client whose
noted composure now seemed ruffled by the sensational and per-
plexing turn given events by the Sebastian inquiry, then under
way, and by Joseph Hamilton Daveiss's persistence despite
popular condemnation.

Was it likely that Daveiss would again invite ridicule by a hastily
prepared case? Was it not probable that he might convert his
earlier charge of misdemeanor into one of treason?

Colonel Burr was courteously importunate; and Clay consented
to appear as his advocate — but not before he had received from
Burr the following categorical and comprehensive disclaimer:

> I have no design, nor have I taken any measure to promote a
> dissolution of the Union, or a separation of any one or more States
> from the residue. I have neither published a line on this subject
> nor has any one, through my agency, or with my knowledge. I

---

[1] In testifying, Innes (then presiding over the second Burr arraignment), had broken
down, 'cried like a child, was attacked with a Vertigo that night, and was under the
necessity of being bled twice. Thus it is that weak men, innocently inclined, feel
ashamed and abashed at the development of their folly,' wrote young Wm. T. Barry,
to John Barry, Dec. 6, 1806, Barry, Wm. T., 'Letters,' ed. I. J. Cox, *Amer. Hist. Rev.*,
XVI, 328–29.

[2] *Session Acts, 1806*, pp. 165–66; also, *Ky. Broadsides*.

[3] Burr to Clay, Nov. 27, 1806, Clay, *Corres.*, p. 13.

have no design to intermeddle with the Government or to disturb the tranquillity of the United States, or of its territories, or any part of them. I have neither issued, nor signed, nor promised a commission to any person for any purpose. I do not own a musket nor a bayonet, nor any single article of military stores, nor does any person for me, by my authority or with my knowledge.

My views have been fully explained to, and approved by, several of the principal officers of Government, and, I believe, are well understood by the administration and seen by it with complacency. They are such as every man of honor and every good citizen must approve.

Considering the high station you now fill in our national councils, I have thought these explanations proper, as well to counteract the chimerical tales which malevolent persons have so industriously circulated, as to satisfy you that you have not espoused the cause of a man in any way unfriendly to the laws, the government, or the interests of his country.[1]

On the following day, December 2, the curtain went up on the last act in Kentucky of this romantic drama so replete with alarums and excursions. The second and final arraignment of Aaron Burr was for Henry Clay's Kentuckians the culmination of a year big with momentous events in Bonapartist Europe and with startling rumors in Jeffersonian America. Throughout the young and gawky republic there was an expectant uneasiness. In the Western World nature had aided in setting the background — there had been an eclipse of the sun in June, and a severe drought continuing into late autumn had withered the crops and caused Providence to be invoked to avert threatened disasters. Western skies were still overcast with war clouds rolling up from the Mexican border, where Wilkinson's troops faced those of Spain, when the proceedings began in the state house at Frankfort.

The courtroom was crowded to the rafters long before Judge Harry Innes made his appearance. Outside, despite the bitter cold and deep snow, people excitedly milled about as reports and rumors were relayed from within by those fortunate enough to get seats or standing room. What was to be the nature of the indict-

---

[1] Burr to Clay, Frankfort, Dec. 1, 1806, Clay, *Corres.*, pp. 13–14. Similar disclaimers were written by Burr to other prominent Westerners — to Andrew Jackson, W. H. Harrison, to Senator John Smith of Ohio.

ment against Aaron Burr and his associates? Would Jo Daveiss now prove his disunionist accusations and reveal that 'conclusive evidence' which he and the *Western World* claimed they possessed?

It was a motley crowd that witnessed the ensuing debates between Henry Clay and Jo Daveiss — Blue Grass planters, cadaverous mountaineers, shaggy Green River men; old gentlemen in smallclothes like Colonel Meade of Chaumière (an ardent Burr admirer); farmers and artisans like John Robert Shaw in striped yarn stockings and loose pantaloons, shirted hunters, and young dandies in the finery of the *Incroyables*; merchants, lawyers, and legislators. Many of these 'free-born sons of the Western World' had fought Indian, Briton, and Hessian; few needed any war-whooping to fight the Spanish Don. They were now curious and excited, for the startling rumors brought into question their own loyalty to the American Union.

Since the Political Revolution of 1800 these men had repeatedly voiced their confidence in 'the United States one and indivisible.' Had they not here in Frankfort during the Louisiana crisis mobbed a wretched fellow who dared suggest disunion? Not inconsistent, surely, with their devotion to the Union was their desire to expand it — into Florida and Mexico, into British Canada and (as General Wilkinson had recently written to Burrite John Adair) into California and the Isthmus of Panama. Not inconsistent with their Republicanism was their desire to give it a wider spread — to give the 'wretched' colonials of insane George the Third and imbecilic Carlos the Fourth 'those inestimable blessings of freedom which we ourselves enjoy.' [1]

With very few exceptions these men were devoted to Thomas Jefferson — the great 'Man of the People' whose purchase of Louisiana, that glorious 'Extension of America's Empire,' had doubled the area of the republic; whose party newspaper at Washington was then stressing the advantages of a more extensive territory; [2] whose foreign policy since 1803 had been centered on

---

[1] Andrew Jackson two weeks before had expressed their views: 'I love my Country and government. I hate the Dons. I would delight to see Mexico reduced, but I will die in the last Ditch before I would yield a foot to the Dons or see the Union disunited.' To Gov. Wm. Claiborne of Orleans Ter., Nov. 12, 1806, Jackson, *Corres.*, I, 153.

[2] *National Intelligencer*, in *Va. Argus*, issues of Nov. 1806.

'his hobby, more Louisiana.' [1] These Children of America had sanction in the highest quarter for their territorial imperialism. They were Kentuckians, the leaders, the very backbone of this adventurous Western World; and 'Kentuckyans are full of enterprise and although not poor, as greedy after plunder as ever the old Romans were,' General Adair had recently written to Burrite James Wilkinson: 'Mexico glitters in our Eyes — the word is all we wait for.' [2] The man who was to give that pregnant word was now here in Frankfort, being investigated ('persecuted,' said the Republicans of Kentucky) by Federalist Jo Daveiss.

And it looked like persecution that opening day, just after Judge Innes with unusual solemnity had charged the jury, when Daveiss arose — and again asked for an adjournment. His witnesses were all present except John Adair and one other, but without General Adair he refused to proceed. A surprised and resentful crowd supported Henry Clay when he at once voiced emphatic protest.

This was the second time Colonel Burr had been forced to dance attendance upon Mr. Daveiss, said Clay. No sooner had he left Kentucky when Daveiss had summoned another grand jury and alarmed the country with 'rumours of an immediate insurrection, the enlistment of men, the purchasing of provisions and military stores, the equipment of gunboats and flotillas, the arrival of boats loaded with muskets, powder and ball, and the issuing of blank commissions; in short, the whole fancy of the Attorney was exerted to muster up every appendage connected with conspiracies, plots and combinations.' Would Daveiss dare repeat his earlier 'farce and pantomime'? [3]

'Is a stranger to be harassed and perplexed in this manner,' demanded Lawyer Clay, now warmed to his subject; 'to have his time and attention diverted from his own affairs, to be tortured and obliged to account to this court for every action, even those of the most trifling nature, in order to gratify the whim and caprice of

---

[1] Taggart, *Letters*, p. 194, March 24, 1806.

[2] Adair to Wilkinson, Dec. 10, 1804, Pratt, J. W., *Expansionists of 1812*, p. 62.

[3] The account of the proceedings here used is from Wood, John, *A Full Statement of the Trial and Acquittal of Aaron Burr, Esq.*, etc. — comparison having been made with the shorter but substantially the same accounts in the *Western World* and Frankfort *Palladium* (both in *National Intelligencer*, Jan. 2, 5, 12, 1807).

the Federal Attorney? God forbid! Let not, for Heaven's sake, such a stigma be affixed to the character of Kentucky. Let it not be said that no stranger can pass through our country without the most atrocious charges being advanced against him. No — we are not so barbarous. Whatever the public attorney may imagine, whatever arts he may use, it will be impossible that he can ever impose so far upon the credulity of our citizens.'

Repeating his motion for an adjournment, Daveiss complained that Burr and his counsel were attempting to obstruct and defeat the investigation. 'They imagine if the jury go out, and no true bill is found, which in the absence of material witnesses will be the case, that their triumph will be glorious, that the popularity of Colonel Burr will increase, and that he will be regarded as the object of a malicious prosecution.' He deeply resented the interference of Mr. Clay. Neither his presence nor that of Colonel Burr, he tartly remarked, had as yet been required by the court.

At once and with great feeling Henry asked how Daveiss could expect Mr. Burr to be indifferent to such enormous accusations. 'No such idea can be entertained but by those who either lost to every sense of honour and shame are callous with regard to public opinion, or who being by nature cold and phlegmatic feel neither for themselves or for others.' After this jab at Daveiss he declared that Burr, alive to the tenderest emotions, attuned to the most delicate sensibilities, and conscious of patriotic intentions, had but one desire: the prompt clearing of his good name. Is such a man, asked Clay, 'to be mentioned with reproach and then made the butt of slander because there is no process out against him, because no deputy Marshal has laid his hand upon his shoulder? Is he on that account to remain idle, is he to have no opportunity of vindication, is he to be treated with scorn and contempt because he has voluntarily presented himself to this grand jury, and because he has not, as probably was expected by the Attorney, run off and endeavoured to escape from investigation?'

After these 'animated and ingenuous' remarks which 'commanded the assent and admiration of the audience,' [1] Burr's advocate turned his oratorical batteries upon Daveiss's 'most

[1] Frankfort *Palladium*, in *Natl. Intelligencer*, Jan. 5, 1807.

singular' attempt 'to force upon the court principles which were never heard of before — to call and adjourn the grand jury at his pleasure,' to make it a weathercock to be turned and twisted at his whim. Were Jo Daveiss given such privileges, said Henry, 'there is no saying when his thirst after power might stop. He might, for aught I know, next take into his head to make presentments as well as to draw indictments; in short, sir, he might proceed to assume and exercise all the rights of the grand jury — in fact, to become a grand jury himself.'

At length the court granted the motion to adjourn. Judge Innes explained, however, that he did so because of the lateness of the hour, and he took the opportunity to express regret that he had discharged the grand jury at the first arraignment when all but one of the thirteen witnesses had been in attendance.

A final skirmish was then fought when Daveiss requested an attachment to secure General Adair's presence on the morrow. Clay contended, and was sustained by the court, that since no hour was designated on the subpoena, Adair fulfilled what the law required if he appeared that day at any time up to midnight. With ill-concealed displeasure Daveiss admitted such to be the practice. Yet he could not resist saying, pointedly, 'that the practice of duellists has always been to name the hour of appointment.' At this Colonel Burr, victor in the duel with Hamilton, rose not to rebuke Joseph Hamilton Daveiss, but to offer him assistance. Standing beside his tall and aggressive young counsel, Little Burr in his mildest tone said that he himself, if it pleased Mr. Attorney, would write General Adair and urge his prompt attendance in court on the morrow. His polite offer was rejected.

The courtroom then disgorged its spectators. Burr and Clay and young John Allen dined with many well-wishers at the Golden Eagle. Daveiss and Marshall and Street in private brooded over the day's proceedings. 'The unusual concourse of people' broke up into earnest groups which discussed the day's events and speculated upon the morrow's. Would Adair appear, and would he and Burr be indicted for a filibuster against 'the Reptile Spaniards' or a treasonable plot against 'the United States one and indivisible'? Would Daveiss and the *Western World* Junto again attempt to deceive Kentucky with trumped-up charges, or would they be compelled to reveal their alleged 'conclusive evidence' as to Burr's Napoleonic ambitions?

Meanwhile the chief figure in the drama moved about Frankfort, the object of curiosity and critical attention. Yet 'there was about him nothing of the restlessness and preoccupation that usually characterizes the manner of those engaged in secret plots,' according to one of the many younger men who gathered about Colonel Burr in respectful and unaffected admiration. 'He was the most perfect gentleman in his manner I ever saw. His mien was not by any means commanding, nor did he try to make it so; but with his sharp, handsome, resolute face, and light, graceful figure, always dressed with scrupulous neatness, his appearance was very striking.'

Young Kentuckians discussed with him the resources and prospects of Western America — 'points so important to one about to embark the wreck of his fortune in land speculations.' They were impressed as were their elders by Mr. Burr's range and originality of ideas, and by his fascinating address. 'Whether it was a dissertation on the English poets, a criticism on the military plans of Napoleon, or an inquiry into the most abstruse branches of metaphysical philosophy, he seemed at home equally in all; and in all displayed the profoundly analytical turn of his genius. No wonder if we boys could not dream of our pleasant companion as a traitor.' [1]

No wonder that frontier romantics should acclaim him as 'the inimitable, the incomparable, Burr.' Or that Daveiss should lament that the enchanting spell he had wrought 'on the whole people' was on young Kentuckians wrought 'with a success at once astonishing and mortifying to a true American.' [2] Or that Henry Clay, in his rôle of advocate, armed with Burr's comprehensive and categorical disclaimer, should on the morrow continue to espouse the cause of his distinguished client with energy and spirit.

On Wednesday morning, December 3, General Adair being present, Daveiss promptly laid before the grand jury an indictment against Adair for having on August 1, 1806, in Mercer County, set on foot an unlawful expedition for the invasion of Mexico and

---

[1] Coleman, *Daveiss*, pp. 352–53.   [2] Daveiss, *A View*, p. 100.

other provinces of His Catholic Majesty, Charles IV of Spain, and
against the peace and dignity of the United States. No charge or
allegation of disunionism was made. The investigating body of
which he asked a presentment was made up of prominent and
most reputable citizens. Even the sardonic Humphrey Marshall
declared that the grand jury was 'then, and since, considered
respectable and intelligent.' ¹ But by no means was the Federal
Attorney willing to allow the jurors to interrogate the witnesses
independently of his aid and direction. This was the key to the
memorable debates between Daveiss and Clay.

A true bill against Adair, and against Burr, is impossible,
insisted Daveiss, 'unless I be present at the [witnesses'] examination
and assist in putting those questions which I know will force the
truth and lead to the disclosure of facts.' No person 'who is a
stranger to the nefarious machinations which are carrying on can
collect together the chain of circumstances that constitute the
necessary proof.' He himself must be present; and upon this point
he insisted with all his power. At the same time, however, privately
he admitted to Madison that 'no authority is appointed in such
cases to examine the witnesses.' ²

Anticipating this maneuver, Clay the day before had contended that the Attorney should go before the jurors only when they
asked his opinion on matters of law, not evidence; and now he
vigorously protested against 'this novelty in the code of criminal
jurisprudence.' When would Mr. Daveiss cease his revolutionizing
attempts to turn the jury 'into a bauble for his fancy to play
upon'? The indictment is sufficiently clear, said Clay. It requires
neither extraordinary judgment nor depth of sagacity for the
Attorney to frame questions to be put to the witnesses. Without
doubt our Kentucky jurors are intelligent enough to exercise their
lawful functions without the aid of Mr. Attorney's ingenious and
dangerous novelties.

'The only novelty which I see in this court is Mr. Clay,' retorted

---

¹ Marshall, *Hist. Ky.*, II, 410.

² Daveiss to Madison, Nov. 16, 1806, Daveiss, *A View*, p. 99. 'I never knew,' he also
remarked to Madison, 'till I made particular examination, that no law forbids an
attempt to disunite the states.'

Daveiss, who plainly showed his irritation. But Henry was undeterred. Daveiss had given him a grand opportunity to put the
affair in the light of a persecution, and to appear as the champion
of republican institutions and the orderly processes of the law.

'I presume, sir,' said Clay, 'that if on this occasion I be thought
to indulge too freely in expressing the honest sentiments of my
mind with regard to the extraordinary request of the Attorney, a
desire of preserving the rights of my fellow citizens will be the only
cause imputed to me. For their rights and for the liberty of my
country I shall never cease to contend.' He would protect the
grand jury, 'that great palladium of our rights,' from being transformed into 'an inquisitorial tribunal for the torturing of virtuous
citizens.' As the Torquemada, the Grand Inquisitor of Kentucky,
Daveiss would 'screw from the witnesses, with instruments he has
previously prepared, such confessions as will best answer his purpose. Such, sir, is the establishment which the Attorney is desirous
of forming in place of the good, old, and found institution of the
grand jury. It is, I confess, a chimerical monster, and one which I
trust will never find a place in this country, except in the brain of
the gentleman who has proposed it. The woods of Kentucky, I
hope, will never be made the abode of inquisitors, or our simple
establishments exchanged for the horrid cells of deception and
tyranny.'

Attacking the request on the ground of legal precedent, Clay
said he would 'even appeal to the courts of Great Britain. There,
where law is tyranny, and its ministers tyrants — when compared
to the mild system and impartial judges of our free constitution —
such a proposal as the one just made by the Attorney of this court
would be rejected with the contempt it deserves.' If his motion 'be
either bottomed upon right or founded upon law, I yield the
argument,' he concluded. 'But, confident as I am that he is supported by neither, and that the principle for which he contends is
subversive both of every right and of every law, and that the
consequences... will lead to the effects of the most dangerous
nature to our liberty and our rights, I regard it my duty not only in
the situation I now stand, but as a citizen of the state, to oppose it.'

Daveiss insisted that his motion did not jeopardize constitutional

liberties — even if a true bill were found the accused could still
have a fair trial. He was unmoved, he said, by Mr. Clay's display
of 'all the figures of rhetoric,' unenchanted by his eloquence.
'What I ask is no novelty; it is the practice, and has been the
practice, in every court with which I am acquainted.'

This assertion was too much for young John Allen, heretofore
silent, who challenged Daveiss to cite 'a single instance where such
a practice was ever tolerated. I know he cannot. The thing never
was done . . . It is against the spirit and laws both of this state and
every other state in the union.'

'I care not with Mr. Allen,' said Clay, again leaping into the
fray, 'in what attitude or capacity I am standing here, whether as
counsel for Colonel Burr or simply as . . . a private citizen combatting for those rights and for those liberties which shall ever be
the objects first in my mind and nearest to my heart. Did I entertain,' he stated, deliberately and earnestly, 'the remotest idea of
Colonel Burr's guilt, or of the truth of those charges which have
been advanced against him, I should instantly renounce both him
and his cause; I should spurn the thought of appearing as his
advocate or countenancing vice, which I trust I hold in equal
abhorrence with the public attorney or any other man. But I
believe the charges have not the smallest foundation in truth; I am
confident they are only founded on idle rumours and the weakest
credulity; that they are the machinations of malice, jealousy, and
suspicion, that have been imposed upon the public attorney, and
which have only assumed a serious shape by the solemnity of an
affidavit.'

The debate continued, with Daveiss insisting upon the propriety of his motion but unable to cite any precedent for it, with
Clay stressing (for the jurors' benefit) the fact that the whole
proceedings rested solely upon Daveiss's affidavit and picturing
freely the awful consequences of his 'novelty in the code of criminal
jurisprudence.' This might well be the precursor of Spain's Inquisition, Britain's Star Chamber, and Robespierre's bloody
tribunal. Plots and conspiracies will be more common than cases
of assault. 'There will be no escaping the claws of the public
attorney; he may indict and persecute whenever his fancy may

direct, or his malice may suggest.' With his catamount eyes flashing, his tall straight form quivering with emotion, Burr's eloquent advocate protested against the importation into republican America, into democratic Kentucky of all places, of the rack, the block, and the lash of a degenerate Old World.

Finally the court settled the heated argument. Daveiss's request was improper, Judge Innes decided. It was unsupported by legal precedent or by the practice of the court, over which he had long presided and of which he had once been the attorney. If the grand jurors should request Mr. Daveiss's opinion on matters of law, he could go to them. Otherwise he must remain in court.

On Thursday morning Daveiss proceeded to read aloud a list of questions to guide the jurors in examining the witnesses. Several of them, he said, were based on information he had obtained from Thomas Read, a young lawyer of Danville, whom Adair had tried to enlist as a Burrite volunteer. No sooner had he said this than Read, who was in court, jumped to his feet and pledged his honor that never had such conversations between him and Daveiss taken place. Giving Daveiss the lie direct, he yelled that this was 'a malicious fabrication . . . to injure the rising reputation of a young man!' Pressing forward to the bar, with fist upraised, he lunged at Daveiss. Innes interposed, stopped their incipient fist fight, and suggested that the two lawyers settle their differences outside of court.

This byplay was not of a nature to convince the audience that Daveiss, even if he had been permitted to control the jury's investigation, would have been much benefited.

About one o'clock that day the grand jury made a report on the indictment against John Adair — 'Not a true bill.' There were shouts from the people, then a prolonged hum of voices. Taking under advisement a similar indictment against Aaron Burr, the jury retired. At five o'clock court adjourned with the charges against the former Vice President still under deliberation.

On Friday, December 5, the last day of the Burr proceedings, about half an hour after the jury had gone to its room a deputy marshal entered, went to the bench, and whispered a few words to Judge Innes. 'A buz ran through the courtroom that the grand jury had sent for other witnesses — witnesses not discovered or offered by the District Attorney. Conjecture and expectation were alive, but were succeeded by astonishment when Messrs. Wood and Street, editors of the *Western World*, were brought into court and sworn as witnesses and severally sent to the grand jury.' [1]

As the door closed upon them, the waiting people asked each other why Daveiss had neglected to call these two men who for months had shaken the republic with their monstrous charges. Repeatedly had they declared themselves possessed of conclusive evidence as to Burr's object — his 'immense revolution.' As early as July they had stated: 'We know the proceedings of his agents in this state, at Orleans, and at St. Louis; we are perfectly informed of the nature of his *contract* with General Wilkinson, as likewise the *articles* agreed to at Frankfort between him and Mr. John Brown.' [2] Now their evidence could be given in court. They could aid in finding a true bill on the indictment drawn by their coadjutor against Aaron Burr.

Probably no Kentucky grand jury ever approached witnesses with greater expectancy than did Foreman Abraham Hite and his colleagues. And probably none ever received such a shock.

With a file of the sensational *Western World* spread before them, the jurors examined the two editors. Astonished, they heard Street under oath declare he could furnish no evidence whatsoever! All his information was rumor or hearsay. Astounded, they heard Wood testify that none of his vast fund of information constituted legal evidence! Indeed, Wood said he was now satisfied that the 'articles' with Brown related only to an Ohio canal; that the 'contract' with Wilkinson, and the activities of Burr's emissaries, concerned only land speculations; and, further, that he himself had come 'to believe that the present designs of Colonel Burr are neither against the government or laws of the United States.'

After this startling testimony by the Junto's fighting and writing editors, other witnesses confirmed the Washita land purchase and revealed that a Mexican filibuster, in event of war with Spain, had

[1] Frankfort *Palladium*, in *Natl. Intelligencer*, Jan. 5, 1807.
[2] *Western World*, in *Ky. Gazette*, July 19, 1806.

been discussed, and that such a project, so they had been assured, was not without the sanction of President Jefferson.[1]

At two o'clock that day the grand jury filed into court and returned the indictment — 'Not a true bill.' The report was unanimous. But the jurors were not content with thus acquitting Burr. 'Considering how greatly the public mind has been agitated,' they took the extraordinary step of making public a signed statement.

'We have no hesitation in declaring,' said Foreman Hite, reading aloud from this unusual document, 'that having carefully examined and scrutinized all the testimony' affecting both Aaron Burr and John Adair, that there has been none 'which does in the smallest degree criminate the conduct of either of those persons; nor can we from all the enquiry and investigation of the subject discover that any thing improper or injurious to the government or the interests of the United States, or contrary to the laws thereof, is designed or contemplated by either of them.'

Wild huzzas greeted this vindication. A cheering people surrounded Colonel Burr and his counsel. 'A scene was presented in the Court-room which I had never before witnessed in Kentucky,' said Henry Clay. 'There were shouts of applause from an audience, not one of whom, I am persuaded, would have hesitated to level a rifle against Colonel Burr, if he believed that he aimed to dismember the Union, or sought to violate its peace, or overturn its Constitution.'[2] No man can imagine the jubilation of this public demonstration, reported Ninian Edwards: 'To have any correct idea of it, a man must have witnessed it.'[3] Clay and Allen 'could scarcely contain their joy,' growled Humphrey Marshall; as for Mr. Burr, he had been given 'an eclat and an elevation . . . which he could not, had he been innocent, ever aspired to.'[4]

In contrast with the people's joy was the Junto's acidulous gloom. The jurors' public statement, said Daveiss, had been con-

---

[1] Richmond *Enquirer*, Jan. 6 (letter from Frankfort), and Jan. 15, 1807. The *Enquirer* of Jan. 10, 1807, has the testimony of Wood and Street similar to that given in John Wood's *A Full Statement*.

[2] Clay to Pindell, Oct. 15, 1828, Clay, *Corres.*, p. 207.

[3] Edwards to Wm. Wirt, Jan. 5, 1807, Edwards, *N. Edwards*, p. 283.

[4] Marshall, *Hist. Ky.*, II, 411.

ceived 'wholly with a personal view — to bury alive a man who should stir a question which brought to the people's mind the old Spanish business, and thwarted our good saviour, Mr. Burr, in his patriotic endeavours to give a wider spread to republicanism.' [1] Snarling at the prejudice of the judge, the craft of the witnesses, and the gullibility of the people, Marshall declared that the jurors' 'MANIFESTO' spoke for itself — it could not better deceive had it been written by Aaron Burr or Henry Clay.[2] 'Why this eulogium?' demanded Street, no longer the amazingly ignorant witness but Marshall's 'fighting editor of sterling mettle,' omniscient as to the Wonderful Conspiracy. Did not the jury 'see every nerve extended by Col. Burr and his counsel to suppress enquiry? Does this look like innocence?' Once again possessed of 'certain proof,' Editor Street declared that the 'altogether unprecedented address' of the jury only strengthened the idea that Burr's project was 'inimical to the perpetuity of the union.' [3]

Now thoroughly discredited, however, were Street and his Federalist coadjutors. Their bubble had been pricked. Upon official inquiry, announced handbill extras on the dramatic day of acquittal, it has been clearly established 'that the rumour circulated throughout the United States, that Col. Burr's project was to divide the union, & to separate the Eastern from the Western states, is totally false and groundless.' [4] Editor Hunter of the *Palladium* expressed his hope and his belief that the great distinction and influence thus acquired by Colonel Burr 'will be used by him in such a manner only as shall promote the honor and interest of the country.' [5]

The Wonderful Conspiracy appeared to be thoroughly punctured. Wood withdrew from the *Western World*, and borrowed enough money from Clay to get back East.[6] Street remained to

---

[1] Daveiss, *A View*, p. 103.   [2] Marshall, *op. cit.*, II, 410.

[3] *Western World*, Dec. 18, 1806, in *Natl. Intelligencer*, Jan. 12, 1807.

[4] *Palladium* extra, Dec. 5, 1806, in *Blennerhassett MSS*.

[5] Frankfort *Palladium*, Dec. 11, 1806, in *Natl. Intelligencer*, Jan. 5, 1807.

[6] On Dec. 4, 1806 Wood wrote Clay (*Clay MSS.*) that Daveiss and Marshall had made a reconciliation with Street impossible; that all his money was tied up in the *Western World*; that Street, who had swindled him out of $1000, would give him on his investment only a note for $70 payable six months hence; and that he would esteem it

continue, aided by Marshall, the anti-Republican campaign. Indignant citizens prepared to file libel suits against the Junto. Henry Clay made hurried arrangements to leave for Washington. Aaron Burr resumed preparations for his expedition — but not before a warm-hearted people had attempted to atone for 'the machinations of malice, jealousy, and suspicion.'

No honor was now too great for the vindicated Burr, who, said Marshall, was 'hailed and huzzaed by the undersized, caressed and feasted by the higher order.' Men acclaimed his courage and courtesy. Women were enraptured by 'that smiling affability, those captivating gestures, that je ne sais quoi, those desolating looks, that soft, sweet, and insinuating eloquence.' At a magnificent ball and supper given in Frankfort on Monday, December 8, Governor Greenup, legislators, lawyers, and other prominent Kentuckians with their wives and daughters formed a hero-worshipping assembly which feasted and toasted 'the inimitable, the incomparable, Burr.'

It was a gala occasion — marred only by a dirk and pistol affray caused by the discovery and forcible ejection of a 'spy,' none other than bellicose Editor Street. Animated groups clustered about the guest of honor, who was elegantly attired in smallclothes, golden knee buckles, dancing pumps with immense rosettes, and a powdered wig which set off those dark eyes which glowed 'with all the ardor of venerial fire.' Fiddles scraped merrily; stately minuets were followed by spirited jigs and contra dances; and the flowing bowl lent its enlivening assistance at this grand festival given by hospitable Kentuckians to the gracious and captivating Little Burr.[1]

Clay regretted his inability to attend these festivities. Anxious to set out for the East and to take his seat in the Senate, he was

---

'the most singular favour' if Clay would advance him money enough to convey him by stage to Richmond, with Street's note for security. See, also, Wood to Editor Wm. Hunter of the *Palladium*, June 22, 1807, *Innes MSS.*, 22. Clay advanced him $70 on Street's note — and for so doing was charged by Marshall with 'seducing' and 'debauching' Wood. Marshall, *Hist. Ky.*, II, 412; *Ky. Gazette*, Jan. 28, 1832.

[1] Marshall, *op. cit.*, II, 411; Trabue, A. E., *A Corner in Celebrities*, pp. 12–13; Lex. *Reporter*, July 9, 1808; *Western World*, in *Natl. Intelligencer*, Jan. 12, 1807 (reporting, also, Street's prejudiced account of a non-partisan 'Union Ball,' held a few days later); and references in *Innes MSS.*, 22.

occupied with matters connected with his law practice, especially with causes he was to argue in the Supreme Court for clients who had already paid him fees amounting to three thousand dollars.[1] On the eve of his departure Colonel Burr came over from Frankfort to thank him once again for his services as counsel, and, as a token of friendship, to give him letters of introduction to acquaintances in Washington.[2] The next day, with a light heart, Henry set out for the Federal City.

Nine years after leaving Richmond he was returning East — a United States senator at the age of twenty-nine, a lawyer whose well-established reputation had only recently been crowned by his successful defense of a former Vice President. As he left the Blue Grass acclamations of Aaron Burr rang in his ears — but the letters of introduction given him by his grateful client, by the fascinating adventurer whom the Western World was now enthusiastically huzzaing, were not presented by the young senator from Kentucky upon his arrival in Washington.

---

[1] Plumer, *Memo*, p. 565.
[2] Clay to Pindell, Oct. 15, 1828, Clay, *Corres.*, p. 208.

Chapter Eight. A Jeffersonian Senator

*Mr. Clay, the new member from Kentucky . . . is quite a young man —
an orator — and a republican of the first fire. (John Quincy Adams.)*

It seems that we have been much mistaken about Burr. When I left Kentucky I believed him both an innocent and a persecuted man . . . (Henry Clay.)

*This is indeed a deep, dark, and widespread conspiracy, embracing the
young and old, the Democrat and the Federalist, the native and the foreigner,
the patriot of '76 and the exotic of yesterday, the opulent and the needy, the
'ins' and the 'outs' . . . I gasconade not . . . (General James Wilkinson.)*

IT WAS at Chillicothe, the capital of Ohio, that Clay first received
intimations of a most startling revulsion of public feeling. High
excitement there prevailed, for the legislators had just enacted
measures for the apprehension of 'Burr's Army,' then on its way
downriver supposedly to seize New Orleans as the first step in the
'immense revolution.' At his Chillicothe tavern, Henry, the
center of a questioning group, stoutly declared the measures wholly
unjustified.[1] But no sooner had he resumed his journey than news
came to him that Jefferson, after months of silence amid sensational rumors, had warned the country of an unlawful expedition
against Mexico and called for the seizure of the conspirators.

---

[1] Clay to Thomas Hart, Feb. 1, 1807, Clay, Thomas Hart, *Henry Clay*, p. 41. These
measures had been initiated by John Graham, Jefferson's confidential agent, who as
late as Nov. 28, 1806 had reported the West decidedly averse to disunion and Burr high
in public favor. *MS. Letters in Relation to the Burr Conspiracy.* For graphic accounts by a
member of Burr's 'army,' see *Silas Brown, Jr. MSS.*

The President's proclamation, based on hysterical dispatches from General Wilkinson, hit the West like a thunderbolt. Burr was not named nor was treason hinted. Yet at once the emotional Jeffersonians, convinced that he must be guilty of more than a patriotic filibuster, violently erupted against 'Aaron Burr, the Traitor!'

The Kentucky Assembly joined in the hue and cry — for Burr's handful of men in a few flatboats now appeared as a Napoleonic host convoyed by a Nelsonian navy. Militiamen in a rage of patriotism sacked the estate of 'Admiral Blennerhassett.' Wilkinson fortified New Orleans against the oncoming armada, imprisoned his former Burrite associates, and carried on a martial reign of terror punctuated by manifestoes on Burr's 'deep, dark, and widespread conspiracy.' [1]

Amid all this melodramatic turmoil one thing appeared certain in the West following Jefferson's proclamation — Aaron Burr was an enemy of the Union. One word from the Man of the People and the adventurer toasted, huzzaed, and caressed as the Son of Destiny who would 'give a wider spread to republicanism' had overnight become despised, detested, and execrated as 'The Republic's Catiline.'

Puzzled and perturbed, Henry Clay pressed on 'amidst bad weather and wretched roads' to Washington, arriving late in December — too late to realize his hopes 'of dining on oysters' in the Federal City on Christmas Day.[2]

Entering the raw and inconsiderable capital from Georgetown, he crossed Rock Creek, rode past the President's white mansion with its post-and-rail fence 'unfit for a decent barnyard,' and continued down poplar-lined Pennsylvania Avenue, his horse's hooves sough-soughing in the muddy slush of that principal thoroughfare. As he neared Capitol Hill he heard the thud of axe and ring of hammer at the new south wing of the unfinished stone pile housing Congress and the Supreme Court — which from afar

---

[1] At the time Wilkinson betrayed Burr he was demanding of Spain more than $100,000 for so doing. McCaleb, *op. cit.*, chap. VI.

[2] Clay to Joseph M. Street, Wheeling, Dec. 17, 1806, Street, J. M., 'Letters,' *Annals of Iowa*, V, 71–72; a short, polite note asking that the *Western World* be sent him — 'Whatever relates to Kentucky will be peculiarly interesting to me.'

THE CAPITOL AT WASHINGTON IN 1807

towered over the infant city like some ruin of Rome or Persepolis. Close by were laborers' shanties, boarding-houses, and grog-shops. Diverging from it were avenue openings on which were widely scattered clusters of houses, 'a jumble of fragments of villages' dotting the shrub plains of the six-year-old Federal City. Not far away were the army barracks and navy yard. Across the broad Potomac were the hazy blue hills of his native Virginia; downriver was the thriving town of Alexandria. In the foreground was sluggish Tiber Creek, formerly Goose Creek but renamed to harmonize with the 'Capitol' and 'Senate' of New World Republicans who dreamed of a seat of national power which would in time equal, nay, outrival, the glory and grandeur of ancient Rome.

No imperial Rome did young Clay find here in Washington on the Tiber. Of this embryonic capital with its 'shrines unbuilt and heroes yet unborn,' grand in theory yet in reality 'as much a wilderness as Kentucky,' it was said that 'every foreigner, after his arrival here, will inquire for fifty years to come, as is now very common, "Where is the city of Washington?" ' [1] With 'everything new, and of course incomplete,' it was but typical of the sprawling, poorly integrated, slowly evolving nation.

In December of 1806 Henry Clay found its atmosphere surcharged with suspense and everyone alarmed and bewildered by rumors of Aaron Burr's plots against the continued existence of the Union.

'Numerous, various, and contradictory' were the conjectures — ranging from a Washita colony, filibuster, disunion aided by Britain or Spain or both powers, to a grandiose New World Empire. 'King Burr and his Freebooters' would seize New Orleans, then Mexico, aided by the navy of a Britain which had just taken Buenos Aires (and was then planning the conquest of Spanish America).[2] Burr would turn Congress neck and heels out of doors,

---

[1] Safford, *Blennerhassett*, pp. 469–70; Moore, T., *Works*, II, 295–302; Janson, *Stranger in America*, pp. 206–07; Story, W. W., *Joseph Story*, I, 148–50; Dunlap, Wm., *Diary*, II, 379–94; Plumer, Wm., *Memo*; Adams, J. Q., *Memoirs*, ed. C. F. Adams; Smith, M. B., *Forty Years of Washington Society*.

[2] Sir Arthur Wellesley, not yet the Duke of Wellington, was then planning the conquest of Mexico, and of Manila, with a force even more motley than Aaron Burr's 'army' — sepoys from the East Indies, black sepoys from the West Indies, British troops from England, British Honduras, Buenos Aires, etc. See Wellesley's memo to Lord Grenville, Jan. 25, 1807, *Dropmore Papers*, IX, 22–25; 481–93.

kill Tom Jefferson, and transform a weak and imbecilic republican government into one of Napoleonic energy, power, and splendor. His was a stupendous plot, worthy of a Corsican Bonaparte, a Roman Caesar, or a British Cromwell, which would elevate him to an imperial throne — or to a republican gibbet.¹

Denunciations and divers suspicions filled the air. The pro-British Pickering Federalists, it was said, would gladly let Burr gobble up the Jeffersonian West: such 'extreme party men, extreme in local attachments,' would welcome such a disunion regardless of the dangers from 'an anti-republican neighbour under the protection of one or more of the great European Nations, the secret cabinets of *all* which are *hostile* to our constitutional principles.' ² Many of the Federalists, in face of 'enigmas that cannot be unriddled' and rumors 'so vague, so improbable, so quixotical, and so contradictory,' declared Burr should be hanged if for no other reason than for frightening the ruling Jeffersonians so horribly.³

'Both amused & perplexed' was cool-headed Senator Plumer, Federalist of New Hampshire, who remarked that the two most unlikely persons in whom 'the cunning, cautious, wily Burr' would have confided were the two most prominent in blowing up this egregious Conspiracy Bubble: the gasconading Wilkinson, Jefferson's tardy informant, and the 'imprudent, wild, & raving' William Eaton. 'Burr is capable of much wickedness — but not so much folly.' And yet each passing day engendered stories which portrayed 'the subtil, cunning Burr' as more visionary than Don Quixote, more odious than Benedict Arnold. 'This state of incertitude is painful, and to the government, disgraceful,' wrote Plumer. 'If Burr has treasonable designs . . . they ought to have been known, & crushed in embryo. If it is a private speculation in lands — the public ought to know it — & be quiet.' ⁴

---

¹ *Natl. Intelligencer*, Phila. *Aurora*, Richmond *Enquirer*, Dec. 1806 ff.

² Tench Coxe to Madison, Jan. 11, and an undated letter of early January, 1807, *Madison MSS*.

³ Taggart, Samuel, *Letters*, pp. 205, 211. 'I know not where all this will end. I think it probable that it will subside for the present but it will without doubt tend to sow the seeds of a separation between the eastern and western section of the Union. It may be suspended for a time but sooner or later it must take place . . .'

⁴ Plumer, *Memo*, pp. 516, 536, 542; and Plumer to Jeremiah Mason, Jan. 4, 1807, *Plumer MSS*.

Such was the atmosphere when Henry arrived. 'The extraordinary circumstances which came out on Sebastian's case, the agitation excited by the movements of Col. Burr, & the vast preparations he is said to have been making on the Ohio & below,' he wrote Judge Innes, 'have thrown the public mind into... consternation.' Even Congress is far from being 'cool, deliberate, & impartial.' [1]

Aware that the new senator from Kentucky had been Burr's counsel, Plumer and other congressmen bombarded him with inquiries as to Burr's alarming yet mysterious projects. What news from the other side of the mountains? What was the temper of the West?

Kentucky was most ardently devoted to Jefferson and the Union, Henry asserted. There was no desire to attack Mexico before war was declared, he said, expressing the general Kentucky view that war with Spain was most probable and that Burr's filibuster had Jefferson's sanction.[2] As for the Ohio measures, in that state a mania had suddenly seized the people: innocence was no longer any security; suspicion alone was equivalent to conviction. As for himself, Clay said he was still convinced that Burr was an innocent and persecuted man — he had yet to see evidence to the contrary.[3]

The evidence that changed his mind came from Mr. Jefferson, when he called at the President's House. 'In a tone of entire confidence' the President assured him that Burr had schemed both to place himself on the throne of Montezuma and to revolutionize the West, using Orleans as his instrument of compulsion. Nothing was more false than Burr's disclaimer to Clay. He showed the Kentuckian some of the many reports and dispatches he had received, among them a letter, in cipher, from Burr to Wilkinson

---

[1] Clay to Innes, Jan. 16, 1807, *Durrett Collection*, Univ. of Chicago.

[2] On this same day, Dec. 29, 1806, the *Kentucky Gazette* stated that up to the time Burr was denounced by Jefferson 'our opinion was, that he meditated an attack on Mexico by the authority of government, should a war take place with Spain, of which there appeared a strong probability. To this opinion, we thought it improper to give publicity... as it might convey notice to the Spaniards... but never hesitated to do so in conversation.' In *Natl. Intelligencer*, Jan. 23, 1807.

[3] Plumer, *Memo*, pp. 548–49; Dec. 29, 1806.

outlining a plan entailing the use of American army commissions and of the British navy. 'Most unquestionably,' asserted Jefferson, Burr had conspired 'the reduction of New Orleans first, the subjugation of Mexico afterwards, and ultimately the Separation of the Western from the Eastern section of the Union.'

Henry became convinced that Burr all along 'had entertained illegal designs.' [1] It appeared that he had been all things to all men, a desperate opportunist to whom no project was unwelcome. His categorical disclaimer now seemed a hollow mockery — a token not only of Aaron Burr's duplicity but of young Clay's gullibility. Most certain was it to Henry that he and his fellow Kentuckians had been outrageously duped by 'the inimitable, the incomparable, Burr.'

On January 22 in an extraordinary message to Congress the President stated that Burr, having found the West unswervingly loyal, had determined to plunder New Orleans before pressing on to Mexico. Two things had produced a general disbelief in his treason: the Washita speculation, and Daveiss's 'premature attempt to bring Burr to justice without sufficient evidence.' Assuring Congress that Burr's guilt was 'beyond question,' he asked its aid in crushing the rebellion by a temporary suspension of the right of habeas corpus.[2]

Following this prejudgment, which removed Plumer's doubts 'as to Burr's seditious & treasonable designs,' the Senate at once rushed through the desired bill. Clay voted for it, but reluctantly. He did not think public safety sufficiently menaced, yet (as he remarked to Plumer) he felt that his position as Burr's late counsel obliged him to sustain the President. The House, however, refused to elevate Burr's intrigue into a rebellion. And later, in view of Wilkinson's conduct, Plumer and doubtless Clay rejoiced that this 'palladium of our civil liberties' had not been suspended.[3]

At New Orleans, so they were informed, 'the whole Country . . .

---

[1] Clay to Innes, Jan. 16, 1807, *Durrett Coll.*; to R. Pindell, Oct. 15, 1828, Clay, *Corres.*, p. 208; to Th. Todd, Jan. 24, 1807, *Innes MSS.*, 18; to Th. Hart, Feb. 1, 1807, Clay, T. H., *Clay*, p. 41.

[2] *Annals of Congress*, 9th, 2nd, 39–43; 1007–19.

[3] Plumer, *Memo*, pp. 589–91. The votes were not recorded in the *Annals*. It has hitherto been said that Clay voted *against* suspension.

is in a Ferment — Commerce stagnated, and the public Indignation great against Wilkinson,' a tyrant Braggadocchio universally despised and distrusted.[1] 'All the talents of the country,' including United States Attorney James Brown, had 'dipped their pens in gall' and were venting their ire at his reign of terror under cover of martial law.[2]

To Washington in February came one of his most abused victims, John Adair, the former Kentucky senator (and future Kentucky governor), whom he had accused of leading two thousand Burrites upon Orleans — a fraction of Burr's huge army over which the bombastic general (formerly Burr's 'most devoted creature') had sworn 'to triumph or perish!' When Adair arrived, alone, unaccompanied, Wilkinson had clapped him into irons and shipped him East. Now, released on a writ of habeas corpus, General Adair lashed out at Wilkinson, 'Burr's infamous co-intriguer,' and at 'the once highly esteemed Jefferson,' who countenanced 'this swaggering demagogue.' If it were wrong to filibuster, asked Adair, then why not prosecute Wilkinson? For only last September this triple-faced deceiver of Burr, Jefferson, and Carlos IV had invited him to 'subvert' Mexico.[3]

It now appeared that 'our great General Wilkinson is as deep in the mud as little Burr is in the mire.'[4] And perhaps the greater rogue was this alleged Spanish pensioner who commanded, and under Jefferson as under Adams, continued to command America's army. Plumer, and others, resented the administration view, as voiced by Giles, that Wilkinson had acted rightly and must be supported. 'This vain, intriguing, haughty infamous Wilkinson,' he said, 'has *created* much of the alarm,' deprived his old Burrite comrades of rights guaranteed 'even to common *convicted* malefactors,' and 'done more to destroy our little feeble military

---

[1] Sen. Buckner Thruston to Innes, Feb. 18, 1807, *Innes MSS.*, 19.

[2] P. T. Schenck to Jas. Findlay, May 8, 1807, 'Torrence Papers,' ed. I. J. Cox, *Qtrly. Pub. Hist. and Phil. Soc. of Ohio*, IV, 126 — 'I can't find a single person but believes' Wilkinson would have joined Burr if he thought Burr might have succeeded. See, also, *Natl. Intelligencer*, Feb. 9, 1807 ff. Although Wilkinson included James Brown in his wholesale charges of Burrism, the administration had 'never for a moment doubted' Brown's loyalty, wrote John Graham to Brown, Sept. 8, 1807, *Jas. Brown MSS.*

[3] Adair, in Richmond *Enquirer*, March 10, 1807; Plumer, *Memo*, p. 614 ff.

[4] Chas. Geirs to Jefferson, Feb. 24, 1807, *Jefferson MSS.*

establishment than its bitterest enemies have been able for years to effect.' [1]

Throughout this session the Wonderful Conspiracy continued to amaze, perplex, and excite Senator Clay and his colleagues.

In February Aaron Burr was captured, in the disguise of a Mississippi planter, and brought East to stand trial for treason. 'The Outlaw Emperor' was now behind republican bars — 'He *might have been* President of the U. States, decked with the wreaths of glory. He *is* a Prisoner, covered with a crown of thorns, degraded by plots of treason, suspected by all.' [2] By all — except Editor John Wood!

For no less a person appeared in Washington to vindicate Burr. Wood had torn him down with his *Western World*; now, amid a general disgust at his colossal impudence, he attempted to build Burr up with his new *Atlantic World*. 'A wonderful task!' exclaimed Senator Mitchill of New York; 'like washing the Ethiopian white.' [3] Yes, 'this vile Wood is here,' reported Senator Thruston of Kentucky: 'what an abominable Countenance the pestilent Dog has!' [4]

In his new 'weekly paper of villainous matter' Wood attacked all 'Intriguers and Conspirators,' with the somewhat notable exception of Aaron Burr, savagely thrusting at Sebastian and Wilkinson, and especially at Jo Daveiss for having through Street made his *Western World* 'the vehicle of the politics of a most daring and desperate faction.' [5] He did his best toward making the Burr extravaganza seem like 'a kind of Waterspout, a terrible Whirlpool, threatening to ingulph every Thing. But it may be,' said former President Adams, 'as the Fable says that [a] single Bullet shot through it will quell it all at once to the level of the sea.' [6]

No single bullet quelled the waterspout in Kentucky. Hysterical letters informed Clay that 'thanks to kind Providence ... Burr & his party are frustrated.' [7] His friends denounced Burr in un-

[1] Plumer, *op. cit.*, pp. 618–19, 624–26, Feb., 1807.
[2] Richmond *Enquirer*, March 20, 1807.
[3] Mitchill, S. L., *Letters*, p. 751; also, Plumer, *op. cit.*, p. 563; Taggart, *Letters*, p. 207.
[4] Thruston to Innes, Feb. 18, 1807, *Innes MSS.*, 19.
[5] *Atlantic World*, Jan. 19, 1807.
[6] Adams to Dr. Benj. Rush, Feb. 2, 1807, *Old Family Letters*, p. 129.
[7] Elijah Foley to Thruston and Clay, Feb. 17, 1807, *Clay MSS.*

measured terms: their 'spirited and patriotic resolutions,' said the Frankfort *Palladium*, 'bespeak the real sentiments of ninety-nine out of a hundred of the citizens of the western country.' [1] Kentuckians would now hang Burr and Blennerhassett 'at one end of a Rope & Wilkinson at the other, & let the world see the fun.' [2] Burr had planned 'a deadly thrust,' said Ninian Edwards, but he is now 'almost universally execrated ... sunk into merited contempt.' [3] In Lexington his once 'warmest advocates declare ... him to be a rascal, villain, thief and highway robber ...' [4]

How would this anti-Burr hysteria affect the political fortunes of Henry Clay? Already, for having been Burr's counsel, and for having so freely expressed his views at Chillicothe, he had been subjected 'to the strictures of some anonymous writer at that place. They give me no uneasiness,' he wrote old Colonel Hart, 'as I am sensible that all my friends and acquaintances know me incapable of entering into the views of Burr.' [5] He neither joined in the popular hysteria against Burr nor gave way to passionate outbursts — like Andrew Jackson's 'My God! How can I express my sentiments!!' [6] These newspaper strictures 'give me no pain,' he wrote Thomas Prentiss, 'as I am conscious of having participated in no illegal projects of Burr, and know that I will not be suspected of having done so by any who know me.' [7]

Clay faced the future with his customary assurance, fortified by the confidence which the administration had in him, personally, and in his fellow Republicans. There seemed to be but one man in all Kentucky — which furnished half of the sixteen congressmen

---

[1] In Phila. *Aurora*, Feb. 3, 1807, on Lexington resolutions.

[2] Nath. Cox to G. Lewis, July, 1807, Cox, *Letters*, p. 187.

[3] Edwards to Wm. Wirt, Jan. 5, 1807, Edwards, *N. Edwards*, pp. 279–84.

[4] *Natl. Intelligencer*, Feb. 2, 1807; one of five such Ky. letters.

[5] Clay to Hart, Feb. 1, 1807, Clay, T. H., *Clay*, p. 41; also, Plumer, *Memo*, p. 565.

[6] *Natl. Intelligencer*, Feb. 11, 1807. Clay, however, plainly showed his feelings when he next met Burr. Upon his return from Europe in 1815 he visited the Federal Court in New York City. 'A small gentleman, apparently advanced in years, and with bushy, gray hair, whom Mr. Clay for an instant did not recognise, approached him. He quickly perceived it was Col. Burr, who tendered his hand to salute Mr. Clay. The latter declined receiving it. The colonel, nevertheless, was not repulsed, but engaged in conversation with Mr. Clay,' who, to his inquiries, 'replied coldly. ... Col. B. expressed a wish to have an hour's interview with him, and Mr. C. told him where he stopped — but the colonel never called.' Greeley, *Clay*, pp. 25–26.

[7] Clay to Prentiss, Feb. 15, 1807, Clay, *Corres.*, p. 15.

from a unanimously Republican West — for whom Jefferson had censure, and that was the 'injudicious' Federalist, Joseph Hamilton Daveiss.

'Everybody here, in, & out, of the administration,' reported James Hughes to Innes, 'does justice to the attachment of Kentucky to the Union.' [1] The true import of her 'patriotic endeavours to give a wider spread to republicanism' was recognized by Jefferson, who declared that Western zeal for Burr's alleged filibuster would in six weeks have given Burr Mexico. Indeed, the President made use of this exuberant expansionism by threatening that Mexico would in truth be conquered unless Spain at once gave up West Florida.[2]

Aaron Burr's star had fallen, this time never to rise again. In September, at Richmond, the former Vice President was acquitted by Chief Justice Marshall upon technical grounds: he had committed no treasonable 'overt act.' Burr was convicted by national opinion, however, and punished by national obloquy. His career was ended.

In the meantime, at Washington, Henry Clay of Kentucky had blithely entered upon his career in national politics.

He was but twenty-nine, lacking four months of the age prescribed by the Constitution, when sworn in a member of the Senate on December 29, 1806. In after years he would smilingly refer to this as one of his 'supposed juvenile indiscretions.' [3] No question was raised as to his eligibility, and he took his seat among the thirty-four Elder Statesmen from the seventeen states of the Union.

Justly renowned was their handsome semi-circular chamber with its elegant appointments, its carpeted floor, cushioned chairs of scarlet leather, wall maps, full-length portraits of ill-fated Marie Antoinette and Louis XVI, and small portrait of General Washington. Yet Henry heard many complaints. The roof leaked, there

---

[1] Hughes to Innes, Washington, Feb. 8, 1807, *Innes MSS.*, 19.

[2] Jefferson to Jas. Bowdoin, Minister to Spain, April 2, 1807, Jefferson, *Works*, X, 381–82. As to West Florida, he said, America expects Napoleon 'will either compel Spain to do us justice, or abandon her to us. We ask but one month to be in... the city of Mexico.'

[3] Winthrop, Robt., *H. Clay*, p. 5.

was a cellar-like dampness, and some of his colleagues were in a constant 'state of fear & uneasiness, least the wall, which is thick & high, should fall on them & either maim or kill them.' [1]

Young Clay, fresh from the state house at Frankfort, found the Senate enveloped in an air of 'solemn stillness.' [2] These 'national gray-beards,' according to young Washington Irving, 'hold all wit and humour in abomination' and declaim the winter away 'in somniferous debates' before deciding 'not to expend a few dollars.' [3] In every respect 'Their High Mightinesses, the Senate,' attracted less attention than the younger, popularly elected, members of the House, where (as Irving noted) such men as Jack Randolph, Mat Lyon, and Josiah Quincy 'were measuring tongues and syllogistically cudgelling each other.' Although the ladies were permitted to sit on the Senate floor, and were restricted in the House to the galleries, they found their favorite orators in the lower chamber. 'Over in the House members have a great propensity to speak to the galleries and for the newspapers,' said Senator Plumer.[4] 'What think you,' asked Senator Mitchill of New York, 'of Congressional beaux uttering in the course of debates, gallant sentiments for their mistresses and sweethearts to amuse themselves with?' [5] Yet this feminine partiality was to be expected. For the House, according to John Quincy Adams, then in the full vigor of his forty years, only emphasized by contrast the Senate's senile apathy.[6]

Senator Adams, stubbornly conscientious, critical of everybody including himself, an able and scholarly man, but 'too stiff & unyielding' (said Plumer of New Hampshire), had recently been

---

[1] Plumer, *Memo*, p. 527, and *passim*.

[2] Clay to James Monroe, Nov. 13, 1810, *James Monroe MSS*.

[3] Irving, W., *Works*, I, 245, *Salmagundi*, No. IX, April 25, 1807.

[4] Plumer to Major D. Plumer, Jan. 10, 1807, *Plumer MSS*. 'I think our country has more to fear from it than from the victorious arms of Napoleon, or the intrigues of the wily Burr.'

[5] S. L. Mitchill to his wife, April 6, 1806, in Washington *Evening Star*, May 27, 1894. On Jan. 31, 1807, *ibid.*, Senator Mitchill stated that while Vice President Burr had 'excluded the ladies from the fires and the floor where the Senators sit, and confined them to the gallery,' Vice President George Clinton now 'admits them to the places they before occupied in the lobby.' Clinton 'has the pretty girls in his eye and enlivens himself by the prospect during a tedious debate, and the Senators themselves now and then leave their scarlet armchairs and relieve their weary limbs while they saunter about in the lobby and pay their respects to the sovereigns of the land.'

[6] Adams, *Memoirs*, I, 452.

appointed Professor of Oratory at Harvard. Yet Professor Clay of Transylvania could hardly rate him more than a mediocre speaker. More effective was William Branch Giles, who at this session hobbled about on crutches, for his carriage had been overturned on the wretched roads. Another Republican of weight was Samuel Smith (brother of the Secretary of the Navy, and of Mrs. George Nicholas), a rich merchant from a Baltimore which now rivalled Boston in population and commerce. Reputedly the best orator was gallant, floridly handsome James A. Bayard, moderate Federalist of Delaware. Timothy Pickering proved to be tall, gaunt, overbearing; like Uriah Tracy of Connecticut, he was able, and choleric, with all the harsher traits of 'rigid' Calvinistic Federalism. Tracy's habit of 'exposing and scourging' had caused Plumer to call him 'that pink of Connecticut politeness.' Buckner Thruston, from 'the wild woods of Kentucky,' Plumer described as an upright, scholarly man, with sensibilities 'exquisitely delicate,' who abhorred the rough give-and-take of politics, and had few of the hardy qualities which had made the late John Breckinridge so prominent a senator.[1]

More typical of the young West was Thruston's new colleague. Clay's fresh and spirited youthfulness was conspicuous among the 'national gray-beards.' On the day he arrived Plumer recorded in his diary: 'I had much conversation with him, & it afforded me much pleasure. He is intelligent, sensible & appears frank & candid. His address is good & manners easy.' Two weeks later the Yankee Federalist recorded that the personable young Kentucky Republican was 'an effective man,' a worthy successor to John Breckinridge.[2]

Clay entered Congress with a characteristic 'rush,' taking his seat on December 29 and making his maiden speech on January 2. It was an appeal for the extension to the West of the Federal Circuit system, and for two District judges each for Kentucky, Tennessee, and Ohio. On this long-deferred matter he asked immediate action, pointing out that in Kentucky, where Innes was the only judge, more than four hundred cases were pending,

---

[1] Plumer, *op. cit.*, pp. 643, 575–76, 371–72, *passim*.   [2] *Ibid.*, pp. 547, 576.

most of them land-title suits in chancery. Before the end of the session the circuit system was extended, and his friend Judge Thomas Todd was appointed to the Supreme Court as the member for the new Western Circuit. His bill as enacted did not wholly please him. But under the circumstances, he wrote Innes, Todd's brother-in-law, 'it was the best I could do.' [1]

'An easy, graceful, & eloquent speaker,' commented Plumer, after hearing Henry's first speech.[2] A few days later Adams remarked that 'Mr. Clay, the new member from Kentucky, made an ardent speech' on the bill abolishing the slave trade. 'He is quite a young man — an orator — and a republican of the first fire.' [3] Perhaps the most interesting comment upon Clay's entrance into Congress — where the feminine audience greatly influenced the style of oratory, and applauded or frowned upon the debaters as upon actors — was Plumer's remark that the youthful Kentucky orator had promptly become 'a great favorite with the ladies.' [4]

Upon his arrival Henry was widely dined and wined by citizens interested in a much-disputed local measure, the erection of a toll bridge across the Potomac. A bill to charter the bridge company was then before the Senate, where the members were about equally divided. For some sessions it had been agitated, but always its passage had been thwarted by the citizens of Georgetown who feared that a Washington bridge competing with their ferry would mean their section's commercial decline. To their chagrin, the new senator declared for the bridge. Its merits, and those of internal improvements in general, were obvious to a Westerner who had spent the best part of the month of December in travelling, 'amidst bad weather and wretched roads,' to the Federal City.

Young Clay promptly plunged into the discussions, which soon became 'as warm and close,' said Adams, 'as I ever witnessed in the Senate.' [5] He advocated the Potomac Bridge with as much vigor as

---

[1] Clay to Innes, Jan. 16, 1807, *Durrett Coll.*; also, *Annals*, 9th, 2d, 27, 1260–62.

[2] Plumer, *op. cit.*, p. 554; Jan. 2, 1807.

[3] Adams, *Memoirs*, I, 444. The debates were not reported.

[4] Plumer, *op. cit.*, p. 608; Feb. 13, 1807.

[5] Adams to Louisa Adams, Jan. 14, Feb. 1, 1807, Adams, *Writings*, III, 157, 160.

if he were at Frankfort, going hammer and tongs after Felix Grundy and the Green River Band. With his 'republican fire' added to Bayard's 'inexhaustible fluency,' Adams thought the bill would pass. But senators in opposition, many of them socially indebted to General Mason, owner of the Georgetown ferry, fought back for two weeks and then called for postponement — 'under the old pretext,' said Plumer, 'want of time & want of information.' This local bill, it was said, had created a tumult rivalling King Burr's.

Vice President George Clinton, in his dotage (a sorry contrast to Aaron Burr), was unable to preserve order. Giles, though personally in favor of the bill, urged its postponement with (said Plumer) a good deal of 'art, intrigue, & deception.' He was supported by Doctor Mitchill of New York — 'always easy pleasant and accommodating, but he has no nerve.' Stephen Bradley of frontier Vermont, and John Milledge of frontier Georgia, satirized the wobbling of the Virginia senators. Pickering and Adams of Massachusetts were zealous for postponement, and flew into 'so great a passion ... that they were utterly unable to speak.' Uriah Tracy, however, provoked by Clay's persistent demands for decisive action, felt called upon to chasten a presumptuous youth, 'in the plenitude of puppyism,' who had but lately arrived from Jacobinic Kentucky.

Obtaining the floor, he urged that the bill be postponed — although not ten minutes before, at the fireplace, he had expressed contrary views to Plumer. While the honest Plumer muttered about Connecticut bigots whose cunning meanness was covered 'under the mask of sanctity' and of rigid Federalists whose 'blind *party* rage' was too much for their honesty or reason, Tracy proceeded to admonish Clay for his puerile views, and for daring to suggest that another postponement would greatly discredit the Senate. His remarks were delivered with the unctuous rudeness customary when he was 'exposing and scourging.'

Tracy's effort at hazing was a boomerang. The veteran scourger was himself scourged — by a youth who really had no constitutional right to be in Congress. Lacking neither experience nor skill in the use of invective, the newcomer from the frontier more than held his own against the bully of the Senate, 'that pink of Connecticut politeness.' No sooner had Tracy taken his seat than he felt Clay's barbs. His mask of sanctimonious omniscience was snatched off, his 'stand by — I am holier than thou!' attitude (as Plumer called it) was ridiculed, and his views were subjected to severe criticism. The Kentuckian concluded his philippic with a verse from Peter Pindar which he thought appropriate, quoting:

> 'Thus have I seen a magpie in the street,
> A chattering bird, we often meet;
> A bird for curiosity well known,
>   With head awry
>   And cunning eye
> Peep knowingly into a marrow-bone.' [1]

With Uriah Tracy rebuked, young Clay continued his advocacy of the Potomac Bridge. The measure, alas, was by a vote of 17 to 16 again postponed — 'after weeks of debate,' said the critical Plumer, by the same men who in a single day had voted to suspend the habeas corpus; and they had postponed it 'under the flimsy pretext of gaining more information.' Clay, however, was not of the great number who 'shrink from the responsibility of acting.' He could be forceful and bitterly sarcastic, as well as 'easy, graceful, & eloquent.' Compared with Bayard, Plumer rated him more the enthusiastic orator than the precise reasoner. One great merit Clay possessed: above all 'he is prompt & decisive.' [2]

These qualities he displayed in urging the claim of William Eaton, of Burr's Conspiracy fame, a somewhat tarnished American hero but a hero nevertheless, a Connecticut Yankee whose adventures rivalled those of the *Arabian Nights*. During the war with piratical Tripoli in 1804, at considerable expense as well as risk, 'General' Eaton had incited an effective revolt among the Bedouin tribes of the ruling Bashaw. The bill reimbursing him was urged by Clay, Bayard, and Bradley, in opposition to Adams and Giles, the administration leader, and was carried by a vote of 16 to 12.[3]

---

[1] Prentice, *Clay*, p. 37; Plumer, *Memo*, pp. 593–96 (and *passim*, on Tracy and other Pickeronians, whose bigoted Federalism had alienated both Plumer and John Quincy Adams); Adams, *Memoirs*, I, 444–48.

[2] Plumer, *op. cit.*, pp. 595–96, and 608.

[3] Adams, *op. cit.*, I, 465; *Annals*, 9th, 2d, 103.

Western affairs claimed his attention — 'I am attempting,' he wrote Colonel Hart, 'several things for the good, as I suppose, of our country.' ¹ He requested indemnities for victims of Indian warfare and various benefits for Indiana and Mississippi Territories. He presented Kentucky's proposed amendment to restrict Federal courts to land-title cases arising only under Federal laws. But his chief interest was internal improvements — Federal aid in developing what Jefferson (reporting on the Lewis and Clark exploration) imperially called 'our continent.' Although such a policy conflicted with a Republicanism which minimized the functions and powers of government, the time seemed ripe for its application.

For these were flush days, for the nation and for the Republican party. Despite dire prophecies in 1800 of Jacobinic misrule, Jefferson's régime had been marked by an unprecedented and widely diffused prosperity. This had resulted, said discomfited Federalists (now reduced to a very slender minority), from the sound foundations laid by Washington, Hamilton, and Adams: 'twas 'all the fruit of Federal toil, though Demo's *riot* in their spoils.' ² Obviously, however, Europe's wars had greatly contributed, as Volney remarked, to this 'lucky and fortuitous concurrence of events.' ³ Jefferson, who had no scruples against milking the cow of wartime profits while one belligerent held her by the horns and the other by the tail, was realizing his hope that 'the new world will fatten on the follies of the old.' ⁴

The New World neutral had become the granary of the Old World belligerents. Though predominantly a republic of farmers, its merchant marine (half of it New England owned) was of meteoric growth and fabulous profits, its tonnage second only to Britain's. So great was the revenue from an expanding commerce that at this session the Treasury was full, the redeemable part of the public debt could not absorb the income, and in the House a committee was appointed to dispose of the surplus. Throughout the thriving republic, recently doubled in area by Louisiana,

---

¹ Clay to Hart, Feb. 1, 1807, Clay, T. H., *Clay*, pp. 45–46.
² Fessenden, T. G., *Democracy Unveiled*, II, 69.
³ Volney, C. F., *A View... of the United States*, p. xv.
⁴ Jefferson to Edward Rutledge, July 4, 1790, Jefferson, *Works*, VI, 88.

plans were being projected, and Federal aid requested, for canals, turnpikes, and other improvements.

Although America's 'splendid prospect of future peace and happiness'[1] was already clouded by foreign difficulties, the young republic was then like some gargantuan cub, stretching its limbs, feeling its present strength, exulting in its future power. No public man better symbolized this youthful buoyancy than the cub senator from Kentucky. Clay's efforts at this session, and his lifelong advocacy of a policy of national aid, entitled him (said ardent admirers) to be called 'The Father of Internal Improvements.'

Jefferson himself, in his opening message of this session, had suggested that the tariff might be maintained and the surplus revenue applied to public improvements. Even this mild suggestion was abhorrent to John Randolph and other champions of States' Rights, of the negative, out-of-power, 'pure Republicanism' of 1798. The President, however, looked to the future, and he adhered to his strict constructionism. For he insisted that the public debt must first be paid, and, moreover, that the Constitution must first be amended so as to give Congress specific powers for internal improvements.[2]

Although a 'Republican of the first fire' and from a West 'bigoted to Jefferson,' young Clay lived in the present, despised legislative 'coasting,' and was imbued with a common-sense opportunism which adapted itself to insistent realities. He was less concerned with the niceties of party dogma than with economic conditions, especially those of the West. Boldly moving ahead of the President and most of his party, he pressed for immediate internal improvements, preferring to find the power (as with the Louisiana Purchase) in the broadly elastic principles of Hamiltonian implied powers than in the narrowly restrictive principles of Jeffersonian amendment. Again, and on a fun-

---

[1] Volney, C. F., A View... of the United States, p. vi. 'Europe in general presented to my view nothing but a gloomy and tempestuous prospect,' said Volney. 'Here I beheld nothing but a splendid prospect of future peace and happiness, flowing from the wide extent of improveable territory; from the facility of procuring property in land; from the necessity and the profits of labour; from the liberty of action and industry; and from the equity of government, a virtue which it owes to its very weakness.'

[2] Annals, 9th, 2d, 14–15; Dec. 2, 1806.

damental policy, he was 'prompt & decisive,' a man who did not 'shrink from the responsibility of acting.' Once again he assailed the citadels of hallowed indecision.

On January 12 he moved that it was expedient and proper to aid in the cutting of a canal at the falls of the Ohio by a grant of public lands at a fixed cash valuation. Such aid, he argued, would ensure the success of a public improvement of great benefit to the Western states and to the nation's vast and undeveloped Western territories. Later in the session, a committee of which he was chairman reported a bill for a commission to determine whether the Kentucky or Indiana side of the Ohio was better suited for the canal.[1]

Clay also served on the committee which favorably reported a bill granting similar aid to a proposed canal connecting Chesapeake and Delaware Bays. 'With great ability and much eloquence,' according to Plumer, the young Westerner joined with Bayard and Samuel White, Delaware Federalists, in arguing a general policy of internal improvements, revealing himself to be not only a Republican of the first fire but a Republican of broadly national views.

He and his colleagues pointed out how common economic interests would bind the several states more intimately within the Federal Union. The hinterland would be opened up for farmer, merchant, and immigrant; the movement of troops in war would be facilitated; and the basis might well be laid for a grand communication system linking the Great Lakes with the rivers of the South, the Ohio and Mississippi with the Atlantic seaboard. Peace and an overflowing Treasury made the time propitious. Plans already projected could be effectuated merely by exchanging for stock in canal and turnpike companies some few of the millions of acres in the uncharted wilderness world of Louisiana. By seizing its present opportunity, government would materially aid in making the republic, now divided by physical obstacles and distracted by sectional patriotisms, stronger and more prosperous, firmly knit by these national economic sinews.

Although opposed at first, Plumer became converted to their

[1] *Annals*, 9th, 2d, pp. 30, 92–93.

views and gave them his 'hearty approbation, as well calculated to aid a great & important & highly useful national object.' Unconverted, and vehement against such a parcelling out of public lands, were Uriah Tracy and James Hillhouse of Connecticut. While roads and canals were more needed for national defense than even ships and forts, Hillhouse was sure they 'would invite invaders and aid their movements against us.' Smith of Maryland would postpone the Chesapeake and Delaware bill: though his state favored it, he himself feared a canal would enrich Philadelphia at Baltimore's expense. 'Violent in his opposition' was irascible John Quincy Adams, who charged that log-rolling was going on between Middle States senators who favored the bill and Western senators who favored Clay's Ohio Canal.[1]

'Mr. White, Mr. Bayard, and Mr. Clay were all roused to reply to me,' wrote Adams, 'which they did with some acrimony.'[2] White stood on the high ground of patriotism and public interest. Clay also spoke from such an oratorical vantage ground, and subjected John Quincy Adams for the first but not the last time to his sarcasm.

Despite Kentucky oratory and Kentucky jibes, the Chesapeake Canal Bill was by a small majority postponed. Neither that canal nor the Ohio Canal was to initiate the grand plans of national domestic development which Clay envisioned. 'There is something insidious about this business of postponing,' growled the forthright Plumer.[3] Nevertheless, Henry carried his bill for a commission to select a site for the Ohio Canal. Its prompt passage, by a vote of 18 to 8, convinced Adams that Clay was not only a fiery orator but an effective politician. His bill 'had obviously been settled out of doors.'[4]

Such golden plans were bottomed upon a belief in the republic's ability to call forth and multiply its resources — a task for which no government 'since the creation of the world,' declared the *National Intelligencer* (with that propensity to boasting typical of adolescent nationalism), was 'so competent as our own.'[5] Alas,

---

[1] Plumer, *Memo*, pp. 628–29; also, *Annals*, 9th, 2d, 55 ff.
[2] Adams, *Memoirs*, I, 460.   [3] Plumer, *op. cit.*, p. 629.
[4] Adams, *op. cit.*, I, 463.   [5] *Natl. Intelligencer*, Feb. 12, 1807.

future sessions, perforce, were to be devoted not to national peace-time improvements but to the maintenance of national integrity against a ruthless Old World — a task for which the republic was far from having the most competent government since Genesis.

Foreign relations were not much agitated, though Clay had anticipated debates as lively as those of the year before when Spain was squeezing our territory and Britain our commerce and seamen. War with Spain did not now seem likely. And from London there was daily expected a treaty respecting British aggressions which in 1805–06 had incited nation-wide roars of protest.

In 1805 Britain had suddenly forbade the indirect West Indian trade, a reexport traffic between Europe and the non-British islands in which the voyage was broken by landing the goods in the United States. This had hitherto been permitted by the Mistress of the Seas. In England, however, there was an ever-growing hostility to an ever-growing neutral competitor that ranged the globe from Cuba to Senegal, Riga to Singapore, everywhere cutting into British profits. Was it only to enrich the Yankee that the Union Jack at great cost had swept the ocean clean of all belligerent flags?

Quite understandably, Britain was provoked by her former colony, which she was not yet psychologically prepared to treat as a full-fledged nation; an upstart republic which 'stole' both her commerce and seamen. She was angered by the thousands of sailors who deserted her marine, the bulwark of her embattled empire, and found refuge in America, or berths in American merchantmen, easily obtaining fraudulent certificates of American citizenship. She was incensed by 'The Frauds of the Neutral Flag,' at which the Yankees were past masters. Her Tory shipping magnates raged with all the self-righteousness of patriots and business men. At the same time, with what Jefferson called 'an inconsistency at which reason revolts,' they had determined to monopolize the rich West Indian trade for themselves, ousting their American neutral rival, and carrying on a 'disguised,' licensed or fraudulent, trade with their French enemy.

Holding the traffic to be in reality a direct trade between

Bonapartist Europe and its Caribbean colonies, a 'War in Disguise' waged against her by an unneutral America, Britain in 1805 without warning had confiscated some one hundred and twenty American ships. Her action had all the precipitancy of highway robbery, whatever the pretext (a British 'Rule of 1756') under a maritime code which seemed ever to be a ruthless 'Rule Britannia!' Moreover, she had intensified her impressment of alleged British deserters, stripping vessels of their crews on the high seas and within sight of their own shores. This in effect meant the enslavement of thousands of American citizens by short-handed British officers who felt duty bound to keep their ships manned — with 'men that speak the same language.' Had not Madison in 1801 pointed out that of some two thousand impressed sailors four-fifths were native Americans and only seventy British subjects? [1]

If Britain's property-plundering enraged the merchants, her man-stealing inflamed the commonalty of Americans. This greatest grievance against Britain, which Minister Liston in 1797 had termed an evil no less alarming in its progress than in its ultimate consequences, was more than ever most galling to national pride and to every humane feeling, regarded as a crime on par with murder. Popular hostility was not abated when fellow Americans met their death at Trafalgar in 1805 — fighting, and dying, for King and Country! Fighting, perforce, for the self-acclaimed 'Defender of the World's Liberties,' the ruthless power that had snatched them from under their own flag, subjected them to the British lash, enslaved them in the stinking and perilous holds of British men-of-war.

Of no avail were popular outcries at England's 'Algerian' rules of force, or sweeping shibboleths as to 'The Freedom of the Seas.'

---

[1] Estimates vary widely, but it appears that during the wars some 20,000 British sailors (as estimated by the Admiralty) deserted, that at least 10,000 sailors were impressed from American vessels, and that out of every ten impressed the British navy retrieved but one *bona fide* British subject. For a general account, see Zimmerman, J. F., *Impressment of American Seamen*; also, Mahan, A. T., *Sea Power in its Relations to the War of 1812*, I, 113–28. Efforts toward adjusting the problem failed because of England's refusal to give up impressing sailors claimed as British out of American ships on the high seas, or to recognize as American any British subject naturalized *after* the Peace of 1783. Liston in 1798 stated that the principle of non-transferable allegiance (then generally recognized) could not be accepted by America as a basis of adjustment, since 'in her present half-peopled... condition, her natural policy must be to encourage the immigration' of foreign-born peoples. Liston to Grenville, Oct. 28, 1798, *F.O.* 5:18.

Or contentions that the right to search for contraband did not permit the enforcement on American ships of English municipal law respecting impressment, with the consequent seizure of both native and naturalized Americans by brutal and indiscriminating press-gangs constituting themselves judge, jury, and jailor. Madison's protest, sneered John Randolph, was but a shilling pamphlet hurled at eight hundred British warships. Yet what else could he hurl? What other weapons would men like Randolph supply their country?

As Senator Clay well knew, retaliation by war had been proposed neither by the farmer-Republicans, who were wedded to peace and economy, nor by the merchant-Federalists, who filled the air with patriotic clamor and partisan jibes, yet preferred submission to the Mistress of the Seas to an entire loss of commerce. Our militia could conquer Canada, said Republicans, our merchantmen could be armed to prey on British commerce, and we could confiscate some forty millions invested here by British capitalists. Even so, war would be self-ruinous. It would destroy our carrying trade, our ships, and Atlantic cities. It would cost us our great revenues from British imports and our great profits from our farmers' exports to Britain. Moreover, it would force a retrogression to the odious Old World system of Federalism — armaments, debts, direct taxes, an expensive and tyrannical central government. War would be 'a very unprofitable business indeed,' Senator Worthington of Ohio had remarked: 'yet it does not follow that we are not to encounter all these difficulties if we cannot obtain justice in another way.' [1]

In the end Jefferson, with his passion for peace and his faith in appeals to an aggressor's self-interest, had applied his favorite weapon of economic coercion. His Non-Importation Act of 1806 was a partial boycott against British imports. It was to go into effect unless England permitted the indirect trade, indemnified the owners of seized ships and cargoes, and, above all, abolished the denationalizing, degrading, and inhumane practice of impressment.

---

[1] Thomas Worthington to Col. Samuel Huntington, March 14, 1806, Huntington, S., 'Letters,' *Tract No. 95, Ann. Rpt. Western Reserve Hist. Soc., 1915*, pp. 107–08.

The weakness of his weapon had been shown just a week later, on April 25, 1806, when the *Leander*, one of the British cruisers blockading New York, 'accidentally' fired on a coastwise vessel, a quarter-mile from shore, and shot off the head of John Pierce, the helmsman.[1] 'The Murder of Pierce' brought to a climax the national disgrace of allowing England, with impunity, in American waters to blockade, to plunder, to impress, and to kill. Compelled by popular clamor to take some sort of action, Jefferson issued a proclamation ordering American harbors to be forever closed to the offending British frigates and to their commanders.

His 'milk-and-water' policy only incited Britain's blockaders from Eastport to Savannah to fresh acts of insolence against a people they despised as 'craven money-grubbers.' In the same spirit British Minister Merry had reported that the Americans, from the weakness of their republic and the uncertainty of their Union, and 'from the prominent passion of avarice . . . and their intolerance under internal taxes,' could not and would not go to war. London should make no concessions to their negotiators. Rather it should send more warships to chastise these Yankee upstarts into 'that respect which they have recently lost toward Great Britain.'[2]

Nevertheless, Senator Clay in January of 1807 was optimistic. 'Our affairs with Britain are stated to be in a train of amicable adjustment,' he wrote Judge Todd, 'and the most favourable result is anticipated. Of those with Spain we still continue in the dark. But War does not seem to be a necessary event — indeed it de-

---

[1] Captain Basil Hall, then a midshipman on the *Leander*, some twenty years later 'was grieved, but not surprised,' to find the *Leander* still heartily detested at New York. 'The blockading service. . . whether legitimate or not, was certainly highly exciting, and sometimes rather profitable to us,' he wrote, but 'the provocation we gave was certainly considerable. . . . Every morning, at daybreak. . . we set about. . . firing off guns to the right and left, to make every ship. . . heave to, or wait, until we had leisure to send a boat on board. . . . I have frequently known a dozen, and sometimes a couple of dozen ships. . . losing their fair wind, their tide, and worse than all, their market, for many hours, sometimes the whole day, before our search was completed.' Sailors 'who were known to be, or supposed to be, British subjects,' were impressed, while a suspicion of French ownership, or of a defect in the ship's papers, led to seizure, a voyage to Halifax, and condemnation; if released, after months of detention, heavy damages, and perhaps loss of market, the ship ran no small chance of being seized and condemned under some new British order. Hall, *Fragments of Voyages and Travels*, etc., series I, pp. 46–48.

[2] Anthony Merry to C. J. Fox, May 4, 1806, Adams, *Hist. U. S.*, III, 202.

pends wholly upon the complexion of the information to be received.' [1]

Young Clay, meanwhile, might well have tempered his optimism by noting that America's army had been starved down to some three thousand regulars and her navy to a dozen warships. National defense, like national improvements, had encountered a formidable enemy in a doctrinaire States' Rights Republicanism. The ruling politicians, men who 'paint the ills which power attend ... but overlook the great propriety of power to guaranty society,' [2] were so zealous in protecting the states from Federal encroachments that they failed to protect the nation from foreign encroachments. The cub senator might well have pondered the paralyzing effects of 'pure Republicanism' not only upon measures designed to call forth and multiply America's resources but upon measures designed to defend her very existence.

Unmindful of disastrous Revolutionary experiences, Clay's fellow Republicans consistently neglected the armed services of the nation and relied upon those of the states, upon short-term militia volunteers, citizen soldiers notoriously lacking in equipment, training, and discipline. Their Jeffersonian economy, according to Washington Irving, was 'a kind of national starvation; an experiment how many ... necessaries the body politic can be deprived of before it perishes.' The Southeastern planters, spend-thrifts in private compared to Yankee Federalists, had disarmed the republic with their 'talismanic word of Economy.' And yet 'to call this nation pacific! most preposterous!' Grand Bashaw Jefferson's 'LOGARCHY, or government of words,' wages war upon the British Empire and most of the world, protecting our citizens from foreign plunderers, impressers, and murderers, and from domestic Bonapartes or Caesars as well; all this by proclamations: 'entirely ... *vi et lingua*; that is to say, by force of tongues.' [3]

---

[1] Clay to Todd, Jan. 24, 1807, *Innes MSS.*, 18.

[2] Fessenden, *Democracy Unveiled* (1806), I, 101.

[3] Irving, *Works*, I, 224, 233–35; *Salmagundi*, March–April, 1807. Bashaw Jefferson 'talks of vanquishing all opposition by the force of reason and philosophy: throws his gauntlet at all the nations of the earth, and defies them to meet him — on the field of argument! Is the national dignity insulted ... the bashaw of America — utters a speech. Does a foreign invader molest the commerce in the very mouth of the harbours ... his highness ... utters a speech. Are the free citizens of America dragged from on

No one was more extravagantly economical, more opposed to 'federalizing influences,' than John Randolph of Virginia, who in the House led the 'constitutional or tertium quids.' At this session only reluctantly did he permit the logocratic mountain to bring forth a litter of inexpensive Jeffersonian gunboats, 'ricketty little bantlings' of one or two guns, which were scorned not only by Britons but by Federalists and maritime Republicans whose constituents ploughed the seven seas.[1] Moreover, Randolph, Eppes of Virginia (Jefferson's son-in-law), and other Southerners rejoiced in America's defenseless condition as a positive good, a deterrent to war, and denounced as perniciously unrepublican the Washington-Federalist doctrine that 'to preserve peace we ought to prepare for war.' They refused to augment the army or to fortify New York, and avowed that in case of attack they would abandon America's commerce ('that fungus of Europe's wars') and the Atlantic cities as well.

Was it any wonder that seaboard Federalists assailed the 'malign envy' and 'puerile phylosophy' of the puissant 'Republican Lords of Virginia' (who had twenty-four congressmen to thirty-five for all New England)? Or questioned the value of the Union in face of such manifest 'disunion of views, interests, & feelings,' and prophesied a dreadful day of reckoning for such sectional bigotry and national folly?[2] Millions could be voted for Louisiana and Florida, they said. Yet the Northeast's commercial 'goose that lays the golden eggs' of revenue was quite unprotected. Adams gave millions for defense but not one cent for tribute. Jefferson, however, would give a two million bribe to Napoleon for bullying

---

board the vessels of their country, and forcibly detained in the war ships of another power — his highness — utters a speech. Is a peaceable citizen killed by the marauders of a foreign power, on the very shores of his country — his highness utters a speech. Does an alarming insurrection break out in a distant part of the empire — his highness utters a speech! — nay, more, for here he shows his "energies"; — he most intrepidly despatches a courier on horseback and orders him to ride one hundred and twenty miles a day, with a most formidable army of proclamations...'

[1] From the first lilliputian gunboat in 1804, which a cyclone had blown eight miles inland from Savannah, opponents derided Jefferson's 'whimsicalities' and 'moonstruck madness' as expressed in these mosquito craft with a waspish sting in their tails: thus, the Baltimore *Federal Republican*, Feb. 19, 1813:

> 'High and dry in cornfield, stood gun-boat No. one,
> Wiggle waggle went her tail, & pop went her gun.'

[2] N.Y. *Herald*, April 23, 26, 1806, and ff.

('our') West Florida out of Spain. How much better to spend two millions in honest 'Federalist' self-protection, they said, bitterly toasting 'The City of New York — Rich and Defenceless' and calling for 'National Honour — Founded not on calculation but in National Sentiment.'[1]

In an epoch which daily demonstrated might to be right the critical realist scoffed at the romantic 'whim-whams' of Henry Clay's fellow Republicans. Would peace be America's lot merely because Americans sincerely wished for peace? Did safety from war lie in a lack of defensive weapons? Surely one could repose little confidence in gunboats against the British Leviathan. Or in logocratic bullets of thrice-valiant editors and orators. Or in Jefferson's 'Quaker-gun diplomacy,' his policy of 'conquering without war,' his philosophic inclination 'to palliate and to endure.' In an armed world, in which weakness invited attack, the Sage of Monticello still believed that '*lying down* disarms a bully,' that '*reason* will supply restraints and make mankind a set of saints.'[2] King Quilldriver, said Federalists, only encouraged the nations small and great in their insults and injuries, by convincing them that the United States under no provocation would ever go to war. Yet most Americans — deluded souls! — still regarded Jefferson 'as a sort of Jupiter the second.' Supported by such patriots as General Wilkinson and Colonel-Editor Duane of the *Aurora*,[3]

---

[1] N.Y. *Herald*, Dec. 27, 1806.

[2] Fessenden, *op. cit.*, I, 83, II, 30, *passim*.

[3] See caricature by Peter Pencil, 1808, entitled *King Quilldriver's Experiments on National Defence*, reproduced opposite page 440 of this volume. In it Napoleon, upper right, blows for war between the United States and Great Britain. Jefferson, center, wearing a huge hat which has a windmill for a cockade, holding the Embargo Proclamation in his left hand and armed with a quill sword in his right, standing behind a fort built of proclamations, with his gunboats at 'Safe Moorings,' is saying: 'And thy will be done! War! War! — Embargo! But — Boney! For the sake of my popularity, do not blow too hard.'

Col. William Duane of the *Aurora*, foreground left, a receipt in his right hand, 'Received from the Emperor £20,000,' a quill sword in his left, is saying: 'I am a hell of a fellow to be sure. "A man that beareth false Witness against his neighbour, said Solomon, is a maul and a Sword, and a sharp arrow." Damme! I think I may take it up with the Pirates.'

General Wilkinson, foreground right, standing upon a barrel of Kentucky Tobacco, trampling upon the Constitution and the right of Habeas Corpus, is saying: 'How do you do! Colonel Billy! I am glad to see you in your Regimentals. Well I got you a Regiment — you may get me now a pension from Napoleon. My friend Carlos IV has not a single Cent to spare now. Devil take it!'

Jefferson with pacific proclamations and palavering tarradiddle
would make —

> 'England cease from war's alarms
> And Buonapart' lay down his arms!' [1]

Just how far these criticisms of the ruling Republicans were
merited by young Clay, only his future career would reveal. It
was obvious, however, that his Republicanism differed appreciably
from that of John Randolph — just as the farmer-democrats of a
dynamic New West differed appreciably from the planter-
republicans of a static Old Dominion. Curiously enough, the
Children of America who were expanding the republic territorially
had much in common with the Northeastern mariners who were
expanding the republic commercially. Equally pioneers 'with
dreams in their heads and iron in their blood,' they displayed the
same speculative enterprise and practical opportunism. Between
farming and trading frontiers the cross-pull of conflicting interests
and prejudices was strong, and to be expected. Yet as a national
Republican Clay could not fail to be concerned by the dangers to
the Union, internal as well as external, resulting from government's pointed neglect of commerce and of national defense.

In contrast with the defeatist pacifism and narrow particularism
of Randolph's stabilized Southeast was the expansive nationalism
of Clay's evolving West. Imbued with the spirit of the gallant
Louisiana Volunteers, ever ready to give a wider spread to
republicanism, his neighbors felt 'an irresistible ardour to maintain
national rights.' They would march to the seaboard, to Mobile, or
to Montreal, against 'the Reptile Spaniards' and against Britishers
who arrogantly 'do as they please with our Ships & Country Men.'
Clay himself would 'evince to the world that Americans appreciate
their rights in such a way as will induce them, when violated, to
engage in War with alacrity and effect.' [2] Obviously, this could
not be done with mere logocratic weapons.

National defense involves 'the good sense as well as the pride of
every American,' said Fielding Turner of Lexington in 1806. Like

---

[1] Fessenden, *op. cit.*, II, 3, 26.
[2] Clay to Breckinridge, Jan. 5, 1806, and others to same, Dec. 1805–Feb. 1806,
Breckinridge MSS.

Clay, he was aware that the outlying settlements from Detroit on the British border to St. Louis and around to the encircling Spanish border were defenseless in their isolation; that most of this wilderness hinterland was held by potential Indian allies of Spain and England. The good sense of maritime as well as territorial defense was appreciated by Judge McDowell — when we had 'No Ships of force to Defend our Trade on which almost our whole Revenue depends and almost no Regular Troops, not even as many as would be a Ralying Post for the Militia.' Yet in 1807 — whatever 'the complexion of the information to be received' from London, from Paris or Madrid — McDowell and other Westerners with good sense as well as national pride could only 'hope if we must have War that Congress will do everything necessary for our defense.' [1]

If young Clay of Kentucky was no devotee of the denationalizing anti-Federalism of John Randolph of Virginia he was even further removed from the denationalizing anti-Republicanism of Timothy Pickering of Massachusetts. No longer a Washington-Hamilton nationalist but an embittered out-of-power sectionalist, Pickering in the Northeast, like Randolph in the Southeast, was the chieftain of 'extreme party men, extreme in local attachments.'

'The session is drawing towards a close,' wrote Pickering in February of 1807, 'and I rejoice at it; sick at heart with the feeble administration of our affairs.' He was sickened not by Jefferson's feeble resistance to the predatory war Britain as far as suited her purposes was waging upon America, but by Jefferson's alleged subserviency to Bonaparte, Emperor of France and King of Italy. The spectacles of localism and Anglo-ism through which he squinted revealed the ruling 'Jacobins' to be vassals of Imperial France. His self-righteousness, his 'stand by — I am holier than thou!' attitude, would have been ludicrous had it not been so dangerous. Though he himself schemed to effect a British-protected Northern Confederacy, Pickering feared that Jefferson schemed to subvert America into a satellite of the Corsican Anti-Christ. The senator from witch-hunting Salem was patriotically

---

[1] F. L. Turner, Jan. 19, 1806, and S. McDowell, Dec. 27, 1805, to Breckinridge, *Breckinridge MSS.*

obsessed with 'the impending prospect of our becoming a province
... of the *Emperor* and *King*.' ¹

No such gloomy fears and morbid obsessions preyed upon young
Clay. Nevertheless, on February 15, he reported his concern over
a measure 'lately taken by Bonaparte of the most gigantic nature'
— the Berlin Decree, which, in alleged retaliation for the British
blockade from the Elbe to Brest, declared the British Isles in a state
of blockade. This economic broadside by a navyless France could
hardly damage the Mistress of the Seas directly. Yet, as Clay fore-
saw, Bonaparte could strike indirectly by seizing, in European
ports, American ships which supplied England with foodstuffs.
'It is said ... that our commerce is not to be affected' by the decree,
he wrote. 'I apprehend, however, that it will subject it to much
embarrassment.' ² The ocean of foreign relations was indeed more
troubled, more foreboding.

Meanwhile he eagerly awaited the treaty negotiated at London
by James Monroe and William Pinkney, hoping that it would
arrive before adjournment. With all Washington he speculated
on the effect an Anglo-American reconciliation would have on
French policy toward America. He shared 'the greatest anxiety
[which] prevails ... relative to the Impressment of American
Seamen on the High Seas' ³ — a grievance (as Madison said) that
'had been taken up as a Point of Honor by the People,' who 'never
would be satisfied until that Point was conceded by Great Britain.'⁴
So eager was Henry that he shocked rigid Calvinists by suggesting
that the Senate sit on Sunday, and thus clear the table for discussion of the British treaty.⁵

Finally, on the very last day of the session, the long-expected
treaty arrived. But Jefferson refused to submit it to the Senate or
to make its terms public. His action was ominous.

In truth the treaty was as bad as John Jay's. For Great Britain,
reported Monroe, 'was evidently prepared to hazard war' rather
than make concessions to an unarmed America, which seemingly

---

¹ Pickering to McHenry, Feb. 9, 1807, Steiner, B., *James McHenry*, p. 534.
² Clay to Thomas Prentiss, Feb. 15, 1807, Clay, *Corres.*, p. 15.
³ D. M. Erskine to Lord Howick, March 3, 1807, *F.O.* 5:52.
⁴ *Ibid.*, same to same, Feb. 2, 1807.   ⁵ Plumer, *Memo*, p. 634.

was wracked by 'Burr's Rebellion' and on the point of war with Spain, the ally of France.[1] Disregarding their instructions, Monroe and Pinkney had abandoned the two major issues: indemnities for illegally seized ships and cargoes, and the abolition of impressment. The latter was 'the great Point' which they 'had been particularly enjoined to press,' said Madison; it was the paramount popular grievance, said Erskine, the new and conciliatory British Minister, and until it was healed 'no Cordiality can be expected from this Country.' [2]

Further, and perhaps more shocking, Monroe and Pinkney had allowed Great Britain to reserve the right to disregard the treaty should the United States fail to resist Napoleon's Berlin Decree, although they had protested that this meant no treaty at all or the treaty and war with France.

Non-violent coercion had humiliatingly failed. And yet Clay might still report that 'War does not seem to be a necessary event.' Even the partial boycott remained in its logocratic scabbard until December of 1807. By that time the murder of Pierce and England's assaults upon the indirect trade had been dwarfed by the 'Murders of the *Chesapeake*' and her assaults upon America's direct trade.

On March 3, 1807, the Ninth Congress adjourned, with Jefferson pigeonholing the British treaty, and with Clay biding his time until he could play a leading rôle in shaping foreign policy.

This session initiated Henry not only into national politics but into the Washington society of which he was to be so conspicuous a member. 'An orator . . . of the first fire' on Capitol Hill, in the

---

[1] Monroe to Madison, Feb. 28, 1808, *A. S. P., For. Rel.*, III, 183.

[2] Erskine to Howick, Feb. 2, 1807, *F.O.* 5:52. Erskine felt it his duty to remark 'that all the Parties in this Country take a warm interest on the Point of the Non-Impressment of Sailors (claimed as British) out of American Ships on the High Seas.' Mr. Madison told me 'that he was confident that America never would consent to abandon that Point, and contended that the Injury that would arise to the American Commerce, from their Ships being liable to be Stript of their Crew and left sometimes without Men enough to navigate them safely, infinitely outweighed the Inconveniences that might be incurred by a few British Sailors being withdrawn from His Majesty's Service for a Short Time, as he said it would be easy for us to recover them when arrived in our own Ports. . . . He further observed . . . that if Justice was done them on that Head, he believed the most friendly and advantageous Intercourse might be established . . .'

salons he was regarded as 'a genteel polite & pleasant companion.' [1] The civilities he accorded others were returned in good measure: his reception, so he wrote Colonel Hart, had far exceeded his expectations. 'Those who are disposed to flatter me say that I have acquitted myself with great credit in several debates in the Senate.' [2]

Among those so disposed was Plumer of New Hampshire, whose first impressions, of a young man courteous, 'intelligent, sensible ... frank & candid,' had been confirmed by a more intimate acquaintance. A lawyer-politician of about fifty, studious and discerning, this Yankee Federalist had rated the Kentuckian eloquent and effective. Outside of Congress he found him 'a man of pleasure — very fond of amusements — gambles much ... a man of honor & integrity.' [3]

They were messmates at Frost and Quinn's near the Capitol. After a day in the Senate they would return to attack a substantial meal, worthy of 'this land of Hog, homminey & hoe-cake,' and to linger about the long table, comfortably established by Plumer's 'Demijohn of Madeira wine, London particular.' A good story-teller, the 'genteel polite & pleasant' young squire of Ashland helped to enliven the winter evenings for a mess composed mostly of Federalists, only one of whom was a bigoted Pickeronian — Doctor Tenney of New Hampshire, whom Plumer dismissed as being 'as destitute of wit, humour & vivacity as lead is of elasticity.' [4] The mess was congenial. Yet Henry had no intention of living as most congressmen were said to do, confined to stuffy boarding-houses 'like bears, brutalised and stupified ... from hearing nothing but politics from morning to night.' [5]

Others might complain of the hackney-coaches that bounced them over the rutted cow-paths of 'this desert-city' to parties three to eight miles from Capitol Hill. Ever-present were the dangers of being overturned or mired — a dreadful dilemma, said young

---

[1] Plumer, *Memo*, p. 608.
[2] Clay to Hart, Feb. 1, 1807, Schurz, Carl, *Henry Clay*, I, 47.
[3] Plumer, *loc. cit.*   [4] *Ibid.*, pp. 570–71.
[5] Foster, A. J., 'Notes on the U. S.,' *The Museum*, XV, p. 32 (printed selections from his MS. 'Notes ... Collected in the Years 1804–5–6–7 and 11–12,' *Foster MSS.*).

Augustus Foster, Secretary of the British Legation, the delicately nurtured son of the Duchess of Devonshire, 'when one can neither go backwards nor forwards, and either loses one's shoes or one's patience.' [1] But these did not deter a circuit-riding Kentucky lawyer eager for the sparkle and gaiety of the capital, the whirl of parties, the games of brag and loo, the polite and generous drinking, the hobnobbing with public men from all parts of the Union, and the charms of feminine society. [2]

'He is a great favorite with the ladies,' recorded the observant Plumer, 'is in all parties of pleasure — out almost every night — gambles much here — reads but little. Indeed he said he meant this session should be a tour of pleasure.' [3]

Henry's tour was pleasingly varied. It embraced dinners and balls at the cabinet ministers' and legations, at Colonel John Tayloe's Octagon House and Daniel Carroll's Duddington Manor. It took him to the Washington Assemblies, to the little theatre where the Great Manfredi and family nimbly cavorted on a tightrope, and to the banquet given Meriwether Lewis, who had explored Louisiana to the broad Pacific — an event warmly patriotic, at which Doctor Joel Barlow read an original poem and Robert Fulton toasted the American Eagle's spreading wings. [4] It brought him to the President's New Year Levee, where, with the scarletcoated Marine Band playing, the sun shining warmly, 'great mirth and good humor' prevailing, and with the sideboard piled high with wines, cakes, and ice cream, the tall, raw-boned, freckled Jefferson greeted with dignified simplicity congressmen, army and navy officers, turbaned ladies, gold-braided diplomats, and blanketed Osage and Mandan Indians — 'our savage brethren from the *Far West.*' [5]

---

[1] Foster, A. J., 'Notes on the U. S.,' *The Museum*, XV, p. 37.

[2] 'Private parties are frequent,' wrote Mitchill of New York, Jan. 31, 1807 (Wash. *Evening Star*, May 27, 1894); 'there is a good deal of high life... a number of families here... delight in gay and fashionable display. The succession of these renders the place agreeable enough for polite strangers of all sorts, and particularly for ladies. A woman of quality who is fond of gayety and carousing need be at no loss for occupation at this place during the session of Congress.'

[3] Plumer, *Memo*, p. 608.

[4] *Ibid.*, p. 534, *passim; Natl. Intelligencer*, Jan. 16, 1807, *passim.*

[5] 'Of the personages present I observed the King and Queen of the Mandanes, a tribe... living about 1,600 miles up the Missouri River. His Majesty was dressed in a

Admittedly the first wonder of Washington was the Virginia aristocrat who led the hosts of democracy, whom a daughter of the Bayard Federalist family, and most Americans, regarded as 'truly a philosopher, and truly a good man, and eminently a great one.' [1] Mr. Jefferson's reddish hair had grayed since Henry had last seen him at Richmond, yet his slow smile and soft manner were still as gracious. He seemed less interested in politics than in his rare plants and music, his many inventions (some of which were more ingenious than practical), his grizzly bears presented him by Lewis and Clark, and his favorite mocking-bird, 'the constant companion of his solitary and studious hours,' that perched on his shoulder and sang among his roses and geraniums. His dinners in the French style, as Clay discovered, were superb — and entertaining. 'The Philosophic Statesman' joked about the half-ton Mammoth Cheese given him by Massachusetts Republicans (which contained not one drop of milk from a Federalist cow — vile stuff, said Plumer); and he freely indulged in what soberly precise John Quincy Adams called 'his itch for telling prodigies.' [2]

Jefferson's itch for 'startling tales' as well as his 'philosophic humility' in manner and dress provoked scornful comments not only from Samuel Tenney of Clay's mess but from British Mr. Foster. 'Excessive vanity and speculative doctrines on imaginary perfection, together with the love of popularity and paradox,' said Foster, 'were his weakness — and to indulge them he flattered the low passions of a mere newspaper-taught rabble...' Foster's Tory

---

sort of regimental coat given him by the Government since his arrival, and her Majesty, wrapped in a blanket, sat on one of the sofas in the great audience-chamber, and received the visits of the ladies and people of quality. ... Besides the smiles of cordiality and welcome which the company received from their generous entertainer, they consumed for him a quarter cask of wine, a barrel of punch and a hundred-weight of cake, besides other knick-knacks to a considerable amount' — and departed 'in high hope that Mr. Jefferson might long continue in the presidential chair. The ladies in particular are charmed with his handsome way of doing things.' Mitchill, Jan. 31, 1807, Wash. *Evening Star*, May 27, 1894. See, also, Plumer, *Memo*, pp. 553–54, Jan. 1, 1807.

[1] Smith, Margaret Bayard (Mrs. Samuel Harrison Smith, wife of the editor of the *National Intelligencer* and cousin of Senator Bayard), *Forty Years*, p. 79; also, pp. 383–412, *passim*. ' "And is this," I said, after my first interview with Mr. Jefferson, "the violent democrat, the vulgar demagogue, the bold atheist, the profligate man I have so often heard denounced by the federalists... this man so meek and mild, yet dignified ... so benignant and intelligent...?" ' *Ibid.*, pp. 5–6.

[2] Adams, *Memoirs*, I, 457–58, 330–31; Plumer, *op. cit.*, p. 212, *passim*.

sensibilities were offended by a Republican Court which was 'raw and rude,' where 'a disgusting democracy' accorded a British Minister no higher rank than a common citizen or a visiting Creek or Osage chieftain.[1]

This Jeffersonian Washington which Clay toured was likewise an inviting target for Tory and Federalist critics who prescribed an Old World subordination of 'the American peasantry,' of 'the puissant tail of the body politic.' To Tom Moore the capital, where 'nought but woods and Jefferson they see, where streets should run and *sages* ought to be,' presented a 'characteristic display of arrogant speculation and premature ruin.' It seemed ample proof that America was no elysian Promised Land but 'the child of Gallia's school,' poisoned and blighted by 'bastard freedom' and 'piebald polity.' It was the embryo capital of a land 'where every ill the ancient world could brew is mix'd with every grossness of the new,' of an embryo nation whose days already 'were done, rank without ripeness, quicken'd without sun, crude at the surface, rotten at the core.'[2]

Quite different were Henry's impressions. His tour made him acquainted with distinguished men who shared his own sanguine faith in the much criticized American experiment. He met not only the executive directory of Jefferson, Madison, and Gallatin, and such men of action as Lewis, the pathfinder, and young Decatur, who at Tripoli had so gallantly carried on the John Paul Jones tradition; but men of science and letters, of versatile genius, sensitive social conscience, and boundless ambition to bring about the greatest good of the greatest number and thus realize the promise of America.

Nevertheless, just as Clay's frontiersmen were scorned by tory-fied critics as the most boorish of Jefferson's 'newspaper-taught rabble,' so were Jefferson's 'pedant throng' scorned as the most fatuous of idealists, men who would 'belie the monuments of frailty past, and plant perfection in this world at last!'[3] With Jefferson, said Foster, they 'lived ... on illusions and mystic philanthropic plans' and 'loved to dream eyes open, or, as the

---

[1] Foster, *Notes on U. S.*, p. 33.   [2] Moore, T., *Works*, II, 284–318 (1804).
[3] Moore, *op. cit.*, II, 285.

Germans say, "zu schwärmen." ' Indeed, this whole nation was 'the paradise for "Schwärmers." ' ¹ No one could gainsay the extraordinary energy and practicality of these 'dreamy' Americans on land and on sea. The jaundiced critic, however, was convinced that any nation that 'wallowed in the mire of democracy' must be 'rotten at the core.' And to him, this fresh American energy was but money-grubbing anarchy, this fresh American idealism but the Jacobinic 'slaver of our frantick times.'

Among the Jeffersonian liberals whom young Clay met were men like Joel Barlow — who was a 'Schwärmer,' and also a shrewd Yankee who had amassed a fortune in business, a diplomat, French revolutionist with Tom Paine, a Western land-promoter, and 'the greatest poet of our country.' ² In the salons Mr. Barlow was congratulated upon his poems, which urged America to lead the world to national liberty and to international peace; he was much interested in government-aided internal improvements, and much distressed that the merchants should be 'raving for war, . . . chiefly as a field of speculation.' ³ His protégé, Robert Fulton, talked about his steamboat, scorned as 'Fulton's Folly,' which in August was to inaugurate a revolution in transportation. Benjamin Latrobe was highly praised for his designs for the new wing of the Capitol, the classic purity of his Bank of Pennsylvania building, and the steam-operated waterworks, a novelty indeed, which he had installed at Philadelphia. Doctor Samuel Mitchill, gallant and gossipy, a senator, scientist, teacher, poet, and the editor of the *Medical Repository*, was quizzed as to 'the laughing philosophers' of (Washington Irving's) *Salmagundi*, who were gaily satirizing everything from Jefferson's 'French red breeches' to British 'travel-mongers,' gunboats, and Yankee bundling.

If the conversation was not always worthy of 'the march of intellect so much vaunted in the present century,' Henry found the ladies charming and Washington already 'one of the most marrying places of the whole continent.' He joined in the gossip — about

---

¹ Foster, *op. cit.*, p. 42. Foster noted, however, that even if Jefferson 'loved to dream eyes open... he was not the less awake or active in taking measures to ensure the triumph of himself and his party.'

² Smith, *Forty Years*, p. 55.

³ Barlow to Jefferson, Feb. 25, 1807, *Jefferson MSS.*

'aged damsels flirting in the gay undress of eighteen,' the excellent snipe shooting close by the Capitol, and John Tayloe's success at the Washington races. Or about Mr. Munn, the Georgetown blacksmith-preacher, who ranted 'in true bathos style' while his frenzied disciples 'sang and danced the Methodist turnabout,' the free-thinking congressmen who made out checks 'To Jesus Christ or bearer,' and the ballroom coquetry which had 'beguiled the tedium' of divine service at the Capitol on Sunday last. They talked of 'the misunderstanding' and of 'the rupture' of the Turreaus; but Aaron Burr, of course, was the chief topic — a fitting topic for a people who, according to Foster, 'love excitement . . . and would imitate, if they could, those heroes in the eyes of all gamblers, a Buonaparte or a Caesar.' As at Olympian Springs, every detail was relished of the latest affair of romantic 'men of the Pistol' — the duel in which Doctor Archer of the navy had been killed by Doctor Smith of the army over 'some ungenerous expressions' upon the daughter of William Eaton.[1]

Akin to the spirit of these quick-triggered hotspurs was the national 'nervous susceptibility as to the opinion foreigners, or rather Englishmen, entertain of America.'[2] At this session it expressed itself in criticism of the low-caliber diplomats Europe sent to a New World republic self-acclaimed as 'the most enlightened country under the sun.' The new British Minister, youthful David Montague Erskine, a Whig, with an American wife, and disposed to be friendly, was by Plumer described as being 'of feeble intellect & very ignorant.' The French Minister, General Turreau de Garambonville, was 'of little learning . . . ferocious disposition, and brutal manners.'[3] This ruffian dignitary was disliked even by 'the French party,' although it was difficult, said a prejudiced Englishman, to shock 'the Irish rebels or butchers and hangmen-sheriffs of Congress.'[4]

---

[1] Foster, *Notes on U. S.*, pp. 37–40, and *MS. Notes*, III, 71; Smith, *Forty Years*, pp. 13–14; Story, *Joseph Story*, I, 196; Latrobe, B. H., *Journal*, pp. 250–57; Taggart, *Letters*, p. 203.

[2] Foster, *Notes*, pp. 44–45. This thin-skinnedness was slight in the seaport merchants but acute in Southerners and Westerners and the recent immigrant, released from Old World restraints, who acted 'like a great cart-horse turned loose upon a plain, kicking and snorting . . . delighted with rolling about in the mire of democracy.'

[3] Plumer, *Memo*, pp. 635–36.

[4] Foster, *Notes on U. S.*, p. 35 (editor's comment).

It was not because Louis Marie Turreau de Garambonville, Marshal of France, red of face, with fierce mustachios, and a uniform heavy with lace, gold braid, and decorations (envied by General Wilkinson, regarded as impertinent by Mr. Jefferson), was 'distinguished by the uncommon size and extent of his whiskers, which cover the greater part of his cheeks.' [1] Or that he was notorious for his Jacobinic infamies during Robespierre's Reign of Terror. Or that he ill concealed his Old World contempt for the village simplicity of Washington, for pacific America's weak republic, or for mild 'Little Madison,' who in his dryly passionate way repulsed the General when he insisted arrogantly that Napoleon would have the United States do this and do that. Rather was it because of the 'barbarous . . . most indecent and scandalous . . . immoral Conduct' of the envoy from Imperial France, who horsewhipped his wife and at this session had driven her to live apart, on republican charity.[2]

The presence of 'Monsieur Whiskerandeau, the cutthroat' (as Federalists openly called him) was enough to convince even the most rabid anti-British democrat that the American from his predominantly British heritage, however modified it had been by other racial elements and especially by the New World environment, retained a good deal of what Mr. Latrobe called his 'practical English unsociability to the French.' [3] This swashbuckling Bonapartist only further disillusioned liberals who with young Clay had once sung *Freedom's Sons Are Frenchmen All.* Whether the anti-British prejudices, so intimately connected with the nascent nationalism of Britain's former colonists, remained constant or increased in emotional intensity, the behavior of Turreau, like that of his imperial master, could only break down earlier pro-French prejudices and provoke spirited young Americans like Clay to cry out, 'A plague on both your houses!'

---

[1] S. L. Mitchill, Jan. 31, 1807, in Wash. *Evening Star*, May 27, 1894.

[2] He would whip Mme. Turreau (a jailer's daughter) while his man played the violoncello to drown her cries. A few months before, in November, 1806, when some sailors by his order tried to spirit her away to a French frigate outward bound from Annapolis, Washington citizens, aroused by her yells, appeared with blunderbusses, defied the General, who stood at the window pistol in hand, and foiled him in this, his latest villainy. Mitchill, *loc. cit.*; Plumer, *op. cit.*, 521, 555; N.Y. *Herald*, Nov. 29, 1806; Foster, *loc. cit.*; also, Merry to Lord Mulgrave, June 30, 1805, *F.O.* 5:45.

[3] Latrobe, B. H., *Journal*, p. 46.

Romantic ladies shivered whenever 'Bluebeard' Turreau appeared, twirling his French mustachios, appraising them with his Latin eyes, and sighed for an earlier day when a Frenchman was chivalry itself. Alas, it was a new age. The modest minuet was yielding to the waltz, this 'loving, hugging dance, this imp of Germany — brought up in France'; pious Bunyan was giving place to 'the lascivious rhapsodies of Moore' and 'novels of a new and rakish race'; buckram fashions to flesh-colored silk stockings and French Empire dresses — '*nudity* being all the rage.' [1] The 'Fig-Leaf' or 'Madam Eve' gowns introduced by Madame Jerome Bonaparte from a Paris where *sans culotte* had given way to *sans chemise*, so thin they could be put in one's waistcoat pocket, were said to be 'astonishingly bewitching.' But Mrs. Josiah Quincy of Boston could only cluck her tongue and cry out, 'What a state of manners and morals!' [2]

'A great favorite with the ladies' and 'in all parties of pleasure,' the tall, slender, fair-haired, and vivacious Henry Clay made many friends. Among them was Mrs. Samuel Harrison Smith, the capital's foremost bluestocking, who at subsequent sessions would have much to say about the Kentuckian's 'soul-speaking eye and persuasive voice,' his 'unrivalled and surpassing talents,' finding in him 'an openness, communicativeness, an affectionateness and warmth and kindness which were irresistibly captivating.' [3] With the renowned Dolly Madison, whose social zest and adaptability matched his own, he talked of Hanover County, where both had spent their childhood. They were soon calling each other 'Cousin Henry' and 'Cousin Dolly.' [4] Congenial also was Mr. Madison, who, if most solemn in public, could be 'incomparably pleasant.' [5] Even Mr. Foster, who thought Madison 'rather too much the disputatious pleader,' found him in private to be 'a social, jovial,

---

[1] Irving, W., *Works*, I, 236, 220; *Salmagundi*, Nos. III, VI, Feb., Mar., 1807. 'The fashion of dressing with a very few clothes is still in vogue, and the delicate belles show even in the coldest weather not only their faces and necks, but their upper bosoms and, indeed, almost all...' S. L. Mitchill, April 6, 1806, Wash. *Evening Star*, May 27, 1894.

[2] Smith, *Forty Years*, pp. 46–47; Baldwin, S. E., *Simeon Baldwin*, p. 345; Quincy, E. S. M., *Memoir*, p. 127.

[3] Smith, *op. cit.*, pp. 304, 286, 325, *passim*.

[4] Clark, A. C., *Life and Letters of Dolly Madison*, p. 461, *passim*.

[5] Benj. Latrobe, in Semmes, J. E., *John H. B. Latrobe*, p. 12.

and good-humoured companion, full of anecdote, sometimes rather of a loose description.' [1]

At the Madisons, as elsewhere, polite gambling was a great resource of an evening; indeed, to many ladies (said Senator Mitchill) 'cards are almost necessaries of life.' Loo was the favorite game of the ladies, who, when *looed*, pronounced the word in a very mincing manner. Brag was Henry's game when he played with such new friends as young Caesar Augustus Rodney of Delaware, the Attorney General, and Bayard of the same state, a man of polished manners and warm feelings — which were sometimes expressed with duelling pistols. Brag, 'the most gambling of all games, as being one of countenance as well as cards,' greatly aided Bayard to bear up under 'the wretched politicks of the day, in the dull seclusion of Washington.' [2] Clay kept a good countenance, whether his favorite goddess frowned or whether she enabled him in triumph to cry out, 'Two bullets and a bragger!' He played for high stakes: the three thousand dollars for cases to be argued in the Supreme Court gave zest to his tour. 'One evening he won at cards $1500,' noted Plumer; 'at another he lost $600.' [3]

These were eventful and enjoyable months. 'But after all I have seen,' wrote Henry to Colonel Hart, 'Kentucky is still my favorite country. There amidst my family I shall find happiness in a degree to be met with nowhere else.' [4] He did not intend to run for Congress upon his return, so he informed Plumer. He was too much interested in his law practice and in his new estate of Ashland; planning the brick house Latrobe was to design, and buying the celebrated Buzzard, that Colonel Tayloe assured him was 'the finest horse upon the Continent.' Two young men whom he met, attracted by the fame and fortune he had attained, and by his warm interest in them, were to accompany him to Kentucky, one to practice law, the other to study law in his office. He did not forget his Transylvania students: he chided them for not writing

---

[1] Foster, *Notes on U. S.*, p. 42.

[2] Bayard, *Papers*, pp. 155, 120; Foster, *Notes*, p. 37; S. L. Mitchill, Jan. 31, 1807, Wash. *Evening Star*, May 27, 1894.

[3] Plumer, *Memo*, p. 608.

[4] Clay to Hart, Feb. 1, 1807, Schurz, *Clay*, I, 47.

more frequently, praised the New Year's ode Thomas Prentiss sent him, and advised them as to their reading. Nor did he, 'a young lawyer of considerable eminence' according to Plumer, forget his business before the Supreme Court.[1]

In February lawyers coming on for the spring term filled Clay's boarding-house to capacity. Among those from Philadelphia was Joseph Hopkinson (who in 1798 had written the Federalist *Hail Columbia*); among those from Maryland was Francis Scott Key (who in 1814 was to write the national anthem). The mess was increased to some thirty men — a group, said Plumer, 'intelligent & highly agreeable.' Even 'General' Eaton, whose heavy drinking and Mussulman antics had been annoying, was 'awed into respect & self-government.' [2]

Henry was pleased to be with these lawyers of national reputation, but he was unprepared for the arrival, at his own lodgings, of a lawyer from Kentucky. None other than Humphrey Marshall!

He found himself in the position of John Brown (one of his clients contributing to the purse of three thousand dollars), when Brown and Marshall had been senators. 'H. M. is here,' John Brown had written his brother James, '& we make out tolerably well to *save appearances*.' [3] Of this Washington meeting Humphrey remarked that there was 'much coldness in our intercourse' but Mr. Clay was 'not uncivil, nor entirely forgetful of our relations as citizens of the same state.' [4]

His arrival, like that of John Wood, recalled vividly to Clay and other Kentuckians the discord blown up by the *Western World* Junto. Had Marshall come East like Wood to contribute further to the all-engulfing Burr whirlpool? Had he come to demand an investigation into the pioneer 'Spanish Conspiracy' and make good his threat to drive Innes, 'the Espaniolized traitor,' from the bench?

To clear his good name, Innes had already requested an im-

---

[1] Plumer, *op. cit.*, p. 565; Clay to Prentiss, Feb. 15, 1807, Clay, *Corres.*, pp. 14–15; Clay to Thomas Todd, Jan. 24, 1807, *Innes MSS.*, 16.

[2] Plumer, *op. cit.*, p. 613.

[3] John Brown to James Brown, Phila., Jan. 14, 1795, *Jas. Brown MSS.*

[4] *Ky. Gazette*, Feb. 18, 1832.

mediate inquiry. Clay had received three letters from the distraught Judge. With Mr. Thruston, Captain Fowler, General Walton, and General Sandford of the Kentucky delegation he had regarded this as unnecessary and, in view of the agitated state of affairs, impolitic. 'We were all of opinion,' wrote Henry, 'that you had acted incorruptly & not so as to subject yourself to impeachment; and that altho' you may have erred in not communicating to the Government the propositions of Spain, you could not thereby have incurred a forfeiture of your office.' [1] Should 'your arch Enemy' attempt any 'Deeds of Darkness,' wrote Thruston to Innes, 'I shall certainly use all my feeble Efforts to Render them abortive.' [2] None were attempted. Humphrey had come to attend the Supreme Court.

In the basement of the Capitol sat the republic's highest tribunal. John Marshall was here dominant. Like Humphrey, his brother-in-law, he was tall and swarthy; like Jefferson, his distant relative and opponent, he was negligent of dress 'in the Virginia style of carelessness.' Clay also recalled from his Richmond days Justice Bushrod Washington, a wizened and beardless man, blind in one eye from study, his face and robe smeared with snuff. With them on the bench were young and capable William Johnson of South Carolina, scholarly-appearing Brockholst Livingston of New York, who in the days of '98 had killed a Federalist under the Code Duello, and Samuel Chase of Maryland, a grumbling Doctor Johnson sort of man, recently acquitted at the impeachment trial presided over by Aaron Burr.

Only two of Clay's cases were heard, both land-title suits on appeal from Kentucky. One, argued against Charles Lee of Virginia, who had been Adams's Attorney General, resulted in a compromise. The other, argued against Humphrey, concerned the

---

[1] Clay to Innes, Jan. 16, 1807, *Durrett Coll.* 'Nothing was to be gained,' wrote John Fowler, 'and some of Marshall's friends if he has any (of this I much doubt) might have seized on such an opportunity of wounding your feelings.' Fowler to Innes, March 4, 1807; also, to same, M. Walton, J. Hughes, Jan.–Feb., 1807, *Innes MSS.*, 19.

[2] Thruston to Innes, Feb. 18, 1807, *Innes MSS.*, 19. 'Being convinced of the Purity of your Heart from...long observation of your Character,' he wrote, '... a Regard for Truth, and a Respect for the inestimable Value of good Fame have urged me to ward off from you...every Imputation which Ignorance Malice or Envy has at any Time been disposed in my Hearing to throw upon you... it has been a rare Thing to hear you spoken of even in Terms of the slightest Disrespect.'

rival claims of James Currie and Thomas Marshall, the father of the Chief Justice.

Henry contended that the Currie entry of August 7, 1784, was valid because the Marshall entry of August 6, 1784, depended upon such vague expressions as 'a *few* poles, a *small* distance, a *branch*,' and that the court was 'now called upon not to give a construction of the law to the words of the entry, but to make a new entry in point of fact.' Nevertheless, just before Congress adjourned, the court decided for the prior Marshall entry.[1] Humphrey was jubilant. But when Henry at once petitioned for a rehearing, he was angered. Marshall was convinced that 'Mr. Clay felt more on the subject than a necessary attachment to his client's interest.'[2]

In this vindictive mood Kentucky's chief Federalist departed for the Blue Grass. There, with public opinion still swirling in the Burr vortex, he was to prove only too well, in the words of 'exquisitely delicate' Senator Thruston, 'that Innocence is not a Shield with a mind of Sensibility, against Vexations which Obloquy is capable of creating.'[3] Humphrey was to vex the 'genteel polite & pleasant' Mr. Clay. That young Republican, 'of the first fire,' was to resort first to goose quills dipped in vitriol and then to pistols charged with the leaden pills of the Code Duello.

---

[1] *U. S. Supreme Court Reports*, Cranch, IV, 171–77; 136–41.
[2] *Ky. Gazette*, Feb. 18, 1832.
[3] Thruston to Innes, Feb. 18, 1807, *Innes MSS.*, 19.

Chapter Nine. Goose Quills and Duelling Pistols

This adventurer Burr has caused more disquiettude in this country than any man ever did in america. (James Taylor.)

Mr. Clay rode the high horse of party, with much gallantry indeed... Had he not run his brute on me, I never should have encountered him. (Humphrey Marshall.)

What, in short, is the whole system of Europe towards America but an atrocious and insulting tyranny? One hemisphere of the earth... is made subservient to all the petty interests of the other, to their laws, their regulations, their passions and wars. (Jefferson.)

UPON his return to Kentucky, where the people on all sides were cursing 'the Modern Benedict Arnold,' praying that 'the tree of Liberty may never produce another Burr,' and wishing both Wilkinson and Burr 'a speedy transportation to Botany Bay,' Clay noted with concern the activities of Marshall's Junto. Burr's conspiracy, they said, was but the culmination of earlier plots, the sponsors of which must also be exposed and punished. Their attack was directed at the older Republicans, the founding fathers of Kentucky. Yet Henry, too, was marked for defamation: these character-assassins, warned Justice Todd, 'have a rod in soak for *even* you.' [1]

It was a rod which the Federalist Junto wielded vigorously, if obliquely. They did not accuse young Clay of participating in

---

[1] Thomas Todd to Clay, May 25, 1807, *Clay MSS*.

any plots — Daveiss, indeed, had termed him 'wholly innocent.'
But they did regard him as the active leader of Kentucky Republicanism, the chief obstacle in their path to revenge and power.
Skilled in covert attack, Marshall held that Clay *'though no
conspirator,* yet, as a warm and intimate friend of theirs,' had
countenanced the Burrites, as well as Nicholas, Brown, and Breckinridge, Innes, Todd, Bradford, and others of the pioneer Democratic Society, whom the *Western World* put on a par with
Sebastian, Wilkinson, and Burr. 'Mr. Clay took the side of the
guilty' and thus 'divested himself of every claim to patriotism,'
said Marshall. 'For the supporter of *disunionists* is a *disunionist!*' [1]

To Henry he applied the same sort of reasoning that irate and
grossly abusive Republicans applied to Chief Justice Marshall for
acquitting Burr.[2] Yet he used his rod on neither 'Burrite' John
Marshall nor Eastern Federalists — who now depicted Burr as the
victim of Jefferson's malice. That pleasure he reserved for 'Burrite'
Henry Clay and Republican enemies — who now cursed 'Catiline
Burr.'

Humphrey Marshall was in a strong tactical position. For the
times had greatly changed since Kentuckians, treated as 'aliens or
enemies,' had been forced to act in self-defense and for self-preservation. Gone was the pronounced sectionalism of the days when
Jay's East tried to barter away the Mississippi; when Marshall's
Federalists enacted the Whiskey Excise, Jay's Treaty, and the
Sedition Law. The pronounced nationalism since Jefferson's
advent to power, now brought to white heat by Burr's 'treason,' [3]
had given Marshall a powerful weapon against the Jeffersonians.
As George Nicholas's brother wrote Harry Innes, the pioneer
leaders would not be judged, alas, from pioneer conditions 'but
from the state of things at this day.' [4]

---

[1] *Ky. Gazette*, Feb. 4, Jan. 28, 1832.

[2] 'Had public sentiment... been heeded... John Marshall would have been
impeached... and... convicted.' Beveridge, *Marshall*, III, 531–32. From New
Orleans in October, 1807, Dr. Sam Brown wrote John Brown: '... How will Mr.
Humphrey Marshall and his backers shape their course now that Brother John is so
directly charged with being a partisan of Burr's and yielding to all Burr's wishes in the
trial...' McElroy, *Ky. in the Nation's Hist.*, p. 313 n.

[3] 'I think it may more thourily serment every part of the union,' wrote James Robertson to Sen. Smith of Tennessee. 'The general voice is *death* to him or them that shall
attempt to disunite the... government.' Jackson, A., *Corres.*, I, 164.

[4] Wilson Cary Nicholas to Innes, May 5, 1807, *Innes MSS.*, 19.

Republican morale was badly shaken. 'I have resided in this Country more than twenty-two years,' wrote Colonel Joseph Crockett, the United States Marshal, 'and in all that period have never known it so much divided and agitated' since the *Western World* was set up 'for the express purpose of changing the politics of this state from warm republican to federalists.' [1] It seemed to be the crisis predicted by James Brown when malcontents would sow 'the detestable doctrines of Yankee federalism amongst us.' [2] Men ventured to criticize Jefferson, complaining that 'Tom's Philosophy will not do for these calamitous times.' [3] In Congress, Mat Lyon and John Rowan were in open revolt. With Randolph's Quids and the Federalists, Rowan was trying to use Wilkinson (as the Junto was trying to use Innes) as a 'hobby-horse to disaffect the people of the West and to ride down the present administration.' [4] Marshall, Daveiss, and their 'base & scurrilous Editor' of the *Western World*, were booted, spurred, and in full cry. 'No man is safe from their malicious attacks,' wrote Justice Todd.[5] 'Col. Nicholas and Mr. Breckinridge being dead,' wrote Crockett to Jefferson, 'they think they have nothing to fear.' [6]

The crisis demanded a bold leader, one who could rally the disaffected and revive the militant spirit of Nicholas and Breckinridge. Young Clay proved to be such a man. Upon his return from the Senate he defied the Junto, and the anti-Burr hysteria as well, by appearing as counsel for Harman Blennerhassett.

Released after imprisonment in Mississippi, the 'Admiral of Burr's Navy' had returned only to be thrown into the Lexington jail by merchants who held him responsible for Burr's protested notes amounting to some forty-two thousand dollars.[7] The erst-

---

[1] Crockett to Jefferson, Jan. 9, 1807, *Jefferson MSS*.

[2] Brown to Breckinridge, Jan. 22, 1805, *Breckinridge MSS*.

[3] Wm. T. Barry to Dr. John Barry, Dec. 6, 1806, Barry, *Letters*, p. 328. Young Barry, friend of Clay and later Postmaster General under Andrew Jackson, on January 2, 1807 (*ibid.*, pp. 329–30; to same) stated that 'there is a great noise here; people are cursing B[urr] and all his adherents,' including Adair and General Jackson of Tennessee. Even 'the would-be Lexington Franklin, alias Bradford, has publicly declared that B[urr] is the greatest rascal in the world... Everything is in commotion here.'

[4] John Pope to N. Edwards, Jan. 9, 1808, Edwards, N., *Papers*, pp. 31–35.

[5] Todd to Clay, May 25, 1807, *Clay MSS*.

[6] Crockett to Jefferson, Jan. 9, 1807, *Jefferson MSS*.

[7] By protesting the bills of exchange which he sold in Lexington, Burr 'will ruin some

while Lord of Blennerhassett's Island was now forlorn, pitiable. Gone forever were fortune and reputation. Gone those halcyon days when he had puttered about with his music and gardening, his books and philosophical apparatus. Former friends (except Colonel Meade of Chaumière) did not dare visit 'the conspirator' in his lonely cell, where he brooded over Burr's duplicity, his shattered dreams of grandeur under Emperor Aaron, and the indignities inflicted upon him 'in this focus of Democracy.'

Before Blennerhassett could be tried on the civil action he was seized by Marshal Crockett to be taken to Richmond, where he had been indicted with Burr for treason. Clay protested, at a hearing before Justice Todd, at this 'unprecedented and illegal' interference. His client, however, wished to leave at once; and Henry was forced to content himself with a request that he be protected from popular abuse on the journey. Mr. Blennerhassett then addressed the crowded courtroom, pleading his innocence with tears streaming down his cheeks. Alas, he won no sympathy. He had already been adjudged an enemy of Jefferson and the Union. On July 20, 1807, escorted by a clattering and heavily-armed cavalcade, the unfortunate Burrite set out for Richmond, his ears ringing with 'the menaces and clamorous yells of the cerebus of Democracy.' [1]

A few weeks later Clay's popularity was put to the test when he stood for the Assembly. Opposed by the Junto, he took to the stump and exercised to the full his oratorical powers — his 'soul-speaking eye and persuasive voice,' his 'catamount eyes' and 'killing countenance.' He denounced the Junto's attacks upon Kentucky's pioneers and upon himself. He recalled how general had been the belief in Burr's innocence up to the moment Jefferson had pricked the Conspiracy Bubble. He had often defended men in court without being accused of being their accomplice. Why

---

of the Merchants here. I shall be sorry for some, but for others I am not. Sanders purchased $15,000, Craig $4,000, Anderson $5,000, and others the balance. The prospect of losing money has touched the Merchants in a tender place. Their country may go to ruin, and they will sit calm in their counting-houses, but touch the strong box, and they will be aroused immediately. It pleases me to think that the servile, sycophantic, parasites of B. are now paying for the honour of his acquaintance.' Wm. T. Barry to Dr. John Barry, Jan. 2, 1807, Barry, *Letters*, pp. 329–30.

[1] Safford, *Blennerhassett*, pp. 260–71; and *Blennerhassett MSS.*, July, 1807.

should he, for giving proper legal aid to Burr, be charged with Burrism?

Fayette returned him to the Assembly. The people, evidently, were still not only 'bigoted to Jefferson' but to Henry Clay. He had 'so *played the orator*,' sneered Marshall, as to make 'the people believe what they were very ready to believe (for Mr. Clay had been high in their confidence, was affecting in speech) . . . Did they want more coaxing? — then nobody better or easier than Mr. Clay would give it to them.' Indeed, 'ninety-nine hundredths needed no speech but an assertion that their orator had measured beards with Mr. Jefferson before he had left Washington City, in order to fraternize as before: and so he was forgiven; innocent soul!' [1]

Despite such acerbity, confidence was generally reposed in the Lexington orator. In discussing the Great Conspiracy the Republican press of the country characterized Clay as a legislator and lawyer of 'powerful talents' whose 'whole life attested his devotions to liberty, to republican principle, to union.' [2] Jefferson's confidence in him was shown in a striking manner. That November, after Burr had been acquitted and before he had fled into exile, the President through Attorney General Rodney requested Clay to serve as government's counsel should it prosecute Burr in Ohio. His request was refused. [3] Yet nothing could be more convincing

---

[1] *Ky. Gazette*, Feb. 18, 1832.

[2] *Natl. Intelligencer*, March 13; Richmond *Enquirer*, March 20, 1807.

[3] In reply to Rodney's request of Nov. 8, 1807, Clay stated: 'I am under no engagement for any of the parties, nor will I in any event appear for Col. Burr. Having deceived me last winter, when I really believed him both innocent, and persecuted by Mr. Daveiss, he shall not deceive me again, now that I believe him guilty and meriting punishment. But it will not be in my power to appear at Chillicothe for the government. The Court there sits just at the moment when our Legislature (of which I am a member) and our Supreme State Court (the most crowded with business of any in the Country) will be in Session; and I could not think of disappointing those who have confided their business to me, by contracting new duties.

'Altho I have no hesitation as it respects Burr about appearing against him, I have some doubt whether I should not by doing so subject myself to the imputation of violating professional honor. Having once appeared for him, it will be supposed, that he imparted to me his projects &c. The fact is however otherwise, but this may not be known to or thought of by the world . . .

'If it should be the intention of the Government to prosecute him in this State, I will in the mean time think of my situation, and determine whether I can consistently with my own honor and reputation act agst him. If Chillicothe is to be the place of trial I cannot attend there.' Clay to C. A. Rodney, Dec. 5, 1807, *Caesar A. Rodney MSS.*

as to the thoroughness with which young Clay had 'measured beards' with Jefferson.

When the President dismissed Jo Daveiss as Federal Attorney,[1] Marshall redoubled his efforts against Kentucky's 'perfidious Catilines and ambitious Caesars.' He was determined 'to try the *moral sense* of the state' on 'the self-convicted and positively guilty Judge Innes.' In August of 1807 he was elected to the Assembly from Franklin County, by eleven votes in a poll of one thousand. Throughout that fall in the *Western World*, 'with an angel's voice' (so he said), he thundered out that only the impeachment of Harry Innes could cure 'the noxious malady of intrigue and disunion.'

His election and his trenchant newspaper articles — 'which brought all hell about my ears,' chortled the malicious Humphrey — caused the excoriated Republicans to concert counter measures, in all of which, said Marshall, the moving spirit was Henry Clay.[2]

Innes, Todd, and others consulted with Henry as to libel suits, and as to measures which would 'prevent any influence of that abandoned & profligate villain in the Legislature.' Scores of pioneers made ready to testify, as a duty 'to Country and injured innocence,' to protect Innes from 'party malice and popular outrage.' John Wood was induced to write (anonymously) a series of articles, timed for the opening of the session, exposing 'the diabolical Marshall.' Justice Todd, Innes's brother-in-law (of high character and, usually, very mild temper) exultantly reported from the Burr trial at Richmond that he had information connecting Humphrey with the Federalist 'British Conspiracies' against Spanish America. Thomas Bodley, Innes's son-in-law, made ready to prove 'the arch Enemy' guilty of gross land frauds, perjury, and mutilation of court records.[3]

In December of 1807 Humphrey took his seat in the Assembly —

---

[1] Daveiss, dismissed, wrote his *A View of the President's Conduct*, lashing out at Jefferson's 'native, constitutional, inherent duplicity,' at Burr, Wilkinson, Innes; and sent out several challenges to duels. Jas. Taylor to Madison, Nov. 13, 1808, *Madison MSS.*

[2] Marshall, *Hist. Ky.*, II, 438–44; *Ky. Gazette*, Feb. 4, 1832.

[3] Todd to Innes, Sept. 23, 27, 1807, *Innes MSS.*, 18; Bodley to same, Jan. 5, 1808, *Innes MSS.*, 19; Preston W. Brown to same, Aug. 9, 1807, *Innes MSS.*, 21; Innes to W. C. Nicholas, Dec. 30, 1807, *Nicholas MSS.*

a detested Federalist, he said, 'among the Jeffersonians and Clayites.' Clay, significantly, was elected Speaker. With young John Allen, Burr's other counsel, he was also elected a director of the Bank of Kentucky.[1] Nevertheless, Marshall was a formidable foe, since opposition to him might be construed as opposition to the general hope that 'all treasons and conspiracies will be exploded and the body politic purged of all its rotten members.'[2] To protect themselves, some members would let him ride his hobbyhorse. Clay, however, promptly took the floor when Humphrey moved that Judge Innes, having convicted himself of disunionist intrigues by his testimony before the Sebastian Committee, should be impeached by Congress.

Henry protested against this prejudication, this attempt to 'fix an indelible stigma ... without the forms of trial or judicial proceedings.' Congress had Innes's testimony, he pointed out; and the Judge rather than opposing was requesting an impartial inquiry of the House, as he had already requested one of Congress. Clay would have the members resolve, instead, that 'the example of a legislative body, before the commencement of any prosecution, expressing an opinion upon the guilt or innocence of an implicated individual, would tend to subvert the fundamental principles of justice.'

'Temperate and just' though they were, Henry's resolutions were negatived. Nevertheless, after some wrangling, the Clayites succeeded in throwing out Marshall's severely criminatory resolutions and in carrying a substitute set. These called for a congressional inquiry, but carefully avoided prejudging Innes.[3]

The House then took up the charges against Marshall made by County Clerk Bodley. A committee of sixteen, eleven chosen by the House and five appointed by Speaker Clay, voted 11 to 4 for Humphrey's expulsion on the ground of moral turpitude. The members, however, were influenced by the idea, as one very frankly expressed it, that if men were expelled for land irregularities Kentucky would 'soon have a thin house.' By a vote of 30 to

---

[1] *Journal of House, 1807–08*, pp. 37, 45.

[2] Pope to N. Edwards, Jan. 9, 1808, Edwards, N., *Papers*, p. 33.

[3] Butler, M., *Hist. Ky.*, p. 325; *Journal of House*, pp. 96–105.

23 the evidence was held insufficient. Humphrey (said Thomas Bodley) was thus *'whip'd and clear'd.'* [1]

Congress that spring, urged on by John Rowan, investigated Judge Innes. It decided that his impeachment was unwarranted.[2]

Thereafter, libel suits galore were filed against the Junto. Clay won Innes's suit against Editor Street for printing the libels of Humphrey Marshall. Innes waived the money award; but when Street moved for a new trial and filed a 'perverting and misrepresenting' affidavit, Clay was so incensed that he advised Innes to release no part of the damages. Both Clay and young Robert Wickliffe, his assisting counsel, significantly remarked that the damages if paid should be borne not by the editorial puppet but by his masters.[3] Other pioneers likewise cleared their names until Street, hounded from one county court to another, fled the state. Innes's libel suit against Marshall dragged on for years. The Judge collected volumes of depositions attesting his patriotism, while Humphrey in 1812 published what he called a *History of Kentucky*, in which he impugned the patriotism of almost every Republican prominent in the early history of Republican Kentucky. Their feud ended only with Innes's death in 1816.

Meanwhile 'the Prince of Devil's Hill' (as Humphrey was sometimes called) blew up the bellows of discord against the Clayites. 'A rank *Federalist*, or in other words a *Monarchist*,' according to Thomas Bodley, he was still determined to bring back 'all the evils and horrors which . . . were so dreaded in the reign of terror.' [4]

The storm raised by Burr did not subside as far as Henry was personally concerned until late in 1808, after he had defended young John Allen and himself in a virulent battle of goose quills. The Junto began its attack on Allen, who had offered for governor,[5]

---

[1] *Journal of House*, pp. 116, 191; Innes to W. C. Nicholas, Feb. 7, 1808, *Nicholas MSS.*; Bodley, Th., untitled pamphlet, Lexington, June 12, 1808; *Ky. Gazette*, Feb. 23, 1808, and Feb. 4, 1832; [Marshall, H.], *Report of the Select Committee Appointed to Investigate Certain Charges against Humphrey Marshall.*

[2] Said Marshall, *Hist. Ky.*, II, 452: Jefferson, 'the grand magician had stretched out his wand over the head of the judge; on it was inscribed: "AN ENEMY TO THE FEDERAL GOVERNMENT — HE HAD BEEN FAITHFUL TO ME" — and impunity was ensured.'

[3] Clay to Innes, April 21, 1812, *Innes MSS.*, 18; and *ibid., passim.*

[4] Bodley, untitled pamphlet against Marshall, June 12, 1808.

[5] Allen, then but twenty-seven, a brilliant lawyer, of high character and popular, lost

but it was forced by Clay to center its fire on him, for it was he rather than Allen who leaped into the fray and bore its brunt.

Street (who later fully, abjectly, apologized to Henry for these 'errors of youth' and his 'entire misconception arising from misinformation'),[1] and Marshall rang all the changes on their charge that Allen and Clay as lawyers and legislators had defended 'disunionists.' They stressed the view that if young Allen were elected, Henry Clay, the 'ambitious Caesar' of Kentucky politics and formerly Burr's chief counsel, would dominate Allen's administration.[2]

In articles signed 'Scaevola' and 'Regulus,' Henry assailed their charges against Allen as 'made from malice, unsupported by facts, and urged for base and electioneering purposes.' The same men slandered the whole Democratic Society, although it was well known that its object had been the opening of the Mississippi and a change in the national councils. He paid his respects to 'the unsullied character of H. Marshall,' and noted that the *Western World* had never attacked Chief Justice Marshall or a single solitary Kentucky Federalist. When Doctor Hunn, editor of the Lincoln County *Lamp*, joined with the Junto, Henry advised him to quit his scurrility: 'Retire into the precincts of your native gallipot, and revel and riot in your proper aliment, asafoetida.' Hunn in reply to 'Scaevola, the raging monster,' condemned the 'all-corrupting lawyer aristocracy' and declared that 'if the card table and punch bowl have left one drop of blood in the face of Mr. Henry Clay, he ought to blush the deepest red' for his 'horrid principles.'[3]

Subversive of justice and humanity, said Henry, was the charge that Allen and himself were Burrites merely because they had been Burr's counsel. At the present time, 'no man entertains a more despicable opinion of Aaron Burr than I do. Whether his object was disunion, revolution in Louisiana, or conquest of Mexico, or all of them, there can be no doubt of his atrocious

---

to General Charles Scott, another Jeffersonian and politically potent as 'A Deserving Veteran of '76.'

[1] J. M. Street to Clay, Vandalia, Ill., Jan. 11, 1827, *Clay MSS.*

[2] Lex. *Reporter*, June–July, 1808.

[3] *Ibid.*, June 11, 1808 ff.; especially June 18, 25, July 2, 1808.

guilt.' Yet in 1806 he was generally regarded as innocent, 'and I repeat that his counsel are to be judged by what was believed *at that time*.' ¹

In this battle of goose quills Marshall's Junto was untiring in its efforts to drive Clay from public life. Yet in 1808 it was not Representative Henry Clay whom Fayette discredited but Representative Hezekiah Harrison. Poor Hezekiah! Although he protested loudly that he was not a friend of the Marshall clan, was not 'double-faced,' and had not absented himself to avoid voting Humphrey's expulsion, he was sent down to defeat. Henry Clay was reelected, at the head of the list of Fayette's representatives.²

'You have carried your election. I am rejoiced at it,' wrote James Brown to Henry. Nevertheless 'I pray you to quit public life, or muster up sufficient philosophy to bear up under all the hard names with which you will be christened,' for 'as long as you retain your brains and your independence you will be abused.' ³

Henry profited little by such advice. He could not, would not, remain silent under fire. Despite warnings that he might needlessly injure himself, he had rushed to Allen's defense.⁴ Neither then nor later did he heed the maxim: 'It was counted Good policy in the Ky Hunters not to disturb a buffelo when he had recd a mortal wound because if they did he would give them much heap of trouble whereas if he was left to himself he would soon die.' ⁵

A wounded buffalo was Humphrey Marshall — an old bull buffalo, tough, valiant, tricky. He was to give young Clay much heap of trouble on issues which foreign relations had forced to the front. These same issues before long were to force 'Harry of the West' forward as the impulsive champion of Young America, eager to lead his beloved country out of the ignominy into which she had been plunged by a war-diseased Old World. Indeed, the first act of 'Mr. Clay's War,' which was formally declared in June of 1812, had already taken place off the coast of his native Virginia.

---

¹ Lex. *Reporter*, 'Regulus,' July 9, and June 11, 1808.
² *Ibid.*, Aug. 6, and issues of July, 1808.
³ Brown to Clay, Sept. 1, 1808, Clay, *Corres.*, p. 16.
⁴ See 'Franklin Penn,' in Lex. *Reporter*, July 9, 1808.
⁵ J. Ficklin to M. Austin, Feb. 18, 1808, *Austin Papers*, I, 145.

In June of 1807 a gross British outrage sounded the very depths of national humiliation. Off Norfolk the British ship-of-war *Leopard* abruptly fired into the frigate *Chesapeake*, killed or wounded twenty-one men, and forced Commodore Barron to give up four of his crew, three of whom were native Americans previously impressed. This man-stealing assault upon a national ship stung Americans of all parties (except Pickering's Junto) into a common anguish of shame and hatred, and put them clamoring 'on tiptoe for immediate war.'

'Without substantial reparation,' said Bayard, Federalist of Delaware, 'whatever the sacrifice, we must go to war.' [1] If we retaliate with 'some thousands of privateers,' wrote Nicholson, Quid Republican of Maryland, 'we shall obtain... an absolute renunciation of impressment.' Strike now! he urged, before 'the merchants begin to calculate,' before manly resentment 'is superseded by considerations of profit and loss.' [2]

'The affair of the *Chesapeake* put war in my hand,' said peace-loving Jefferson: 'I had only to open it and let havoc loose.' [3] Yet he clenched his hand tightly, passionately. Resisting the nation-wide clamor, and by delay cooling it, he ordered all British warships excluded from American ports, and, sending out the dispatch ship *Revenge*, he asked of England '*reparation* for the past, & *security* for the future, that is to say an end of impressments.' [4]

The *Revenge* limped back with grim and provocative news. Goose quills had not pierced the singularly tough hide of John Bull.

---

[1] Bayard to C. A. Rodney, July 24, 1807, Bayard, J. A., *Letters*, p. 9. 'To be an American and not to feel ... this atrocious act ... committed ... against our honour rights and independence ... would be impossible.... The nation ... will not be satisfied [as in past incidents of British naval insolence] with empty apologies or the mockery of a trial which ends in a promotion of the offender.'

[2] Joseph H. Nicholson to Gallatin, July 14, 1807, Adams, H., *Gallatin*, p. 360. 'But one feeling pervades the nation. All distinctions of federalism and democracy are vanished. The people are ready to submit to any deprivation ... I trust to God that the Revenge is going out to bring Monroe and Pinkney home.'

[3] Jefferson to James Maury, April 25, 1812, Jefferson, *Works*, XI, 239–44.

[4] *Ibid.*, X, 470; Jefferson to John Page, July 17, 1807. 'Never since the battle of Lexington have I seen this country in such a state of exasperation, and even that did not produce such unanimity,' he wrote Dupont de Nemours, July 14, 1807, *ibid.*, X, 460–61. 'The federalists themselves coalesce with us as to the object, tho' they will return to their trade of censuring every measure taken to obtain it.'

While the act of the *Leopard* was disavowed, England refused to connect 'the murders of the *Chesapeake*' with the subject of impressment; refused even to consider reparations for the slain, and restoration of the enslaved, until Jefferson first withdrew his 'hostile' order excluding British warships. Foreign Minister George Canning only poured salt into the wound so wantonly inflicted. A Tory Parliament urged the most dictatorial coercion of an upstart competitor. A chauvinistic London press approved the murderous attack, applauded when those responsible were promoted, reminded the 'cowardly Yankees' that might was ever right, and called for their further chastisement by the mighty and ever righteous British navy.

In October of 1807 Tory England gave unarmed America the brutal alternative of war or submission to impressments from merchant ships. Impressments continued, perforce, a deep and festering wound. And for years the *Chesapeake* atrocity remained unredressed, a rankling national insult, a badge of shame and a cry for revenge.

These were smashing blows; yet before America could recover she was assailed by edicts which threatened to annihilate her commerce or her nationality. To the 'painful recollection of past injuries' was now added the 'imminence of incalculable dangers.' [1]

By November of 1807 England in successive orders-in-council had declared all Europe blockaded from the Baltic to the Adriatic. Yet she was most anxious to promote her own trade with Europe, which Napoleon would exclude by his Continental System; and she was determined to monopolize that of neutrals. She permitted a highly restricted traffic, provided neutrals first entered a British port, paid British duties, took on British goods, and obtained British licenses. [2] On his part, Napoleon by his Milan Decree declared all ships thus denationalized to be British, and subject to seizure.

---

[1] Coxe, Tench, *An Examination of the Conduct of the British Respecting Neutrals* (Phila., 1807), p. 72.

[2] Canning indulged America to the extent of asking whether, as to cotton brought into England for re-export, she preferred an absolute interdict or a prohibitory duty! As Madison bitterly commented, Britain was 'not only violating our rights, and stabbing our interests, but superadding, under the name of indulgences, a blow at our national independence and a mockery of our understandings.' *A. S. P., For. Rel.*, III, 221.

America was marked for plunder: by Britain on the seven seas and in American waters; by France, in Europe. The Leviathan would force her commerce, on pain of confiscation, through British channels, taking toll and tribute of it as under the Navigation Laws which had helped to bring on the Revolution of '76. The Mammoth would confiscate all commerce going through such channels. Each wielded a double-edged sword, one sharp edge of which cut at the United States.

With pleas of 'retaliation,' of 'Liberty of the Seas against British Tyranny' and 'The Liberties of Mankind against Gallick Despotism,' the ruthless Titans rode a hurricane which blasted the world physically and morally. The law of the jungle alone prevailed. Defenseless America might well fear 'incalculable dangers' when she beheld, in 1807, the fate of Europe's remaining neutrals. When Portugal refused to make war on England, Napoleon occupied the country. When Denmark refused England's ultimatum, a British fleet in September bombarded Copenhagen, destroyed the town piecemeal, killed two thousand non-combatants, and confiscated the Danish navy and merchant marine. The Old World had decreed: No More Neutrals!

Did the *Chesapeake* murders (which seemed a calculated act of terrorism),[1] followed by Britain's impressment ultimatum and her new orders-in-council, presage for America the bloody fate of Denmark? War seemed inevitable; with England, or with both England and France. How else defend our ships, cargoes, and seamen —

> 'While Europe's mad powers o'er creation are ranging,
> Regardless of right, with their bloodhounds of war:
> Their kingdoms — their empires, distracted and changing;
> Their murders and ruins resounding afar'?[2]

---

[1] Such might be inferred, wrote Jefferson to Thomas Paine, Sept. 6, 1807, from its being 'so timed as to find us in the midst of Burr's rebellion as they expected, from the contemporaneousness of the Indian excitements, and of the wide & sudden spread of their maritime spoliations.' Jefferson, *Works*, X, 493.

[2] 'Freedom and Peace — or, the Voice of America. A National Song,' in *The Gleaner; or Monthly Magazine*, I (Lancaster, Penna., Sept. 1808), 27–29; reprinted in the Lexington *Reporter*, Oct. 3, 1808. Expressing the general opinion of his peace-loving countrymen, the anonymous poet stated that America should make war only if every other expedient failed —

> 'The demons of discord are roaming the ocean,
> *Their* insult and rapine and murder are law;

Jefferson's answer, his escape from a cruel dilemma, was neither war nor submission and tribute, but the Embargo — a self-sacrificing Quaker weapon which shut off American commerce with all the world. Enacted by Republican farmer-exporters over the protests of Federalist merchant-shippers, it would withhold America's grain and cotton and other produce from the British Shark and the French Tiger until they revoked their anti-neutral edicts.

In Kentucky the news of the *Chesapeake* murders provoked unprecedented cursing of Britain's 'bloody sea-robbers' and heady talk of retaliating upon Britain's Canada. In the Assembly Speaker Clay made fiery speeches, for which fresh fuel was given by the impressment ultimatum, and the open defiance of Jefferson's proclamation by the *Leopard* and other British blockaders infesting American waters. With his fellow legislators Clay pledged blood and treasure in support of war or of any other weapon government might apply 'to chastise and bring to reason our haughty and imperious foe.' In this spirit Kentuckians, though deprived of markets for their produce, most ardently supported Jefferson's 'commerce-protecting Embargo.' [1]

To maritime Federalists, however, this 'commerce-destroying Embargo,' this sudden stunning blow at their means of livelihood, at their profits as the carriers not only of American produce but of British imports and a good share of the world's trade, was stark Virginia madness, worse than war, 'cutting one's throat to cure the nosebleed.' They were willing to risk British blockades, or to

---

From scenes so atrocious of blood and commotion,
  'Tis great — it is godlike — awhile to withdraw!
Perhaps when the hand that had fed is suspended,
  When famine's pale spectres their steps overtake,
The firm VOICE of TRUTH may at last be attended,
  And JUSTICE and REASON may once more re-awake.'

[1] *Journal of House, 1807–1808*, p. 63; also, Lex. *Reporter* and *Ky. Gazette*, July, 1807 ff. There were complaints, however: see, Cox, N., *Letters*, 189; *Austin Papers*, I, 148; S. Brown to Ephraim Brown, June 13, 1808, *Silas Brown, Jr. MSS*. A few merchant-shipbuilders joined in the Eastern lament (Hulbert, *Western Ship-Building*, p. 732):

  'Our ships all in motion
  Once whiten'd the Ocean
  They sailed and returned with a cargo;
  Now doomed to decay
  They have fallen a prey
  To Jefferson, worms, and embargo.'

submit to British monopoly and risk French seizures. Greater risks meant greater gains: if one ship out of three reached its goal handsome profits would be realized. Few in number but exceedingly articulate, they denounced the Embargo as unconstitutional and pro-French. They evaded it by wholesale smuggling, vilified Jefferson, urged States' Rights (as violently as Kentuckians had done in '98), and threatened to secede unless an end were put to this 'dreadful war of depredation, of Jacobins against the nation,' this *blow* which aim'd against Great Britain, recoiling has our vitals smitten.' [1]

In the Embargo Pickering's Federalists had an issue that might have won them agrarian support; for in the long run the farmer-producer was perhaps harder hit than the shipper-capitalist, who could more readily exchange the trident of commerce for the distaff of manufacturing. They had many other issues — in Republican neglect of national defense, legislative incapacity, and diplomatic bungling. But by failing to use them on purely American grounds, by failing to offer any counter-program other than submission to England in preference to a 'commerce-destroying Embargo' (and, later, to its alternative, a 'commerce-destroying war'), the die-hard Federalists, as Josiah Quincy of Boston himself admitted, by the great mass of Americans came to be 'hated for British affinities, and for their willingness . . . to abandon to that nation every right.' [2]

Assailing the majority as Napoleonic vassals, they ignored America's British-inflicted wounds for the sake of profits and the moral issue — Britain against Bonaparte for a world made safe for 'the rich, wise, and well-born,' a world freed of Revolutionary Caesars and Jacobinic 'newspaper-taught rabbles.' Yankee farmers no less than Clay (and future Americans) marvelled, and winced, at their localism, 'Carthaginian cupidity,' and an Anglomania which at times surpassed that of the stoutest and goutiest British Tory.

America's Tories held it folly to prate of 'National Honor' as

---

[1] Fessenden, T. G., *Pills, Poetical, Political*, pp. 28, 18. For effects of Embargo, see Sears, L. M., *Jefferson and the Embargo*, and Jennings, W. W., *The American Embargo, 1807–1809*.

[2] Quincy to his wife, early in 1812, Quincy, *J. Quincy*, p. 239.

long as the nation was enthralled by Jeffersonian Democracy. Self-styled 'the aristocracy of talents & of property,' they palliated impressment — common sailors could be replaced with British deserters; sentiment must not interfere with business. They were willing to take out denationalizing British licenses (in 1809 a total of fifteen thousand were granted)[1] to engage in a trade prohibited by their hard-pressed country, and to smuggle British goods into Europe. While Britain scoured the coast, committing brutal outrages, Pickering brandished the bugbear of invasion by a navyless France.[2] In Congress he defended British orders that British Whigs in the House of Lords declared 'would have disgraced the darkest ages of monopoly,' orders that had perverted language and common sense so that 'if A [France] strikes me, I may retaliate by striking B [America].'[3]

New England Republicans valiantly combatted the 'seditious purse-proud Junto of Boston Rebels,' Pickering's 'Lobster Princes and Tory priests,' who would 'sacrifice honor, independence, internal industry to maritime craft, smuggling, and all the evils of disunion so much reprobated by Washington!'[4] Republican editors praised the self-sacrificing patriotism of Marblehead's non-smuggling merchants and sailors; emphasized 'the INHUMAN VILLAINY of IMPRESSMENT'; and printed indignant letters of Revolutionary Heroes who asserted that they had fought for Independence and the Rights of Man, and against this same self-interested Toryism now embodied in Pickering's 'British money-changers.' Yet in vain was the 'True Spirit of Bunker Hill' opposed to the 'British Influence' of the bar, the pulpit, and the counting-room. For the Pickeronians in 1808 won political control of Massachusetts. 'Devilism reigns!' shouted a Yankee democrat. 'Civil War seems imminent, unavoidable! Unless the Farmers in

---

[1] Channing, E., *History of U. S.*, IV, 386.

[2] Yankee Nathaniel Ames raged at such attempts 'to bring back this country to court, caress, and hug that corrupt old whore of a step-mother that ... had starved and poisoned about 11,000 of her children on board the Jersey prison-ship' during the Revolution; to set up 'as a barrier to Bonaparte who keeps his distance' this tyrant that daily comes into our ports 'to insult, kidnap, press, rob, plunder, and murder...' Warren, *Jacobin and Junto*, p. 236.

[3] Adams, *Hist. U. S.*, IV, 319–20, q. Lords Erskine and Grenville.

[4] Warren, *Jacobin and Junto*, p. 221 (Jan. 1808).

Massachusetts threaten to beat their ploughshares into swords to support their own laws and Government.' ¹

Citizens otherwise intelligent shuddered at Pickering's Bonapartist phantoms and accepted his dogma, the dogma of politicians who desperately sought to revive Federalism and to reassert the power of New England, that England had done us no essential injury. Even Chief Justice Marshall pronounced his speeches 'excellent' ² — and thus furnished most Americans 'undeniable proof of the bad state of morals in our country.' ³ John Adams, however, was enraged by the 'Calves of John Bull' who justified even the *Chesapeake* murders, and deluded people into an unaccountable eagerness 'to rush into the arms of Great Britain ... as if the lamb ... should seek the friendship and protection of the wolf.' With his son John Quincy, with Plumer of New Hampshire, and others, Adams turned violently against a Federalism that had denationalized itself.⁴ Other Federalists, while retaining the party label, could but acknowledge that the British orders were 'Acts of Hostility against our neutral rights,' and that Americans at this crisis should 'show to the world that we are a united people, and that our Independence and Sovereignty are Paramount to any other Considerations.' ⁵

It was as obvious to most Americans (i.e., the Republicans) as it was to John Adams that French tyranny kept pace with British in principle but not in power and extent of injury. They condemned Bonaparte's wholesale sequestrations of 1808 and 1810, in Europe; but they condemned more the greater 'piracies' of Britain, and

---

¹ Warren, *Jacobin and Junto*, pp. 221, 243; and Salem *Essex Register*, 1808–09; and, also, for the views of a New England Republican, Bentley, Rev. Wm., of Salem, *Diary*.

² Marshall to Pickering, Dec. 19, 1808, Beveridge, *Marshall*, IV, 14. Chief Justice Marshall's partisan, anti-Jacobin, last volume of his *Life of Washington* ('that five-volume libel,' said Jefferson), which came out in 1807, greatly augmented the Federalist writings which enabled British writers to draw what they called 'A True Picture of the United States.' See *British Critic* magazine, London, Nov. 1807, for review of various anti-American pamphlets, including *A True Picture* etc., (based on Marshall's *Washington*), *Softly Brave Yankies!!!*, and *The Lie Direct!!! — A Refutation of the Charges in the Proclamation of President Jefferson.*

³ Gov. John Tyler of Va. to Jefferson, May 12, 1810, Tyler, L. G., *The Letters and Times of the Tylers*, I, 246–47.

⁴ Adams, J., *Corres. with Wm. Cunningham*, pp. 83, 168 ff. (1808–09).

⁵ Jas. I. Van Alen to Wm. P. Van Ness, Wash., Dec. 14, 1808, *Wm. P. Van Ness MSS.* Van Alen, a Federalist congressman, was a half-brother of Martin Van Buren.

impressments as well, in home waters and on the high seas.[1] They scorned an alliance with Napoleon, whom they had come to detest as the arch-Judas to Republicanism.[2] Although Pickering cried out 'French Influence,' French Minister Turreau denounced the Jeffersonians as British in heritage, in affections, in 'sordid avarice,' and in 'aversion' to France.[3] A similar tribute to their independent Americanism had earlier been paid by a minister from Republican France: 'Jefferson, I say, is an American, and as such, he cannot sincerely be our friend. An American is an enemy of all the peoples of Europe.' [4] It was only natural, however, that Americans should hope, just as long as Great Britain robbed, enslaved, and killed fellow citizens, that 'Bonaparte will drub and frighten the British into the appearance, at least, of good humour with us.' [5]

Of America's two enemies, as Clay himself often said, peace was especially desired with England. Yet proffers which might well have led to a common front against France smashed, again and again, on the rocks of Tory indifference, greed, and arrogance. The events of these years only confirmed most Americans in the view Jefferson in 1807 expressed: 'I never expected to be under the necessity of wishing success to Buonaparte. But the English being equally as tyrannical at sea as he is on land, & that tyranny bearing on us in every point of either honor or interest, I say "down with

[1] As Erskine reported in Oct., 1807, more ill will was incited by 'a few illegal captures' and impressments in American waters than by 'the most rigid enforcement' elsewhere. Adams, *Hist. U. S.*, IV, 143.

[2] 'How did all Americans stand on tiptoe, during his brilliant campaigns in Italy [for] the republic! With what rapture did . . . our bosoms bound at the prospect of an emancipated world! Yet see in what it all ended! The total extinction of European liberty, and the too probable prospect of an *enslaved* world!' Wm. Wirt, July 2, 1808, Edwards, *N. Edwards*, p. 462. At the same time Wirt (*ibid.*, Nov. 26, 1808, p. 435) lashed out at Americans 'so tame and so mean as to reward Great Britain for the slaughter of our brethren on board the "Chesapeake," for the captivity of the thousands whom she holds in her ships, for the unprincipled tyranny by which she has driven our seamen from the ocean, and the thousand wrongs and insults which she is daily offering us, by making her a present of the complete monopoly of our whole carrying trade and surplus produce!'

[3] Turreau to Talleyrand, Sept. 4, 1807, Adams, *op. cit.*, IV, 140–42.

[4] P. A. Adet, Dec. 31, 1796, Turner, F. J., ed., 'Corres. of the French Ministers to the U. S., 1791–1797,' *Ann. Rpt. of the Amer. Hist. Assoc., 1903*, II, 983.

[5] Wirt to Dabney Carr, Sept. 8, 1807, Kennedy, *Wirt*, I, 222. The same idea was expressed to Clay by Breckinridge in the spring of 1806: Napoleon's victories would most probably make Great Britain less hostile towards the United States, and perhaps force her to do America justice in order to gain our friendship. Breckinridge to Clay, March 26, 1806, *Clay MSS*.

England" and as for what Buonaparte is then to do to us, let us trust to the chapter of accidents, I cannot, with the Anglomen, prefer a certain present evil to a future hypothetical one.' [1]

During this critical and rancorous period, filled with rumors of war and of disunion, Clay exerted every effort in support of 'the illustrious Jefferson.' He ardently supported Madison for President, as against George Clinton, the candidate of disaffected Northern Republicans, and James Monroe, the candidate of Southern Quids.[2] As a pamphleteer he distinguished himself against 'trimming, quiddical Republicans' and Humphrey Marshall's Junto.[3] As Kentucky's foremost orator he led the people in resolving that never would they hew wood for Napoleon or draw water for King George the Third.

With Clay, in public meetings and in the press, Kentuckians assailed Federalism's pocketbook patriotism, and denounced Napoleon's wholesale seizure of American ships in French ports: they had violated the Embargo, but was that any excuse to hold them as British ships in disguise? The people demanded reparations for the *Chesapeake*, commiserated with 'our fellow citizens, prisoners on board British ships of war,' praised former President Adams for his public letters on 'the Inadmissible Principles of British Impressment,' and cheered George Washington Campbell of Tennessee, who in combat with a Tory congressman had refreshed the nation's honor with his duelling pistol. They railed at such Federalist sentiments as 'The Potomac the Boundary: the Negro States by Themselves,' and, pointing out that Napoleon had abolished the Spanish Inquisition, said that any man who believed George III was fighting God's battles must wish 'to make the Deity as whimsical as himself.' They toasted the Union, the Freedom of the Seas, and spiritedly declared: 'The French decrees

---

[1] Jefferson to Th. Leiper, Aug. 21, 1807, Jefferson, *Works*, X, 483–84.

[2] At a meeting of the legislators at the Eagle Tavern, Frankfort, Feb. 17, 1808, 'Mr. Clay, Speaker of the House... in an animated speech, called... attention... to an address to the freemen of Kentucky, which he had prepared, and which being read, was unanimously approved of, and signed.' The address called for the election of James Madison. *Ky. Gazette*, March 2, 1808.

[3] As against Jo Daveiss, who as 'Citizen' wrote anti-Embargo articles for the *Western World*, Clay was considered a pamphleteer with 'point and force enough to blow forty such *citizens* out of the water.' Wm. Wirt to N. Edwards, Nov. 26, 1808, Edwards, *Edwards*, p. 433.

and British orders-in-council — the American who would submit to either deserves a halter.' [1]

Yet by the fall of 1808 they were fearfully apprehensive. 'Congress,' reported a Westerner, 'hardly know what is best to be done. For we can't make successful war against either of the damn'd nations who have so wantonly and grossly insulted & invaded our rights & sovereignty. And the operation of the Embargo, it seems, has not brought and is not likely to bring either to a right sense of justice.' [2] Bonaparte was adamant. Though Whig manufacturers were hard hit, Canning, backed by the Tory squires and shipping magnates, strengthened by the opening of Spanish-American markets, and confirmed in his view that '*Republican* and *fool* are synonymous,' officially derided a republic that was committing economic suicide.

At home, the effects of the Embargo were only too evident. Exports had dropped from $108,343,150 in 1807 to $22,430,960 in 1808. Imports had dropped from $138,500,000 to $56,990,000, cutting the revenue down from $16,000,000 to about $10,000,000. The republic groaned under the weight of hard times — yet, in 1808, elected Madison by more than two-thirds of the electoral vote. In spite of this striking proof of Republican strength, New England had become a 'hot-bed of treason' and her town meetings 'eggs of sedition.' British secret agents were active, and Pickering's British-protected Northern Confederacy threatened to become a reality.

'If the Embargo be raised,' wrote an Ohio senator, 'vessels must be permitted to arm, & war will be inevitable with some foreign nation or nations. If the Embargo be kept on, there is imminent danger, from the east and north, of civil war and a dissolution of the Union . . . God knows what is before us.' [3]

---

[1] *Ky. Gazette*, Lex. *Reporter*, 1808–09.

[2] Geo. Hoffman to F. Bates, Nov. 15, 1808, Marshall, *Bates*, II, 41.

[3] S. Griswold to Huntington, Nov. 12, 1808, Huntington, *Letters*, pp. 125–26. Boston's Federalists for the past year, wrote John Adams, have shown nothing but 'a blind devotion to England and a disposition to sacrifice to her, our rights and a headlong inclination to go to war with France, and for the sake of these *blessings* to hazard if not sacrifice the Union.' Boston is in the hands of Loyalists — 'shapen in toryism, and, in British idolatry, did their mothers conceive them.' Adams, *Corres. with Cunningham*, pp. 84, 66.

On March 1, 1809, the Embargo was superseded by the Non-Intercourse Act. This reopened trade with all nations but England and France, and authorized intercourse with them only when they revoked their edicts. It was a victory for New England Federalism, and for Old England Toryism — for England, unlike France, could now get America's produce indirectly. Yet it was a questionable victory. In their 'selfish sectionalism and blind heedlessness,' the Federalists had forced a measure which was incapable of doing what the Embargo might ultimately have done: avert war with England.[1] Non-Intercourse, predicted an English Whig, will likewise 'be equally insufficient as a measure of offence to us, or as security to [America], but this does not change the question as to the folly of our Orders in Council . . . which ultimately must bring us to a state of actual war, in which our commercial interests . . . have everything to lose.'[2]

To avoid such an outcome, Minister Erskine (going beyond Canning's instructions) on April 19, 1809 effected an agreement with President Madison and announced that the orders 'will have been withdrawn as respects the United States on the 10th day of June.' Federalists lauded Madison, and counted on war with France. Yet no sooner had hundreds of ships sailed for England than news came that England, instead of revoking her orders-in-council, had issued new ones, brazenly extended her illegal paper blockades,[3] and levied new duties on cotton. Non-Intercourse was revived, perforce, when Canning repudiated Erskine, and brought matters to a fresh crisis.

Even Federalists raged at Canning's arrogant farce of *Who's the Dupe?* — surely England could not expect that 'she can crop off our noses and that we will remain content because our heads are spared?'[4] Between England and France, said Bayard, it now

---

[1] Sears, *Jefferson and the Embargo*, pp. 195–96.

[2] Buckingham to Grenville, Feb. 12, 1809, *Dropmore Papers*, IX, 277.

[3] The orders of April 26, 1809, 'blockaded' Europe from the Ems to and including Northern Italy — 'as if the same were actually blockaded by His Majesty's naval forces.' *A. S. P., For. Rel.*, III, 241.

[4] Wm. Cunningham, Adams, *Corres. with Cunningham*, p. 149. 'Americans without number rush into Bull's throat,' said Dr. Ames. 'British Government got supplied, then refuse to perform agreement with Erskine and put even Fudderalism [*sic*] to blush for their baseness!!' Warren, *Jacobin and Junto*, p. 234, June 31, 1809.

'seems left to us only to chuse our enemy.' [1] Pickeronians censured Madison, but most Americans with young Editor Niles of Baltimore fervently prayed: 'From British "*honor and magnanimity*," Canning's *sincerity*, Castlereagh's *mercy* . . . British advocates . . . the impressment of our seamen, the plunder of our property, and the murder of our people — The Spirit of Seventy-Six deliver us!' [2] Old John Adams, who had 'never hoped for mercy from *British Bears and Tory Tigers*,' likewise prayed that America might free herself of British shackles that made the War of '76 seem but a prelude to a War for Independence. '*Poor Democrats, Republicans and still poorer Americans, are at the feet of John Bull and his Calves*,' lamented Adams, although it was now thirty-three years since he with Jefferson and other Revolutionary radicals had forced through Congress and upon George III the Declaration of '76.[3]

It appeared that Canning was deliberately inciting 'Revolution No. 2,' if not goading the United States into the arms of Bonaparte. For he replaced Whiggish Mr. Erskine with Francis James Jackson, whose notorious brutality at Copenhagen in 1807 had caused even George III to say that he should have been kicked downstairs. Armed with instructions which of themselves 'might well have justified a declaration of war,' [4] Copenhagen Jackson started in to bully America as he had bullied Denmark. Madison curtly dismissed him.

Although Republican cartoonists pictured 'the Copenhagen Monster' as muzzled by Madison, Jackson, very much unmuzzled, for a year stayed on. A Tory envoy who disdained a nation-wide demand for 'Justice from England or War,' he was confirmed in his view that America's 'blackguard and ferocious' mobocracy must be chastised into a proper respect for British supremacy.[5] A British Genêt, he subsidized Pickeronian writers to the sum of seven hundred pounds, and had his own insulting pamphlets

---

[1] Bayard to A. Bayard, July 3, 1809, Bayard, *Papers*, p. 177.

[2] Baltimore *Evening Post*, in Salem *Essex Register*, Sept. 6, 1809.

[3] Adams, *Corres. with Cunningham*, pp. 151, 168; and *passim*.

[4] Channing, E., *The Jeffersonian System*, p. 237. Canning again 'challenged . . . an instant declaration of war from a people who had no warmer wish than to be permitted to remain his friends.' Adams, *Hist. U. S.*, V, 105.

[5] Jackson, Sir George, *Diaries and Letters, 1809–16*, I, 44, 109.

printed by Pickeronian editors (notably Hanson of Baltimore) and franked out by Pickeronian congressmen.[1] Chief Justice Marshall was indignant, not at this 'old game of Genêt played over again' (as Justice Story called Jackson's 'infamous' appeals to Americans to overthrow their own government); Marshall was indignant at Republican 'servility' to France.[2] Nothing, however, could match the servility of seaport Anglo-Federalists, who banqueted Jackson, reviled Madison, and at Boston drank Pickering's toast: 'The world's last hope — Britain's fast-anchored isle!'[3] And nothing could have been more revealing than the Tory envoy's comment that the Yankees were all alike, 'except that some few are less knaves than others.'[4]

'Dishonorable, treacherous, and infamous' — such was the verdict of the huge Lexington Market Meeting addressed by young Henry Clay in August of 1809 on Canning's repudiation of Erskine. Against a 'perfidious' England that violated 'solemn national contracts,' irate Kentuckians affirmed their readiness to fight for 'the American character . . . the honor and dignity, and the neutral and national rights of our country.'[5] Their passions were further heated by Copenhagen Jackson, by Pickering's 'Internal British Faction,' and by fresh British captures and impressments. So heated, indeed (at the Shelbyville tavern), were two of Lawyer Clay's colleagues, Isham Talbot and William Cook, that they were presented for violating the profanity law: Talbot for yelling 'God damn Mr. Jackson; — the President ought to . . . have him kicked from town to town until he is kicked out of the country. God damn him!' Cook for yelling 'God damn Timothy Pickering — he ought to be hung!'[6]

---

[1] Fisher, J., 'Francis James Jackson and Newspaper Propaganda in the U. S., 1809–1810,' *Maryland Hist. Mag.*, XXX, 93–113.

[2] Beveridge, *Marshall*, IV, 23–25.

[3] Pickering, O., *Timothy Pickering*, IV, 170. John Quincy Adams could only pray that a new British Minister 'will spare his country's partisans in Congress and in the Massachusetts legislature the degradation of proclaiming themselves the satellites of his insolence, and that he will not undertake to instruct the Ancient and Honorable Artillery Company of Boston, at a public dinner... to draw their swords... against their own government.' Adams, *Writings*, IV, 65.

[4] Jackson, G., *Diaries*, I, 29; *passim.*

[5] *Ky. Gazette*, Aug. 15, 1809. Clay sponsored the resolutions.

[6] 'If our *pious* New England men were as attentive to enforce the laws against profan-

Angels and saints would have been provoked, let alone emotional, direct-action frontiersmen. Having borne themselves with more than Christian forbearance, it seemed that Clay's compatriots would now strike back at America's 'haughty and imperious foe.' And it was no anomaly that the war fever should flame highest in Clay's West, the section most removed from Britain's *Leopards* and press gangs. 'Uncontaminated' by the seaboard's intimate British ties, cultural and commercial, its spirit was peculiarly American.[1]

Nationalism and democracy both had a deeper meaning to the Free Sons of the West, with their vision of an America distinct from the Old World and the past; with their exaltation of 'The Union, one and indivisible'; and with their exaltation of the common man — even the impressed common '*American Sailor in Durana Vili,*' those Sons of the Seas who suffered on 'the "*Floating Hells of Old England*" such cruelties as would have disgraced the national character of the Algerines!' [2] It was no anomaly that they should join with the common citizens of Baltimore and Philadelphia, of Boston and Pickering's Salem, in complaining of government's failure (after Britain's ultimatum of 1807) to emphasize this paramount grievance, asking, 'Why are thousands impressed and enslaved by Britain, totally forgotten?' [3] Uncommonly sensitive to slights upon personal character and rights, they tended to personify the nation in their own image, and to expect from it their own hot resentment at assaults, 'unprovoked and unredressed,' upon the American character and national rights.

The Children of America were still for 'Freedom and Peace.' To preserve both they had most loyally supported Jefferson's Embargo, which required of hot-tempered Kentucs a Quaker-like

---

ity as these "*southern infidels*" are, how many of the Essex Junto would have been *presented* last year for God Damning Mr. Jefferson and his administration!' *Essex Register*, Nov. 11, 1809.

[1] It was frequently remarked how pervasive and 'baneful' was even 'unconscious English influence' among the people on the coast. 'We on the seaboard are more infected than the people of the interior, who less frequently come into contact with it, in the shape of a *bale of goods*, a newly printed British *volume*, a fresh imported *Lunnun* blood, or a flippant *Manchester* rider.' *Niles' Register*, May 9, 1812, and 1811 ff. Also, *Essex Register*, Jan. 4, 1809 ff.

[2] Salem *Essex Register*, Nov. 1, 1809, Jan. 16, 1811, *passim.*

[3] *Ky. Gazette*, July 11, 1809; also, Jan. 24, 1809, *passim.*

meekness and passive self-sacrifice. Yet a change came when, intimidated by Anglo-Federalism, 'the ever odious Tenth Congress' repealed the Embargo, then flinched from war, and substituted a temporizing 'cobweb submissive system' of indirect trade with Britain. Their natural instinct to return blow for blow was not much longer to be suppressed. Their seething volcano of resentment was soon to erupt, violently, and with little calculation as to the consequences. It was to overcome even their repugnance to direct taxes, to Federalism's armaments and 'odious Stamp and Still excises.' With the repeal of the Embargo, Kentuckians were in a desperate mood, so Humphrey Marshall reported to Pickering. 'Much as they might dislike the Embargo, they prefer'd it to War. But should it [Non-Intercourse] become intolerable, the transition to war would be easy, and even desirable.' [1]

By 1810 such men as young Clay found outright war preferable, and even desirable, to a mongrel peace in which America, left naked and unarmed by a logocratic Congress, was assaulted and robbed with impunity, subjected to a Canning-Jackson insolence, and taunted by Pickeronians (who frustrated all efforts to avoid both war and outright submission) with being so craven that she could never even be 'kicked' into war. Clay would never agree with the Tories that America was 'rotten at the core.' Yet his young republic did seem sick, enervated by a prolonged abasement, demoralized by a stock-jobbing cupidity.

'Submission only encourages oppression,' said Lexington's *Reporter*, pointing to Britain's issuance of new orders seven days after Madison in good faith had accepted Erskine's revocation and lifted the Non-Intercourse.[2] 'We *have* deliberated too long; we *have* talked too much,' agreed the Baltimore *Whig*. 'When we have received blows *behind* and *before*, are we to listen to a debate in congress on a resolution that *we have* been insulted? that two and two make four, &c? Must we be governed by *fear* and *avarice*?' [3]

Retaliation by war, after all, was not altogether hopeless. France was out of reach. Not so Britain, the greater aggressor.

[1] Marshall to Pickering, March 17, 1809, *Pickering MSS*.
[2] Lex. *Reporter*, July 1, 1809; and *passim*.
[3] Baltimore *Whig*, in Alexandria *Gazette*, Alexandria, Va., Jan. 20, 1810.

No nation could gall her so much by privateers; no nation could more readily strike at her American provinces.[1] With forces scattered from rebel Ireland to rebel India, even the British Colossus could not spare men and money for extended American operations. And surely America's great resources, her courage and skill in peace time, could be brought to bear successfully in spite of war's novelty. At the very least, war would fuse quondam British colonists into an American nation, and arrest this degeneration into a mongrel race of stock-jobbers, despised by the world — and by themselves.

As in the psychological prelude to the Revolution of '76, and all social upheavals, an overwrought people for years had expressed their resentment in words — and failed to get relief. With government paralyzed, and with the 'haughty and imperious foe' providing the provocative incidents that accelerate revolt, the people had reached the point where they demanded relief in direct action.

Such general considerations are basic to an understanding of the forces which impelled the United States into its 'Revolution No. 2.' The grievances were many, and long-standing. They were voiced by all sections of an America which was overwhelmingly Republican and overwhelmingly agrarian. Most determinedly were they voiced from 1810 on by young men of the hinterland. Since 'Mr. Clay's War' was nominally for 'Free Trade and Sailors' Rights,' though brought about by Republican farmers, their grievances — and their interests — deserve further and more particular analysis.

From an economic viewpoint it was no anomaly that the agrarian West and South should be most clamorous in demanding 'Free Trade or War!' The determining factor in the foreign commerce of the United States, where in 1810, as in 1800 and in 1790, about ninety per cent of the people were farmers, was the

---

[1] At Washington, reported a British secret agent, 'they frankly say we cannot if disposed, injure France, nor can she attack us. Her territory is out of our reach, and she has no Commerce on the Ocean. But they say, we can take the British Provinces of Canada, Nova Scotia, and New Brunswick... [with] extreme facility... No Man of either Party seems to imagine there would be any difficulty in effecting the Object.' Howe, John, 'Secret Reports of, 1808,' Nov. 27, 1808, *Amer. Hist. Rev.*, XVII, 342–43.

exportation of agricultural surpluses. A free commerce was as essential to the Republican producers as it was to the few Federalist middlemen-shippers, though the tendency to view commerce as merely the concern of the carrier caused much confusion then and later. A 'free trade' to Clay's Republicans meant a free outflow of exports: they drew a sharp distinction between the carrying trade, an indirect traffic in foreign produce (so profitable to Federalist shippers) which concerned only a small part of the nation, and the direct trade in America's own grain, flour, tobacco, cotton, and other produce, which was of vital concern to all sections and interests of the farmer republic.

Agrarian discontent was intimately and fundamentally connected with the rising war fever against England. When economic distress became more severe, even after America receded from the Embargo, even after she abolished all restrictions, war came to be regarded as the only weapon left to end an intolerable situation involving not only 'National Honor' but also, as Western and Southern spokesmen frankly and realistically stated, 'National Interest.'

After enjoying a boom prosperity following the Louisiana Purchase and the renewal of the great wars in 1803, the West suffered increasingly from hard times. After an unprecedented boom in cotton, the South likewise suffered. The closing of foreign markets greatly accentuated a decline in commodity prices which by 1808 had brought about an acute depression. In that year the prices of produce at New Orleans had fallen twenty per cent since 1805. The growing pains accompanying rapid settlement and mounting surpluses, and frontier problems in transportation and financing, contributed to the economic ills which prostrated the hinterland from 1808 to 1812. Yet the chief cause, it was asserted, was a monopolistic Mistress of the Seas that restricted the West Indian trade, excluded America's grain, flour, animal products, tobacco, and cotton from the Continent (thus slashing down America's purchasing power, and thereby depressing severely the price of hemp, provisions for the cotton country, and other home-consumed products), placed high duties on imports into Great Britain, and, in general, shackled the farmer republic economically and placed her (as John Adams would say) *'at the feet of John Bull and his Calves.'* [1]

The Westerner had opposed any recession from the Embargo as long as the British orders-in-council forbade a direct trade with Europe and confined his exports to the British market alone. Submission would only profit England and the Federalist shippers, he contended, while the farmer would be only further distressed by the glutting of the sole British market, by ruinously low British prices, high British taxes, and other evils of a British monopoly that was even more disastrous now than when Americans were British colonists.

Such were the predictions and arguments of Western congressmen and editors, especially of the Lexington *Reporter*, bellwether of hinterland journalism, which from the repeal of the Embargo in 1809 had urged government 'to cast aside all temporizing,' to eschew all submission, and to act before 'our chains are fully riveted.' [2] Despite some temporary relief in 1809 and 1810, these predictions were realized, and the arguments for direct action gained added force. By 1811 prices were below even those of 1808. Tobacco and hemp, Kentucky's two staples, were at disastrously low levels. Cotton, the great staple of the Lower Mississippi Valley, had fallen as much as fifty per cent. The very serious plight of the farmer was accentuated, moreover, by the unchanging or increasing costs of production and of imported goods. As the depression deepened, stronger grew the desire to strike off Britain's economic shackles.[3] Pacific coercion had failed to force a free

---

[1] See the excellent studies by Taylor, G. R., 'Agrarian Discontent in the Mississippi Valley Preceding the War of 1812,' *Jour. Pol. Econ.*, XXXIX, 471–505, and 'Prices in the Mississippi Valley Preceding the War of 1812,' *Jour. Econ. and Business Hist.*, III, 148–63. In the latter study Taylor charts (p. 149) the disastrous declines in wholesale prices of Western products at the port of New Orleans, taking the average of 1805–06 as equalling 100. The yearly averages were : 1804, 87; 1805, 102; 1806, 98; 1807, 95; 1808, 81; 1809, 84; 1810, 88; 1811, 79; 1812 (Jan. to May), 76.

[2] Lex. *Reporter*, July 1, 1809, and ff.

[3] The gist of the agrarian argument was given in a letter of a Louisiana planter, July 25, 1811 (Taylor, *Agrarian Discontent*, pp. 499–500) — 'Upon the subject of cotton we are not such fools, but we know that... the British are giving us what they please for it — and ... we happen to know that we should get a much greater price for it, for we have some idea of the extent of the Continent, and the demand there for it; and we also know that the British navy is not so terrible as you would make us believe; and, therefore, upon the score of lucre, as well as national honor, we are ready.'

trade for the products of American soil and industry. The sword alone remained against a relentless enemy who had on so many fronts and 'often enough, God knows, given us cause for war.' [1]

Allied with fundamental economic grievances were territorial grievances — and interests — which fanned the fires of war, and interwove a Republican expansionism (which Burr had so easily capitalized) with the general desire for retaliation and security.

On the disputed southern border, even before the Anglo-Spanish alliance of 1808, England appeared to the frontiersman in her familiar rôle of world-grasping villain, threatening (as Jefferson said) to seize the Floridas 'as a *point d'appui* to annoy us' on the south as Canada did on the north.[2] 'It is presumed if War Takes place,' wrote a Westerner, an old Revolutionary officer, in February of 1808, 'That one of the Earliest British Expeditions Will be To Take the Floridas and New Orleans — If they Succeed in this They will no doubt Excite the Indians To Take up the Hatchet against us . . .' [3] Since '75 Americans had said that the Canadas voluntarily would one day be annexed to the republic, and that 'they become ours the first war that takes place between us and England.' [4] By 1810 Clay's Westerners were hotly demanding the conquest of both Florida and Canada.[5]

---

[1] Jefferson to Duane, July 20, 1807, Jefferson, *Works*, X, 471.

[2] *Ibid.*, X, 467, Jefferson to John Armstrong, July 17, 1807. To Madison on Aug. 16, 1807 (*ibid.*, X, 476–77) he wrote that Spain's Western intrigues, maritime spoliations, and retention of American lands sufficed for reprisals on the Floridas. 'I had rather have war against Spain than not, if we are to go to war against England. Our southern defensive force can take the Floridas, volunteers for a Mexican army will flock to our standard, and rich pabulum will be offered to our privateers in the plunder of their commerce & coasts.'

[3] Judge Thomas Rodney (father of C. A. Rodney) to Geo. Poindexter, Feb. 3, 1808, Swearingen, *Poindexter*, p. 101 n. On May 21, 1808 John Patterson from New Orleans wrote W. C. Nicholas (*Nicholas MSS.*) that: 'The Floridas ought to be ours, & there will be no difficulty in taking possession of them, if we should have war with France.' After a study of Mississippi opinion in 1808, which fluctuated with the changes in Spain, Swearingen (*op. cit.*, p. 102) states: 'Be the enemy France, Spain, or England, there was an inescapable necessity of gobbling up all the neighboring colonies!' After England went to the aid of the Spanish people and the deposed Bourbons in 1808, men 'could be loyal to national policy, enjoy their traditional dislike of England, and make sheep's-eyes at West Florida — all with one gesture. Thus the hostile fixation shifted from Spain to England, though Spain was still involved.'

[4] Th. Worthington of Ohio, March 14, 1806, Huntington, *Letters*, p. 107.

[5] See Lex. *Reporter*, Jan. 30, Feb. 10, 1810, and ff.

The problems of the Northwest involved rivalry in the fur trade, expansion into America's own territories, and a revival of Indian warfare. Britain's removal of her forts in '96 had checked but not ended her intrigues among America's Indians — which she justified, as did Spain on the south, on the ground of self-defense against an aggressively expanding America. Not until 1815 did England give up hope of erecting a vast neutral Indian barrier state, north of a line drawn from the Ohio's mouth to San Francisco. In reality a British protectorate, this would have brought the results of the American Revolution within bounds, and in time seen Chicago arise the metropolis of a British Upper Mississippi Valley empire.[1]

From the *Chesapeake* year of 1807 on, the British courted the savages, held powwows at Fort Malden on Lake Erie, liberally dispensed gunpowder, and stressed their common interests. Pioneer fears and hatreds were thus revived — against a Britain that in the past had incited savage fiends 'year after year to inflict agony and torture, death and destruction.'[2] The 'massacrees of whole families' after 1807 but deepened the conviction that these, too, were committed 'under the influence of and by the orders of Great Britain.'[3]

Yet, as Clay himself frankly admitted, there were other causes 'sufficient to account for Indian hostilities, without returning to that most fruitful source of them, British instigation.'[4]

Chief of these was the inexorable westward advance. For years Governor Harrison of Indiana Territory had been extinguishing Indian land titles, bringing in pioneers, and transforming hunting grounds into cultivated fields. From 1807 on, a halt was demanded by two remarkable Indians: the Prophet, who preached and exhorted, and his brother, Tecumseh, who worked to confederate

---

[1] 'Such is one of the might-have-beens of history which threatened to become a tremendous reality.' Bemis, *Jay's Treaty*, p. 110.

[2] Littell, Wm., *Political Transactions* (1806), p. 9.

[3] Gen. A. Jackson, orders to Tennessee militia, April 20, 1808, as to the recent 'horrid Massacrees' of 25 whites by Creeks led by white men, presumably British. Jackson, *Corres.*, I, 188.

[4] Clay to Monroe, Sept. 21, 1812, *Monroe MSS*. Other sources, said Clay, were 'the progression of the Whites Westward — the death of the old warriors — the springing up of a new race of young ones — the natural propensity of savage man to War...'

all the tribes from the Great Lakes to the Gulf. Nevertheless, Harrison in 1809 from petty chiefs made pliable by his usual 'judicious liberality' obtained (for the usual pittance of one or two cents an acre) the cession of two million more acres, including Tecumseh's village on Tippecanoe Creek. In so doing he precipitated a crisis, and drove the savages into the welcoming arms of the British.[1]

Thus by 1810 the Indians' 'alliance' with Britain formidably menaced the settlements and barred further expansion. The West had become convinced that territorial security, as well as the redress of maritime grievances, could be achieved only by striking at British Canada. American independence was in jeopardy, it was contended, as long as 'the British retain either their possessions in Canada or possess their present influence over our commerce.' [2]

Parallel to these demands for freedom in territorial expansion and in the exportation of foodstuffs, tobacco, and cotton, was a revolt against the monopoly of imports long held by Britain. Lexingtonians gave nine cheers for 'The plough, the spindle, and the loom — what the sword of the Revolution achieved, it remains for them to perpetuate — national independence.' [3] Five years of non-importation, asserted Westerners in 1807, will make America self-sufficient. 'Our planters, too, will hereafter find their markets at home; and the British navy, if Britain and her navy should continue to exist, will at length find that her tyranny on the ocean has given *commercial independence* to those confederated States which British tyranny on the land first led to *political independence.*' [4]

Despite mounting complaints at hard times and the scarcity of money, Lexington's industries in eleven years, it was estimated in 1810, had increased forty-fold. Numerous newspaper articles appeared on textile and other manufacturing, on merino sheep, and labor-saving machines. There were demands for 'permanent

---

[1] See Pratt, J. W., *Expansionists of 1812*; also, Goebel, D. B., *Wm. H. Harrison*; *Michigan Pioneer and Hist. Collections*, XV, XXV; *A. S. P., Indian Affairs*, I; Brymner, D., *Report on Canadian Archives, 1892* and *1896*.

[2] Judge Coburn of Ky. to John Graham, Jan. 23, 1812, Marshall, *Bates*, II, 215. An interesting diagnosis of the Western war fever.

[3] *Ky. Gazette*, July 11, 1809; and *ibid.*, 1808 ff.

[4] Washington County, Miss. Ter., resolves, *A. S. P., Misc.*, I, 481–82.

and heavy tariff duties.' And constantly reiterated was the argument that as long as America depended upon the British manufacturer and his agent, the Federalist importer, independence was but a fiction — 'only a NAME, as the wealth and industry of America must go to THEM for their manufactures.' The United States must no longer permit itself to be duped, fleeced, degraded, and terrorized like another Ireland or India. Lexington must lead 'in this patriotic business' of emancipating the New World from a Great Britain whose known principles now as in '76 were 'Avarice, Pride, Hypocrisy, and Monopoly.' ¹

At their meetings the people toasted 'Homespun — may its use become general and supplant the fabrics of Europe,' and recommended 'Hemp cravats and a coat of homespun' for Pickeronian importers.² British cloth was a badge of shame; American cloth (though 'more wretched Stuff can not be conceived,' said Erskine) ³ a badge of patriotism. As befitted the Jeffersonian leader, Clay had cloth woven from the wool of his merino sheep at Ashland. He strongly advocated American manufactures — and it was this that brought his feud with Marshall to a head, and to 'the tribunal of ten paces.'

During these troubled years, according to Marshall, 'Mr. Clay rode the high horse of party, with much gallantry indeed; but also with much pride, and some frowardness.' So ardent was his Republicanism, or, so aspiring for distinction was this young fighting-cock, 'of superior talents and eloquence,' said Old Humphrey, that his conduct was often that of a flaming Jacobinic demagogue.⁴

Yet Henry hardly deserved this title when in 1807 he opposed the attempt of Kentucky's legislators, incited by the *Chesapeake* atrocity, to prohibit in the courts any British legal citation whatsoever. The bill was overwhelmingly popular, in tune with the frontier's prejudices and its freshly fired fury. Passionate speeches

---

¹ *Ky. Gazette*, Sept. 25, 1810; Sept. 18, Dec. 25, 1810, *passim.*

² Lex. *Reporter*, March 7, April 1, 1809; and *ibid.*, March 19, 1808 ff.

³ Erskine to Canning, Nov. 12, 1808, *F.O.* 5: 58. Cloth from buffalo wool — truly an American cloth! — was also advocated. St. Louis letter, Alexandria *Gazette*, Jan. 9, 1810.

⁴ *Ky. Gazette*, Feb. 18, 1832.

were made against the 'rags of despotism' cast off by the judicial prostitutes of Tory England, that nation of murderous pirates. Only a miracle could defeat the bill, it seemed, when Speaker Clay took the floor.

Although he gave credit to his colleagues' patriotism, Clay struck hard at the impassioned ignorance, the blind zeal, that would destroy an unrivalled legal system which was as much America's heritage as England's. It was a scene dramatic in its sheer audacity as 'the bell-wether of Republicanism' (according to Marshall) exerted all his powers to stay this 'blow' at 'our haughty and imperious foe.' One of those who witnessed it said 'every muscle of the orator's face was at work, his whole body seemed agitated, as if each part were instinct with separate life, and his small white hand, with its blue veins apparently distended almost to bursting, moved gracefully, but with all the energy of rapid and vehement gesture.' He swayed the emotions, so much so that tears were shed. Tears from 'wild Kentucs' over England's common law, in this year of England's murders of the *Chesapeake*! A miracle indeed!

Before the House could recover from Henry's 'impetuous and moving eloquence,' it had consented to the compromise bill he proposed. This prohibited only those British decisions rendered since July 4, 1776. It was a remarkable achievement, a striking example of what Marshall called 'the seductive arts of the Kentucky orator.'[1]

Although Henry's 'demagoguery' on this occasion was not entirely displeasing to Humphrey, partisan feeling had sharpened the hatred between the two men. During the Burrite controversy Henry, it was said, had threatened to use weapons more dangerous than goose quills.[2] Since then Humphrey's waving of the banners of Federalism, banners which had come to bear a close resemblance to the Union Jack, was not calculated to dampen Henry's resentment. The *Western World*, according to William Wirt, in its anti-Embargo articles was 'as truly British as if we had already gone

---

[1] Prentice, *Clay*, pp. 40–42; and Marshall in *Ky. Gazette*, Jan. 28, Feb. 11, 1832. In 1808 Clay was enjoined by Chief Justice Ninian Edwards from citing a decision of Lord Ellenborough. *Ky. Reports*, Hardin, p. 372.

[2] Lex. *Reporter*, July 9, 1808.

back to the darkest ages of our colonial servitude.' Such Anglicized scribblers as Marshall and Daveiss were 'firebrands of faction who have chosen this perilous and fearful crisis to foment disunion and discontent, and to erect themselves upon the ruins of republicanism and the Union.' [1]

In truth, Kentucky's self-appointed scourge of Gallicized and Espaniolized 'traitors' had himself entered the twilight zone of disunionism with Timothy Pickering. 'The unsullied H. Marshall' held Pickering's Essex Junto to be 'the source of reformation, or should that be unattainable, of disunion,' and agreed with his old colleague (at the very moment Madison was eagerly seizing Erskine's olive branch) that 'the ruling demagogues' were slaves of Bonaparte. 'I am almost the only person who gives the democrats here any disturbance,' he wrote, 'and truly they are a formidable host.' [2]

Yet the Prince of Devil's Hill was in himself as formidable a host as in the days of Jay's Treaty and the Sedition Act, when men asked, 'For God's sake . . . tell us what *materials* this man is made of,' who, instead of '*palliating* the infamy of his conduct . . . fills the public prints . . . and . . . attacks every individual and every meeting of *free men*?' [3] As 'the libertine father of that bastard paper,' the *Western World*, the 'modern Catiline' whose principles were ever 'Blackguardism and Billingsgate scurrility,' his powers were unimpaired. He was still capable of saluting his foes in the pleasing style of Junius: 'I will not call you liar, villain, or scoundrel, but, with all the politeness imaginable, I could prove you so.' [4]

At the 1808–1809 session Henry's friends, it was said, did not reelect him Speaker because they wished to have him on the floor in a better position to counter Marshall's expected attacks on Jefferson. Humphrey, however, scouted the idea that any member declined to vote for Clay 'lest it might embarrass him as a fighting fowl,' or was disposed to make the chamber 'a *cock pit*.' [5]

---

[1] Wirt, Nov. 26, 1808, Edwards, *N. Edwards*, pp. 434–36.
[2] Marshall to Pickering, March 17, 1809, *Pickering MSS.*
[3] *Ky. Gazette*, Oct. 10, 1795.
[4] *Ibid.*, Aug. 29, Oct. 10, 1809; Sept. 11, 1810.
[5] *Ibid.*, Feb. 11, 1832. Clay was defeated for the Speakership by William Logan, receiving 31 votes to 36 for Logan. *Journal of House 1808–09*, p. 1.

After Governor Scott in his opening message had directed attention to Jefferson's order for the militia to be in readiness for possible war with either France or England, Clay sponsored resolutions of confidence in the national administration. But before they were put to a vote almost a month was consumed by the objections and dilatory motions of Humphrey Marshall. Under the circumstances, the restraint of the Clayites was exemplary.

Marshall assailed the Embargo as a tyrannical, self-immolating folly, and advocated its repeal. He ridiculed the resolutions — only to have Clay vary their phrasing, 'somewhat extending their *spirit*.' In reply to his 'misrepresentations and misconstructions,' Clay was 'pertinent, severe, and eloquent.' At length, confident that 'the house were prepared finally to decide — were prepared when the resolutions were first introduced, and would, in their unanimous decision, draw the line between American Whig and Tory,' Henry called for a vote. His resolutions were carried 64 to 1, Marshall voting in the negative.

They declared the Embargo an honorable and judicious expedient for avoiding both war and Europe's 'piratical depredations.' Kentuckians, they said, 'would view with the utmost horror' any submission to the French decrees or British orders. Being sensible that 'the alternatives are — *a surrender of liberty and independence, or a bold and manly resistance*,' they would support government 'whether war, a total non-intercourse, or a more rigid execution of the Embargo system be determined on.' Finally, it was resolved 'that THOMAS JEFFERSON is entitled to the thanks of his country for the ability, uprightness and intelligence which he has displayed in the management both of our foreign relations and domestic concerns.' [1]

Henry then introduced his 'homespun resolution.' He would have the legislators 'clothe themselves in the productions of American manufactures, and abstain from the use of cloth or linens of European fabric, until the belligerent nations respect the rights of neutrals by repealing their orders and decrees as relates to the United States.' It was in accord with public sentiment, yet

---

[1] Lex. *Reporter*, Dec. 22, 26, 1808; *Journal of House, 1808–09*, pp. 30–33.

Marshall termed it the clap-trap of a demagogue. 'Mr. Clay,' said Humphrey later, 'then dressed in belligerent cloth, British I believe, declaimed most manfully, and patriotically, against the use of it.'

Their hostility now came to a head, in debates which were exceedingly abusive. Clay, with the invective that had left scars on Uriah Tracy, questioned the patriotism of men who opposed American manufactures, and failed to support government in times of grave peril. Humphrey complained, later, that being 'the only Federalist present, probably, gave me a peculiar exposure.' It was an exposure, however, which he himself invited, and one which gave him full opportunity of employing his matchless powers of vituperation.

At length Marshall lost his head, and bluntly called Clay a liar. Henry, then ten or twelve feet away, darted forward with arm uplifted. Members interposed. Beside himself with anger, Clay struggled to get free. In the scuffle he accidentally gave old Colonel Garrard a severe blow on the head ('a mighty thunderbolt,' said Marshall, with the force of 'a ball of soaped cotton'). They were separated (it was said) by General Riffe, a giant of a man, of German extraction, who entreated, then threatened. 'Come poys,' he said, holding them off, 'no fighting here, I vips you both.'

Turning to the House, Henry apologized. He would not have taken the liberty, he said, had his opponent been a man of honor. This was too much for Humphrey, who rose and yelled: 'It is the apology of a poltroon!' That night Clay challenged Marshall.[1]

'After the occurrences in the House of Representatives on this day, the receipt of this note will excite with you no surprize,' wrote Henry, hurriedly, his agitation revealing itself in his scrawled and blotted letter. 'I hope on my part I shall not be disappointed in the execution of the pledge you gave on that occasion, and in your disclaimer of the character attributed to you. To enable you to fulfill these reasonable and just expectations my friend Maj. Campbell is authorized by me to adjust the ceremonies proper to

---

[1] *Journal of House*, p. 93; Lex. *Reporter*, Jan. 19, 1809; *Ky. Gazette*, Jan. 24, 1809, Feb. 11, 18, 1832; Quisenberry, *Marshall*, pp. 100–03.

Sir ~~·~~ 4 Jan. 9.

After the occurrences in the House of Representatives on this day, the receipt of this note will excite with you no surprise. I hope on my part I shall not be disappointed in the execution of the pledge you gave on that occasion, and ~~in your~~ disclaimer of the character attributed to you. To enable you to fulfill these reasonable and just expectations my friend Maj. Campbell is authorized by me to adjust the ceremonies proper to be observed

I am Sir
Yr. &c
H. Henry Clay

~~Frankfort~~ Jan'y. 4th 1809

Sir ~~&c.~~

Your note of this date was handed me by Major Campbell, the object is understood, and without deigning to notice the insinuation, it contains as to character, the necessary arrangements are, on my part, submitted to my friend Colo. Moore.

Yours Sir &c.

H. Marshall

CLAY'S CHALLENGE AND MARSHALL'S
ACCEPTANCE, JANUARY 4, 1809

be observed.' Humphrey's acceptance was prompt and tart. 'Your note of this date was handed me by Major Campbell, the object is understood, and without deigning to notice the insinuation it contains as to character, the necessary arrangements are, on my part, submitted to my friend, Colo. Moore.' [1]

On that same evening of January 4, 1809, Henry, by special messenger, advised his brothers-in-law, Thomas and Nathaniel Hart, that Marshall had used language 'to which I could not submit, & I attempted to chastise him on the spot, but was prevented by the interference of the House. I have since challenged him, and there is a prospect of his accepting it. Should he do so I shall want a brace of pistols, and know of none . . . on which I would rely, except Morton's . . . procure some of the best powder adapted to such occasions . . . at any rate let the bearer return with them by tomorrow evening, or in the course of the night.' [2]

His haste was needless, since they did not meet until January 19. Meanwhile the legislators speculated upon the affair, recalled Humphrey's numerous brawls, and reflected upon young Clay's inexperience. Perhaps Henry himself wondered if his Goddess of Chance would bless Morton's pistol as she had the hunter's Old Bess.

Meanwhile, his 'linsey-woolsey resolution' was enthusiastically carried, with only Marshall and one other opposed. All now appeared in 'patriotic garb' — all except Humphrey. Although he afterwards said he had been throughout 'circumspect and inoffensive,' dressed in a new suit of British broadcloth, he strutted about in supreme disdain of the homespun 'Clayites and Jeffersonians.' [3] Both in its provocative contempt and in its downright bravery, this action was characteristic of Humphrey Marshall's relations with a people who on American Independence Day

---

[1] These notes of Jan. 4, 1809, the rules adopted, and an account of the duel by the seconds are in the *Clay MSS*. They were all printed in the *Ky. Gazette*, Jan. 21, the Lex. *Reporter*, Jan. 26, 1809. Both MS. notes of Jan. 4, 1809 have the word 'Frankfort' carefully blotted out, presumably as a precaution against the Kentucky law of Dec. 13, 1799 — 'An Act more effectually to suppress the practice of gambling and duelling.'

[2] Clay to Th. Hart or to N. G. Hart, Jan. 4, 1809, *Clay MSS*.

[3] Quisenberry, *op. cit.*, p. 101; *Journal of House*, p. 101.

uttered such threatening sentiments as — 'May he that despiseth home manufactures be stripped round the world.' [1]

Meanwhile, with all the formality usual with Kentucky gentlemen when acting under the Code Duello, Major John B. Campbell and Colonel James F. Moore, a Federalist senator, in punctilious conferences arranged very business-like rules. Their principals were to meet at ten paces, and at the word of command 'to fire at their leisure.' A snap or flash was to be equivalent to a shot. The man who fired first must hold his position and await the fire of the other. 'A violation of the above rules by either of the parties (accidents excepted) shall subject the offender to instant death.'

At last came the fatal day. On Thursday, January 19, in the nipping cold of early morning, the principals with their surgeons, seconds, and a few friends crossed the Ohio River at Louisville, and selected 'an eligible spot of ground' just below Silver Creek. The surgeons stood by with cases open, the seconds consulted together gravely, pistols were examined, ten paces measured off, and, amid awesome silence, slender, fair-haired Henry Clay faced in mortal combat tall and swarthy Humphrey Marshall.

A moment of suspense, a tightening of the trigger finger, then shots came quickly upon the words 'Attention! Fire!'

Clay remained steady, but Marshall staggered. Henry's ball had grazed his abdomen, and given him a slight wound. On the second round Clay's pistol snapped: there was only one shot, but Marshall fired without effect. On the third Henry staggered — and his shot went wild. Marshall had given him a flesh wound in the thigh.

'Mr. Clay insisted on another fire very ardently,' said the seconds, 'but his situation, resulting from the wound, placing him on unequal grounds, his importunate request was not complied with.'

Puffs of smoke drifted lazily through the cold morning air toward Silver Creek. The affair was over.

'We deem it justice to both gentlemen,' reported Colonel Moore and Major Campbell, 'to pronounce their conduct on the occasion,

---

[1] *Ky. Gazette*, July 8, 1806.

cool, determined, and brave in the highest degree. Mr. Clay's friend was under the impression that Mr. Marshall, at the third fire, violated a rule which required that he who fired first should stand in the position in which he was when he fired; but Mr. Marshall's friend, being convinced that Mr. Clay had fired previous to Mr. Marshall's moving from his position, this circumstance is considered as one in which gentlemen may be mistaken on such occasions, and is not to be noticed in this affair.' [1]

'I have this moment returned from the field of battle,' wrote Henry, from a friend's house near Louisville. 'We had three shots. On the first I grazed him just above the navel — he missed me. On the second my damned pistol snapped, and he missed me. On the third I received a flesh wound in the thigh, and owing to my receiving his fire first, etc., I missed him. My wound is in no way serious, as the bone is unhurt.' [2] Doctor Ridgley, who attended him as surgeon, declared that Marshall on all three rounds had fired first. 'Tell Mrs. Clay,' he wrote Thomas Hart, 'on my honor, 'tis only a simple wound & no danger but a few of the first days, say 4 or 5, I expect some pain & inflammation. . . . Mr. Clay wishes to come up in a Carriage tomorrow but I shall not assent to it.' [3]

While Mrs. Clay quietly repeated 'Thank God, he is only slightly wounded,' [4] Henry's friends in fervent letters praised his courage, and regretted that his pistol had missed on the second fire. James Johnson, who signed himself 'Yours until death,' said such 'heroism' would 'stop the mouths of all snivel faced Tories.' [5] William Barry, who offered to look after his law business, reported that 'nature & art combined cannot keep pace in healing your wound with the wishes and solicitude of your friends. Fortune, who has hitherto accompanied you thro' life, seems to have left you on the second fire — but no! perhaps she never was more

---

[1] Campbell and Moore's report, Jan. 19, 1809, *Clay MSS.*
[2] Clay to Jas. F. Clarke, Jan. 19, 1809, Quisenberry, *op. cit.*, p. 103 n.
[3] Fred. Ridgley to Th. Hart [Jan. 19, 1809], *Clay MSS.*
[4] Clay, T. H., *Clay*, pp. 50–51.
[5] Johnson (a member of the Assembly from Scott County; a brother of R. M. Johnson) to Clay, Frankfort, Jan. 28, 1809, *Clay MSS.*

careful of her darling son. She interfered,' said Barry, 'to save the
life of a miserable sinner and give him time for reformation. And
thereby has saved a feeling mind from the unpleasant reflections of
hurrying into the other world a poor soul in all probability not
prepared to meet his God.' [1]

As fortune's darling and the miserable sinner nursed their
wounds, Kentucky excitedly discussed every detail of an encounter
which became a part of frontier lore, and in the retelling tended to
become a conflict of Titans, a saga approaching the fantastic.[2]
Humphrey later characteristically snorted: 'We were kept on the
ground, trying to kill each other, until a skilful duellist would have
killed both, with less powder and fewer balls.' [3] Clay's friends, it
was said, had planned to welcome him from the field with a
banquet. Instead, Henry gave them card parties; and enemies
later charged that while he was laid up he repaid the tender
courtesies of his Louisville host by winning from him large sums at
brag.[4]

By February 9 Henry was sufficiently recovered from his wound
— his patriotic wound, said his friends — to return for the final
week of the session. Upon adjournment he resumed his law
practice, but found that politics took up more and more of his
time. His influence with the Madison administration was requested by his friends.[5] His oratory was considered indispensable
at the many mass meetings of that year. At Lexington's annual
Saint Patrick Day's banquet, in the Kentucky Hotel, where
Hibernian patriots were praised, English Tories denounced, and
the Union of the Harp and the Eagle acclaimed, Clay toasted 'the
genuine Irish character: frank, brave, and generous.' On Independence Day he himself was toasted. Six cheers were given

---

[1] Wm. T. Barry to Clay, Frankfort, Jan. 29, 1809, *Clay MSS*.

[2] One legend told of an encounter, shortly after, between Clay and an aggrieved
cousin of Humphrey, Eli Marshall, Ohio desperado and horse thief, 'a giant in stature
and every inch a villain,' whom Henry in melodramatic fashion overawed, forced to
apologize, and to sign himself a coward. Peck, C. H., *Jacksonian Epoch*, pp. 31–33.

[3] *Ky. Gazette*, Feb. 11, 1832.

[4] Washington *Globe*, Jan. 24, 26, 1832.

[5] On April 10, 1809 he recommended Ninian Edwards to Pres. Madison, and to Sec.
of State Robt. Smith, for the governorship of Illinois Territory. Edwards, *N. Edwards*,
pp. 27–28.

'Henry Clay, the Kentucky orator, patriot, and philanthropist,' and six more hailed 'Henry Clay, our next Senator in Congress.' [1]

In December he entered the Assembly for his sixth, and last, term. He distinguished himself by a cogent, precedent-setting, report on a much disputed election in Hardin County. He heard old Governor Scott review Europe's degrading and destructive aggressions, and point out — significantly, in view of the fiery speeches of hot-triggered young Kentuckians — that only one-fifth of the militia was armed. He was in full accord with resolutions which unanimously condemned British Minister Jackson for conduct 'insidious and insulting,' and pledged support in asserting the nation's rights against England 'whatever may be the consequences,' warlike resolutions which contained (said Massachusetts' *Essex Register*) 'the true sense of the U. States.' [2] On January 4, 1810, his final session came to an end when the Assembly elected him by a two-to-one vote to serve out Buckner Thruston's term in the United States Senate.

In submitting his resignation to Speaker William Logan, his rival on several occasions, whom he had defeated for Thruston's seat, Henry wrote: 'It is in vain, sir, to attempt to express my gratitude to a partial country for this new mark of esteem. No language would do justice to the sensibilities excited on the occasion. I cannot, however, refuse to myself this opportunity of bearing testimony to the frank, liberal, and honorable manner, in which, on your part, the competition between us has been conducted.' [3]

It was a gracious gesture to his competitor, and to his colleagues in state politics. He was now within three months of his thirty-third birthday, a Kentucky lawyer, politician, orator, planter, horse-breeder — and duellist. Proceeding to Washington, he at once commanded national attention by voicing at a most depressing period the impassioned demands of Young America and the New West.

---

[1] *Ky. Gazette*, March 21, July 11, 1809.   [2] Salem *Essex Register*, Feb. 24, 1810.

[3] *Journal of House, 1809–10*, p. 121; also, pp. 8–10 (for the disputed Haycraft-Thomas election in Hardin County), and pp. 119–20 (for Clay's election to the Senate). Clay defeated Logan by a House vote of 44 to 20, by a joint vote of 61 to 31. Thruston had been appointed to the U. S. Circuit Court of the Dist. of Columbia.

Chapter Ten. The Cock of Kentucky

I am for resistance by the sword . . . *for war with Britain.* (*Henry Clay.*)

I admit the outrages of both France and England; but I dread the Power of neither. I dread nothing but the disease of the Mind in my own dear beloved Nation. But that must and will be cured. (*John Adams.*)

Vigour and Despatch are not the properties of a Republic. (*John Dickinson.*)

ON FEBRUARY 22, 1810, young Clay, newly arrived from Kentucky, ventured to address the Senate in a speech which was both a rebuke and a prophecy. 'When the regular troops of this House,' said the impetuous Westerner, 'disciplined as they are in the great affairs of this nation, are inactive at their posts, it becomes the duty of its raw militia, however lately enlisted, to step forth in defence of the honor and independence of the country.'

For three months Congress, incited by a pro-British minority, had been impotently ranting against Copenhagen Jackson, avoiding, then fumbling, its most pressing problem — a substitute for the generally discredited Non-Intercourse Act, which was to expire at this session. After much wrangling the House had sent up a measure drafted by Gallatin called 'Macon's Bill.' This modified and weakened the Non-Intercourse so as to permit American ships to import British and French goods, in order to gain revenue for a depleted Treasury. A further recession from both Embargo and war, it enabled Britain, indirectly, not only to continue her monopoly of America's exports but to regain her control of America's imports.

Both this administration measure and the Eleventh Congress were severely criticized. The Baltimore *Whig* raged at the 'imbecility, impolicy and *meanness*' of Gallatin's 'Submission Bill,' and at a Congress 'governed by *fear* and *avarice*.' Boston's *Patriot*, Salem's *Register*, Philadelphia's *Aurora*, and Baltimore's *Evening Post* denounced both '*British apologists*' and Republican moderates.[1] Congress will never rouse from its 'lethergy and temporiseing,' said an irate Tennessean, until Minister Jackson 'Copenhagens' our seaports.[2] 'We have lost our resentment for the severest injuries a nation ever suffered, because of their being so often repeated,' wrote an irate Virginian. In failing to retaliate in kind upon Britain's goods and men, our American character has 'degenerated into a system of stock-jobbing ... By the God of Heaven, if we go on in this way, our nation will sink into disgrace and slavery.' [3]

Feeble as Macon's Bill was, a factious Senate on February 21 emasculated it. By a vote of 16 to 11 nothing was left but a clause excluding British and French warships from American waters.

It was this that had stirred young Clay into action. Fresh from the frontier where people were demanding retaliatory war in place of a 'cobweb submissive' Non-Intercourse, he was shocked by these senescent 'regular troops' who dropped even the pretense of commercial retaliation. And no one protested! — until the Kentuckian, on Washington's Birthday, moved to recommit the mutilated bill.

The House measure 'was a crazy vessel,' he said, but, 'taken from us without a substitute, we are left defenceless, naked, and

---

[1] Baltimore *Whig*, and other Republican papers, in Alexandria *Gazette*, Jan. 20, 1810; *Essex Register*, Dec. 23, 1809 ff.

[2] A. Jackson to Sen. Whiteside, Feb. 10, 1810, Jackson, *Corres.*, I, 200.

[3] John Tyler to Madison, Jan. 15, 1810; also, to Jefferson, May 12, 1810, Tyler, *Tylers*, I, 235, 246. 'I would,' Gov. Tyler wrote Madison, 'not only interdict the trade with G. B., but I would seize British goods ... and if another impressment should take place, I would make prisoners of every British subject in the States.'

exposed to all the rage and violence of the storm.' [1] Non-Importation, Embargo, Non-Intercourse — all were '*peaceful* resistance of the law. When this is abandoned,' he cried in his vibrant young voice, 'I am for resistance by the *sword*. No man in the nation wants peace more than I; but I prefer the troubled ocean of war . . . with all its calamities . . . to the tranquil and putrescent pool of ignominious peace.

'If we can accommodate our differences with one of the belligerents only,' continued Clay, 'I should prefer that one to be Britain; but if with neither, and we are forced into a selection of our enemy, then I am for war with Britain.' On the score of property spoliations 'we have just cause of war with both,' he said. But Britain stands prior and preeminent in her atrocious outrages upon us — 'by her violation of the sacred personal rights of American freemen, in the arbitrary and lawless imprisonment of our seamen, the attack upon the Chesapeake . . .' He would not dwell 'on the long catalogue of our wrongs' which had been 'repeated until the sensibility of the nation is benumbed by the dishonorable detail.' He would insist, however, that America had the means of redress, and that there were objects attainable 'by war with Great Britain.'

We have abundant means of carrying on war, he confidently asserted, scorning those who 'triumphantly appeal to the vacant vaults of the Treasury.' Indeed, 'is it not astonishing that despondency itself should disparage the resources of this country?' Our public credit is unimpaired, and 'the boundless territories of the West' will secure loans to any extent. At Orleans alone we have public property enough to extinguish 'the celebrated deficit.' Is it nothing that the people have so often pledged us their last cent, their last drop of blood? 'Or are we to be governed by the low, grovelling parsimony of the counting-room, and to cast up the actual pence in the drawer before we assert our inestimable rights?'

'We are to estimate,' said Clay, 'not only the benefit to be derived to ourselves, but the injury to be done the enemy. The conquest of Canada is in your power. I trust I shall not be deemed presumptuous when I state that I verily believe that the militia of

---

[1] *Annals*, 11th, 2d, 579–82; Feb. 22, 1810.

Kentucky are alone competent to place Montreal and Upper Canada at your feet. Is it nothing to the British nation; is it nothing to the pride of her Monarch, to have the last of the immense North American possessions held by him in the commencement of his reign wrested from his dominion? Is it nothing to us to extinguish the torch that lights up savage warfare? Is it nothing to acquire the entire fur trade connected with that country, and to destroy the temptation and the opportunity of violating your revenue and other laws?

'War with Great Britain will deprive her of those supplies of raw materials and provisions which she now obtains from this country,' he said. War will be a complete non-intercourse. 'She will not have the game, as she will if you press this bill without an efficient system, entirely in her own hands.' While our soldiers scale the heights of Montreal and Quebec, 'the enterprise and valor of our maritime brethren will participate in the spoils of capture.' War will unify the nation, purify it, strengthen it, revive the ardor of the Revolutionary Fathers, and produce a new race of American heroes 'to preserve inviolate what they achieved.' At the very least a manly resistance, as in '76, will 'gain the approbation of our own hearts. If we surrender without a struggle ... we forfeit the respect of the world, and (what is worse) of ourselves.'

And yet 'we are often reminded that the British navy constitutes the only barrier between us and universal dominion. When resistance to Britain is submission to France, I protest against the castigation of our colonial infancy being applied in the independent manhood of America. I am willing, sir, to dispense with the parental tenderness of the British navy. I cannot subscribe to British slavery upon the water that we may escape French subjugation on land. I should feel myself humbled, as an American citizen, if we had to depend upon any foreign Power to uphold our independence; and I am persuaded that our own resources, properly directed, are fully adequate to our defence. I am therefore for resisting oppression by whomsoever attempted ... whether maritime or territorial.'

'What ought to be the substitute [for Macon's Bill], I confess I have not satisfied myself — not expecting that it would fall to my

lot to make you this motion ... I would suggest two for consideration — either a total non-importation, which our laws can doubtless enforce, or to arm our merchantmen, and authorize convoys ... This latter measure may lead to war,[1] but ... let those
who attempt to molest us take to themselves the consequences.'

Above all there must be no submission, he said in conclusion.
Into this 'lifeless skeleton' of a bill the Senate must 'breathe vigor
and energy.' Our precious independence won by the Fathers
must not be abandoned without a blow. 'I entreat the Senate ...
I call upon the members of this House ... I beseech them not to
forfeit the esteem of the country,' not to disgrace America and
themselves by a base and 'ignominious surrender of our rights.'

It was a flaming speech — heralding a new epoch. In the
Senate at the precise moment that body had reached the lowest
depths of futility and despair Clay voiced the rising spirit of a
Young America and a New West, both of which had come into
existence since '76. The Kentuckian's speech of youthful 'energy
and courage ... marked the appearance of a school which was for
fifty years to express the national ideals ... drawing elevation of
character from confidence in itself, and from devotion to ideas of
nationality and union, which redeemed every mistake committed
in their names. In Clay's speech almost for the first time the two
rhetorical marks of his generation made their appearance ... the
Union and the Fathers.'[2]

Britain was not only the preeminent aggressor but the hereditary
enemy, to this Kentucky orator who had begun life amid the
blackened ruins left by Tarleton, entered manhood declaiming
Patrick Henry's Liberty or Death speeches, and lived on the scene
of past, and probably future, British-savage warfare. Against 'our
haughty and imperious foe' war was the only alternative to pacific
coercion, the only escape from a prolonged colonial servitude.
Never had the issue been stated so eloquently, so decisively. And
never had there been such a need of energy and courage.

---

[1] 'If you authorize merchant vessels to arm and resist visitation and search,' wrote
Rufus King to Pickering, Jan. 26, 1810, 'the matter will not demand six hours delibera-
tion in England — it must and will be treated as an aggression to be repelled by arms.'
King, R., Corres., V, 189.

[2] Adams, Hist. U.S., V, 190.

Emotionally exhausted, cowed, without initiative, Congress was in a mood to submit. To submit — with 'Apostate' Matthew Lyon, who would repeal all restrictions and thus raise the price of Western produce at New Orleans ten to twenty per cent.[1] To submit — with seaport Federalists, who argued that to resist further by self-ruinous boycotts, or even to resent Copenhagen Jackson's insults, would incite Britain to war and to the complete destruction of American commerce.[2] To submit — when Britain and France daily added to their millions in plundered property; and Britain daily added to her thousands of impressed Americans, having enslaved over fourteen hundred in the past seventeen months.[3] To submit — when Federalist congressmen championed Jackson and franked out his anti-American pamphlets; when Editor Hanson of Baltimore, exulting that 'every mail is charged with some dozens of the pamphlets,' called upon the dismissed British envoy for 'a constant supply of ammunition' so that Pickeronian editors might 'keep up a brisk and effectual fire' upon their own American government at 'Sansculottesville.' [4]

In the House a few 'war Republicans' had demanded 'energetic measures' in place of a Non-Intercourse they held to be ruinous to the farmer and favorable only to Britain and British-licensed Federalist shippers; as giving 'our inveterate, rapacious, and relentless enemy' a monopoly of our carrying trade, 'a monopoly of our cotton at eleven cents, and . . . of broadcloths at fourteen dollars the yard.' [5] These young insurgents were disorganized, leaderless. But from now on they were boldly to press Clay's 'resistance by the sword.' The conquest of Canada, noted Josiah

---

[1] *Annals*, 11th, 2d, 1648.

[2] *Ibid.*, pp. 943, 1336, 1161, 1221, 1229, House speeches of Quincy, Wheaton, Livermore, of Mass., Haven (N.H.), Sturges (Conn.).

[3] Madison's report, April 4, 1810, *A. S. P., For. Rel.*, III, 348.

[4] Fisher, *Jackson and Newspaper Propaganda*, pp. 99–104. Editor Hanson's fire with his duelling pistol, at least, was 'brisk and effectual' — in a duel, January 1810, he had killed Capt. Gordon, an officer of the *Chesapeake* when it was attacked by the *Leopard* in 1807.

[5] See speeches by Desha (Ky.), Anderson (Tenn.), Poindexter (Miss. Ter.), Fisk (N.Y.), Sawyer (N.C.), McKee (Ky.), *Annals*, 11th, 2d, 1301, 1327, 1600, 1512, 1166, 1724; also, on 'British monopoly,' and the recurrent theme: 'The non-intercourse co-operates with the Orders in Council' to the detriment of the Southern and Western farmer, Troup (Ga.) to Gov. Mitchell, March 17, 1810, Harden, E. J., *George M. Troup*, p. 95.

Quincy, 'now for the first time . . . began seriously to be agitated.' [1]
And from now on the 'raw militia' of the nation were to be increasingly importunate.

In the Senate, however, Clay failed to rally the regular troops.
The Elder Statesmen resented being lashed by an imperious
stripling, the youngest man in the chamber, scarcely two weeks
from the backwoods. Ignominious surrender indeed! This boy
with his drum-and-trumpet rhetoric about the sword of honor
knew nothing of the Revolution's hardships. His duellist's courage
only invited disaster. Conquer Canada! with an empty Treasury,
a navy of Jeffersonian gunboats, a Wilkinsonian army literally
decimated by death and desertions? [2] By a vote of 20 to 13 Clay's
motion was killed.

Dispirited, Henry thought the lower chamber would concur in
this abject submission.[3] But the House insisted upon its original
bill. Again the Senate rejected it. A deadlock ensued, with
Congress more indecisive, more deeply embogged, than in
November.

'Here all is still & torpid,' reported a Westerner: 'the patriotism
& honnor of the Country is gone.' Nothing will stir Congress but
'a direct attack on our territory by Great Britain . . . the people in
the N. E. States have become sordidly avaritious & the Government
is paralized.' [4] Everyone seemed inclined to wait upon
London and Paris. But the months-old European news, 'a jumble
of Probabilities, Possibilities, and Lies,' only augmented the indecision. With war out of the question, said Bayard, the Republicans can only cultivate England's good will, 'and that their
Stomachs are not yet prepared for.' [5] And yet our 'sap-ient,' 'sapskulled' orators cry for war, sneered John Randolph: 'it must be

---

[1] Quincy, *Quincy*, pp. 203–04.

[2] At New Orleans, in 1809, 523 soldiers were dead, 745 sick, 499 absent, and only
414 fit for duty. *Natl. Intelligencer*, Feb. 16, 1810. 'This country is now without a cent,
with a deficit of four millions,' with an effective army of some 4000 'despicable men,'
and a navy 'reduced to some eight or nine frigates,' reported Luis de Onis, unrecognized envoy of the (Bourbon-British) Spanish Junta, on Feb. 4, 1810. Nevertheless, it
has designs on Spanish possessions, and can be brought to reason '*but by energy, by force,
and by chastisement.*' *A. S. P., For. Rel.*, III, 404.

[3] Clay, Feb. 23, 1810, in *Ky. Gazette*, March 6, 1810.

[4] Elisha Tracy, Feb. 25, 1810, Huntington, *Letters*, p. 141.

[5] Bayard to A. Bayard, March 5, 1810, Bayard, *Papers*, p. 179.

against the pismires for the pigmies & cranes ... would be too formidable.' [1]

Government was demoralized. President Madison complained that Congress was 'unhinged,' [2] but he himself, with neither the force nor the inclination to drive the car of state, had thrown the reins on the necks of a distracted and leaderless majority. When the House, on motion of Randolph and led by Macon of North Carolina, actually resolved to reduce the 'unrepublican' and expensive army and navy such raw militiamen as Dick Johnson of Kentucky and Troup of Georgia concurred — out of sheer disgust at this 'everlasting degradation' when America's wounds were 'fresh bleeding.' [3] Never were men 'more completely divided, bewildered, and disorganized.' [4] Randolph himself felt the dangers of this chaos: with the Cabinet 'all to pieces, and the two Houses ... tumbled about their own ears,' there was a paralysis, an impotence, and a confusion that in other countries had invariably precursed 'mighty changes.' [5]

In this spring of 1810 — when Henry Clay, 'the Cock of Kentucky,' as Randolph called him, so audaciously and lustily crowed for 'resistance by the sword' — both the nation and the majority party suffered sorely from shattered morale and mutinous factions. A crisis had indeed occurred, and mighty changes were imminent.

The few Federalists had gained an undue weight, 'by superior intelligence, by cunning, by stratagem,' [6] and by assailing every proposal as another step in yielding 'our political virginity' to 'Napoleon, Our King.' [7] They clamored for naval defense — against French privateers; deplored the clamor about British

---

[1] Randolph to Jos. H. Nicholson, Feb. 15, 1810, *Nicholson MSS.*

[2] Madison to Jefferson, April 23, 1810, Madison, *Writings*, II, 472.

[3] Johnson, like Clay, in vain tried to infuse Western confidence and energy. See speech of April 16, 1810, *Annals*, 11th, 2d, 1867–70.

[4] Samuel Taggart, *Letters*, p. 347; April 27, 1810.

[5] Randolph to Nicholson, May 2, 1810, Adams, *Hist. U.S.*, V, 209; Randolph to R. K. Randolph, April 8, 1810, *John Randolph MSS.*

[6] Geo. M. Troup to Mitchell, March 17, 1810, Harden, *Troup*, p. 95.

[7] *Independent American*, Georgetown, D.C., April 21, 1810. The editor, one of Minister Jackson's co-workers, in a five-column editorial listed thirty-five considerations to prove the Republicans sold out to France, one of them being American writers and editors in the pay of France.

impressments made by Kentucky politicians and Irish-American editors; and lamented the people's continued submission to Republican tyranny: 'Though our soil is fertile in *Caesars*, it seems incapable of bearing *Brutuses*. If our British ancestors had been made of such stuff, the Stuarts would ... have ground the nation under their iron sceptre.' [1]

More important than the spleen of Federalists, who would 'rule the nation if they could, but see it damned if others should,' was the inertia of the majority party — oppressed by the dead weight of Old Republicanism, hampered by Executive weakness, split into Madisonians, Clintonians, Randolph-Monroe Quids, and anti-Gallatin 'Invisibles.' The last group, consisting of Senators Giles, Smith of Maryland, Leib of Pennsylvania, and Robert Smith, the Secretary of State, was supported by the warlike Philadelphia *Aurora* and Baltimore *Whig*. The Federalists themselves were no more violent than Editor Irvine of the *Whig*, 'the Smiths' paper,' who reproached Madison for 'hearkening to the ruinous counsel of that *arch-apostate* ALBERT GALLATIN' as to that '*most feeble* and *despicable* measure' called Macon's Bill. 'While he (or any one led by him) sways our councils, the nation will continue in an eclipse,' said Irvine: for Gallatin 'has gone over to the Philistines,' as shown by Treasury reports which are 'chiefly calculated to strike a panic into the ignorant; to conceal our great resources; to make foreign enemies deride us; or to favour ... rapacious speculators.' [2]

Clay was on good terms with Mr. Madison — and remained so, even if his political course often was commended by the *Aurora* and *Whig*. At this session Giles sponsored the resolutions condemning Copenhagen Jackson. Leib on March 8 moved to recall Minister Pinkney from London unless England complied with Erskine's agreement, atoned for the *Chesapeake*, and released impressed Americans. Smith on March 19 urged naval convoys. All these proposals, ostensibly, were in keeping with the Kentuckian's demand for vigor and energy. Yet neither now nor later did Clay join this small but powerful Senate group in its anti-administration petty politics and personal animosities.

---

[1] Boston *Centinel*, in Alexandria *Gazette*, Jan. 31, 1810.

[2] Baltimore *Whig*, in Georgetown, D.C., *Spirit of 'Seventy Six*, April 6, 1810.

Nevertheless, younger Republicans like Clay who supported the administration were most critical of the old guard leaders of their party, not excluding Mr. Madison. The President's messages, said young Senator Crawford of Georgia, were so cautiously worded as to be as obscure as Delphic oracles.[1] Young George Poindexter of Mississippi, with whom Clay became very friendly, in private stated that 'the President has crept into a nutt-shell from whence he is sometimes heard to speak indistinctly, but no one in either house of Congress ventures to pronounce what course would be acceptable to the Executive. . . . we have been Scuffling, during a four months session,' discussing everything 'from Torpedoes to Convoys and all the intermediate grades of resistance, protestations, and averments . . . without even the poor Consolation of opposing any thing like resistance to Foreign aggression.'[2]

Clay was still a 'democrat' — as were Crawford and Poindexter; all three young frontiersmen, indeed, had in their native Virginia drunk deeply of Jeffersonianism. Clay admired Jefferson, and the latter regarded him as one 'in whose friendly disposition I have confidence.'[3] But the harsh realities of the times were jolting him out of the pattern of Jeffersonian theories, which, while nobly postulated, did not allow for the elemental fact that men and nations will eventually, perhaps in blind desperation, strike back at an 'inveterate, rapacious, and relentless enemy.'

Sharp was the contrast between Clay's war speech and Jefferson's serene view, written a few days later, that the maniac Old World, while giving us 'the blue devils at times,' could not vitally wound America because 'happily for us the Mammoth cannot swim, nor the Leviathan move on dry land.'[4] Still believing it 'sheer Quixotism in us' to employ the sword of defense, the Sage of Monticello for another year was to expound his familiar gospel:

---

[1] Crawford, Jan. 1810, Adams, *Hist. U.S.*, V, 179–80.

[2] Poindexter to Cowles Mead, April 20, 1810, *Poindexter MSS.* (in the *Claiborne Papers*, Mississippi State Archives). The lack of Executive leadership was only too evident, when 'the Majority as they are called in Congress are divided and sub divided into Sections, half, quarter, and fractional Sections, and each is too wise to be led by the other.'

[3] Jefferson to John W. Eppes, Nov. 12, 1810, *Jefferson MSS.* He wanted Clay's legal advice on the famous New Orleans batture case.

[4] *Ibid.*, Jefferson to Walter Jones, March 5, 1810.

remaining in peace, despite insult and injury, America grows rich and strong and in time *'hors d'insulte,'* while the bedlamite Old World wars itself into either reason or ruin.[1] 'Our difficulties are indeed great,' he wrote in March of 1810, 'but when viewed in comparison with those of Europe . . . they are the joys of Paradise.' [2]

At this crisis John Adams more nearly approximated the feelings prompting Clay's speech. With a passionate faith in 'this over-grown Colt of a Nation' that equalled the Kentuckian's, this old Revolutionary radical (never a John Bull but always a John Yankee, as he would say) did not shrink from a second war with England. Unlike Jefferson, he could not compare injured rights and insulted sovereignty to the joys of Paradise, or, in face of the *Chesapeake* atrocity, still preach 'the ruinous folly of a navy.' [3] He welcomed the changes heralded by Clay. As in '76 Adams was convinced — had he not proved it in '98 against France? — that security and peace could be had only by a strong national government and the sword.[4]

The Kentucky 'Jacobin' who in '98 had won his spurs by his anti-Adams declamations was now veering away from Jefferson's pacifism to Adams's militancy. Clay was to travel a new road and to urge America to travel it with him. He came to symbolize a new National Republicanism, a merging of the practical Adams's nationalism with the idealistic Jefferson's democracy. The necessity for this was generally sensed. Jefferson himself saw the need of entrusting the Ship of State 'to the young and robust.' [5] Before long Clay and other robust Young Republicans were to seize the helm; to lighten the distressed vessel of its anti-national prejudices — leaving them to Randolph's Quids and Pickering's Anglomen; and to cause Adams to remark that ' *"the Hyper-Federalists are become Jacobins, and the Hyper-Republicans are become Federalists."* ' [6]

At this session Clay was engaged on more than 'a tour of

---

[1] Jefferson to Kosciusko, April 16, 1811, *Jefferson MSS.*
[2] *Ibid.*, Jefferson to Walter Jones, March 5, 1810.
[3] Jefferson to Th. Paine, Sept. 6, 1807, Jefferson, *Works*, X, 493.
[4] Adams to Rush, June 28, 1810, *Old Family Letters*, pp. 258–59.
[5] Jefferson to John Armstrong, Dec. 13, 1810, *Jefferson MSS.*
[6] Adams to Waterhouse, July 12, 1811, Adams, *Corres. with Benj. Waterhouse*, ed. W. C. Ford, p. 64.

pleasure.' He argued for internal improvements. He called for increased garrisons for the frontier. And he urged a liberalizing of land grants to encourage migration to Lower Louisiana. His interest in the last subject was whetted by James Brown, who beseeched him to help Americanize a Franco-Spanish Louisiana by such legislation, and by the annexation of the already Americanized province of West Florida.[1] Congress, however, remained a Castle of Indolence. From it Henry sought relief in 'the dissipated circles of the City.'

Since his tour in 1807 the Potomac Bridge had been built and a canal at Great Falls had made Washington, now with a population of eight thousand, accessible to the fur trade of the Upper Mississippi. But the Federal City was still raw and crude: 'commenced on a huge, unwieldy scale . . . the enormous joints fall asunder before they can be well knit together.'[2] The domeless Capitol, two wings without a body, likewise seemed symbolical of a huge, unwieldy republic — where the people's disunity and impotence of government, remarked Minister Turreau, 'renders their independence at least problematical.'[3]

Henry attended the social 'crushes and squeezes' with such good friends as Caesar Augustus Rodney and William Armistead Burwell; friends who in themselves revealed the Kentuckian's social tastes, both being Southern democrats who were 'great aristocrats in their domestick habits, if not in their Politicks.'[4] They presented themselves at the Wednesday evening levees of 'Presidentess' Madison; drove to Great Falls and to the Spa at Bladensburgh; and visited the barnlike theatre, where, when *The Forest of Bonday, or the Dog of Montargis* was given, one speculated as to whether the concealed sausage would cause the heroic dog to ring the alarm bell.[5]

At salon and mess they discussed the increasing number of

[1] Brown to Clay, New Orleans, Feb. 26, 1810, *Clay MSS*.

[2] Ingersoll, C. J., *Inchiquin, the Jesuit's Letters* (1810), pp. 31, 35.

[3] Turreau, *Aperçu sur la Situation Politique des États Unis d'Amérique* (1811), pp. 112–13.

[4] Foster, A. J., *MS. Notes*, I, 136. Taggart (*Letters*, pp. 119, 355), rigid Yankee Federalist, described Atty. General Rodney as 'distinguished. . . polite. . . of correct ideas and great candor,' and young Burwell of Virginia, formerly secretary to Mr. Jefferson, as 'one of the most sensible candid' Republicans in the House.

[5] Semmes, J. E., *John H. B. Latrobe*, p. 36.

American ships that were smuggling British goods into the Continent; and the increasing number that were being captured by French and Danish privateers. In his efforts to exclude British wares from Europe by his Continental System (a monopolistic navigation system similar to that which had enriched Britain for centuries), Napoleon was being driven on to fresh conquests. Great Britain was being driven deeper into a system of licenses which was shot through with fraud and perjury; a system under which the Tory oligarchy, though still excluding American exports from France, permitted Britons a trade that gave Bonaparte British-made army apparel and sustained England with French grain! [1] There were revolts in South America, and rumors of revolt in Canada and Florida. Aaron Burr, an exile in Paris, was said to be asking Bonaparte's aid for his 'disunionist plots.' [2] General Wilkinson was in the Federal City with 'two committees . . . in operation on his conduct,' noted Poindexter. 'He must kick the beam, Old Tom to the contrary notwithstanding.' [3] Robert Fulton was assuring Clay and his friends that the United States would succeed in its revolt against the Old World if it but adopted his torpedoes, his aquatic incendiaries, for with them rowboats could sink British ships-of-the-line. [4]

Mme. Jerome Bonaparte, 'very handsomely dressed . . . very saucy and pretty,' [5] no longer disturbed rigid Calvinists by French gowns of thinnest sarcenet. Nevertheless, the Reverend Samuel

---

[1] *Natl. Intelligencer*, March 16, 1810 ff., Alexandria *Gazette*, Feb. 5, 1810 ff. Also, Adams, J. Q. (Minister to Russia), *Writings*, IV, 82 ff.; and Hall, Capt. Basil, *Fragments of Voyages*, etc., series I, p. 46, on England's licensed trade, 'the very essence of which,' wrote Hall in 1831, 'was false swearing, false papers, and the most unprincipled collusion of every kind.' From our English merchants 'the base contamination has not yet quite washed away.' It was under this system, 'culminating in 1810 with the granting of over 18,000 licenses,' says Heckscher, E. F., *The Continental System*, p. 205, 'that the greater part . . . of the maritime trade of the whole world was carried on . . .'

[2] *Natl. Intelligencer*, April 13, 16, 1810.

[3] Poindexter to Mead, April 20, 1810, *Poindexter MSS*.

[4] *Natl. Intelligencer*, Feb. 26, March 14, 1810; Feb.–May, 1810.

[5] Mrs. F. J. Jackson, Jackson, *Diaries*, I, 59, Nov. 21, 1809. Writing of her two months in Washington, where her husband, the dismissed British Minister, had failed in his negotiations ('being accustomed to treat with the civilized Courts and governments of Europe and not with savage democrats, half of them sold to France'), Mrs. Jackson said that Mrs. Madison, 'Madame la Présidente' (who with other ladies copied her toilettes), was *'une bonne grosse femme, de la classe bourgeois*, very fit to grace the President's table; *sans distinction* either in manners or appearance, but, to be just, *elle est aussi sans prétentions.' Ibid.*, I, 57.

Taggart (who boasted that 'he had no short sermons') and other Pickeronian congressmen were now convinced that her infant son had been designated by the French Anti-Christ as America's future sovereign.[1] Tokens of Bonapartist Influence, also, were Madame la Présidente's 'French sauces and flum-flumeries.' British Influence, on the other hand, was damned by none more thoroughly than by the Republican Sons of Saint Patrick, who on March 17 'drowned their Shamrocks' in patriotic toasts, one of which was to Home Manufactures.[2]

A few days later Henry joined in a general discussion of this subject, begun when Lloyd of Massachusetts opposed requiring the navy to give preference to American hemp. Clay said he would not encourage manufactures at the expense of agriculture, or have the wretched poverty of England's factory workers. But he would have America supply her own wants. 'The nation that imports its clothing,' said the young Kentuckian, 'is but little less dependent than if it imported its bread.' Dame Commerce, 'a flirting, flippant, noisy jade,' would keep us in perpetual dependence upon British muslins and broadcloth. He was confident, however, that she would no longer seduce 'the yeomanry of the country, the true and genuine landlords of this tenement called the United States.' [3]

For years after gaining political independence, said Clay, 'a gentleman's head could not withstand the influence of solar heat unless covered with a London hat; his feet could not bear the pebbles, or frost, unless protected by London shoes; and the comfort or ornament of his person was only consulted when his coat was cut by the shears of a tailor "just from London." ' Lately, however, a *wonderful* discovery has been made — manufactures are not beyond the reach of American enterprise. Fostered by government, and aided by household exertions, they will soon free us from British dependence.

Encouragement might be given by bounties or tariff duties, he said. Unquestionably in time of war we should be independent of

---

[1] Taggart, *Letters*, pp. 345, 114; *Independent American*, April 21, 1810.
[2] *Natl. Intelligencer*, March 21, 1810.
[3] *Annals*, 11th, 2d, 626–30; also, *Natl. Intelligencer*, April 6, 1810.

foreign cordage and sailcloth, articles which the Western country
can supply with but little aid from government. Of all practicable
aids surely this one under consideration should escape opposition,
unless everything proposed in Congress is doomed to futility. 'We
have had before us,' Clay scornfully concluded, 'a proposition to
afford a manly protection to the rights of commerce, and how has
it been treated? Rejected! You have been solicited to promote
agriculture, by increasing the facilities of internal communication
through the means of canals and roads, and what has been done?
Postponed! We are now called upon to give a trifling support to
our domestic manufactures, and shall we close the circle of congressional inefficiency, by adding this also to the catalogue?'

The regular troops voted, 22 to 9, to give this trifling support.
Their circle of inefficiency was to close on a House measure
termed 'Macon's Bill No. 2' — the weakest and most mischievous
phase of the policy of defense by commercial coercion.

All restrictions were removed by this bill, which was introduced
in the Senate on April 27. It provided that if either belligerent
before March 3, 1811 revoked its edicts, three months thereafter
Non-Intercourse would be restored against the power that continued its predatory system at America's expense.

This was neither resistance by the law nor by the sword, but for
the time being was outright submission to England. It opened our
markets to her, and gave her control of our commerce 'as far as
she may wish to distress her adversaries, to cramp our growth as
rivals, or to prevent our interference with her smuggling monopoly.' [1] Yet it was hoped that this very partiality to England,
instead of inciting Bonaparte to war, would induce him to revoke
his decrees, and thus compel England to revoke her orders. 'An
apprehension that France may take this politic course,' said Madison, 'would be a rational motive with the British Government to
get the start of her.' [2]

The few war men were disgusted — 'for certainly,' wrote
Poindexter, 'there never has been, since the establishment of the
American Government, a party in power who acted with so little

---

[1] Madison to Jefferson, May 7, 1810, Madison, *Writings*, II, 474.
[2] Same to Wm. Pinkney, May 23, 1810, *ibid.*, II, 475-76.

energy or dignity.' ¹ Yet all those whom Clay regarded as steeped in 'counting-room cupidity' were overjoyed. 'Whilst the Yankees,' declared young Troup from the southern frontier, 'can freight their vessels to smuggle British property into the continent, they care not two straws about the rest.' ²

In the bill as it came to the Senate there was but one coercive provision (forced by young Johnson of Kentucky), an additional duty of fifty per cent on British and French imports. Clay favored this virtual non-importation. Yet as he predicted,³ the Senate rejected it as too radical. For it a naval convoy clause was substituted. This the House rejected. And another deadlock ensued.

On May 1, 1810, the Eleventh Congress found itself within a few hours of adjournment, and of the expiration of Non-Intercourse, with no action taken. Low in spirits, in courage, and in self-respect, the regular troops eliminated both the convoy and the additional duty clauses. With all its teeth extracted, Macon's Bill late that evening was enacted into law — and America was left deeper than ever in 'the putrescent pool of ignominious peace.'

'Congress has adjourned, and has completed my triumph,' exulted Jackson, the dismissed British envoy, 'by repealing without any concession on our part, the famous non-intercourse law by which they were to coerce England and France, and for the repeal of which Erskine agreed last year to sacrifice our Orders in Council. Thus ends this famous session. It began in "blood and thunder" and ended in a drunken frolic. . . . One thing, however, is certain — they have covered themselves with ridicule and disgrace.' ⁴

It was a sentiment echoed by many Americans.

---

¹ Poindexter to Mead, April 20, 1810, *Poindexter MSS.*

² Troup to Mitchell, March 17, 1810, Harden, *Troup,* p. 95.

³ Clay to Adam Beatty, April 23, 1810, Clay, *Corres.,* p. 46. 'One of its valuable effects, if it passes,' wrote Clay, 'will be the encouragement of our manufactures. As the increase is not contemplated, however, to be permanent, I should prefer a smaller augmentation, and that it should be durable.' The additional duty, and tariff protection in general, was opposed not only by importing New England but by sections exclusively agrarian. Poindexter (letter cited above) called it a '*Yankee*-bantling... a specific tax on...the cotton of the Southern planter... for the advancement of the Manufacturing Interest' of the North and East. Macon also opposed it; earlier Macon had declared that while the present Constitution remained 'it was utterly impossible for the United States to become a manufacturing nation.' *Annals,* 11th, 1st, 186.

⁴ Jackson, G., *Diaries,* I, 116–17, New York, May 7, 1810.

Against such a background young Clay stood out conspicuously. Rodney, Burwell, and others (who like Plumer in 1807 were 'disposed to flatter' him) urged him to forsake the Senate for the House. Already in Kentucky a campaign had opened to elect him in place of Benjamin Howard, who had become Governor of Upper Louisiana. 'Farmer,' 'Citizen,' and 'Mechanic' declared that 'HARRY CLAY should fill the more honourable and important appointment of an immediate Representative of the People.' [1] Henry's wishes accorded with theirs. He preferred, so he said, the accustomed 'turbulence' of a lower house to the 'solemn stillness of the Senate.' [2]

Upon his return he announced his candidacy. He would serve out his Senate term and, if elected, enter the House in the fall of 1811. 'All that I dare promise,' he said in his open letter, 'is that those political principles which have hitherto directed me shall continue to be my guide; and that in honest zeal to promote the welfare of the nation I yield to no one.' [3] There were other aspirants; but they withdrew when he announced his candidacy. Unopposed, Clay that August was elected to the Twelfth Congress.[4]

The Kentucky orator had truly been a precursor of a new epoch. At the polls in 1810 nascent nationalism took the form of a political revolt. Both Anglo-Federalism and the Eleventh Congress's 'eunuch politicians' were rebuked. Almost half of the House was retired, and young 'pepperpot politicians' were elected. When the Twelfth Congress met in the fall of 1811 Henry Clay was to lead a host of raw militia. Fresh from exhorting the people as he had exhorted the Senate, these Young Americans were eager to emulate the Fathers, who 'prayed — petitioned — remonstrated; and, when all was unavailing, indignantly shook off the yoke of a tyrant!' [5]

In Kentucky, where 'turncoat' Mat Lyon was politically guil-

---

[1] *Ky. Gazette*, May 1, 8, 1810.

[2] Clay to Monroe (for whose saline lands on Goose Creek he was agent), Nov. 13, 1810, *Monroe MSS.*; also, Clay to Rodney, May 27, 1810, *Rodney MSS.*; to Beatty, May 31, 1810, Clay, *Corres.*, p. 47.

[3] *Ky. Gazette*, May 15, 1810.   [4] *Ibid.*, Aug. 14, 1810.

[5] *Niles' Register*, Sept. 28, 1811.

lotined, Humphrey Marshall at this 'unsuspecting moment' established a new journal, the *American Republic*, from the masthead of which he flaunted a defiant rattlesnake. With all the 'sweetness' of his genius (said Editor Hanson) he tried to enlighten democrats who for free grog 'throw up their hats, and huzza their demagogues.' [1] But 'the abandoned Tory miscreant' prevailed not. Jo Daveiss, whom he championed, was crushingly defeated despite 'stump speeches many a score.' Alas! jeered the *Gazette*, 'that all the men of talents should be doomed to stay at home! *These cursed republicks!*' [2]

'What news from abroad?' asked Henry of Attorney General Rodney shortly after his return from Washington. How has Macon's Bill been received? 'I feel great solicitude for our Country & for our cause.' [3]

England, with the game entirely in her own hands (as Clay predicted), seemed wedded to her orders. Lord Wellesley, Canning's successor, approved by Tories who longed to give the Yankees 'a good drubbing,' [4] carried on with the viceregal air he had acquired in India. Why yield when the United States after captures, impressments, the *Chesapeake* attack, the Erskine and Jackson affronts, but threatened to revive her Non-Intercourse? Concessions seemed particularly gratuitous when America's difficulties with France were such, it appeared, as to preclude her from ever going to war with England.

France, indeed, promised to give Macon's Bill a violent reception, judging from her alleged reprisal that spring against the Non-Intercourse Act of 1809. Although that act merely threatened the confiscation of French ships entering American ports, Napoleon, resenting every recession from the Embargo as submission to England, had suddenly (as in 1808) swept up some two hundred American ships. Property valued at about ten million dollars, exclusive of British goods disguised as American, was thus 'sequestered' and held. Bonaparte's rapacity threatened to equal that of

---

[1] Baltimore *Federal Republican*, Oct. 23, 1811.
[2] *Ky. Gazette*, Aug. 14, July 3, 1810.
[3] Clay to Rodney, May 27, 1810, *Rodney MSS*.
[4] Jackson, G., *Diaries*, I, 30–31.

Britain. Indeed, by 1812 France since 1803 had seized 558 vessels to Britain's 917.[1]

While the Federalists cried for war with France, Madison angrily demanded the release of the ships, declaring that Bonaparte's seizures 'comprise robbery, theft, and breach of trust, and exceed in turpitude any of his enormities not wasting human blood.'[2] There was the usual lament that 'we can't make successful war against either of the damn'd nations who have so wantonly and grossly insulted & invaded our rights & sovereignty.' And there was the usual enervating bickering 'about which government injured us most; just as if one should openly contend,' said John Tyler, 'that three was more than two; for full that much, or more, has Great Britain done beyond all the nations of the earth put together.'[3]

Bonaparte's 'act of infamous treachery, if not of open robbery,' wrote Clay to Rodney, 'affords us just cause of reprisal . . . But I scarcely know of an injury that France could do us, short of an actual invasion of our Territory, that would induce me to go to War with her, whilst the injuries we have received from Great Britain remain unredressed. That the Feds. should endeavor to precipitate us into a War with France, whilst they are totally regardless of British aggressions, is perfectly consistent with the uniform tenor of their conduct. What will they say,' he asked, 'of the repetition upon the Vixen of the outrage committed on the Chesapeake?'

Henry was fairly boiling at the wanton attack in June of 1810 upon the naval brig *Vixen*, en route to New Orleans, by the British warship *Moselle*. It was one of those recurring acts of British

---

[1] *Annals*, 12th, 1st, 2045. See, also, Clauder, A. C., *American Commerce as Affected by . . . the French Revolution and Napoleon*. The spoliation claims against Great Britain disappeared in the War of 1812. Those against France, of over $10,000,000 for the period 1803–15, were adjusted in 1831, and were paid by France (under pressure by President Jackson) in 1836.

[2] Madison to Jefferson, May 25, 1810, Madison, *Writings*, II, 477–78.

[3] Gov. Tyler to Jefferson, May 12, 1810, Tyler, *Tylers*, I, 247. His Revolutionary ire was aroused by 'Judge Marshall and Mr. Pickering & Co.' who claimed England 'had given us no cause of complaint.' John Adams raged at both French and British pirates, but pointed out that while Britain hammered America and the world, France was 'a Hammer to Europe only and to America when she sends her sons and Ships to Europe.' *Old Family Letters*, p. 258, June 28, 1810.

insolence in American waters which, as Erskine reported, were far more inciting than wholesale captures in remote parts of the globe.[1] The flag and public character of the *Vixen* were recognized only after the *Moselle* had shot away the main boom, wounded young Rodney, the Attorney General's son, and endangered the lives of crew and passengers, among whom was Clay's friend Poindexter (with his family), the delegate from Mississippi. What incensed Henry most was the failure of Lieutenant Trippe, like that of Barron in 1807, promptly to return the fire of his British assaulter.

'Is not it provoking in the extreme,' he asked Rodney, 'that Trippe should have imitated so exactly the conduct of Barron? After receiving two shot, that he should have stooped to ask an explanation, parleyed, or hesitated for a moment... is to me astonishing. A man receives a fillip on the nose, and instead of instantly avenging the insult, inquires of the person giving it what he means!'[2]

Clay's pepperpot views found a popular echo that summer at the courthouse, at Fowler's Gardens and the Coffee House. His neighbors abhorred the 'villainy of the French.' But they resented most, British 'rascality and deception,' British fillips on the nose, and the British torch that was lighting up savage war — through the agency of such men as British Captain Elliott, who had announced to Tecumseh's hostiles (so Governor Harrison reported): 'My tomahawk is now up — be you ready — but do not strike untill I give the signal.'[3]

Never had a Fourth of July been more spirited. On the march to Maxwell's the Liberty Pole and Cap was carried by Major Morrison, once a Virginia Rifleman. At Postlethwaite's there were toasts to 'The Crisis — If we mean like men to assert our maritime rights, now is the time,' to 'The army and navy — reduced if not used in avenging their country's wrongs,' and to the Spanish-American patriots — 'It is high time that the new world was totally disenthralled from European chains.' Six cheers greeted 'Henry

---

[1] Erskine to Canning, Oct. 5, 1807, Adams, *Hist. U.S.*, IV, 143–44.

[2] Clay to Rodney, Aug. 6, 1810, *Rodney MSS.*; and see *Natl. Intelligencer*, July 23, 1810.

[3] Harrison to Sec. of War Eustis, July 18, 1810 (one of his many alarmist letters), *Madison MSS.*; also, *Michigan Pion. and Hist. Coll.*, XXV, 272, XV, 53; and *Ky. Gazette*, July 3, 10, Sept. 11, 1810, *passim*.

Clay — our worthy member in Congress, the friend of Liberty and man.' Clay's Senate speech was reflected in deprecations of a 'tweedle dum, tweedle dee' foreign policy, and in such toasts as 'The starry flag of Columbia — Before the next anniversary of Independence, may it float triumphant on the ramparts of Quebeck,' and 'Florida and Canada — A fee simple in the one, a mortgage upon the other.' [1]

Shortly after this eruption of Western patriotism American troops occupied West Florida. Since 1808, when Napoleon usurped the Spanish throne and England espoused the deposed Spanish Bourbons, complete anarchy had there reigned. Claimed under 'limitless' Louisiana treaties by King Joseph Bonaparte, King Ferdinand VII, and the United States, the province was already American in race, being 'entirely settled' by Kentuckians and Tennesseans, who were eager for 'an union with their parent country.' [2] When the settlers declared their independence that summer, Madison ordered the occupation of the region from the Mississippi to the Perdido River.

Clay and his friends were jubilant at this long-awaited thrust to the Gulf, 'our natural boundary.' Westerners were eager to aid their 'brave countrymen in taking possession of that Elegant part of this country, which our non-energetic government long since purchased.' [3] In securing this country from both France and Britain, James Brown had written Henry, 'you serve Kentucky more effectually than by raising Cavalry there to fight the British Navy' — and you win for yourself 'solid fame and lusty distinction.' [4]

In Congress that December the Federalists denounced the occupation of West Florida as instigated by Bonaparte, and as likely to involve us in war with England. Our claim is highly questionable, wrote Josiah Quincy of Boston. Bonaparte robbed Spain of Louisiana, and we bought the stolen goods. 'But here is

---

[1] *Ky. Gazette*, July 10, 1810.

[2] John Patterson to W. C. Nicholas, New Orleans, May 21, 1808, *Nicholas MSS.* See, also, *Ky. Gazette*, July 31, 1810.

[3] W. H. Overton to Jackson, Sept. 26, 1810, Jackson, *Corres.*, I, 205.

[4] Brown to Clay, Feb. 26, 1810, *Clay MSS.*

the difficulty — the title deed we thus obtained, although it contained more than we wanted, yet did not contain exactly what we wished. And so administration have ever since been consulting how to make the title deed cover more than it does.' The Republicans argue: 'We want West Florida. Our Western brethren will have West Florida. By G—— we will take West Florida. By G—— it is in the title deed.' [1]

In the Senate Clay made himself the outstanding champion of annexation by a notable speech 'On the Line of the Perdido.' [2] He plunged into the debates when Outerbridge Horsey, Federalist of Delaware, denied America's claim, warned of Britain's anger, and all but wept over the fate of Spain. After paying his respects to Horsey's 'more than Aristidean justice,' Clay said he would give the American view. He would not go into the deposition of Charles IV and his son Ferdinand, or the revolts against Joseph Bonaparte. Federalists could mourn 'the fallen Charles. I have no commiseration for princes. My sympathies are reserved for the great mass of mankind, and I own that the people of Spain have them most sincerely.'

He then made a detailed exposition of our 'indisputable' title to West Florida. Originally a part of French Louisiana, extending to the Perdido, it had been ceded to England in 1762, while Louisiana west of the Mississippi had been ceded to Spain. When England ceded it to Spain in 1783, old French Louisiana, he contended, was thus once more an entity. West Florida, consequently, was included in the cession of Louisiana by Spain to France in 1800, and by France to us in 1803. This was obvious, for both treaties defined the cession as 'Louisiana with the same extent it had in the hands of Spain, and that it had when France possessed it.'

This plausible argument was confirmed by Congress and the Supreme Court, though Spain denied she had ceded West Florida

---

[1] Quincy to Wm. Sullivan, Dec. 21, 1810, *Washburn MSS.*, Mass. Hist. Soc. Senator Bradley of Vermont defended the title, said Quincy; but Bradley 'also thought that we had a right to West Florida on another principle. That it was destitute of government and as our ancestors took this country from the Savages, we had a right to take that country and for aught he saw East Florida into the bargain.'

[2] *Annals*, 11th, 3d, 55–64, Dec. 28, 1810.

to France in 1800.[1] More effective was Clay's argument of expediency.

A peaceful nation, we have been content to negotiate, he said. But with Spain strife-torn and her empire disintegrating, this is no longer possible. Moreover, England has projected herself into Spain's affairs, and war with England is not improbable. Shall we remain idle when our rights are thus jeopardized? When this Gulf coast in British hands would endanger the entire Mississippi Valley, two-thirds of the United States? Are we to neglect this auspicious moment and permit some other nation to get a fatal foothold on our southern frontier, by seizing what incontestably belongs to us?

Clay would unhesitatingly lay down this governing principle: If chronic disorders persist in a colony adjacent to us, thereby menacing our peace; if misrule and anarchy invite that colony's annexation by another power, thereby threatening the integrity of the Union, 'we have a right, upon the eternal principles of self-preservation, to lay hold upon it. This principle, alone, independent of any title, would warrant our occupation of West Florida.'

After this forthright — and prophetic — declaration, he turned upon the Federalists, who earlier had urged the conquest of Florida and Mexico, and in 1805–06 over this same West Florida had denounced the Republicans as cowardly pacifists who compelled America 'to suffer with humility insults from Spanish imbecility.'[2] The Federalists, Clay noted, wanted war only when Spain was the ally of France. Now, when 'we attempt a peaceful possession of the country to which we are fairly entitled,' they weep over Spain and parade their fears that England, her present ally, will make war upon us. Against this ever-present 'British Influence' he hotly protested.

'Is the time never to arrive,' asked the young Kentuckian, 'when we may manage our own affairs without the fear of insulting his

---

[1] See Cox, I. J., *The West Florida Controversy*, on this subject complicated by 'foreign invasions and filibustering... foreign and domestic wrangling, and evasive treaty provisions.'

[2] Fessenden, *Democracy Unveiled*, II, 68 (1806).

Britannic Majesty? Is this rod of British power to be forever suspended over our heads? Does Congress put on an embargo to shelter our rightful commerce against the piratical depredations committed upon it on the ocean? We are immediately warned of the indignation of offended England. Is a law of non-intercourse proposed? The whole navy of the haughty mistress of the seas is made to thunder in our ears. Does the President refuse to continue a correspondence with a minister who violates the decorum belonging to his diplomatic character, by giving and deliberately repeating an affront to the whole nation? We are instantly menaced with the chastisement which English pride will not fail to inflict.

'Whether we assert our rights by sea, or attempt their maintenance by land,' continued Clay, 'whithersoever we turn ourselves, this phantom incessantly pursues us. Already has it had too much influence on the councils of the nation. It contributed to the repeal of the embargo — that dishonorable repeal ... I have before said on this floor, and now take occasion to remark, that I most sincerely desire peace and amity with England; that I even prefer an adjustment of all differences with her before one with any other nation. But if she persists in a denial of justice to us, or if she avails herself of the occupation of West Florida to commence war upon us, I trust and hope that all hearts will be united in a bold and vigorous vindication of our rights.'

After appealing once more for action sustaining Madison, reiterating his belief that the people were ready to 'retrieve the lost honor of the nation, in the case of the Chesapeake,' Clay ended on the frontier note of expansion, of Manifest Destiny. 'I am not, sir, in favour of cherishing the passion of conquest,' he said. 'But I must be permitted to conclude by declaring my hope to see, ere long, the *new* United States (if you will allow me the expression) embracing not only the old thirteen States, but the entire country east of the Mississippi, including East Florida, and some of the territories to the north of us also.'

Once again this fighting cock from Kentucky, this young Patrick Henry, had defiantly sounded the war trumpet against England. At a time when the national spirit was at lowest ebb, young Clay audaciously called for a strong, expanded '*new* United States.'

By Republicans he was hailed as 'The Western Star,' as a long-awaited leader, eloquent, decisive, thoroughly American. Federalists, however, deplored and ridiculed his '*new* United States,' which meant new Republican states and, probably, a ruinous war with Britain. Why, in time, we might even embrace California — or Patagonia! Like the British at Copenhagen, jibed Editor Hanson, he urges self-preservation! 'Mr. Clay, who is cried up as another luminary,' takes the same ground that Canning took in 1807.[1] Like 'Murat, Robespierre, and other philanthropick worthies,' he professes sympathy for 'the *great mass of mankind*,' jeered Philadelphia's *United States Gazette*. Like Bonaparte, the Kentucky orator professes tenderness for a Spanish people he would despoil. Mr. Clay blusters — yet why do our wordy 'anti-submission men' year after year *submit* to this selfsame rod of British power? [2]

Incensed by Clay's critics, Kentuckians hotly refuted the charge of 'British hireling editors' that he was a backwoods Robespierre, and asserted, in answer to rumors that England had already seized West and East Florida, 'Let the sabre decide.' [3] Both Canada and Mexico, said Salem's *Register*, would be only a just recompense for property plundered and seamen impressed.[4] If our '*men of moderation*' take no notice of insults that they '*dared not* resent' Britain's depredations, said the *Aurora*, then 'Britain is fully *justified* in every future *insult*, capture, *impressment* and murder.' [5]

Clay's speech was held by Republicans generally to be conclusive as to our right to West Florida, and to be expressive of the general desire for a New World independent of the Old. Massachu-

---

[1] Baltimore *Federal Republican*, Jan. 18, 1811.

[2] *U.S. Gazette* (country edition; giving Clay's speech), Jan. 21, 1811. 'West Florida ours,' they say (*ibid.*, Jan. 17, 1811). 'East Florida has no owner... Care not if the Cham of Tartar or emperour of the Hindoos is offended... Vast advantages... Must have it... Kentucky and Tennessee boys defend it. Spanish segars there — sea island cotton, green turtles. Make the United States of all climes... Be hundred million in a century. Greatest nation in the world. Must own all North America — South too.'

[3] Lex. *Reporter*, Feb. 9, 1811; Ky. letter in Phila. *Aurora*, Feb. 27, 1811.

[4] *Essex Register*, Jan. 23, 1811; and Dec. 1810–Feb. 1811 *passim*.

[5] Phila. *Aurora*, March 15, 1811; and Baltimore *Evening Post*, Dec. 12, 1810 ff., for attacks on Hanson's 'Pickering's Gazette' at Baltimore.

H Clay

'THE COCK OF KENTUCKY'

setts democrats, who acclaimed his address as singularly lucid and eloquent, exulted in the spirit manifest in both South and North America to 'break all European shackles.' [1] Western democrats likewise applauded Clay's defiance of England, and gave thirteen cheers to the toast: 'South America — May success crown her struggles for freedom — and may the Eagle of Liberty extend his wings from Hudson's Bay to Cape Horne.' [2]

'In learning, argument, and eloquence' this speech 'has seldom been surpassed in America,' said Irvine of the Baltimore *Whig*, who had looked forward to the day 'when Mr. Clay would be hailed as one of the brightest luminaries of his country; when the republick would greet him as one of the most powerful champions of her liberties and independence.' This young orator, this 'noble patriot,' he said, 'is all that becomes an American republican — a sacred reverence for the publick liberties; love of country; an ardent zeal, tempered with prudence and wisdom for its honour and welfare.' His soul is Roman but his oratory is that of Demosthenes, 'bold and vigorous, inestimably convincing.' Nervous in style, correct in language, chary of gestures and of classical allusions, he 'is infinitely superior . . . to the great mass of congressional orators . . . His prominent aim is to command attention and enforce conviction. The hearer is not permitted to infer anything, every feeling is assailed, no argument is left untouched . . . Mr. Clay is often keenly sarcastick. Federalism writhed under the agonizing severity with which he adverted' to its excessive sensibility not for our much-injured country but for haughty and imperious England.[3]

The foe writhed but was not silenced. For the Kentucky Demosthenes was confronted by Pickering, 'The Lion of Federalism.'

Young Clay and old Pickering — they were of different worlds. Sharp-eyed, bald, tight-lipped, calculating, Pickering despaired of the republic and schemed for its dissolution. 'Envious of every superior and impatient of obscurity,' he always reminded John

---

[1] Dr. N. Ames, Jan. 1811, Warren, *Jacobin and Junto*, p. 238.
[2] *Ky. Gazette*, Feb. 26, 1811.
[3] *Ibid.*, Jan. 29, 1811, q. Baltimore *Whig*; also in Phila. *Aurora*, Jan. 8, 1811.

Adams of a 'coal-pit, covered with red earth, glowing within.' [1]
Sandy-haired, wide-mouthed, impulsive, as spirited as one of his
Blue Grass colts, Clay that summer had been raging at British
outrages while 'the man Timothy' had been giving Copenhagen
Jackson at Boston a reception more warmly loyal than that given
him at Montreal. [2] Clay beheld a man whom most Americans
damned along with Arnold and Burr; who did much to foster the
prejudice that Yankees were cunning and unctuous, 'that they
wear leather breeches, and smell of onions and train oil,' and have
an 'air of artless simplicity, while, at the same time, they are artful
enough to cheat the devil.' [3]

Advancing the stock argument of 'French Influence,' Pickering
artfully enough attempted to use France itself to cudgel down
America's title to West Florida. He triumphantly produced a
letter of Talleyrand declaring the claim unfounded, which Jefferson in 1805 had sent to the Senate in confidence. His triumph was
short-lived, for Clay, though warned 'there would be danger in
taking the lion by his mane,' [4] was quick to move that Pickering
be censured for thus violating the Senate's pledge of secrecy. A
great wrangling ensued. But the Kentucky militiaman pressed his
charge, and by a party vote the Massachusetts veteran was
censured. [5]

The snarling Lion of Federalism had been 'tented to the quick.'
Clay had seized upon his 'indecent and unexampled procedure'
and held up to public scorn this Anglomaniac who had 'the
turbulence of Catiline without his talents.' [6] Pickering's friends
attempted to soften the censure — 'dictated by grovelling, vile,
jacobin malice,' said Editor Hanson. Clay himself should have
been censured for his impudence, he wrote, expressing his hope
that the rotten-ripe state of the Union might soon enable Federal-

---

[1] Adams, *Corres. with Cunningham*, p. 56. 'A greater Egotist never existed,' said a
Salem neighbor. 'Tim was always in the newspapers & he is determined to finish as he
began.' Bentley, Rev. Wm., *Diary*, IV, 14, March 25, 1811.

[2] So Jackson himself reported, Jackson, G., *Diaries*, I, 154.

[3] Wm. Wirt to Dabney Carr, [1810], Kennedy, *Wirt*, I, 281.

[4] Boston *Gazette*, Jan. 10, 1811.

[5] *Annals*, 11th, 3d, 66, 83.

[6] Boston *Patriot*, Jan. 9; Boston *Independent Chronicle*, Jan. 10; Phila. *Aurora*, Jan. 8,
1811.

ism to 'convert the Scoffs and revilings of the knaves into tears and lamentations.' [1]

Clay had exaggerated neither Florida's anarchy nor Spain's impotence. On January 3, 1811, five days after his speech, Madison sent in a letter in which the Spanish governor of West Florida offered to turn his chaotic province over to the United States unless he were speedily reenforced. Since similar conditions prevailed in East Florida, the adage 'in for a penny, in for a pound' seemed to apply. By occupying it as well as West Florida we could give Europe no more offense, while its possession would strengthen us in any future negotiations over boundaries and spoliation claims.

In spite of British protests, and in spite of Quincy's deliberate threat in the House that further expansion, nay, even the admission of new states from the Louisiana Purchase, would force the Northeast to secede, 'amicably if they can, violently if they must,' [2] Congress was impelled in the direction of Clay's 'new United States.' It sanctioned the occupation of West Florida, and permitted part of that province to be incorporated with the proposed state of Louisiana. Secretly it authorized the President to occupy East Florida, subject to future negotiations, if the Spanish officials assented or if any foreign power (i.e., England) attempted to seize it.[3]

Congress had been forced into action by the people's revolt at the polls, and not a little perhaps by Henry Clay. If it continues to act 'upon the policy recommended and doctrines defended by your Clays,' wrote a Federalist, 'the conquest of South America may become a popular measure.' [4] If Adams ten years back had tried to seize New Orleans, said Hanson, 'both he and his army would have been thrown into the Potowmac.' After this, 'little more is wanting to land Aaron Burr with a few thousand French

---

[1] Baltimore *Federal Republican*, Jan. 5, 1811; and Alexander C. Hanson to Pickering, Jan. 7, 17, 1811, *Pickering MSS*.

[2] *Annals*, 11th, 3d, 524 ff.

[3] Neither Madison nor Monroe (who became Secretary of State that spring) was loath to act under this authorization. By June of 1812 not only was the region to the Perdido (except Mobile) occupied, but footholds had been obtained on the Florida peninsula. In event of war with England, Spain's ally, the South and West were primed to take all Florida. See Pratt, *Expansionists*, chap. II.

[4] *U.S. Gazette* (country ed.), Jan. 31, 1811.

soldiers & veteran Generals to aid "the sons of Frenchmen" [in Louisiana] to establish a separate empire.' [1] A democracy militant had revived the Federalist fear that

> 'Some Buonaparte or Robespierre
> Will close the jacobinic career,
> Our precious liberty will wreck,
> And set his foot upon our neck.' [2]

While Clay expressed his satisfaction at this 'proper energy' on the momentous subject of creating new states in the West,[3] the mortification of Quincy and Pickering was shared by John Philip Morier, the British chargé. For Morier had reported that 'it would be difficult to expect any Energy, except what may be displayed in Words, from a Government with an Army of five thousand Men & with an empty Treasury.' His suggestions, 'if the taking of West Florida should produce War,' would have interested Clay. England, said Morier, should blockade the mouth of the Mississippi, and distress the West perhaps to the point of disunion. Spain should send in her Negro regiments to incite America's slaves to revolt — 'at the Thought of which all the People of the South Tremble.' [4]

On their part, the Pickeronians trembled no less at war with England than at the prospect of being ruled not only by Kentuckians and wild Irish democrats but by 'Anglo-Hispano-Gallo Americans,' uncouth and motley hordes from the trans-Mississippi West. If Easterners permit this expansionism, wrote Quincy, 'they deserve to be what they will be, *slaves*, and to no very desirable masters' — backwoodsmen 'violent, overbearing, and insolent.' Surely Clay's *new* America was not the America of the Fathers! Surely Clay's pioneers had little in common with Yankee merchants 'educated in the strictness and under the laws which regulate New England' [5] — a seaboard gentry more familiar with the quays of Canton and Feejee cannibals than with farmer-

---

[1] Baltimore *Federal Republican*, Jan. 18, Feb. 27, 1811.

[2] Fessenden, *Pills, Poetical, Political*, pp. 45–46.

[3] Clay to Rodney, Jan. 11, 1811 [misdated, 1810], *Rodney MSS*.

[4] Morier to Wellesley, Jan. 12, 1811, *F.O.* 5:74. He enclosed a copy of Pickering's speech, exposing the 'immaculate Republicans.'

[5] Quincy, *Quincy*, pp. 187–88, 212–13.

democrats of Chillicothe or New Madrid; who were nearer both in time and in spirit to a London and Liverpool of Old England than to a Lexington and Nashville of Clay's New West.

In the House Quincy continued to fume and rage, less picturesquely but more dangerously than Randolph of Roanoke, who shared the Bostonian's prejudice against expansion, and in his rôle of Tory squire was not above remarking that Kentucky was 'the Botany Bay of Virginia.' [1] Quincy said his disunion speech incited yells of 'Burr's fate' from 'bullies and blackguards... using language learnt in the backwoods or among their slaves.' He had religious scruples against duelling, and disdained the threats of 'Georgia and Kentucky ruffians' (as Fessenden put it), who when vanquished by 'a Fed for logick substitute cold lead.' Nevertheless, aware how violently these 'demagogues tremble at the word "separation," ' the Federalist leader vowed he would continue to 'make their ears tingle with it.' [2]

America's Tories applauded Quincy's 'noble stand in the House,' and assured him that posterity would acclaim his disunion threat.[3] 'For my part, I say without reserve that *the union was long ago dissolved*,' wrote Editor Hanson to Pickering. State conventions should confirm the fact, for certain it is 'that if the question was barely *stirred* in N. England, some States would drop off from the Union like fruit, *rotten-ripe*.' [4] Publicly Hanson stated that if Madison, intent solely upon reelection in 1812, 'does not keep his eye to it, there may be *no next President of the American Union*.' [5]

In face of the rising power of Clay's New West would Northeastern maritime Federalists, who regarded themselves as already ruined by an agrarian Republicanism, remain passive? Or would they, especially in event of war with Britain, resort to Secession

---

[1] Thomas, F. W., *John Randolph*, etc., p. 19. 'We are the first people that ever acquired provinces, either by conquest or purchase (Mr. Blackstone says they are the same), not for us to govern, but that they might *govern us*, — that we might be ruled to our ruin by people bound to us by no common tie of interest or sentiment.' Randolph to Quincy, Oct. 18, 1813, Quincy, *Quincy*, pp. 337–38.

[2] Quincy, *op. cit.*, pp. 212–13, 235; Fessenden, *op. cit.*, pp. 31–33.

[3] See John Lowell, chief pamphleteer for the Essex Junto, to Quincy, Feb. 13, 1811, Quincy, *op. cit.*, p. 215.

[4] Hanson to Pickering, Jan. 17, 1811, *Pickering MSS.*

[5] Baltimore *Federal Republican*, Feb. 27, 1811.

Conventions and to Pickering's British-protected Northern Confederacy?

In the meantime, with the clearing of an atmosphere he described as 'dense, heavy, & disagreeable,'[1] Senator Clay had plunged into the debates on a domestic issue — the United States Bank.

In contrast with his strong nationalism on foreign affairs and his liberalism on internal improvements, the young Kentuckian now reverted to Old Republican dogmas. His speech against renewing the charter of the bank, which was to expire in March of 1811, was eloquent and powerful. Yet it was an effort rash and harmful.

For twenty years Hamilton's semi-public national bank had issued a uniform currency, floated loans for the Treasury, and served as a depository for public funds. No better measure of its utility could be had than that Jefferson, though detesting it as being 'of the most deadly hostility against the principles and form of our Constitution,' with a power sufficient in wartime to 'dictate to us the peace we should accept,' had retained it and even enlarged it.[2] The bank's dissolution, it was said, would contract the currency by five millions, send seven millions abroad to redeem stock chiefly held by Britons, and bankrupt thousands by the calling in of loans. And this, too, when America was feeling the effects of a world-wide financial depression, and war with England was possible.[3]

Secretary Gallatin strongly urged the need of this sound engine of national finance. But Madison held himself aloof from a Congress which was about equally divided. As a Chief Executive and party leader, said a pro-bank Federalist, he was 'but little

---

[1] Clay to Rodney, Jan. 11, 1811, *Rodney MSS.*

[2] Jefferson to Gallatin, Dec. 1803, Adams, H., *Gallatin*, p. 321.

[3] This 'is no boyish experiment of killing a goose that lays golden eggs... nor yet is it the female frolic of Hogarth's drunken trollop.... It partakes more of the inhuman spirit of the Feejee Cannibal, who stabs an affrighted female prisoner and tears her heart from her mangled and still heaving bosom...' Baltimore *Federal Republican*, Jan. 26, 1811. Kentuckians scoffed: 'Why this downfall of the bank is as revolting to nature as the request of a lady to her lover to cut his whiskers!' Prices will fall so low, they say, that with cheap bargains from Philadelphia 'our wives and daughters [will] shine forth for nothing at all at all.' *Ky. Gazette*, Jan. 8, 1811.

better than a man of straw,' with not 'half the independence of an old clucking hen.' ¹ His equivocal silence had encouraged the enemies of this 'Federalist' and 'British' aristocratic 'Money Monster,' the most hostile of which were the country's state and local banks.

The Bank of Kentucky (of which Clay had been a director) and the Lexington Bank (which he had saved from Grundy's 'assassins') had joined with the banks of other states in clamoring for the death, and the profits, of their powerful and conservative national rival. Attuned to popular sentiment, Kentucky's legislators had joined with the legislators of other states — of Virginia and of such capitalistic states as Massachusetts, Maryland, and Pennsylvania — in instructing their congressmen against recharter.

The issue was sidestepped by the House, which on January 24 voted 65 to 64 for indefinite postponement. In the majority was 'every representative of the great commercial towns' except Quincy and one other.² With broadcloth thus allied with home-spun, it was 'impossible to guess what will or will not, be done.' ³ With such a 'nice division' of the House, wrote Clay, 'it is not un-likely . . . that the corporation may yet accomp[lish] its object.' ⁴

In February, to crowded galleries, the Senate debated the fate of the bank. Speeches in its favor were made by Federalists and by Republicans, notably Pope of Kentucky and William H. Crawford of Georgia. The latter ably argued its expediency and constitution-ality, and savagely attacked the vandalism of selfish local interests. Against him Clay took the floor. The debates between these two young Republicans, both Virginia-born frontier lawyers, were said to have equalled any ever heard in the Senate.⁵

After first satirizing the speech in which Giles 'had instructed and amused us,' by proving the bank both 'constitutional and un-constitutional,' Clay chided Crawford and other deserters to

---

¹ Samuel Taggart, *Letters*, p. 354, Feb. 4, 1811. While in favor of renewal, Madison by his timidity defeated it, said Taggart.

² Taggart, *op. cit.*, pp. 352–53.

³ Randolph (writing from 'Babel,' i.e., Washington) to Nicholson, Feb. 5, 1811, *Nicholson MSS.*

⁴ Clay to Adam Beatty, Jan. 24, 1811, *Misc. MSS.*, N.Y. Hist. Society.

⁵ Macon to Nicholson, Feb. 20, 1811, *Nicholson MSS.*

Federalism's 'Macedonian phalanx.' [1] With barbed humor he noted that men objected to their states' instructions yet kowtowed to the bank lobbyists, whose woes Lloyd of Boston had so 'pompously detailed.' Then, in arguments reminiscent of Grundy, he denied the utility of this 'splendid association of favored individuals . . . invested with exemptions, and surrounded by immunities and privileges.' State banks were as good, and safer, he contended, scoffing at the idea that the bank's discontinuance meant universal and lasting distress, of which the recent failures in New York were premonitory. 'As well might you ascribe to that cause the failures of Amsterdam and Hamburg, of London and Liverpool,' he said. 'The embarrassments of commerce, the sequestrations in France, the Danish captures; in fine, the belligerent edicts are the obvious sources of these failures. Their immediate cause is the return of bills upon London, drawn upon the faith of unproductive or unprofitable shipments.'

Imperiously brushing aside Crawford's argument that the bank was constitutional on the basis of implied powers, Clay declared that in cases where the Federal Government must act on implied powers 'the implication must be necessary, and obviously flow from the enumerated powers with which it is allied. The power to charter companies is not specified . . . and I contend is of a nature not transferable by mere implication . . . It is mockery, worse than usurpation, to establish [this bank] . . . for the ostensible purpose of aiding in the collection of the revenue, and, whilst engaged in this, the most inferior and subordinate of all its functions,' to allow it 'to diffuse itself throughout society, and to influence all the great operations of credit, circulation, and commerce. Like the Virginia justice, you tell the man whose turkey had been stolen, that your books of precedent furnish no form for his case, but that you will

---

[1] *Annals*, 11th, 3d, 200–19, Feb. 15, 1811. Giles reminded him, said Clay, of how Patrick Henry once by mistake made a masterly courtroom speech in behalf of his opponent. 'His distracted client came up to him . . . and, interrupting him, bitterly exclaimed, "you have undone me! You have ruined me!" "Never mind, give yourself no concern," said the adroit advocate; and, turning to the court and jury, continued his argument, by observing, "may it please your honors, and you, gentlemen of the jury, I have been stating to you what I presume my adversary may urge on his side . . ." The skilful orator proceeded, satisfactorily refuted every argument he had advanced, and gained his cause! — a success with which I trust the exertion of my honorable friend [Giles] will on this occasion be crowned.'

grant him a precept to search for a cow, and when looking for that he may possibly find his turkey! You say to this corporation, we cannot authorize you to discount, to emit paper, to regulate commerce, &c. No! Our book has no precedents of that kind. But then we can authorize you to collect the revenue, and, whilst occupied with that, you may do whatever else you please!'

Was there not grave danger when the nation's purse was controlled by a single corporation, amenable only to its stockholders, and they chiefly foreigners? All history warns us that republics ought most seriously to guard against foreign influence, 'and yet gentlemen contend that we are benefited by ... this foreign capital!' Has the influence of 'Englishmen holding seven-tenths of the capital of this bank,' asked Clay in conclusion, 'released from galling and ignominious bondage one solitary American seaman, bleeding under British oppression? Did it prevent the unmanly attack upon the Chesapeake? Did it arrest the promulgation, or has it abrogated the orders-in-council — those orders which have given birth to a new era in commerce? In spite of all its boasted effect, are not the two nations brought to the very brink of war?'

On February 20, when the decision was made, every senator was in his seat. Seventeen voted yea, seventeen nay. Thereupon Vice President Clinton, repeating Clay's strict-construction argument almost verbatim (indeed, his address was written by Clay),[1] threw his casting vote against recharter. The first United States Bank was destroyed. Henry Clay as much as any man could be held responsible. Since the bill lacked but one vote of a majority in each house, his vote, influence, and eloquence might well have saved it — to the great benefit of the nation in war years, and to his own peace of mind later when States' Rights champions turned his arguments against him.

In Kentucky Henry was wildly acclaimed; while John Pope, for voting for 'Britain and Aristocracy,' was abused as no other man had been since Humphrey Marshall was in the Senate.[2] In the

---

[1] 'Mr. Clay said he ... had written it, but under Mr. Clinton's dictation, and he never should think of claiming it as his own composition.' Adams, J. Q., *Memoirs*, VII, 64, Nov. 1825.

[2] See *Ky. Gazette*, Lex. *Reporter*, March–July, 1811.

anti-Gallatin, anti-British, press there was high praise of Clay's 'strong and perspicuous arguments' which had 'chained the attention of the senate, and of crowded galleries ... Such a display of forceful oratory I have never witnessed in a legislative body,' said one auditor, whose report of 'this matchless oration' was widely reprinted.[1] Senator Clay's 'shining talents and patriotic course,' it was predicted, 'will one day raise him to the highest honors.'[2]

Henry Clay is 'one of the finest orators in the Senate, though I believe the youngest man in it,' wrote Washington Irving, and 'is one of the finest fellows I have seen here.' The urbane New Yorker, down for the social season, at once had acquired a 'great personal regard' for the Kentuckian.[3] In the salons Margaret Bayard Smith likewise acclaimed 'the admired orator.'[4] As ever, Henry was a favorite with the ladies and, with Washington Irving at this session, in all parties of pleasure.

With dinners and balls and levees, 'brilliant and crowded with interesting men and fine women,' reported Irving, 'you meet with so many intelligent people that your mind is continually and delightfully exercised.' He enjoyed the blazing splendor of Mrs. Madison's drawing-room, and fell in love with the Presidentess, 'a fine, portly, buxom dame, who has a smile and a pleasant word for everybody ... but as to Jemmy Madison — ah! poor Jemmy! — he is but a withered little apple-John.'[5] With Clay he joined in the gossip about John Pope's long-winded apology to the ladies for his unconscionably long Senate speeches; the alleged conversion of the Prince of Wales from debauchery to Methodism; and madcap

---

[1] Wash. letter, Feb. 15, to Baltimore *Whig*, in Phila. *Aurora*, Feb. 22, 1811.

[2] Richmond *Enquirer*, March 12, 1811; also, *Aurora*, March 20, 1811.

[3] Irving, *W. Irving*, I, 272; to Wm. Irving, Feb. 16, 1811.

[4] Smith, *Forty Years*, pp. 84–85. She was then a temporary resident at Mrs. Wilson's, the boarding-house where Clay, his wife, his children and nurse, and his niece, Eliza Price, were lodged. She found Mrs. Clay to be 'of strong natural sense, very kind and friendly.'

[5] Irving, *op. cit.*, I, 263, 268–69. Madison, wrote a Federalist, Dec. 29, 1810, 'is a short man, his forehead full of wrinkles, a face which has the appearance of the mid-night lamp... by no means indicating... firmness and wisdom.' Bigelow, Abijah, 'Letters of... to his wife,' *Proc. Amer. Antiq. Soc.*, XL, 313. Justice Story in 1808 had described Madison as 'a most agreeable, modest, and unaffected man, of a short stature, and of a mild countenance,' easy in conversation, famed as a scholar. Story, *J. Story*, I, 152.

Jack Randolph's latest tantrums — his caning of Mr. Alston, who had objected to the dogs he brought into the House, and his near duel with Mr. Eppes. If Clay failed to understand why '*no one dared*' expel Randolph's dogs, he 'could not but admire the felicity' with which Randolph somehow settled disputes which 'admitted of but one mode of adjustment.' [1]

Young Irving appreciated a companion who could help him 'wonder, admire, and laugh,' one who, like himself, could be 'in ten minutes ... hand and glove with half the people in the assemblage.' Irving, though of Federalist leanings, became 'great cronies' even with Monsieur Whiskerandeau Turreau. Clay, with his 'certain reckless, good-natured look,' [2] was as 'genteel polite & pleasant' when with such Federalists as Bayard and even young Outerbridge Horsey [3] as when he was with Burwell and Poindexter. Few politicians were as socially adaptable, for a party spirit was poisoning the atmosphere. 'One day I am dining with a knot of honest, furious Federalists,' wrote Irving, 'who are damning their opponents as a set of consummate scoundrels, panders of Bonaparte, etc., etc. The next day I dine, perhaps with some of the very men I have heard thus anathematized, and find them equally honest, warm, and indignant; and if I take their word for it, I had been dining the day before with some of the greatest knaves in the nation, men absolutely paid and suborned by the British government.' [4]

The angry charge of French Influence had become most furious because of the crisis produced by Macon's Bill. That mischievous attempt to play off one belligerent against the other had entangled the republic in the mazes of Napoleonic diplomacy, and run her full tilt against the rock of John Bull stubbornness.

France had accepted the proffer, but informally and in ambiguous terms. On August 5, 1810, Napoleon had announced that his decrees as to America were revoked, effective November 1, 'it

---

[1] Clay to Rodney, March 7, 1811, *Rodney MSS.*; Wm. Duane to Jefferson, Jan. 25, 1811, *Jefferson MSS.*

[2] Preston, Mrs. Wm. C., *Diary*, III, 334.

[3] See Clay to Rodney, Jan. 11, 1811, *Rodney MSS.*

[4] Irving, *op. cit.*, I, 268, Feb. 7, 1811; and I, 263–73.

being understood' that Britain would revoke her orders or that
America would cause Britain to respect her rights. Accepting this
promise, Madison on November 2 had given England the stipu-
lated three months' warning that Non-Intercourse would be revived against her.

As in the Erskine affair, Madison's eagerness to get America
clear of bedlamite Europe exposed him to foreign humiliation and
domestic opposition. Intent upon peace, since if he wanted war
he could have placed America's cause upon impressment and
other very substantial grounds, Madison was willing to gamble to
obtain it. It was a dangerous gamble, however, since it depended
upon Napoleon's good faith as well as upon the coercing of Britain
by economic pressure. It was dangerous, also, in that it confused
the issues, subordinated and obscured clear-cut and fundamental
grievances, and gave color to the Federalist charge of French
Influence.

Madison realized, of course, that the revocation came in
questionable shape. Yet he hoped to make it the means of a
diplomatic triumph; the means of putting an end, without war,
to 'embarrassments which have been as afflicting as they have been
unexampled. It promises us,' he wrote Rodney, 'at least an
extrication from the dilemma, of a mortifying peace, or a war with
both the great belligerents. The precise course which G[reat]
B[ritain] will take, remains to be seen. Whatever the immediate
one may be, it is probable that we shall ultimately be at issue with
her, on her fictitious blockades.' [1]

Although England had promised to revoke her orders as to
America whenever France revoked her decrees, her Tory Ministry
stubbornly refused, upon legalistic grounds, to meet the French
'revocation' by any relaxation either real or nominal. This refusal
was 'much more important' than Bonaparte's revocation, wrote
Senator Clay, since England's power for good or evil was so much
the greater.[2] He was convinced that her illegal system would
stand as long as George III reigned. Since it was possible, however,

---

[1] Madison to Atty. Genl. Rodney, Sept. 30, 1810, *Rodney MSS*.
[2] Clay, Jan. 30, in *Ky. Gazette*, Feb. 12, 1811.

that the Prince of Wales might become Regent for his insane father, and a new ministry might come in, Clay was of the opinion
that, as yet, 'we ought not to lose all hopes of an abandonment of
her iniquitous policy.' [1]

As the session advanced, the seizure of an American ship at
Bordeaux caused Clay to question whether Napoleon aimed to
dupe and deceive America precisely as Canning, through Erskine,
had done.[2] Moreover, it now appeared that France had substituted
for her decrees a new system of tariffs and licenses designed to
control American imports and to prevent the smuggling in of
British goods. In form this did not violate neutral rights. Yet in
substance it bore heavily upon American commerce. Together
with continued predatory seizures in one guise or other, the new
system tended to reduce the dispute over the repeal of the decrees
to a mere cavil upon words.

With Jefferson, men wondered what Congress would do in face
of the wily Bonaparte's new trick of 'opening the seas to us &
shutting his ports to us, as well as on the immoveableness of the
British.' [3] Would Non-Intercourse be revived against England
alone? Or would it be revived against both England and France?
Then and thereafter, Madison protested and threatened retaliation unless Bonaparte gave both formal and actual proof of
his revocation, removed his new restrictions, and made compensation for all sequestered ships.[4] Yet then and thereafter, despite
evasion of these demands, Madison, having publicly accepted the
conditional revocation and made it a technical ground against
England, having, lawyerlike, assumed a position necessary for his
policy of obtaining relief without war, publicly insisted that
France had satisfied the terms of Macon's Bill. [5]

---

[1] Clay to Adam Beatty, Jan. 24, 1811, *Misc. MSS.*, N.Y. Hist. Soc.

[2] If ships have been seized in spite of the revocation, we have only additional 'mortifying proof of the total want of good faith on the part of [both] the belligerents.' Clay,
Feb. 1, in *Ky. Gazette*, Feb. 12, 1811.

[3] Jefferson to John Hollins, Jan. 20, 1811, *Jefferson MSS.*

[4] Americans a generation later discovered that Bonaparte on Aug. 5, 1810, the very
day of his 'revocation,' had signed a secret Trianon Decree which confiscated and
ordered the sale of sequestered American ships. See Channing, *Hist. U.S.*, IV, 414–15,
427.

[5] Madison on March 18 wrote Jefferson that while Bonaparte was influenced by
'his want of money and his ignorance of Commerce, he has also distrusted... our

Clay, too, believed that France, technically, had fulfilled the contract.[1] But the Federalists, furiously angry, with Britain denied that the decrees were revoked, and denounced French policy as a gross and palpable fraud. Madison was Bonaparte's cat's-paw! The agrarian democrats were Napoleonic hirelings, or at best hoodwinked fools, who would embroil us in war!

Clay and his colleagues were neither blind nor silent as to the outrages of a treacherous France. But they were more concerned with England's arrogant rejection of their olive branch, her man-stealing and property-stealing outrages, her torch of savage war, and her possible aid to Anglo-disunionists. Above all were they concerned with England's denationalizing and ruinous world monopoly.

With Macon's Bill, duties on British imports had replenished the Treasury. The Federalist shipper had profited: his foreign carrying-trade tonnage had reached an unprecedented high despite pillage and confiscation. Yet America as a whole suffered from a deepening economic distress. As a result, resentment against England had increased in all parts of the farmer republic, and was especially violent in the pioneer communities of the South and West.

Exports had flooded out — very largely, perforce, to the British market. But cotton, tobacco, and hemp (as Clay was informed by angry Kentuckians) were now falling to even more disastrous levels than in 1808. 'Unprecedented hard times' caused by Britain's illegal monopoly was the constant theme of distressed

---

pledge to renew non-intercourse... and has wished to execute his in a manner that would keep pace only with the execution of ours.' On May 3 he wrote that 'from the jumble of accounts from France, it is probable that the repeal... is professedly adhered to; and that an exchange [of American and French products] is permitted by the municipal laws, under vexatious precautions against British forgeries and American collusions...' Madison, *Writings*, II, 491, 508.

[1] 'In respect to France,' wrote Clay, 'her failure to restore the property seized under the Rambouillet decree [of March 23, 1810], but more particularly her new tariff, which amts to a prohibition of some valuable articles of our produce, creates some embarrassment as to the line of conduct we ought to pursue. Nevertheless, ascribing the latter measure to that municipal power of regulating commerce which belongs to all nations, and trusting to negotiation on the subject of the former, I shall be disposed on our part faithfully to enforce the Non-intercourse agst G. Britain, unless she repeals her orders in Council, and with them her paper blockades.' Clay to Adam Beatty, Jan. 24, 1811, *Misc. MSS.*, N.Y. Hist. Society.

farmers.[1] Grain still commanded good prices. Yet England, as she boasted, in 1810 had imported twice as much grain from her French enemy as from neutral America. She thus made it obvious that her 'envy of American enterprise has really created War in disguise, to discourage our agriculture and rather promote that of open enemies,' said a Yankee Republican.[2] The envy and hatred of her Tory rulers was such, wrote John Quincy Adams, 'that they will force America into a war against them, though they might see as clearly as you and I do, that in this policy they make themselves the tool of Bonaparte.' [3]

To Senator Clay it still seemed that nothing but a French invasion could equal the wrongs inflicted and threatened by England. And surely it was but common sense to take one enemy at a time, and that the more oppressive; the enemy against whom war, if need be, could be waged on our own continent, and from whom we could exact reparation for the past and security for the future, on land and on sea.

Only a few members dared contemplate Clay's 'resistance by the sword.' Indeed, he himself had not lost all hope, as yet, in the weapon of self-sacrificing non-violent coercion. It was clear, however, that the majority had selected the chief enemy — with a

---

[1] *Ky. Gazette*, Lex. *Reporter*, Nov. 1810–March 1811, and ff.; Jas. Taylor to Madison, Nov. 28, 1810, Feb. 20, 1811, *Madison MSS.*; Clay to Beatty, Jan. 24, 1811, *Misc. MSS.*, N.Y. Hist. Soc.; Taylor, *Agrarian Discontent*, and *Prices in the Mississippi Valley*. Although Britain was held responsible, directly or indirectly, for the agricultural crisis of 1811–1812, renewed Russian competition was the direct cause of the precipitous fall of hemp prices early in 1811, from an average of $7.00 per cwt. to $4.50, and thence to the ruinously low level of $3.00 early in 1812. Clay informed Beatty, *supra*, that he was attempting, with little success, to get higher duties on foreign hemp, and assured him that he felt 'all the solicitude that belongs to this great staple of our Country.' Hemp growers met at Clay's Kentucky Hotel and resolved not to sell until they got $6.00 per cwt. *Ky. Gazette*, Jan. 22, 1811; also, Feb. 5, 1811. Britain was held directly responsible for the radical and long-continued price declines in tobacco — which from an average before 1808 of $6.00 per cwt. had fallen to $3.37½ in May of 1811, and thence to a record low of $2.87½ in 1812 — and cotton, the chief staple of the Southwest, by far the most valuable export at New Orleans, which had fallen from an average of 22 cents a pound in 1805–06 to below 10 cents a pound, an unprecedented low, by April of 1812.

[2] Dr. Nathaniel Ames, Jan. 1811, Warren, *Jacobin and Junto*, p. 239. In the summer and fall of 1810, however, grain and flour in unprecedented quantities had begun to flow to Britain's armies in Spain and Portugal. See Galpin, W. F., 'The American Grain Trade to the Spanish Peninsula, 1810–1814,' *Amer. Hist. Rev.*, XXVIII, 24–27; and, by the same writer, *The Grain Supply of England During the Napoleonic Period*.

[3] Adams (then Minister to Russia) to Geo. Erving, St. Petersburg, Aug. 13, 1811, Adams, J. Q., *Writings*, IV, 175–76.

sense of danger as to injuries Britain might further inflict, and with a sense of relief from vain efforts to keep both enemies at arm's length. With Madison they saw in the professed repeal the promise 'at least of an extrication from the dilemma, of a mortifying peace, or a war with both the great belligerents.'

Macon's Bill, contended the Republicans, was a solemn contract with the power that revoked its edicts; France had done so, despite her new customs regulations; and retreat was in honor impossible. They would keep their pledged word, if only to direct America's energies against the more reprehensible of her enemies. Indeed, some members would shut off provisions to Britain's armies in Spain and Portugal, and obtain the release of impressed Americans, before they would ever again open America's markets to England.

Of no avail was Quincy's and Randolph's derision of this 'one-sided contract' with Bonaparte, this 'first fruit of French allegiance.' Of no avail outcries at the return of a commercial warfare which would ruin the maritime section, and perhaps force it into disunion. Of no avail filibustering and gross disorders on the floor of the House. For by large majorities, on March 2, 1811, the Non-Importation Bill was enacted. By it, non-intercourse was revived against England alone, operative until she revoked her orders-in-council as to America.

With the adjournment of the Eleventh Congress on the following day there closed an era in American history. The stage was cleared for a new drama in which Clay of Kentucky was to play a prominent rôle. The prologue, heralding the entrance of new forces and new actors, was provided by the rising war fever of the people.

Chapter Eleven. Chief of the War Hawks

*T*he Winds begin to rustle, the Clouds gather, it grows dark: will these airy Forces rear up the ocean to a foaming Fury? (*John Adams.*)

We are to have war, then? I believe so, and that it is necessary. Every hope from time, patience, & the love of peace is exhausted, and war or abject submission are the only alternatives left us. I am forced from my hobby, peace. (Jefferson.)

War, dreadful as it is, will not be without its benefits in giving us a NATIONAL CHARACTER, and separating us from the strumpet governments of Europe. (Hezekiah Niles.)

FROM March of 1811 to the reassembling of Congress the sentiment for Clay's 'resistance by the sword' steadily mounted, impelled by Britain's threatening demands, incited by a series of provocative events. After years of ignominious and self-flagellating peace, the sprawling and amorphous republic — this infant Hercules that Britain had spawned — was stirring itself, preparing itself (psychologically at least), to fight for full-fledged nationhood.

Outspoken and general was criticism of a resistance of the law against lawless belligerents, France as well as England, which had degenerated into a quibbling futility. 'Angling for trade, we offered an *if* to England, an *if* to France, and caught *ifs* from both,' said the Baltimore *Whig*. 'In the tedious, disgustful diplomacy of the last seven years, how conspicuous this *if* has been!' [1]

---

[1] Baltimore *Whig*, in Phila. *Aurora*, March 14, 1811.

Even the administration's *Intelligencer* admitted the force of such criticism.[1] 'People of America,' exhorted the *Aurora*, 'you must rouse from your apathy.' You must eschew avarice, fear, and indecision. Against Britain especially you must now affirm with the 'plain, hardy western people' that a truly independent nation 'is bound to protect the lives, liberty and property of its citizens.'[2]

Despite Federalist cries of 'French Vassalage' and threats of disunion, the Republicans that spring scored a smashing victory in Massachusetts. They reelected Governor Gerry, gained full legislative control, and replaced Pickering in the Senate with Varnum, the Speaker of the House. Clay's raw militiamen were greatly encouraged, and national public opinion was powerfully stimulated.

Both John Adams and Jefferson (united now as in '76) exulted in this blow at Pickering's 'herd of traitors.' Federalism was now reduced to a mere Anglo-monarchical clique, said Jefferson. Yet he warned that it was still 'powerful & profuse in the command of money, & backed by a nation, powerful also & profuse, in the use of the same means.' As in '76 all Americans must unite against 'enemies within and without,' he wrote Duane, recalling the fate of divided Poland and declaring that 'the last hope of human liberty in this world rests on us.' Republican dissensions must cease, he chided the anti-Gallatin editor of the *Aurora*. 'If we move in mass, be it ever so circuitously, we shall attain our object.' But 'if we schismatize on either men or measures, if we do not act in phalanx ... I will not say our *party* ... but our *nation* will be undone. For the republicans are the *nation*.'[3]

To keep the harassed Gallatin from resigning, Madison that spring dismissed Secretary of State Smith. He replaced him with James Monroe. A Quid, who had criticized recent policy as partial to France, Monroe was at first hesitant. But he accepted when assured that the President's chief desire was still a cordial

---

[1] *Natl. Intelligencer*, March 21, 1811.

[2] Phila. *Aurora*, March 1, 29, 1811.

[3] Jefferson to Dearborn, Aug. 14; to Duane, March 28, July 25, 1811, *Jefferson MSS.*; Adams, *Corres. with Waterhouse*, pp. 56, 58–63.

accommodation with England. Madison, who made no war preparations, still flattered himself that his *if* policy could be the
means of 'closing the scene of rivalship in plundering and insulting
us, and turning it into a competition for our commerce and friendship.' [1] Jefferson, too, assured Monroe that the great mass of the
people were for peace — until, 'indeed, peace shall become more
losing than war.' [2]

In April Monroe took up the skein of diplomacy and found it
more tangled than ever. At London in February the Prince of
Wales became Regent for insane George III, and had disappointed
all friends of peace by retaining the Perceval-Wellesley Ministry.
In the same month Minister Pinkney, after years of rebuffs, had
boldly demanded the repeal of the orders and the restoration of
friendship by all just and necessary acts. When Wellesley brushed
aside his virtual ultimatum, Pinkney in hostile fashion departed
from England.

Hopes for conciliation were further dashed by intensified
British depredations in American waters, following America's
refusal to buy British goods.[3] An explosive situation came to a
head one night in May, when the frigate *President* was fired on by a
warship thought to be His Majesty's frigate *Guerrière*, notorious for
her recent captures and impressments. Unlike Barron in 1807,
and Trippe in 1810, Commodore Rodgers did not mortify Clay
by 'stooping to ask an explanation' for this fillip on the nose. He
returned the fire, and after a fifteen-minute battle silenced his
assaulter. The next morning disclosed the insolent stranger to be
the British sloop-of-war *Little Belt*, with a loss of thirty-two
wounded or killed.

Great was the popular excitement — and elation. Rodgers had
all but blown out of the water a British pirate that had tried to do
what the *Leopard* had foully done in 1807. The *Chesapeake* murders
had at last been avenged — and by American cannon! Force was

---

[1] Madison to Jefferson, March 18, 1811, Madison, *Writings*, II, 491.

[2] Jefferson to Monroe, May 5, 1811, *Jefferson MSS.*

[3] 'British war vessels, swarming on our coast, annoy our coasting trade intolerably.
They press even passengers, and seem to threat to send their press gangs into our
streets next!' Dr. N. Ames, May, 1811, Warren, *Jacobin and Junto*, p. 240.

the only weapon, it was said, to 'beat off these beasts of prey that infest our coast.' We must now do what we did to the British Lion in '76, when with 'our hay forks, pitch forks and grubbing hoes . . . we knocked down his teeth and scowered his blackhell throat.' [1] Incited and emboldened, the people in all sections that July Fourth called for 'more fire and less smoke,' for 'less talk and more cider,' for no treaty until England released our impressed citizens, and for 'open war in preference to peace on its present terms.' [2]

In the midst of this furor Augustus J. Foster, formerly Secretary of Legation, arrived as the new British Minister. His instructions, alas, made peace with honor and independence impossible.

He was permitted only an all too tardy reparation for the *Chesapeake* atrocity — which he offered that fall when Congress assembled. Although English Tories were mortified that Foster even to this extent 'should have so knuckled down to the Yankees,' [3] his restoration of the two surviving seamen of the four impressed in that rusty affair but took one splinter out of America's wounds, and wore the appearance of a diplomatic ruse. 'Presented at *such a time*,' said the Baltimore *Whig*, it 'is like restoring a hair after fracturing the skull.' [4] It is *'only a sop, to stop the mouth of Congress*,' said Lexington's *Reporter*. 'This DECEPTION is exactly what we expected, and we expect a dozen more such. They cost Britain nothing — they muzzle Congress, and Britain continues in full sweep all her piracies, murders and impressments. Good God — Reparation!!!!' [5]

While there was a superfluity of causes for war, Monroe narrowed discussions down to the British orders. He insisted that the French decrees as to America had been revoked — a precarious position, since he was then angrily demanding of Louis Serurier,

---

[1] 'Lenitas,' in Phila. *Aurora*, July 2, 1811. In marked contrast, Hanson declared that 'the pimping, prevaricating jacobins' were inciting war in order to make the whole country 'catspaws of these French monkeys.' Baltimore *Federal Republican*, May 24, June 7, 1811.

[2] *Essex Register*, July 27; *Natl. Intelligencer*, July 16, 18; and Phila. *Aurora*, July 27, 29, 1811, for nation-wide July 4 toasts.

[3] Jackson, G., *Diaries*, I, 313.

[4] Baltimore *Whig*, in New York *Eve. Post*, Nov. 19, 1811.

[5] Lex. *Reporter*, in N.Y. *Eve. Post*, Dec. 12, 1811.

the new French Minister, that France live up to her promise in letter and spirit. Foster not only denied their revocation, but he took new and high ground. Regardless of whether the decrees as to America were repealed nominally or actually, Britain, anyhow, would never repeal her orders as to America until France repealed her decrees as to Britain. Her aggressions upon the United States would continue until France freely admitted British goods into Europe!

Such a basis for amity was impossible, unjust, insulting. Neutral America had neither the right nor the power to commit the folly of trying to force Britain's goods upon Britain's enemy, to pull her chestnuts from the French fire. Yet until that was done, that is, until France was defeated, England's lawless edicts (which she herself justified only on the plea of 'self-preservation') would operate against America. To them America must submit, and in effect be recolonized. Such terms, as English Whigs said, were fitter for ridicule than for refutation — other than by a war for independence.[1]

Tory Britain was stupidly arrogant when wisdom as well as fair play dictated conciliating an America that was pathetically anxious for peace. Both Madison (of whom Foster reported: 'decision is not a feature of his character') and Monroe (whom Foster found to be 'of the most mild & conciliatory nature') keenly felt Bonaparte's duplicity and thievery; while the most rabid democrat raged at a French perfidy which 'disgusts all, and dissolves confidence in any but our own Government.'[2] On the other hand, Foster found 'even among the warmest of the Federalists a disposition to resist our pretention' that the repeal of the

---

[1] 'We have violated the rights of America as a neutral state,' wrote Wm. Cobbett, Whig publicist, on September 5, 1811; 'we have carried, and still carry into execution, *an interdict against all trade on the part of America, except as we choose to license.*' Now, faced by a Non-Importation, which is justified as war is justified, we say: ' "We will cease to violate your rights; we will cease to do you wrong; we will cease to confiscate your vessels in the teeth of the law of nations; but not unless Napoleon will suffer the continent of Europe to purchase our manufactures and commerce." If my neighbour complains to me for a grievous injury and outrageous insult committed against him, am I to answer by saying, that I will cease to injure and insult him, when another neighbour with whom I am at variance will purchase his clothing and cutlery from me?' *Natl. Intelligencer*, Nov. 12, 1811. See, also, Cobbett, Wm., *Letters on the Late War*, etc., pp. 12–26, and *passim*.

[2] Dr. Ames, June 30, 1811, Warren, *Jacobin and Junto*, p. 241.

orders-in-council as to America must wait upon the repeal of the French decrees as to England.

The new British envoy was soon convinced that a reconciliation could be had if England unbent only slightly — if England made only some 'apparently generous act,' such as a nominal or partial repeal of the orders 'as far as concerns the American Coasts.' [1]

Alas, Foster was compelled by his instructions to browbeat and frighten. Employing what he termed 'decisive, unbending language,' he solemnly protested against the occupation of West Florida as 'contrary to every principle of public justice, faith, and national honor.' And he threatened retaliation in good earnest if the United States persisted in its Non-Importation.[2] John Bull, as even a Boston Federalist some months before had ruefully admitted, was indeed 'a bad negotiator.' [3]

Britain's inflexibility, her outrageous demands, and her threats, together with well-timed concessions by France as to imports and as to ships seized since November of 1810, brought matters to an impasse. Monroe, the peace-loving Quid, confessed himself unable to promote an accommodation short of unconditional and abject submission. Madison thereupon issued a call for Congress to meet on November 4, 1811, a month earlier than usual. The crisis had come!

In flaming words the press denounced 'this new species and system of British insult and injury,' this brazen and wholly undisguised maritime monopoly, and hotly reviewed British wrongs past and present. Editors and correspondents dilated upon the demands and threats of Foster, criticized government's 'imbecilities' of the past, and beseeched the new Twelfth Congress to secure independence by retaliating upon British commerce and British

---

[1] Foster to Wellesley, July 2, 12, Nov. 5, 9, 23, 1811, *F.O.* 5:76, 77.

[2] *A. S. P., For. Rel.*, III, 435 ff.

[3] H. G. Otis to Harrison Gray, April 30, 1811, Morison, S. E., *Harrison Gray Otis*, II, 36–37. In this letter, the first of a series, to his Loyalist uncle at London, Otis declared that the repeal of the orders would prevent war, enhance Anglo-American trading profits, and oust the Republicans (who were 'knaves & fools... though not corrupted by France') in favor of the Federalists, 'the most intelligent and respectable men,' who 'tremble for the prosperity and fate of Britain, and consider her justly as the Bulwark of the liberties of this country and mankind.' The letter was published in the London *Morning Chronicle*, June 24, 1811.

Canada. 'The President,' significantly remarked Monroe to Serurier, the new French Minister, 'does indeed hold the rudder of the Ship of State; he guides, but it is public opinion which makes the vessel move.' [1]

Public opinion was further inflamed by British measures for 'humbling the Yankees,' and the fear that a British squadron daily expected might execute Foster's threats by 'Copenhagening' the seaport towns. Public excitement mounted with fresh cases of 'British plunder and impressments,' off New York by the *Guerrière* and within the Chesapeake by the *Tartarus*; the sale of prize ships at Halifax; and especially the wholesale condemnations in England of American provision vessels merely for having been bound to France, with the consequent casting upon British shores of several hundred American sailors as victims for the brutal press gangs of George the Third.

'I look upon War with G. Britain as inevitable,' wrote Clay from Kentucky; assuming, he said, that 'France is honest and sincere in her recent measures,' and 'that a total & absolute revocation of the French decrees will alone satisfy' Britain. [2] War seemed utterly unavoidable to John Quincy Adams, in Russia, who noted that it was 'the usual caution of the British to begin their Wars without declaration, by a general and indiscriminate capture of merchantmen.' [3] May this new Congress *act*, prayed the American chargé at London: 'We shall never *write* ourselves into the character and reputation our temporizing and cringing policy has lost us.' [4]

'War with England!' cried the Philadelphia *Aurora*. 'Let the people and the government look to it — war or submission are now the only alternatives.' [5] Nothing remains but 'such decisive acts . . . as will meet the hostility of England with effect,' said the Boston *Chronicle*. With patience exhausted, 'moderation is inflamed — *and the voice of every American is FOR WAR.*' [6] Significantly, even

---

[1] Serurier to Bassano, Oct. 23, 1811, Adams, *Hist. U.S.*, VI, 121.
[2] Clay to Rodney, Aug. 17, 1811, *Rodney MSS*.
[3] Adams to John Spear Smith, Aug. 25, 1811, *Samuel Smith MSS*.
[4] *Ibid.*, J. S. Smith to Sen. S. Smith, Oct. 20, 1811 (author's italics).
[5] Phila. *Aurora*, Aug. 8, 1811.
[6] Articles by 'Wallace,' reprinted in *Essex Register*, Sept. 18, Oct. 2, 5, 1811.

Jefferson, erstwhile proponent of passionate pacifism, now agreed that peace had indeed become more losing than war; that it would be sheer quixotism longer to endure Britain's one-sided war without some effort 'towards indemnification and retaliation by reprisal.' [1]

Exception was taken, however, by Republican moderates who urged the old Jeffersonian arguments, and by Quids who urged their old colleague, Monroe, not to join in this 'War of Words and Shilly Shally pretences.' [2] The Anglo-Federalists, who also urged Monroe to dissociate himself from Madisonian 'putridity and corruption,' [3] alternately deplored and ridiculed public sentiment — and greatly encouraged John Bull in his stubbornness.

With the country penniless, defenseless, despised and hated by Britain, by France, and every nation, 'war is the greatest and most fatal calamity that could happen,' said Editor Hanson of 'Pickering's Gazette.' After all, 'there is scarcely an act of tyranny and oppression complained of against George the Third which has not been committed or attempted by Jefferson and his political pimp . . . whiffling Jemmy.' [4] These satellites of Bonaparte 'sicken at the sight of our towering cities,' and as ever seek to ruin the commercial section. If war does come, 'we pray God that the sword of civil war may be permitted to remain sheathed.' [5]

Yet this war clamor is a mere bugbear, said Hanson. The Republicans only wish to incite party spirit and reelect 'Mounseer Madison.' They know full well that a bungling, quixotic war would turn them out of office, 'blast their management and defeat their impostures.' The ruling Virginians have no heart for Canada's conquest: they 'never would consent to prepare in the North the instrument of correcting Southern preponderance.' Indeed, the Federalist merchants themselves would prefer 'a short

---

[1] Jefferson to Eppes, Sept. 6, 1811; to C. Caine, Sept. 16, 1811, *Jefferson MSS.* His letters reveal the wrench it took to divorce him from his hobby, peace; and the eagerness with which he seized upon rumors that America might yet be permitted, in honor, to avoid war.

[2] Matthew Lyon to Monroe, Sept. 26, 1811, *Monroe MSS.*

[3] *Spirit of Seventy-Six,* in Pittsburgh *Gazette,* Sept. 20, 1811.

[4] Baltimore *Fed. Republican,* July 4, 6, Aug. 31, 1811.

[5] *Ibid.,* Aug. 29, Sept. 9, 1811.

war to another embargo or the continuance of the continental system which palsies everything.' For 'a six months war will give democracy to the dogs.' [1]

Decrying as abominable Anglicism all arguments that the republic was too weak to hit back, too divided, too avaricious, too cowardly to defend itself, editors generally with young Niles of Baltimore and young Ritchie of Richmond called for a united and militant Americanism, 'a spark from the altar of Seventy-Six.' [2] As summer advanced they gave increasing space to the horrors and galling disgrace of impressment, 'this greatest of outrages,' of itself 'more than sufficient cause for war,' under flaming headlines of 'Another list of Slaves, Not Africans but Americans!' [3] And higher rose the clamor with accounts of Tecumseh and the Prophet, of murderous raids by the Indians, and of an imminent 'Anglo-Savage War.'

'If plunder on the ocean must be united with the cruelty of the tomahawk,' declared Salem's *Register*, 'then let freemen do their duty.' [4] England is indeed 'kicking' us into war, said the Baltimore *Sun*, for 'even in our western wilds the savage is stirred on to imbue his hands in American blood.' [5] Only the prospect of a new British Ministry (resulting from the death, then rumored, of George III) ought to delay the conquest of Canada, wrote Jefferson. Only its conquest will forestall the British and Indians, and 'put an everlasting end to their aggressions.' [6] We must annex the British provinces and 'fraternize' their people, said 'Wallace' in the Boston *Chronicle*. Only by the conquest of Canada, which 'policy requires, right demands, retaliation promotes,' can we defend and make secure our own Northwest, where, at this very moment,

---

[1] Baltimore *Fed. Republican*, May 24, Sept. 28, Oct. 3, 10, 1811.

[2] *Niles' Register*, Oct. 26, 1811, *passim*.

[3] Portland, Maine, *Eastern Argus*, in *Essex Register*, Aug. 7, 1811; and *Essex Register*, Phila. *Aurora*, *Natl. Intelligencer*, et al., *passim*.

[4] *Essex Register*, Oct. 23, 1811.

[5] Baltimore *Sun*, in Phila. *Aurora*, Aug. 1, 1811. The wampum belts sent to the various tribes by Tecumseh and the Prophet were linked with the *President-Little Belt* affray: '*Belts*,' ran a popular toast, '*whether Indian, French or British* — If sent as emblems of peace, the *President* will clasp them; as tokens of war, may the *President* ever make them *buckle to*.' *Natl. Intelligencer*, July 16, 1811.

[6] Jefferson to Eppes, Sept. 6, 1811, *Jefferson MSS*.

Britain's officials are '*systematizing assassination* among the savage tribes.' [1]

An ominous background for these alarums was furnished by Nature herself. For she, too, had been roused from her apathy, and gave violent evidence of it that fall and winter by earthquakes, hurricanes, and floods. In September there was an eclipse of the moon, an eclipse of the sun, and the Comet made its appearance —

> 'From its horrid hair,
> Shaking pestilence and war.' [2]

'The Americans grow warm very slowly,' wrote French Minister Serurier in the same month, 'but at last they are heated; and at any moment the least spark can light up a conflagration from the Gulf of Mexico to Canada.' [3] Would that incendiary spark appear on the seaboard, where even now Britain's *Leopards* and *Guerrières* waged undeclared but actual war on American shipping, seamen, and agricultural exports? Or in the Northwest, where even now Britain's Indian 'allies' waged sporadic war on American pioneer farmers?

Meanwhile Henry Clay was in Kentucky, at the pulse of a Western opinion so bellicose that Eastern submission-men regarded it as portending 'ghastly deeds of mischief and blood.' [4] Regarding agriculture as ruined and negotiation no longer possible, national honor outraged and national interest strangled, Clay's neighbors had come to look upon war with Great Britain not only as inevitable but as 'indispensably necessary.' Their demands for resistance by the sword, for 'Free Trade or War,' were augmented and quickened not only by the agricultural crisis of 1811, with its disastrous decline in commodity prices, but by a territorial crisis which menaced their Western peace and safety.

---

[1] Boston *Chronicle*, in Phila. *Aurora*, Sept. 25, 1811. There were many such articles. The Canadians, on their part, inveighed against America's 'lawless & obtrusive' Jacobins, who had all 'the ferocity... of starving tigers.' They feared that American emigrants would attempt a revolt like that 'lately acted in West Florida.' *Ibid.*, June 28; *Natl. Intelligencer*, July 27, 1811, q. Montreal *Gazette*.

[2] Baltimore *Fed. Republican*, Sept. 26, 1811.

[3] Serurier to Bassano, Sept. 8, 1811, Archives des Affaires Étrangères, Paris, *Correspondance Politique, États-Unis*, Vol. 66. (Library of Congress photostats.)

[4] Baltimore *Fed. Republican*, Oct. 18, 1811.

Across the Ohio, in Indiana and Illinois, and above in Michigan Territory, and across the Mississippi in Upper Louisiana, outlying settlers were fleeing to blockhouses before savages, who were 'loaded with British presents and ammunition,' incited by 'hostile Indians and traitorous British Indian agents,' exhorted and given belts of wampum by the 'British Prophet,' Tecumseh's brother. 'War is the language of all the red people,' it was said; already they commit ghastly murders on our defenseless farmers, their wives and children.[1] The tomahawk is up because of 'the too successful intrigues of British emissaries,' declared Lexington's *Gazette*. Tecumseh's Confederacy, the powwows at the British fort of Malden, Foster's threats, and the arrival of British regulars in Canada, all point to war upon us on both maritime and territorial frontiers.[2]

This crisis has been expected ever since the *Chesapeake* murders, said Frankfort's *Argus*, but we have avoided war because we have relied upon commercial restrictions, which the Federalists have frustrated, and because, up to now, we have been pressed by both France and England. After reviewing 'unendurable' British maritime hostilities, the *Argus* emphasized the horrors of earlier border hostilities — when 'British gold and British influence provoked . . . and continued for twelve years, the most cruel, savage, Indian murders and butchery . . . In conformity to the same practice, an Indian war of indiscriminate carnage is threatened the people of the northwestern territories . . . *The probability of a war with Great Britain is great.* Nothing but a *retraxet* on her part can prevent it.'[3]

Above the bellicose uproar rose the lone but strident voice of Humphrey Marshall, who denounced 'Madison and his imps' for blowing up a war clamor to conceal their bungling incompetency.[4] Jo Daveiss, however, was in harmony with public opinion in its support of the expedition Governor Harrison of Indiana Territory was preparing against the Prophet's Town on Tippecanoe Creek,

---

[1] St. Louis letter, July 4, in *Natl. Intelligencer*, Aug. 3, 1811.
[2] *Ky. Gazette*, Aug. 27, 1811.
[3] Frankfort *Argus of Western America* in Phila. *Aurora*, Sept. 19, 1811.
[4] *American Republic*, in Baltimore *Fed. Republican*, Oct. 23, 1811.

in the Wabash Valley. Federalist though he was, no son of the West more ardently desired to drive the savages from the lands purchased in 1809, to crush Tecumseh's Confederacy, and to march into British Canada if necessary. Political aspirations thwarted, he gave rein to his military ambitions, and by Harrison had been made colonel of the Mounted Volunteers.

That fall Kentucky dispatched one group of young patriots to Washington and another to Harrison's army. Henry Clay and his fellow congressmen were fighting cocks, 'good game and will take the pit freely.' They would hear Madison's message as to war, submission, or perpetual embargo. 'As no American can or dare submit, war or Embargo is the question,' wrote a Kentuckian, who believed that 'a little blood-letting would relieve the system.' [1]

Booted and spurred, well-mounted and well-armed, in blue coatees and bearskin caps, the Kentucky Volunteers galloped away amid fervent huzzas. No 'silk-stockings or chicken-glove patriots' these, said the *Aurora*, urging seaboard dandies to emulate their spirit.[2] The Volunteers swore they would not return until they had given the British-armed Indians 'a good drubbing,' and brought them to 'by fair means or hard knocks.' Like Mad Anthony Wayne on his first campaign, Jo Daveiss was most zealous. 'He is all for glory,' wrote Colonel John Scott: 'He will do wonders, or be killed.' [3]

On November 7, 1811, a frontier skirmish was fought at Tippecanoe which had implications as big as the frontier skirmish of 1754 which began the Seven Years War. Three days after Congress had assembled, Harrison in a badly managed campaign was surprised by a ferocious attack. The Prophet's people were repulsed, but not until they had killed or wounded sixty-eight of the whites, and forced them back to the Indiana settlements. Jo Daveiss and other gallant Kentuckians had impetuously rushed forward to their deaths.

'War! War! War!' screamed the press of Western America.

---

[1] Anthony Butler to A. Jackson, Oct. 12, 1811, *Jackson MSS.*

[2] Phila. *Aurora*, Sept. 17, 18, 1811.

[3] *Ibid.*, Nov. 15, 1811 (Scott to the Frankfort *Argus*, Vincennes, Oct. 23, 1811); also, *Natl. Intelligencer*, Oct.–Nov., 1811.

'BRITISH-SAVAGE WAR! THE BLOW IS STRUCK!' The real murderers are the British! shouted enraged frontiersmen. The Indians are only 'hired assassins,' England's savage hell-hounds. '*The blood of our murdered heroes must be revenged*,' thundered Jackson of Tennessee.[1] 'Upon our frontier the work of blood has commenced,' cried a Kentuckian. 'After this, will any doubt? Will any waver? ... Whoever hesitates may be set down to George III.'[2]

'Well, war we now have,' said the *Kentucky Gazette*, 'and when we consider that the blow is struck in the western woods at the same moment that Great Britain is sweeping our vessels off the ocean, and her minister is making demands which he knows cannot *possibly* be indulged or acceded to — we cannot but consider these events as proceeding from one common source — the English cabinet.'[3]

This assumption that Britain directly as well as indirectly had incited the savages was general; and it hardened into implacable conviction. The Western people were in no mood to listen to the denials of British officials,[4] or to consider dispassionately the inciting effect upon the Indians of Harrison's land policy. In Lexington, Frankfort, and throughout the Northwest Harrison was banqueted and toasted as 'one of the most faithful gallant and accomplished defenders of the Republic,'[5] as the man who had

---

[1] Jackson to Harrison, Nov. 30, 1811, *Jackson MSS*.

[2] Letters from Kentucky in Phila. *Aurora*, Dec. 14, 1811. A typical letter, one from a soldier who had fought at Tippecanoe, read: 'We took above 90 fusees and rifles from the enemy, most of them new and of *English* manufacture.' Similar letters and accounts appeared in the *Natl. Intelligencer*, Nov. 28, Dec. 5, 1811 ff.

[3] *Ky. Gazette*, Nov. 19, 1811.

[4] Foster denied it when the charge was made in Congress by Grundy and others, *A. S. P. For. Rel.*, III, 483; Foster to Wellesley, Dec. 11, 1811, *F.O.* 5:77. The policy of British officials in Canada was not to precipitate war but to be sure to have the Indians as allies if war took place. In 1811 Sir James Craig, the Governor General, had ordered his Indian Department agents to use all endeavors to prevent a rupture between the Indians and the United States — and at the same time to keep them friendly to the British. Singularly revealing, however, is the comment of General Isaac Brock, of Feb. 1811 (q. Channing, *Hist. U. S.*, IV, 458 n.): 'Our cold attempt to dissuade' the Indians from making war on the United States could scarcely be expected to prevail 'after giving such manifest indications of a contrary sentiment by the liberal quantity of military stores with which they were dismissed.'

[5] C. S. Todd to Gen. Thomas Bodley, Jan. 30, 1812 [misdated 1811], Ky. S. Hist. Soc., *Misc. MSS*. Todd, writing from Frankfort, wanted 'the German band of musicians' sent over from Lexington, since the legislators and citizens (except Humphrey

begun the movement of armed resistance against both Britain and her savage 'allies' which marked the end of a pusillanimous epoch in American history.

'*The War on the Wabash is purely British*,' declared Lexington's *Reporter*. 'The British scalping knife has filled many habitations both in this state as well as in the Indiana Territory with widows and orphans.' This is what comes of 'dignified moderation.' On both land and sea Britain with impunity violates sacred personal rights. The crisis in the West does not affect ships and cargoes, or '*British agents or importing merchants*,' or '*British callicoes or bags of coffee*' but something 'ten thousand times more valuable... *The lives of the women and children on the frontiers* are at stake, and the settlement of the western territories is deeply involved.'

The two great popular grievances against England, and England alone, were now combined in the cry of — 'Look to the Wabash, look to the impressed seamen!' Of one piece were 'the cause of the impressed seamen and the LIVES and wounds of hundreds of American FARMERS... Will Congress treat the citizens of the *Western country* as they have treated the seamen of the United States?... *One case is not more interesting, or ever has been more important, than the other*. But congress *must* now move and they dare not but *move*.' [1]

In warlike speeches Kentucky's legislators, wearing black armbands in honor of 'The Heroes of the Wabash,' called for the immediate redress of national wrongs, maritime and territorial. Their long indictment of England included such charges as 'imprisoning and torturing our fellow citizens,' insulting our national honor, 'inciting the savages to murder... furnishing them with arms and ammunition lately, to attack our forces, seeking to dispose of our whole strength and resources, as may suit her unrestrained ambition or interest.' Their resolutions concluded on the note Clay almost two years before had sounded: 'Should we tamely submit, the world ought to despise us — we should despise ourselves — she would despise us.' [2]

Marshall, and others, who criticized Harrison for unnecessarily sacrificing Jo Daveiss), are 'disposed to do him every honor.'

[1] Lex. *Reporter*, in Phila. *Aurora*, Dec. 10, 13, 28, 1811.

[2] *Niles' Register*, Dec. 28, 1811, Jan. 11, 1812.

This cry havoc of the hinterland resounded in the East, where newspapers and state legislatures voiced the impassioned demands of an aroused people. With 'the blood of our best citizens flowing on the Wabash,' fourteen of the seventeen states resolved that government must cast aside its pacifism and futile diplomacy. Retaliation by the sword is now certain, declared the *Aurora*, reciting anew the 'oppression of our commerce on the high seas — the piratical seizure and the unprecedented code of piracy established in the British admiralty courts — the manstealing outrages on our citizens — the letting loose of the savages with arms.' [1] But one sentiment prevails, said *Niles' Register*: Congress must rescue our impressed seamen 'from a worse than Algerine bondage; ... secure our frontiers from the tomahawk of the savage; ... maintain our right to carry the productions of our own soil to the proper market for them, and redress many other just causes for complaint.' [2]

War's black clouds had gathered in portentous mass. Fierce, ever-mounting winds, blowing strongest from Clay's West, were lashing national opinion to 'a foaming Fury,' and driving forward the republic's unwieldy Ship of State. All eyes turned to the new Twelfth Congress, as with unabated violence Britain's 'storm of war ... howls along our coasts and hovers over our habitations.' [3]

Even before the news sped east from the Wabash, the Boston *Chronicle* had declared that never in our history 'did the American congress assemble under circumstances of greater interest and responsibility.' [4] Its deliberations, said the *National Intelligencer* on the day before Tippecanoe, 'will, perhaps, do more to stamp the character of genuine republican governments than has been effected since the creation of the world.' [5] With this new House 'we shall divest ourselves of the livery of disgrace,' said the Boston *Patriot*.[6] 'The people, the times, and the government,' said Salem's *Register*, 'all require DECISION.' [7]

---

[1] Phila. *Aurora*, Dec. 31, 1811.   [2] *Niles' Register*, Jan. 4, 1812.
[3] *Ibid.*, Jan. 4, 1812; speech of the Governor of Pennsylvania.
[4] Boston *Chronicle*, in Phila. *Aurora*, Oct. 9, 1811.
[5] *Natl. Intelligencer*, Nov. 6, 1811.   [6] *Ibid.*, Nov. 2, 1811, q. Boston *Patriot*.
[7] *Essex Register*, Oct. 30, 1811.

Even Editor Hanson of 'Pickering's Gazette' professed to hope that a stand would be taken after 'years of self-immolation upon visionary experiments.' [1] Yet, to the question of 'What course will Congress pursue?' Hanson's Anglo-Federalists, Randolph's Quids, and not a few Republican regular troops cynically answered:

> 'Will they lay an embargo? — No!
> Then to war they'll go! — Not so.
> They'll build a navy tho' — Poh! Poh!
> Raise an army e'en so! — Oh! No.
> Have non-intercourse with France? — Whieu!
> What then will they do? — Remain in statu quo!' [2]

Such men reckoned without Henry Clay and his raw militiamen. Editor Tom Ritchie of the Richmond *Enquirer*, who knew full well Clay's detestation of 'narrow and dastardly *coasting*,' and who praised the young Westerner whose genius was carrying him 'from the sequestered vale to the towering summit,' anticipated a spirit quite different from the 'flinching' Tenth and Eleventh Congresses. [3] Likewise, Editor Irvine of the Baltimore *Whig* harbored 'the cheering hope' that Clay of Kentucky would infuse into the new Twelfth Congress 'a portion of his manly and independent spirit' and amply supply 'the want of wisdom, of energy, of honourable feeling.' [4]

Meanwhile, by saddle-horse, gig, stage, and packet-boat, aided by good weather and impelled by the crisis, congressmen were arriving at Washington well in advance of November 4, 1811. There was a buzz of speculations. Would it be open war, an embargo, or a more rigid non-intercourse? Should action against England be delayed until Joel Barlow, the new Minister to France, sent home a treaty providing reparations for sequestered ships and adjusting all differences with Napoleon? Merchants were already petitioning for the repeal of restrictions against British imports, and dreading a return to Jefferson's Embargo. Mr. Gallatin and his old guard followers seemed to favor putting teeth into the exist-

---

[1] Baltimore *Fed. Republican*, Oct. 29, 1811.
[2] *Ibid.*, Nov. 13, 1811, q. *Farmer's Cabinet*.
[3] Richmond *Enquirer*, March 22, 1811.
[4] Baltimore *Whig*, in *Ky. Gazette*, Jan. 29, 1811.

ing non-intercourse. If such men maintained their sway, 'I fear we shall have *Non intercourse* until the nation will be overrun with *Old maids* and witches,' said young Poindexter. 'No one has suggested a specific measure; but all agree *that something must be done.'* [1]

Who was to be the new Speaker? That was a recurrent question. Macon, and other veterans, were mentioned. It was also suggested that one of the some seventy new members might be chosen. But no, that would violate precedent, and besides, most of the new members were only inexperienced boys. It was 'hardly to be presumed that a *new* man will be elected Speaker.' [2]

Precedents, however, were to be smashed by the new pepper-pot politicians. A new and invigorating spirit pervaded Capitol Hill with the arrival of such men as Felix Grundy of Tennessee, John Adams Harper of New Hampshire, William Lowndes, Langdon Cheves, and John C. Calhoun of South Carolina, Richard M. Johnson and Henry Clay of Kentucky. They were largely from the West and the lower South, from the new states or the frontier regions of the Old Thirteen. Their revolt of 1810 (like other insurgent movements in American history) was a Western movement. And they brought to the East all the aggressive qualities, all the fresh emotional strength, all the courage of convictions that characterized the 'Children of America.'

Their youth was most striking. Calhoun and Lowndes were but twenty-nine, Johnson thirty, Harper thirty-one, Cheves a year older, while Grundy, thirty-four, was the same age as Clay; all of them had been born after July 4, 1776. With leaders and aspirations drawn from a militantly American hinterland, the republic's first-born generation was making its debut in national politics.

These insurgent 'War Hawks,' these 'Liberty Boys of the West,' represented a revolt of youth against cautious age; a protest against the conservative seaboard; an upsurging of nationalistic fervor. They embodied, it appeared to John Adams, 'a Spirit of Contrition and Shame at our long Apathy and Lethargy; a Spirit of Resentment of Injuries; a Spirit of Indignation at Insolence.' [3]

---

[1] Poindexter to Mead, Nov. 11, 1811, *Poindexter MSS.*

[2] Washington letters in Baltimore *Fed. Republican*, Phila. *Aurora, U.S. Gazette*; and the *Natl. Intelligencer*, Oct. 31–Nov. 16, 1811.

[3] Adams to Rush, Dec. 19, 1811, *Old Family Letters*, p. 367.

Coming into power on the upward swing of the pendulum, away
from their elders' 'ignominious surrender,' they were likely to be
more passionate than prudent, to display youth's defects as well as
youth's virtues. Yet they had faith, and were unafraid. Through
them Young America and the New West were to speak — and to
act.

Before them, however, were many obstacles in a government
notorious for its incapacity. These were mainly to be encountered
in their own strife-torn party, for the Federalist minority numbered
but 7 members in a Senate of 34 and but 37 in a House of 142.[1]
Could these raw militiamen infuse their spirit into the Madison-
Gallatin regular troops? Could they master factious Quids and
Clintonians, and such wavering moderates as Worthington of
Ohio and John Pope ('the Apostate,' who 'mis-represented Kentucky')? Could they, with such allies in the Senate as Crawford of
Georgia, Bibb of Kentucky, and Campbell of Tennessee, rely upon
the pro-war but anti-administration Giles, Leib, and Smith?
Could 'these boys,' these 'junior apprentices,' themselves remain
united as to methods and objectives? Above all, could they convince a contemptuous Old World, and their own long-submitting
country, that when the republic threatened war it meant, really
meant, actual war by the sword?

These grave questions, together with the new men's youthful
inexperience and innocence of political discipline, called for a
leadership adroit, tactful, and bold, persuasive and commanding.

Upon arrival, whether by accident or design, Clay, Lowndes,
Grundy, Cheves, Bibb, Calhoun, and a few others took up lodg-
ings together. With good reason they were soon dubbed 'The War
Mess.' Canvassing the situation, they found themselves agreed as

---

[1] In the Senate the Federalists were Goodrich and Dana of Connecticut, Howell and
Hunter of Rhode Island, Horsey and Bayard of Delaware, and Lloyd of Massachusetts.
In the House, Connecticut (7), Rhode Island (2), and Delaware (1) had unanimous
Federalist delegations, 10 in all; Massachusetts had 7 Federalists (out of a delegation
of 17), Virginia 6 (out of 22), New York 5 (out of 17), Maryland 3 (out of 9), North
Carolina 2 (out of 12), New Hampshire 2 (out of 5), Vermont 1 (out of 4), Pennsylvania 1 (out of 18). In his excellent study, *Expansionists of 1812*, pp. 126–32, Professor
Pratt analyzes the membership, stresses the importance of Republican factionalism,
and points out that 'nothing could better demonstrate the frontier character of the war
spirit than to observe its progressive decline as we pass from the rim of the frontier
crescent to its center at the national capital,' and that 'it is near the center too that we
find all that remained of Federalist strength outside its northeastern stronghold.'

to the need of 'some controlling or at least some concentrating influence,' which Madison did not, and apparently could not, exercise. The President frankly looked to the people's representatives for his policy or for the limits of policies already forced upon him, and seemed willing to follow their lead. This new House, then, must take the helm and provide the popular leadership demanded by the crisis. And the man best fitted by talents and experience to lead the House, to urge and drive, to conciliate and persuade, appeared to be Clay of Kentucky — that 'clever man,' Lowndes reported, 'whom they call "the Western Star." ' [1]

Such was the opinion of the War Mess. And such was the opinion of the Young Republicans who met in caucus on Sunday evening, November 3, and brought Clay forward as their candidate for the Speakership. [2]

When the House assembled on the following day Henry Clay was elected Speaker on the first ballot by a two-to-one vote over his nearest rival. [3] It was without precedent, this election of a new member on his first day in the House. A tribute to Clay personally and to the growing importance of the West, it was peculiarly significant of the temper of the new Twelfth Congress. The revolt of 1810 had borne first fruit. Control had passed from cautious temporizers to a compact minority of insurgent young hotspurs.

So unexpected was this upset of precedent that the new Speaker was at first confused with Matthew Clay (his distant relative), the veteran Virginia representative. But the country was soon informed that the man selected was young Mr. Clay of Kentucky, formerly of the Senate; a new man but capable and accustomed to legislation; a proper man at this crisis to conduct public business with dignity and dispatch. 'The new Speaker is quite popular,' reported a Federalist. 'He possesses fine talents and presides with dignity.' [4] Plumer of New Hampshire, who knew 'the necessity of

---

[1] Lowndes, Nov. 2, 7, 1811, Ravenel, Mrs. St. J., *Wm. Lowndes*, pp. 84–86.

[2] John Adams Harper to Plumer, Feb. 6, 1812, *Plumer MSS.*; and Wash. letter, Nov. 4, in *Relf's Philadelphia Gazette*, Nov. 6, 1811, which stated (as did other accounts) that Clay's name was not mentioned for the Speakership until the eve of the election, and, also, that the caucus was held presumably to prevent the election of Macon, who, it was feared, might reappoint his friend Randolph as chairman of the Ways and Means Committee.

[3] *Annals*, 12th, 1st, 330. The vote was Clay 75, Bibb (Ga.) 38, Macon (N.C.) 3, Nelson (Va.) 2, Bassett (Va.) 1. Phila. *Aurora*, Nov. 7, 1811.

[4] Boston *Columbian Centinel*, Nov. 9, 13, 16, 1811.

having a man of talents, extensive information, & prompt decision,' warmly congratulated Clay, being confident that he would 'reflect back upon the house with usury, the honor they have conferred upon you.' [1]

For the tall, slender son of Kentucky who briskly advanced to the Speaker's rostrum, pounded the gavel, and crisply called the House to order, it was a moment of triumph — his first day in the House of Representatives and already its chosen leader!

Dramatic was the occasion, and colorful. Morning sunlight played upon the blond hair and mobile face of the new Speaker as he sat in his ornate chair under a magnificent canopy, a potentate 'surrounded with the richest scarlet and green velvets and gold fringe,' more like 'the trappings of royalty than the seat of republicanism.' [2] High above him was an enormous stone eagle, with outspread wings; a fighting eagle, fiercely defiant. Before him in the elliptical chamber, its Corinthian pillars of fluted sandstone draped in crimson, sat the nation's representatives, in long-tailed, short-waisted coats of rich blues, of green, black, and plum. On the floor were Turkey carpets. Above was the painted ceiling with its alternate squares of inch-thick skylights. In the semicircular, green-draped galleries, reached by spiral stone steps, were crowds of visitors — their eyes fixed on Mr. Speaker Clay, who on this and succeeding days observed and estimated his new colleagues upon whom the fate of America so largely depended.

No longer need William Wirt lament 'a most miserable and alarming dearth of talents . . . among the young men of the U. S.' Evidently the great convulsion had taken place which, 'like our revolutionary war,' Wirt in 1810 thought necessary to rouse the nation. [3] Even British Minister Foster, though he said the House still had 'too many low and uneducated Individuals who are too ignorant to have any opinion of their own,' remarked upon the 'considerable accession . . . of men of talents and respectability.' [4] It was hard for Clay (and future Americans) to understand how a

---

[1] Plumer to Clay, Nov. 20, 1811, *Plumer MSS.*
[2] Hooker, Edward, 'Diary,' *Ann. Rept. Amer. Hist. Assoc. 1895*, I, 927.
[3] Wirt to Benj. Edwards, May 8, 1810, Kennedy, *Wirt*, I, 285.
[4] Foster to Wellesley, Dec. 21, 1811, *F.O.* 5:77.

nation with such sons could have remained so long in 'putrescent peace.'

Most of these Young Americans, indeed two-thirds of the House, were lawyers. Many of them, unlike the new Speaker with his meager years in the Old Field School, had received in formal training the best the country afforded. All had learned bitter lessons during long years of national degradation. All were resolved upon regaining national liberty and national self-respect. Most of them came from the frontier crescent from Maine around through Kentucky and Tennessee to Georgia. In a conflict with England (and, presumably, with Spain), they would obtain what their pacific elders had long demanded, '*reparation* for the past, & *security* for the future,' by breaking down menacing barriers on sea and land, and by bringing into reality Henry Clay's truly independent '*new* United States.'

Peter B. Porter from western New York, four years older than Clay, lived within gunshot distance of the British Canada he longed to conquer. Young John Adams Harper and his New Hampshire mountaineers would retaliate in the same quarter. Auburn-haired Dick Johnson, born in the Dark and Bloody Ground while his father fought off Britons, Tories, and Shawnees, like Clay was eager to secure the frontiers north and south. Samuel Ringgold from western Maryland was said to carry a declaration of war about in his pocket. Joseph Desha of Mays Lick, Kentucky, with Mad Anthony Wayne had fought England's 'red and white savages.' Irish-born Stephen Ormsby of Louisville had been a general in the Ohio Valley wars, while Virginia-born William Butler from the Carolina mountains in '76 had fought invading Britons and Cherokees from British Florida.

Felix Grundy had seen members of his family killed and scalped. Ezekiel Bacon from western Massachusetts, a man skilled in finance, was born in Boston in '76. Impetuous Carolinians were David R. Williams, a year older than Clay; Israel Pickens, three years younger; and William R. King, nine years younger than the Speaker. George Michael Troup of Dublin, Georgia, a Princeton graduate, born on the Tombigbee River just above Spanish Mobile, was two years younger than Clay. Both Troup and

William Wyatt Bibb, a Virginia-born Georgian three years younger than Clay (a physician, like young Condict of New Jersey and Seybert of Philadelphia), believed that Georgia's safety rested on East Florida's annexation. Stevenson Archer of Maryland, far from being a war-monger or chauvinist, as sincerely anxious for peace as he was sincerely convinced that Britain would grant peace only when compelled by force, was the son of a distinguished Revolutionary officer, a graduate of Princeton, and but twenty-five years old.

Allies of 'these boys' were men who had known Revolutionary hardships yet were willing to fight England again. At sixteen, both Thomas Moore of South Carolina and Bolling Hall, a Virginia-born Georgian, had fought the redcoats. Anthony New of Elkton, Kentucky, as a Virginia colonel had fought Tarleton's Dragoons. Alexander McKim of Baltimore had been a cavalryman in Hanover under Lafayette. Virginia-born John Sevier of Knoxville, the famous border warrior and first governor of Tennessee, with Irish-born John Rhea of Sullivan in the same state, at King's Mountain had whipped Britons and Tories. James Fisk from frontier Vermont had opposed invading Britons, Hessians, and Indians. Democratic Green Mountain Boys, also, were William Strong and Doctor Samuel Shaw. William Widgery, Devon-born ship-builder of Portland, one of the four all-Republican members from Massachusetts' frontier district of Maine, in '76 had commanded a privateer. Robert Wright, for years governor of Maryland, a fierce little old veteran, with powdered hair, flashing eyes, and curling lip, notoriously quick with his tongue, pen, and duelling pistol, had long urged war on impressment alone.

Quick with his pistol, also, was George Poindexter of Natchez. Two years younger than his friend Clay, and like him a Richmond law student who had gone West, Poindexter in a duel had just killed an Anglo-Federalist. Mississippi Territory's sole delegate, he had no vote. Yet in the many caucuses that were held his effective talents and strong will were influential; and on the floor, with a voice which had been raised against Quincyism in 1811, and since 1808 against a British monopoly which impoverished his cotton-growing constituents, he more than made up for Sevier and

LANGDON CHEVES   JOHN C. CALHOUN

GEORGE POINDEXTER   RICHARD M. JOHNSON

others, who voted silently the same way their long rifles had so often pointed. Samuel McKee of Kentucky, another Virginia-born lawyer, also hotly voiced the exasperation of frontier farmers at delay in striking off all British shackles. For decisive action were quick-tempered Langdon Cheves, who had been born in '76 at Bulltown Fort on the Cherokee-ravaged border, and William Lowndes, gentle, learned, six feet six and thin to emaciation. Five years younger than Clay, educated at Yale and Litchfield Law School, slender, with piercing dark eyes, strong chin, and a mind logical and keen, was John Caldwell Calhoun from the Carolina hill country.

The moderate Republicans for the most part were elderly and mediocre men. Typical of many New Yorkers, who vacillated between DeWitt Clinton and Madison for President in 1812, was Doctor Samuel Mitchill, one of New York City's two members, whom Clay found as in 1807 to be pleasant but timid, a straw in the wind. 'Ancient and devoted partisans of the administration' were old John Smilie and old William Findley, Irish-born Pennsylvanians, erstwhile radicals become standpatters. Ebenezer Seaver, Richard Cutts, and Isaiah Green of Massachusetts, all Harvard graduates, had all shown a self-sacrificing devotion to Jefferson-Madison policies. Zealously cautious were Hugh Nelson (the son of Nelson of Offley), Matthew Clay, and Thomas Gholson of Virginia; Adam Boyd of New Jersey; and Nathaniel Macon of North Carolina, an honest round-faced planter, bald and gray, in navy-blue coat and cambric stock, his pantaloons always carefully — and economically — tucked within his white-top boots.

At one side of the Speaker's chair was the small but able group of Federalists led by Josiah Quincy, Boston's sole member, a man who cared little for a nation that rejected his ideas — and never forgave him his threat of disunion and taunt that America could not even be 'kicked' into war. From his state came business-like William Reed of Marblehead, gloomy Abijah Bigelow, and the Reverend Samuel Taggart, corpulent and stern, with a Federalist disdain (not unlike his Calvinistic dogma of the sainted few and the damned many) for the many Yankees who now sung out that 'Columbia's God' rather than 'New England's God forever reigns.' [1] Connecticut's seven members, all born before 1776, were all grimly against war. With them were personable Harmanus Bleecker and dapper James Emott of New York, icy-stiff James Breckinridge from the Valley of Virginia, and Philip Barton Key of Maryland, who in '76, in those earlier 'times that tried men's souls,' had worn the red coat of King George the Third.

Close allies of Quincy were such Quids as Richard Stanford of North Carolina, who jeered at Speaker Clay's 'bubble of National Honor' as in '98 he had jeered at John Adams's selfsame bubble, and Daniel Sheffey from the Valley of Virginia, an able and frequent speaker whom Foster described as 'very deep in Adam Smith's principles — he is very fair about Impressment.' [2] Their leader, the famous 'moon-struck' Randolph of Roanoke, sat swathed in sundry greatcoats and silk cravats, his long black hair negligently ribboned, his pipestem legs thrown over a desk. This freakish, emaciated, girlish-voiced, beardless eccentric had been a 'meteor of Anti-Federalism.' Since breaking with Jefferson, refusing longer to be governed by 'the old red breeches of that Prince of Projectors, St. Thomas of *Canting*bury,' he had become a 'mad genius of discord,' a superbly insolent and destructive freelance. To Jefferson, he was 'the outcast of the world.' To John Adams, who also had felt his malignity, he was 'A Boy with a mischievous syringe full of dirty water.' [3]

An unrivalled bully, whose sadistic nature delighted in envenomed displays, Randolph was irritated by the incoming 'horde of upstart patriots.' And especially was he irritated by the fighting cock from Kentucky, who had, he sneered, 'strided from the door of the Hall as soon as he entered it to the Speaker's Chair.' [4]

In accepting the office Clay in a terse yet gracious speech promised every facility in his power for the transaction of business

---

[1] Massachusetts Republicans had changed the old New England song against tyranny to read thus (*Essex Register*, March 14, 1812):

> 'Let Federals shake their iron rod,
> Let Tories clank their galling chains,
> WE FEAR THEM NOT — WE TRUST IN GOD
> Columbia's God forever reigns.'

[2] Foster, A. J., *MS. Diary*, April 21, 1812.

[3] Jefferson to Duane, April 30, 1811, *Jefferson MSS.*; Adams to Rush, May 14, 1810, *Old Family Letters*, p. 256; Bruce, W. C., *John Randolph*.

[4] Perry, B. F., *Reminiscences*, p. 53; and, also, Randolph to Nicholson, Dec. 20, 1811, *Nicholson MSS.*

'in the most agreeable manner.' [1] He gave no hint that he considered his duty other than that of preserving order. But he was to be far more than a presiding officer in the British tradition of his predecessors. Determined to be the leader of the House and his party, and ready as always to shoulder the burdens of leadership, he was to exercise to the full the Speaker's prestige and latent powers. Repeatedly was he to give force and direction to legislation, not only by informal conferences but by bringing to bear in the Committee of the Whole House his 'bold and vigorous, inestimably convincing eloquence.' From young Clay's advent the Speakership (when in strong hands) had an importance second only to the Presidency. [2]

The crisis had given national leadership to the House; and in the House Clay characteristically seized the chance to exert 'a controlling influence.' Just as this new Congress differed in age, in spirit, and in ability from the 'flinching' Tenth and Eleventh, so did the young Kentuckian differ from previous Speakers.

At first, in view of the notorious disorders which had often turned the House into a turbulent cock-pit, 'a spouting club or bear garden,' there was some question as to whether young Clay would uphold 'his reputation for superior acquirements.' [3] Neither 'Father Macon' (Speaker from 1801 to 1807) nor 'superannuated' General Varnum (Speaker from 1807 to 1811) had been able to contend with Quincy's tactics or to prevent Randolph from acting like 'a petted, vindictive schoolboy,' an escaped maniac, 'a malignant monkey.' At the last session, within three days Randolph had provoked a challenge from Mr. Eppes, and, in defense of his hound dogs, with his hickory stick had pummelled Mr. Alston, as he himself boasted, 'with all the nonchalance of Sir Harry Wildair.' [4]

All this was well known to the new Speaker, who as 'a mere matter of taste' had preferred the turbulent House to the solemn Sen-

---

[1] *Annals*, 12th, 1st, 332–33, Nov. 4, 1811.

[2] See Follett, M. P., *The Speaker of the House of Representatives*, and Brown, G. R., *The Leadership of Congress*.

[3] Baltimore *Fed. Republican*, Nov. 15, 1811; also, *ibid.*, March 13, and Richmond *Enquirer*, in Phila. *Aurora*, March 14, 1811.

[4] Bruce, *Randolph*, I, 256, 364.

ate,[1] and who had no doubts as to his ability to get the momentous business before the House done 'in the most agreeable manner.'

Such cocks-of-the-walk as Randolph and Quincy, said John Adams, had now 'better hold their Tongues.' [2] Quincy, for reasons best known to himself, at present was willing to be silent. Randolph, however, did not intend to hold his mordant tongue when these fledgling War Hawks, these backwoods Yahoos, threatened to 'Federalize' government and to plunge the republic into a disastrous war. The nationalistic ardor, the fervent patriotism, of Calhoun and Clay he attributed to selfish ambition. These men, and especially the Kentuckian who had taken the unprecedented first-day 'stride,' he remarked, shortly after the session had opened, have 'their eyes on the Presidency, and mark my words, sir, we shall have war before the end of the session!' [3]

Unfriendly to France, unmistakably hostile to England, Madison in his message of November 5 did not call for war, but he did call upon Congress to put the republic 'into an armor and an attitude demanded by the crisis.' In this spirit Clay organized the House. He appointed, as chairmen, Porter to the all-important Foreign Relations Committee, Williams to Military Affairs, Cheves to Naval Affairs, and Bacon to the Ways and Means Committee. He saw to it that on each the War Hawks predominated. Old Republicans resented his neglect; Randolph sneered at the boy dictator; and Federalists lamented the Speaker's 'monstrous' power that permitted a new man thus to chart a course for Congress and for the nation.[4]

---

[1] Clay to Monroe, Nov. 13, 1810, *Monroe MSS*.

[2] Adams to Rush, Dec. 19, 1811, *Old Family Letters*, p. 367.

[3] Garland, Hugh A., *John Randolph*, I, 306. Interesting in this connection is a letter from Washington, Nov. 4, 1811 (Phila. *Aurora*, Nov. 7, 1811), which described the election of Clay to the Speakership, termed him 'a young, intelligent, capable gentleman, accustomed to legislation and the practice of the bar; [who] will readily fall into the business of the house,' and went on to state that the election had been 'with a view to *other events*, which are to arise out of the womb of time. . . what would you think of taking measure for a pair of breeches for your grandson yet unborn; how would you go about it; I assure you that the election has been conducted upon the idea of a full suit for a child that is to be born in 1816 or 1817; and if your grandson should turn out to be a *fine girl*, how would you contrive to get over it?'

[4] Taggart, *Letters*, p. 361, Nov. 7, 1811; Macon to Nicholson, Nov. 21, 1811, *Nicholson MSS*.; *Annals*, 12th, 1st, 333, 343. On Porter's committee Clay placed Calhoun, Grundy, Harper, Desha, War Hawks; Smilie and Seaver, moderates; Key, Federalist; Randolph, nondescript.

While Porter's committee prepared its eagerly awaited report, Republican editors (even Duane of the *Aurora*) hailed the message as confidence-inspiring. Federalist and British editors, however, derided it as 'whiffling and whimpering' in the imbecilic spirit of the past. Dodging behind abstract generalities, and throwing the reins to Congress as usual, the President had announced a 'hollow and deceitful policy.' It was understood and approved, they said, by the 'old democrats.' It was understood and despised by Giles, chairman of the Senate Foreign Relations Committee. It was misunderstood by the new men, but only at first, for they too were now cursing Madison and his Cabinet for their timidity and insincerity.[1]

Distrust as to the Executive's war pulse, openly voiced by Giles,[2] was in truth privately expressed by Clay's War Hawks. Quite naturally, they could not dissociate the Madison-Gallatin old guard from the humiliating past. Desiring definite assurances, through their House Foreign Relations Committee they demanded a pledge that if they voted arms Madison would use them against England.[3]

Neither President nor Cabinet wanted war, yet they did not seem disposed to thwart the people's representatives. Through Monroe, the insurgents were given 'the strongest assurances that the President will cooperate zealously with Congress in declaring

---

[1] N.Y. *Herald*, Nov. 19; N.Y. *Eve. Post*, Nov. 26; Baltimore *Fed. Republican*, Nov. 12; Boston *Columbian Centinel*, Nov. 16, 1811.

[2] Criticizing Madison, Giles in the Senate (*Annals*, 12th, 1st, 42) introduced a Quebec account which revealed, he said, how thoroughly convinced all the world was that the United States would always talk about but never defend its rights. The Canadian editor contrasted 'the imbecility of the United States, with their dozen ships,' with John Bull's thousand warships, which had checked 'the violent inclinations of Dame Columbia to extend her arms to cherish, aid, and assist her admired hero, Napoleon.... Unpardonable is the grievance that the Leviathan is not as powerless as the Cod; that the Jackall, whom nature meant for the Lion's provider, is not permitted to divert its provender to the support of the Tiger...' Madison's message, said the editor —

> 'With syllogisms 'twill make a clatter,
> With abstract rights three-deckers batter;
> An empty purse at millions shake,
> And no trade 'gainst a free trade stake:
> Of rotting produce count the gain,
> A seaboard boast shut from the main;
> To seamen recommend the loom,
> And on each mast to fix a broom;
> Merchants, for lack of foreign wares,
> To retail apples, plums, and pears.'

[3] Grundy to A. Jackson, Nov. 28, 1811, *Jackson MSS.*

war, if our complaints are not redressed by May next.' [1] Yes, 'the executive is pledged for War,' exulted young Johnson of Kentucky. 'Before we adjourn therefore, War measures will be taken; viz. letters of Marque etc. & taking the Canadas.' [2] Confident also was young Poindexter of Mississippi, who reported: 'We shall assuredly have war.' [3]

Their apprehensions, however, were not entirely quieted. 'Rely, on one thing,' wrote truculent Felix Grundy, 'we have War or Honorable peace before we adjourn or certain great personages have produced a state of things which will bring them down from their high places, If there be honest men enough to tell the truth loudly.' [4]

If Madison intended Congress to blow the trumpet he could not have been disappointed in the warlike blast on November 29. After a scathing review of Britain's relentless hostilities, 'with a full determination to report in favor of actual War, at a given period,' [5] Porter's committee recommended filling the ranks of the army, adding ten thousand regulars and fifty thousand volunteers, arming merchantmen, and outfitting existing warships. 'The great bomb' had at last exploded. The cry was now loudly raised for 'Revolution No. 2.'

In the strain of Clay's Senate speeches the War Hawks argued the necessity of getting ready to fight and of fighting when ready. They would redeem America's character, vindicate her rights, protect her seamen, secure her territory, force a free trade for her produce, and indemnify her losses by attacking British commerce and by conquering Canada (for the North) and Florida (for the South).

Against them Randolph, who furnished most of the opposition, unloosed a sheaf of arrows brightly colored and sharply barbed. This is not a war for maritime rights, he said, but 'a scuffle and scramble for plunder' urged on by 'agrarian cupidity.' But one

---

[1] Lowndes to wife, Dec. 7, 1811, Ravenel, *Lowndes*, p. 90. See, also, Harper to Plumer, Dec. 2, 1811, *Plumer MSS.*; Wm. A. Burwell to W. C. Nicholas, Dec. 29, 1811, *Nicholas MSS.*

[2] R. M. Johnson to Jas. Barbour of Va., Dec. 9, 1811, *Barbour MSS.*, N.Y. Public Library.

[3] Poindexter to Mead, Dec. 12, 1811, *Poindexter MSS.*

[4] Grundy to Jackson, Nov. 28, 1811, *Jackson MSS.*   [5] *Ibid.*

cry is heard — 'Canada! Canada! Canada!' Though he himself
in 1807 had raised the same cry, he now tried to split the war
party by repeatedly warning that 'this tid-bit Canada' would give
such a preponderant power to the North as would force the slave
South to secede.[1]

A weird and garrulous Cassandra, he shrilly denounced everything and everybody — from ruinous war to ruinous embargoes,
from Khouli Khan, Jefferson, Cromwell, Tom Paine, Tamerlane,
Caesar, and female gadabout cardplayers to Yankee peddlers and
slave-inciters. He rhapsodized British genius, contemned the
American character, and refused to be 'bound to France as Sinbad
the sailor was bound to the putrifying corpse of his deceased wife.'
Thrusting his scrawny forefinger at Speaker Clay and his 'unfledged political pedagogues,' he repeatedly accused them of
adopting Hamilton's merchant-Federalism, and John Adams's
'profligate instruments of despotism,' for the base purpose of conquest and for raising the price of hemp and cotton. Never would
the people pay taxes, he shouted, for a predatory war, waged by
Wilkinson's hireling troops and by plundering privateersmen,
against 'the only Power that holds the arch-enemy of mankind in
check.' Never would they permit old-fashioned Republicanism to
be scourged out of us by these power-infatuated, war-mad, boys.

For the first time the new men felt the tomahawk of the mad
genius from Virginia, who could spellbind his audience even if he
could not convince it. For the first time they saw 'the satanic fire on
his swarthy face,' and 'the sneering devil that lurked in his tone
and look.'[2] Yet they were undaunted. In a strongly nationalistic
speech, young Calhoun with cold logic dissipated his rhetorical
fogs, riddled his brilliant inconsistencies, and emphasized the

[1] *Annals*, 12th, 1st, 422, 441, 525; Dec. 9, 10, 16, 1811. A North-South sectional dispute had flamed up at the opening of the session over the reapportionment of congressional seats under the 1810 census, which benefited the North and West. See Pratt,
Expansionists of 1812, chap. II.

[2] 'Fickle, wayward, and overbearing... haughty and wedded to Southern supremacy,' said Quincy, 'he had the temper... of his savage ancestress, Pocahontas. His
tomahawk was continually in his hand... Enemies he could not destroy he never
failed to cripple.' Quincy, *Quincy*, pp. 94, 459. 'There is no speaker in either house
that excites such universal attention as Jack Randolph,' wrote Washington Irving in
February of 1811. 'But they listen to him more to be delighted by his eloquence and
entertained by his ingenuity and eccentricity, than to be convinced by sound doctrine
and close argument.' Irving, *Irving*, I, 273.

essential issue of war or submission, independence or recoloniza-
tion. He spoke of the Union and the Fathers, and he flatly turned
his back on Republican agrarian-particularism. National protection and national patriotism were reciprocal, he declared. No
real Union or great nation could ever be achieved unless government protected every citizen in the lawful pursuit of his business —
protected commerce no less than agriculture, the New England
merchant no less than the Southern and Western farmer. He
refused to reply in kind to Randolph's gross abuse. Yet he warmly
repudiated 'the stale imputation of French partiality' and the
charge of 'agrarian cupidity,' though quite frankly contending
(as did his fellow War Hawks) that national interest as well as
national honor was at stake. Dismissing as absurd the idea that
British Canada bore no relation to a war of defense, and retaliation,
he minced no words in holding Randolph's (and Jefferson's) old-
fashioned, 'economical,' States' Rights Republicanism responsible
for America's dire unpreparedness, which alone prevented immediate war.

Other War Hawks, incited by Randolph, inflamed by the news
of 'British-Savage War on the Wabash,' and disgusted by the
quibbling of such moderates as Macon, poured forth a torrent of
passionate oratory. They ceased only when Troup and others
sharply reminded them that the day of mere logocratic fighting
had long passed. The people now demanded defense by bayonet
and gunpowder. It is not necessary to talk the republic into war,
said Poindexter. 'The fact is far otherwise: — the National Spirit
is alive and every eye is directed, every finger pointed to the same
object.' [1] With 'the people ... indignant ... to the last degree,'
said Archer of Maryland, surely it is 'our imperious duty *to act.*' [2]

By December 19 every recommendation of the warlike report
had been carried, and by immense majorities. In no case did the
opposition muster more than twenty-two votes. It was a striking
initial success. Yet the War Hawks had but scratched the surface.
After ten years of Jeffersonianism, the road leading to effective

---

[1] Poindexter to Mead, Dec. 12, 1811, *Poindexter MSS.* 'These considerations,' he
wrote, 'have kept me quiet in my seat, against many violent impulses to repel the
anomalies of John Randolph.'

[2] Stevenson Archer to Dr. Elijah Davis, Dec. 4, 1811, Maryland Hist. Soc., *Misc. MSS.*

resistance by the sword was one of great difficulties, filled with vexatious delays. As Speaker Clay well knew, the mills of republican government ground slowly, and often turned out a poor product.

While bills to transmute warlike resolutions into realities were being prepared, these preliminary debates provoked extended comment which revealed in both parties schism and uncertainty.

Singular indeed was the attitude of the radical Federalists led by Quincy. All had been silent; yet all had voted for the warlike resolutions. Underestimating Clay's raw militia and public sentiment, convinced that Republicans could never even be kicked into war, they had concocted a scheme which the British Minister, their confidant, considered perverse, 'strange and dangerous.'

The idea of actual war is ludicrous, they said. Madison plays a game of brag in which all is staked on coercing England by threats of war. Even if Clay's insurgents force him into war, in its 'political effects,' wrote Quincy, war is preferable to non-importations and embargoes. Inevitably short and ruinous, war will oust the Republicans and ensure a solid Federalist peace. On the other hand, as will undoubtedly be the case, costly preparations and blustering threats without concessions by England, and without being followed by war, will be equally fatal to Republican popularity. 'Poor fellows they are in a sad dilemma,' exulted the Reverend Mr. Taggart. Whether submission or war 'the administration must sink.' [1]

Thus intent upon gaining party advantage by stabbing the Republicans (and the republic) in the back, by throwing democracy to the dogs, Quincy's Tories had voted with Clay's Young Americans.

Yet the Federalists were by no means united. Some were indignant at a British policy 'so foolish and unjust that it was no longer possible to defend it without betraying one's country.' [2]

---

[1] Foster to Wellesley, Dec. 11, 1811, *F.O.* 5:77; Quincy to Otis, Nov. 26, 1811, Morison, *H. G. Otis*, II, 33–34; Quincy, *Quincy*, p. 239 ff.; Taggart, *Letters*, pp. 372, 364–74.

[2] Serurier to Bassano, Dec. 20, 1811, *Aff. Étr.*, vol. 66.

Some honestly voted for defense measures. A few even turned 'War Federalists.' In private many merchants (to the disgust of Copenhagen Jackson) beseeched British friends and partners to repeal the orders.¹ Against them indignation 'is loud and universal from both parties,' reported Harrison Gray Otis. Even granting that Bonaparte's revocation was but nominal, and that Madison was his willing dupe, wrote this Boston Federalist, why should Britain 'not embrace any pretence for restoring harmony . . . especially *as it will, of consequence, be followed by hostility on the part of France*' which will force America into the war against Napoleon? This 'quite incomprehensible' and 'unscrupulous adherence of your Cabinet to an empty punctilio,' warned Otis, 'will too probably . . . sever for generations, perhaps forever, interests that have the most natural ties of affinity, and men who ought to feel and love like brethren.' ²

Even so, most Federalists still regarded war with England, whatever the provocation or the ultimate partisan advantage, as the worst possible evil. With Timothy Pickering they palliated English wrongs, feared their own 'pro-French' and 'anti-commercial' countrymen, and opposed all defense measures. Quincy himself, oddly enough, soon complained that most Federalists had indeed lost '*their national character*.' ³

---

¹ 'The wish for the removal of the Orders in Council is become general in America, and I have had several letters from federal friends to that effect — men who are amongst the most sensible politicians of that country. But the fact is, they can support no principle against the operation of their own interest and the prospect of that interest being much more materially affected. I do not say they are wrong, as merchants; but their credit, as politicians, suffers not a little by their conduct.' F. J. Jackson, Feb. 12, 1812, Jackson, G., *Diaries*, I, 327.

² H. G. Otis to H. Gray, Jan., 1812, Morison, *op. cit.*, II, 37–39. Otis's letter, and the reply of Prime Minister Perceval that the orders were 'absolutely essential,' became public in April–May, 1812 — at which time Otis was violent against war. 'Otis' circular to excite the prejudices against our Government in this state,' wrote Rev. Wm. Bentley, April 27, 1812, 'appeared at the same time with his Letter printed in England & used as a circular there. It leaves no just doubts that a most infamous game has been played.' Bentley, *Diary*, IV, 94.

³ Quincy, *Quincy*, p. 241. That these bullying War Hawks and 'their leaders, Jefferson & Madison, . . . do not intend active war with Great Britain I perfectly believe,' wrote Pickering; 'but that a war of *mere endurance* on our part . . . that should only destroy our commerce would be unwelcome to Jefferson I am far from thinking . . . such a passive war would save him and his party a world of trouble in contriving miserable and disgraceful shifts to soothe their Lord Napoleon and to impoverish the commercial states . . .' Pickering to Sen. Dana of Connecticut, Jan. 16, 1812, Prentiss, *Pickering*, pp. 79–80.

At this time, however, Federalist seaport editors echoed Josiah Quincy's idea that 'something *may* be gained and nothing *can* be lost by war.' They urged 'the anti-submission men, so valiant of tongue,' not to rely upon Madison's warlike manifesto and their own bloody resolutions — which the sloop-of-war *Hornet* was taking abroad, to flatter France (innocent France!) and to terrify England. Instead, the Liberty Boys should give a truce to 'whiffling and whimpering . . . and enable the nation to place itself in some other "armour and attitude" than that of the grovelling tortoise in its shell.' They deplored 'the interposition of Western tongues' and ridiculed the uncouth buckskin lawyers and tavern orators who thumped the tub of maritime rights, spouted drivel about the 'British massacre' of their 'shirt-tailed neighbors on the Wabash,' and by bluster conquered Canada while their vaunted militia ran away from an Indian war which their own agrarian cupidity had incited.

As for mousy Little Jemmy, they said, 'he is scared by the sound he himself has made.' His message was an electioneering device, but Speaker Clay's war hounds took him seriously! And what a tremendous barking we have had! But it is all bark and no bite. Madison already quiets them by tossing them now and then a snug bone of patronage. Speaker Clay's fiery young colts 'may strut and foam' but 'the little man in the white house' will keep a taut check-rein. In truth, jeered Editor Hanson, 'this glorious 12th congress . . . is of the same *kidney* as every other democratic congress — blown bladder-like, vapouring, pusillanimous, impotent, contemptible.' [1]

Denouncing such 'venal writers and editors' as Loyalist dregs of colonial days, the press generally acclaimed the new Congress. Significantly, Federalist editors of the hinterland declared that 'if they *will* give us war . . . we will not be backward in the cause of our country.' [2] This was not the odious Jefferson policy of embargoes and proclamations, said the Pittsburgh *Gazette*, but the true Washington policy, and if boldly pursued 'the United States

---

[1] Baltimore *Fed. Republican*, N.Y. *Eve. Post*, N.Y. *Herald*, *Connecticut Courant* (Hartford), Dec. 1811–Jan. 4, 1812.
[2] *Western Spectator*, in Baltimore *Fed. Republican*, Dec. 16, 1811.

may once more become respectable as an independent nation.' [1] Even the Federalist *United States Gazette* of Philadelphia hailed the new 'spirit of determined independence.' [2] Congress has found the spark, said the Boston *Patriot*: 'the fire of patriotism will blaze as pure in 1812 as in '76,' and a new band of heroes 'shall lead us to Quebec and conquest.' [3] Not in fifty years had Americans shown 'a Spirit of greater Unanimity,' said John Adams.[4] 'It will truly be a war of the *people of America* against the *government of England*,' said Editor Niles. Regardless of our 'too contemptible' Anglomen, 'from all quarters of the country,' from almost every state legislature, 'we have a common expression . . . almost universal . . . for war.' [5]

British Minister Foster, who had known only the submissive if prudent America of Jefferson, Madison, and Gallatin, was disconcerted and alarmed. Clay's raw militia had driven the regulars forward. They might yet, and soon, drive a timorous Madison-Gallatin Executive to 'ulterior measures' — even though 'to any man of sound understanding the absolute want of means in this Country to make war on us is so palpable that the very idea seems almost ridiculous.'

To offset these young fellows of eloquence and 'extreme want of calculation,' Foster violated his instructions by encouraging among 'persons who are the most exposed to be worked upon on every side, namely, the moderates of all parties,' the hope that the orders-in-council would soon be repealed. He did this, he said, 'as if by tacit agreement' with Madison, who on his part 'suffered the conjecture to spread that Mr. Monroe and myself had some understanding.' Madisonian indecision, War Hawk impetuosity, and Federalist perversity forced the British Minister to conclude 'that unless we change our system this Country,' though with few troops and only four frigates fit for sea, 'is disposed to go to war with us.' Indeed, this new Congress 'may not wait to hear if we shall change it.' [6]

---

[1] Pittsburgh *Gazette*, Dec. 13, 1811.   [2] *U.S. Gazette*, Dec. 6, 1811
[3] Boston *Patriot*, in Lex. *Reporter*, Feb. 1, 1812.
[4] Adams to Rush, Dec. 19, 1811, *Old Family Letters*, p. 367.
[5] *Niles' Register*, Dec. 7, 1811, Jan. 11, 1812.
[6] Foster to Wellesley, Dec. 11, 18, 1811, *F.O.* 5:77.

Murky and uncertain, however, was the situation into which Clay's Young Republicans were advancing, holding aloft the torch of war. Within the overwhelming majority that had voted for the warlike resolutions there existed every variety and degree of opinion as to 'the ulterior measure,' as to if, when, and how war should be made. The only certain elements were the left-wing War Hawks and the right-wing submissionists. In the shuffling center were not only 'moderates of all parties' but the Executive itself.

Despite assurances of cooperation for war, if Britain did not recede, the administration inspired little enthusiasm or confidence. From Gallatin, who was against war, to Monroe, who had become the most warlike (though with Pinkney, the new Attorney General, he beseeched British friends to repeal the orders),[1] the Cabinet officers were too optimistic as to England's yielding to war threats and the Non-Importation; too pessimistic as to America's ability to fight; too sluggish as in the past in preparing for an 'inevitable war.' Between old guard Executive and raw militia Congress were vital differences in age, temperament, and viewpoints.

Even though Madison was jibed at as a tool of the anti-war Gallatin, a politician 'pimping for reelection,' an old woman in Queen Dolly's French petticoat, he had backbone, talents, and a deep sense of responsibility. A closet statesman, however, by his caution even in normal times he provoked charges of timidity. There was about the hard-pressed, hard-working, Chief Executive a scholarly aloofness and dry coolness, an indirectness, and a prudent reluctance to return in kind Britain's fillips on the nose, which were peculiarly irritating to pepperpot youngsters, 'piping hot for war.'

As in the past, the President was enmeshed in the tortuous '*if* policy.' Neglecting impressment and other popular issues, Madison and Monroe stressed the British orders. To sustain their

---

[1] Loyal to Madison, whom he hoped to succeed, Monroe was distrusted by his former anti-Madison friends. His share in taking the country into war has been stressed (too much, it seems) by Joseph Gales, an editor of the *National Intelligencer*, who in 1857 wrote for that journal 'Recollections of the Civil History of the War of 1812' (nine numbers in *Natl. Intelligencer*, June 9–Sept. 12, 1857; see, especially, the last number), and in 1854 a memoir which has been printed by Hunt, G., 'Joseph Gales on the War Manifesto of 1812,' *Amer. Hist. Rev.*, XIII, 303–10. See, also, J. W. Pratt's sketch of Monroe in Bemis, S. F., ed., *The American Secretaries of State and their Diplomacy*, III, 201–77.

position they felt compelled to demand of a France of 'crafty contrivance and insatiate cupidity' [1] unmistakable proof that the decrees had been revoked, and a speedy adjustment of all grievances. Everything depended on France, Monroe constantly and angrily informed Serurier: when America had perfect amity with France, then America would proceed against England.[2] Such maneuvering by the President and his Foreign Secretary, both of whom had for years been devoted to a circuitous Jeffersonian diplomacy, engendered uncertainty and delay.

It was difficult for impatient young War Hawks to accept the Madison-Gallatin-Monroe view that England was thus given more time 'to reflect further and to change her policy,' [3] or that war preparations were *an appeal to the feelings of the foreign Gov[ernments]* ... accompanied with the most friendly explanations,' [4] or that Foster must not regard Congress's 'use of angry terms as a threat on the part of the Government.' [5] It was difficult, also, to appreciate the Executive view of a small-scale, inexpensive war. Even while appreciating Mr. Gallatin's task of financing war (a war to which he was averse), it was difficult to agree with his narrow bookkeeping dogma, which insisted that 'the means ought to be accurately squared with the object,' when the object to his mind was such that he could say that we ought 'not prepare to strike a blow with the violence of a Giant when the vigor of an ordinary man can accomplish the end.' [6] It was difficult, also, to see eye to eye with Mr. Monroe, who (not uninfluenced by his sectional prejudices, and by his former Quid Old Republicanism) remarked that 'in case of War it might be necessary to invade Canada, not as an object of the war but as a means to bring it to a satisfactory conclusion.' [7] It was a view which clashed with that of Porter and Johnson, Harper and Grundy, and with the popular demand, insistent after Tippecanoe, that Canada must be con-

---

[1] Madison to Barlow, Nov. 17, 1811, Madison, *Writings*, II, 519–20.
[2] Serurier to Bassano, Sept. 29, 1811 (and ff.), *Aff. Étr.*, vol. 66.
[3] Monroe to John Taylor of Caroline, June 13, 1812, *Monroe MSS.*
[4] Monroe to House For. Rel. Committee, March 31, 1812, Memo in *Samuel Smith MSS.*
[5] Foster to Wellesley, Dec. 18, 1811, *F.O.* 5:77.
[6] Wm. A. Burwell to W. C. Nicholas, Dec. 29, 1811, *Nicholas MSS.*
[7] Monroe to Taylor, June 13, 1812, *Monroe MSS.*

quered and retained; that, indeed, no peace should be made without this guaranty of security even if England restored impressed seamen and indemnified property losses.[1] The war party had different views and planned (complained Monroe) on 'a very different scale.'[2]

Of the regular troops in Congress, some would go along with Madison, some would lag far behind. All resented the 'infuriated' Young Republicans who would go far ahead. They quibbled about being pledged for war, canvassed its 'dreadful consequences,' and exhorted 'great caution & circumspection.' Such views, said Nelson of Virginia, 'were precisely those of the Executive.'[3] They indulged in sickly hopes, and would spin out negotiations. They feared the presidential candidacy of DeWitt Clinton, feared Giles, Smith, and other anti-Madison 'intriguants,' feared the strong national government war entailed, feared the preponderance Canada might give the North, feared (as Clay 'with some naïveté' admitted to Quincy)[4] that war might turn them out of office. Many of them feared that Madison, in trying to coerce England by the threats of those 'who think War is indispensably necessary,' might 'prime Congress up so high' that in the end he would be unable to 'prevent an explosion.'[5]

Throughout that winter — that winter of alarums and excursions, discontent, intrigue, and suspense; that winter of quakes and floods when, as John Adams remarked, 'not only "a slight Speck," but a black Cloud of War with England hangs over us'[6] — the old guard in Congress and in the Executive were to hamper the raw militia, retard preparations, damp the people's ardor, and thwart the 'golden opportunity' of a quick Canadian conquest. They blunted the edge of national expectations, and brought about at home and in England an uncertainty that was insidious — and most dangerous.

---

[1] See Phila. *Aurora*, Dec. 30, 1811 ff.; Lex. *Reporter*, Jan. 21, 1812 ff.

[2] Monroe to Taylor, June 13, 1812, *Monroe MSS.*

[3] Hugh Nelson to Dr. Chas. Everett, Dec. 4, 16, 1811, *Hugh Nelson MSS.*

[4] Quincy to H. G. Otis, Nov. 26, 1811, Morison, *Otis*, II, 33–34.

[5] John Taylor of Caroline to Monroe, Jan. 2, 1812, *Monroe MSS.*; Nelson to Everett, Nov. 13, Dec. 4, 16, 1811, *Nelson MSS.*

[6] Adams, *Corres. with Waterhouse*, p. 75; March 11, 1812.

If England only believed us to be in earnest, wrote Senator Cutts of New Hampshire to Plumer, she would unbend enough to prevent war. Yet for years we have submitted to her tyranny, and, such is the character of our government and people, we shall probably continue to submit. 'Resolutions . . . & some violent war speeches will satisfy the public mind for the present, time will allay its heat, and we shall calmly wait for some new outrage before we begin to bluster again.' [1] Such, too, was the British view. 'America fluctuates between her inclinations and her apprehensions,' said the ministerial London *Courier*. 'She seems always to stand TREMBLING and HESITATING on the slippery verge of a war; and to be incessantly tossed about at the mercy of every event; a condition which, of all others, most directly tends to *palsy* the spirit, and to destroy the confidence of a nation. Of all evils which can befall a people, the first is a government *without any fixed principles or plan.*' [2]

Throughout that winter there was friction between old guard Jeffersonians and insurgent Young Nationalists, which the Federalist, Quid, Clinton, and Giles-Smith factions on every occasion tried to capitalize. Madison had failed to weld 'the Majority, as that motley group in Congress is called.' [3] Could the unfledged politicians succeed? Could they weld together and make effective their fledgling nation's human and natural resources? Could they overcome their republic's deep-rooted pacifism, and offset peace-at-any-price Old Republicans who warned Madison against war-mongers 'destitute of honor as of genuine patriotism' and urged him to send a peace mission to London; [4] who exhorted — 'Oh Madison! in every Act beware!

---

[1] Charles Cutts to Wm. Plumer, Dec. 11, 1811, *Plumer MSS.*

[2] London *Courier*, Dec. 5, 1811 (much quoted by war editors) in Phila. *Aurora*, Feb. 12, Lex. *Reporter*, Feb. 29, *Niles' Register*, March 7, 1812.

[3] Randolph to Nicholson, Jan. 22, 1812, *Nicholson MSS.*

[4] Dr. Geo. Logan to Madison, Dec. 17, 1811, *Madison MSS.* Logan, Pennsylvania Quaker and former Republican senator (whose private attempt to end the French war of 1798 provoked the Logan Act), continued to urge Madison to throw America on the mercies of the Prince Regent. Curiously enough, this Quaker had formerly preferred war to Jefferson's Embargo, which he termed 'dastardly attacking the humble cottage, the comforts, the subsistence of unoffending women & children, instead of meeting in an open & honorable conflict the armed battalions of the enemy.' Logan, D. N., *Dr. George Logan*, p. 170.

For *one wrong step may spoil an Age of Care!*' and who questioned —

> 'Can War with all its hideous train
> Our reconcilement prove?
> Can ships destroy'd upon the main,
> Or desolation on the Plain,
> Or flaming roof, or bleeding vein,
> Or thousands of our brethren slain,
> Our injuries remove?' [1]

Even this early, the War Hawks were openly disgusted, and stung into a more passionate temper, by the old guard's shuffling conduct. With England continuing her piracies and atrocious impressments, 'it is extremely difficult to perceive how war can be avoided, without degrading the national character, still lower,' wrote Campbell of Tennessee. Yet 'many who vote for armies . . . will vote against war with England!!' [2] The loss to our children of the independence won by our fathers, wrote Grundy, can be prevented only by 'a firm & manly effort now.' [3] Indeed, so firmly convinced were many War Hawks that Britain would not recede, and so strongly insistent were they upon 'war without delay,' upon war now with preparations to follow, that even Johnson of Kentucky reported that such too-fiery spirits 'will have to be restrained for the present.' [4]

As chief of the War Hawks, Speaker Clay was in a key position of great power — and great responsibility. He was against further parleying with England, and he was confident that the republic could meet this crisis. But he would first prepare, speedily and wholeheartedly, augmenting the militia and privateers with regular troops and men-of-war, cost what they might. If he was forced to whip forward such timid moderates as Hugh Nelson and old John Smilie, he was at the same time forced to restrain such imprudent 'marplots' as Grundy. 'The most dangerous

---

[1] Saml. Harrison of Vt. to Madison, May 11, 1812, *Madison MSS.*

[2] Geo. W. Campbell to A. Jackson, Dec. 24, 1811, *Jackson MSS.* See, also, Poindexter to Mead, Dec. 12, 1811 and ff., *Poindexter MSS.*; letters of Bibb (Ky.), Dec. 29, 1811, in Richmond *Enquirer*, Jan. 25, 1812; Bibb and Hall (both of Ga.), Dec. 1, 11, 1811 in Phila. *Aurora*, Jan. 21, 1812.

[3] Grundy to A. Jackson, Dec. 24, 1811, *Jackson MSS.*

[4] R. M. Johnson to Jas. Barbour, Dec. 9, 1811, *Barbour MSS.*; also Washington letter of Dec. 20, 1811, in Pittsburgh *Gazette*, Jan. 10, 1812.

man in Congress for the administration and perhaps no man defies them more,' the bellicose Felix repeatedly declared to all and sundry that Madison and his old guard politicians 'should either fight or quit talking about it, or he would expose them in their true colours.' [1]

Thus, with schism and uncertainty on all sides, most discerningly did old John Adams remark that more to be dreaded than Old World outrages was 'the disease of the Mind in my own dear beloved Nation.' That this paralysis would be cured, and a militant Americanism achieved, the venerable patriot said he 'so wishes, so prays, so hopes and so undoubtedly believes.' [2]

Speaker Clay had perhaps been sensible in allowing Randolph free play for his ranting — for the odor of a noxious bug when crushed, said Adams, was more nauseous than its stings could be painful.[3] Yet Republican editors tried to crush 'England's sole advocate' with ridicule, depicting 'Milord' Randolph as a voodoo soothsayer, a petulant opera girl, a fishwife ' *"reeling it off"* in the true style of Xantippe.' They were pleased that Mr. Clay, who 'unites the qualities of a statesman with the manners of a gentleman, has lately called Randolph to order for his pert effrontery.' [4]

'Our Speaker is a fine man, gives universal satisfaction, and not even Randolph himself has as yet attempted to embarrass him,' reported John Adams Harper. 'He is a gentleman who commands respect and esteem, & keeps good order . . . *Mr. R. has brought his dog into the House only once this Session*, and then the Speaker immediately ordered the Doorkeeper to take *her* out.' [5] It was a revealing incident: in the past '*no one dared* turn the dogs cut.' [6]

---

[1] Taggart, *Letters*, pp. 375–76, Dec. 30, 1811.

[2] Adams to Rush, Jan. 15, 1812, *Old Family Letters*, pp. 293–94.

[3] *Ibid.*, same to same, Jan. 8, 1812, p. 368.

[4] Boston *Chronicle*, in Phila. *Aurora*, Jan. 21, 1812. 'This moody little gentleman is trying to frighten all the old women in the land out of the notion of encouraging their sons to battle, because, forsooth, there has been a comet, an earthquake, a storm and other natural events.... Even the Ethiopian, whose mind is dim and rayless as his complexion, would smile contemptuously on Mr. Randolph for his miserable augury.' Petersburg, Va., *Republican*, in *Aurora*, Feb. 18, 1812.

[5] Harper to Plumer, Dec. 2, 1811, *Plumer MSS.*

[6] Duane to Jefferson, Jan. 25, 1811, *Jefferson MSS.* The eccentric Virginian had other ways of provoking. He would arise, stare insolently about, deliberately lay aside

Clay so far had preserved his reputation for 'superior acquirements.' A critical Federalist grudgingly admitted that his appointments to committees were 'judicious,' though not exactly 'the images of clay of the administration,' and paid tribute to the new Speaker when he promptly set 'about to establish some new rules in the house, to give it, if possible, a little dignity.' Speaker Clay had made old Mr. Smilie take his seat, when that gentleman persisted in being out of order, with a polite request that was so firmly stated as to cause the Pennsylvania veteran to drop his spectacles in bewildered surprise; 'he sent to one member [who was] asleep, a message, either to go home to bed, or keep awake; and to others to take down their legs stretched on their tables.' The young Kentuckian seemed 'to have at present the respect of both parties.' Indeed, it was even a matter of regret, said the Federalist writer, referring to the 'very considerable accession ... of talents, in the person of the new members, of whom Mr. Clay is, perhaps, the foremost,' that the Speakership will prevent him from displaying those talents, 'in debate, which many have been anxious to witness.' [1]

Even Josiah Quincy from the floor praised Clay's efficiency and impartiality.[2] John Randolph was not then present, and one could only guess what he might have said about the upstart patriot from Virginia's Botany Bay. But neither the new Speaker nor the raw militia feared or much respected '*the great Mr. Quincy and the still greater Mr. Randolph.*' [3] Unlike the 'eunuch politicians' of the past, they were not men whom Randolph — or Tory Britain — could pummel at pleasure and 'with all the nonchalance of Sir Harry Wildair.'

---

buckskin gloves and riding whip, ostentatiously unwind and spread on the floor one after another of his silk neckerchiefs, then spread over them one after another of his topcoats, finally pointing with his bony forefinger and shrilling out, 'Mis — ter Speak — er!' would launch upon one of his abusive and rambling harangues. Binns, John, *Recollections*, p. 240; also, p. 211; Nov.–Dec., 1811. Binns, editor of the influential Philadelphia *Democratic Press*, had come to Washington 'to ascertain, as far as I was able, the probability of war ... and as well as in my power, by an honest representation of the public opinion in Pennsylvania, to encourage the declaration.'

[1] Wash. letters, Nov. 4, 8, 9, 11, Dec. 12, in *Relf's Phila. Gazette*, Nov. 6, 11, 14, Dec. 16, 1811.

[2] *Annals*, 12th, 1st, 576; Dec. 23, 1811.

[3] Harper to Plumer, Dec. 2, 1811, *Plumer MSS*.

In the following weeks Randolph, with his spleen against 'new men and new doctrines,' found much to criticize in Clay both as Speaker and as chief of the horde of young political Goths, who had swept east from the mountains and steppes of the hinterland, intent upon making good the demand for 'resistance by the sword.'

Chapter Twelve. Bloody Battles on Paper

A great many Gentlemen express themselves anxious for war, but they don't know how to get at it. (*Bayard.*)

Clay, Cheves, Lowndes & Calhoun ... confessedly the best informed & most liberal men of their party ... have regardless of the wishes of & consequences upon the administration uniformly declared themselves for War ... for a general & effective system. (*William Reed.*)

With great truth did Randolph say, 'the Speaker of the House ... was the second man in the nation.' (*Cheves.*)

'IN MEASURES relating to war, it is wisest, if you err at all, to err on the side of the largest force.' So asserted Clay on the last day of December, 1811, when he addressed the Committee of the Whole House in an effort to drive through the Additional Army Bill, the most important of effectuating measures.

This was an anti-administration bill, framed in the Senate by Giles and carried with Federalist votes. It called for twenty-five thousand additional five-year regulars instead of the ten thousand enlisted for three years that Madison wanted. Giles in sponsoring it had savagely attacked the Executive's sincerity and capacity for war, terming its proposals so feeble as to be 'as much trifling with the energies of the nation as inefficient commercial restrictions had heretofore been.' [1] To many it seemed that the Giles-Smith faction had joined with Quincy's Federalists 'in their object

---

[1] *Annals*, 12th, 1st, 41, Dec. 17, 1811.

of promoting war as a means to overthrow Mr. Madison and his administration.' [1] While 'deadly hostile to Mr. Monroe, and not much in *love* with Mr. Madison,' Giles, said such an ardent War Hawk as Harper, 'is not so *bad* a man as many suppose.' [2] Congress, at least, means war, said Smith (whose brother Robert had been ousted in favor of Monroe): it intends to call Madison's bluff, and 'will adopt such measures as will force the Executive into war.' [3]

In the House Giles's bill was greeted by a gust of passion. The moderates, joined by Porter and some of the older war men, argued that this increased force was not only contrary to the President's wishes but that it was unnecessary, too expensive, impracticable of enlistment, 'unrepublican,' and decidedly dangerous to civil liberties. Clay, however, contended that the force of ten thousand recommended by Madison was 'too great for peace, yet too small for war.' With spirit, yet not without tactful appeals for 'a candid and dispassionate' discussion, he undertook to demolish arguments based on Jeffersonian economy and abhorrence of 'Federalist' national armies. In 'the language of an independent patriot' (said young Niles), he insisted that even twenty-five thousand trained regulars added to the army (on paper) of ten thousand were not too many for the object in view: war — war with Britain and the conquest of her Canadian provinces.[4]

We must have regulars, said the Kentuckian, since our gallant militia are unsuited for long campaigns, for siege and garrison duty. And we must have a sufficient number actually in the field; enough to take, and to hold, Montreal and Upper Canada, Quebec and Lower Canada. Let us not underestimate the British regulars and Canadian militia, said Clay. Let us not delude ourselves that either the French or British inhabitants will treasonably fraternize with their invaders. Wisdom and true economy imperiously demand this larger force. It means all the differ-

---

[1] Foster to Wellesley, Dec. 18, 1812, *F.O.* 5:77; also Monroe's indignant letter on Giles to John Taylor, June 13, 1812, *Monroe MSS.*; and, for an account sympathetic to Giles, see Anderson, D. R., *Wm. Branch Giles*.

[2] Harper to Plumer, June 14, 1812, *Plumer MSS.*; also, Wm. C. Preston to F. Preston, Feb. 10, 1812, *Campbell-Preston MSS.*, on Giles, whom young Preston acclaimed as 'the Fox of America.'

[3] P. N. Nicholas to W. C. Nicholas, Dec. 13, 1811, *Nicholas MSS.*

[4] *Annals*, 12th, 1st, 596–602; and *Niles' Register*, Jan. 4, 1812.

ence between 'a short or protracted war, a war of vigor or a war of languor and imbecility.'

This is no peace-time army, he assured the older Jeffersonians, but a fighting army intended solely for this war. It is absurd to say that this 'petty force' might menace civil liberties. We have sufficient safeguards against any usurper or invader, in our state governments, in the American character — though Europe's 'tourists, whether on horse or foot, in verse or prose, have united in deprecating it,' and in the boundless reaches of our great Western Country, where Liberty and Union will always find refuge and support.

At the same time Clay proposed a compromise amendment which lessened the immediate strain upon the Treasury, as he was at pains to point out to such administration stalwarts as Smilie, who constantly avowed they would never spend one shilling unnecessarily. By it the officers of but eight of the thirteen new regiments could be at once commissioned, and paid. Only when their regiments had been recruited could the remaining officers be commissioned, and paid.

His maneuver, his apparent concession, caused Federalists to scoff. 'Even Mr. Speaker Clay, the new bantling of the day, from whom so much was expected,' said Hanson, 'has taken the side of "economy and cheapness."'[1] The new bantling, however, was a practical politician. His amendment was a wedge which split the opposition, and in the end brought about the passage of the bill.

Clay had deserted the Speaker's chair not only to drive through the Army Bill but to give an impetus to the whole war program. For the old guard's war pulse had noticeably weakened, so much so that Foster, convinced that the Executive will not allow itself to 'be pushed into a War with us,' reported that 'there never was a more favourable moment for Great Britain to impose almost what terms she pleases.'[2] Popular feeling was strong against

---

[1] Baltimore *Fed. Republican*, Jan. 4, 1812.

[2] Foster to Wellesley, Dec. 28, 1811, *F.O.* 5:77. 'All idea of war is abandoned,' reported Taggart — the administration men spread the report that the British orders will soon be repealed; Attorney General Pinkney and others are writing British friends urging repeal; while DeWitt Clinton's candidacy 'has already struck terror into... Madison ...Monroe, Gallatin & Co.' Taggart, *Letters*, Dec. 28, 30, 1811, pp. 370–75.

France, and vented itself when two French privateers were burned in November at Savannah, after a brawl in a brothel had caused street-fighting between French and American sailors. Continued captures by French privateers, 'hostilities as pronounced as were those of England,' complained Madison,[1] greatly embarrassed a President who based his technical system on Napoleon's professed revocation, and was paraded by his enemies as the dupe or hireling of France. Varied fears, hopes, rumors, and intrigues had already made the atmosphere 'turbid and unwholesome.'

Now, and throughout the session, the War Hawk leader felt the need for purging away this infectious indecision. He would convince timid moderates that the manifesto which the *Hornet* had taken to London was by no means an end in itself. He would convince carping editors (Duane and Irvine no less than Hanson) and the British Minister, who with his secretary often sat in the House gallery,[2] that this was truly 'Revolution No. 2' and no mere 'Resolution-ary War.'

With this in mind, Speaker Clay proceeded to make what he called general observations. For two hours he held the floor, 'animated and eloquent,' reported a Federalist; making an address upon which, said young Hezekiah Niles, 'eulogium is useless.' [3] He commanded the undivided attention of the House — no mean achievement at any time, and truly notable in a group of speechmakers already restive under their own patriotic verbiage, bombast, and bickering.[4]

Less floridly declamatory than Grundy or Johnson or Williams, or old Governor Wright, who was sometimes 'so infuriate as to

---

[1] Serurier to Bassano, Jan. 2, 1812, *Aff. Étr.*, vol. 67. Only the repeal of the orders can relieve poor Madison 'from the noose which Bona has so craftily wound round his delicate neck,' said a Wash. letter, Dec. 30, 1811, in the Clintonian N.Y. *Columbian*, Jan. 23, 1812.

[2] Nelson to Everett, Dec. 16, 1811, *Nelson MSS.*; and Foster, *MS. Notes*, I, 146. Later on Mr. Baker, Foster's secretary, alone attended the war debates — even though he thus provoked abusive comments.

[3] N.Y. *Eve. Post*, Jan. 3, 1812; *Niles' Register*, Jan. 4, 1812.

[4] 'Words, words, words appear still to be the rage. I am so much disgusted with the repetition of our wrongs and the *windy* storm which is sped from Capitol Hill to Canada, Novescotia, and even to Halifax, that I am sick to loathing if the most eloquent attempt to present them in a new dress to the imagination.' Poindexter to Mead, Dec. 12, 1811, *Poindexter MSS.*

be totally unintelligible,'[1] less abstract, more dramatic, more warmly persuasive than Calhoun or Lowndes or Cheves, the Kentucky orator was bold, exciting, convincing. His speech was well calculated to rouse the vigorous, to shame the timid. He spoke of *the* war; definite, immediate war, to regain peace and prosperity, to resist England's undeclared war, and to end the bastard ignominy of half-war, half-peace. To the question, 'What are we to gain by the war?' he made the ringing reply, 'What are we not to lose by peace? — Commerce, character, a nation's best treasure, honor!'

Clay said he would not dwell upon our long catalogue of wrongs. But he could not overlook impressment, an enormity which aroused every American to an indignation words could not adequately express. 'Not content with seizing upon all our property which falls within her rapacious grasp,' England violates 'the personal rights of our countrymen — rights which forever ought to be sacred.'

Yet 'if pecuniary considerations alone are to govern,' he asserted, 'there is sufficient motive for the war.' Under the orders-in-council we annually lose ten millions in revenue. Remove them and our revenue, now reduced to six millions, will again mount up to the sixteen millions of 1807. Some merchants would have us repeal the Non-Importation. Yet even if we were capable of such 'perfidy, the revenue would not be restored to its former state, the orders in council continuing. Without an export trade, which these orders prevent, inevitable ruin would ensue. . . . A nation that carries on an import trade, without an export trade to support it, must, in the end, be as certainly bankrupt as the individual would be who incurred an annual expenditure without an income.'

Obviously, said Clay, 'the real cause of British aggression is not to distress an enemy but to destroy a rival.' Surely Britain would not relinquish her trade with us, which has always so greatly favored her, and push us into war, if it were her sole purpose to deprive her enemy of a trade with us, which is of no vital consequence to France, and which has always been in our

---

[1] W. C. Preston to F. Preston, Feb. 10, 1812, *Campbell-Preston MSS.*

favor. 'No, sir; you must look for an explanation of her conduct in the jealousies of a rival. She sickens at your prosperity, and beholds, in your growth — your sails spread on every ocean, and your numerous seamen — the foundations of a power which, at no distant day, is to make her tremble for her naval superiority.'

We were but yesterday contending for the indirect West Indian trade, he said. Today we are asserting our right to the direct American trade, our right to export America's produce in America's ships to America's markets. 'Yield this point, and tomorrow intercourse between New York and New Orleans — between the planters on the James River and Richmond, will be interdicted. For, sir, the career of encroachment is never arrested by submission.'

With impassioned eloquence he emphasized that this was an assertion of American nationality, an American war. He scoffed down the submissionist view that since England was fighting 'the arch-enemy of mankind' we should not weaken her exertions. England *our* friend? asked Clay. England fighting for *our* rights and liberties? England the champion of that international law she repeatedly and avowedly violates? What absurdity! Must we Americans continue to bear the actual cuffs of British arrogance and greed that we may escape a chimerical French subjugation? Must we drink British poison that we may avoid an imaginary Napoleonic dose?

'We are called upon to submit to debasement, dishonor, and disgrace — to bow the neck to royal insolence, as a course of preparation for manly resistance to Gallic invasion! What nation, what individual, was ever taught in the schools of ignominious submission these patriotic lessons of freedom and independence?' Surely our American republic was not so achieved. The anti-submission men of '76 'nobly fronted encroachment on its first appearance' in the form of petty taxes. A petty tax on tea, with all the monopolistic tyranny it implied, was enough to stir the Fathers into action. And they were much worse prepared than we — we, their sons, who are now compelled to fight, to resist colonial servitude, if we are to keep for ourselves and our children their hard-won independence.

The young Speaker asserted his confidence not only in America's resources but in her ability to call them forth and give them a fighting edge. Keenly sarcastic, he assailed the contention of Randolph and many others that republics could not stand the shock of war, and should defend themselves only when invaded. Is it not equivalent to invasion, he demanded, when Britain scours our coast, enslaves our seamen, plunders our merchants, and prevents the produce of our farmers from finding their natural markets? When essential rights are thus invaded, shall we submit? 'When the burglar is at our door, shall we bravely sally forth and repel his felonious entrance, or meanly skulk within the cells of the castle?'

Yet it is said that we dare not defend ourselves. For war, say our alarmists, will oust the Republicans and make for a disgraceful peace. Craven and unwarranted fears! 'What! shall it be said, that our *amor patriae* is located at these desks; that we pusillanimously cling to our seats here, rather than boldly vindicate the most inestimable rights of the country? Whilst the heroic Daveiss and his gallant associates, exposed to all the perils of treacherous savage warfare, are sacrificing themselves for the good of their country, shall we shrink from our duty?'

The speech of this 'new bantling of the day,' of 'the celebrated Mr. Clay,' was widely reprinted, praised, censured, and generally discussed. But the printed words could not revivify his peculiar dramatic powers, the deep hush that fell upon the chamber, or the eagerness with which those on the floor and in the galleries leaned forward. The audience heard again the heroic strains of America's Revolutionary Seventies, and were thrilled as their fathers had been thrilled by Patrick Henry.

Our Speaker has given us 'a flow of eloquence and animation seldom equalled,' said a veteran member of the House, with 'facts and truths not to be denied or gainsaid.' [1] His speech, said young Niles, breathes patriotism in 'every line and word.' [2] Our own party annals, reported a Federalist, should be proud to record this address: it 'breathed not *submission, nor aught of Commercial*

---

[1] Adam Boyd, *Annals*, 12th, 1st, 604.
[2] *Niles' Register*, Jan. 4, 1812. Also, N.Y. *Columbian*, Jan. 16, 1812.

restrictions to subdue our enemies to justice; but *open, manly old fashioned war.*[1] From the British Isles, later on, came the report that Mr. Speaker Clay had made it plain to all the world that America now had a party 'neither French nor British, but genuinely American,' a party determined to defend by war its neutral and national rights unless the Tories speedily changed their policy.[2]

Clay had set the tone for the ensuing debates on the Army Bill — and on the question of war. His arguments were reiterated by the War Hawks. They were quibbled over by the moderates, who insisted upon caution, the selfsame emasculating caution of the past. They were criticized by Quids and Federalists, whose theme was submission, prudent submission to the British Colossus, mistress of the seas and vast possessions; a power unhumbled by Napoleon, a power which thrived on war and was much stronger now than in '76.

Although the peace men noted that the cry for maritime rights was loudest in the hinterland; contended that a war over impressment meant fighting for British deserters as well as for enslaved Americans; asserted that Western land-hunger rather than British intrigue was responsible for the Indian war; and held France equally culpable with England, none, not even Randolph, denied that cause for war existed, and for years had existed. When stripped down, their argument (as with Jeffersonians formerly) was that war, however just, was inexpedient.

Our means are inadequate, they contended, our objects unattainable; our present evils will increase a thousand-fold. A war which will destroy our seaports is too high a price to pay for liberty in Mr. Clay's backwoods; Canada's frozen wilds are too drab a lure. A war with England to force a relatively insignificant export trade to France would be suicidal. We were better pre-

---

[1] N.Y. *Eve. Post*, Jan. 3, 1812. Editor Coleman on second reading felt compelled to differ with his 'respected correspondent at Washington' as to 'the celebrated Mr. Clay.... The truth is ... this Mr. Clay understands playing the demagogue as well as the best of 'em, and he employs the old, but not worn out, machinery of prejudice against England and partiality for France, with as daring and perhaps as adroit a hand as the best of 'em.' *Ibid.*, Jan. 10, 1812.

[2] *Monthly Magazine*, Belfast, in Richmond *Enquirer*, May 22, 1812.

pared to fight in 1807, before the Embargo and its ruinous train. Why fight now, when our Treasury is empty; when Spain, and Russia too, it appears, have become mighty Britain's allies; when we are so unprepared that the administration, admitting its failure to keep up commercial coercion or to make war, is asking us to lift the Non-Importation so as to import essential British blankets.[1]

There is no dishonor in submitting to insuperable evils, said the peace men. Yet our impetuous young Speaker, a chivalrous Quixote, a heedless duellist, for this 'bubble of National Honor' would thrust us into a bloody conflict which will annihilate all commerce, embog us in taxes and debts, and perhaps subject us to the former British colonialism. Because of Bonaparte's enmity for us and his lust for world dominion, even victory would mean the destruction by him, eventually, of our independence. Shall we, then, plunge to our ruin merely to say that we acted like men of spirit?

Yet to avoid war, countered Clay's Young Republicans, we have receded until England's debasing system of submission and poverty, so notorious in Ireland and India, is already gangrening America's heart and soul. The paw of the British Lion crushes us even more than in '76. A free export trade is but one object of the war, they said, discussing the long-continued and 'crying enormity of impressment' (the horrors of which came home when impressed Americans on the *Little Belt* in May had been compelled by their British enslavers to fight against their own country, one of them being killed); the ever-mounting millions in property plundered under the orders-in-council (surely a far less 'quixotic' cause for war than the 'pitiful tax on tea' in '76); the revival of savage atrocities by British-armed Indians; and the 1811 crops of

---

[1] That the Executive should be so generally criticized for its incapacity and indecision was not surprising, said *Niles' Register*, March 7, 1812. Although our manufacturers are begging for orders, this ' "ridiculous mouse" comes out of the WAR DEPARTMENT,' this pernicious request by Secretary Eustis, 'the very "god of war" himself,' for British blankets for our Indians. Presumably, he will next want British army equipment admitted. See, also, Lex. *Reporter*, Jan. 21, 1812, ff. Francis James Jackson's remark, of Feb. 12, 1812, was revealing as to the effect in England: 'The Yankees you see are giving in, amidst all their bluster and outcry, and cannot do without some of our manufactures.' Jackson, *Diaries*, I, 327.

the great staples of tobacco and cotton, which were 'rotting at home, waiting for the repeal of Britain's monopolistic orders-in-council.' America's flag, they insisted, must protect America's farmers, seamen, and legitimate non-contraband produce. Even if we export less to France — and much less now because of Britain's illegal monopoly, be it noted — are we therefore to abandon our neutral and national rights? Or are we to give the world a lasting memento that American liberties are not to be invaded with impunity?

A war for national character is not quixotic, nor are its objects unattainable, come what may. Honor to us, individually, means more than mercantile profits; why not to us as a nation? Let us have done with the yardstick of sordid avarice! Let us have done with craven fear! If this unwelcome war be just, as is universally acknowledged, if this war of defense be necessary, as the nation is convinced, then let it be commenced and aggressively prosecuted.

And war is not inexpedient, they asserted. There is no danger of a land invasion: Britain is occupied abroad, while at home, her manufacturers are protesting bitterly at being deprived of our markets by the Non-Importation, and her unemployed and starving people have begun to riot. Her naval depredations cannot be much greater than at present. On our part, a single campaign will give us Canada and crush forever Britain's Indian allies. War has its evils, to be sure. But a continuance of our 'temporizing and vibrating policy,' our wordy, do-nothing, '*if* policy' which unnerves and paralyzes, will bring about a debasement more calamitous than war's temporary evils — 'a lasting and mortal disease, national ignominy.' If we but unite and exert ourselves, if we but do justice to ourselves and future Americans, this second struggle for independence will be no less glorious than the first.

Carried back to the days when he deserted Princeton to fight Cornwallis and Tarleton, 'Father' Macon astonished everybody by a fiery war speech. Other moderates were swept along. Young Pickens fairly throbbed with passionate idealism; old Rhea was angry and rambling; Williams blustering; Lowndes coolly intellectual. Stanford, the Quid, groaned that the anti-war Republican dogma of '98 was being jettisoned. Sheffey unloosed heavy batteries of trade statistics, and talked of 'practical' as opposed to 'romantic' ideas of national honor. Smilie, Findley, and Boyd hesitated, twisted, and cautioned. Old Widgery of Maine, hardly 'a Herculean adversary to Mr. Clay in debate,' [1] opposed the Speaker's regulars, yet he spiritedly declared that New England's militia alone would take Canada. As spirited but more realistic were young Harper, Calhoun, and Troup. Reiterating Clay's argument that the war would be no holiday militia campaign, they insisted that liberal and energetic preparations now would in the end be true economy of blood and treasure, and make all the difference between 'a war of vigor' and 'a war of imbecility.'

Undermined by Clay's compromise amendment and routed by impetuous arguments, the old guard at last gave way — 'contrary to the known wishes of the President.' Only a small group led by Smilie still heeded (as Federalists put it) the 'confidential and private' tones of Madison's 'twofold language,' which called upon Congress 'disgracefully to tread back their steps.' [2] On January 6 the amended Army Bill was passed by a vote of 94 to 34. Its amendments were rejected by the Senate; but the House had so committed itself that on January 9 it accepted Giles's original twenty-five thousand bill.

Would Madison accept this 'anti-ministerial' measure? Though he still privately objected to it,[3] he gave way — and his action was promptly termed base subservience to a violent faction whose support was necessary for his renomination. On January 11 he signed the bill sent him by a Congress whose leaders (said Foster)

---

[1] Phila. *Aurora*, Jan. 8, 1812.

[2] Baltimore *Fed. Republican*, Jan. 7; *Connecticut Mirror*, in Pittsburgh *Gazette*, March 6; *Connecticut Courant*, April 8, 1812.

[3] From a 'mixture of good and bad, avowed and disguised motives,' Congress, 'to enable the Executive to step at once into Canada... have provided, after two months delay, for a regular force requiring twelve to raise it.' Madison to Jefferson, Feb. 7, 1812, Madison, *Writings*, II, 526. Later, on April 8, 1812, the act was amended so as to allow enlistments up to 15,000 for 18 months, instead of 5 years, thus meeting the objection that long-term enlistments (despite the ample land bounties, which Clay considered strong inducements) were well nigh impossible in an America of cheap lands and high wages.

seemed to be 'pushing for measures so decisive as to leave him no retreat,' no escape from outright war.[1]

'The *Rubicon is passed*,' exulted Niles. 'A strong indication of expected war,' said the Lexington *Reporter*, bellwether of Western opinion: 'the blood of our farmers on the Wabash, and the blood of our impressed seamen' cries out against further '*over cautious deliberation*' on economy, and against further submission based on hopes of some 'plausible *deceptious* propositions' England might make. Congress, it was generally said, 'gives elasticity to the hopes and expectations of the people.' With the valor of peace, stated the Boston *Patriot*, for years 'we have repeatedly wiped the spittle from our face.' Now, after England's 'continued series of aggressions that could not be endured were we her colonies,' we are forced to say ' "*What mean ye?*" and to prepare for "broken heads and bloody noses" if the answer is uncivil.'[2]

The Army Bill, reported Serurier, was decisive proof that the Americans, while differing as to method, were united as to object. The people and their representatives, who were most concerned with England's aggressions upon their dearest interests, had outstripped a President who seemed most concerned about France's failure to sustain his system of diplomacy. An adjustment with France, which now seemed imminent, would mean war 'as soon as some Corps can march into Canada,' he wrote. 'They take to arms with regret; they take them slowly; but they will not quit them easily.'[3]

The Young Republicans were elated over their victory and the people's response, although aware (as Lowndes said) that many of the old guard had not been so much disposed as obliged 'to vote rightly.'[4] The Army Bill, Clay informed his constituents, was 'the strongest war measure that could be adopted short of an actual declaration of war.' He had no doubt but that Congress before it rose would declare war on England, unless England

---

[1] Foster to Wellesley, Jan. 16, 1812, *F.O.* 5:84.

[2] *Niles' Register*, Jan. 11; Lex. *Reporter*, Jan. 18, 25, and Feb. 1 (q. Boston *Patriot* and Cincinnati *Liberty Hall*); Richmond *Enquirer*, Feb. 6, 1812.

[3] Serurier to Bassano, Jan. 12, 1812, *Aff. Étr.*, vol. 67.

[4] Lowndes to wife, Jan. 12, 1812, Ravenel, *Lowndes*, p. 92.

ceased her aggressions.[1] Significantly, Macon now agreed with the Speaker and his bold, hard-driving lieutenants as to war before adjournment: 'The return of the Hornet must settle the question.' [2]

While Clay's raw militia had measurably offset the uncertainty engendered by an Executive which seemed less intent upon harnessing the chariot of war than upon driving the old coach of diplomacy, Randolph, a diabolical gadfly, declared they could not muster forty-five votes for actual war. He asked if the House, having forced on Madison this huge unrecruitable army, would now place Mr. Speaker in command of the fire-eating colonels and hireling dragoons who were to win the liberty of the seas in the snows of Canada. It was as easy to go to war as to get a wife, shrilled Randolph. But many an ardent blockhead after vast exertions finds that he has married a shrew.[3] Equally provoking was Hanson, who in his journal of 'moral depravity and malicious slander' [4] ran a cartoon depicting the war men as monkeys in full regimentals, brandishing swords, mounted on terrapins which carried coals of fire on their backs, all making their ' "Rapid Descent Upon British Possessions." ' Henceforth submission men jeered not only at Madison's 'scarecrow plan of warfare' but at the War Hawks' 'Galloping Terrapins' and 'crustaceous Rosinantes.' [5]

---

[1] Clay, Jan. 4, 1812, Lex. *Reporter*, Jan. 18, 1812.

[2] Macon to Judge Nicholson, Jan. 7, 1812, *Nicholson MSS*.

[3] *Annals*, 12th, 1st, 707–16, and 719–28, Jan. 9, 10, 1812. Grundy, Wright, and others protested furiously that Randolph was 'drivelling out the debates,' but Clay allowed him to proceed. Randolph in melodramatic manner, asked if Cromwell was already knocking at the door of the hall, and in general conducted himself as dramatically as did Sheridan and Burke at the trial of Lord Hastings. All this was in the usual strain of Randolph — 'a man choleric, ardent, ambitious, bizarre,' said Serurier, 'of an eloquence harsh and savage, like his origin which is said to be Indian; a restless mischief-maker... who throws himself as by instinct into opposition... Such is the sole advocate' of England. Serurier to Bassano, Dec. 20, 1811, *Aff. Étr.*, vol. 66.

[4] Norfolk *Herald*, in N.Y. *Columbian*, Feb. 5, 1812.

[5] Baltimore *Fed. Republican*, Jan. 2, 4, 1812. A popular Federalist verse, from Hanson's journal (N.Y. *Eve. Post*, Feb. 4, 1812), ran:

'Huzza for our liberty boys
These are the days of our glory —
The days of true national joys,
When Terrapins gallop before ye.

Such critics were highly pleased at the furor caused by the Volunteer Bill, which was taken up on January 10. The great question here was whether the President could dispatch the fifty thousand one-year volunteers from the militia against Canada when the Constitution did not expressly empower him to use militia outside the country. It was a question on which Madison was equivocally silent; one which caused disheartening confusion; one which encouraged Foster to report that a slight British concession, 'a little management,' or better still a threatened attack on the seaports would 'bring them to our terms.' [1]

War Hawks joined with strict-constructionist 'old democrats' in this 'idle debate,' despite fervid assurances by citizen soldiers of their readiness to march into Canada at once — 'our swords leap, flaming from their scabbards, and cannot be returned unappeased.' [2] Porter, who first raised this issue, would expressly designate the volunteers for foreign service. But this provoked the objection that Congress should not try to circumvent that which (as Porter himself contended) the Constitution forbade. Bacon would get the consent of the states. Others would get the consent of the volunteers. Grundy and Johnson opposed any nationalization of the states' troops. It was even suggested by Republican doctrinaires that the volunteers might be held in check until the enemy invaded; then, to repel invasion, with all legality they could chase — and follow — the enemy over the Canadian border.

Taking high nationalistic ground, and advocating what Jefferson himself, oddly enough, called the 'common sense view,' [3] Clay and Cheves argued that the supreme national power of

---

> There's Porter and Grundy and Rhea
> In Congress who manfully vapour,
> Who draw their six dollars a day,
> And fight bloody battles *on paper!*
> Ah! this is true Terrapin War.'

[1] Foster to Wellesley, Jan. 16, 1812, *F.O.* 5:84.

[2] Lex. *Reporter*, Jan. 28, Feb. 29, 1812, quoting resolutions of Virginia, Vermont, and New Hampshire militia. The Green Mountain Boys, 'determined to submit no longer to *diplomatic chicanery, insult and injury*,' would repeat their glorious victories of the Revolution.

[3] Jefferson, whose dogma was the great stumbling-block, assured Madison (Feb. 19, June 6, 1812, *Jefferson MSS.*) that as to fighting in Canada or Florida the militia had none of 'those doubts which puzzle the lawyers of Congress & astonish common sense.'

TWO FEDERALIST CARICATURES, 1808 AND 1812

King Quilldriver's Experiments on National Defence. By Peter Pencil, 1808. (See page 286.)
Rapid Descent upon British Possessions. Baltimore 'Federal Republican,' January 4, 1812

declaring and making war carried with it the right to employ the volunteer militia in any way coextensive with the objects of the war. The conquest of Canada was essential, said Clay, since it was the one certain means of operating upon our enemy. Futile indeed would this sovereign war power be, he declared, if we did not exert the nation's every energy and resource to make vigorous and effective war.[1]

Such broad 'eternal principles of self-preservation' were roundly denounced. Porter and Grundy objected to an unlimited war power. Old Republicans were horrified by such Hamiltonian heresy. Federalists declared, ominously, that the sovereign states never would permit their militia to be sent, willy-nilly, to conquer Canada or Florida or Paraguay or China. Such high-toned doctrines, piped up Randolph, would disarm the states against a national army, enlisted from brothels and boozing kens, which might not only embark on this 'windmill Quixotic expedition to Quebec' but afterwards install their Burr or Wilkinson in yonder Presidential Palace.[2]

For a week the wordy lawyers milled about in a dense constitutional fog, with Clay and Cheves urging them boldly to leap the barrier of Jeffersonian States' Rights. Madison, they asserted, would unhesitatingly send the volunteers against Canada. The President neither confirmed nor denied their assertions. Yet he did give point to their demands for prompt action by a curt message, accompanied by notes exchanged with Foster, which indicated Britain's unabated hostility.[3] At length quibbling ceased — even if constitutional doubts persisted. On January 17 the 'common sense' insurgents carried their Volunteer Bill.

---

[1] *Annals*, 12th, 1st, 733, 743, Jan. 11, 1812.

[2] And all these evils were to be risked, he said, for the sake of conquering Canada — 'a barren, frozen wilderness — a country — so help me God! which, if the British Minister would make me a present of, I would not accept.... a wretched territory, filled with tories and refugees, who would soon prove a curse to the Union, by bringing new forces and allies to that party which is known by the name of the Essex Junto.' *Annals*, 12th, 1st, 774.

[3] Randolph (and others) regarded Madison's message of January 16, like his signing of the Army Bill, as bids for the support of his renomination by the War Hawks. 'He is whipping up & seems not disposed to be thrown out in the chase of *Patriotism*! Some however think that he is too late — that the die is cast — & that he stands not much better with his (nominal) friends, than with his enemies.' Randolph to Nicholson, Jan. 17, 1812, *Nicholson MSS*.

Turning to naval defense, Clay's National Republicans succeeded in overcoming the opposition of Smilie, Macon, and Boyd to the outfitting of existing warships. But when Cheves and Lowndes tried to add twelve ships-of-the-line and twenty frigates to the little navy of fifteen effective vessels they were overwhelmed, submerged, by agrarian Old Republican prejudices. Smilie's standpatters, emphasizing that Madison did not want these new ships, declared that a navy would be useless against Britain's thousand warships, would pauperize the country, involve us in constant war, and subvert civil liberties. Equally prejudiced were Western War Hawks. Grundy and Rhea abhorred all 'water animals.' McKee hotly insisted that the great mass of farmers would be oppressed for the benefit of a few pro-British merchants. While 'Kentucky' Johnson declared that only when our Second Revolution had been won, Canada annexed, commerce restored, and the Treasury filled to overflowing, would he even consider 'this ruinous system of a great navy.'

It was a violent flare-up, yet not unexpected. Speaker Clay well knew that the aversion to 'John Adams's Federalist navy' was even stronger than the aversion to 'Federalist standing armies.' He well knew that the Kentucky press, while red-hot against the Mistress of the Seas, was opposing a navy out of fear that it would 'give an overwhelming influence to the commercial interest.' [1] In view of these deep-rooted prejudices, sectional and partisan, there was much speculation as to what course Clay would take.

Here was 'the *real* Rubicon,' said Washington observers, the critical test for the Liberty Boys. Would Clay of Kentucky dare support an enlarged navy? Would the new bantling of the day join his backwoods colleagues and thus confirm the charge that agrarian cupidity alone urged a war which would enrich and populate the West in proportion to the injuries suffered by the seaboard? Or would he continue his rôle of independent patriot?

Speaker Clay crossed this Rubicon on January 22 when he 'spoke at length in favor of a navy, which was very unexpected.' [2]

[1] *Ky. Gazette*, in *Natl. Intelligencer*, Nov. 12, 1811; Lex. *Reporter*, March 21, 1812.
[2] Washington letter, in N.Y. *Columbian*, Jan. 25, 1812.

'The source of alarm is in ourselves!' he cried, assailing the 'chimerical apprehensions' of those who failed to see that 'every argument in favor of a power of protection on land applies, in some degree, to a power of protection on the sea.' [1] Even after we take Canada, if our enemy fails to do us justice, how can we continue the war without a navy? It is on the ocean that England's edicts operate, and it is on the ocean that America's rights in the end must be maintained. What was Federalist naval folly in 1798 might well be Republican naval wisdom in 1812, when our commerce is greatly expanded, our population and territory doubled, our national wealth tripled. The United States, he confidently asserted, needs 'only resolution, and a proper exertion of its immense resources, to command respect, and to vindicate every essential right.'

'In his usual masterly manner,' [2] he argued that the proposed force was not only essential but practicable. Such a navy could defend our maritime frontier from any single British ship-of-the-line or small squadron of frigates. Aided by privateers, it could inflict great injury upon British commerce. While far from viewing Britain's thousand warships with 'a despondent eye,' he insisted that construction towards this minimum force should begin at once. Have we so soon forgotten the lesson of the *Chesapeake*? asked Clay. Shall we withhold these inconsiderable additions only to reproach ourselves if New York is bombarded by a single British seventy-four? 'If we are not able to meet the wolves of the forest, shall we put up with the barking impudence of every petty cur that trips across our way? Because we cannot guard against every possible danger, shall we provide against none?'

Then, with what Randolph called his 'Kentucky suavity,' he appealed to his fellow Westerners, asserting that New Orleans, and with it the entire Western export trade, was at the mercy of a single British ship-of-the-line. He recalled how the West had agitated for its solitary outlet to the sea, and he looked into the future, stating that the convulsions of South America were far more challenging than those of Europe. If England should ac-

[1] *Annals*, 12th, 1st, 910–19; also, Mallory, *Clay*, I, 230–39.
[2] *Niles' Register*, Jan. 25, 1812.

quire not only East Florida but Cuba, thus making an English lake of the Gulf of Mexico, through which Western exports must pass, all Americans must tremble for the integrity of the Union, said Clay. How could Westerners, especially, 'contemplate such possible, nay, probable, events without desiring to see at least the commencement of such a naval establishment as would effectually protect the Mississippi?'

In a fitting climax to a splendid speech, Clay emphasized the interdependence of agriculture and commerce, and envisioned a powerfully knit Union made possible by a truly national government.

Commerce is a national interest, as broad as the Union, he said, referring with pride to the Ohio Valley's seafaring pioneers. And surely commerce is worth protecting, when, with but trifling aid from other sources, it has defrayed all the expenses of government since 1789 and extinguished half of the national debt. A navy is essential for its protection, for 'neglect to provide the one and you must abandon the other.' Let us protect it, he pleaded, not by taxing the land but by 'drawing from the sea itself, the resources with which its violated freedom should at all times be vindicated.' Diversified as our interests are, 'how admirably do they harmonize and blend together! We have only to make a proper use of the bounties spread before us, to render us prosperous and powerful. Such a navy as I contend for will form a new bond of connexion between the States, concentrating their hopes, their interests, and their affections.'

Alas, the Kentucky orator failed to win over Smilie's old guard faction or his own Western colleagues. With their opposition augmented by Gallatin's report on finances (truly an untimely and 'very bitter pill'), they continued to scoff at this 'Federalist scheme of permanent armaments and taxes.' Could Mr. Speaker's navy, they asked, repulse Tecumseh's hostiles or conquer Canada? Would it not invite on our shores the infamous British rape of Copenhagen? Even Williams, chairman of the Military Affairs Committee, who blustered about the army's 'sweeping over Canada with the resistless impetuosity of Niagara,' insisted that a navy would be 'of no use in the approaching contest.'

Of no avail were reductions in the number of proposed ships, or denunciations of 'violent geographical' prejudices, or frank reminders of the bruises in sovereignty and pocketbook suffered from Jefferson's neglect of the navy. The opposition was only further augmented when Josiah Quincy joined with Speaker Clay in emphasizing 'the essential connexion between such a naval force and the safety, prosperity, and existence, of our Union.' His arguments might have aided if most of his fellow Federalists had supported rather than opposed a navy, 'once their pride and hope,' and if he had presented them in a manner less open to the interpretation that 'Mr. Quincy threatens separation again, peaceably if we can, forcibly if we must — "a navy or separation." ' [1]

On January 27 the additional war vessels were rejected by the close vote of 62 to 59. With the sole exception of Clay, whose independence was thus clearly focussed, every Western member was against an increased navy. The shift of two votes — of a Grundy, so suspicious of Madison's sincerity for war, and a Johnson, so loudly concerned about impressed sailors; or of two New Englanders, Republican or Federalist — would have spelled victory. And victory here was important; psychologically, very important.

A few new frigates, wrote John Adams to Jefferson, enough to indicate a rejection of your deplorable policy of 'total neglect and absolute refusal of all maritime protection,' would have gone far in lessening New England's 'contumacious' anti-war spirit, in maintaining Republican supremacy in Massachusetts, and in assuring the merchants that the Union was much more than 'a brittle China vase, a house of ice, or a palace of glass.' [2] On the other hand, Quincy privately declared that the Federalists, 'so unnerving has this apprehension of war with England become,' had lost 'their national character.' Though we clamor against the Republicans 'for protecting us, as they call it, by commercial restrictions, we are

---

[1] J. Q. Adams to John Adams, July 13, 1812, Adams, J. Q., *Writings*, IV, 371. Also, *Annals*, 12th, 1st, 949–68; Quincy, *Quincy*, p. 239.

[2] Adams to Jefferson, June 28, 1812, Adams, John, *Works*, ed. C. F. Adams, X, 20; also, Adams to Rush, May 14, 1812, *Old Family Letters*, pp. 382–83. In reply to his old Revolutionary colleague Jefferson wrote of Indian customs, bones of mammoths, etc.

not willing to accept from them anything else,' not even a 'Federalist' navy. As a result the great mass of people are more deeply prejudiced against us as men who would basely yield every right to England, 'without struggle or preparation.' [1]

The navy debates brought clearly into view the tremendous obstacles confronting Clay and his colleagues when they set out to organize America's resources, to vitalize government, and to realize a nation strong in its union of states and capable of maintaining its independence. While 'everybody is persuaded that war is just, inevitable,' reported Serurier, the young House leaders are convinced that they must 'create in this nation that which is perhaps more indispensable yet than a navy, a national spirit.' [2] Yet they had already made a notable advance. The reduction of the anti-navy party to a bare majority of three, remarked Justice Story, showed how strongly traditional prejudices had been buffeted by these 'men of talents, of great talents.' [3]

Not unexpected was the 'contemptible ribaldry' of London's press on ' "the *lengthy* debates, whether six or two frigates shall be built to cope with the Navy of England," ' [4] but peculiarly interesting were Federalist comments on the pro-navy War Hawks.

'Clay, Cheves, Lowndes & Calhoun,' wrote Reed of Marblehead, 'are confessedly the best informed & most liberal men of their party, and from the commencement of the Session, have regardless of the wishes of & consequences upon the administration uniformly declared themselves for War.' They have refused to become the puppets of Gallatin, 'the arch Jugler,' who directs the Executive's scarecrow warfare. Cheves 'begins to manifest disgust and coldness towards the administration,' wrote Taggart. These men have 'too much talent, honour, and independence to keep up with this system of political juggling.' These new leaders have risen above party prejudice and 'the false glare of Democracy,' said Reed, 'are gentlemanly and apparently at least candid Men . . . in earnest for War . . . for a general & effective system.' They

[1] Quincy, *Quincy*, pp. 239, 241.
[2] Serurier to Bassano, Jan. 21, 1812, *Aff. Étr.*, vol. 67.
[3] Story, *Joseph Story*, I, 215–21; Feb. 16, 18, 1812.
[4] *Natl. Intelligencer*, Apr. 14, 1812, q. London *Courier*.

have 'so notoriously outstripped the administration,' both men reported, that the Republicans more than ever are in a woeful dilemma. Without concessions by England, they cannot now retreat without irretrievable disgrace. Yet if they go ahead, they will ruin their party by an inevitably disastrous war.[1]

Speaker Clay and his Young Nationalists were determined to go ahead. They hammered out bills for ordnance, bills for equipment and supplies, bills for Mounted Rangers on the frontier, bills for coastal defense; organizing bills, supplementary army, militia, and naval bills. They were often forced back or to the side, often compelled to compromise, to modify, to omit, and to revise. Yet with persistent energy and indomitable courage, they went ahead.

In February, however, their majority had become fluctuating, uncertain, and with morbid pleasure the anti-war men painted a gloomy picture. The old guard, they said, were resentful at the successive demands of these rough-riding boys, and had a deadly fear of taxes. Paper soldiers were yet to be recruited by Secretary Eustis, 'the little god of War & Company,' and yet to be commanded by 'Granny' Dearborn, whom Madison had appointed 'Generalissimo of the Terrapin Army.' Everyone was looking in fear and hope to Foster. The President, they said, was delaying war measures, intriguing for renomination, and trying to escape his dilemma by proposing the rejected Monroe-Pinkney Treaty of 1806. The Cabinet was divided, with peace sentiment dominant. Congress, without confidence in Madison, was split into many factions.

It was a gloomy picture that the Federalists painted, but the young War Hawks were confident, especially those like Speaker Clay, Poindexter of Mississippi, and Troup of Georgia, who had had some experience with the vagaries and fears and complexities of legislators. In the same vein of light sarcasm which the Kentuckian had used with Quincy, as to regular troops who feared losing their seats in Congress, George Poindexter reported: 'We are jogging on with our war measures, not precisely with the Celerity of a Napoleon, but with a full determination, as expressed

---

[1] Wm. Reed to Pickering, Feb. 18, 1812, *Pickering MSS.*; Taggart, *Letters*, pp. 376–82, Jan. 20, 22, Feb. 6, 1812.

by many able Orators in Debate, to give a dreadful blow when we do strike; or as Mr. Rhea of Tennessee very eloquently observed, "we will not go about a thing 'till we are ready to do a thing." And besides, we have not forgotten the trite adage of our Great Grand Mothers, "There is luck in leisure"; by the strict observance of which sage Maxim many honest people have saved their necks, and, what is better, many old maids their virginity. Do not be disheartened at this *grave* account of our deliberations. We really do intend to pull John Bull by the nose, that is if he had rather be pulled by the nose than to open his ears and grant us our humble petition for indemnity for past wrongs and security against their repetition.' [1] George Troup, more serious in his complaints of a hesitant and fearful old guard, declared that 'for myself, I denounce all further temporizing or indecision; and, our Foreign relations continuing the same, nothing but a declaration of war or an open abandonment of the contest will satisfy me.' [2]

It was admitted by Federalists that 'the scarecrow or Presidential party' was still outweighed by those whom 'nothing short of War will satisfy.' [3] Convinced that in a war with Britain 'more is to be apprehended from the barrenness of the country — from thirst & famine, than from the shafts of the Enemy,' Randolph was alarmed by the persistency of those 'hot-headed enthusiasts who have run the Government into the most serious difficulties by their rash precipitation.' [4] Of the war majority, said Foster, some forty to fifty House members 'wish for War at all events; and about

---

[1] Poindexter to Mead, Jan. 25, 1812, *Poindexter MSS.*

[2] Troup to Mitchell, Feb. 12, 1812, Harden, *Troup*, p. 107. 'Nothing short of this,' said Troup, 'can satisfy the just expectations of the Southern people, who have been bearing the brunt of the restrictive system from the beginning.'

[3] Reed to Pickering, Feb. 18, 1812, *Pickering MSS.*; Taggart, *Letters*, p. 376 ff. Federalist editors still jeeringly said, N.Y. *Eve. Post*, Feb. 4, 1812 —

> 'Poor Madison the tremors has got,
> 'Bout this same arming the nation,
> Too far to retract, he cannot
> Go on — and he loses his station...
> As to powder and bullets and swords,
> For as they were never intended,
> They're a parcel of high sounding words
> But never to *action* extended...
> O! this is *great* Terrapin War!'

[4] Randolph to R. K. Randolph, Feb. 7, 1812, *Randolph MSS.*; and same to Nicholson, Dec. 20, 1811, *Nicholson MSS.*

the same number' would welcome concessions sufficient to enable them with propriety 'to *back out.*' [1]

The British Minister was disturbed by a persistent rumor that the House Committee on Foreign Relations was about to report in favor of immediate war. Since early in the session Grundy had been scheming to force the great issue, it was said, in concert with Federalists 'who wish to expose the Government.' Porter, the chairman of the committee, had become more of a Madisonian than an insurgent; yet such members as Grundy, Calhoun, Harper, and Desha might not wait longer either for England's answer by the *Hornet* or for a presidential message recommending war. The Executive, however, forestalled these men, reported Foster, by making known through 'two Members of the Government' that Madison 'would not consider himself authorized to send out of the limits of the Country the Volunteers from the Militia already voted,' and, through Porter, by 'amusing them with propositions for raising a more Effective force.' [2]

With the war men in the saddle and England unbending, yet with the Executive retarding decisive measures, Bayard was 'obliged to think that we shall have the war, not instantly but before the year goes round.' [3] They 'find it almost as difficult to get men and money as to get the Orders in Council taken off,' he said.[4] 'Shall we have War? That is the question you want answered. *So, do, I,*' wrote Felix Grundy to Andrew Jackson, venting his disgust at a temporizing Executive. 'I thought sometime ago, there was no doubt. But, if in six weeks only one man [Dearborn] out of 25,000 is furnished, how long will it take to furnish 25,000?' [5]

---

[1] Foster to Wellesley, Feb. 13, 1812, *F.O.* 5:84.

[2] *Ibid.*, same to same, Jan. 30, Feb. 13, 29, 1812; also, N.Y. *Eve. Post*, Jan. 6, 1812 on 'marplot' Grundy. Foster was kept well informed by Key (and Randolph, perhaps) of the Foreign Relations Committee.

[3] Bayard to A. Bayard, Feb. 13, 1812, Bayard, *Papers*, p. 192.

[4] Bayard to Rodney, Jan. 26, 1812, Bayard, *Letters*, pp. 13–14. The war men, said a satirist, were like mice discussing, bombastically and vainly, how to bell the British cat (N.Y. *Commercial Advertiser*, in Pittsburgh *Gazette*, Feb. 23, 1812) —

> 'One *Wright* good Mouse would break his jaws,
> If he could only slit his paws;
> Another mov'd, who look'd like *Clay*
> To tear his whiskers right away.'

[5] Grundy to Jackson, Feb. 12, 1812, *Jackson MSS*.

It will take the President at least a year to recruit the regulars, answered no less a person than Porter, in the House on February 18. As for the volunteers, Madison cannot, and will not, march them outside the country, despite the Hamiltonian nationalistic doctrines of Cheves and Clay. He proposed a new army of twenty thousand regulars and volunteers, expressly designated for foreign service. His motion, without debate, was dismissed that day by a vote of 58 to 49. While the vote showed, in general, a North-South cleavage,[1] it appeared that most of the war men considered the forces already voted, while open to changes, to be sufficient if only the Executive energetically exercised its powers.

Foster reported that Porter's administration-inspired maneuver had failed to check the war spirit.[2] Yet this vote was seized upon as proof that 'there will be no war.' Mars's thermometer, it was said, has fallen to 49 degrees, far below fever heat. It will not rise again 'on account of the chilling blasts from the Treasury.'[3]

The great question of 'scraping together the chink, the ready rhino,' had taken the stage in disconcerting fashion. Mr. Gallatin, with Smilie and other moderates, was determined to have, if war came, 'the smallest possible quantity of debt, perpetual taxation, military establishments, and other corrupting or anti-republican habits or institutions.'[4] He had at first given the impression that existing revenues aided by loans would suffice. But with the passage of the twenty-five thousand Army Bill he had changed his mind. He now wanted in addition to a loan of ten millions and doubled imposts, five millions from direct taxes.

Recoiling in dismay from the 'Federalist' excise, license, stamp and still duties proposed by Gallatin, the one-time Whiskey Rebel, Smilie's moderates bitterly reproached the Secretary for not informing them of his plans before they had committed themselves so deeply. Clay's War Hawks were 'excessively irritated.' They regarded this about-face on war financing as unexpected, and as evidence of what Grundy called 'rottenness in the state of

---

[1] See Pratt, *Expansionists*, pp. 146–47.
[2] Foster to Wellesley, Feb. 29, 1812, *F.O.* 5:84; see also, *Niles' Register*, Feb. 22, 1812.
[3] N.Y. *Eve. Post*, Feb. 21, 1812.
[4] Gallatin to Jefferson, March 10, 1812, Adams, *Gallatin*, pp. 455–56.

Denmark.' Old Governor Wright raged at Gallatin, and refused to drink 'the deleterious draught' of taxes which in 1800 had destroyed Federalism. Privately Harper and Grundy were almost as abusive as the anti-Gallatin editors who accused this 'Rat in the Treasury,' this 'dishonest apostate,' of betraying Cabinet secrets to Foster, of exerting a sinister influence over Madison, of attempting to chill the nation's ardor, *frighten the war-hawks*, and *blow up the cabinet.*[1]

Chortling with delight, Federalists reported that Pandora's box had been opened and the very devil let loose. Gallatin's budget, they said, is 'very chokey meat' for our war hounds. 'They had rather Old England should exist than pay a tax on Whiskey! Glorious patriots these!' Madison's mask is off! — Clay's hotspurs now see that Little Jemmy never intended war. By means of 'Mounseer' Gallatin's odious taxes he has crushed the mad war people. 'The wordy thunder of war resounds no more in Congress Hall. . . . Gallatin's *damper* seems to have entirely put out the fire.' Our gasconading Liberty Boys have concluded that

> 'A war of words, by wind, or paper,
> Than war with taxes, is much cheaper.'[2]

Mr. Gallatin's budget has had the expected effect of 'damping the military ardour,' wrote Foster. Furthermore, his report on last year's exports, which showed a trade with Britain and her allies of $38,000,000 and a trade with France and Italy of not much above $1,000,000, 'has served to expose the immensity of the sacrifice required by the advocates for Hostilities with Great Britain' — these quixotic patriots who insist, nevertheless, that national honor demands a war to free their exports from British monopoly and to secure their citizens from British impressment.[3]

Direct taxes, abhorred by an America of isolated farmers who had revolted against the tax collectors of King George, of President

---

[1] Harper to Plumer, Feb. 6, 17, 1812, *Plumer MSS.*; Grundy to Jackson, Feb. 12, 1812, *Jackson MSS.*; *Annals*, 12th, 1st, 846, 997 ff.; and Phila. *Aurora*, N.Y. *Columbian*, Jan.–Feb., 1812.

[2] N.Y. *Eve. Post*, Feb. 15, March 3, 1812; Pittsburgh *Gazette*, Feb. 23, 1812; Taggart, *Letters*, pp. 375–86; Bigelow, *Letters*, p. 323 ff.

[3] Foster to Wellesley, Jan. 31, 1812, *F.O.* 5:84.

Washington, and of President Adams, these were regarded as
the real test, the decisive Rubicon. Since our people for ten years
have been relieved of internal taxes by the 'sage of Monticello'
(for 'he with his empyrical phylosophy — his utopian politics . . . is
the cause of this disgusting, this frightful situation of the country'),
wrote the son of Senator Samuel Smith, 'no party, no administration that would impose a tax, would stand three months.' [1] That
was the view of many congressmen, as Troup reported. 'What —
you will ask — men ready to go to war who are not ready to vote
taxes? Yes; the very name is more terrible than 50,000 British
bayonets,' he wrote. 'There are only two alternatives: the expenses
being already authorized by law, we must repeal the law [creating
the Additional Army] or raise the money. To repeal the laws, will
be to abandon, in the most deliberate manner, the contest . . .' [2]

A climax had been reached, reported Bayard. If the majority
agree to lay taxes 'I shall believe them in earnest and determined
upon war, but till then I shall consider the whole as a game of
juggling in which the presidency and the loaves and fishes belonging to it are the objects.' [3]

Eager to meet this test, Speaker Clay with his usual confidence
and energy applied himself to whipping the motley majority
forward. War loans were not sufficient, he argued. Taxes were
necessary to pay the accruing interest on loans, to sustain government's credit, to avoid expedients which had made the Revolutionary paper not worth a Continental. 'Taxes must be laid . . . are
indispensably necessary,' said Clay. Some of those recommended
were 'not of the most agreeable description.' But the House would
select those least burdensome, apportioning them justly according
to the sections of the Union. And the people, he insisted, would
unquestionably support their representatives. 'The nation would
be unfaithful to itself if it withheld the requisite supplies. . . .

---

[1] John Spear Smith to S. Smith, Jan. 23, 1812, *S. Smith MSS.*

[2] Troup to Mitchell, Feb. 12, 1812, Harden, *Troup*, p. 107.

[3] Bayard to A. Bayard, Jan. 25, 1812, Bayard, *Papers*, p. 190. Senator Bradley,
typical old guard Republican, Bayard thus described to Rodney (Bayard, *Letters*,
pp. 13–14, Jan. 26, 1812) — 'Bradley says he has no objection to go to war, but . . . he
is against taxes, or loans, and he wishes to God that it was part of the constitution, that
Government should neither tax nor borrow, for the purpose of making war!'

Surely no man will hesitate to contribute his just *part* when *all* is at hazard.' [1]

Clay's views were accepted by most of the War Hawks. Even Grundy and Harper were induced to overcome their 'excessive irritation,' and to argue that the sanctioning of taxes now, to be voted upon the declaration of war, was a necessary pledge of government's financial capacity and earnestness. The young insurgents were consolidated behind the Executive's budget. But could the Executive's regular troops be driven across this most formidable Rubicon?

Supported by such Young American editors as Niles and Ritchie,[2] and, after an initial anti-Gallatin outburst, by Western editors, Clay and his lieutenants resolutely undertook the task of persuading and coercing Congress. The regular troops, with Porter and such older war men as Widgery, Fisk, and Wright, twisted and squirmed and flinched. They tried for a postponement. They objected strenuously to taxes bearing most heavily upon their particular sections. They talked of adjourning to get the advice of their constituents, of waiting for dispatches from London, of 'anything and everything' that might delay a decision.

All of Clay's Kentucky boldness and suavity was called into play to dispel their fears, to smooth over violent sectional jealousies, and to get them in the mood of Gholson of Virginia, who at length declared he would swallow the whole patriotic draught of taxes even though it proved to be political hemlock at the 1812 elections. Randolph protested against 'out-of-door influences,' and said the older Republicans were being bludgeoned into war. But the young leaders persisted, and by force of character, intellect, and emotional conviction they succeeded in driving through Gallatin's budget, the last major item of the preparedness program.

---

[1] Clay, in Lex. *Reporter*, Feb. 4, 22, 1812. Western sentiment was at first hostile: a Lexington toast on Feb. 22 was to 'Albert Gallatin and his budget — A friend to the country or not?' But Clay's views prevailed: the *Reporter*, March 14, 1812 ff., stated there was no objection 'to the paying of taxes. If any taxes are unequal and oppressive this year, alter them the next. *But no submission to Britain.*'

[2] While holding no love for Gallatin or his methods, Ritchie's Richmond *Enquirer*, Jan. 25, Feb. 8, 1812, urged Congress to 'Be Just and Fear Not!' *Niles' Register*, March 14, 1812, in the same strain declared the people would gladly bear taxes 'to defend their lives from the *tomahawk*, their persons from the *pressgang*, their government from TREASON, and their property from *theft* . . .' This was preeminently a war of the people: 'THE CAUSE IS THEIR OWN.'

On February 25 a loan of eleven millions, at six per cent, was carried by a vote of 92 to 29. On February 26 the Committee of the Whole accepted, 'without any change whatsoever,' fourteen resolutions bearing a heavy load of direct taxes. The House wrangled and quibbled. But by March 4 all the taxes had been approved, to be formally enacted into law upon the declaration of war 'against a European nation,' or, as Clay put it, in the event 'of the war into which we are about to be driven by the aggressions of England.'[1]

It was an impressive victory. 'If no Concessions be made,' reported Foster, 'War may ensue in the course of a Fortnight.' Not one regular has been recruited, yet the impatient war men place great reliance upon the militia and privateers.[2] Bayard said he would not be surprised if the great question was debated within that time. 'No war, no taxes, not a bad combination,' he wrote Rodney. 'How results the specific gravity — will the war float the taxes, or the taxes sink the war?' Speaker Clay's clever and importunate young men had as little respect for the people's money as the Federalists of '98. This being the case, 'you know what may be the consequences.'[3]

Despite rumors that the insurgents, their preparedness bills enacted, were about to stampede the administration and its regular troops into war, actual preparations were far from reassuring, and on this ground alone some delay seemed unavoidable. While the Executive was making 'all the necessary preparations for War, in case it should be necessary,' said Monroe, it would take months to recruit the army. During that time (so he informed Barlow) the door of negotiation would still be open to Britain.[4] The re-

---

[1] Clay, Feb. 28, in Lex. *Reporter*, March 7, 1812. He assured the West that the still tax was 'free from the vexatious incidents of an Excise,' that the stamp tax was 'confined to bank notes... and negotiable paper, leaving the great body of country transactions exempt from its operations.' See also, *Annals*, 12th, 1st, 1088–1155.

[2] Foster to Wellesley, Feb. 26, 1812, *F.O.* 5:84. Also, *U.S. Gazette*, March 7, 1812, for rumor that war would be voted by substantial majorities in both houses. On March 6, however, Foster reported to Wellesley (*F.O.* 5:84) that the rumor of war was perhaps being spread in order that Britain might 'strike the first Blow and thereby create the Irritation absolutely necessary... to raise an Army. The important fortress of Detroit is left unprotected... as a temptation...'

[3] Bayard to Rodney, March 6, 9, Feb. 27, Bayard, *Letters*, pp. 16–18.

[4] Monroe to Barlow, Feb. 24, March 21, 1812, *U.S. Ministers, Instructions 1808–1815* (State Dept.).

luctance of the administration to close that door, even though it
admitted that 'there never was a more hopeless prospect of an
amicable accommodation with Great Britain,' [1] was in itself a
formidable impediment to preparations. War men still complained of the torpor caused by the Executive's *if* policy, while the
Baltimore *Whig* and 'the violent War Hawk editors of the West'
increasingly cried out: 'How much of *dignity*, of *wealth* and *ir-
revocable time* have been sacrificed, by looking ever and anon across
the waves, instead of looking at home, and acting the part we
ought to have acted!' [2]

It was generally held by the people that Minister Barlow's
negotiations at Paris, as Clay reported on February 28, 'wore a
favorable aspect.' [3] Yet the Executive was far from sharing their
optimism, or their view that French wrongs and the embarrassments of Madisonian diplomacy should not obscure the essential
merits of the case against Britain, or delay action against the
greater aggressor. To Madison, Napoleon's evasive delays, continued depredations, and refusal to include the paramount subject
of indemnities in the projected (but never concluded) commercial
treaty which he dangled before Barlow, were peculiarly humiliating. With Executive hopes as to France dwindling, Monroe
constantly appealed to Serurier to sustain a President who, upon
the basis of Napoleon's 'revocation,' had selected the orders-in-
council as his one technical issue against Britain. Any delay in
preparing or in declaring war, reiterated Monroe to the French
Minister, would be 'due to the fact that we come to no conclusion
with France.' [4]

Speaker Clay, however, was not to be thus delayed. A few days
later when the Executive sent further admonitions to Barlow by the
dispatch ship *Wasp*, the War Hawk leader informed an impatient
Kentucky that there was 'not the slightest intention of delaying our
declaration of WAR until her return [from France].' [5]

---

[1] *Natl. Intelligencer*, Feb. 13, 1812; also, Madison to Jefferson, Feb. 7, March 6, 1812,
Madison, *Writings*, II, 525, 530.

[2] Baltimore *Whig*, in N.Y. *Columbian*, March 2, 1812; see, also, Geo. Bibb to Gov.
Scott, Feb. 23, 1812, in Lex. *Reporter*, March 7, 1812; and Bibb to Scott, Dec. 29, 1811, in
Richmond *Enquirer*, Jan. 25, 1812.

[3] Clay, in Lex. *Reporter*, March 7, 1812.

[4] Serurier to Bassano, March 2, 1812, Adams, *Hist. U.S.*, VI, 188.

[5] Clay, March 15, 1812, in Lex. *Reporter*, March 24, 1812.

Since the Executive departments now had before them the great (and little appreciated) task of transmuting congressional measures into the realities of men and money, it was generally understood that the final decision would not be attempted until the return, from England, of the long overdue *Hornet* — winged either with peace or war. At the same time it was possible that the issue might be forced before her arrival by impatient War Hawks, who with Desha of Kentucky were 'tired waiting' and believed both expediency and honor demanded 'acting.' [1] Clay himself in February had publicly hinted at circumstances which might well 'accelerate a declaration of war.' [2] Even so, the delay which now ensued was to become a long period of painful, insidious, and dangerous suspense.

For four months Speaker Clay and his 'boys' had struggled to put the republic 'into an armor and an attitude demanded by the crisis.' This had meant changing pacifist and partisan attitudes; modifying the dogma that power was always the enemy of liberty; forcing a merger of agrarian democracy with early Federalist nationalism — in short, an internal revolution. It was a gigantic task for such a short period, and for inexperienced legislators. Yet not since the First Congress had there been such vigor and energy. Despite the patchwork legislation enacted, a surprising degree of success had been attained after years of Jeffersonian 'utopian politics' and Madisonian 'whiffling and whimpering.'

The unprecedented number of measures, said the administration's *Intelligencer* with bland optimism, sufficiently rebuked all those who had 'exulted in their country's reputed imbecility and nakedness.' [3] Yet the great question, retorted both insurgent and Federalist editors, was the implementing of these bills by the Executive. Could any man truthfully say, asked Duane and Irvine, that Madison had kept pace with Congress, was pushing preparations, or that he was unequivocally for war? [4] Even the

---

[1] *Lex. Reporter*, March 24, 1812, letter of General Desha, March 10, 1812.
[2] *Ibid.*, Feb. 22, 1812, letter of Clay, Feb. 9, 1812.
[3] *Natl. Intelligencer*, March 19, 1812.
[4] Phila. *Aurora*, March 24, 1812, and *passim*; also, N.Y. *Eve. Post*, March 25, 1812. In a typical editorial Irvine of the Baltimore *Whig* ('the Smiths' paper') stated that

'non-partisan' Niles, with 'bitter mortification,' said that such savage jibes were justified by Madison's 'timid and temporizing management.' [1] Critical also of both Congress and the Executive were the many poets spawned by Revolution No. 2, who stressed the people's readiness for 'the glorious hap of war' and their impatience for 'the inspiring summons.' [2]

From Speaker Clay's district of Lexington, the focus of Western opinion, came angry condemnations of all 'Quid' (i.e., lukewarm or anti-war) Republicans, and impatient demands for 'CANADA and our arms!' Calling for 'either *federal* or democratical energy,' and an end to all 'half-way, *quid*, execrable measures and delays,' the Lexington *Reporter* said that from now on it would speak out boldly, just as long as government seemed to flinch, to be, 'as the British prints remark, tossed about by every wind which blows....
Fifteen states have supported congress, what more do congress wait for?' [3]

The West was importunate, and clear as to objectives. '*For what are we going to fight?*' thundered Andrew Jackson on March 7. Not for Britain's loot-swollen Tory aristocracy, France's 'apostate republican general,' or an Old World of assassin kings and exclusive privileges. 'But we are going to fight for the reestablishment of our national charector ... the protection of our maritime citizens, impressed on board British ships of war ... to vindicate our right to a free trade, and open a market for the productions of

---

Madison 'keeps as Secretary of the Treasury a dishonest apostate... retains a Secretary of War unfit for his station, and *detested* by the little army, which is distracted by his imbecility and intrigue... is reported to have nominated for Commander in Chief a gentleman who could hardly manoeuvre a regiment...' In *U.S. Gazette*, Feb. 7, 1812.

[1] *Niles' Register*, March 7, 1812.

[2] For example, the 'Spirit of America,' from Pittsburgh *Mercury*, in *Natl. Intelligencer*, March 24, 1812 —

> 'Why droops each ardent youth his head?
> Is it for fitful courage fled?...
> It is for endless dull debate
> That wastes occasion, while they wait
> The signal word to send them bound
> For British battlement and mound —
> Oh! for Montgomery's arm, they cry,
> To plant the eagle standard high,
> Wherever red-cross flag before
> Wav'd, from Au-Plait to Labrador.'

[3] Lex. *Reporter*, March 14; and, also, Jan. 21, 25, Feb. 29, 1812.

our soil, now perishing on our hands . . . in fine, to seek some indemnity for past injuries, some security against future aggressions, by the conquest of all the British dominions upon the continent of north america.' [1]

Our wordy warriors at Washington, said Federalist maritime
editors, are afraid to go ahead, and afraid to go back. The *Hornet*
has obviously failed to sting the British Lion into submission, yet
no sane person expects war. Our ships still go out, insurance rates
remain the same, and no one enlists for this mad anti-commercial
war to force a worthless trade with France, to please Bonaparte,
and to conquer the barren wastes of Canada. If government really
intends a war of bullets and blood, 'why is our shipping allowed to
run into certain capture?' But an embargo is also inconceivable:
after Jefferson's ruinous experiment 'you might as well talk of a
gallows to a widow whose husband has been hanged, as to talk of
an Embargo.'

Obvious even to the most Frenchified democrat, they said, is the
absurdity of a war conducted by Little Jemmy and such Revolutionary 'grannies' as Dearborn, who as Jefferson's Secretary of
War cut down and ruined our army; Wilkinson, who is generally
denounced as a traitor; and Doctor Eustis, who has not yet even
begun to recruit the Terrapin Army. Though it be part of
Madison's 'hollow and deceitful policy' to jockey the War Hawks
into supporting his renomination, he abhors a war which will
defeat his reelection. Through Gallatin and his 'back-stairs' men'
in Congress, the President will, and must, restrain the 'Mad Men
of Kentucky and Tennessee.' [2]

---

[1] Jackson, *Corres.*, I, 220–23; call for volunteers, March 7, 1812. 'The hour of national vengeance is now at hand [against] the eternal enemies of american prosperity,'
said Jackson. '*Who are we?* . . . are we the titled Slaves of George the third? the military
conscripts of Napoleon the great? or the frozen peasants of the Rusian Czar? No —
we are the free born sons of america; the citizens of the only republick now existing in
the world . . . *a free people compelled to reclaim by the power of their arms the right which god
has bestowed upon them, and which an infatuated King has said they shall not enjoy* . . . the free
sons of the west will never *submit to such degradation*.'

[2] N.Y. *Eve. Post*, Feb. 12, 18, March 10, 25, 1812; *Conn. Courant*, Apr. 8, 1812, *passim*.
The *Courant* on April 15 gave a Federalist summary of events: '*Memoranda*. Congress
in session five months — six dollars a day — "Time is money" — President sends
a gun-powder speech, but not in earnest — employs his back-stairs' men, as usual,
to give hints of his secret views and wishes — hard luck this time — Congress refractory
— war hawks ungovernable — vote to raise an additional army of twenty-five thousand
men and one . . . tremendous clatter of tongues . . . Treasury examined — found

Public opinion generally, as Speaker Clay well noted, daily became more fretful at a government which seemed, as in the past, to be '*waiting* to be driven by Britain' — a ruthless Tory Britain, said the legislators of New Jersey, with which 'further negotiation becomes idle and vain.' [1] Unquestionably '*peace as we now have it*, is disgraceful,' said the legislators of Virginia. While our inveterate enemy daily makes 'war upon us of the most aggravated species, a further indulgence of hope...is criminal.' [2] Yet why does government 'continue the farce of dispatch-vessels' and thus keep 'a degraded and indignant people in the labyrinth of affliction and despondency?' asked the Clintonian New York *Columbian*. [3] ' "Hope deferred maketh the heart sick," ' said Niles, inveighing against the 'extreme folly' of waiting further upon London after having for years in vain sent 'line upon line, and remonstrance upon remonstrance...message after message,...bundles of paper, mountains high, like Pelion upon Ossa.' [4]

The *Hornet* was 'sting enough!' cried the Lexington *Reporter*. Yet it now appears that the *Wasp* is being sent out 'with another *sting* in her tail — Mr. Gallatin's budget of taxes!!' And with it goes an account of how *war men* like Porter and Fisk opposed *war taxes*! Influenced by our few mercantile nabobs, 'British agents and the United States aristocracy,' it said, our '*quid* representatives and *quid* members of the administration... *who have never been able to form an opinion one way or the other... are now gaping for more deceptions*,' and are 'encouraging the British by their disgraceful delays.' And this, too, when British monopoly (depressing hemp to three dollars, cotton to twelve dollars, and tobacco to nine shillings), British press gangs, and British tomahawks daily wage cruel war upon the great mass of Americans. Our seamen continue to be

---

empty — great puzzle of politics — Senator Giles scolds the President... vote to lay on John Adams' taxes, with ample additions... War fever subsides — spirits wasted ... throats and lungs sore — take aim long, but dare not pull trigger — wait and gape for news from Europe... President contriving ways and means to secure his own election... terribly haunted by the ghost of the N. Yorker, DeWitt — fears him worse than John Bull... thinks of him by day, dreams of him by night...'

[1] *Annals*, 12th, 1st, 907–09, New Jersey Resolutions.
[2] *Ibid.*, pp. 112–14, Virginia Resolutions.
[3] N.Y. *Columbian*, March 13, 1812.
[4] *Niles' Register*, March 7, 1812; Dec. 7, 1811, ff.

impressed, and our farmers 'continue to be *ruined* and *murdered*.' [1]

Meanwhile the popular demand for Canada was quickened by fresh and harrowing accounts of Indian violence; by Canadian assertions that England would reject as allies neither America's redskins nor black slaves; [2] and by reports (little relished by Clay) that British officers at Malden on Lake Erie, when remonstrated with on the barbarity of employing Indians, had 'coolly replied, that if there was war, the American government would employ the *Kentuckians*!!!' [3]

'Our frontiers are deluged with blood,' read a St. Louis dispatch. 'NINE WOMEN . . . murdered . . . the SCALPING KNIFE and TOMAHAWK of *British savages, is now, again, devastating our frontier.*' [4] Government delays 'though every mail records some new circumstance of British villainy and cruelty,' raged Lexington's *Reporter*. 'On the ocean, British licenses are the only passport for our navigating . . . "*On our own territory, close by our own forts,* AMERICAN CITIZENS *are compelled to deny their country as the only safeguard from* BRITISH *tomahawks!*" Because "*the Indians receive a high price for the* SCALPS *of every* AMERICAN"!!' [5] The savages are 'instigated . . . by the British in Canada, any official declaration to the contrary notwithstanding,' said Niles of Baltimore: 'As it was in 1776 and 1794 — so it is now.' [6] Britain's ' "allies" ' will be rendered impotent only when Britain's Canada falls to our arms, '*and fall it will, and* MUST.' [7]

Meanwhile the people had pushed impressment — British 'indignity, abuse, and destruction of our seamen, and through

---

[1] Lex. *Reporter*, March 14, 21, 1812; see, also, Phila. *Aurora*, April 8, 1812.

[2] Montreal *Herald*, in Phila. *Aurora*, Feb. 5, 1812.

[3] Lex. *Reporter*, April 25, 1812; also, *Niles' Register*, March 7, 1812.

[4] Lex. *Reporter*, March 14, 1812; also, Phila. *Aurora*, Feb. 21, April 8, 1812 ff.; *Natl. Intelligencer*, March 3, 1812 ff.

[5] Lex. *Reporter*, April 4, 1812, q. 'a Kentuckian at Fort Madison.' Its accounts of 'MORE SCALPS PURCHASED!' were widely reprinted.

[6] *Niles' Register*, March 7, 1812.

[7] *Ibid.*, April 4, 1812. After noting that Governor Scott of Kentucky had approved the requests of Governors Benj. Howard and Ninian Edwards of Upper Louisiana and of Illinois Territories to raise volunteer soldiers in Kentucky, Niles stated: 'So far as the physical force of the savages is adequate to the object, an extensive war may be anticipated, until *Upper Canada*, at least, the very heart and soul of this nefarious business, shall be subjugated by the United States. *The evil will cease with the cause.*'

them of the sovereignty of our country' — into its proper place at the head of the causes which made war 'indispensably necessary.' This one grievance alone (as was noted by a British Whig) had become so unbearable that 'the whole country cries out war! war! or an end to impressment!' [1] Foster, like his predecessors, found that this grievance 'certainly creates more irritation than any other.' Even the Federalists, privately, 'do not fail on all occasions to complain of the interruption of their direct trade with France and of the practice of impressment exercised by us on board American ships.' The release of fifty or a hundred impressed Americans, he reported, 'would be better than any bribe and would wonderfully assist us with the Multitude.' [2]

To America's multitude, to her press and legislators national and state, impressment more than ever was 'a great sea mark towering above the horizon higher than a lighthouse or the pyramids of Egypt.' It was a British offense 'for which the Roman Republic would have laid the world in ruins,' a British crime 'which has no parallel for ferocity or extent but the business of negro-stealing on the coasts of unfortunate Africa.' It was a vestige of colonialism incompatible with American nationality and with every humane feeling.

In huge black type America's journals, from Portland to Savannah and from Baltimore to Lexington, printed the figures 6257, the number of impressed fellow citizens officially recorded as of January, 1812. Under this symbolical black badge of national shame, and headlines of 'More Impressments!' and 'Prison Ships of England,' there appeared harrowing accounts of fellow Americans kidnapped, chained to British gun-decks, kicked, flogged, and murdered while attempting to regain their freedom; heart-wringing letters about citizens enslaved, many of them since 1803; prose and verse on the sanctity of human lives and human rights — those 'sacred personal rights' which Clay in Congress emphasized. No American was immune. Not even the nephews

---

[1] *Cobbett's Weekly Register*, Feb. 1, 1812, in *Niles' Register*, May 23, 1812. Cobbett stated that Lyman, the agent at London for impressed Americans, estimated the number of impressments at 14,000.

[2] Foster to Castlereagh (Wellesley's successor) April 23, May 5, 22, 1812, *F.O.* 5:85, 86; and Foster, *MS. Diary*, March 27, 1812 ff.

of Senator Reed of Maryland; not even the grandnephews of George Washington, as Speaker Clay in March reminded Minister Foster, stressing this greatest of popular grievances which by itself imperiously demanded resistance by the sword.[1]

Imploring the Soul of Columbia 'to rest in guilty peace no more,' but to 'rouse, rouse thy Lion's heart and fire thy Eagle's eye,' to heed 'thy tortured seamen's cries' and 'the babes and mothers screaming, mix'd with hideous savage yells,' the people satirized government's apparent concern over such comparative 'tare and trett' as the orders-in-council. They said that to be enslaved for life by a British press gang or to be tomahawked to death by British-Indian murderers was no less disagreeable than to have property stolen by British pirates. They approved of Wright's 'scalping bill' for impressment reprisals upon British subjects; acclaimed the (administration-inspired) attempts that spring to 'revolutionize' East Florida,[2] and insisted upon Canada as a *sine qua non* to any peace. With fervor they echoed this 'solemn and reverential malediction — *Accursed be the American government and every individual of it who . . . shall agree to make peace with Great Britain until ample provision shall be made for our impressed seamen, and security shall be given for the prevention of such abominable outrages in future.*'[3]

Editors and correspondents asserted that the republic had

---

[1] Foster, *MS. Diary*, March 25, 1812. Foster, of course, on all occasions countered with the usual argument that Britain did not claim the right to impress native Americans (and only did so by mistake), and that the Americans aided British deserters and furnished them with fraudulent certificates. Typical of the frauds, he recorded, *Notes*, p. 45, was that practiced by 'an old woman, in one of the sea-port towns, who kept a cradle, made for the purpose of rocking full-grown British subjects, who were to be converted in a hurry into American citizens, that, when testimony should be called for to prove their birth, she might with a safe conscience swear she had known them from their cradles.' Even so, the infamous press-gang continued to man Britain's warships with British seamen, and with those 'that speak the same language.' British officers, with the first lieutenant of H.M.S. *Immortalité* in *Jacob Faithful*, p. 331, by Captain Marryat (who himself had helped to scour the American coast), continued to justify the press gang: 'Men we must have, and get them how we can, and where we can, and when we can. Necessity has no law; at least it obliges us to break through all laws.'

[2] *Essex Register*, April 12, Lex. *Reporter*, April 14, May 9, 1812; and Pratt, *Expansionists*, chap. II. In May, when the popular feeling against France had reached a high pitch, the *Whig* stated that both the great sea robber and the great land robber were our enemies, yet 'with the Canadas and the Floridas in our possession, we may defy the hostile attacks of "a world in arms" — without them we are never free from danger.' (Balt. *Whig*, in Lex. *Reporter*, June 6, 1812.)

[3] *Niles' Register*, April 18, 1812.

never been better prepared, especially as to militia and privateers; that a declaration of war would recruit more regulars in a week than could be had in a month of indecision; that the act of war, by forcing upon England the prospect of adding one third to her enormous war expense, might in itself compel her to do us justice. They drew the most sanguine comparisons between America's strength in 1776 and in 1812. 'The odds are greatly in our favor,' said young Niles; 'we shall obtain justice if we deserve it ... the issue will compensate the temporary injury.' [1] As in 1776 so in 1812, said Worsley: despite alarmists and Tory traitors 'our privateers swept the ocean ... the armies of the British tyrant were captured — his Indian allies were subdued, and Britain acknowledged our independence.' [2]

Repeatedly stressed were not only the military but the psychological dangers of further delay, of the painful indecision which was fast driving the nation to 'a pining, lingering, and inglorious death.' Even the Federalist *United States Gazette* of Philadelphia, on March 12, agreed that 'war is a terrible remedy; but it is better than none; and a remedy must be had.' [3] That war was not already declared, said War Hawk editors who incessantly jibed at 'Madison, Gallatin & Company,' was largely because of the 'stupefactious current of intrigue' in this presidential year of 1812. How can Madison speedily prepare and speedily go to war, asked Irvine, when he 'is occupied in contriving ... those *Italian* schemes that render everything involved, circuitous, profound, perplexed, and mysterious?' [4]

---

[1] *Niles' Register*, April 4, 1812; and *passim*. 'A British army will never tread our soil... some of our seaports may be attacked; but we have a million of tons of shipping, and more able seamen than all Europe... whithersoever a keel can be driven she will be vexed and retaliated upon. Besides, she is surrounded by enemies and her internal peace destroyed by the lack of bread for her people...'

[2] Lex. *Reporter*, May 2, 1812; and *passim*.

[3] *U.S. Gazette*, March 12, 1812. The present self-ruinous Non-Importation, admittedly, is no defense. Yet if 'crimes for which a poor American would be hanged by his own government are to be punished in John Bull only by denying to ourselves the use of his cloths and his blankets, his hats and his hosiery, let us so understand it and make no more vauntings about Upper Canada, Quebeck, and Nova Scotia.'

[4] Baltimore *Whig*, in Phila. *Aurora*, March 4, 1812. Instead of decisively acting, and 'doing only what the people wish,' said the *Aurora* (Feb. 24, 1812; and ff.), he pursues 'an *Italian system* of policy... by which the ostensible energy of the executive is palsied, and the congress is distracted by underhand dealings, calculated to deceive the public, and to deceive even their own colleagues.'

Such criticism, however justified, only whetted the people's impatience. Our government, said Niles on March 7, seems like a schoolboy, who, when beaten by a bully, began 'threatening and THREATENING and THREATENING to retaliate, but *turning* and *twisting* ten thousand ways to avoid *an appeal to his own strength* — until, at last driven into a corner, and literally "KICKED INTO WAR," he was compelled to fight a hard battle which would have been avoided, had he respected himself in the beginning. . . . Procrastination *must* come to a close: It is generally agreed that war is inevitable — and if so, the sooner it is commenced, or, at least *actively* prepared for, the better; because it will be the sooner ended.' [1]

Extricate us from this mongrel condition, demanded the New York *Columbian*, on March 9: New York 'wishes either for war or peace, and is disgusted with a state which is *both* and *neither* — which is despised abroad and ridiculed at home, and is ruining the country while it disgraces the administration.' Let us have action! 'In the name of all that's base and all that's honorable,' shouted Philadelphia's *Democratic Press*, 'let us determine either to submit or to resist — to crouch or to stand erect. This shilly shally, he-would-and-he-would-not kind of conduct, is more fatal to our interests, more deadly to our honor, than any other conduct could possibly be. The people "stand like greyhounds in the slips straining upon the start" yet will not congress do its duty.' [2]

Several times that winter the Young Republicans had been on the verge of forcing a decision as to whether America was to crouch or to stand erect. But in each case they had been prevented by the 'shuffling conduct,' said Foster, of Madison and his regular troops. Although the rumor persisted that the raw militia would soon force the ulterior measure, Foster by March 9 was inclined to believe that the Executive upon receipt of unfavorable news by the *Hornet* would still seek to avoid the issue of war or submission. Despite the popular clamor, 'the impotency of the Government' and its dread of war were such, he said, that Madison would probably yield to the older democrats and in the end send peace

---

[1] *Niles' Register*, March 7, 28, 1812.
[2] *Democratic Press*, in N.Y. *Columbian*, Feb. 22, 1812.

commissioners to London to get what terms Great Britain might deign to grant.[1]

No one more keenly felt the dangers and disgrace of this paralyzing irresolution than young Henry Clay. With the preparedness program enacted and the President empowered for the crisis, the Madison-Gallatin Executive must be brought to a decision. At this extraordinary first session of the Twelfth Congress, with its revolutionizing 'new men and new doctrines,' the ultimate Rubicon was to be crossed. But not until Mr. Speaker Clay had fully displayed those qualities of 'physical and moral courage and of readiness to assume responsibility' with which the Cock of Kentucky, the new bantling of the day, was amply, even 'superabundantly endowed.' [2] Only then was the trumpet to give its 'inspiring summons.'

---

[1] Foster to Wellesley, March 6, 9, 12, 1812, *F.O.* 5:84. On May 12 he reported that Dr. Logan, the Quaker pacifist, had been called to Washington, and might be one of the peace commissioners. Logan was urging such a mission: Logan to Madison, March 31, 1812, *Madison MSS.*
[2] Van Buren, Martin, 'Autobiógraphy,' ed. J. C. Fitzpatrick, *Ann. Rpt. Amer. Hist. Assoc. 1918*, II, 634, 662.

Chapter Thirteen. 'Mr. Clay's War'

Henry Clay was the man whose influence and power more than any other produced the war of 1812. (Josiah Quincy.)

I have thought it both just and necessary for five or six years ... not for conquest or ambition, but for our injured Rights, for our freedom, and the security of our independence. (John Adams.)

That this may end in indemnity for the past, security for the future, & compleat emancipation from Anglomany, Gallomany, and all the manias of demoralized Europe ... is the sincere prayer of —— Th. Jefferson.

IN THE crowded little capital Clay's Liberty Boys mingled with army and navy officers, editors, political bosses, seekers after commissions and contracts, old Indian fighters, 'spies,' and foreign adventurers. There was a Don Alvarez de Toledo who was printing Tom Paine's *Rights of Man* for Spanish-American Whigs; a mysterious wound-scarred little Frenchman, with 'monstrous thick legs' and 'large whiskers,' styled Count Crillon, who swindled Capt. John Henry, a British secret agent, out of a sensationally earned $50,000; an unctuous English cleric, Mr. Andaine, who said unconscionably long prayers at dinner and cheated Randolph at whist. Redcoated Captain Coore had 'just come from Canada,' Foster blandly said, 'to see whether War was really brewing or no.' General Jean Victor Moreau, the exiled French Revolutionist, was on his way to fight for the Czar. Simon Bolivar, dark, fiery, and twenty-eight, was on his way to fight Bourbon-British Spain for New World Liberty. Old Parson Weems was preaching 'God is Love,' yet with Henry Clay and Stephen Decatur, who was gallant, competent, and thirty-three, the Parson agreed that America must again 'fight the British into their better senses.' [1]

There was a coming and going of carriages and saddle-horses — to Capitol Hill and the President's House; to parties at the Marine Barracks, in the sail loft of the Navy Yard (where the smell of tar made ladies ill, and the Secretary of the Navy overindulged in his favorite beverage), and on board the *Constitution* and the *Enterprise*, the guns of which Congress heard from time to time. Serurier, at Joel Barlow's Kalorama, and Foster, at the Seven Buildings, gave rival entertainments. Young women (and Foster 'never saw prettier girls') more fervidly sang that 'man-trap' *Just Like Love is Yonder Rose*. Gambling was intensified: a child was born that winter, it was said, '*marked* with the five of clubs.' [2] A feverish excitement prevailed, even among Randolph and his Federalist messmates at Georgetown's Union Tavern, who lumbered down to the Capitol each day in the *Royal George* omnibus. A new spirit, animating and disturbingly youthful, had been imparted by Speaker Clay's boys, whom 'nothing short of War will satisfy.'

These were the men who 'filled the public attention and contested the public admiration,' said eighteen-year-old William Preston, a White House guest. 'My heart bounded as I looked upon . . . Clay, Calhoun, Cheves and others.' But his heart sank when he looked upon the temporizing and distrait old guardsmen about Mr. Madison.[3]

Old John Smilie was 'most in the Confidence of the President.' [4] His friend Mr. Gallatin, Madison's ablest and most influential adviser, was 'the Old Fox,' thin, of medium height, with dark bushy hair, long nose, 'hideous mouth & teeth, but a black,

---

[1] M. L. Weems to Madison, Jan. 17, 1812, *Madison MSS.*; Foster, *MS. Diary*, Jan. 20, 1812, ff., and *MS. Notes*, I, 101, 133 *passim*; Foster to Hamilton (describing Crillon), May 5, 1812, *F.O.* 5:85.

[2] *Natl. Intelligencer*, Jan. 25, 1812.

[3] Preston, *Reminiscences*, pp. 7–9; also his 'Personal Recollections,' *The Land We Love*, V, 337.

[4] Foster, *MS. Diary*, April 8, 1812.

intelligent & piercing eye.' [1] Dr. Eustis of Boston, a surgeon in '76 but now the overworked 'little god of War & Company,' smarted at demands for his dismissal. Old General Hull, freshly arrived from Detroit, inordinately proud of his gaudy new regimentals, was in hopes of supplanting Eustis as Secretary of War. General Wilkinson, ruddy-faced and gold-braided, freshly acquitted of Burrism, Spanish pensions, and army graft, was in truth 'the knight of the golden spurs, macaroons and comfits.' [2] General Dearborn of Boston, Madison's intimate, a heavy unwieldy veteran of '76, had not yet donned his '$500 Coat Militaire.' Not until April 4 did he accept the chief command; and even then only on condition that his port collectorship at Boston should be held open for him 'until war be actually commenced or abandoned for the present.' [3]

Indecision such as this confirmed cynics in the belief that a tragi-comedy was being played, and made the winter one of discontent and torturing doubt. It was a strange winter, of war and rumors of war, when comets glared, earth tremors shook Washington, and Boston's Tory clergy shouted that God was angry at Henry Clay. Aaron Burr quietly returned from exile, and Timothy Pickering frantically threatened the disunion of New England should America go to war with Old England. Colonel Duane of the *Aurora* praised the martial qualities of General Wilkinson, sniped at the jaw-bone Gascon Knights of Congress, and bombarded a Gallatinian Executive that prepared for war like a man who would 'run a race with his legs in his pockets.' [4] Wellington's Spanish army depended upon American grain, and the New World forged arms against Britain and Spain. Though hard-pressed for means to defend themselves, Americans voted $50,000 for the relief of Venezuelan earthquake sufferers; tried to spread the blessings of republicanism to East Florida;

---

[1] Dunlap, Wm., *Diary*, II, 384.

[2] N.Y. *Eve. Post*, April 13, 1812. Wilkinson drank heavily, boasted, talked much of New Orleans, where 'Yellow Balls are fashionable... the Ladies shoot Champagne bottle corks across the Table... & there is a vast deal of Intrigue...' Foster, *MS. Diary*, April 27, 1812.

[3] Henry Dearborn to Madison, April 4, 1812, *Madison MSS*. Dearborn's son, a customhouse officer, succeeded his father as Collector of the Port of Boston.

[4] *Aurora*, Jan. 17, 30, March 9, 24, April 8, 1812, *passim*.

lamented the execution of Mexican patriots who had rebelled against Divine Right of Kings and the Holy Inquisition; and satirized Anglo-Federalists who 'to resist *Bonaparte*, the *"tyrant!"* ' would unite with 'the liberty-loving *English* . . . in a crusade to restore "ORDER, RELIGION AND LAW" to the fertile regions of "Spanish America!" ' [1]

Black Americans that winter huzzaed 'Negro Henry King of Haiti,' and tried to burn down Clay's Lexington. Red Americans killed with 'the British tomahawk,' and the press teemed with 'British atrocities' past and present, on sea and land. Yet at the moment the savage warwhoop resounded in Western Wilds the first steamboat floated on Western Waters, the first contracts were let for a National Highway to the West, and the first state from Jefferson's Purchase entered the Union. While men planted the advance-post of Astoria on the distant Pacific, and planned a grand Erie Canal to hasten Western settlement, Bonaparte's Grand Army prepared to march into Russia, Bolivar's 'Exaltados' battled fresh armies from Bourbon-British Spain, and Clay's Liberty Boys of the West launched Revolution No. 2.

It was a strange world, and strangely managed. Abroad, the Age of War had degenerated into an Age of Smuggling and Corruption, 'into a huge system of jugglery on both sides.' [2] At home, war was demanded by Republicans whom it was England's best interest to conciliate, as Foster agreed with Gallatin, since 'the old Democratic party' was for economy, States' Rights, and peace; since America, overwhelmingly agrarian and Republican, was England's best market and best source of raw materials. War was opposed by Federalists who were for 'Glory . . . large navies and armies,' and were England's greatest maritime rivals.[3]

---

[1] *Niles' Register*, March 28, 1812. Niles stated that 'it is more than probable that the *United States* will soon acknowledge the republics of south America, as free, sovereign and independent states. If so, our western citizens can and *will* give such aid to the patriots of *Mexico*, as may enable them to expel their bloody tyrants. It would be a "harvest of glory," aye, *and of profit too*, to the hardy republicans resident beyond the Alleghanies; and its success would open a trade for themselves, and for their fellow citizens of the Atlantic states . . . a vast field for enterprize, would be opened, and we naturally should enjoy its first fruits.'

[2] Heckscher, *Continental System*, p. 214. See his chap. III, 'Smuggling and Corruption; Fiscalism and Licensing.'

[3] Foster to Wellesley, Jan. 16, 1812, *F.O.* 5:84.

'*British Bears and Tory Tigers*,' as John Adams remarked, had forced Jeffersonian pacifists into militant nationalists. 'They will force us,' said Jefferson, 'to become a nation of souldiers; & then the more woe to them.' [1] Their conduct was such that young Samuel Morse in England, where he had quickly shed his parental coat of Pickeronianism, longed for some sort of telegraph by which he could urge his compatriots to fight.[2] Young Clay needed no urging: the British news he discussed in the War Mess or reflected on when he took his daily canter through Georgetown only sustained him in his course.

British Toryism was unyielding, despite serious rioting for food by a 'seditious' proletariat; despite British Whig protests against such a 'revolting pretext' for an American war as illegal orders-in-council based on 'profit and monopoly, and not retaliation or self-defence.' [3] The Tory oligarchy of squires and shipping magnates, as John Quincy Adams said, seemed intent upon kicking the United States into war, even 'though they may see as clearly as you and I do, that in this policy they make themselves the tool of Bonaparte.'

Wellesley had been succeeded as Foreign Minister by Lord Castlereagh, notorious for his work in Ireland — 'cold-blooded, smooth-faced Castlereagh' (according to Byron), whose job was 'cobbling at manacles for all mankind.' [4] London's ministerial press (embarrassing Foster by its 'contemptuous language') continued its might-makes-right fulminations on the theme of 'No More Neutrals!' [5] Britons openly sold forged American ships'

---

[1] Jefferson to Chas. Pinckney, Feb. 2, 1812, Jefferson, 'Papers,' *Mass. Hist. Soc. Collections*, 7th s., I, 169.

[2] Morse, E. L., *Samuel F. B. Morse*, I, 41 ff.

[3] [Brougham, Henry], 'Review of *The Crisis of the Dispute with America*,' *Edinburgh Review*, XXXVIII (Feb. 1812), 290–317. As to Brougham's authorship, see Aspinwall, A., *Lord Brougham and the Whig Party*, p. 259. The excuse is given that '*this war*' is unlike any other war, said Brougham, and that for a neutral like America 'to take no part... in *this* grand contest, is highly criminal.' Yet the same excuse has been applied to all wars, 'from contentions about a few acres of snow — or a fishing or fur station — to the Polish partition, and the French and Spanish revolutions... Surely, if an American war is so dear to our rulers — if they must at all risks have a rupture with the only free people beside ourselves now left in the world — if they are quite resolved upon finally shutting up the best and safest market which yet remains to our industry — they may find some less revolting pretext...'

[4] Byron, *Don Juan*, dedication.

[5] Foster to Castlereagh, May 5, 1812, *F.O.* 5:85. The London *Courier* on March 19,

papers, smuggled British goods (and American produce, which
their navy had confiscated) into the Continent under the American flag, and carried on a licensed trade of enormous proportions
with the French enemy.[1] At the same time the *Guerrière* (her sails
provocatively marked: 'This is NOT the Little Belt'), the *Belvidera*,
and other blockaders 'retaliated' upon the French enemy by
seizing American ships laden with such 'contraband' as hides and
fish. A strange world indeed! As Madison tartly remarked to
Foster, 'it seemed quite necessary to become a belligerent in
order to enjoy the advantages of Commerce.' [2]

No one seemed less perturbed than Foster — until 'the Insolence
of the War Party had passed all bounds,' until Speaker Clay, 'the
head of the advocates for war,' had forced a decision.[3] The British
Minister saw a great deal of Clay socially, and found the tall, fair-
haired young Kentuckian always polite yet always warlike, a
spirited man of action, unlike Monroe ('a very mild moderate
man') and most old-school Virginians, who 'are flattered in their
own Minds with the Existence of a Plan to be put off sine die.' [4]
He marvelled at the 'immensity' of the economic sacrifice required
by the Clay-Calhoun men, who had injected into Anglo-American
relations their quixotic and highly explosive element of national
honor. Nevertheless, two years younger than Clay and irked by
sneers at his own boyishness, his own 'juvenile looks,' [5] he sensed

---

reprinted in *Natl. Intelligencer*, May 2, 1812 under the headline of 'The Mask Thrown
Off,' stated that the orders and decrees 'may be regarded as a sort of *tacit agreement*
between France and England, that *neutral trade shall no longer be carried on*... *Though
the French decrees never existed*,' Britain 'from her naval superiority... must have *a right
to enact laws for the regulation of its own element*...'

[1] Heckscher, *op. cit.*, 210–13, quotes Brougham's fiery speech in Parliament of March
3, 1812 against the licensing system, and states: 'That British licenses were openly
bought and sold, not only in Great Britain, but also all over the Continent, was a fact
known to all the world; they were a mere trade commodity not only in Gothenburg
and Norway but even in French maritime towns, such as Bordeaux and Amsterdam.'

[2] Foster, *MS. Diary*, Jan. 30, 1812.

[3] Foster to Castlereagh, May 3, June 9, Aug. 25, 1812, *F.O.* 5:85, 86.

[4] Foster, *MS. Diary*, May 8, 1812.

[5] Foster to his mother, the Duchess of Devonshire, Jan. 2, 1812, *Foster MSS*. Taggart, who seemingly preferred the blustering arrogance of Copenhagen Jackson to
the conciliatory manner of Foster, and said 'an Erskine game' was probably being
played upon the youthful envoy by Madison, described Foster as 'a very pretty young
gentleman... too much... of a boy for a Minister Plenipotentiary. He looks as if
he was better calculated for a ball room... He is probably older but his appearance
does not indicate more than 25.' Taggart, *Letters*, p. 374, Dec. 30, 1811.

something of the psychology of an internal struggle in which 'young men seem pitted against the old ones.' He had some glimmering of what impelled Clay's 'boys' from the democratic and nationalistic 'mountains and the West' to be 'constantly urging on the President.' [1]

Foster appreciated in some degree the political revolt which had taken place. A new generation, with leaders from the New West, had aggressively thrust itself into the national scene. An upstart frontier section was asserting its rising power, and of that section the older seaboard north and south entertained 'the greatest jealousy.' [2]

Clay's hinterland democracy, he noted, differed from the plantation Southeast, with its tobacco and cotton gentry who, if 'democrats abroad,' were 'tyrants at home, for the most part.' John Randolph, for example, who outdid the squires of England in his true-blue Toryism, who assured him 'that the possession of slaves was necessary to the formation of a perfect gentleman, which he held himself to be,' and insisted that he was a member not of the American Protestant Episcopal Church but of the Established Church of England — Randolph, said Foster, 'would have made an excellent Russian nobleman.' [3] The West with its motley immigrants, and un-English 'rowing, noisy, bullying ways,' contrasted strongly with Quincy's New England. 'Never did land answer better to its name' than New England, truly 'a scion from its parent tree,' where the people derived their industrious and religious qualities from their 'purer descent from English ancestry, unmixed and uncontaminated with French, German, Dutch, or any other foreign blood.' In Connecticut, the most Federalist of states, Foster did not find 'brawling ostentation, or the Utopian nonsense of ultra-political ranters.' There, as in Old England, the common people 'take off their hats in passing you, which one meets with nowhere else on the American side of the

---

[1] Foster, *MS. Notes*, I, 156–57; *MS. Diary*, May 28, 1812, and *passim*.

[2] Foster to Wellesley, Dec. 18, 1811, *F.O.* 5:77.

[3] Foster, *Notes*, p. 47; Foster to Quincy, July 18, 1839, Quincy, *Quincy*, p. 459; and Quincy, *Figures of the Past*, p. 211. When Randolph went to Russia as Andrew Jackson's envoy to the Czar, he 'presented his letters of credence to the Emperor at St. Petersburg on his knees,' wrote Foster to Quincy (*loc. cit.*). 'It is a positive fact.'

Atlantic,' and not, most assuredly, 'among the liberty-boys of the west.' [1]

Foster did not consider all Americans (as did Copenhagen Jackson and his Prussian wife) 'knaves' and 'savage democrats, half of them sold to France,' nor did he (as did General Moreau) repeat Talleyrand's remark 'that he could not bear America, because it was a country where a man would sell his favorite dog.' In the seaports he found merchants who 'might have made one forget one was not in England, if it had not been for the occasional pronounciation of some common word.' [2] In Washington he found 'many sensible worthy men,' and reported that 'never was radical attachment to us ... more strongly proved than on the present occasion.' [3] He was censorious, however, of Clay's un-English Children of America; and his views were shared by such intimates as Josiah Quincy, Key of Maryland, who in '76 had fought for King George, and Randolph, who disliked and feared Clay's '*Kaintuck*' and the New West of 'Clay, Grundy & Co' — that 'Yahoo's paradise' where the common emigrant from the East and Europe 'can get dead drunk for the hundredth part of a dollar.' [4] Foster liked Clay personally, and in after years asked to be remembered to him.[5] Yet with the American 'friends of England,' he too believed that it was in Clay's war-inflamed Western World that one found 'the greatest Degree of Immorality and recklessness, the States beyond the Alleghenies being notoriously full of gamblers, Speculators, and adventurers of all Sorts, with scarcely any Check from a Religious Establishment, far removed, moreover, from the Censure of Europe or even of the Atlantic Cities.' [6]

Speaker Clay, remarked the British Minister, possessed 'much influence as being a Man of great weight in the Western States, as well as from his Station and Talents.' He 'was of an enterprizing Spirit and ever ready to trust to Chance ... just as he was to Stake

---

[1] Foster, *Notes*, p. 47.   [2] *Ibid.*, pp. 36, 45.

[3] Foster to the Duchess of Devonshire, Jan. 2, 1812, *Foster MSS.*

[4] Randolph to Dr. John Brockenbrough, June 2, 1813, Garland, *Randolph*, II, 15, and *passim*.

[5] Foster to Bayard, Jan. 27, 1815, Bayard, *Papers*, 376.

[6] Foster, *MS. Notes*, I, 128.

his Money at the Game of Brag.' Mr. Clay and his friends 'always
talked to me of war as of a duel' that was as necessary to their
young nation as to a young man of honor 'to prevent his being
bullied and elbowed.' Clay would say that, when over, it 'would
probably leave them both better Friends than they had ever before
been.' ¹

They had some provocation, Foster later admitted, for this duel
for national honor into which they 'pushed' an Executive that
made 'the most earnest though secret struggles to avoid it.'
Indeed, it took great provocation to incite the United States to
war, he said. The disunity of interests and the great power of the
states, which differ from each other as much as England from
Holland, and Russia from Germany, must ever give a slowness to
national proceedings 'and incline the Government to preserve
peace as long as they can without exposing themselves to a total
loss of credit. The President of the day, if he looks to re-election,
must dread the reaction which may be produced in the feelings
of the public by the chances of War.' ²

Foster was impressed by the assurance with which the Kentuckian and his 'most resolute' South Carolina lieutenants demanded
war — for maritime rights, though 'they affected to despise the
Merchants as Men who suffer any Degree of wrong in their Search
after Gain.' He was impressed, too, by such a warlike former
Federalist as Charles Ingersoll of Philadelphia, the son of a
Loyalist, polished by residence in England, yet withal an impetuous
Young American who detested Federalist hat-doffing to England,
admired 'the fervid and fearless' Speaker, and thought an ounce
of impulse was worth a ton of caution.³ In contrast were the

---

¹ Foster, MS. Notes, I, 3–4, 148–49, 160–62.

² Ibid., I, 1–3, passim. 'The truth is, they had very good reason to be annoyed,'
wrote Captain Hall of the British navy in 1831; 'and if the guiding maxim amongst
nations be, that "might makes right," as I conceive it always has been, and ever will
be, so long as powder and shot exist, with money to back them, and energy to wield
them — then we really cannot pretend to find fault with the Americans, because they
took advantage, or tried to take advantage, of that moment when our "right" being
the same, our "might" appeared to be waning... Now, let us be candid to our rivals;
and ask ourselves whether the Americans would have been worthy of our friendship,
or even of our hostility, had they tamely submitted to indignities which, if passed upon
ourselves, would have roused... the whole country into a towering rage of nationality?'
Hall, Fragments of Voyages, etc., series I, pp. 48–49.

³ Ibid., I, 156, and MS. Diary, Feb. 12, April 15, 1812; also Ingersoll, C. J., Hist.
Sketch of the Second War, etc., I, 122, Meigs, W. M., C. J. Ingersoll, chap. II.

cautious waverers, whom Foster assiduously cultivated: 'Old Democrats' like Worthington, who was most concerned about impressment (he himself had once been impressed) and 'the Point of Honour,' who said 'he would rather live on a Crust in the Interior than live degraded,' and yet, worried about war's expediency, to the very end tortuously debated with himself and (of all persons) the British Minister whether he should vote for war or not.[1]

A colonial sense of inferiority persisted despite a boastful defiance of the Old World. 'They talk more loudly than before of war,' Foster wrote home in April; war against both France and England. 'A great many people here are afraid of being laughed at if they don't fight. It is really a curious state of things. They even refer to me occasionally to ask what we shall think of them.' [2]

Yet it was this very concern for the respect of the world and of themselves which motivated Clay's 'hot-headed enthusiasts.' With young Morse they might even wish England success against Bonaparte — 'against everything but *my* country.' Yet with Morse they had been humiliated into the conviction 'that the only way to please John Bull is to give him a good beating, and ... the more you beat him, the greater is his respect for you.' [3] They were impulsive, these boys who would 'fix a National Character' by a Second Declaration of Independence; as impulsive as Jefferson when at Clay's age he had written the First Declaration. Yet Jefferson himself could but agree as to the necessity of 'this second weaning from British principles, British attachments, British manners and manufactures.' He too had 'no fear of the award ... a spirit of nationalism and of consequent prosperity, which could never have resulted from a continued subordination to the interests and influence of England.' [4]

Notwithstanding his mortifying official position, Foster, so he wrote, was accorded the greatest personal consideration.[5] He

---

[1] Foster, *MS. Diary*, Dec. 7, 1811, May 13, 24, 1812, *passim*.

[2] Foster to the Duchess of Devonshire, April 18, 1812, *Foster MSS.*

[3] Morse, *S. F. B. Morse*, I, 72, 87, 110.

[4] Jefferson to Duane, April 20, 1812, *Jefferson MSS.*

[5] In the House 'when a member abused me and called me an opiate (bye the bye no great abuse either) Baker [his secretary] says he could perceive almost an inclination to hiss in the gallery.' Foster to the Duchess of Devonshire, Jan. 2, 1812, *Foster MSS.*

soon gave up attending the war debates, but he was constantly at the President's House. He dashed about in his curricle and in his coach and four with two outriders; parried remarks that he must soon be packing by observing that the declaration of war that men had carried so long in their pockets must be quite worn out; and kept his aplomb when many of the five hundred persons whom he had to dinner that winter mistook his caviar (made from Potomac sturgeon by his maître d'hôtel) for black raspberry jam, and 'spit it out very unceremoniously as a thing excessively nasty.' Even at the banquet on April 15 celebrating Louisiana's admission as a state, where Wright in his old-school manner 'sung a b — y song and gave a b — y toast,' and 'the Landlord sat in a Corner drawing Corks' in order to bring forth more boasts about 'The Republic one & indivisible,' Foster, sitting between the 'very warlike' Clay and the 'cool decided' Calhoun, maintained a superior British tranquillity.[1]

Thus did he bravely carry on, despite London obstinacy and Washington irresolution, doing his best 'to make a consistent story of what is passing' when there was 'so much lying and so much intrigue.' He stood firm despite the impressment evil, which subjected him to the violent clamor of a press 'principally conducted by Irishmen,' the sharp-tongued complaints of 'Mrs. Custis, Surrurier's bonne amie,' the protests in private of Federalists, and the abuse of Wright, whose 'scalping bill' made the practice a felony on par with piracy and murder, and provided for retaliation upon British subjects and their property. He dismissed lightly, as Jacobinic mobs 'principally composed of Irishmen of the lowest order, Negros, and Boys,' monster mass meetings in Philadelphia, Baltimore, and other seaports, in which the newspaper-taught rabble of the cities joined with the homespun farmers of the frontier crescent, from Harper's Yankee mountains around to Calhoun's Carolina hills, in demanding prompt, vigorous, and open war.[2] He believed that he had 'most triumphantly' refuted the charge that Governor General Craig of

---

[1] Foster, *MS. Diary*, April 15, 1812; and *MS. Notes*, I, 30–31, *passim*.

[2] Foster to Castlereagh, May 5, *Private*; May 26, 1812, *F.O.* 5:85, 86; and *MS. Diary*, Jan. 3, 1812 (on Mrs. Custis and impressment of George Washington's relatives), *passim*.

Canada 'employed Indians to scalp & massacre' — by presenting, said Lexington's *Reporter*, 'a letter from Craig, three years old, to prove that he had no hand in the transaction of yesterday.' [1] He was annoyed that the men whom he lavishly entertained should continue to drink Serurier's brandy and to vote war bills. Yet it pleased him to think that he had 'by the little intricacies of social life' staved off an embargo, which, in view of the flow of grain to Britain's armies in Spain and Portugal would be 'one of the most injurious measures that could be adopted against us.' [2]

By April he was bored by an interminable session and by talk of an 'inevitable' war which became less certain the longer it was delayed. He was diverted, however, by 'Brent, the drunken Senator from Virginia,' who swears 'he likes me 1000 times better than Surrurier . . . is a perfect sieve . . . but he is useful to put Reports about.' [3] He paid court to Mrs. Madison, who to cheer him would ask him 'to have some of the sprightly Bottle in a Joking Tone,' and he was fascinated by Mme. Jerome Bonaparte, who 'told me Turreau had proposed to her.' [4] He was amused, yet puzzled, by Randolph with his sparkling epigrams and bad champagne, his tears over Miss Lee's marriage to Horsey, and his bagnio songs sung 'with a voice that spoke of Chastity.' [5] He was amused, yet fearful, when entertaining Ormsby of Kentucky and other 'hot-headed Irishmen in Congress,' who in the liquor of the British Legation damned 'the Mother Country,' shouted that 'Men's Minds must be sufficiently made up,' and 'would have desired no better sport than to shoot at Randolph and any other leading Member of the Opposition.' [6] He was amused, too, by the Philadelphia innkeeper-congressman who,

---

[1] Foster, *MS. Notes*, I, 123–24; *Reporter*, April 4, 1812; also *A.S.P.*, *For. Rel.*, III, 483. As proof of non-incitement Foster had referred to a warning by Craig in 1810 that the savages intended war. The *Reporter*, and Republicans generally, did not fail to point out that while Sir James Craig might write a '*friendly* letter' about the Indians he also had sent agents into New England 'to promote a separation of the states!' *Niles' Register*, March 14, 1812.

[2] Foster to his mother, April 18, 1812, *Foster MSS.*; Foster to Wellesley, Nov. 9, 1811, *F.O.* 5:77.

[3] Foster, *MS. Diary*, Jan. 30, April 19, 1812.

[4] *Ibid.*, Dec. 17, 1811, April 2, 1812.

[5] *Ibid.*, Dec. 22, 1811, April 20, 1812.

[6] *Ibid.*, May 6, 1812; and *MS. Notes*, I, 143.

at his brilliant Queen's Birthday Ball, by 'an act of great impropriety' in his drawing-room chimney provoked the Federalists for months to cry out 'BLUSH DEMOCRATS — if you can!' [1]

The attendance of Speaker Clay and the entire War Mess at this notable British ball greatly incited Duane of the *Aurora*. Shortly afterward, however, 'the strongest war mess in Congress' and 'a pleasant one, the most so, perhaps in the place,' risked the Colonel-Editor's cry of overt treason by having the British Minister in to dinner. [2] The Kentuckian and such young and 'fiery Democrats' as Cheves, Calhoun, George Bibb, and Lowndes, even invited Mr. Gallatin, whom Duane detested no less than he did George III. It was a pleasant party, yet as usual (so Foster noted) 'the Speaker was very warlike.' [3]

The War Hawk leader no less than Foster utilized 'out-of-door influences' during these months of 'suspence, *ennui*, & anxiety,' [4] when Congress had little to do but to wait for the Executive's preparations, and for men's minds to be made up. Socially active, and adaptable, Clay was gallant when exchanging confidences and snuff with Mrs. Madison; earnest when exhorting Gholson or Nelson; convivial when playing brag with young Poindexter or old John Sevier, 'Nolichucky Jack of the Border,' or when feasting with Bayard on Delaware terrapins, grenadiers of their species, sent down by Rodney. Though Quincy (a 'very inaccurate' partisan, said Lowndes) pictured him as a bully; and Federalists, when he met with an accident while riding, were quick to hint of 'some fiery rencounter' with duelling pistols; the members were, as Foster noted, much 'courted by Clay.' [5] In the very nature of

---

[1] N.Y. *Eve. Post*, Oct. 23, 1812; Foster, *Notes*, p. 34. 'On the company going to supper, he thought (poor fellow!) that he was alone and unobserved but two stray *federal* members... espied [him] and the joke was too good to be lost, so they had it... all over the States in prose and verse, ringing the changes on the extinction of the British fire. My poor guest wrote me an humble letter... and I most graciously answered, and hoped to have gained his vote for peace by my soothing; but the graceless dog voted all the same for war.'

[2] Ravenel, *Lowndes*, pp. 100–01, 86.

[3] Foster, *MS. Diary*, Feb. 11, 1812. On the following day (*ibid.*, Feb. 12, 1812) 'I dined with Mr. Bayard, Mr. Clay, Randolph, Tayloe, Ingersoll, Milligan [the last two] Philadelphians.'

[4] George Bibb to John J. Crittenden, May 21, 1812, *Crittenden MSS.*

[5] Ravenel, *Lowndes*, p. 84 (Nov. 1811); *U.S. Gazette*, May 22, July 20, 1812, Foster, *MS. Diary*, April 17, 1812.

things the Kentuckian relied much on his 'seductive' persuasive arts as well as his 'singular power of at once firing men's hearts, and of coercing them by his ever furious will.' [1]

As Speaker, against the wishes of the more violent men in respect to Randolph, he had allowed the utmost freedom of debate. Yet with the issue thoroughly thrashed out, he did not shrink from his 'onerous, and absolute, if not arbitrary, functions.' [2] As the proponent of a '*new* United States' extending both north and south, undoubtedly Speaker Clay did much to keep united behind a joint Canada-Florida program Southerners who wanted Florida yet feared the weight Canada might give the North. [3] His tactful management was needed not only with resentful and timid old guardsmen but with such men as young Harper — who demanded a pledge that Canada once conquered must be retained, raged at Federalists who 'frequently hold caucuses ... at Foster's,' and denounced Gallatin, Smilie, and such 'wise Senators' as Pope and Worthington, whose time-spinning projects could only mean 'no war but complete disgrace.' [4]

At mess and salon and the President's House Clay displayed both force and finesse, even though he appreciated the feelings of Poindexter, who was most sarcastic about the abortive fruits of Mr. Madison's solemn consultations 'with his wise and Magnificent Cabinet Council,' [5] or of truculent Felix Grundy, who threatened to expose the Madisonian Executive, to expose 'certain great personages,' unless they made up their minds for actual war. Of Speaker Clay during these rancorous months Cheves said he had 'never heard him say a harmful word of any one, and that he thought him remarkably circumspect and generous in that

---

[1] *Atlantic Monthly*, LX, 562 (1887) — a review of Schurz's *Clay* by one who had known and admired Clay, and recalled 'that graceful form... that marvellous voice.'

[2] Ingersoll, C. J., *Hist. Sketch of Second War*, I, 210. As to Randolph, Clay had resolved never to receive an insult 'without giving immediate notice... Their mode of intercourse or non-intercourse was most singular. Sometimes weeks, months would pass without their speaking to each other. Then, for an equal space of time, no two gentlemen could treat each other with more courtesy and attention. Mr. Randolph, on entering the house in the morning, while these better feelings prevailed, would frequently approach the chair, bow respectfully to the speaker, and inquire after his health.' Greeley, *Clay*, p. 41.

[3] See Pratt, *Expansionists*, chap. III, 'Sectional Politics.'

[4] Harper to Plumer, Feb. 6, 17, April 13, 29, May 13, 1812, *Plumer MSS.*

[5] Poindexter to Mead, Jan. 25, 1812, *Poindexter MSS.*

respect.'[1] Others paid tribute not only to the Kentuckian's 'genteel polite & pleasant' qualities but to his oratory, his moral and physical courage, his bold and adroit leadership. 'We looked up to him as the Ajax Telamon; and by his counsel we were guided,' said Richard M. Johnson. 'Clay was always the master-spirit.'[2]

There were many honest differences of opinion and many impediments in a republic that was described by General Moreau in April as a sprawling young giant without bone or nerves.[3] Yet the 'greatest impediment,' Calhoun in April was 'sorry to say,' was the President himself. Though of 'amiable manners and great talents,' he lacked 'those commanding talents' necessary to unify his divided Cabinet, control his old guard friends, and to energize preparations in a manner which would permit Congress to proceed. It was not that Mr. Madison actively opposed war; rather was it, said Calhoun, that 'he reluctantly gives up the system of peace.'[4]

No matter how boldly the young congressional leaders sounded the call to arms, the Chief Executive gave a peculiar appositeness to Saint Paul's question: 'If the trumpet give an uncertain sound, who shall prepare for the battle?' His regular troops seemed 'bewildered, half blind, dizzy and weak,' while public sentiment 'lost tone' by being subjected in turn to 'fear, hope, doubt, expectation and disappointment.'[5] In vain did Senator Crawford, among others, urge upon the President the necessity of making his intentions unequivocally clear by 'frequent & candid communication.'[6] In vain did Grundy and other young War Hawk militia-

---

[1] Perry, *Reminiscences*, pp. 241–42. About 1831 when Cheves was politically opposed to Clay.

[2] Johnson, later in life when he was a supporter of Andrew Jackson, said he had known many great men but Clay in his opinion was second only to Jefferson. 'In moral courage, in physical courage, in oratory, in patriotism... he is without a superior... If the rest of the committee assembled before him, and were in doubt how to proceed, when he made his appearance, all eyes were turned upon him — and we were certain to be right when we followed his opinion. He is a great man — a very great man!' Greeley, *Clay*, p. 318, quoting the Richmond *Whig*.

[3] Foster, *MS. Notes*, I, 96. Moreau said 'he did not think that they were "assez fous" to go to War with us, tho he had been positively assured they meant to fight both us and the French.'

[4] Calhoun to James MacBride, April 18, 1812, *MacBride MSS*.

[5] Wash. letter, April 14, to Baltimore *Whig*, in *Aurora*, April 20, 1812.

[6] Crawford to Madison, March 28 (also May 2), 1812, *Madison MSS*.

men, who were determined 'to pull John Bull by the nose,' fret and
fume at a Chief Executive who seemed even more than at past
sessions to have 'crept into a nutt-shell.' In private Poindexter
agreed with the Federalists that 'Mr. Madison is afraid to go to
war or to be at peace; and the course he pursues really deserves
ridicule.' [1]

As suspense became more enervating the idea deepened that the
President would never abandon 'Old Tom' Jefferson's logocratic,
quilldriving, Quaker-gun system of national defense. 'Madison is
a good little man,' observed Commodore O'Brien to Foster, 'but
. . . he goes by the long Tiller at Monticello.' [2] Like Jefferson
when in power, it was said, 'Little Jemmy' would never give up
the '*if* policy' to ride the whirlwind of Mars.

Madison's reluctance was understandable — either as a diplo-
matist keenly embarrassed by Bonaparte's deceit, a politician
apprehensive of reelection, or a President devoted to peace, who
realized his country's unpreparedness as well as its wrongs, was
irked and depressed by his grave responsibilities, and not unmoved
by frenetic appeals to '*Pause — before you take the dreadful plunge.*' [3]
It was with considerable understatement that one of Mr. Madison's
very few editorial defenders remarked that 'the President of the
United States is placed in a disagreeable situation.' [4]

Young William Preston, who was staying at the White House,
'an avowed pet of Mrs. Madison,' and a spirited lad who was
proud of being 'a good deal' with the War Hawks, noted with
others that Mr. Madison was not in good health. Indeed, he went
outside but twice in seven months.[5] At the levees and formal dinners he was taciturn, his countenance was 'pallid and hard,' his
'manners somewhat cold and stiff.' His 'toils and vexations' were

---

[1] Poindexter to Mead, Jan. 25, 1812, *Poindexter MSS.*

[2] Foster, *MS. Diary*, April 8, 1812. It was not generally known that Jefferson considered war not only inevitable but imminent.

[3] Samuel Harrison to Madison, May 11, 1812, *Madison MSS.*

[4] Wilkes-Barre *Susquehanna Democrat*, in *Democratic Press*, April 14, 1812. He must
bear the blame for all sins of commission and omission, those of Congress and of the
European belligerents; is accused of cowardice if he recommends peace, and of war-
mongering if he recommends the maintenance of our rights; 'and if he sits down,
stands up, or walks about, in all he is pronounced guilty by the disaffected and discord-
sowing miscreants, who disgrace the name and prostitute the blessings of Liberty. . . .'

[5] Foster, *MS. Diary*, June 7, 1812.

many: often he would be 'at his desk by candlelight in the morning.' Of his intimates he asked many questions: What had Congress done? What did John Marshall think of its doings? For the diplomatic corps (i.e., young Foster and young Serurier) he had 'the most thorough contempt.' Of Randolph 'he would pettishly say, "The damned rascal! I wonder how he would conduct the government. It is easy for them to make speeches."'

The President, wrote Preston later, 'was exceedingly harrassed and manifestly defective in that vigour of character demanded ... He wanted a talent for affairs, was deficient in tact, and in persistence of purpose. The opposition ... was a source of daily annoyance ... exciting him to petulance and querulousness ... Amidst the perplexity of his public affairs he did not see clearly and therefore did not step firmly ... His judgment was not clear about the war or the mode of conducting it, nor had he about him friends whose pertinacity and firmness might supply his own defects in these qualities.' [1]

Madison's old guard friends, especially those of the Senate, only augmented his reluctance by their welter of fears, and their welter of arguments for any scheme which might avoid this 'inevitable' war, or at least delay it until, with adequate preparations, 'the word and the blow might go together.' [2] Nor did his Cabinet nerve him for decisive leadership.

Gallatin and Pinkney were not for war. Secretary Hamilton of the Navy, like Doctor Eustis, was a mediocre man, notoriously inadequate. Postmaster General Granger, politically powerful though not strictly of the Cabinet, secretly worked for Clinton and that spring reputedly was the author of an anti-war pamphlet.[3] Secretary of War Eustis not only 'never made up his mind to war' but tried to circumvent the will of Congress by recruiting the

---

[1] Preston, *Reminiscences*, pp. 7–9; and *Recollections*, pp. 338–40. Preston (1794–1860), a Virginian, later was president of South Carolina College and Calhoun's colleague in the U.S. Senate. 'Mr. Madison,' he wrote (*Reminiscences*, p. 6), 'treated me with a kindness beyond his usual wont and Mrs. Madison with cordiality and even affection. She called me her own boy. She had been present at my birth and had nursed me in my cradle. The most affectionate relations existed between us all her life.'

[2] Sen. Gregg (Penna.), in *U. S. Gazette*, June 15, 1812; also, Worthington, *MS. Diary*, 1811–12; and Pope, in N.Y. *Eve. Post*, Sept. 22, 1813.

[3] Foster, *MS. Diary* and dispatches (especially May 3, 12, 23, 1812), *passim*; Adams, J. Q., *Madison and Monroe*, pp. 148–49.

Additional Army of 25,000 'in a way which would make little real deviation' from the administration's plan of an Additional Army of but 10,000.[1] Secretary of State Monroe, however, stood out from his colleagues. Even though he seemed equivocating to brash young hotspurs, was distrusted by his former Quid associates, and hated by Giles, Monroe, in comparison with the rest of the Cabinet, was most warlike. In the many conferences held with the congressional leaders, 'Mr. Monroe was decidedly of opinion that we ought to make a "forward movement," ' Lowndes recorded, but, alas, 'the problem of the admin[istration] seemed to be how to make this without going to war.' [2]

A thorough reorganization of the Executive departments was already obviously needed. Yet Madison characteristically hesitated and delayed, until forced to it by the pressure of men and events. If war came it would be fought not by its young and energetic proponents but by unwarlike Cabinet members, 'fighting Secretaries' (said Macon) unfit 'for real war,' and by Madisonian generals as suitable 'as the Indian Prophet would be for Emperor of Europe.' [3] Even the sanguine Poindexter was apprehensive when he considered that the republic's 'national cocks and fire locks' would be commanded by 'Field Marshal Henry Dearborne... whose martial qualities have been looked into by Doct. Mitchell, who reports that they are in a state of decay from original imbicility to rapid debility and not worthy of repair.' [4] Even

---

[1] Eustis 'himself told me that he was determined . . . not to appoint at first more than ½ the Officers. Giles &c were de[ceived] . . . they supposed themselves passing a bill for 25,000 men &c — But the material error was Mr. Eustis — He wished to avoid war, & when Congress in its *ignorance* believed it had provided for a large army, they were satisfied that war might be made safely & they made it.' Lowndes, in his 'Common Place (Historical)' notebook, written in 1819, *Lowndes-Pinckney MSS*.

[2] *Ibid*. This entry, also written in 1819, like the entry cited above is on the page which, if numbered, would be page 9. Editor Gales of the *Natl. Intelligencer* stated in 1854 (when his memory was such that he classified Porter as not a Republican) that Monroe's influence was 'less publicly exerted, but not less potent' than that of Clay, Calhoun, and their associates; that Monroe 'in frequent private consultations . . . constantly repeated the deep conviction . . . "Gentlemen, *we must fight*. We are forever disgraced if we do not." ' Hunt, *Gales on the War Manifesto*, pp. 306–09. On June 13, 1812 Monroe wrote John Taylor of Caroline (*Monroe MSS*.) that he was inclined to think that actual fighting would be unnecessary: that a mere declaration of war would force a change of ministry, and cause Britain to yield.

[3] Macon to Nicholson, April 22, March 25, 1812, *Nicholson MSS*.

[4] Poindexter to Mead, Jan. 25, 1812, *Poindexter MSS*. After weeks of solemn consultation with his Cabinet, Madison has nominated Dearborn. 'The Senate have laid

the sanguine Cock of Kentucky, while appreciating Mr. Madison's 'mild & amiable virtues,' was more apprehensive than he cared to admit of the Chief Executive's fitness for 'the rough and rude blasts which the conflicts of Nations generate.' [1]

'There is much to disappoint us at Washington,' wrote Lowndes; 'many follies which we cannot conceal from ourselves, and which in the state of the country we cannot with prudence publicly censure.' [2] Macon — whose rash Old Republicanism was a root evil — criticized not only an inept and laggard Executive but an inept and rash Congress: 'We shall I apprehend get to war not half fixed for it, under the belief that then we shall do things as we ought to do.' [3] On the other hand, the men who in November had urged 'war without delay,' before the old guard's 'temporizing and vibrating policy' could exert its baneful influence, now argued with added force and numbers that war alone could cut ꞏthe Gordian knot of suspense, rally the people, and give decisive effect to preparations. Such were the ravages made by this 'disease of the Mind,' which was more formidable than the power of Britain, that John Adams was inclined to agree that war in November might well have been the wiser course.[4]

Contributing greatly to the progress of this disease, and one of Madison's sources of daily annoyance, was the charge that his selfish political concern was largely responsible for the Italian policies and 'Gallatinian intrigues' which kept the nation in a 'moral and political labyrinth' worse than war. 'His re-election engrosses nine tenths of his time, dreams and study,' reiterated the *Whig*.[5] 'A change of rulers,' threatened the *Aurora*, 'will be the least of the public evils.' [6] Such malcontents cast their eyes on

---

the great personage on the shelf, for inspection. The Military epicures pronounce him too fat for wasting and therefore they say *boil him*. The cooks declare that he is quite too tough for anything but a coachman's whip.* The Ladies are out of patience ... *Mem. This great man was horse whipped by a stable driver while he was Secretary at War.'

[1] Clay to Rodney, Dec. 29, 1812, *Simon Gratz Collection.*
[2] Lowndes to wife, March 23, 1812, Ravenel, *Lowndes,* p. 103.
[3] Macon to Nicholson, March 31, 1812, *Nicholson MSS.*
[4] Adams to Rush, May 14, 1812, *Old Family Letters,* p. 383.
[5] Baltimore *Whig,* in Phila. *Aurora,* March 4, 1812.
[6] *Aurora,* Jan. 25, May 13, 1812, *passim;* N.Y. *Columbian, passim.*

DeWitt Clinton of New York,[1] who had appeared in Washington earlier in the session, ostensibly to get aid for a canal to Lake Erie, yet much interested in electioneering a road to the White House.

'A bold designing man' who 'spares no means to effect his purpose,'[2] Clinton sought support in all quarters — from Federalists, Northern Republicans, Southern Quids, the Giles-Smith Senate Invisibles, and from Western Republicans who were ripe for revolt, it was said, from the terrapin, do-nothing, Virginia dynasty. There was much talk of a North-West alignment. The Clintonians had turned to the leading state of a West which at this session (effective in 1813) had more than doubled its congressional strength. In their 'tea-pot caballings' they had suggested as Clinton's running mate in 1812 the Kentuckian who had been elected Speaker on his first day in the House.[3]

Late in January, after Clay's Navy speech, their trial balloon was released when the Federalist press broadcast the report that a Republican congressional caucus had rejected Madison and nominated a Clinton-Clay ticket. No caucus was held. Clay's colleagues and friends, notably Editor Ritchie, branded it an infamous lie designed to sow discord.[4] In Grundy's opinion Madison was in 'a very delicate' position.[5] If he retains Gallatin he will lose many friends, said Harper; nevertheless 'at this time there is no doubt but Mr. Madison stands fair enough to be again supported.'[6]

Federalists still doubted whether he could command a Republican majority for his renomination. 'Certain it is,' said Randolph, that he is shown 'very little deference . . . by the *leaders*, in the two houses of Congress, or even by their *humble* followers.'[7] This lack of cordiality was offset by the lack of a strong rival about whom the insurgents could rally. Monroe, who might have com-

[1] See *Democratic Press*, April 14, 15, 1812, on anti-administration Republican editors.
[2] Foster to Castlereagh, April 24, 1812, *F.O.* 5:85.
[3] N.Y. *Eve. Post*, Dec. 28, 1811; Baltimore *Fed. Republican*, Jan. 10, 1812.
[4] Richmond *Enquirer*, Jan. 28, 30, Feb. 4, 1812, ff.; *Natl. Intelligencer*, Jan. 25, 1812, ff.; N.Y. *Columbian*, Feb. 10, March 23, 1812, *passim*.
[5] Grundy to Jackson, Feb. 12, 1812, *Jackson MSS*
[6] Harper to Plumer, Feb. 6, 1812, *Plumer MSS*.
[7] Randolph to Nicholson, Jan. 22, 1812, *Nicholson MSS*.

manded their support, was 'too timid' (remarked Key in April) to cut loose from the falling star of Madison, although he 'should & could get away even now.' [1]

Meanwhile Clinton's candidacy was boomed in the Northeast by 'peace-and-commerce men' of both parties. The demand for an energetic, decisive, 'Northern President' became more threatening the longer the people, and the War Hawks, waited in suspense for convincing proof that the Executive had taken an unequivocal stand. By supporting Madison's nomination in the usual congressional caucus the insurgents might well have attested their belief that he would definitely take the plunge into war. But that caucus was deferred. It was not held until well into May. Meanwhile the uncertainty was 'productive of the best effects,' said Foster, as to public and congressional distrust of a shuffling Executive.[2] The Federalists regained Massachusetts and the Clintonians secured New York, there was 'much caballing' at Washington,[3] and the importunate War Hawks made Congress a 'sleeping Aetna' that might at any moment erupt.[4]

Republican intrigues made the Washington air as fetid as that of any Old World court, said Federalists, who declared that a dangerous and desperate game of brag was being played in which 'all is staked on a single throw.' It was a game of 'bluster and look, and talk big,' of cursing 'the British by bell, book and candle' and roundly asserting 'the repeal and inoperation of the French decrees,' a din of warlike preparations which would frighten the British Leviathan to its very marrowbones. Yet even in this game of brag Madison played a hesitant and bungling hand, and offset the War Hawk clamor, they said, more convinced than in November that the old guard Executive did not want war but only 'a loud noise about it,' that 'Little Jemmy' was as likely 'to scale the moon' as to go to war with England. Brag most assuredly was not Madison's game. Indeed, 'it is probable that proposals sufficiently

[1] Foster, MS. Diary, April 17, 21, 1812; also May 14, 1812, ff.
[2] Foster to Wellesley, March 22, 1812, F.O. 5:85.
[3] Crawford to Madison, March 28, 1812, Madison MSS.
[4] Quincy to wife, Mar. 20, 1812, Quincy, Quincy, p. 252.

low and humiliating are made in private and transmitted by Mr. Foster.' [1]

In truth, the 'low and humiliating' proposals came from the Federalists themselves. If Republicans were playing a dangerous and desperate game to avert war with England, some of 'the friends of England' were playing a game even more dangerous and desperate in which the object was not to avert but to bring about war with England.

By February Federalist intrigues with the British Minister had reached the border of treason. In secret conferences at the British Legation, almost in the shadow of the President's House, Federalist leaders urged Foster to 'concert measures' with them, insisting that Britain must push Madison 'to the Edge of the Precipice, by an unbending attitude,' and leave him no alternative but ruinous war or ruinous submission. The Tory Ministry must remain inflexibly firm, must 'neither revoke our Orders in Council nor modify them in any manner,' since the Executive would eagerly seize the slightest concession, the smallest loophole, to escape going to war. Either submission or war, they assured Foster, would crush anti-British democracy and ensure Federalist supremacy, put an end to embargoes and non-importations, and bring about a lasting peace, 'a thorough amalgamation of interests between America and Great Britain.' [2]

'You clearly discern that you have in your hands the fate of the party now in power,' wrote an unnamed 'Federalist of influence' to Foster on February 10. 'You can oust them if you will it . . . The threatened war is not even a bug bear . . . and it is *admitted* that the militia cannot be marched out of the Country. Canada is therefore safe if it were not so from its internal defences . . . The federalists . . . wish for the *extinction*, as they have already witnessed the *humiliation*, of the Virginian faction, the greatest enemy you as well as they and this Country have to provide against. This faction is linked to France through all its mutations; and its leaders so far

---

[1] Taggart, *Letters*, Dec. 30, Nov. 30, 1811, Feb. 6, 1812, pp. 375, 364, 383, and ff.; Wash. letters in Boston *Columbian Centinel*, Nov. 16, Balt. *Fed. Republican*, Dec. 25, 1811, and N.Y. '*Royal Gazette*,' q. in Phila. *Aurora*, Feb. 14, 1812.

[2] Foster to Wellesley, Feb. 2, 1812; also to same, Dec. 11, 1811, Jan. 16, March 12, 1812, *F.O.* 5:77, 84; also Foster, *MS. Diary*, 1811–12.

from feeling a patriotic impulse are not even free agents when the wishes and interests of France cross their way.' [1] Even if our ruling demagogues plunge America into war on the side of Emperor Napoleon, war could last only 'until the People feel the Weight of Taxes,' said merchant-Federalist congressmen, who asserted of the American people 'that nothing would bring them to a right sense of their Interests but touching their purses, and that if we did go to war for a time we should be better friends afterwards.' [2]

War would make America and Britain better friends — these were the selfsame words which Clay and his quixotic young enthusiasts used, so Foster noted, in justifying their determination to resist Britain by the sword. Clay's Young Americans would compel Britain to recognize the United States as an independent and sovereign member of the family of nations, and thereby win, perhaps, a friendship based upon mutual respect. Quincy's Federalists envisioned a friendship based upon a colonial dependence upon Britain, which was to come from a war disgraceful, humiliating, and disastrous to American democracy and nationalism: 'in short,' so Foster reported, 'they seemed to think that Great Britain could by management bring the United States into any connexion with her that she pleased.' [3]

Future Americans might be amazed by the audacity of Henry Clay's Young Nationalists in plunging their unprepared nation and peace-loving Executive into a David-and-Goliath contest with the powerful, war-experienced, peculiarly cold-blooded and tough-hided British Leviathan. They would be more amazed by the calculation of the merchant-Federalists; by the intensity of the hatred both of Napoleonic despotism and of Jeffersonian Democracy which linked together the Tories of Old and of New England; by the extremes to which economic interests and partisan prejudices could push men who considered themselves the most respectable of Americans; and by the singular lack in such men of a national consciousness and a national patriotism.

Yet the views of these 'extreme party men, extreme in local attachments,' had for years been publicly expressed, obliquely and

---

[1] Letter enclosed with Foster to Wellesley, March 12, 1812, *F.O.* 5:84.
[2] Foster to Wellesley, Feb. 2, 1812, *F.O.* 5:84.   [3] *Ibid.*

directly. At the last session during the West Florida debates
Quincy of Boston had deliberately, ominously, threatened the
disunion of the Northeastern states, 'amicably if they can, violently
if they must,' should Louisiana be admitted to the Union as the
forerunner of Clay's *new* United States.' Poindexter of Mississippi
had charged him with outdoing Aaron Burr 'in all the ramifica-
tions of his treasonable projects,' and had noted that the Federalists for four years had constantly linked together 'a war with
England and a separation of the Eastern States from the Union . . .
Why these subjects have gone hand in hand, I leave the gentlemen
who are in the secret to explain . . . He who deliberately wields
"the mischief-meditating" hand of civil commotion, will seldom
hesitate as to the means which he employs to accomplish . . .
political parricide.' [1]

The Union was still intact in April of 1812, although in that
month Louisiana was admitted as a state, an inspired 'revolution'
had taken place in East Florida, and in Massachusetts Pickering's
politico-ecclesiastical oligarchy had regained control. The Pickeronians were uttering such 'NAKED ANGLO–FEDERALISM' as
'it behooves us to Speak, for STRIKE WE MUST, if speaking does
not answer'; we hope for *an eternal separation* between the northern
states and the nabobs of the south'; and 'Have we no Moses to *lead
us out of Egypt*?' [2] With war against England imminent, and with 'a
certain quarter of the Country disposed to fly off' (as Speaker Clay
phrased it),[3] Americans could but be apprehensive of 'enemies
without and enemies within.'

If war came the Anglo-Federalists should be held responsible,
said Republicans, who with Senator Smith of New York (as Foster
noted) complained 'bitterly of the federalists who have pushed

---

[1] Swearingen, *Poindexter*, pp. 110–12. At the session of 1808–09, when Quincy was
assailing the pacifistic Jefferson ('a dish of skim milk curdling at the head of the nation'), threatening disunion, and declaring that no insult could ever be gross enough
to 'kick' America into war, Troup of Georgia had pointed out that Quincy's policy,
obviously, was to force 'an unpopular war,' and had denounced the Anglo-Federalists
as 'men who cry out, away with your honor, your independence, your neutrality. . .
give us gold!. . . men who would sacrifice. . . the nation for a little trade in codfish
and potash!' Harden, *Troup*, pp. 34–36.
[2] *Democratic Press*, April 13, 1812, quoting such Boston journals as the *Gazette,
Repertory*, and *Centinel*.
[3] Clay to Monroe, March 15, 1812, *Monroe MSS*.

them into it.'¹ In the past the minority had clamorously opposed and thwarted Jefferson's non-violent methods of national defense. In the present crisis Quincy's faction, after first voting for war-like preparations, publicly (but not privately with Foster) opposed war, while Pickering's oligarchy by their editorials, sermons, and letters in the British press were 'invigorating' the British Ministry in its 'spirit of insolence and hostility' by picturing the Americans as a weak and divided people.² Americans in England indignantly reported that the self-styled 'rich, wise, and good' confirmed the Tory belief that America would never go to war, and materially offset the agitation there for the repeal of the orders-in-council. Since 'there is scarcely any hope of their repeal,' wrote Morse from England as late as June 8, 'I sincerely wish that America will declare war.' ³

Perhaps the Federalist congressmen would not have so freely urged upon Foster a concert of measures had they foreseen the John Henry disclosures of March 9, an explosive affair which, in Clay's opinion, was powerfully to 'accelerate a declaration of war.' ⁴

On that day Madison laid before Congress the instructions and dispatches of Captain Henry, a secret agent whom Governor Craig of Canada had sent into New England during the Embargo discontent, as evidence that Britain had intrigued 'for the purpose of bringing about resistance to the laws, and eventually, in concert with a British force, of destroying the Union and forming the

---

¹ Foster, *MS. Diary*, April 1, 1812.

² Baltimore *American*, in Lex. *Reporter*, March 7, 1812.

³ Morse, *Morse*, I, 76–77; also, Lex. *Reporter*, May 16, 1812, and Jas. Maury to Madison, Liverpool, April 20, 1812, *Madison MSS*. 'What Lord Castlereagh said at a public meeting a few days ago ought to be known in America,' wrote Morse, the quondam Federalist (*loc. cit.*). 'Respecting the Orders in Council, when some one said unless they were repealed war with America must be the consequence, he replied that, "*if the people would but support the Ministry in those measures for a short time, America would be compelled to submit, for she was not able to go to war.*"... Great Britain is jealous of us and would trample on us if she could, and I feel ashamed when I see her supported through everything by some of the Federal editors... for it is *their* violence that induces this Government to persist in their measures by holding out hope that the parties will change, and that then they can compel America to do anything. If America loses in this contest and softens her measures towards this country, she never need expect to hold up her head again.'

⁴ Clay, Feb. 9, in Lex. *Reporter*, Feb. 22, 1812. The Henry documents were purchased by the Executive on Feb. 10, 1812.

eastern portion thereof into a political connexion with Great Britain.'

In the House there was a tremendous uproar. Foster's secretary hurriedly left the gallery, but the New England friends of Old England remained — 'in the greatest agony and distress.' Pitkin of Connecticut 'began to kick and *squirm* . . . Quincy looked pale — walked the floor in haste,' and on the flushed faces of others appeared great drops of sweat.[1] Although Quincy said there was a difference between threatening and attempting disunion, and although Henry had deleted the names of his Federalist friends, Widgery and other Yankee democrats recalled the adage that wounded pigeons are best discovered by their fluttering, and declared that everyone knew too well the 'Boston rebels' who had attempted to hatch the Embargo 'eggs of sedition,' threatened a British Northern Confederacy, caressed Copenhagen Jackson, and now opposed war as wicked and pro-French. 'Struck with horror' at this plot 'not to stab an individual but to stab a nation,' Macon and others called for an immediate declaration of war.

Under headlines of 'The Plot to Dismember the Union!' the Republican press urged unity against the inveterate enemy, who had been 'stirring up rebellion . . . feeling for the vitals of the Republic, to which she might . . . direct her poisoned dagger.'[2] From now on 'the TORIES will stand alone,' for no American 'federalist or democrat' can desire the blessings of British friendship: 'the TOMAHAWK and the SCALPING KNIFE for the *farmer* of the western country . . . CIVIL WAR for the citizens of the eastern states.'[3] Not content with impressment and plunder,

---

[1] Harper to Plumer, March 11, 1812, *Plumer MSS.*; and, *Annals*, 12th, 1st, 1162 ff.; Lex. *Reporter*, April 7, 1812 (re Foster's secretary).

[2] *Natl. Intelligencer*, March 10, 1812. That the British Ministry, reputedly 'the vilest and weakest' in British history, should have attempted to dissever the Union was not surprising, said Niles; nor was it surprising that 'this horrible intrigue' failed, for 'the high-handed measures in *Boston* and its neighborhood in 1809, alarmed no body but the *tenth congress*. We said then — and we repeat . . . Massachusetts in herself — nay, *Marblehead* and a few neighboring towns, contained physical force enough to disperse the whole contemplated "*northern confederacy*.' ' *Niles' Register*, March 14, 1812.

[3] Lex. *Reporter*, March 28, 1812. 'A civil war . . . is contemplated!!! . . . for the sole purpose of her *commercial interests!!*' Citizens, consider well Henry's Letter XI. '"*A war would produce an incurable alienation of the eastern states, and bring the* WHOLE COUNTRY *in* SUBORDINATION *to the* INTERESTS OF ENGLAND, WHOSE NAVY WOULD *PRESCRIBE* AND *ENFORCE* THE TERMS UPON WHICH THE COMMERCIAL STATES *SHOULD* CARRY, AND THE AGRICULTURAL STATES EXPORT THEIR SURPLUS PRODUCE."'

England 'must lay her bloody hand, which blasts all things, on the holy bond of our AMERICAN UNION!' [1]

It was impossible to deny that Britain had sent Henry 'into the houses of the "Boston rebels" to . . . fan the fuel of their opposition,' or, as Henry himself described the purpose of his mission, to concert measures 'with the English party in the United States for an effective resistance to the general government, which would probably terminate in a separation of the northern states.' [2] Yet Foster made a lame disavowal,[3] and the Federalists angrily accused Madison of squandering $50,000 upon Henry in order to win the Northeast spring elections and to incite a clamor which might frighten Britain, and induce France, into making concessions. His 'political torpedo,' they said, would have little effect. His base insinuations of Federalist disloyalty were so unjustified by the Henry letters that even 'the democrats, altho' at first they thought it a wonderful thing, are sorry it was ever meddled with.' [4]

While Serurier reported that Madison aimed to incite the nation into war,[5] Duane said that if Madison had any war fever 'it must be a species of *intermittent*, what is vulgarly called the *shaking ague*,' and sneered at his '*fooling away time* and *money* — and public character.' [6] Madison curtly informed Foster that the Henry exposure might 'produce a good effect by bringing matters in a more peremptory manner before His Majesty's Government.' [7] To Jefferson the President and Gallatin expressed their hopes that a check would

---

[1] *American Mercury* (Hartford, Conn.) in Phila. *Aurora*, March 23, 1812.

[2] *Democratic Press*, in N.Y. *Columbian*, March 26, 1812; Henry's memorial to Lord Liverpool, Letter VI. Henry was recalled when Erskine's Agreement presaged peace, although Canadian officials were 'cruelly out of spirits at the idea of old England truckling to such a debased and accursed government as that of the United States.' H. W. Ryland to Henry, May 1, 1809, Letter V, in *Annals*, 12th, 1st, 1177.

[3] 'Foster must really be now on a bed of roses — growing on a dunghill,' commented F. J. Jackson. Henry 'has turned out a very pretty scoundrel,' but our government should not have neglected to pay him. 'I am very glad he has not introduced my name...' Jackson, G., *Diaries*, I, 370–71, May 8, 1812.

[4] Abijah Bigelow to wife, March 22, 1812, Bigelow, *Letters*, pp. 332–33; also, Taggart, *Letters*, p. 389 ff. 'Bayard says the People have been so abused with Lies & Stories of every kind that Henry's Disclosures will produce but small effect.' Foster, *MS. Diary*, March 19, 1812.

[5] Adams, *Hist. U.S.*, VI, 181.　　　　　　[6] *Aurora*, March 11, 24, 1812.

[7] Foster to Wellesley, March 12, 1812, *F.O.* 5:84. Foster regarded it as an electioneering device, aimed at the Northeast and at the choosing of presidential electors. He reported that Dr. Logan had been invited to Washington, and that it was probable that peace commissioners would be sent to London.

be given to the Anglo-Federalists and to Clinton's 'new focus of opposition at Albany.' ¹ Yet Postmaster General Granger, canny Connecticut politician, thought so little of their hopes that in conversation with Foster he attempted to defend the Henry mission as one merely to gain information.² Some Republicans feared that the political effect would be outweighed by a further incitement of a war spirit already too violent.³

The Henry letters failed to meet the Executive's hopes as to their political effect in the Northeast, yet for weeks the press and people used them as tom-toms for war. Joined with atrocity stories from a now widespread 'Anglo-Savage War,' they furnished an added reason for the conquest of Canada — the British source both of Indian incitements and of intrigues to dissever the Union. Further, the apparent indifference of the anti-war 'Tories of Boston and New York' to Henry's 'damning proofs of British perfidy' convinced most Americans that 'Henryism' was still rampant. War alone could purify and unite the nation, it was said. 'War alone can furnish a remedy for this deplorable malady of the body politic' as well as for the 'insufferable insults daily heaped upon us by the enemy.' ⁴

Why does government wait another moment? asked the Baltimore *Whig*, asserting with the *Aurora* that Madison recruited voters rather than soldiers, criticizing his preparations as inadequate, and at the same time demanding instant war.⁵ When thousands of our seamen have been for years abandoned, 'of what use is it to complain?' asked the Lexington *Reporter*.⁶ Energy is alone required, said the Pittsburgh *Mercury*: the people themselves could supply it, but 'our *government will not* — nay through want of spirit *cannot* . . .' ⁷ While 'nothing remains but *submission* or *resistance*,' said Niles on March 14, obviously 'something is wanted to enspirit our government, timorous of reciprocating the confidence the

¹ Adams, *Gallatin*, p. 455; Madison, *Writings*, II, 530.
² Foster, *MS. Diary*, March 12, 1812.
³ John Taylor of Caroline to Monroe, March 12, 1812, *Monroe MSS*.
⁴ Jas. G. Jackson to Madison, March 30, 1812, *Madison MSS*.; also, John Adams to Jefferson, May 1, 1812, *Jefferson MSS*.
⁵ *Whig*, in Phila. *Aurora*, March 25, April 8, 14, 1812.
⁶ Lex. *Reporter*, April 4, 1812; in Phila. *Aurora*, April 22, 1812.
⁷ Pittsburgh *Mercury*, in Phila. *Aurora*, April 9, 1812.

people have placed in it.' Some impulse is still required to give it *immediate* energy.' [1]

On the evening of March 15, Clay and Cheves solemnly assured the skeptical Bayard that war would shortly be declared. Bayard was impressed. 'Clay is certainly in confidence,' he wrote Rodney, '& I believe both are & they spoke in entire sincerity.' [2]

On that very day Clay in talks with Monroe, and then in writing, had set forth a War Hawk plan for decisive and *'immediate* energy.'

Calling upon the President to exercise his executive and 'constitutional duty,' the Speaker urged him to recommend a thirty-day embargo and at its end, if Britain persisted, to recommend a declaration of war. A short embargo preliminary to war, said Clay, would be 'a measure of some vigor upon the heels of Henry's disclosure.' A definite warning of war, it would 'give tone to public sentiment,' shelter ships and cargoes 'before the storm,' and, 'above all, powerfully accelerate preparations for the War.' [3]

Of necessity, this enspiriting impulse took the form of a continuing pressure. For a week passed, and still another, before any action was taken on Clay's plan of war within four weeks.

On March 21 Foster received the long-awaited news from London. Although war editors cited the Erskine and Henry affairs, and warned against any 'deceptious' repeal of the orders, rumor at first had it that Britain had yielded.[4] Alas, Foster was instructed to reiterate with greater menace that the Tory Ministry never would give way: the orders must stand, whether the French repeal

---

[1] *Niles' Register*, March 14, 1812.

[2] Bayard to Rodney, March 16, 1812, Bayard, *Letters*, p. 20.

[3] Clay to Monroe, March 15, 1812, *Monroe MSS*. 'Altho the power of declaring War belongs to Congress,' wrote Clay, 'I do not see that it less falls within the scope of the President's constitutional duty to recommend such measures as he shall judge necessary and expedient than any other which, being suggested by him, they alone can adopt.' He further urged Madison to recommend a short-term volunteer force of 10,000, with officers commissioned by the President: this 'will get rid of all constitutional embarrassment, furnish a force in itself highly useful, and leave a certain quarter of the Country disposed to fly off without even a pretext for dereliction.'

[4] Lex. *Reporter*, March 31, 1812. 'The truth is; it is a disgrace to the United States to treat with the present ministers —— see more from Henry: "*The important changes that occur in Europe might render it inconvenient for her to* ADHERE *to any stipulations in favor of neutral maritime nations.*" Britain might remove the orders for a month or two, but she never would, with an intention of adhering to any stipulations — her only aim is more deceptions.'

was genuine or not, until France in effect freely admitted British goods into Europe.

It now seemed that paralyzing indecision must cease. Foster believed that there was a House majority for war. Serurier found the Executive seriously talking of an embargo preliminary to war.

On March 23, however, the technical ground Madison had selected seemed to be cut away from under him by the report that a French squadron, which had burned two ships supplying grain to Wellington's army, had done so under open orders. If the President now recommended embargo or war, fumed Monroe at Serurier, all his enemies would rise 'and demand why we persist in making war on England for maintaining the Orders in Council when we have proofs so recent and terrible that the French Decrees are not withdrawn.' [1]

While Madison and Monroe hotly reiterated to Serurier that their whole system against England depended on the French repeal, Clay and many Republicans hotly declared that they might include France in their declaration of war against England.[2] The War Hawks were still credited with a House majority 'for Embargo & War.' [3]

At this crisis, and thereafter, many moderates still caught at 'every plea on which they might with propriety retract.' [4] Pope and others pressed upon the President the view that 'French Perfidy' made necessary the repeal of the Non-Importation and, if war there must be, war against both aggressors. Only thus could Madison, they said, win Federalist mercantile support and get clear of the mortification of being paraded as Bonaparte's dupe or tool.[5] It was but a step from this to argue, as did Pinkney in the Cabinet (so Foster reported), that since war against both enemies

---

[1] Serurier to Bassano, March 22–23, 1812, *Aff. Étr.*, vol. 67.

[2] At the President's on March 25 Clay told Foster 'if it be true the French have burned their ships... he will be for war on France as well as England (in a softer Tone).' At the same time Clay stressed impressment. On March 27 Sec. Eustis 'thought all might be settled if Impressment were put a stop to.' Foster, *MS. Diary.*

[3] Senator Smith, Memo of March 30–31, 1812, *S. Smith MSS.*

[4] Foster to Wellesley, April 1, 1812, *F.O.* 5:85. He noted that Quincy's faction, after voting war preparations, now opposed war so that Madison might not escape 'from either disgrace or complete loss of popularity.'

[5] See Pope, in N.Y. *Eve. Post*, Sept. 22, 1813. Also, Worthington, *MS. Diary*, May, 1812; and Foster, *MS. Diary*, April–May, 1812.

was alone logical, and this meant an impracticable war against most of the world, Madison should submit to England.[1] On the other hand, the gross inexpediency of such a 'triangular war,' however justified and however logical on the issue selected by Madison, caused John Adams angrily to demand a united front against England in the name of 'common sense and common courage.'[2] Jefferson, too, denounced this quixotic 'sublimated impartiality' as an obvious snare of the submissionists.[3] Both Foster and Serurier scoffed at the idea of triangular war. Federalists privately termed it 'topping the climax of folly.'[4]

Although threatening war upon France, Clay's War Hawks and most Americans were not to be deflected from their policy of taking one enemy at a time, and that the greater aggressor, and the one against whom war could be effectively waged on sea and land. Public opinion, then engrossed in Britain's 'Disunion Plot,' took indignant but relatively incidental notice of French depredations upon ships furnishing grain (much of it purchased by Foster) to Britain's Peninsula armies.[5] The people were primarily concerned with Britain's wholesale captures — some twenty ships in the past month alone; with the Indian war, of which Lexington's *Reporter* thundered: 'Britain has commenced war in the Western Country, equally so as France would have done, was she to burn

---

[1] Foster to Castlereagh, May 23, 1812, *F.O.* 5:86.

[2] Triangular war would 'essentially and fundamentally divide us,' make for a British Northern and a French Southern Confederacy, stop the war loan, make all ships and seamen British, prevent trade with all the world, and 'drive the whole Continent, but especially the Northern half of the Nation to desperation.' Adams to Rush, May 14, 1812, *Old Family Letters*, pp. 382–83.

[3] It would preclude privateering and alienate Eastern capitalists and seamen, deprive our farmers of every market, and make all nations our enemies at any peace conference. Jefferson to Jas. Maury, April 25, to Madison, May 30, 1812, Jefferson, *Works*, XI, 239–44, 248.

[4] Serurier said he must 'concert measures' with Foster to protect France 'against so alarming a power.' Foster to his mother, April 18, 1812, *Foster MSS.* Also, Taggart, *Letters*, May [27], 1812, p. 400.

[5] Foster early in 1812 received £304,881 to buy grain and flour for direct shipment to Britain's armies in Spain and Portugal. Before his departure he had completed these purchases, and had issued 180 licenses. Galpin, *American Grain Trade to the Spanish Peninsula*, pp. 25–30. The trade was profitable to New England shippers and to the producers of the Middle States, Maryland, and Virginia; yet, as to French depredations upon it, the *Connecticut Courant*, April 28, 1812, complained that even the Federalist press, like the Republican, seemed disposed 'to bury in oblivion all the atrocious deeds of Bonaparte... and to give him moreover the credit of friendly intentions for the time to come.'

New York';[1] and with impressment, of itself considered sufficient cause for war. They were concerned with the late news of a hot press for seamen in England, which might precurse sudden hostilities in the manner of Britain's undeclared war upon Denmark in 1807 and earlier upon Holland and Spain. Most of all were they concerned with the answer Britain through Foster had made to America's threat of a Revolution No. 2.

With inflexible determination Britain had pushed America 'to the Edge of the Precipice.' The British Lion (as Foster remarked) had not been awed or frightened: he had contemptuously sniffed, then fiercely snarled. There was to be no cessation of present wrongs, let alone indemnity for the past and security for the future; no concession real or nominal from a Tory Ministry adhering to Dr. Johnson's dogma: 'Sir, they are a race of convicts and ought to be content with anything we allow them short of hanging.'

If Congress now flinches, and turns traitor to the people as in 1809, said the Richmond *Enquirer*, 'there is not a petty nation in Europe, but will despise us. The Dey of Algiers or Tripoli will again insult us. And as to France or Great Britain (let us hide our heads in shame!) they will spit upon us, and treat us as the vilest caitiffs breathing.'[2] The people have declared for war, said Philadelphia's *Democratic Press*. 'We never shall be better prepared. Though ill provided with ramparts and citadels, we have hearts and hands, raised high for action.'[3] Nothing remains but the sword, said Niles of Baltimore, despite 'all that sophistry can devise, the fear of popularity invent, or personal pusillanimity dictate.... Every eye is fixed on Congress for the impulse. Let it be given with spirit, and *peace* will be coerced on honest and honorable terms through war.'[4]

We must have war, asserted Giles on March 25. On the same day Livingston of New York, a war Federalist, declared that war within thirty days was now certain. We will fight England for twenty years if need be, said old Varnum of Massachusetts. The

---

[1] Lex. *Reporter*, May 30, 1812. [2] Richmond *Enquirer*, March 27, 1812.
[3] *Democratic Press*, in N.Y. *Columbian*, March 26, 1812.
[4] *Niles' Register*, April 4, 1812.

House would pass a presidential recommendation of war, Foster was told; and it was not likely that the Senate moderates would reject it, for fear of ruining their party.[1] Nevertheless, Foster was optimistic. Since what Congress would do seemed to depend upon what Madison would recommend, he thought it 'not unlikely that the Session may terminate favourably to our interests after all.'[2] It was well known that Dearborn had yet to accept command of the army, and the President (as Crawford complained) by maintaining an equivocal silence fostered diversity of opinion and encouraged all those who would delay the inevitable decision 'untill it might be equally useless & pernicious.'[3]

The enspiriting impulse, perforce, was again imparted to the Executive, still stunned apparently by the blow France had given its badly managed diplomacy. On March 28, while Crawford was urging upon Madison the 'imperious' necessity of divulging his views, and while Gallatin was assuring Bayard that an embargo 'was entirely out of the question,'[4] young Johnson informed Kentucky that 'we are determined to declare war . . . in a few weeks. . . . Nothing but the want of troops in the north prevents a declaration of war at this moment.'[5] The raw militia adhered to Clay's embargo plan, but in order to prod the old guard forward they pressed for immediate war.[6]

Taking the initiative, on March 30 through their House Com-

---

[1] Foster, *MS. Diary*, March 25, and April 1, 2, 3, 1812.

[2] Any measure Madison recommends, depend upon it, will be with a view to his reelection — 'be it Embargo, Non-Intercourse, war, repeal of the Non-Importation Act (which is not improbable), or reconciliation... and many members who would otherwise be against any one of these measures will for the sake of the party vote in its favour.' Foster to Wellesley, Apr. 2, 1812, *F.O.* 5:85.

[3] Crawford to Madison, March 28, 1812, *Madison MSS*. He divided Congress into those who demanded immediate war; those who would submit; those who would temporize indefinitely; and those who 'would meet & support the views of the executive, when divulged,' who were for war yet believed the state of preparations made necessary 'a short delay' by means of 'a short embargo' preliminary to war with England. As to France Crawford, significantly, made no mention whatsoever.

[4] Bayard, *Papers*, p. 196. Later Bayard told Foster he 'thought Gallatin a terrible Liar, & that the Government was carried on by downright lying.' Foster, *MS. Diary*, June 7, 1812.

[5] R. M. Johnson, March 28, 1812, in *U.S. Gazette*, May 8, 1812.

[6] So insistent were they, wrote Senator Gregg (Penna.) on June 4, that 'their succeeding in their object... was only prevented by the embargo. That measure would not have been adopted at the time, had it not been to prevent war until the state of preparations would render us more competent to meet it.' *U.S. Gazette*, June 15, 1812.

mittee on Foreign Relations they informed Monroe that they were
ready to report ulterior measures. Did the Executive, they asked,
believe that its preparations warranted the step they contemplated? [1]

On the following morning Monroe assured the committee that
the President still thought war necessary unless Britain receded,
and of that there was little hope. He would not recommend
immediate war in view of the tardiness of preparations. But he
would, in spite of 'constitutional scruples,' recommend a sixty-day
embargo. This would be preparatory to war. In the meantime,
said Monroe, the *Hornet* will have arrived from France. If France
does us justice, 'it will increase the pressure upon England; if not,
we must resort to measures against her also.' Such an embargo
will leave 'the ultimate policy' as to both England and France in
our own hands. [2]

Monroe's remarks about 'the ultimate policy' convinced Com-
mitteeman Randolph that the Executive did not intend war but
planned to coerce Britain by stopping the flow of grain to Wellington's army. [3] Chairman Porter himself stated that war before
September would be disastrous, and that 'he was for a short
adjournment, letting our preparations go on, and at our succeeding meeting, laying an Embargo as preparatory to a War.' [4]
Impatient of further temporizing, Calhoun, Harper, Desha, and
Grundy approved the embargo as preliminary to war, and only
as such did they support it.

On April 1 Madison recommended a sixty-day embargo in a
curt message stating that he thought it 'expedient under existing
circumstances and prospects.' After hearing Clay's impassioned
appeals for it as a measure unquestionably precursing war with
England, the House overrode moderates who wanted an embargo
of one hundred and twenty days, cut off Randolph's abusive
tirades by the rule of the previous question, and carried it by a
vote of 70 to 41. On April 2 the Senate passed it by a vote of

---

[1] Resolution of committee, March 30, 1812, *S. Smith MSS.*
[2] *Ibid.*, Memo of remarks of Monroe and committeemen, March 31, 1812.
[3] Randolph to R. K. Randolph, March 31, 1812, *Randolph MSS.*
[4] Porter's remarks in committee, March 31, 1812, Memo in *S. Smith MSS.*

20 to 13 — but not before the moderates had extended it to ninety days; and the Giles-Smith faction had opposed it as a measure designed not to give Madison's administration more time to prepare for war but 'a fair occasion to Sneak out of War.' [1]

In the House Smilie moved its adoption. The War Hawks opposed the Senate's extension, then reluctantly gave their consent. On April 4 the Embargo Act, of ninety days yet presumably the first step in Clay's war program, was signed by Madison.

Hailing the Embargo as 'the signal for battle,' the press and people declared that the spell of indecision had been broken, and urged the Executive to make amends for past delays by energetic preparations for war on if not before July 4 — Independence Day. '*War* is inevitable,' exulted Clay's Kentuckians: '*The die is cast!*' [2]

Federalist maritime editors, however, echoed the assertions of Randolph and Quincy that the Executive intended the Embargo as an escape from war.[3] This 'palsying Embargo,' this 'miserable Terrapin Trap,' they said, is Madison's ultimate goal: a substitute for war which is worse than war, a pro-French and self-ruinous Jeffersonian Embargo No. 2 instead of the vaunted Revolution No. 2. 'The whole war fire evaporates in smoke!' Congress will now adjourn, then meet again to prolong the Embargo.[4] Madison will now send a peace mission to London — just as Jay was sent in '94 on the heels of a similar 'war' embargo.[5] 'Alas! Mr. Henry Clay . . . we cannot believe you, when you say that the embargo leads directly to war.' [6]

---

[1] Senator Smith's comment on memo of March 31, 1812, *S. Smith MSS.*

[2] Lex. *Reporter*, April 11, 14; Boston *Patriot*, in *Natl. Intelligencer*, April 23; Baltimore *Whig*, in N.Y. *Eve. Post*, April 8; *Niles' Register*, April 11; *Democratic Press*, April 17; Richmond *Enquirer*, April 7, 1812.

[3] Debates April 1–3, 1812, *Annals*, 12th, 1st, 1587–1611 (also, *ibid.*, pp. 1384–1411, May 6, 1812, a further discussion, Randolph vs. war men, on Madison's real intentions). 'If we must perish, let us perish by any hand except our own!' cried Quincy, who openly boasted that he had sent advance notice that merchants might put to sea — might 'escape into the jaws of the British lion, and of the French tiger, which are places of refuge, of joy and delight, when compared with the grasp and fangs of this hyena . . . which destroys under the mask of preserving.'

[4] N.Y. *Eve. Post*, April 4, 7; also *U.S. Gazette*, April 7; *Conn. Courant*, April 8; Trenton *Federalist*, in Pittsburgh *Gazette*, May 1, 1812.

[5] Baltimore *Federal Gazette*, April 3, 1812, enclosed in Foster to Wellesley, April 3–4, 1812, *F.O.* 5:85.

[6] *Connecticut Mirror*, in *U.S. Gazette*, April 21, 1812.

In propelling this 'war measure' through the House, and in defending Madison against Randolph and Quincy, Speaker Clay (said a member) 'was a flame of fire. He had now brought congress to the verge of what he conceived to be a war for liberty and honour, and his voice, inspired by the occasion, rang through the capitol, like a trumpet-tone sounding for the onset.' [1] The Kentuckian vehemently asserted that those who protested want of preparations were not for war. Our grievances against France (whom America would fight, too, if need be) should not embarrass our efforts against England, he said. There was complete proof that the enemy selected would do anything to destroy not only our shipping and the products of our soil but our seamen, our Western farmers, our Union itself. Against that enemy this temporary preparatory Embargo precursed open retaliatory war.[2] This opinion Speaker Clay and the War Hawks maintained in and out of Congress, even asserting that war would be declared before the end of the Embargo period.[3]

In private to Jefferson, Madison stated that since Britain preferred war to a repeal of her orders, nothing was left but to make ready for war, and that he had recommended the Embargo 'as a step to it.' [4] Unfortunately, the President by his cryptic public message had caused all factions to place varying interpretations on just why he considered the Embargo 'expedient,' and once again seemed to have (as Poindexter phrased it) 'crept into a nuttshell from whence he is sometimes heard to speak indistinctly.'

In private to Foster, both Madison and Monroe stated that while war was justified the Embargo was not war, that 'one Embargo might be inoculated on another,' that the door of negotiation was still open, and a reconciliation might well lead to war with Napoleon — with whom an adjustment was not expected.[5] To Serurier they declared that war with Britain was

---

[1] Prentice, *Clay*, p. 82. [2] *Annals*, 12th, 1st, 1589–91, April 1, 1812.

[3] Clay to Editor Worsley, April 4, 1812, *Reporter*, April 14, 1812; also, R. M. Johnson, April 4, 1812, *ibid.*, April 18, 1812. To Worsley, Clay declared: 'This measure is not designed as the substitute of War, but as a component part of that system which government is deliberately forming.'

[4] Madison to Jefferson, April 3, 1812, Madison, *Writings*, II, 531.

[5] Foster to Wellesley, April 1, 2, 3, 1812, *F.O.* 5:85; Foster, *MS. Diary*, April 1, 2, 3, 1812.

inevitable — if France did America justice; if she did not, the administration 'would infallibly succumb, or would be obliged to propose war against both Powers.' [1]

Unfortunately, these diplomatic equivocations found public expression in the *National Intelligencer*. Madison's 'court gazette' blew hot and cold, justified war against both powers, stressed French aggressions, and in shilly-shally fashion informed the country, on April 9, that the Embargo 'is not war, nor does it inevitably lead to war.'

The situation was further bedeviled by speeches, beginning April 9, on the propriety of a recess while preparations went forward, and of a suspension of the Non-Importation to allow the entry (and thus, perhaps, obviate war taxes) of American-owned British goods. The House War Hawks managed to postpone both proposals on the ground that they would seem to be 'giving the go-by to war.' The recess project (on which Madison refused to commit himself) continued to be pressed, however, by all those opposed to war; by 'every federalist with Foster at their head,' by Gallatin, and by those Senate moderates whose '*fears* and *apprehensions*' seemed to overcome 'their *resolution* and *judgment*.' [2]

Joined with the *Intelligencer's* editorials, and with the Executive's ostensible withdrawal from its badly managed East Florida 'revolution' (after Foster's strong protest in the form of 'a *paper broadside*'),[3] these 'symptoms of flinching' tended to confirm the view that the Embargo was a negotiating rather than a war instrument, and gave point to the rumor that Madison was about to send a mission to London headed by Bayard to cringe and beg for peace.[4]

Prompt, clamorous, and threatening was the public protest.

---

[1] Serurier to Bassano, April 9, 1812, Adams, *Hist. U.S.*, VI, 200–201.

[2] G. W. Campbell to Jackson, April 10, 1812, *Jackson MSS.*; Harper to Plumer, April 13, 29, 1812, *Plumer MSS.*; also Foster, *MS. Diary.*

[3] *Aurora*, April 15, 1812; *Democratic Press*, April 11, 13, 1812; and see Pratt, *Expansionists*, pp. 110–11. This intrigue became somewhat embarrassing in face of Foster's protests and Federalist outcries against it as 'a Plot more atrocious than Henry's.'

[4] *Poulson's American Daily Advertiser* (Phila.), March 30; *Natl. Intelligencer*, March 31 (a congressman's indignant letter against the idea); Lex. *Reporter*, April 14, 1812. Dr. Logan was urging such a mission; and men applied for the position of peace commissioner: Logan to Madison, March 31, and F. Corbin to same, April 6, 1812, *Madison MSS.*

These signs of continued indecision seem to lead, said the irate Lexington *Reporter*, to 'a total submission to the British government.' [1] The *National Intelligencer* was savagely attacked for hinting that war might yet be avoided. 'Come! Come! let's have no *backing out*, nor the cant of 1808,' retorted the Baltimore *Whig*.[2] Only as a prelude to war can the Embargo be justified, said the Albany *Register*.[3]

'The Intelligencer may talk of negociation . . . with England,' sneered the *Kentucky Gazette*, 'but . . . we should much like to know the price which the "Intelligencer" would receive as a compromise for the scalps of *Western Farmers*.' [4] By talking of a ridiculous triangular war, said the Petersburg *Republican*, the administration's gazette but deadens public ardor and nullifies every measure against England.[5] What is behind these 'doings and undoings,' it was asked; this talk of repealing the Non-Importation; of adjourning and of further negotiation? Is it to mollify our anti-war Tories, to reelect Madison, or to prepare the people for the sending of a submission agent to London? Or does it merely reveal a lack of 'plan, project or system?' [6]

Meanwhile, behind the scenes at Washington, a crisis had been reached in the struggle between the War Hawks and the men who tried by every means, as Madison himself remarked, 'to put off the day of war as long as possible, if ultimately to be met.' [7]

By April 9, according to Senator Worthington, Madison had yielded to the pressure of the moderates of both parties, and agreed to send a mission to London headed by Bayard in a last effort to prevent war.[8] It was on April 9 that the administration's journal,

---

[1] Lex. *Reporter*, April 18, 25, 1812.

[2] Baltimore *Whig*, in N.Y. *Eve. Post*, April 13, 1812.

[3] Albany *Register*, in N.Y. *Eve. Post*, April 17, 1812.

[4] *Ky. Gazette*, April 21, 1812, in Pratt, *Expansionists*, p. 57.

[5] Petersburg, Va., *Republican*, in *Aurora*, April 22, 1812.

[6] Washington letter, April 11, in *Aurora*, April 15, 1812.

[7] Madison to Jefferson, April 24, 1812, Madison, *Writings*, II, 533.

[8] Worthington's comments to Abraham Shepherd, of Shepherdstown, Va., on April 10, 1812, as reported by Shepherd to Timothy Pickering, Feb. 20, March 9, 1814, *Pickering MSS.* (vol. 30). The time of Worthington's talk with Shepherd (given by the latter as 'sometime in the beginning of April 1812') is fixed as April 10 by Worthington's *MS. Diary*: he left Washington April 9, arrived at Shepherdstown April 10, and returned to Washington late on April 13, 1812.

with its morale-shattering equivocations, informed the country that the Embargo 'is not war, nor does it inevitably lead to war.' Nevertheless, on April 14 the *National Intelligencer* made a sensational about-face. In a vigorous editorial which, significantly enough, was attributed to Speaker Clay, and was the Kentuckian's 'in style, manner and sentiment,' [1] the administration's gazette came out boldly and confidently and imperiously for immediate war!

This was a decisive stroke, unexpected, dramatic in its timeliness and effect. It heralded the Executive's definite commitment to the war party and the end of paralyzing indecision.

Why further delay? asked the *National Intelligencer* on April 14. Since England has crushed all hopes of an accommodation, 'let war therefore be forthwith proclaimed against England ... Any further discussion, any new attempt at negotiation, would be as fruitless as it would be dishonorable.' As to France, whatever the result of negotiations, which are said to be progressing favorably, 'we shall still be at liberty to pursue the course which circumstances may require.' If we now yield to England, whose pretensions are of no transient nature, we must forever be silent, mortified, disgraced. Only the timid and pusillanimous will falter. 'Our preparations are adequate to every essential object ... Our wrongs have been great; our cause is just, and if we are decided and firm, success is inevitable ... The final step ought to be taken; and that step is WAR.' [2]

This clarion call to courage and decisive action, in the Executive's journal and in the midst of 'milky-silky' equivocations, had 'an astonishing effect' upon 'the drooping spirits of the people.' [3] Foster, at first, could not believe that the Madison-Gallatin Executive approved this editorial 'Clay wrote.' [4] He could not believe that the President and the Secretary of State who a few days back

---

[1] Wash. letter, April 14, in N.Y. *Eve. Post*, April 17, 1812; Foster, *MS. Diary*, April 14, and Foster to Castlereagh, April 23, 1812, *F.O.* 5:85.

[2] *Natl. Intelligencer*, April 14, 1812. The editorial, under the American Eagle woodcut, was in large type, leaded, and ran about two columns, taking up most of the editorial page.

[3] Petersburg *Republican*, in *Aurora*, April 23, 1812.

[4] Foster, *MS. Diary*, April 14, 1812. Stanford, North Carolina Quid, and Milnor, Philadelphia Federalist, assured him, however, that they now believed war inevitable.

had assured him that the 'Embargo is not war' could approve Speaker Clay's 'very vehement exhortation to Congress to declare war against us immediately.' Yet neither the British envoy nor the anti-war men could disguise their alarm, for 'the sensation created by it was very great, not only here, but in the principal cities of the Union.'[1] Nor could they disguise their growing conviction that Madison and his old guard adherents had come under the 'complete ascendancy' of young Clay's war junto.[2]

On April 14 the 'great mist' of indecision began to lift.[3] Henceforth reports persisted that Madison had 'brought himself up to the "sticking place," ' and that war would be declared in a few days, a few weeks, certainly by June.[4] The *Intelligencer* no longer equivocated. Smilie said that war was against his conscience, 'but yet he must vote for it.' Porter, 'after being for war, then against it, then for it and against it,' had made up his mind and was off with a contract to supply the troops and, if possible, 'to save Madison's influence' in Clintonian New York.[5] Even Secretary Gallatin and Dr. Eustis now said that war was inevitable; to Foster, Gallatin remarked, rather significantly, that he was 'against the Game of Brag in Politicks — it argues a want of Self Respect.'[6] Exultingly, the Baltimore *Whig* declared that 'the Goal — to which the English cat-o'-nine-tails has been whipping us ever since 1783 — is at last in view!'[7]

By April 16 it seemed obvious to Taggart that Madison, in order to ensure his renomination, had given up his 'crooked insidious policy,' accepted the views of Clay's ruling junto, and was being 'driven by them like chaff before the wind.'[8] While still critical of a President who 'reluctantly gives up the system of peace,'

---

[1] Foster to Castlereagh, April 23, 1812, *F.O.* 5:85.

[2] Taggart, *Letters*, p. 394, April 26, 1812; also, *ibid.*, p. 393, April 16, 1812.

[3] Wash. letter, April 14, to Balt. *Whig*, in Phila. *Aurora*, April 20, 1812.

[4] Wash. letters, April 16 ff., in N.Y. *Columbian*, May 1; *U.S. Gazette*, April 20; Boston *Columbian Centinel*, April 25; Lex. *Reporter*, May 2, 1812; and Foster, *MS. Diary*, April 15, 1812, ff.

[5] Foster, *MS. Diary*, April 17, 1812; Foster to Castlereagh, April 21, 1812, *F.O.* 5:85.

[6] Foster, *MS. Diary*, May 6, 1812; Bayard to A. Bayard, May 2, 1812, Bayard, *Papers*, p. 196.

[7] Baltimore *Whig*, in Phila. *Aurora*, April 28, 1812.

[8] Taggart, *Letters*, p. 393, April 16, 1812.

Calhoun on the 18th reported that 'war is now seriously determined on.' [1] On the 21st Clay wrote that he expected to get home in June.[2] On the 25th and again on the 29th the House rejected a Senate resolution for a recess, on the ground that war would be declared before the Embargo's termination. Notwithstanding continued efforts of 'the British party' to alienate Senate Republicans — whom Harper regarded as being 'afraid that the ulterior measures will be brought forward too soon' by the 'rash and inconsiderate young men' of the House — Sevier on April 26 declared that there could not now be 'a shadow of doubt remaining of war.' [3]

Foster's dispatches revealed the gradual dissolving of the great mist. Republicans stopped coming to the Legation. Federalists in alarm now urged a 'concert of measures' in which British war activities would be confined to the South and West. Smilie's old guardsmen resented being superseded in the confidence of the Executive, noted Foster, but Clay's young War Hawks, who had postponed the nominating caucus because of 'the uncertain line of conduct hitherto pursued' by Madison, counted on a certain House majority for war, and were so impatient that if refused 'pabulum to their rage they must burst with the Violence of it.' Madison and Monroe gradually took on a firmer tone. By the end of April Foster was compelled to believe that Madison had been forced to give up his expressed intention 'to hook on one Embargo to another.' By May 3 it appeared that the President had 'at length come to a decision' and would take the plunge into war — a war 'principally on the point of honour,' brought about by young men 'who are either blinded by their passions, or whose Interests are embosomed in the back woods.' [4]

Yet to prevent war, Madison, so Foster still reported, would seize upon even a mere change in the name of the orders-in-council.

[1] Calhoun to Jas. MacBride, April 18, 1812, *MacBride MSS.*

[2] Clay to Innes, April 21, 1812, *Innes MSS.*, 18.

[3] Sevier to G. W. Sevier, April 26, 1812, Sevier, John, 'Journal,' *Tennessee Hist. Mag.*, VI, 65; Harper to Plumer, April 29, 1812, *Plumer MSS.*

[4] Foster to Castlereagh, April 21, 23, 24, May 3 *Most Secret*, May 3, 4, 5, May 5 *Private*, *F.O.* 5:85. Also, same to same, May 22, June 9, 21, 1812, *F.O.* 5:86, for his belief that the War Hawks of the South and West made war a condition for their support of Madison.

Perhaps indignation at France (and no one seemed angrier at Bonaparte than Speaker Clay) [1] might reduce everything to the absurdity of a triangular war. Perhaps it would all end in a nominal declaration of war or the issuing of letters of marque and reprisal, and a quasi war on sea like America's war against France in 1798. Perhaps Madison, still 'very loth to come to a rupture with us, and yet being pushed to it . . . as a Condition of his Re-election,' might try, by issuing letters of marque and reprisal to American merchantmen, to incite the British cruisers to some bloody action which would make an outright declaration of war popular in the Northeast. Foster himself tried, in vain, 'to put the Federalists upon insinuating that they will support him, if he agree to give up the advocates for war.' [2] He worked harder on the waverers, tried to soothe them on impressment, and urged Pope 'to suggest sending another Envoy to London.' [3] Nevertheless, the war current was strong. Even Senator Chauncey Goodrich, stalwart Federalist from Connecticut, when asked 'what was required of us by men of fair Views,' gave Foster in private this answer: 'Take off the orders in Council & come to some Arrangement about Impressment.' [4]

While uncertainty persisted up to the moment war was declared, undoubtedly the enspiriting impulse had been imparted to the Executive and its old guard adherents, who, as Serurier said, had been in a state of 'perpetual oscillations.' [5] And it was indicated that this had been accomplished or successfully initiated

---

[1] On May 8 Clay told him that if the *Hornet* failed to bring indemnities for spoliations by France, ten days thereafter war would be declared against France as well as England. Foster, *MS. Diary.*

[2] Foster to Castlereagh, May 3 *Most Secret*, May 3, *F.O.* 5:85; and Foster, *MS. Notes*, I, 147. In his *MS. Diary*, April 26, 1812, Foster recorded: 'Called on Eustis; he says Letters from the Eastward say, they don't want war with Canada, but only on the High Seas, and if that lead to general Hostility let it come. They are for Letters of Marque and Reprisal which I observed to Eustis were about the same as War. The Executive he said had done what they conceived their Duty and the remainder rested with Congress, which had to decide.'

[3] Foster, *MS. Diary*, May 19, 1812. On the preceding day, May 18, Foster wrote (*ibid.*): Senator Goodrich 'wants us to solicit that a Minister should be sent out. They cannot propose it from hence and it should be asked for as if to restore Equality . . . between the Two Countries.'

[4] *Ibid.*, May 18, 1812.

[5] Serurier to Bassano, April 15, 1812, *Aff. Étr.*, vol. 67.

between April 9 and April 14 — between April 9 when Madison allegedly had consented to send out a temporizing peace mission, and the *Intelligencer* had termed the Embargo neither war nor the inevitable precursor of war, and April 14 when the *Intelligencer*, in the dramatic editorial attributed to Speaker Clay, had stated that 'any new attempt at negotiation would be as fruitless as it would be dishonorable,' and had advocated 'the final step . . . and that step is WAR.'

What had caused this change, this new state of affairs which Giles petulantly described as 'every thing being given into the Hands of Boys'? [1] Could it have been the reports from France, alluded to yet not emphasized by Clay?

On April 11 Postmaster General Granger had received from Joel Barlow a private letter of March 3 informing him that Barlow was detaining the *Hornet* (already months overdue) 'a few days longer' to take out a commercial treaty with France. [2] Although Barlow officially on March 3 had written that he was 'under the painful necessity' of detaining the *Hornet* longer, [3] Republican editors seized upon this unofficial news, distorted it, used it to augment their demand for decisive action against Britain. [4] Anti-administration editors ridiculed it as a 'clumsily fabricated . . . hum-bug story.' [5] The news did not end threats of triangular war: only momentarily did it relieve Serurier from the angry attacks of Republicans upon an evasive and treacherous France. [6] It was

---

[1] Foster, *MS. Diary*, May 13, 1812.

[2] Clay on April 11 reported the story, without comment, Lex. *Reporter*, April 25, 1812; also, Wash. letter, April 11, *Democratic Press* (Saturday Evening) April 11, 1812.

[3] Barlow to Monroe, March 3, 1812, *U.S. Ministers, Dispatches*.

[4] 'This for ever and for ever puts a period to doubt, difficulty or procrastination. Folly can hardly miss the only honorable path there is now left for the United States.' *Democratic Press*, April 11, 1812. The same journal on April 15, 1812 reported (as did others) the rumor that the *Hornet*, hourly expected, had on board not just a commercial treaty but a treaty settling the southern boundaries, and, especially, a treaty providing indemnities for sequestered ships.

[5] Boston *Columbian Centinel*, April 29, 1812, jeering at 'Barlow's *cargo of Treaties*,' and asking, what many Republicans in private asked, why Barlow had chosen Granger — of all persons! — for his correspondent and not the Secretary of State. Also, Wash. letter, April 11, N.Y. *Eve. Post*, April 14, 1812 (stating that Madison, 'our great Magician, stirs the witch-pot full merrily'); Wash. letter, April 11, in Phila. *Aurora*, April 15, 1812.

[6] Serurier to Bassano, April 9, 15, 24, May 4, 14, 1812, *Aff. Étr.*, vol. 67. At Mrs. Madison's on April 15 Anderson, the veteran senator from Tennessee, a 'decided

discounted by Madison and Monroe, who were only further exasperated at France and at this time-spinning commercial treaty for which Barlow had no instructions, and with which he was 'burning his fingers.' [1] Reparation for sequestered property was Barlow's primary object, as Madison had reminded him in February. Without indemnities 'there can be neither cordiality nor confidence here; nor any restraint from self-redress in any justifiable mode of effecting it; nor any formal Treaty on any subject.' [2]

To Madison and the old guard Republicans, France was still pursuing a policy 'of crafty contrivance and insatiate cupidity.' The decisive change in tone in April was to be explained by something other than the Barlow-Granger story of April 11.

Between April 9 and 14, according to Worthington, a 'Caucus Committee' of 'hot headed Violent men,' including Grundy and captained by Speaker Clay, had forced Madison to give up the peace mission. Unless the President committed himself to their views, and 'nothing less than Open and direct War with England would satisfy that committee,' this 'set of hot headed fools... Clay at their head' had declared that 'they would forsake him and be Oposed to him.' Madison himself (said Worthington) told me 'that his friends had waited upon him' and that he felt 'bound to comply with their wishes.' [3]

Madisonian,' who was alarmed by the 'violent Measures' of young hotspurs, and had voted to extend the Embargo to ninety days, angrily denounced France: 'He was a little tipsy, spoke loud & in the hearing of Serrurier.' Foster, *MS. Diary*, April 15, 1812; also May 23, 1812. At 'Madame Jerome's' on April 16, Mme. Bonaparte 'tells me Serrurier says he hears they mean to make War on France as well as England in which Case he says he Shall solicit an Interview with me to concert Measures for attacking them. Mad. B thinks Serrurier has some Sense.' *Ibid.*, April 16, 1812.

[1] Madison to Jefferson, April 24, 1812, Madison, *Writings*, II, 533–34. In a letter to Mr. and Mrs. Barlow, Mrs. Madison stated: 'you will pardon me if I say aught that gives you pain, in preparing you for the disappointment expressed at Mr. Barlow's having told the state of his negotiations to Mr. Granger, who directly gave it circulation. ... The objection to this communication is — "that you may yet be disappointed; the anticipations of such a treaty might cause improper speculations"; "that Mr. G. was not a proper channel," and much of the same kind. All this from the people, not from the Cabinet, yet you know everything vibrates there.' The letter (misdated '1811') is in [Cutts, Mrs. L. B.], *Memoirs and Letters of Dolly Madison*, p. 87.

[2] Madison to Barlow, Feb. 24, 1812, Madison, *Writings*, II, 529; also, Monroe to Barlow, Feb. 23, 24, March 21, and his very sharp instructions of April 23, 1812, *U.S. Ministers, Instructions*.

[3] Senator Worthington, as reported by Shepherd to Pickering, Feb. 20, March 9, 1814, *Pickering MSS*. Immediately upon his return from Shepherdstown (i.e., April 13–14, 1812), so he told Shepherd July 6, 1812 (both dates fixed by Worthington's

In truth, friends of Madison both in and out of Congress were urging him to take a decisive stand. War was the next step demanded by the nation, wrote a Virginia friend on April 13; 'if the Government were now to succumb — what with the pressure from abroad & at home — it would be crushed to annihilation.' [1] Likewise the congressional committee, with Clay as its spokesman, urged upon the President arguments similar to those of the *Intelligencer's* editorial of April 14. Asserting that the Anglo-Federalist and 'peace-and-commerce' opposition could not be reconciled whatever policy was pursued, and stressing the national disgrace and obvious political dangers of further temporizing, of further efforts at fruitless negotiation, Clay urged upon him the imperious necessity of more 'vigorous preparation, and of a speedy declaration of hostilities.' The Kentuckian was confident that the people and their republican form of government were capable of preserving American independence. No people or government had ever tried so desperately to avoid resort to the sword. But by now, 'surely we have exhausted the argument with Great Britain. Let us do what we sincerely believe to be right, and trust to God and the goodness of our cause.' [2]

Using his utmost persuasion, the Speaker overcame the President's reluctance to give up the system of quasi peace — enough

---

MS. Diary), Worthington heard that during his absence, since April 9, the War Hawks had threatened and prevailed over the coalition of temporizing and anti-war Federalists and Republicans.

[1] J. G. Jackson to Madison, April 13, 1812, *Madison MSS.* Editor John Binns was friendly to Madison, and defended him against Duane, Irvine, and other Republican critics; yet, most insistent for action, he constantly reiterated: 'Every man... ardently wishes for *decision*. Every man... calls for *decision*. The honor and interest of the Union and the conservation and prosperity of the democratic party, demand *decision*. The Nation expects and too long has expected *decision*. There is no point from which Patriotism can view our national position without being impressed with the necessity of *decision*. *Irresoluteness*, and it alone can feed faction and unman the nation. It alone can degrade us in the eyes of other nations and make us loathesome in our own.' *Democratic Press*, April 28, 1812.

[2] Clay's early biographers (and it may be noted, in the case of Colton's *Life and Times*, that Clay read the proof-sheets) agree that 'this formal meeting' of the caucus committee was held after the Embargo, and that it was decisive: Clay 'inspired him with determination and boldness,' and 'nothing remained but the formal act of war.' Coercive threats are not mentioned, yet all agree that 'powerful influences' were exerted to overcome 'Mr. Madison's well known moderation,' his 'extreme caution, bordering on timidity,' and to counteract the powerful influence over him of Secretary Gallatin. Colton, I, 153, 161; Mallory, I, 63, 67; Sargent, Epes, *Life and Public Services of Henry Clay*, p. 14; *Life and Speeches of Henry Clay*, Anonymous, N.Y., 1843, I, 67; and, also, Adams, J. Q., *Madison and Monroe*, pp. 148–49; Ingersoll, C. J., *Recollections*, p. 350.

so that Calhoun (on April 18) could report that 'war is now seriously determined on.' [1]

Then and thereafter the submission men (in varying versions) asserted that Clay and his War Hawks had bullied Madison into war, using the nomination as their club. Not until they had bluntly told Little Jemmy that he had to fight or quit the palace did 'the old gentleman screw up his courage to the sticking place,' relax his 'grasp of death' on the peace system, accept the Embargo as a war measure, and promise to send in a war message. Henry Clay was most responsible, said Quincy: that bold, aspiring, overbearing young Westerner, the imperious Speaker of the House, 'was the man whose influence and power more than any other produced the war of 1812.' [2]

The bald partisan charge that Madison had been coerced by Clay, and in base betrayal of his principles had made war in order to secure his reelection, was belied by the esteem in which Madison and Clay always held each other; and, indeed, by the affectionate relations always existing between Mrs. Madison and Clay. It ran counter to the good-humored though earnest spirit in which the President and the Speaker discussed the subject — not whether there should be war but when war should begin. [3] It was contrary to the Chief Executive's pledge of cooperation for war given at the

---

[1] Calhoun to James MacBride, April 18, 1812, *MacBride MSS.*

[2] Quincy, *Quincy*, pp. 255, 259; also, N.Y. *Eve. Post*, June 20, Oct. 3, 1812; *U.S. Gazette*, June 30, July 6, Aug. 1, 1812. On May 5, 1812, the *Connecticut Courant*, quoting the Baltimore *Fed. Republican*, stated that (in late April, apparently) 'Mr. Madison was waited upon by the committees of both Houses, selected to consider of an adjournment, who... called upon him for the measures which it was understood the embargo was to introduce.' Editor Hanson in June of 1813, on the floor of the House asserted that a committee had twice waited upon Madison, coercing him the second time. *Annals*, 13th, 1st, 254.

[3] 'By way of illustrating the difference between speaking and writing, and *acting*, Mr. Clay related to Mr. Madison an anecdote of two Kentucky Judges. One talked incessantly from the Bench. He reasoned every body to death. He would deliver an opinion, and first try to convince the party that agreed with him and then the opposite party. The consequence was that business lagged, the docket accumulated, litigants complained, and the community were dissatisfied. He was succeeded by a Judge, who never gave any reasons for his opinion, but decided the case simply, for the plaintiff or the defendant. His decisions were rarely reversed by the appellate Court — the docket melted away — litigants were no longer exposed to ruinous delay — and the community were contented. "Surely," said Mr. Clay, "we have exhausted the argument with Great Britain."
'Mr. Madison enjoyed the joke, but, in his good-natured, sly way, said, he also had heard an anecdote, of a French Judge, who after the argument of the cause was over, put the papers of the contending parties into opposite scales, and decided according to the preponderance of weight.' Sargent, *Clay*, p. 14. See, also, Mallory, *Clay*, I, 67.

beginning of the session; contrary to the spirit of his public messages, and of his private letters (and those of Mrs. Madison), which
recognized the probability if not the inevitability of war.[1] It
clashed with the view expressed by Editor Gales of the *Intelligencer*,
that Madison's hesitation, which was overcome by a formal 'dep-
utation of Members of Congress, with Mr. Clay at their head,' was
caused by his uncertainty 'as to the House sustaining the Executive
in a declaration of war.' [2] It clashed with the view held by such a •
critical and insistent young War Hawk as Editor Niles. Noting that
men had charged President Adams 'with a temporizing policy . . .
with a view to a *re-election*; that is, that he sacrificed *principles* to
popularity,' Niles declared that 'the same things are alleged by some
in regard to president *Madison*; — but certainly not with the same
plausibility, for in the *public* acts of that gentleman we observe
only one sentiment — an uniformly *non-submitting* spirit.' [3]

The allegations of the submissionists were not supported by
confidential letters of the War Hawks, not even by those of Poindexter, who to intimates had most freely expressed his irritation,
and in January had declared: 'Mr. Madison is afraid to go to war
or to be at peace; and the course he pursues really deserves ridicule.' On April 10 the Mississippi War Hawk reported that 'the
Executive is much censured by all parties for the tardiness of its
advances to meet the *tug of war*, and the tenure of Mr. Madison's
continuance in the presidential chair, in my opinion, depends on
the success of our hostile preparations.' Poindexter did not picture
the President as being dead set against war. Yet, like Calhoun,
he did criticize his lack of vigor in preparing for war and his
reluctance in entering war. And like Calhoun, Poindexter confidently declared, on April 10, that 'the close of the embargo will
open a new scene — *War* in all its moods & tenses (as Gov. Wright
says).' [4]

---

[1] An interesting supplement to the *Madison MSS.* (which are pretty well thinned on
this period) are the intimate letters of Mrs. Madison to her sister Anna, the wife of Rep.
Rich. Cutts of Maine (some of them unfortunately misdated), in Cutts, *Memoirs and
Letters of Dolly Madison*, pp. 73–89.

[2] Hunt, *Gales on the War Manifesto*, p. 309. Gales, writing in 1854, placed the time of
this conference very roughly, stating that it was held when 'More than six months had
passed since Congress met, and the question of actual war was still in suspense.'

[3] *Niles' Register*, May 23, 1812.

[4] Poindexter to Mead, April 10, 1812, *Poindexter MSS.*

Even the indefatigable Timothy Pickering could not substantiate the charge that Speaker Clay and his War Hawk committee, using the nomination as a club, had bludgeoned President Madison into 'a wicked and unjust war.' [1] By the War Hawks it was ignored or denied. When Quincy made it in the House in January of 1813, Clay contemptuously dismissed it as having but an 'imaginary existence,' and directed Quincy's attention to such notorious and treasonable realities as 'Henryism' past and present. The Kentuckian might also have directed Quincy's attention to Federalist efforts in promoting hostilities in order to defeat Mr. Madison's reelection; Federalist schemes urging Britain to bully America into war, which the Tory *Quarterly Review* of London thought 'dangerous and doubtful,' and the British Minister himself termed 'strange and dangerous.' John Randolph, who appreciated the inconsistency, and the irony, said Quincy's 'crooked scheme' merited its fate, even though 'great allowance is to be made for men under the *regime* of Clay, Grundy & Co.' [2]

One thing however was certain. War Hawk pressure had been applied, and applied ever since Clay's election as Speaker. The enspiriting impulse demanded by the people had been imparted to Congress and then to a President who did not actively oppose war, yet was reluctant to take the final step. Whatever the degree to which that pressure had been exerted, there could be no question but that Madison had been powerfully influenced, and brought to a decision.

The tide had turned, and by the first of May was running swiftly. The *National Intelligencer* spoke the language of the War Hawks; [3]

---

[1] The charge of coercion is dismissed by Smith, T. C., 'War Guilt in 1812,' *Proc. Mass. Hist. Soc.*, June 1931, LXIV, 319–45. On the evidence at his command, Smith concludes that Clay imparted the necessary impulse to Madison possibly in May, after the nomination, rather than in April, before the nomination, as above indicated.

[2] Randolph to Francis Scott Key (Federalist, who had condemned the Quincy extremists, stating that 'the Quarterly Reviewers say well that the expedient of driving the administration into the war for the purpose of making them unpopular was "dangerous and doubtful" '), Sept. 12, 1813, Garland, *Randolph*, II, 18, 20. The Federalists, he wrote Key, had borne more from the 'pettifoggers of the West than they would ... from Lord North ... there is no common tie of interest or of feeling between them and their upstart oppressors.'

[3] 'The truth, then, is, the undoubted truth, that the Embargo is meant to be the precursor of war, and that so soon as the physical resources of the nation can be arranged, war will ensue...' *Natl. Intelligencer*, April 28, 1812.

Monroe on May 5 informed the chargé at London of the 'great probability of a rupture';[1] and even the moderates agreed that war with Madison's approval would be declared early in June.[2] So far from being unprepared, stated Calhoun on May 6, the administration within four weeks of the declaration would have part of Lower Canada and all of Upper Canada.[3] Sustained by letters from the East and from the West, Speaker Clay was most confident as to the people's 'fortitude and firmness' in coping with 'this new & untried experiment to which the only free government on earth is about to be subjected . . . God grant us a happy result.'[4] He was proud of Kentucky, where 'Volunteer Corps are going out *daily* to the protection of Indianna.' Even Humphrey Marshall, Dr. Louis Marshall, and the whole Marshall clan could not resist the wave of all but hysterical martial ardor which had engulfed democratic and nationalistic Kentucky. 'Humphrey Marshall,' so Robert Wickcliffe reported, 'has volunteered this morning in Capt., Doctor, Marshall's *Troop*.'[5]

At Washington, John Randolph and Quincy's Federalists raged most furiously, demanded the repeal of the Embargo, reiterated that war without an army, a navy, or money would be a gross and treasonable folly, and for the first time cavilled at the Speaker's 'intolerance.'[6] On May 12 the Senate summarily dismissed, by a vote of 15 to 8, the attempt of Pope, Worthington, and the Federalists to repeal the Non-Importation and place France and England on an equal footing — and thus prepare the ground for

---

[1] Monroe to Jonathan Russell, May 5, 1812, *U.S. Ministers, Instructions.*

[2] Bayard to A. Bayard, May 9, 1812, Bayard, *Papers*, p. 198; and Washington letter, May 15, in Lex. *Reporter*, May 30, 1812.

[3] *Annals*, 12th, 1st, 1397.

[4] Clay to Thomas Bodley, May 12, 1812, Ky. S. Hist. Soc., *Misc. MSS.* M. McKim, Jr., Baltimore merchant and Clay's client, declared: 'We are an Humbled & degraded Nation and If the Stand that is now Taken is departed from, Without bringing England to Justice, we may as well give up our Republican Government & have a Despot to rule over us.' McKim was enraged at speculating merchants, who were clamoring about their property or money in England (which 'with their Eyes open . . . calculating on our Government submitting' they had bought or sent there, despite the non-intercourse), and urged that such men not 'be Indulged at the Expense of every thing Dear to the United States.' McKim to Clay, May 13, 1812, *Clay MSS.*

[5] Robt. Wickcliffe to Clay, May 31, 1812, *Clay MSS.*

[6] *Natl. Intelligencer*, May 14, 1812 (defense and praise of Clay); *Democratic Press*, May 11, 1812 (attack on Randolph).

triangular war, or no war at all.[1] On May 13 the House recalled its absent members in order to have them present by June first to vote on the ulterior measure. Both Senate and House stand fast, it was reported; 'the Executive, likewise, is firm, fixed, & immovable as Atlas.'[2]

Against this background, on May 18 the long-delayed nominating caucus was held, with Speaker Clay and his War Hawks prominent among the eighty-three congressmen present. Eighty-two votes were cast, and all for Madison. Even Pope voted for him.[3] The unanimity of both the moderates and the uncompromising war men was most striking. At the same time the old guard was warned by young Niles that 'a thousand such nominations will not retain the good opinion of the people in favor of Mr. *Madison*, or induct him a second time to the presidential chair, unless the country is released from the present *quasi* state of war — by an honest peace or open hostilities.'[4]

Foster regarded it as a 'sine qua non' that Madison would now exert his whole influence to keep his old guard adherents in line with the young War Hawks, and would send in a presidential message recommending war.[5] In truth, by May 21 Madison was

---

[1] Pope's resolution was generally reprobated. Said the indignant Lexington *Reporter*, May 30, 1812, it 'would have been a total submission... to the British, and this at the moment when that savage government are devastating and murdering on all our frontiers.' Under the headline of 'FRENCH WAR' Editor Worsley stressed the popular grievances against Britain alone; stated that 'citizens of the Eastern States, and members of Congress, may abandon 7,000 seamen — they may term it, a *trifling impropriety* on the part of England,' but not so Western Americans; and vehemently declared: 'The Government MUST not abandon the Western Country to the British.'

[2] Richmond *Enquirer*, May 19, 1812. Ritchie decried Pope's 'submission resolution,' and the tactics, as to Madison, of the *Whig, Aurora,* and Albany *Register* — which 'once led the Republican party to victory; but who, like Elephants in eastern battles, are now turning upon the very ranks, which they formerly assisted' — and called upon all Americans for 'a long pull, a strong pull, & a pull all together.'

[3] To Foster he lamely explained why he had voted for Mr. Madison by saying 'Mrs. Madison made a very good President & must not be turned out.' Foster, *MS. Diary*, May 19, 1812. On May 14, 1812 Foster recorded (*ibid.*) of Morgan Lewis, leader of the Lewisites or New York Quids, whom Madison had just appointed Quartermaster General of the army: 'Lewis says Madison has no Personal Friend and if he be reelected it will not be because he personally is approved of, but because they dont know what other Candidate to put up. He thinks they cannot alter, they will be for War & carry it.'

[4] *Niles' Register*, May 23, 1812. 83 members attended; 82 voted for Madison; Rep. Sammons of New York did not vote. Elbridge Gerry, defeated that spring by a close vote for reelection as governor of Massachusetts, was chosen vice presidential candidate on June 8, 1812. At this second caucus Clay had the ballot opened for ten members not present at the May 18 caucus; all ten voted for Madison. *Ibid.*, June 27, 1812.

[5] Foster, *MS. Notes*, I, 166.

preparing such a message, and Congress was at work on a declaration of war.[1]

Meanwhile, from the middle of April on, Federalist editors in the Northeast increasingly assailed 'Mr. Clay and his Western brethren,' these hot-brained young backwoodsmen who 'have bounced, and blustered, and foamed, and swore, that war we must and shall have,' these 'Kentucky hot-heads' who have vaulted into power over the weakness of Virginia, dragooned Madison, and tied down the majority hand and foot. 'We tell them plainly *we will not go to war*,' said the New York *Evening Post*; we will not have our commerce ruined, our cities destroyed, and ourselves driven 'into the western wilds . . . as recommended by Mr. Speaker Clay and other great orators' in order 'to save the credit of a few rash men in Congress!'[2] They discouraged recruiting, and refused to subscribe to the war loan. '*Let every highwayman find his own pistols*,' said the Boston *Gazette*. We must 'chastise the INSOLENCE of those MAD MEN of *Kentucky and Tennessee*,' said the New York *Commercial Advertiser*, declaring that 'Old Massachusetts is as TERRIBLE to the AMERICANS now as she was to the British Cabinet in 1775.' By all means let us prepare our arms for war, said the Pickeronian Boston *Repertory*: 'We must use them for the EMPEROR of FRANCE or for OURSELVES.'[3]

Denouncing the 'Henryism' of the hydra British party composed of 'old tories and modern traitors,' and threatening to punish 'pert Sedition, snarling Treachery, and deep-mouthed Treason,'[4] editors and correspondents reiterated the familiar grievances, emphasizing impressment. With young Niles they agreed that 'war dreadful as it is, will not be without its benefits in giving us a NATIONAL CHARACTER, and separating us from the

---

[1] Geo. M. Bibb to John J. Crittenden, May 21, 1812, *Crittenden MSS.*

[2] N.Y. *Eve. Post*, April 30, May 4, 16, 18, 19, 1812, *passim.*

[3] N.Y. *Commercial Advertiser*, and Boston *Gazette*, in *Natl. Intelligencer*, April 23, 28; Boston *Repertory*, in Lex. *Reporter*, May 16, 1812. No journals more vehemently denounced such 'Henryism' than the Boston *Patriot* and the Boston *Chronicle*, which warned of the fate meted out to the Tory aristocracy of New England in '76 by the common people of Massachusetts, the squatters of Maine, and the Green Mountain Boys.

[4] *Democratic Press*, April 28, 1812.

strumpet governments of Europe.' [1] Admitting that detestable France gave just but not equal cause for war, they discussed and in the end rejected triangular war because of the manifest absurdity of fighting all Europe at one and the same time.[2] They confidently asserted that energetic action would soon recover the ground lost by protracted forbearance, swell the ranks of the army, and fill the loan of eleven millions, six millions of which had been subscribed on the first two days of May.[3] They acclaimed the mass meetings demanding immediate war held in Philadelphia, Baltimore, Richmond, Charleston, and hundreds of smaller towns; and reported the movement of troops to the frontiers, the brisk recruiting, the eagerness of privateersmen. The Kentucky Volunteers were ready to march at once 'to the Lakes or to the Plains of Abraham, or the consecrated field of Tippecanoe; alike indifferent whether they face the mercinary soldiers of the Royal Maniac in Canada or their Savage allies on the Wabash.' [4]

Although war was opposed by a powerful and wealthy minority, the people were better united than in '76, John Adams Harper was informed by Plumer, who that spring was elected Republican governor of New Hampshire.[5] Despite 'the Tories of Boston and New York,' John Adams was as confident as Harper or Clay that the great mass of Americans wanted and would have this just

---

[1] *Niles' Register*, May 9, 1812, ff.

[2] 'It is ... unavailing to regret that we did not resist England early enough: Both as the London Courier says, seem to have made a tacit agreement to wrong us,' stated the Baltimore *Whig*, in Lex. *Reporter*, May 23, 1812, and ff. 'Tyrannical governments hate free ones. IF, therefore, the Hornet bring no treaty or news of settlement with France, we hope our government will instantly renew the non-importation law with her, and declare war against England. The heinous sin of *impressment* justifies the discrimination. Let us then cultivate all our own resources, *protect our manufactures*, and secure the friendship and commerce of our *Spanish American neighbours*, which appear more important than any precarious intercourse with European nations.... Let us sequester *French funds*, &c. while we bend our united forces against the *original* aggressor, the great disturber of the world ... the *first* to light the torch of war and make a bonfire of neutral rights.... It is to England (and her faction here) we owe nine tenths of our wrongs and sufferings.'

[3] On the failure of wealthy capitalistic New England to subscribe to the loan, the *Democratic Press* (in *U.S. Gazette*, May 9, 1812) deplored the fact that the books were confined to the Atlantic cities: 'Those only have been invited to subscribe who are like swine at their wash — give them trade — their aliment — and the dogs may worry them as they will; — they will grunt and swill, and swill and grunt, but never turn on their tormentors.'

[4] *Ky. Gazette*, in Lex. *Reporter*, May 23, 1812.

[5] Plumer to Harper, May 11, 1812, *Plumer MSS.*

and necessary Second Revolution. The vote for war might be close, yet 'all the great critical questions about Men and Measures from 1774 to 1778 were decided by the vote of a single state, and that vote was often decided by a single Individual,' reassuringly declared the old patriot. 'Jumble and Chaos as this Nation appears at this moment, I never knew it better united.' [1]

Madison had been renominated, and the ulterior measures were being prepared by the President and Congress, when on May 22 the long-delayed *Hornet* brought news from uncompromising Tory London which gave the final impulse to the long-smouldering volcano.

There was no question as to its eruption; no question as to war with England. Yet the *Hornet*, alas, failed to bring from France indemnities or even a commercial treaty, and the indignant Republicans raised the cry of triangular war. Only 'some few' (as Foster noted) seriously advocated it, however.[2] Madison himself had come to realize the 'thousand difficulties' which made triangular war, while justified, grossly and dangerously inexpedient.[3] 'The universal sentiment was,' wrote Clay, ' "we will go on in our intended course as to England, and wait a little longer with France." ' [4] After silencing 'the insolence of British cannon . . . we can then speak to the hushed batteries of French aggression.' [5] As planned, Madison would send in his war message on June 1.

---

[1] Adams to Rush, June 12, 1812, *Old Family Letters*, p. 393.

[2] Foster to Castlereagh, June 9, 1812, *F.O.* 5:86, and Foster, *MS. Diary*, May 22, 1812, and ff.

[3] Madison to Jefferson, May 25, 1812, Madison, *Writings*, II, 535. It is possible that Madison was again reassured by a committee headed by Clay, as suggested by Smith, *War Guilt in 1812*, above cited. See, also, Hunt, G., *Gales on the War Manifesto*, p. 309.

[4] Clay, May 24, 27, in Lex. *Reporter*, June 6, 13, 1812. See, also, Clay to Crittenden, May 28, 1812, *Crittenden MSS.*; Geo. M. Bibb to Jas. Morrison, May 24, 1812, *Clay MSS.*; Poindexter to Mead, May 24, 1812, *Poindexter MSS.*

[5] Clay, June 18, in Lex. *Reporter*, June 27, 1812. 'France. . . has forebore, except as to her Tariff, which we cannot complain of as an infraction of the public law,' he wrote. 'The balance with her is struck, though not paid. England has a running account with us which every passing moment swells with the most enormous items. The blows of the one, though heavy and severe, are at least intermitted. With regard to the other, behind and before us is exhibited but one boundless proof of wrong and of insult.' Another letter of the same date (*ibid.*) stated: 'As to France, the negociation is not yet absolutely broken off, however hopeless we may be of a favourable result. As to France we have no complaint, on the score of violation of neutral rights,

On May 29 Randolph attempted to precipitate an open discussion in advance of the President's message by 'conjuring up the Gorgon head of Bonaparte,' [1] in one of the many abusive and discursive tirades with which he had worried the patience of Congress and the nation for seven long months. He held the floor for over an hour. Then Calhoun hotly called him to order: there was no motion before the House. Clay under a little-used rule required him to submit his motion in writing. Randolph became enraged, and strenuously objected.[2] But the House sustained Clay, refused by a vote of 72 to 37 to entertain Randolph's motion that it was inexpedient to resort to war, and forced him from the floor. The Cock of Kentucky, 'the dictator of the House,' had used beak and talons. Never before in his fourteen years in the House had 'the *great* Mr. Randolph' been mastered and muzzled. He had been utterly crushed, and with him Freedom of Speech, so he asserted, by 'the *sic volo* of one tyro on the floor and the *sic jubeo* of another in the chair.' [3] Republicans praised Clay, and said he would be equal to the filibuster the submission men in caucus were reported to have planned against the declaration of war. 'It is a subject of pride and congratulation to the nation that at such a session the House has a Speaker so prompt and vigorous, so well acquainted with the rules of the House and so resolute in enforcing them as Mr. Clay.' [4]

On June 1 Madison's message recounting the many causes just-

---

but of the past. Of England we have to complain in all the tenses. The one has in some measure ceased her blows, the other is everywhere pounding us. The one we can strike, the other we cannot reach...' See, also, *Natl. Intelligencer*, May 30; Richmond *Enquirer*, June 2, and *Niles' Register*, May 30, 1812, and ff.

[1] Denouncing his 'miserable manoeuvre,' the Richmond *Enquirer*, June 12, 1812, asked: 'Do YOU seriously believe... that Nathaniel Macon is a tool of the Emperor... Crawford & Troup and Bibb... Williams & Lowndes and Cheves and Calhoun... Henry Clay & all the representatives of the West and East, the minions of France?'

[2] 'My lord has been indulged so much in his humors that, like a spoiled child, he kicks and squeels monstrously on being forced to discipline' by a Speaker 'equal to his duty.' Washington letter, May 29, in *Democratic Press*, June 2, 1812.

[3] Bruce, *Randolph*, I, 381, 417; *Annals*, 12th, 1st, 1451–79, for debates and public letters of Clay and Randolph. Cheves on July 30, 1812 (Clay, *Corres.*, pp. 18–19) advised Clay not to dispute further, and above all not 'to put it on any other footing than that of argument.' In sending his public letter, replying to Randolph, of June 17, Clay cautioned Editor Worsley to avoid the (minor) mistakes made by Editor Gales in the *Intelligencer* — because 'One hates to be mangled!' Clay to Wm. W. Worsley, June 18, 1812, Lexington Public Library, *Misc. MSS.*

[4] *Democratic Press*, June 3 (also, June 19), 1812.

ifying war, and stressing not only British monopoly but the 'crying enormity' of impressment,[1] was received by the House. On June 3 the war bill was reported, supported by an able summary of the long-sustained evils which made this war forced by England on the United States 'radically' a struggle for national character and sovereignty, a second war for independence. Speaker Clay, Calhoun, and some others wanted open discussions, but mainly upon the advice of Madison the proceedings were secret.[2] Randolph and Quincy vainly attempted obstructionist tactics, then subsided into silence. After months of war debates 'there was no more really to be said on the subject,' remarked Calhoun, and the measure went through 'without discussion, except upon some incidental points.'[3] An effort to include France in the declaration was defeated: only ten votes, of which but two were Federalist, were cast for triangular war.[4] Overriding Federalists, Quids, Clintonians, peace-at-any-price Republicans, and 'war Republicans' who would declare war in the indefinite future when preparations were further advanced, the House on June 4 passed the war bill 79 to 49. With this majority of thirty votes ('exclusive

---

[1] 'Against this crying enormity, which Great Britain would be so prompt to avenge if committed against herself, the United States have in vain exhausted remonstrances and expostulations.' *Annals*, 12th, 1st, 1625. As long as the impressment practice is continued, said the House report, 'it is impossible for the United States to consider themselves an independent nation. Every new case is a new proof of their degradation. Its continuance is the more unjustifiable, because the United States have repeatedly proposed to the British government an arrangement which would secure to it the control of its own people.' *Ibid.*, p. 1551.

[2] Calhoun, in a Senate speech, July 17, 1841. Speaker Clay, myself, and others 'were of opinion that the war question should be discussed with open doors; but there were others of the party (among them... Grundy...) who differed with us.' Clay, Grundy, and myself 'waited upon the President, and the result of the interview was, that the discussion should be with closed doors.' *Congressional Globe*, 27th, 1st, 215. Doubtless this conference, along with others, aided in giving color and variety to the charge of 'coercion.' Secret proceedings, said Editor Duane (who at the same time cried out for 'open, honest, unsophisticated war, such as Rome made in the days of her virtue'), were as imperative as in the days of the Revolutionary Congress, and for the same reason: to avoid dangers from Tory 'apostles of *discord*.' Phila. *Aurora*, June 12, 16, 1812.

[3] Calhoun, in 1841, *loc. cit.*

[4] Clay to Adam Beatty, June 21, 1812, Boston Public Library *Misc. MSS*. 'It is in vain by such a step [war or hostile measures against France], to attempt the conciliation of the Feds.'

In a speech of January 1813 Clay stated that when McKee of Kentucky moved in the Committee of the Whole to make war against France as well as England, 'there appeared but ten votes in support of it, of whom, seven belonged to this side of the house, and three only to the other!' Mallory, *Clay*, I, 249.

of my own, and of others who were absent,' wrote Clay), the House sent the ulterior measure to the Senate.[1]

Here it was delayed, on various grounds. At first the war party waited for absent colleagues, fearing a coalition with the Federalists of the Clintonians, of such uncertain moderates as Pope and Worthington, and of the malcontents — Giles, Leib of Pennsylvania, and Smith, who since November (wrote the fretful Monroe) had contrived and managed 'every pestilent scheme' to embarrass and ruin the administration.[2] There were speeches for postponement by Bayard and by German, Republican of New York, on the ground of war's inexpediency. There were calls for information on the state of preparations, by Worthington, who assured Madison that while war was 'unavoidable' three months should elapse before its declaration,[3] and by Gregg of Pennsylvania, who would also wait until fall, if the causes for war persisted, since 'we are *totally unprepared*, as yet, to carry such declaration into effect.' [4] As Bayard wrote, much depended upon 'management in giving a direction to wavering and balancing opinions,' and in providing 'a good cover . . . for those who are disposed to retreat.' [5]

An attempt to provide a cover for retreat was made when Pope,

---

[1] Clay to Worsley, June 20, 1812, Lex. *Reporter*, July 1, 1812. The following states voted unanimously for war: Kentucky, Tennessee, Ohio, South Carolina, Georgia; total of 20. Unanimously against: Connecticut, Rhode Island, Delaware; total of 10. Predominantly for: New Hampshire, Vermont, Pennsylvania (16 to 2), Maryland, Virginia (14 to 5), North Carolina (6 to 3); total of 48 for war, 16 against. Predominantly against: Massachusetts (8 to 6), New York (11 to 3), New Jersey (4 to 2); total of 11 for war, 23 against. North of Virginia the vote was 39 for war, 41 against; Virginia, the South, and West, 40 for war, 8 against. *Annals*, 12th, 1st, 1637. Poindexter of Mississippi Territory was allowed to register that if he had a vote it would have been cast for war.

[2] Monroe to John Taylor of Caroline, June 13, 1812, *Monroe MSS.*

[3] 'Conversed near an hour & half with the president on indian affairs and the subject of war . . . candidly stated to him towit that we are unprepared that 3 months must elapse before any invasion [of Canada] can take place that in the meantime the administration will be exposed to the attacks of its enemies the people will be disheartened . . . That although I may differ with my friends on this question or with him I will be the very last to agree to a disgraceful peace & will rise or sink with my political associates. That I believe war is unavoidable but as we have it compleatly in our power to choose our own time to make it I cannot take the responsibility on me of entering into it in an unprepared [state].' Worthington, *MS. Diary*, June 14, 1812.

[4] Gregg, June 4, in *U.S. Gazette*, June 15, 1812. Gregg (who in the end voted for war) stated that the Senate would probably defeat the war bill, and substitute for it letters of marque and reprisal against Britain, and, possibly, against France also.

[5] Bayard to A. Bayard, June 4, 1812, Bayard, *Papers*, p. 198.

on June 12, and Giles, on June 17, moved that letters of marque and reprisal be issued against France as well as Britain. Both motions were defeated, but by close votes; the first 17 to 15, the second 18 to 14.[1] Another cover for retreat, and one which had even stronger support, was a nominal declaration of war against Britain, with a proviso that it should be limited to letters of marque and reprisal that the President would issue at some future period, if Britain still persisted in her depredations. This plan had many political advantages, and would probably succeed, reported Foster, since 'the Whole question of war is merely looked upon by many of its advocates as a party question on which depends the election to the next Presidency.'[2] An attempt was made, on June 12, to change the House bill from outright and absolute war against Britain to the issuing of letters of marque and reprisal; and it almost succeeded. The original bill was resumed, however, when the Senate divided equally, 16 to 16.[3]

It was not surprising that the old guard moderates in the Executive, like those in the Senate, should have weakened under the strain. Nor was it surprising that such determined Young Republicans as Clay, Calhoun, and Crawford should have continued, perforce, to infuse their 'enspiriting impulse.' According to Lowndes, not one member of the Cabinet, with the possible exception of Secretary Hamilton, was averse to this project to reduce the House bill from a direct declaration of war to one of reprisals. Indeed, 'a considerable effort was made [by] the Executive to prevent a declaration of war ... to substitute something else & less — letters of marque &c.' But 'a good many' senators and representatives discussed it, and flatly rejected it, said Lowndes. 'We determined to adjourn. go home. doing nothing — or have a War in common form.'[4]

---

[1] *Annals*, 12th, 1st, 270, 297.

[2] Foster to Castlereagh, June 9, 1812, *F.O.* 5:86. 'Such a step,' he reported, 'would supercede the Embargo and Non-importation Acts, would be going nominally beyond what they supposed themselves engaged to by their pledge to France, would gratify their spleen against England, would gain them time till the Election is decided, and above all would be in character with the shuffling proceedings which have distinguished the present Administration.'

[3] *Annals*, 12th, 1st, 267–71.

[4] Writing in 1819, Lowndes termed this 'one of the most curious anecdotes connected with the declaration of war,' and timed it as 'after the President's message was sent

For almost two weeks the Elder Statesmen debated, quibbled, amended, and delayed, encouraging hopes that the young War Hawks of the South and West might yet be checked, that cold water might yet be poured on 'Clay, Calhoun, Grundy & Company.' The uncertainty and anxiety, the cross-currents of intrigue, the 'perpetual oscillations,' and the paralyzing disease of the mind of this long session were here epitomized.

Meanwhile the people threatened and implored, and swamped Congress with petitions — for war, against war, and some (by merchants who had condemned and evaded the measure) for an extension of the Embargo.[1] 'God grant to the Senate the same Wisdom and fortitude' as the House in crossing the Rubicon; 'our anxiety is great, in a State of such awful suspense,' wrote Elbridge Gerry of Massachusetts.[2] 'Delay is Death!' reiterated the Boston *Chronicle*. '*Submission*, that ugly monster which held us spell-bound for so many years,' must be made 'to breathe its last,' said the Baltimore *Whig*. 'The wrath of Western America is in a flame,' said Kentuckians; 'you must breathe our spirit, and speak our sentiment,' and write this 'SECOND DECLARATION OF INDEPENDENCE.'[3]

Meanwhile out-of-door influences were exerted, and rumors conflicting and inspired were rife. Madison, it was said, had counted upon the measure's failing in the Senate. The navy would incite Britain to some hostile act to precipitate a decision. The Giles-Smith faction would vote for war, or against war, to turn out Madison, Monroe, and Gallatin. New England would

---

in.' Attorney General Pinkney 'came from Baltimore & was anxious for this plan,' and even 'Grundy was brought over' by its advocates. Lowndes stated that he himself, with Crawford, and a good many others of both houses, joined in rejecting it. Lowndes's 'Common Place (Historical)' notebook, pp. 11–12 (if pages were numbered), *Lowndes-Pinckney MSS*. See, also, on efforts 'to substitute something else & less,' and to gain minority votes by reprisals against France as well as Britain, Wash. letters in *U.S. Gazette*, June 4, 6, 8, 15, 1812.

[1] The 'Speculators of both parties' (whose ships 'crowded from our ports' in April at advance news of the Embargo) 'have refused no arts to evade our Laws & to profit above their neighbours by the violation of them. Their clamours are great as their ruin is sure. These events give us not a favourable opinion of the Mercantile character & prove how much gain predominates over their boasted patriotism. We might be tempted to doubt while with such men, whether patriotism was in the world.' Rev. Wm. Bentley of Salem, *Diary*, IV, 10, June 12, 1812.

[2] Gerry to Madison, June 12, 1812, *Madison MSS*.

[3] Lex. *Reporter*, June 6 (q. *Chronicle* and the *Whig*), 13, 1812, *passim*.

secede; and New York, where the Republican legislators had all
but unanimously nominated Clinton for President, would remain
neutral. The British-Savage war had created a panic throughout
the West: Vincennes, Indiana, and other towns had been taken,
and the people massacred.

England would yield, or had yielded, it was said. The assassination of Prime Minister Perceval at London on May 11 spelled
the end of the predatory war Britain had long waged on neutral
America, not for interfering with Britain's belligerent rights, not
for supplying the wants of her French enemy, which she herself
supplied, but for interfering with British profit and monopoly.
Great Britain had at last been forced to suspend or repeal the
orders-in-council! But this rumor was vigorously combatted by
Foster, who maintained (on May 23, June 10, and again on June
14) the selfsame uncompromising stand: never would Britain
yield until France revoked her decrees not only as to America
but fully, generally, and unconditionally. At the same time
Foster did his best to strengthen the anti-war men and persuade
the moderates. Hoping to prevent at least one vote for war, he
instructed his aide, Lieutenant Moore, 'to be sure to make Senator Brent . . . drunk every day — which was no difficult matter.' [1]

But the end of the fitful drama was in sight. On the morning
of June 17 the British Minister was informed by Pope that it was
too late to pour cold water on the patriotic blaze. Worthington
was of the same opinion. That evening at the President's House
Foster noted that Mr. Madison 'looked ghastly pale — he made
me three bows — he was remarkably civil — talked of Lord
Selkirk and of Russia, of our successes in Spain, Bernadotte &ca.,
&ca.' Flanking the little President, towering above Madison's
five feet four, and flushed with triumph, were Calhoun and Speaker
Clay. Both War Hawk leaders had been observed to shake hands
as if good news had been announced; and both talked very freely
with Foster on all but the one absorbing subject. 'I staid near two
hours,' recorded the British Minister, '& on going home found
a letter saying that the Bill had passed.' It mattered not that 'Lt.
Moore came in tipsy & swore he had converted Brent.' [2]

---

[1] Foster, *MS. Diary*, June 15, 1812.   [2] *Ibid.*, June 17, 1812.

On June 17 the Senate passed the war bill, 19 to 13. Giles, Leib, and Smith voted for it; Pope, Worthington, and four other Republicans voted against it.[1] The House concurred in the Senate's unimportant amendments, and repelled a final attempt to defeat it by a vote of 85 to 44. On that same day, June 18, 1812, Madison signed the act declaring that between the United States and Great Britain there existed a state of war.

---

[1] Joined with the seven Federalist senators, two each from Connecticut, Rhode Island, and Delaware, and one from Massachusetts, were six Republicans: Pope of Kentucky, Worthington of Ohio, Gilman of New Hampshire, Reed of Maryland, Lambert of New Jersey, and German of New York. Two Republicans were absent: Bradley, of frontier Vermont, and Campbell, of frontier Ohio. *Annals*, 12th, 1st, 297.

Bibliography

I. Manuscript Sources: Official and Private Papers.
II. Printed Sources: Documents and Writings of Contemporaries.
III. Newspapers.
IV. General: Books and Magazines.

I. Manuscript Sources

a) Official Papers

Archives des Affaires Étrangères, Paris — photostats at Library
of Congress: Correspondance Politique, États-Unis. (*Aff. Étr.*)
Fayette County Courthouse, Lexington, Kentucky:
Fayette County Deed Books. (Deed Book F, 1802, is at the office
of the Clerk, Court of Appeals, Kentucky Capitol, Frankfort.)
Fayette County Will Books.
Fayette Circuit Court, and Lexington District Court, Order Books
and File Records.
General Index to Deeds, Mortgages, etc.
Kentucky State Historical Society, Frankfort, Kentucky:
Fayette County Tax Lists.
Woodford County Tax Lists.
Lexington, Kentucky, City Hall:
Trustees' Books for the Town of Lexington, 1781–1810.
Public Record Office, London — photostats and transcripts at
Library of Congress:
Foreign Office, Instructions, Dispatches. (*F.O.*)
Admiralty.
State Department Archives, Washington:
U.S. Ministers, Instructions, Dispatches.
Domestic Letters.
Virginia Archives, Richmond, Virginia:
Hanover County Records:
Court Records, 1733–35, 1783–92.

Land Tax Books, 1782–1802.
Public Claims, 1780–81.
Taxable Property Lists, 1782–99.
Vestry Book, St. Paul's Parish, 1705–85.
Virginia Land Grants.

b) *Private Papers*
(In MSS. Division, Library of Congress, unless otherwise noted.)

Barbour, James. New York Public Library.
Blennerhassett, Harman.
Boston Public Library, Miscellaneous Manuscripts.
Breckinridge, John.
Brown, James.
Brown, Silas, Jr.
Burr Conspiracy, Letters in Relation to.
Campbell-Preston.
Clay, Henry.
Clifford, Thomas and John. The Historical Society of Pennsylvania, Philadelphia.
Crittenden, John J.
Dreer, Ferdinand J., Collection. The Historical Society of Pennsylvania.
Durrett Collection, Miscellaneous Manuscripts. University of Chicago Library.
Foster, Augustus John:
    Letters.
    Notes on the United States of America. Collected in the Years 1804–5–6–7 and 11–12. 3 volumes.
    Diary, July 1, 1811–July 12, 1812.
Gratz, Simon, Collection. The Historical Society of Pennsylvania.
Harrison, James O.
Innes, Harry.
Jackson, Andrew.
Jefferson, Thomas.
Kentucky State Historical Society, Miscellaneous Manuscripts.
Lexington, Kentucky, Public Library:
    Miscellaneous Manuscripts.
    Records of the Orders, Resolutions and Proceedings of the Sharers and Directors of the Lexington Library. 3 volumes.
Lowndes-Pinckney.
MacBride, James.
Madison, James.
Maryland Historical Society, Baltimore, Miscellaneous Manuscripts.

Monroe, James.

Nelson, Hugh.

New York Historical Society, New York, N.Y., Miscellaneous Manuscripts.

Nicholas, Wilson Cary.

Nicholson, Joseph H.

Pickering, Timothy. Massachusetts Historical Society, Boston.

Plumer, William.

Poindexter, George. In the Claiborne Papers, Mississippi State Archives, Jackson, Mississippi.

Randolph, John.

Rodney, Caesar Augustus.

Smith, Samuel.

Thornton, William.

Transylvania College Library, Lexington, Kentucky:
Miscellaneous Manuscripts.
Records of the Proceedings of the Board of Trustees of the Transylvania University. 3 volumes.

Van Ness, William P. New York Public Library.

Washburn Papers. Massachusetts Historical Society.

Whelpley Autograph Collection. Historical and Philosophical Society of Ohio, Cincinnati.

Worthington, Thomas. Diary 1801–13.

II. PRINTED SOURCES: DOCUMENTS AND WRITINGS OF CONTEMPORARIES

a) Documents

American State Papers. Documents, Legislative and Executive, of the Congress of the United States. Selected and edited under the Authority of Congress. 38 volumes. Washington, 1832–61. (Cited as *A.S.P.* References in this work are to *Finance, Foreign Relations, Indian Affairs, Miscellaneous.*)

Annals of Congress. Debates and Proceedings, First Congress, First Session, March 3, 1789, to Eighteenth Congress, First Session, May 27, 1824. 42 volumes. Washington, 1834–56.

Brymner, Douglas, Editor. *Reports on Canadian Archives, 1892,* and *1896.* Ottawa, 1893, and 1897.

Calendar of Virginia State Papers and Other Manuscripts. Preserved in the Capitol at Richmond. Volumes I and II. Richmond, 1875–93.

Congressional Globe. Containing Sketches of the Debates and Proceedings of ... Congress. From Dec. 2, 1833 to March 3, 1873. 46 volumes. Washington, 1834–73.

Force, Peter, Compiler. *American Archives, consisting of a Collection of*

Authentick Records, State Papers, Debates, and Letters and other Notices of Publick Affairs. 4th series, 6 volumes; 5th series, 3 volumes. Washington, 1837–53.

[Howe, John.] 'Secret Reports of John Howe, 1808.' Contributed by D. W. Parker. *American Historical Review,* XVII (N.Y., 1911–12), 70–102, 332–54.

Journals of the House of Representatives of the Commonwealth of Kentucky. 1804–10. Published annually by the Public Printer, Frankfort, Kentucky.

Kentucky Law Reports:

Bibb, George M. *Reports of Cases at Common Law and in Chancery, argued and decided in the Court of Appeals . . . from fall term 1808 to spring term 1809.* Louisville, 1904.

Dana, James G. *Reports of Select Cases Decided in the Court of Appeals . . . during the year 1833.* Volume I, Century Edition. Cincinnati, Ohio, (no date).

Hardin, Martin D. *Reports of Cases argued and adjudicated in the Court of Appeals . . . from the Spring Term 1805 to the Spring Term 1808.* Louisville, 1899.

Sneed, Achilles. *Reports of the Decisions of the Court of Appeals . . . March 1, 1805 to January 18, 1805 inclusive.* Edited by Harvey Myers. Louisville, 1898.

[Marshall, Humphrey.] *Report of the Select Committee Appointed to Investigate Certain Charges against Humphrey Marshall.* 27 pp. [Frankfort, 1808.]

Michigan Pioneer and Historical Collections. Copies of Papers on File in the Dominion Archives at Ottawa. Volumes XV and XXV. Lansing, Michigan, 1889–

Minor, Benjamin Blake, Editor. *Decisions of Cases in Virginia by the High Court of Chancery.* Richmond, 1852.

North Carolina Colonial Records, 1662–1776, 11 volumes, and *State Records,* 15 volumes. Raleigh, N.C., 1886–

Robertson, James Rood, Editor. *Petitions of the Early Inhabitants of Kentucky to the General Assembly of Virginia, 1769 to 1792.* Filson Club Publications, No. 27. Louisville, 1914.

[Sebastian, Benjamin.] *Report of the Select Committee to whom was referred the Information communicated to the House of Representatives charging Benjamin Sebastian . . . with having received a Pension from the Spanish Government.* Frankfort, Ky., from the Press of J. M. Street, 1806.

Session Acts of the General Assembly of Kentucky. 1803–10. Published annually by the Public Printer, Frankfort, Ky.

Tansill, Charles Callan, Compiler. *Documents Illustrative of the Formation of the Union of American States.* Washington, 1927.

Turner, Frederick J., Editor. 'Correspondence of Clark and Genêt.' *Annual Report of the American Historical Association for the year 1896.* Volume I, 930–1107. Washington, 1897.

    'Correspondence of the French Ministers to the United States, 1791–1797.' *Ann. Rpt. of the Amer. Hist. Assoc. for 1903.* Volume II. Washington, 1904.

U.S. Supreme Court Reports:

Cranch, William, *Reports of Cases Argued and Adjudged in the Supreme Court of the United States in the years 1807 and 1808.* 2d ed. 6 volumes. New York, 1812.

Dallas, Alexander J. *Reports, Supreme Court of the United States.* Volume III. Newark, N.J., 1882.

Wood, John. *A Full Statement of the Trial and Acquittal of Aaron Burr, Esq., Containing all the proceedings and debates that took place before the Federal Court at Frankfort, Kentucky,* etc. Printed by Cotton and Stewart, Alexandria, Va., 1807.

b) *Writings of Contemporaries*

Adams, Henry, Editor. *Documents Relating to New-England Federalism 1800–1815.* Boston, 1877. (Mainly letters of Pickering and his extremist friends.)

Adams, John. *Correspondence between the Hon. John Adams . . . and the Late Wm. Cunningham, Esq.* Boston, 1823.

    Letters of John Adams Addressed to his Wife. Edited by Charles Francis Adams. 2 volumes. Boston, 1841.

    Statesman and Friend — Correspondence of John Adams with Benjamin Waterhouse, 1784–1822. Edited by Worthington Chauncey Ford. Boston, 1927.

    Works. Edited by C. F. Adams. 10 volumes. Boston, 1856.

Adams, John Quincy. *Memoirs.* Edited by C. F. Adams. 12 volumes. Philadelphia, 1874–77.

    The Lives of James Madison and James Monroe. Boston and Buffalo, 1850.

    Writings. Edited by W. C. Ford. 7 volumes. New York, 1913–

Alsop, Richard. *The Echo, with Other Poems.* [By Richard Alsop, Theodore Dwight, et al.] Printed at the Porcupine Press by Pasquin Petronius. [New York], 1807.

    The Political Green-House for the Year 1798. Hartford, Conn., 1799.

Ames, Dr. Nathaniel. See Warren, Charles.

Anburey, Thomas. *Travels through the Interior Parts of America.* 2 volumes. London, 1789.

Asbury, Rev. Francis. *Journal, 1771–1815.* 3 volumes. New York, 1821.

Audubon, John James. *Delineations of American Scenery and Character.* Introduction by Francis Hobart Herrick. New York, 1926.

Austin, Moses. 'Journal, Dec. 1796–Mar. 1797.' Edited by George P. Garrison. *Amer. Hist. Rev.*, V (April, 1900), 523–42.

Austin, Moses and Stephen F. 'The Austin Papers.' The Papers of Moses and Stephen F. Austin. Edited by Eugene C. Barker. *Ann. Rpt. of the Amer. Hist. Assoc. for 1919.* Volume II, parts one and two. Washington, 1924.

Barry, William Taylor. 'Letters.' Selected by I. J. Cox. *Amer. Hist. Rev.*, XVI (Jan., 1911), 327–36.

Bayard, James Asheton. *Letters of James Asheton Bayard 1802–1814.* (Written to Caesar A. Rodney.) Wilmington, Delaware, 1901.

'Papers of James A. Bayard 1796–1815.' Edited by Elizabeth Donnan. *Ann. Rpt. of the Amer. Hist. Assoc. for 1913.* Volume II. Washington, 1915.

Beatty, Erkuries. 'Diary of Major Erkuries Beatty, Paymaster of the Western Army, May 15, 1786 to June 5, 1787.' *Magazine of American History*, I (N.Y., 1877), 235–41, 309–15, 380–84, 432–38.

Bentley, William. *Diary of William Bentley, D.D. Pastor of the East Church, Salem, Massachusetts.* 4 volumes. The Essex Institute. Salem, Mass., 1914.

Bigelow, Abijah. 'Letters of . . . to his wife, 1810–1815.' *Proceedings of the American Antiquarian Society*, n.s., XL (Worcester, Mass., 1930), 305–406.

Binns, John. *Recollections . . . Written by Himself.* Philadelphia, 1854.

Bishop, Robert Hamilton. *An Outline of the History of the Church in the State of Kentucky, During a Period of Forty Years, containing the Memoirs of Rev. David Rice.* Lexington, 1824.

Bodley, Thomas. Pamphlet written against Humphrey Marshall, title page missing, 7 pages, dated Lexington, Ky., June 12, 1808.

Brissot de Warville, Jean Pierre. *New Travels in the United States of America, performed in 1788.* Dublin, 1792.

Brooke, Francis T. *Narrative of My Life.* Richmond, 1849.

[Brougham, Henry. Baron Brougham and Vaux.] 'Review of *The Crisis of the Dispute with America* by a Merchant of the Old School, London, 1811.' *Edinburgh Review*, XXXVIII (February, 1812), 290–317.

[Brown, John.] 'Glimpses of Old College Life' — Letters of John Brown to William Preston, his Uncle, 1779–1780. *William and Mary College Quarterly Historical Magazine*, IX (Williamsburg, Va., 1900–01), 18–23, 75–83.

Butler, Mann. *A History of the Commonwealth of Kentucky, from its exploration and settlement by the whites to the close of the northwestern campaign, in 1813.* Cincinnati, 1836.

[Carrington, Mrs. Betsy Ambler.] 'An Old Virginia Correspondence,
1780–1823.' *Atlantic Monthly*, LXXXIV (Boston, Oct. 1899),
535–49.

Cartwright, Peter. *Autobiography*. Edited by W. P. Strickland.
Cincinnati, 1859.

Cass, Lewis. *France, Its King, Court, and Government*. New York, 1848.

Chastellux, Marquis de. *Travels in North America, 1780, 1781 and 1783*.
2 volumes. Dublin, 1787.

Clark, Louis Gaylord. 'Henry Clay, Personal Anecdotes, Incidents,
etc.' *Harper's Magazine*, V (N.Y., 1852), 392–99.

Clay, Henry. *Speeches of... with a Biographical Sketch*. Anonymous.
Carey and Lea, Philadelphia, 1827.

   Speeches of. See Mallory.

   The Life and Speeches of. Anonymous. 2 volumes. Copyrighted
      1842 by James B. Swain. Published by Greeley and McElrath,
      New York, 1843.

   The Private Correspondence of. Edited by Calvin Colton, LL.D.,
      Prof. of Political Economy, Trinity College. New York, 1855.

   Works, Life, Correspondence, Speeches. Edited by Calvin Colton.
      Federal Edition. 10 volumes. New York, 1904.

Cobbett, William. *Letters on the Late War between the United States and
Great Britain*, etc. New York, 1815.

   Porcupine's Works, 1783–1801. 12 volumes. London, 1801.
   (Cobbett, *Works*.)

Colton, Calvin. *The Last Seven Years of the Life of Henry Clay*. New
York, 1856.

   The Life and Times of Henry Clay. 2 volumes, New York, 1846.

Condict, Lewis. 'Journal of a Trip to Kentucky in 1795.' *Proceedings
of the New Jersey Historical Society*, n.s., IV (Newark, 1919), 108–27.

Cox, Nathaniel. 'Letters of... to Gabriel Lewis.' *Louisiana Historical
Quarterly*, II (New Orleans, Apr. 1919), 179–92.

Coxe, Tench. *An Examination of the Conduct of Great Britain, Respecting
Neutrals*. Pamphlet signed 'Juriscola.' Phila., 1807.

Cuming, Fortescue. *Tour to the Western Country* (1807–09). In volume
IV of Thwaites, R. G., Editor, *Early Western Travels*. See Thwaites.

Daveiss, Joseph Hamilton. *A View of the President's Conduct Concerning
the Conspiracy of 1806*. Frankfort, from the Press of Joseph M. Street,
1807. Reprinted in *Quarterly Publication of the Historical and Philosophical Society of Ohio*, XII (Cincinnati, 1917), 53–154. Edited,
with introduction, by Isaac Joslin Cox and Helen A. Swineford.

Davis, John. *Travels of Four Years and a Half in the U.S., 1798–1802*.
Edited by A. J. Morrison. New York, 1909.

[Dropmore Papers.] *The Manuscripts of J. B. Fortescue, Esq. Preserved at
Dropmore. Appendices to the Reports of the Royal Historical Manuscripts
Commission*. 10 volumes, London, 1892–1927.

Dunlap, William. *Diary of William Dunlap* (1766–1839). 2 volumes. New York Historical Society. New York, 1930.

Edwards, Ninian. *The Edwards Papers.* Edited by E. B. Washburne. *Chicago Historical Society Collection.* Volume III. Chicago, 1884.

Espy, Josiah. *Memorandums of a Tour in Ohio and Kentucky in 1805. Ohio Valley Historical Series Miscellanies.* No. 1. Cincinnati, 1870.

[Fessenden, Thomas Green.] *Democracy Unveiled, or Tyranny Stripped of the Garb of Patriotism. By Christopher Caustic* ... Third Edition with Large Additions. 2 volumes in one. New York, 1806.

Pills, Poetical, Political, and Philosophical. Prescribed for the Purpose of Purging the Public of Piddling Philosophers, of Puny Poetasters, of Paltry Politicians, and Petty Partisans. By Peter Pepper-Box, Poet and Physician. Philadelphia, 1809.

Fifthian, Philip Vickers. *Journal and Letters, 1767–1774.* Edited for the Princeton Historical Association by John Rogers Williams. Princeton, N.J., 1900.

Flint, Timothy. *Recollections of the Last Ten Years.* (Boston, 1826.) Edited with an introduction by C. Hartley Grattan. New York, 1932.

Foster, The Right Hon. Sir Augustus J., Bart. 'Notes on the United States. London, 1841 (unpublished).' In *The Museum*, n.s., XV (Phila., 1841), 31–48. Reprinted from *The Quarterly Review*, LXVIII (London, 1841), 20–57.

[Gales, Joseph.] 'Recollections of the Civil History of the War of 1812. By a Contemporary.' Nine articles in the *National Intelligencer*, Washington, D.C., June 9–Sept. 12, 1857.

Gallatin, Albert. *Writings.* Edited by Henry Adams. 3 volumes. Philadelphia, 1879.

Graydon, Alexander. *Memoirs of a Life*, etc. Harrisburgh, Pa., 1811.

Greeley, Horace. *The Life and Public Services of Henry Clay, down to 1848 by Epes Sargent. Edited and Completed at Mr. Clay's Death by Horace Greeley.* New York, 1860.

Hall, Captain Basil, *Fragments of Voyages and Travels*, etc. First, Second, and Third Series. London, 1860.

Hamilton, Alexander. *Works.* Edited by John C. Hamilton. 7 volumes. New York, 1851.

Works. Edited by Henry Cabot Lodge. Federal Edition. 12 volumes. New York, 1904. (Citations to this edition unless otherwise noted.)

Harrison, James O. 'Henry Clay, Reminiscences by His Executor.' *Century Magazine*, XXXIII (N.Y., Dec. 1886), 170–82.

Henry, Patrick. See Henry, Wm. W.

Hooker, Edward. 'Diary of ... 1805–1808.' *Ann. Rpt. of the Amer. Hist. Assoc. 1895.* Volume I, 842–929. Washington, 1897.

Huntington, Samuel. 'Letters from the Samuel Huntington Correspondence 1800–1812.' (Part II.) *Tract No. 95, Annual Reports of the Western Reserve Hist. Society*, pp. 57–151. Cleveland, Ohio, 1915.

Hutton, James, Editor. *Selections from the Letters and Correspondence of Sir James Bland Burges, Bart., sometimes Under-Secretary of State for Foreign Affairs*, etc. London, 1885. (*The Bland Burges Papers.*)

Imlay, Gilbert. *A Topographical Description of the Western Territory of North America*, etc. 3d edition. London, 1797.

Ingersoll, Charles Jared. *Historical Sketch of the Second War Between the United States and Great Britain.* '3 volumes' (two volumes published). Philadelphia, 1845–49.

    Inchiquin, the Jesuit's Letters, During a Late Residence in the United States, etc. New York, 1810.

    Recollections, Historical, Political, Biographical, and Social. Philadelphia, 1861.

Irving, Washington. *Letters.* See Irving, Pierre M.

    Works. With a Life of Irving by Richard Henry Stoddard. 3 volumes. New York, 1883.

Jackson, Andrew. *Correspondence.* Edited by John Spencer Bassett. 6 volumes. Washington, 1926–33.

[Jackson, Sir George.] *The Bath Archives. A Further Selection from the Diaries and Letters of Sir George Jackson, K.C.H., from 1809 to 1816.* Edited by Lady Jackson. 2 volumes. London, 1873. (Jackson, G., *Diaries.*)

Janson, Charles William. *The Stranger in America.* London, 1807.

Jarratt, Devereux. *Life of ... written by himself.* Baltimore, 1806.

Jay, John. *Correspondence and Public Papers.* Edited by Henry P. Johnston. 4 volumes. New York, 1890–93.

Jefferson, Thomas. 'Papers.' *Collections of the Mass. Hist. Society.* 7th series, volume I. Boston, 1900.

    Works. Edited by Paul L. Ford. Federal Edition. 12 volumes. New York, 1904.

    Writings. Andrew A. Lipscomb, editor-in-chief; Albert E. Bergh, managing editor. Monticello Edition. 20 volumes. Washington, 1904–05.

Kendall, Amos. *Autobiography.* Edited by William Stickney. Boston, 1872.

Kentucky Broadsides. In the MSS. Division, Library of Congress.

Kilby, John. 'Narrative of John Kilby — Quarter-Gunner of the U.S. Ship "Bon Homme Richard," under Paul Jones.' With introduction and notes by Augustus C. Buell. *Scribner's Magazine*, XXXVIII (N.Y., July 1905), 23–41.

[King, Rufus.] *The Life and Correspondence of Rufus King.* Edited by his grandson, Charles R. King. 6 volumes. New York, 1894–1900. (King, R., *Corres.*)

Lambert, John. *Travels Through Canada and the United States . . . in the Years 1806, 1807, & 1808.* 2 volumes. London, 1814.

La Rochefoucauld-Liancourt, François Alexandre Frédéric, Duc de Liancourt. *Travels Through the United States . . . in the Years 1795, 1796, and 1797.* 2 volumes. London, 1799.

Latrobe, Benjamin Henry. *The Journal of Latrobe. Being the Notes and Sketches of an Architect, Naturalist and Traveller in the United States from 1796 to 1820.* With an introduction by J. H. B. Latrobe. New York, 1905.

Leland, John. *The Virginia Chronicle.* Fredericksburg, Va., Printed by T. Green, 1790.

Littell, John S. *The Clay Minstrel.* Philadelphia, 1842.

Littell, William. *Festoons of Fancy, consisting of Compositions Amatory, Sentimental, and Humorous, in Verse and Prose.* From the Press of William Farquar, Louisville, Ky., 1814. (A copy at the Kentucky State Hist. Society, Frankfort.)

> *Political Transactions in and concerning Kentucky from the first settlement thereof until it became an Independent State in June, 1792.* From the Press of William Hunter, Printer to the Commonwealth, Frankfort, 1806.

Lowndes, William. See Ravenel, Mrs. St. Julien.

McAfee, Robert B. 'The Life and Times of Robert B. McAfee and his Family and Connections, written by Himself.' *Register of the Kentucky State Historical Society,* XXV (Frankfort, Ky.; 1927), 5–37, 111–43, 215–37.

McBride, James. 'Journey to Lexington, Kentucky, in 1810.' *Qtrly. Pub. of the Hist. and Phil. Soc. of Ohio,* V (1910), 21–27.

McCullough, Samuel D. 'Reminiscences of Lexington.' *Reg. Ky. S. Hist. Society,* XXVII (Jan. 1929), 411–32.

Mackintosh, James. *Vindiciae Gallicae — Defence of the French Revolution and its English Admirers against the Accusations of the Right Hon. Edmund Burke.* Dublin, 1791.

Madison, James. *Letters and Other Writings . . . Published by Order of Congress.* 4 volumes. Philadelphia, 1865. (Madison, *Writings;* references to this edition unless otherwise noted.)

> *Writings.* Edited by Gaillard Hunt. 9 volumes. New York, 1900–10.

Mallory, Daniel. *The Life and Speeches of the Hon. Henry Clay.* 2 volumes. Fifth Edition. Van Amringe and Bixby, New York, 1844.

Marshall, Humphrey. *The Aliens; A Patriotic Poem by H. Marshall, a Senator of the United States, Occasioned by the Alien Bill now before the*

Senate, May 15, 1798. With dedication to George Washington. Reprinted, for Charles F. Heartman. Metuchen, N.J., 1925.

    The History of Kentucky. 2 volumes. Frankfort, 1824.

Marshall, Thomas F. *Speeches and Writings.* Edited by W. L. Barre. Cincinnati, 1858.

Melish, John. *Travels Through the United States, 1806–1811.* 2 volumes. Philadelphia, 1815.

Michaux, F. A. *Travels to the Westward of the Allegheny Mountains, 1802.* In Volume III of Thwaites, *Early Western Travels.*

Mitchill, Dr. Samuel Latham. 'Letters from Washington, 1801–1813.' *Harper's Magazine,* LVIII (April 1879), 740–55.

Moore, Thomas. *Memoirs, Journal and Correspondence.* Edited by Lord John Russell. 6 volumes. London, 1853.

    Poetical Works, collected by himself. 10 volumes. London, 1853.

Morris, Gouverneur. *Diary and Letters.* Edited by Anne Cary Morris. 2 volumes. New York, 1888.

Morse, Jedidiah. *The American Gazetteer.* Boston, 1798.

Morse, Samuel F. B. See Morse, E. L.

Munford, Col. Robert. *Plays and Poems.* Printed for William Prentiss, Petersburg, Va., 1798.

Munford, William. *Poems and Compositions in Prose.* Printed by Samuel Pleasants, Richmond, 1798.

Murphey, Archibald Debow. *Papers.* Edited by William Henry Hoyt. Publications of the North Carolina Historical Commission. 2 volumes. Raleigh, N.C., 1914.

Nicholas, George. *A Letter from George Nicholas of Kentucky, to his friend in Virginia, Justifying the conduct of the citizens of Kentucky, as to some of the late measures of the general government; and correcting false statements, which have been made in the different States, of the views and actions of the people of Kentucky.* Nov. 10, 1798. From the Press of John Bradford, Lexington, 1798.

Old Family Letters. Copied from the originals for Alexander Biddle. Series A. Philadelphia, 1892.

Paine, Thomas. *Selections from the Writings of Thomas Paine.* Edited with an introduction by Carl Van Doren. New York, 1922.

Perry, B. F. *Reminiscences of Public Men.* Philadelphia, 1883.

[Peters, Richard.] 'Selections from the Correspondence of Judge Richard Peters of Belmont.' *Pennsylvania Magazine of History and Biography,* XLIV (Phila., 1920), 325–42.

Plumer, William. *Memorandum of Proceedings in the United States Senate 1803–1807.* Edited by Everett Somerville Brown. New York, 1923.

Prentice, George D. *Biography of Henry Clay.* Hartford, Conn., 1831.

[Preston, Mrs. Wm. C.] 'Personal Recollections of Eminent Men — Extracts from My Diary. By a Virginia Matron.' Signed 'Lois.'

The Land We Love, Charlotte, N.C., 1867–68, III, 334–36, 419–22, 512–14; IV, 402–04; V, 119–22. (Preston, Mrs. Wm. C., *Diary*.)

[Preston, William Campbell.] 'Personal Recollections of Eminent Men.' *The Land We Love*, V (Aug. 1868), 337–40.

Preston, William Campbell. *The Reminiscences of William C. Preston*. Edited by Minnie Clare Yarborough, Ph.D. Chapel Hill, N.C., 1933.

Quincy, Mrs. Eliza S. M. *Memoir of the Life of Eliza S. M. Quincy*. Boston, 1861.

Quincy, Josiah. See Quincy, Edmund.

Rankin, Adam, Pastor at Lexington, a Member of the Associate Reformed Synod. *A Review of the Noted Revival in Kentucky commenced in the Year of Our Lord 1801*. [Lexington], 1803.

Reynolds, John. *My Own Times*. Chicago, 1879.

Riedesel, Frederike C. *Letters and Journal*. Translated by William Stone. Albany, N.Y. 1867.

Ritchie, Thomas. *Reminiscences of Henry Clay and the Compromise*. Reprinted from the Richmond *Enquirer*, Sept. 10, 1852. [Richmond], 1852.

Robertson, George. *An Outline of the Life of George Robertson, Written by Himself, with an Introduction and Appendix by His Son*. Lexington, 1876. (Robertson, *Autobiography*.)

Rodney, Thomas. 'Letters of... from Mississippi Territory.' Edited by Simon Gratz. *Penna. Mag. of Hist. and Biog.*, XLIV (1920), 47–72, 170–89, and ff.

Safford, William H. *The Blennerhassett Papers*. Cincinnati, 1864.

Sargent, Epes. *The Life and Public Services of Henry Clay*. New edition, revised, enlarged and brought down to the year 1844, by the author. New York, 1844.

Schoepf, Johann D. *Travels in the Confederation, 1783–1784*. Translated by A. J. Morrison. 2 volumes. Philadelphia, 1911.

Semple, Robert B. *A History of the Rise and Progress of the Baptists in Virginia*. Richmond, 1810.

Sevier, John. 'Journal... 1790–1815.' Edited by John H. DeWitt. *Tennessee Historical Magazine*, VI (Nashville, 1920), 18–68.

Shaw, John Robert. *A Narrative of the Life and Travels of John Robert Shaw, the Well-Digger, now resident in Lexington, Kentucky. Written by himself*. Lexington, Printed by Daniel Bradford, 1807. Reprinted, Louisville, 1930.

Smith, Margaret Bayard. *The First Forty Years of Washington Society. Portrayed by the Family Letters of Mrs. Samuel Harrison Smith (Margaret Bayard) from the Collection of her grandson, J. Henley Smith*. Edited by Gaillard Hunt. New York, 1906.

Smyth, J. F. D. *A Tour in the United States of America*, etc. 2 volumes. London, 1784.

Stevens, Benjamin Franklin, Editor. *The Campaign in Virginia, 1781. An exact reprint of six rare pamphlets on the Clinton-Cornwallis controversy*, etc. 2 volumes. London, 1888.

Street, Joseph M. 'Letters.' *Annals of Iowa*, V, 3d series (Des Moines, Ia., 1901–03), 71–72.

Sutcliffe, Robert. *Travels in North America, 1804–1806*. Philadelphia, 1812.

Taggart, Samuel. 'Letters... 1803–1814' — written to Rev. John Taylor. Introduction by George Henry Hayne. *Procs. of the Amer. Antiq. Soc.*, XXXIII, n.s. (1923), 113–226, 297–438.

Taul, Micah. 'Memoirs.' *Reg. Ky. S. Hist. Soc.*, XXVII (1929), 343–80, 494–517, 601–27.

Taylor, James B. *Virginia Baptist Ministers*. Series I, Richmond, 1838. Series II, Edited by J. B. Jeter, New York, 1860.

Thomas, David. *The Observer trying the Great Reformation in This State and Proving it to have been originally a work of Divine Power with a survey of Several Objections to the contrary as being chiefly comprised in Mr. Rankin's Review of the Noted Revival lately published*. Printed by John Bradford, Lexington [1803].

Thwaites, Reuben Gold, Editor. *Early Western Travels 1748–1846*. 32 volumes. Cleveland, 1904.

[*Torrence Papers*.] 'Selections from the Torrence Papers, V, — The Transfer of Louisiana and the Burr Conspiracy, as illustrated by the Findlay Letters.' Edited by Isaac Joslin Cox. *Qtrly. Pub. of the Hist. and Phil. Soc. of Ohio*, IV (1909), 93–138.

Turreau, General. *Aperçu sur la Situation Politique des États-Unis d'Amérique*. Paris, 1815.

Van Buren, Martin. 'Autobiography.' Edited by John C. Fitzpatrick. *Ann. Rpt. of the Amer. Hist. Assoc. for 1918*, Volume II. Washington, 1920.

Volney, Constantin François. *A View of the Soil and Climate of the United States*, etc. Translated with occasional remarks by Charles Brockden Brown. Philadelphia, 1804.

Washington, George. *Writings*. Edited by W. C. Ford. 14 volumes. New York, 1889–93.

Watson, Elkanah. *Men and Times of the Revolution*. Edited by his son, W. C. Watson. New York, 1857.

Weld, Isaac. *Travels Through the States of North America in 1795, 1796, and 1797*. 3d edition. 2 volumes. London, 1800.

Whitaker, Arthur Preston, Editor. 'Harry Innes and the Spanish Intrigue; 1794–1795.' *Mississippi Valley Historical Review*, XV (Cedar Rapids, Ia., 1928–29), 236–48.

Winthrop, Robert C. *Memoir of Henry Clay*. Cambridge, Mass., 1880.

III. Newspapers

(At the Library of Congress unless otherwise noted)

Alexandria, Va., *Daily Gazette, Commercial and Political*. City Hall, Alexandria, Va.

Baltimore, Md., *Evening Post*.
    Federal Republican and Commercial Gazette.
    The Weekly Register. (*Niles' Register*.)

Boston, Mass., *Columbian Centinel*. Library of Congress and Goodspeed's Book Shop, Boston.
    Gazette.
    Independent Chronicle.
    Patriot.

Georgetown, D. C., *Independent American*.
    Spirit of 'Seventy-Six.

Hartford, Conn., *Connecticut Courant*.

Lexington, Ky., *Kentucky Gazette*. Lexington Public Library, Kentucky State Historical Society, Library of Congress, Cincinnati Public Library.
    Reporter. Lexington Public Library and Library of Congress.

New York, N.Y., *Columbian*.
    Evening Post.
    Herald.

Philadelphia, Penna., *Aurora*.
    Democratic Press.
    Pennsylvania Packet and Daily Advertiser.
    Poulson's American Daily Advertiser.
    Relf's Philadelphia Gazette.
    United States Gazette. Daily, and semi-weekly for the country.
    (References are to the daily unless otherwise noted.)

Pittsburgh, Penna., *Gazette*.

Richmond, Va., *Enquirer*.
    Richmond and Manchester Advertiser.
    Virginia Argus.
    Virginia Gazette.

Salem, Mass., *Essex Register*.

Washington, D. C., *Atlantic World*.
    Evening Star.
    Globe.
    National Intelligencer.

IV. GENERAL: BOOKS AND MAGAZINES

Adams, Henry. *The Life of Albert Gallatin.* Philadelphia, 1879.
  *History of the United States of America during the Administrations of
  Thomas Jefferson and James Madison.* 9 volumes. New York,
  1889–91. Reprinted, New York, 1930, in 4 volumes (of 9 books).

Ambler, Charles Henry. *Thomas Ritchie — A Study in Virginia Politics.*
  Richmond, 1913.

Anderson, Dice Robins. *William Branch Giles: A Study in the Politics of
  Virginia and the Nation from 1790 to 1830.* Menasha, Wis., 1914.

Aspinwall, Arthur. *Lord Brougham and the Whig Party.* Manchester,
  England, 1927.

Atlantic Monthly. LX (Boston, 1887), 556–66. Unsigned review of
  'Schurz's *Life of Henry Clay.*'

Bagot, Capt. Josceline, Editor. *George Canning and His Friends.* 2 volumes. London, 1909.

Baldwin, Simeon E. *Life and Letters of Simeon Baldwin.* New Haven,
  Conn., [circa 1919].

Beard, Charles A. *Economic Origins of Jeffersonian Democracy.* New York,
  1927.

Bemis, Samuel Flagg. *Jay's Treaty. A Study in Commerce and Diplomacy.*
  New York, 1923.
    Editor. *The American Secretaries of State and Their Diplomacy.* 10 volumes. New York, 1927.

Berryman, Florence Seville. 'Kentucky's "Rubens" and Some of His
  Subjects.' *Daughters of the American Revolution Magazine,* LXIV (Wash.,
  D.C., April, July, 1930), 220–28, 414–22.

Beveridge, Albert Jeremiah. *The Life of John Marshall.* 4 volumes.
  Boston, 1916–19.

Birney, William. *James G. Birney and His Times.* New York, 1890.

Boswell's Life of Johnson. 2 volumes. Oxford University Press. London,
  1927.

Bradford, Daniel, Editor. *The Medley, or Monthly Miscellany for the Year
  1803.* Printed by Daniel Bradford, Lexington, Ky.

Bradford, Gamaliel. *As God Made Them. Portraits of Some Nineteenth-
  Century Americans.* Boston, 1929.

Bradford, John. *Kentucky Almanac for the Year of our Lord, 1795.* Lexington, Ky.

British Critic Magazine. London, November 1807, Volume XXX.

Brown, Charles Raymond. *The Northern Confederacy according to the Plans
  of the 'Essex Junto' 1796–1814.* Princeton, N.J., 1913.

Brown, George Rothwell. *The Leadership of Congress.* Indianapolis,
  1922.

Bruce, William Cabell. *John Randolph of Roanoke, 1773–1833.* 2 volumes.
  New York, 1922.

Byron, George Gordon (Lord). *Don Juan.* Edited with an introduction by Frank H. Ristine. New York, 1927.

Caldwell, Charles (M.D.). *Discourse on Rev. Horace Holley, LL.D., Late President of Transylvania University.* Boston, 1828.

Channing, Edward. *A History of the United States.* 5 volumes. New York, 1929.
  The Jeffersonian System, 1801–1811. New York, 1906.

Channing, W. H. *Memoir of William Ellery Channing.* 3 volumes. Boston, 1848.

Charless, Joseph. *Directory of Lexington, Kentucky . . . for the Year 1806.* Published by Joseph Charless, Lexington, Ky.

Clark, Allen C. *Life and Letters of Dolly Madison.* Washington, 1914.

Clauder, Anna Cornelia. *American Commerce as Affected by the Wars of the French Revolution and Napoleon, 1793–1812.* Philadelphia, 1932.

Clay, Mrs. Mary Rogers. *The Clay Family.* Part I, 'The Mother of Henry Clay,' by Z. F. Smith. Part II, 'The Genealogy of the Clays,' by M. R. Clay. Filson Club Publications, No. 14. Louisville, 1899.

Clay, Thomas Hart. *Henry Clay by his grandson, Thomas Hart Clay, completed by Ellis Paxson Oberholtzer, Ph.D.* Philadelphia, 1910.

Cleveland, Catharine C. *The Great Revival in the West 1797–1805.* Chicago, 1916.

Coates, Robert M. *The Outlaw Years — the History of the Land Pirates of the Natchez Trace.* New York, 1930.

Coleman, R. T. 'Jo Daveiss, of Kentucky.' *Harper's Magazine,* XXI (Aug. 1860), 341–56.

Conway, Moncure Daniel. *Omitted Chapters of History disclosed in the Life and Papers of Edmund Randolph.* New York, 1888.

Cox, Isaac Joslin. *The West Florida Controversy, 1798–1813. A Study in American Diplomacy.* Baltimore, 1918.

[Cutts, Mrs. Lucia B.], *Memoirs and Letters of Dolly Madison.* Edited by her Grand-Niece. Boston and New York, 1886.

Davis, Matthew L. *Memoirs of Aaron Burr, with Miscellaneous Selections from His Correspondence.* 2 volumes. New York, 1836–37.

Dufour, Perret. 'Early Vevay.' *Indiana Magazine of History,* XX (Bloomington, Indiana, March 1924), pp. 1–36.

Duke, Basil W. *History of the Bank of Kentucky 1792–1895; including an interesting account of early banking,* etc. Louisville, 1895.

Eckenrode, H. J. *The Revolution in Virginia.* New York, 1916.

Edwards, Ninian W. *History of Illinois, from 1778 to 1833; and Life and Times of Ninian Edwards.* Springfield, Ill., 1870. (Edwards, *Ninian Edwards.*)

Faÿ, Bernard. *The Revolutionary Spirit in France and America — a Study of the Moral and Intellectual Relations between France and the United States at the End of the Eighteenth Century.* Translated by Ramon Guthrie. New York, 1927.

Fisher, Josephine. 'Francis James Jackson and Newspaper Propaganda in the United States, 1809–1810.' *Maryland Historical Magazine,* XXX (Baltimore, June, 1935), 93–113.

Follett, M. P. *The Speaker of the House of Representatives.* New York, 1896.

Galpin, W. Freeman. 'The American Grain Trade to the Spanish Peninsula, 1810–1814,' *Amer. Hist. Rev.,* XXVIII (Oct. 1922), 24–44. *The Grain Supply of England During the Napoleonic Period.* New York, 1925.

Garland, Hugh A. *Life of John Randolph of Roanoke.* 2 volumes in one. New York, 1854.

The Gleaner; or Monthly Magazine. Lancaster, Penna., edited by Stacy Potts, Jr., and printed by William Greer, Volume I, Sept. 1808–Aug. 1809.

Goebel, Dorothy Burne. *William Henry Harrison. A Political Biography.* Indianapolis, 1926.

Griffith, Elmer C. 'Early Banking in Kentucky.' *Proceedings of the Mississippi Valley Historical Association,* II (Cedar Rapids, Ia., 1908–09), 168–81.

Grigsby, Hugh Blair. *Discourse on the Life and Character of Hon. Littleton Waller Tazewell.* Norfolk, Va., 1860.

Gross, Samuel D., Editor. *Lives of Eminent American Physicians and Surgeons of the Nineteenth Century.* Philadelphia, 1861.

Harden, Edward J. *The Life of George M. Troup.* Savannah, Ga., 1859.

Harper, Lillie DuPuy Van Culin. *Colonial Men and Times.* Philadelphia, 1916.

Harper's Magazine. VI (Jan. 1853), 270. Editorial on Henry Clay.

Harrell, Isaac S. *Loyalism in Virginia.* Durham, N.C., 1926.

Harvey, Peter. *Reminiscences and Anecdotes of Daniel Webster.* Boston, 1882.

Hazen, Charles Downer. *Contemporary American Opinion of the French Revolution.* Baltimore, 1897.

Heckscher, Eli F., *The Continental System. An Economic Interpretation.* London, 1922.

Henderson, Archibald. *The Conquest of the Old Southwest.* New York, 1920. 'The Creative Forces in Western Expansion: Henderson and Boone.' *Amer. Hist. Rev.,* XX (1914–15), 86–107.

Henry, William Wirt. *Patrick Henry — Life, Correspondence, and Speeches.* 3 volumes. New York, 1891.

Herrink, L. S. 'George Wythe.' *The John P. Branch Historical Papers of Randolph-Macon College,* III (Richmond, Va., 1901), 281–333.

Historical Sketch of Christ Church Cathedral, Lexington, Kentucky. By the

Altar Guild, Easter, 1898. Press of the Transylvania Printing Company, Lexington, Ky.

Hovey, Alvah. *Life and Times of Rev. Isaac Backus.* Boston, 1859.

Hulbert, Archer B. 'Western Ship-Building.' *Amer. Hist. Rev.,* XXI (July 1916), 720–33.

Hunt, Gaillard. 'Joseph Gales on the War Manifesto of 1812.' *Amer. Hist. Rev.,* XIII (Jan. 1908), 303–10.

Irving, Pierre M. *The Life and Letters of Washington Irving.* 3 volumes. New York, 1862.

James, James Alton. 'Some Phases of the History of the Northwest, 1783–1786.' *Procs. of the Miss. Valley Hist. Assoc.,* VII (1913–14), 168–95.

Jameson, J. Franklin. *The American Revolution Considered as a Social Movement.* Princeton, N.J., 1926.

Jennings, Walter Wilson. *The American Embargo 1807–1809 — with Particular Reference to its Effects on Industry.* Iowa City, Ia., 1921.

Jillson, Willard Rouse. *Early Frankfort and Franklin County.* Louisville, 1936.

    The First Printing in Kentucky. Some Account of Thomas Parvin and John Bradford and the Establishment of the Kentucky Gazette, etc. Louisville, 1936.

Johnson, Lewis Franklin. *History of Franklin County, Kentucky.* Frankfort, Ky., 1912.

Jones, Howard Mumford. *America and French Culture, 1750–1848.* Chapel Hill, N.C., 1927.

Kennedy, John Pendleton. *Memoirs of the Life of William Wirt.* 2 volumes. Philadelphia, 1849.

    Swallow Barn or A Sojourn in the Old Dominion. Edited with an introduction by Jay B. Hubbell. New York, 1929.

Kent, William. *Memoirs and Letters of James Kent, LL.D., Late Chancellor of the State of New York,* etc. Boston, 1898.

Kerr, Charles, Editor. *History of Kentucky.* 5 volumes. American Historical Society, Chicago and New York, 1922. Volumes I and II, historical, by William Elsey Connelly and E. M. Coulter.

Kimball, Sidney Fiske. *Domestic Architecture of the American Colonies and of the Early Republic.* New York, 1922.

Levin, H., Editor. *The Lawyers and Lawmakers of Kentucky.* Chicago, 1897.

Little, Lucius Powhatan. *Ben Hardin: His Times and Contemporaries, with Selections from his Speeches.* Louisville, 1887.

Logan, Deborah Norris. *Memoir of Dr. George Logan of Stenton.* Philadelphia, 1899.

McCaleb, Walter Flavius. *The Aaron Burr Conspiracy.* New York, 1903.

McDougle, Ivan E. *Slavery in Kentucky 1792–1865.* Worcester, Mass., 1918.

McElroy, Robert McNutt. *Kentucky in the Nation's History.* New York, 1909.

McIlhany, H. M. *Some Virginia Families.* Staunton, Va., 1903.

McLaughlin, J. Fairfax. *Matthew Lyon, the Hampden of Congress.* New York, 1900.

Mahan, Alfred Thayer. *Sea Power in its Relations to the War of 1812.* 2 volumes. Boston, 1919.

Marryat, Captain Frederick, *Jacob Faithful.* (London, 1833–34.) With an Introduction by Douglas Veale. London, 1936.

Marshall, Thomas Maitland. *The Life and Papers of Frederick Bates.* 2 volumes. St. Louis, 1926.

Martin, Asa Earl. *The Anti-Slavery Movement in Kentucky Prior to 1850.* Filson Club Publications, No. 29. Louisville, 1918.

Meigs, William M. *The Life of Charles Jared Ingersoll.* Philadelphia, 1897.

Mordecai, Samuel. *Richmond in By-Gone Days.* Richmond, Va., 1856.

Morison, Samuel Eliot. *The Life and Letters of Harrison Gray Otis, Federalist, 1765–1848.* 2 volumes. Boston, 1913.

Morse, Edward Lind. *Samuel F. B. Morse, His Letters and Journals.* 2 volumes. Boston, 1914.

Munford, George Wythe. *The Two Parsons; Cupid's Sports; The Dream; and The Jewels of Virginia, with Biographical Sketch of the Author.* Richmond, Va., 1884.

[Norwood, J. W.] *Concise History of Lexington Lodge No. 1, F. and A. M., 1788–1913.* Lexington, Ky., 1913.

Ord, George. *Sketch of the Life of Alexander Wilson, Author of the American Ornithologist.* Philadelphia, 1828.

Page, Rosewell. *Hanover County — its History and Legends.* [Richmond, Va.], 1926.

Parrington, Vernon Louis. *Main Currents in American Thought. An Interpretation of American Literature from the Beginnings to 1920.* 3 volumes. New York, 1927–30.

Paxson, Frederic L. *History of the American Frontier, 1763–1893.* Boston, 1924.
'Influence of Frontier Life on the Development of American Law.' *Proceedings of the State Bar Association of Wisconsin for the Years 1919, 1920, 1921,* Madison, Wis., pp. 477–89.

Peck, Charles H. *The Jacksonian Epoch.* New York, 1899.

Pelzer, Louis. 'Economic Factors in the Acquisition of Louisiana.' *Procs. of the Miss. Valley Hist. Assoc.,* VI (1912–13), 109–28.

Perrin, William Henry. *The Pioneer Press of Kentucky.* Filson Club Publications, No. 3. Louisville, 1888.

Peter, Dr. Robert and Johanna. *The History of the Medical Department of Transylvania University.* Filson Club Publications, No. 20. Louisville, 1905.

    Transylvania University. Its origin, rise, decline, and fall. Filson Club Publications, No. 11. Louisville, 1896.

Pickering, Octavius [and Upham, Charles Wentworth]. *The Life of Timothy Pickering. By his son.* 4 volumes. Boston, 1867–73.

The Port Folio Magazine. VI (Phila., Aug. 1811), 109–12. Letter of 'Incola' [William Littell?] in reply to the critique of Lexington by Alexander Wilson.

Pound, Roscoe. *The Spirit of the Common Law.* Boston, 1921.

Pratt, Julius W. *Expansionists of 1812.* New York, 1925.

Prentiss, Hervey Putnam. *Timothy Pickering as the Leader of New England Federalism, 1800–1815.* [Salem, Mass.], 1934.

Price, Samuel Woodson. *The Old Masters of the Blue Grass.* Filson Club Publications, No. 17. Louisville, 1902.

Purviance, Levi. *The Biography of Elder David Purviance.* Dayton, Ohio, 1848.

Quincy, Edmund. *Life of Josiah Quincy, by his son.* Boston, 1874.

Quincy, Josiah. *Figures of the Past. From the Leaves of Old Journals. By Josiah Quincy (Class of 1821, Harvard College).* Boston, 1883.

Quisenberry, Anderson Chenault. *The Life and Times of Hon. Humphrey Marshall,* etc. Winchester, Ky., 1892.

Railey, William E. 'Woodford County Notes.' *Reg. of the Ky. S. Hist. Society,* XIX (Jan. 1921), 39–115.

Ranck, George W. *History of Lexington, Kentucky.* Cincinnati, 1872.

Ravenel, Mrs. St. Julien. *Life and Times of William Lowndes of South Carolina, 1782–1822.* New York, 1901.

Reed, Alfred Lantzinger. *Training for the Public Profession of the Law.* Carnegie Foundation for the Advancement of Teaching. Bulletin No. 15. New York, 1921.

Rogers, Joseph M. *The True Henry Clay.* Philadelphia, 1904.

Rothert, Otto A. *The Outlaws of Cave-in-Rock.* Cleveland, 1924.

Rusk, Ralph Leslie. *The Literature of the Middle Western Frontier.* 2 volumes. New York, 1925.

Schurz, Carl. *Life of Henry Clay.* 2 volumes. Boston, 1887.

Sears, Louis Martin. *Jefferson and the Embargo.* Durham, N.C., 1927.

Semmes, John E. *John H. B. Latrobe and His Times 1803–1891.* Baltimore, 1917.

Simpson, Elizabeth M. *Bluegrass Houses and Their Traditions.* Lexington, Ky., 1932.

Smith, M. V. *A History of the Executives of Virginia.* Washington, D.C., 1893.

Smith, Theodore Clarke. 'War Guilt in 1812.' *Mass. Hist. Society Proceedings,* LXIV (June 1931), 319–45.

Smith, Zachary F. 'Henry Clay.' Volume III, 937–77, of *Library of Southern Literature*, etc. Edited by E. A. Alderman and Joel C. Harris. 16 volumes. Atlanta, Ga., 1908.

> See Clay, M. R., *The Clay Family.*
> *The History of Kentucky.* Louisville, 1895.

Speed, Thomas. *The Wilderness Road.* Filson Club Publications, No. 2. Louisville, 1886.

Stanard, Mary Newton. *Richmond; Its People and Its Story.* Philadelphia, 1923.

Steiner, Bernard C. *The Life and Correspondence of James McHenry, Secretary of War under Washington and Adams.* Cleveland, 1907.

Story, William W. *Life and Letters of Joseph Story.* 2 volumes. Boston, 1851.

Swearingen, Mack. *The Early Life of George Poindexter. A Story of the First Southwest.* New Orleans, La., 1934.

Taylor, George Rogers. 'Agrarian Discontent in the Mississippi Valley Preceding the War of 1812.' *Journal of Political Economy*, XXXIX (Chicago, Aug. 1931), 471–505.

> 'Prices in the Mississippi Valley Preceding the War of 1812,' *Journal of Economic and Business History*, III (Cambridge, Mass., Nov. 1930), 148–63.

Terhune, M. V. H. (Marion Harland). *More Colonial Homesteads and Their Stories.* New York, 1899.

Thom, William Taylor. *The Struggle for Religious Freedom in Virginia: The Baptists.* Baltimore, 1900.

Thomas, F. W. *John Randolph of Roanoke and other Sketches of Character, including William Wirt, together with Tales of Real Life.* Philadelphia, 1853.

Townsend, John Wilson. *Kentuckians in History and Literature.* New York and Washington, 1907.

Townsend, William H. *Lincoln and His Wife's Home Town.* Indianapolis, 1929.

Trabue, Alice Elizabeth. *A Corner in Celebrities.* Louisville, 1922.

Tyler, Lyon Gardiner. 'George Wythe.' Volume I, 49–91 of *Great American Lawyers*, etc. Edited by W. D. Lewis. 8 volumes. Philadelphia, 1907–09.

> *The Letters and Times of the Tylers.* 3 volumes. Williamsburg, Va., 1884–96.

Verhoeff, Mary. *The Kentucky River Navigation.* Filson Club Publications, No. 28. Louisville, 1917.

Virginia Magazine of History and Biography, Richmond, Va., XXI (Oct. 1913), 436; XXXIII (Oct. 1925), 395. Notes on the Hudson family.

Warfield, Ethelbert Dudley. *The Kentucky Resolutions of 1798.* New York, 1887.

Warren, Charles. *A History of the American Bar.* Boston, 1911.

Jacobin and Junto, or Early American Politics as Viewed in the Diary of Dr. Nathaniel Ames 1758–1822. Cambridge, Mass., 1931.

The Supreme Court in United States History. Revised edition. 2 volumes. Boston, 1932.

Whitaker, Arthur Preston. *The Mississippi Question 1795–1803. A Study in Trade, Politics, and Diplomacy.* New York, 1934.

The Spanish-American Frontier, 1783–1795; the Westward Movement and the Spanish Retreat in the Mississippi Valley. Boston and New York, 1927.

White, Elizabeth Brett. *American Opinion of France. From Lafayette to Poincaré.* New York, 1927.

Williams, Thomas J. C. *A History of Washington County, Maryland ... including a History of Hagerstown.* 2 volumes. Hagerstown, Md., 1906.

Wirt, William. *Patrick Henry.* 15th edition, corrected by the author. Hartford, Conn., 1854.

Young, Mrs. Sarah S. *Genealogical Narrative of the Hart Family.* Memphis, Tenn., 1882.

Zimmerman, James Fulton. *Impressment of American Seamen.* New York, 1925.

Index

Index

DATE DUE

GAYLORD			PRINTED IN U.S.A.